The Evolution of Management Thought

NINTH EDITION

Daniel A. Wren
David Ross Boyd Professor Emeritus
The University of Oklahoma

and

Arthur G. Bedeian
Boyd Professor Emeritus
Louisiana State University and A&M College

WILEY

PUBLISHER	Lise Johnson
EDITOR	Jennifer Manias
SENIOR EDITORIAL ASSISTANT	Campbell McDonald
SENIOR MANAGING EDITOR	Judy Howarth
PRODUCTION EDITOR	Mahalakshmi Babu
MARKETING COORDINATOR	Jessica Spettoli
COVER PHOTO CREDIT	© David Charouz/Getty Images

This book was set in 10/12 Times LT Std by Straive™.

Founded in 1807, John Wiley & Sons, Inc. has been a valued source of knowledge and understanding for more than 200 years, helping people around the world meet their needs and fulfill their aspirations. Our company is built on a foundation of principles that include responsibility to the communities we serve and where we live and work. In 2008, we launched a Corporate Citizenship Initiative, a global effort to address the environmental, social, economic, and ethical challenges we face in our business. Among the issues we are addressing are carbon impact, paper specifications and procurement, ethical conduct within our business and among our vendors, and community and charitable support. For more information, please visit our website: www.wiley.com/go/citizenship.

ISBN: 978-1-394-20231-7 (PBK)

Library of Congress Cataloging-in-Publication Data:

Names: Wren, Daniel A., author. | Bedeian, Arthur G., author.
Title: The evolution of management thought / Daniel A. Wren, David Ross Boyd Professor Emeritus, The University of Oklahoma, and Arthur G. Bedeian, Boyd Professor Emeritus, Louisiana State University and A&M College.
Description: Ninth edition. | Hoboken, NJ : Wiley, [2024] | Includes index.
Identifiers: LCCN 2023017108 (print) | LCCN 2023017109 (ebook) | ISBN 9781394202317 (paperback) | ISBN 9781394202287 (adobe pdf) | ISBN 9781394202294 (epub)
Subjects: LCSH: Management—History. | Management—Philosophy.
Classification: LCC HD30.5 .W73 2024 (print) | LCC HD30.5 (ebook) | DDC 658.009—dc23/eng/20230530
LC record available at https://lccn.loc.gov/2023017108
LC ebook record available at https://lccn.loc.gov/2023017109

The inside back cover will contain printing identification and country of origin if omitted from this page. In addition, if the ISBN on the back cover differs from the ISBN on this page, the one on the back cover is correct.

SKY10054664_090523

To Leon, Maude, and Karen
my links with the past;
To Jonathan, Laura, and Lynda;
and to another generation,
Karen Nicole, Tanner Main, Ethan Daniel, Sarah Lynn, Caitlyn Claire, and Aria Charlotte
my links with the future.

To Varsenick and Arthur Bedeian
for reasons lost to history;
To Lynda, Katherine, and TAB
for every reason;
To Anna-Kennon, Kate McGee, Laura Gabrielle, and Elizabeth Jane
for making me so very happy.

Contents

PART III The Social-Person Era

About the Authors

Daniel A. Wren, PhD, the University of Illinois, is David Ross Boyd Professor of Management *Emeritus* and Curator *Emeritus* of the Harry W. Bass Business History Collection at The University of Oklahoma. He has served as president of the Southern Management Association, as chairman of the Management History Division of the Academy of Management, is a Founding Fellow of the Southern Management Association, and a Fellow of the Academy of Management. He has been honored as a member of the Oklahoma Higher Education Hall of Fame and has received the Distinguished Educator Award from the Academy of Management for his contributions "as the foremost management historian of his generation." His research has appeared in numerous scholarly journals, and he is the author of *Collegiate Education for Business Administration at The University of Oklahoma: A History; White Collar Hobo: The Travels of Whiting Williams*; and coauthor with Ronald G. Greenwood of *Management Innovators: The People and Ideas That Have Shaped Modern Business.*

Arthur G. Bedeian, DBA, Mississippi State University, is a Boyd Professor *Emeritus* and former Ralph and Kacoo Olinde Distinguished Professor of Management at Louisiana State University and A&M College. He is a past president of the Academy of Management, the Foundation for Administrative Research, the Southern Management Association, and the Southeastern Institute for Decision Sciences. A former Dean of the Academy of Management's Fellows Group, he is a Fellow of the American Psychological Association, the Society for Industrial and Organizational Psychology, the Association for Psychological Science, the International Academy of Management, and the Southern Management Association. He has been honored with the Richard M. Hodgetts Distinguished Career Award, Ronald G. Greenwood Lifetime Achievement Award, Academy of Management Distinguished Educator Award, Academy of Management Distinguished Service Award, and, for his contributions to the field, membership in the Society for Organizational Behavior. In addition to having been an editor of the *Journal of Management*, he has served on 18 editorial boards, including the *Academy of Management Review, Journal of Applied Psychology, Leadership Quarterly, Journal of Vocational Behavior, Organizational Research Methods, Journal of Management History, Management & Organizational History,* and *Academy of Management Learning & Education.* He has chaired the J. William Fulbright Foreign Scholar Board and been an external reviewer for the National Science Foundation, the National Academy of Science, and the National Research Council of Canada.

Preface

Iter fac in praeteritum ut praesentia et futura intellegas
"Journey into the past to understand the present and the future"

Over half a century has passed since *The Evolution of Management Thought*'s first edition, and throughout those intervening years, the authors have come to more fully appreciate that everything about management as an academic discipline—its language, its theories, its models, and its methodologies, not to mention its implicit values, its professional institutions, and its scholarly ways—comes from its inherited traditions. Our aim has been to understand these inherited traditions by revealing their origins in the past. Simply stated, we believe that to better understand the present and the future, it is necessary to know the past.

Our challenge as we have prepared each edition of *The Evolution of Management Thought* has been to recognize that, like all historians, we are a product of our own personal interests and biases. We make no claim to possessing a monopoly on truth. Subjectivity is inherent at every stage of historical study, as history is always written backwards and historical meaning can only be established in retrospect; even "historical 'facts' are strongly embedded in interpretation."[1] Acknowledging that absolute truth in analyzing the past is impossible, however, does not relieve the historian from the duty of striving for objectivity or from recognizing that "interpretations change from generation to generation," as new scholars view history from their own set of prejudices.[2] Thus, before moving ahead, we forewarn our readers that, because history is not an objective science, how things "really were" can never be fully known.

As a further complication, given that it is impossible to rewind time, the historical record is inescapably spotty and fragmentary; there are many missing links. It is hence seldom (if ever) possible to establish an unquestioned chain of antecedents and consequences leading to a specific event. There are those who argue that to "see the world truly" one must "survey the whole stream of time in one comprehensive vision."[3] We find that efforts to do so all too frequently make history medicinal, reducing historical knowledge to a drab meshing of abstract and impersonal forces. The study of history need not be a slog through time. To avoid pointless excess associated with a mere chronicling of past events and to give texture to the people and ideas discussed, we have attempted to offer flecks of color when appropriate.

We strongly believe that contemporary scholarship within the management discipline suffers to the extent that it lacks an appreciation of the past's impact on modern thinking. To learn that others in the past have traveled the same intellectual byways offers reassurance that progress in scholarship is a multigenerational endeavor. Joining us in an appreciation of the "past as prologue," James G. March argued that the pursuit of knowledge involves the improvement of ideas "as they evolve through generations of individual scholars and scholarly communities, each building on those who went before and providing a base for those who follow." Further echoing our own sentiments, March has exulted "the benefits and beauties of being connected to a boundless past of cumulative scholarship that can anticipate a boundless future in which the ideas of

[1] Geoffrey Jones and Tarun Khanna, "Bringing History (Back) into International Business," *Journal of International Business Studies* 37(4) (July 2006), p. 465.
[2] Sidney Pollard, *The Genesis of Modern Management: A Study of the Industrial Revolution in Great Britain* (Cambridge, MA: Harvard University Press, 1965), p. 1.
[3] Bertrand A. W. Russell, "Mysticism and Logic," *Hibbert Journal* 12(4) (July 1914), p. 795.

today mature and develop into complex wonders of future knowledge."[4] At the same time, as the future chapters will attest, we do not mean to suggest that the present is the culmination of an ascending and historically inevitable march of progress. Furthermore, we acknowledge that progress is a moral concept measured with regard to some set of varying assumptions about which all may not agree.[5]

Like its predecessors, *The Evolution of Management Thought*, Ninth Edition seeks to capture the "benefits and beauties" of this past as a basis for expanding our intellectual horizons. Acknowledging the tendency to view history from the perspective of our own era, Seymour B. Sarason warned that "we can be unfortunate prisoners of time and place unless our education builds into us schemata that aid us in taking distance from our time and place."[6] Toward this end, to convey an appreciation of the narrative past underlying the evolution of management thought, every chapter in this edition has once again been rigorously reviewed and systematically updated. Our intent has been to place various theories of management in their historical context, showing how they developed as thinking about the nature of work, the nature of human beings, and the nature of organizations changed across time.

With this in mind, we caution readers to avoid the folly of gauging the past by the standards of the present; as has been noted, "Doing history with integrity requires us to interpret elements of the past not through the optics of the present but within the worlds of our historical actors."[7] Although previous generations lacked the foresight to match our contemporary hindsight, it is an illusion to think we are any more able to see the present in a perfect light than were our predecessors during their time. In this sense, in discussing history, people have all too often fallen victim to what Herbert Butterfield has called the "pathetic fallacy," abstracting events and ideas from their historical context and judging them without regard to the social and intellectual fabric of the era or period within which they occurred or existed.[8] Interpreting the past through the context of present-day values or projecting features of today's world back in time invariably results in previous generations falling short. As will become evident in the coming chapters, finding fault with our forebears is generally more informative if contrasted with actual historical experience rather than a utopian ideal.

History may be portrayed using any number of complementary approaches. The following account presents a chronological rather than topical history of management thought. In doing so, it makes no claim at being encyclopedic; our aim was not to write a history of everything that has happened within the management discipline since the beginning of time. Indeed, as John H. Elliott wrote, "No narrative is ever fully comprehensive, no explanation total, and the balance between description and analysis is painfully elusive."[9] Concerning the latter point, within a four-part chronological structure (Early Management Thought; The Scientific-Management Era; The Social-Person Era; and Moving Onward: The Near Present), we move back and forth through time, highlighting unsuspected connections. Though we exhort readers to eschew what might be called "straight-line thinking" in associating individual factors with specific events, at the same time, we also reject the notion that history is simply a sequence of disparate events and personalities that careen through time and space.

Although the chronological structure we have chosen is not universal and varies across countries, we have chosen this approach because we believe a "consideration of time sequences

---

[4] James G. March, "Research on Organizations: Hopes for the Past and Lessons from the Future," *Nordiske Organisasjons-studier* 1(1) (1999), pp. 80, 81.

[5] Immanuel Wallerstein, "A Theory of Economic History in Place of Economic Theory?" *Revue économique* 42(2) (March 1991), p. 178.

[6] Seymour B. Sarason, *The Making of an American Psychologist* (San Francisco, CA: Jossey-Bass Publishers, 1988), p. 277.

[7] James H. Sweet, "Is History History? Identity Politics and Teleologies of the Present," *Perspectives on History* 60(6) (September 2022), p. 8.

[8] Herbert Butterfield, *The Whig Interpretation of History* (London: G. Bell and Sons, 1931), p. 30.

[9] John H. Elliot, *History in the Making* (New Haven, CT: Yale University Press, 2013), p. 94.

is crucial to any kind of history writing[10] and it best creates a feeling for the *zeitgeist* of the people and ideas that compose the management discipline's intellectual heritage. Moreover, toggling back and forth in time and from one theme or topic to another can prove frustrating and confusing compared to a smooth narrative flow. We also realize that, in distinguishing between various eras or periods in time, different boundaries could have been employed; that historical eras or periods rarely fit dates precisely; and that shifting from one period to another is never neat or easily explained. As Cheryl A. Logan has observed, "History has few 'natural' lines of fracture." We thus remind readers that the boundaries we have selected "are not the boundaries of what really happened at a given place or time; rather, they are boundaries [we have chosen] about that place and time—a story that has a workable beginning and end."[11]

In addition, we should perhaps comment once again on the title *The Evolution of Management Thought*. It has been said, "A teacher must either treat history as a catalogue, a record, a romance; or as an evolution."[12] We have selected the latter. Our use of the term "evolution" in both title and text is meant to refer to the historical development of management thought over time. We do not intend to call to mind Charles R. Darwin's theory of evolution by natural selection "in which randomly generated traits survive and spread because they provide some edge in the competition for survival and reproduction."[13] We have no Darwinian theory of evolution to promulgate and find it impossible to manhandle the facts to fit one.

The continuing interest of scholars who care about the evolution of management thought and the students who find value in the lessons that history provides made this edition possible. Over the years, the authors have had the privilege of training several generations of gifted graduate students who have gone on, as eminent historians, to shape the study of management thought. We are proud of their contributions to our knowledge of the past and the leadership they have provided in chairing the Management History Division of the Academy of Management. This latter group is comprised of Paula Phillips Carson, the late Kerry David Carson, Shawn M. Carraher, Franz T. Lohrke, Milorad M. Novicevic, Roland E. Kidwell, Stephanie Case Henagan, Leon C. Prieto, and Jeffrey Muldoon. Several esteemed colleagues who propelled management history into the limelight as a scholarly endeavor and from whom we learned so much live only in our memories. We wish to remember Claude S. George, Jr., John F. Mee, Richard J. Whiting, W. Jerome Arnold, Ronald G. Greenwood, James C. Worthy, Richard M. Hodgetts, Alfred A. Bolton, William B. Wolf, William F. Muhs, Charles D. Wrege, and Peter B. Petersen. Their unique insights and contagious enthusiasm continue to inspire us. We remain indebted to John D. Breeze, W. Jack Duncan, and David D. Van Fleet for their decades of friendship and contributions to expanding our knowledge about the management discipline's past.

It was a pleasure working with Regina Scannell Greenwood and the late Julia Kurtz Teahen in developing PowerPoint slides to accompany this and past editions. The slides feature photographs, charts, and other visual materials that enliven and augment the companion text. In preparing the current edition, it has been a special bonus to work with Elizabeth "Ashley" Gilly. As an editorial assistant with LSU Press, Ashley is an eagle-eye wordsmith of uncanny talent. Her quick wit and encouragement made collaborating a blessing. At John Wiley & Sons, we wish to express our appreciation to Jennifer Manias, Portfolio Manager, Business, and Judy Howarth, Senior Managing Editor, who cheerfully saw the present edition through its various stages from manuscript to print. Mahalakshmi Babu and Manimaran Edward Johnson at Straive provided indispensable support. Finally, we want to acknowledge Melba K. Staub, Elizabeth L. Allen, and

[10] Ernst Mayr, *The Growth of Biological Thought: Diversity, Evolution, and Inheritance* (Cambridge, MA: Harvard University Press, 1982), p. 2.
[11] Cheryl A. Logan, "Shaping and Owning the Boundaries of a Book," *History of Psychology* 16(3) (August 2013), pp. 217, 218.
[12] Henry Adams, *The Education of Henry Adams* (Washington, DC: Privately printed, 1907), p. 261.
[13] John R. McNeill, [Review of the book *A Foot in the River*], *Wall Street Journal* (February 29, 2016), p. A11.

Larissa K. Elliott at the Louisiana State University Libraries for obtaining material through the Interlibrary Loan Service, as well as their colleague Thomas E. Diamond, Collections and Materials Selector Librarian, for fulfilling—at record speed—countless acquisition requests. Melba, Elizabeth, and Larissa possess magical skills in locating even the most elusive materials and doing so without breaking stride. We thank them both for their tireless efforts on our behalf.

No book fully achieves the intentions of its creators. We would thus welcome being told of any discrepancies in the following pages, as well as receiving additional information or materials that might be incorporated into a future edition. In closing, we remain grateful for the suggestions and encouragement of the many people who have used previous editions of *The Evolution of Management Thought* in the classroom and in their own research.

DANIEL A. WREN — ARTHUR G. BEDEIAN

NORMAN, OKLAHOMA — BATON ROUGE, LOUISIANA

July 24, 2023

About the Instructor Companion Website

This book is accompanied by an instructor's companion website: www.wiley.com/go/wren/evolutionofmanagement9e

This website includes:

- Instructor Manual and Test Bank
- Computerized Respondus Test Bank
- PowerPoint Slides
- Image Gallery.

Early Management Thought

PART I

Part I traces developments in management thought up to the scientific-management era in the United States. In a brief introduction, it is noted that management thought is a product of a society's culture and to be understood requires an appreciation of the cultural context within which management as an activity and as an academic discipline is rooted. Chapter 2 examines management in early civilizations preceding the Industrial Revolution. It also discusses the changing cultural values in these civilizations that led to the Industrial Revolution. Chapter 3 reviews the main features of the Industrial Revolution, the management challenges it created, and the resulting cultural consequences. Chapter 4 highlights the contributions of four pioneers who were instrumental in sowing the seeds of the management discipline. Chapter 5 focuses on the Industrial Revolution in the United States, the industries it spawned, and the work of various management pioneers from this era. Finally, Chapter 6 outlines the continued growth of U.S. industry following the conclusion of the War Between the States, traces the accompanying emergence of systematic management, and describes the nation's economic, social, political, and technological environment on the eve of the scientific-management era.

A Prologue to the Past

CHAPTER 1

The practice of management is ancient, but the formal study of management, based on an evolving body of knowledge, is relatively new. As has been remarked, "[r]arely, if ever, . . . in human history has a new institution" arisen as swiftly as management or "proven indispensable so quickly."[1] For a broad working definition, *management* may be viewed as the activity whose purpose is to achieve desired results through the efficient allocation and utilization of human and material resources. *Management thought*, the evolution of which is our primary focus, encompasses the existing body of knowledge about management as an activity *and* as an academic discipline.

OUR GOAL

The goal of this book is to trace the many roots of modern management thought. In doing so, we aim to explore how ideas about the nature of work, the nature of human beings, and the nature of organizations have changed throughout history. Our methodology is *analytic*, *synthetic*, and *interdisciplinary*. It is *analytic*, in that it examines the backgrounds, experiences, and beliefs of people *who* made significant contributions to management thinking. It is *synthetic*, in that it weaves developmental trends, social movements, and environmental forces into a conceptual framework for understanding *how* management thinking has evolved within and across generations. It is *interdisciplinary*, in that it draws insights from economics, history, political science, psychology, and sociology to explain *why* management thinking has developed as it has.

We thus study the past to illuminate the present. A smattering of courses on the *whos, hows,* and *whys* of current management thought is taught at the baccalaureate and graduate levels, though the instruction generally lacks depth, direction, and unity—elements necessary to comprehend the past and illuminate the present. In his 1838 poem "A Psalm of Life," Henry Wadsworth Longfellow said, "Let the dead Past bury its dead!"[2] but there is much to be said for resurrection. We live and study in an age characterized by myriad approaches to management—students encounter quantitative, behavioral, and functional approaches, amongst others, in their various management courses. Although such a variety may be intellectually stimulating, it presents students with a fragmented picture of the management discipline and assumes that they have the insight to unify these different approaches for themselves. In many cases, this burden is far too great.

[1] Peter F. Drucker, *The Practice of Management* (New York: Harper & Row, 1954), p. 3.
[2] Henry Wadsworth Longfellow, "A Psalm of Life," *The Knickerbocker* 12(4) (October 1838), p. 189.

A mindfulness of the evolution of management thought contributes to a more logical, coherent picture of the present discipline through providing a historical backdrop for unifying the different approaches to management. Without a knowledge of the past, individuals have only their own limited experiences as a base for thought and action. Making sense of the current status and prospective evolution of management thought, therefore, requires a recognition of its origins and development over time. In this way, history is a "universal experience—infinitely longer, wider, and more varied than any individual's experience."[3] The study of history equips students with an awareness of past answers and, in turn, viable alternatives to the challenges of contemporary life. Going further, social theorist Barbara S. Lawrence has offered that a historical perspective "pushes thinking about alternative explanations for phenomena, helps identify more or less stable concepts, and expands research horizons by suggesting new ways of studying old questions."[4] To which management educator George E. Smith has added: "Reading, exploring, and discussing history can provide students with opportunities to acquire knowledge of their field and its practices, gain wisdom, and develop and use judgment."[5]

A CULTURAL FRAMEWORK

History is more than a series of past events. It is also a record of a society's culture. An understanding of how our ideas about the nature of work, the nature of human beings, and the nature of organizations have changed throughout history requires an appreciation of the cultural framework within which management as an activity and as an academic discipline is situated. Culture is the whole of a society's "knowledge, belief, art, morals, law, custom, and any other capabilities and habits" that has been transmitted across generations.[6] Implicit in this definition is the realization that culture influences the decisions people make and, therefore, their behavior. By extension, culture determines a society's success. Like a society's culture, management as an activity and as a discipline is a product of the past and present—it is not static or fixed in time.

Culture is a very broad subject. The chapters that follow are limited to a consideration of those specific economic, social, political, and technological facets of culture that influence management as both an activity and academic discipline. In practice, these facets constantly interact and are each reinforced by the others, so inseparably entwined and closely braided that the boundaries among them can be difficult to determine exactly. Although the facets are treated individually here and throughout the coming chapters for descriptive purposes, they should not be viewed as independent; rather, they should be viewed as a seamless, interacting whole. Thus, for example, the technological facet cannot be understood without taking into consideration the economic, social, and political processes in which technological advances are embedded.

THE ECONOMIC FACET

The economic facet of culture concerns the allocation of scarce resources to produce and distribute goods and services necessary to ensure the smooth functioning of society. As "scarcity" implies, choice is at the heart of economics. In an environment of scarcity, choices must be made among options that are seldom perfect and whose future outcomes are rarely known. To this end, economic historian Robert L. Heilbroner identified three different methods for allocating

---

[3] Basil H. Liddell Hart, *Why Don't We Learn from History?* (London: G. Allen & Unwin, 1944), p. 7.

[4] Barbara S. Lawrence, "Historical Perspective: Using the Past to Study the Present," *Academy of Management Review* 9(2) (April 1984), pp. 307, 311.

[5] George E. Smith, "Management History and Historical Context: Potential Benefits of Its Inclusion in the Management Curriculum," *Academy of Management Learning & Education* 6(4) (December 2007), p. 524.

[6] Edward B. Tylor, *Primitive Culture: Researches into the Development of Mythology, Philosophy, Religion, Art, and Custom,* vol. 1 (London: John Murray, 1871), p. 1.

resources: *by tradition*, *by command*, and *by market forces*.[7] The *traditional method* allocates resources based on custom and belief. Occupations are passed down from one generation to the next, agriculture predominates over industry, and social and economic systems remain essentially closed to change. The *command method* is based on authority imposed by an economic "commander-in-chief." Resources are allocated based on the decree of a monarch, dictator, or central planning agency. In situations involving monarchs and dictators, one-man rule allows a single individual's interest to trump national interests. The *market method* relies on marketplace competition to maintain equilibrium between the supply and demand of resources and, in turn, automatically adjusts price levels, wages, and employment. As we will see in Chapter 2, the "market ethic" is associated with an intellectual movement (known as the Renaissance) that began in late fourteenth-century Italy and, subsequently, spread throughout Western Europe. The Renaissance saw a profound change in prevailing values toward people, work, and profits.

THE SOCIAL FACET

The social facet of culture concerns the patterns of behavior that develop between and among members of a society. "Humans have survived as a species not because [they] have physical advantages like size, strength, or speed, but because of [their] ability to connect in social groups."[8] Within these groups, humans exchange ideas, coordinate goals, and share unique information and experiences. Out of these social connections, a shared set of beliefs, values, and patterns of behavior must develop if a society is to achieve mutual understanding and a consensus among its members. Within societies, shared beliefs and values not only deepen social bonds, but define standards of acceptable behavior. Such standards vary within and across societies, as well as over time. As will be noted at several points throughout the coming chapters, questions of acceptable behavior and, particularly, ethical business behavior, have occupied theologians and philosophers since antiquity.

THE POLITICAL FACET

The political facet of culture concerns the relationship between individuals and sovereign states and includes institutional arrangements for establishing social order and protecting life and property. The absence of social order is anarchy; unless there is some provision for protecting rational from irrational actors (i.e., individuals or groups), economic, social, and political chaos will prevail. Political institutions that provide stability take various forms, ranging from representative governments to absolute dictatorships. Correspondingly, assumptions about the nature of humanity range from the belief that the citizens of a nation-state are capable of democratic self-government to the conviction that people cannot, or will not, govern themselves and, thus, require a governing elite to determine what is in their best interests. Provisions for property, contracts, and justice likewise vary according to the character of a nation's political institutions. In a democracy, people have private property rights, the freedom to enter or not to enter contracts, and an appeal system for justice. By contrast, in a dictatorship, the right to hold and use private property is severely restricted, freedom to contract is limited, and justice depends on the whims of one person. Management as an activity is affected by the character of a nation's political institutions, and the subsequent right of its citizens to hold or not hold property, to engage in contracts for the provision of goods and services, and to petition government for a redress of grievances.

---

[7] Robert L. Heilbroner, *The Making of Economic Society* (Englewood Cliffs, NJ: Prentice-Hall, 1962), pp. 10–16.
[8] Vivek H. Murthy, *Together: The Healing Power of Human Connection in a Sometimes Lonely World* (New York: HarperCollins, 2020), p. 65.

THE TECHNOLOGICAL FACET

The technological facet of culture concerns "the information, skills, processes, and procedures" used by a society "for accomplishing tasks."[9] The etymology of the English word "technology" may be traced back to the seventeenth century and the Greek words *technē* (art, craft, skill) and *logos* (knowledge) and, thus, may be interpreted to mean "knowledge about skillful practices."[10] Technology is, thus, more than computers, cell phones, and circuity. It also includes everything from recombinant DNA and artificial-intelligence software to engineering designs and specifications. Over the centuries, technology has changed the world, sometimes rapidly, other times more slowly, permeating every corner of modern life. As we will see in the next few chapters, "[t]echnological change is a dynamic and multidimensional phenomenon involving invention, innovation, transfer and diffusion of technology."[11] Because technological stagnation is generally a harbinger of economic decline, and prosperity, a quest for new technologies through advancements in scientific knowledge is never ending, impelling us to learn, to do better, to live better. In his First Annual Message to Congress on January 8, 1790, U.S. President George Washington urged his "Fellow Citizens of the Senate and House of Representatives" to encourage "exertions of skill and genius" in introducing "new and useful inventions" and to promote both science and literature, saying, "Knowledge is, in every country, the surest basis of publick happiness."[12] Washington understood that innovation and a nation's greatness are born from free enterprise, and believed that government exists to protect that freedom. He knew from history that, unless there is investment in innovation, a nation cannot grow, with the result being poverty, repression, civil discord, and ruin. Indeed, research has since shown that the best predictor of a nation's prosperity is its history of technological development.[13] As we will discuss in Chapter 3, the economic prosperity we enjoy today is a direct result of an increase in the rate of technological advancement that began in mid- to late-eighteenth-century Great Britain, soon spreading to continental Europe and the United States.

An appreciation of the foregoing economic, social, political, and technological facets, as they unite to form an expressive whole, is necessary for understanding how our ideas about the nature of work, the nature of human beings, and the nature of organizations have changed throughout history. Moreover, a consideration of the interactions among these facets highlights the wide variety and often dizzying complexity of the forces with which managers must contend in striving to accomplish desired goals.

PEOPLE, MANAGEMENT, AND ORGANIZATIONS

We now turn to a consideration of basic elements underlying the study of management as an activity and as an academic discipline. Even before people began to record their activities, they found it necessary to coordinate their combined efforts as they worked together to fulfill their shared needs. As an overview, Figure 1.1 places humans in a "state of nature" characterized by a relatively harsh environment and general scarcity of resources. Acknowledging that all people have a shared set of needs, it traces the quest for need satisfaction through the formation of economic, social, and political organizations. Management, an activity essential to organized endeavors, facilitates the satisfaction of people's needs.

---

[9] Stephen J. Kline, "What Is Technology?" *Bulletin of Science, Technology & Society* 5(3) (June 1985), p. 216.

[10] For a conceptual history of technology, see Eric Schatzberg, *Technology: A Critical History of a Concept* (Chicago, IL: Universality of Chicago Press, 2018).

[11] Govindan Parayil, "Models of Technological Change: A Critical Review of Current Knowledge," *History and Technology* 10(2/3) (1993), p. 105.

[12] George Washington, "Speech of the President of the United States to Congress," January 8, 1790, in *State Papers and Publick Documents of the United States from the Accession of George Washington to the Presidency: 1789–1796*, vol. 1 (Boston, MA: T. B. Wait and Sons, 1815), p. 15.

[13] Garett Jones, *The Culture Transplant: How Migrants Make the Economies They Move To a Lot Like the Ones They Left* (Stanford, CA: Stanford University Press, 2023), pp. 466–554.

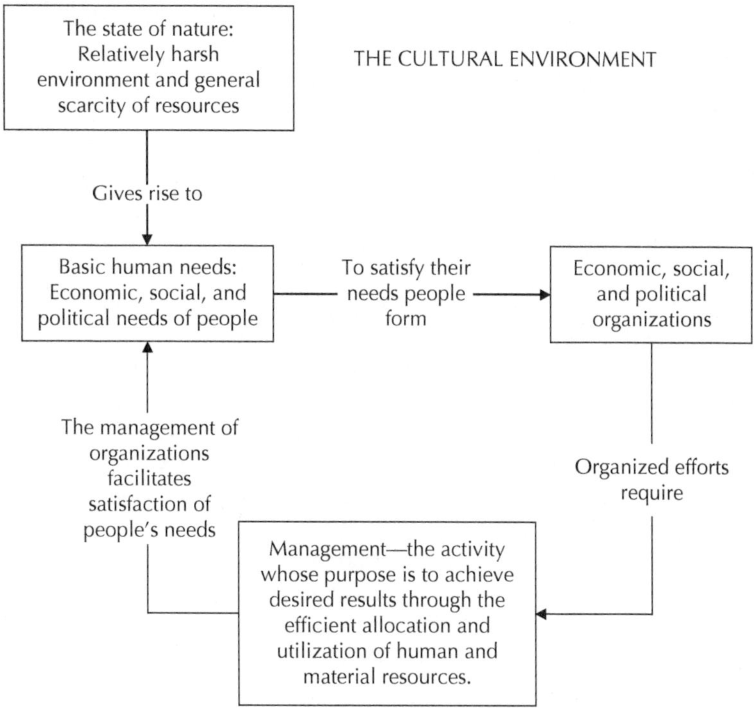

FIGURE 1.1 People, management, and organizations

HUMAN ACTIVITY

Human activity is the fundamental unit of analysis in the study of history, the study of organizations, and the study of management. Humans have historically faced a relatively hostile world characterized by a scarcity of food, inadequate shelter, and limited material resources with which to satisfy their many needs. By comparison, as noted, humans are biologically weaker than many other species. To explain their survival, we must look beyond physical prowess for other characteristics that have enabled humans to control and manipulate their environment.

The answer to the question of why humans have survived is found in their ability to reason. In the long evolutionary process, it was not always the most physically fit who survived; rather, it was the most cognitively capable who fashioned tools and weapons, mastered the use of fire, developed the ability to think conceptually, advanced their power of communication, and engaged in group activities that required a marked degree of planning and coordination. These were the people who fashioned clubs and spears for defense, created implements for tilling the soil, and cooperated with one another to give humans a differential advantage over their natural enemies.

Anthropologists have pushed our knowledge of humankind further and further into the past.[14] They have studied the origins of *Homo habilis,* "handy man," who fashioned tools; *Homo erectus,* who possessed bipedal ability; and *Homo sapiens,* the thinker. Humans are thinkers, doers, and makers; they are active, creative, and ever changing in their quest to better themselves and their species. Their most basic needs are physiological: food, water, shelter, sleep, and oxygen necessary for physical survival. Beyond these fundamental needs, social needs most probably arose out of the drive to reproduce and, thus, to select a mate. In turn, families became the most elementary unit forming human groups. With time, humans found that it was to their mutual advantage in gathering food, defending themselves, and arranging childcare to form kinship

[14] Jamie Shreeve, "Mystery Man," *National Geographic* 228(4) (October 2015), pp. 30–57.

groups, generally relatives of one another. As they grew larger, kinship groups were replaced by bands, whose members claimed descent from a common ancestor. Recognizing that they could better protect and enhance their welfare, bands formed tribes, which could embrace thousands of people. In historian Allen C. Guelzo's telling, for tribes to subsist, they had to be on the move to obtain food by hunting game or gathering seeds, nuts, berries, and wild fruits. Humans were hunter-gatherers for 100,000 years. Between 10,000 and 12,000 years ago, however, "tribes discovered that there was an easier and more secure way to feed and clothe themselves, and that way was agriculture."[15] This required that tribes remain in a fixed and secure location and gave rise to settled societies. Over time, individual tribe members developed occupations that served agriculture, including metalworking, weaving, stone-quarrying, and building. With the movement to settled farming, in due course, "the tribe became a nation associated with a fixed territory and a fixed religion and language."[16] In management historian Bradley G. Bowden's estimation, "The transition from hunter-gathering to an existence based around settled agricultures was one of the defining shifts in the human experience. It was upon the raising of crops . . . that the civilizations of the Old World and the New were built."[17] Biologist Jacob Bronowski has concluded with regard to our social relations: "We human beings are joined in families, the families are joined in kinship groups, the kinship groups in clans, the clans in tribes, and the tribes in nations."[18] This is humanity's primordial structure, linking generation to generation from the past to the present. As will be discussed beginning in Chapter 3, it has only been within the last few centuries that economies centered on agriculture have transitioned to industrial societies based on manufacturing and, even more recently, information technology.

ORGANIZATIONS AND MANAGEMENT

As humans have evolved, so have organizations. Early humans found that they could magnify their own abilities by working with others to better satisfy their respective needs. Differences in natural skills and abilities led to the observation that some people were better at certain tasks than others. Tasks, thus, were logically differentiated; that is, there was a division of labor to take advantage of inborn talents.[19] Once labor was divided, some agreement had to be reached about how to structure and interrelate various activities to accomplish desired goals. As the activities required to accomplish a task grew in number, it became necessary to combine similar tasks and develop a hierarchy of authority to assure adequate coordination across activities. Perhaps the wisest, the strongest, the eldest, or the most articulate group member became its leader, assigning tasks based on skill and ability. In any case, group members had to achieve some agreement about what was to be done, how it was to be done, and who would be responsible for expending the required effort. Indeed, as has been observed, "if left free of exogenous forces, any affinity group will naturally evolve a hierarchal network inherently structured to maximize the desired output of the group."[20]

The elements leading to the initial emergence of organizations are essentially the same throughout history. First, there must be a goal, a purpose, an objective, or something to be accomplished. Perhaps for our ancestors this was an annual berry harvest, a bison hunt, the harvesting of spring crops, or mounting a common defense from marauding nomads. Second, people must be sufficiently attracted to the goal. They must perceive that it is in their best interest to cooperate

[15] Allen C. Guelzo, "From Tribal Warfare to the Managerial State," *National Review* 73(24) (December 27, 2021), p. 19.
[16] *Ibid.*
[17] Bradley G. Bowden, *Slavery, Freedom and Business Endeavor: The Reforging of Western Civilization and the Transformation of Everyday Life* (Cham, Switzerland: Palgrave Macmillan, 2022), p. 45.
[18] Jacob Bronowski, *The Ascent of Man* (Boston, MA: Little, Brown and Company, 1973), p. 95.
[19] Emilio Depetris-Chauvin and Ömer Özak, "The Origins of the Division of Labor in Pre-Industrial Times," *Journal of Economic Growth* 25(3) (September 2020), pp. 297–340.
[20] Tim G. Jaeger, "Letters to the Editor: Constructal Law Faces the Deconstructalists," *Wall Street Journal* (February 9–10, 2019), p. A14.

in its accomplishment. The genesis of organized group activities can be found in people's attraction to others as a means of satisfying their own individual needs. Third, those joining in a group activity must possess the skills and abilities, weapons, tools, and other implements necessary for goal attainment. Fourth, the actions of group members must be structured in such a way as to further goal accomplishment. Proceeding without coordinating separate activities nurtures chaos. Finally, as undertakings became complex, groups soon discovered that goal accomplishment was more likely if someone was assigned the task of keeping everyone on course. Some central authority had to resolve differences of opinion, decide on strategy and timing, and, in a word, manage the people and activities necessary to succeed. This emergence of managing as a distinct role was to become an essential aspect of all cooperative endeavors.

Since the dawn of time, people have participated in organizations (whether families, kinship groups, clans, tribes, nations, mom-and-pop groceries, or *Fortune* 500 companies) to satisfy their needs. Different means for satisfying needs are reflected in arrangements for transmitting knowledge from one generation to the next, for protecting life and property, and, in general, for providing a seemingly unlimited variety of goods and services. As the human species has evolved over millions of years, people have sought to efficiently allocate and utilize human and material resources to achieve desired results. We call this art "management."

SUMMARY

Our ideas about the nature of work, nature of human beings, and nature of organizations have evolved throughout history. Likewise, our knowledge of how to manage has also developed within a cultural framework comprised of economic, social, political, and technological facets. As management thought is a product of a society's culture, it must be examined within this framework to be understood. Organizations naturally form as individuals seek to satisfy their needs through group action. In doing so, people expand on their own specialized talents to enrich their lives and the lives of others.

CHAPTER 2

Management Before Industrialization

Industrialization is a relatively recent phenomenon. Humans existed for eons before the great advances in power, transportation, communication, and technology that came to be known as the Industrial Revolution took place. Prior to the Industrial Revolution, organizations were primarily family-, church-, military-, or government-related. Some individuals engaged in economic undertakings (e.g., barbers, bakers, blacksmiths, cabinetmakers, cobblers, millers, tailors, wheelwrights), but not on a scale comparable to what emerged during the Industrial Revolution, starting in the mid-eighteenth century and accelerating thereafter. Nevertheless, there was still a need for management in conducting military campaigns and administering household, civic, and religious affairs. In this sense, as observed long ago, the art of management "is as old as the human race."[1] This chapter examines management in early civilizations preceding the Industrial Revolution. It also discusses the changing cultural values in these civilizations that led to the Industrial Revolution, the focus of Chapter 3.

MANAGEMENT IN EARLY CIVILIZATIONS

THE MIDDLE EAST

As group affiliations evolved from families to nations, the establishment and management of authority became a challenge. In families, authority rested in a patriarch or a matriarch, but in nations, there was often a conflict between chiefs and priests, the former claiming secular power and the latter heavenly dominion. From this struggle and divided authority came the idea of a priest-ruler or divine king. A king was not a King until ordained by priests, a tradition that long endured. One such divine king was Hammurabi (circa 1811–1750 BCE), who ruled over Babylon, located in the Middle East between the Tigris and Euphrates rivers and near modern Baghdad—an area that is often referred to as the Cradle of Civilization. Hammurabi believed his right to rule emanated from the sun-god, Shamash. In circa 1754 BCE, Hammurabi issued 282 laws he claimed to have received from this solar deity. The laws governed business dealings, personal behavior, interpersonal relations, punishments, and other societal matters. Law 104, for

[1] Edward D. Jones, "Military History and the Science of Business Administration: I. The Utility of the Study of History," *Engineering Magazine* 44(1) (October 1912), p. 1.

example, is the first historical reference to a form of accounting.[2] It required an agent acting on behalf of a merchant to provide the merchant with a receipt for the monetary value of any goods with which the agent was being entrusted and, in turn, to be given a receipt for any money the agent returned the merchant for the sale of the goods. Hammurabi's Code, as the laws came to be known, also regulated wages and fees, such as what a physician might charge for a broken bone, and what shepherds, field-laborers, boat builders, navigators, brickmakers, tailors, carpenters, stonecutters, and milkers might be paid.[3] By contrast, in 2000 BCE, at the Temples of Ur (near the mouth of the Tigris and Euphrates rivers), women weavers were paid with food rations in proportion to the amount of cloth they produced.[4] This possibly influenced the later biblical notion, "If anyone will not work, let him not eat" (2 Thess. 3:10); or, in the words of the Prophet Muhammad (circa 570–632 CE), "He who neither worketh for himself, nor for others, will not receive the reward of God."[5] In the case of the Ur weavers, the reason for working was clear. In Hammurabi's Code, however, there was no incentive to do more than the minimum a job required because wages and fees were regulated. Thus, here were early examples of bureaucratic authority and differing ideas about incentives, motivation, and workplace performance.

THE FAR EAST AND SOUTH ASIA

The ancient Chinese civilization occasionally opened its doors to let Westerners peek in. The Chinese general Sun Tzu (544–496 BCE) authored the oldest known military treatise. He wrote of marshaling an army into divisions; establishing gradations of military rank; and using gongs, flags, and signal fires for communications. Sun Tzu advocated lengthy deliberations and sound plans before going into battle: "Thus do many calculations [i.e., plans] lead to victory, and few calculations to defeat."[6] He commented on the distinct roles of line and staff managers and boldly advised: "The general that hearkens to my counsel and acts upon it, will conquer: . . . The general that hearkens not to my counsel nor acts upon it, will suffer defeat."[7] It appears that the challenges of managing line and staff relations are over 2,500 years old. Sun Tzu also provided strategic decision-rules for generals:

> This is the art of offensive strategy. . . .When ten to the enemy's one, surround him. . . . When five times his strength, attack him. . . .If double his strength, divide him. . . . If equally matched you may engage him. . . .If weaker numerically, be capable of withdrawing. . . . And if in all respects unequal, be capable of eluding him.[8]

If the rivalry among business competitors to achieve goals such as increased market share and higher profits is considered a surrogate for war, "competitive strengths" can be compared to "forces," and "competitor" to "enemy," and we can see an early pillar of modern management strategy.

Chinese philosopher Confucius (circa 551–479 BCE) and his followers have also had a lasting influence on Eastern thinking. His ideas on virtuous behavior, including tenets such as benevolence toward others, applying practical wisdom in making sound decisions, avoiding extremes, and living an exemplary life resonate even today. In Confucius's time, the highest goal

---

[2] Tom B. Jones, "Bookkeeping in Ancient Sumer," *Archæology* 9(1) (March 1956) pp. 16–21; Douglas Garbutt, "Modern Mesopotamian Accounting," *Accounting Historians Notebook* 8(1) (Spring 1985), pp. 10–11.

[3] Robert F. Harper, *The Code of Hammurabi, King of Babylon* (Chicago, IL: University of Chicago Press, 1904), pp. 77–95. Written circa 1755–1750 BCE.

[4] C. Leonard Woolley, *The Excavations at Ur and the Hebrew Records* (London: G. Allen & Unwin, 1929), pp.145–146.

[5] Prophet Muhammad, *The Sayings of Muhammad*, ed. Abdullah al-Māmūn al-Suhrawardy (London: A. Constable, 1905), p. 2.

[6] Sun Tzu, *Transcription of the Text of Sun Tzu on the Art of War: The Oldest Military Treatise in the World*, trans. Lionel Giles (London: Luzac, 1910), p. 27. Written circa 513 BCE.

[7] *Ibid.*, p. 26.

[8] Sun Tzu, *The Art of War*, trans. Samuel B. Griffith (Oxford, England: Oxford University Press, 1963), pp. 79–80. Written circa 513 BCE.

one could pursue was service in the Chinese government: merchants ranked only slightly above convicts in social esteem. The competition for governmental posts was severe, and Confucius believed that only those of proven ability should hold public offices. Written examinations to identify the empire's most talented subjects and bring them to the emperor's court as *mandarins* had been administered as early as 165 BC during the Han dynasty.[9]

Beginning in 650 CE, competitive exams were used to select candidates for the Chinese civil service based on merit rather than political or family connections.[10] After some 1,255 years, the exams were abolished in 1905 in the belief that they placed too much emphasis on outdated content (classical literature and philosophy) rather than modern technical knowledge in areas (engineering and science) deemed vital to China's economic development.[11] In addition to being aware of the importance of recruiting based on ability, there is evidence that the Chinese were familiar with the division of labor and departmentalization, or the grouping of activities, as early as 1 CE. For example, an inscription on a rice bowl from this period indicates that it was made in a government workshop where there was specialization among artisans divided into various departments. The workshop was subdivided into three departments: accounting, security, and production.[12] Such artifacts enable us to understand the earliest roots of management.

In ancient South Asia, Kautilya (also known as Chanakya; circa 350–275 BCE) was a noted and feared minister to Chandragupta Maurya, the greatest statesman of Hindu India.[13] Kautilya's *Arthaśāstra*, a treatise on statecraft, contained advice on establishing and maintaining economic, social, and political order. Kautilya cautioned that it was difficult to find competent public officials because humans "are naturally fickle-minded, and like horses at work exhibit constant change in their temper." He further warned that "it is impossible for a government servant not to eat up, at least, a bit of the king's revenue."[14] To maintain order, he advised tight controls, severe punishment, the use of workplace spies, and various ploys to test employee loyalty. Kautilya's assumptions about human nature are as modern as they are ancient, as are the prescriptions he provided on maintaining order. Although he was largely unknown in the Western world, his advice is reflected in the words of others. Kautilya also wrote on the desired traits for administrators ("of high family . . . wise . . . eloquent . . . intelligent, possessed of enthusiasm . . . affable") and how to select employees using interviews and by checking references. He commented further on consulting staff advisers ("consult three or four"), establishing departments with directors, and preparing detailed job descriptions for various offices.[15] Kautilya's writings highlight the antiquity of many management concepts and assumptions.

EGYPT

The ancient Egyptians developed extensive irrigation projects as an adjunct to the annual overflowing of the Nile River. Their engineering feats in building the Great Pyramids of Giza and the Canal of the Pharaohs (forerunner of the modern Suez Canal) were marvels superior to anything the Greeks and Romans later constructed. Mining and most engineering projects were government monopolies and required developing an extensive civil service to administer them. The

[9] Pan Ku, *The History of the Former Han Dynasty*, vol. 2, trans. Homer H. Dubs in collaboration with P'an Lo-chi and Jen T'ai (Baltimore, MD: Waverly Press, 1944), p. 343. Written between first-century and second-century CE.

[10] Benjamin A. Elman, "Civil Service Examinations (*Kējǔ* 科举)," in Linsun Cheng, ed., *Berkshire Encyclopedia of China: Modern and Historic Views of the World's Newest and Oldest Global Power*, vol. 5 (Great Barrington, MA: Berkshire Publishing Group, 2009), pp. 405–410.

[11] By Ying Bai and Ruixue Jia, "Elite Recruitment and Political Stability: The Impact of the Abolition of China's Civil Service Exam," *Econometrica* 84(2) (March 2016), pp. 677–733.

[12] Rodger D. Collons, "Factory Production – 1 A.D.," *Academy of Management Journal* 14(2) (June 1971), pp. 270–273.

[13] Jawaharlal L. Nehru, *The Discovery of India* (Delhi: Oxford University Press, 1946), pp. 125–126. See also Sandeep Singh, "Wise Leadership in Kautilya's Philosophy," *Philosophy of Management* 15(1) (February 2016), pp. 35–49.

[14] Kautilya, *Arthaśāstra* [*The Science of Political and Economic Relations*], trans. Rudrapatna Shamasastry (Bangalore: Government Press, 1915), pp. 77, 79. Written between second-century BCE and third-century CE.

[15] *Ibid.*, pp. 16, 32.

labor force for such projects consisted of both slaves (selected from war captives and subject peoples) and simple peasants. Strong cultural traditions bound individuals to occupations, and chains and whips suppressed other labor problems.[16]

There is evidence that the early Egyptians were aware of limits to the number of laborers one overseer could supervise. Excavated engravings suggest a ratio of about ten laborers to one overseer. Excavations have also revealed distinctive dress for overseers and laborers. Overseers wore kilts or robes, whereas laborers were dressed to represent their trade or occupation.[17] The "rule of ten" as a limit on an overseer's "span of control" was an Egyptian practice that can be found in numerous civilizations, as we shall see shortly.

The most important official in ancient Egypt was the *vizier*, who served the pharaoh as chief political advisor and supervised the administration of the country. It is from the word *vizier* that we derive the word *supervisor*. The existence of a *vizier* was recorded as early as 1750 BCE. One of the best-known *viziers* was the Hebrew-Israelite named Joseph, son of Jacob, who had been sold into Egyptian bondage by his brothers (Genesis 37:2–36). Because of Joseph's ability to forecast the future, Pharaoh made him *vizier*. This was a clear delegation of authority, leaving spiritual matters in his own hands and secular matters in Joseph's care. As *vizier*, Joseph was the second most powerful person in ancient Egypt. He was an organizer, coordinator, and decision-maker. Under Joseph's direction, an elaborate bureaucracy was developed to measure the level of the Nile River—on which every part of the economy depended—to forecast grain production and revenues, allocate these revenues to various governmental units, and supervise all industry and trade. This involved some rather sophisticated (for the times) management techniques, including forecasting, planning, division of labor and departmentalization, and a well-trained "professional" bureaucracy to function.

THE HEBREWS

The Old Testament is a story of a people in the quest of a land. In addition to Joseph, other Hebrew leaders combined spiritual and secular powers, including Abraham (circa 1900 BCE), Moses (circa 1300 BCE), and David (circa 1000 BCE). After these great leaders had passed away, tribal leadership became the task of judges, who led by virtue of possessing spiritual power, or what has come down to us as "charisma"—in this case, a gift of the Holy Spirit. The Book of Judges in the Bible tells how 12 judges, in successive reigns amounting to 410 years, held sway over Israel.

It is very likely, however, that the Egyptians provided the seeds for management concepts found in the Bible. Joseph was sold into slavery, rose to be Pharaoh's *vizier*, and gained valuable administrative experience. Moses, while in captivity in Egypt, observed the Egyptian "rule of ten." The Bible tells us that on the advice of his father-in-law, Jethro (thus making Jethro the first known management consultant), Moses "chose able men from all over Israel and made them judges over the people—thousands, hundreds, fifties, and tens. They were constantly available to administer justice. They brought the hard cases to Moses but judged the smaller matters themselves" (Exod. 18:25–26). Thus, Moses employed the most fundamental control technique, management by exception, as well as established a more orderly structure for tribal management. Other managerial advice can be found in the Bible: "Without deliberation, plans come to nothing; where counselors are many, plans succeed" (Prov. 15:22). This bears a marked resemblance to the advice of Sun Tzu, who was a continent and many years away. For controlling, we are told: "Where there are many hands, lock things up" (Eccles. 42:6).[18] Leadership, delegation,

---

[16] For a further discussion of Ancient Egypt's economy, see Jean-Loup Richet, "A Loose Coupling Perspective on Ancient Egypt Economy and Society," *Business History* 64(6) (September 2022), pp. 1149–1171.

[17] William. M. Flinders Petrie, *Social Life in Ancient Egypt* (Boston, MA: Houghton Mifflin, 1923), pp. 21–22.

[18] For other examples, see Sterling R. McLean, "The Evolution of Principles of Organization Structure" (Doctoral dissertation, University of Texas, Austin, TX, 1961); Robert L. Hagerman, "Accounting in the Bible," *Accounting Historians Journal* 7(2) (Fall 1980), pp. 71–76; William Ritchie, David Cavazos, Justin Barnard, and Charles White, "The Ancient Hebrew Culture: Illustrations of Modern Strategic Management Concepts in Action," *Business History* 54(7) (December, 2012), pp. 1099–1117.

span of control, planning, organizing, and controlling were managerial practices found among ancient peoples.

GREECE

Philosopher Will Durant captured the essence of the rise and fall of many civilizations in writing: "A nation is born stoic, and dies epicurean."[19] In the stoic phase of this cycle, adversity breeds cohesion, and deprivation fosters initiative. Self-control, thrift, hard work, and an orderly life bring prosperity. As affluence reigns, self-control becomes self-indulgence, thrift becomes a vice, industry and perseverance yield opportunism, and social order breaks down. With no thought for tomorrow, collapse begins. Commenting specifically on the breakdown of ancient Greece, historian Arnold J. Toynbee argued that its decline was "a case of suicide and not a case of murder."[20] Echoing this theme, military theorist B. H. Liddell Hart noted, "the downfall of civilized States tends to come not from the direct assaults of foes, but from internal decay."[21] This cycle was true for Greece and Rome.

The institutions, art, language, drama, and literature of ancient Greece form a significant part of Western culture. Greek economic philosophy, however, was antibusiness. Trade and most commerce were considered beneath the dignity of Greek aristocrats. Profit-making was seen as dishonorable, as were those who pursued it. As Greek philosopher Aristotle (384–322 BCE) explained, for the greatest happiness "citizens . . . must not live the life of mechanics or tradesmen, for such a life is ignoble and inimical to virtue."[22] Prestige was directly proportional to the amount of time a person spent engaged in leisurely pursuits. The liberation of the mind was considered the highest ideal of human development. Manual labor was for slaves, brought back as prisoners of war, and the working classes.[23] Business and agriculture were for "freedmen" (i.e., former slaves) and resident foreigners. Affairs of state were controlled by an oligarchy of privileged citizens and their descendants. All others were denied the privileges and immunities of citizenship.

Socrates (469–399 BCE), one of the greatest of Greek philosophers, believed in the transferability of managerial knowledge: He held that "the conduct of private affairs differs from that of public concerns only in magnitude; in other respects they are similar . . . neither of them are managed without men . . . and those who know how to employ them, conduct either public or private affairs judiciously, while those who do not know, will err in the management of both."[24] Plato (circa 428–348 BCE), a pupil of Socrates, remarked on human diversity and how this led to the division of labor:

> . . . I am reminded . . . that we are not all alike; there are diversities of natures among us which are adapted to different occupations. . . . And, if so, we must infer that all things are produced more plentifully and easily and of a better quality when one man does one thing which is natural to him and does it at the right time, and leaves other things.[25]

---

[19] William J. Durant, *The Story of Civilization*, vol. 1: *Our Oriental Heritage* (New York: Simon and Schuster, 1935), p. 259.
[20] Arnold J. Toynbee, *A Study of History*, vol. 4: *The Breakdowns of Civilization* (London: Oxford University Press, 1939), pp. 68, 63.
[21] Basil H. Liddell Hart, *Why Don't We Learn from History?* (London: G. Allen & Unwin, 1944), p. 49.
[22] Aristotle, *The Politics of Aristotle*, vol. 1, trans. Benjamin Jowett (Oxford, England: Clarendon Press, 1885), p. 221. Written in fourth-century BCE. See also Denis Collins, "Aristotle and Business," *Journal of Business Ethics* 6(10) (October 1987), pp. 567–572.
[23] Rodolfo Mondolfo, "The Greek Attitude to Manual Labour," trans. David S. Duncan, *Past & Present* no. 6 (November 1954), pp. 1–5.
[24] Xenophon, *The Anabasis, or Expedition of Cyrus, and The Memorabilia of Socrates*, trans. John S. Watson (London: Henry G. Bohn, 1854), p. 433. Originally written circa 421 BCE.
[25] Plato, *The Dialogues of Plato*, 2nd ed., vol. 3, trans. Benjamin Jowett (Oxford, England: Clarendon Press, 1875), pp. 240–241. Written circa 380 BCE.

The notion that a division of labor optimized productivity would persist for nearly 2,000 years, forming the basis for organizing work and determining how to best use individual differences in knowledge, skills, and abilities.

Despite his disparaging view of profit-making, Aristotle, Plato's most famous student, provided numerous insights into management and organization. Examples from his classic *Politics* (circa 350 BCE) include:

> On the specialization of labor: "[E]very work is better done which receives the sole, and not the divided attention of the worker."
>
> On departmentalization: "[E]very office should have a special function [and one question is] should offices be divided according to the subjects with which they deal, or according to the persons with which they deal?"
>
> On centralization, decentralization, and delegation of authority: "We should also know when local tribunals are to have jurisdiction over many different matters, and when authority should be centralized; for example, should one person keep order in the market and another in some other place, or should the same person be responsible everywhere?"
>
> On synergy: "The whole is naturally superior to the part."
>
> On leadership: "[H]e who has never learned to obey cannot be a good commander."[26]

Aristotle's *Nicomachean Ethics* (circa 350 BCE) guided Western thought for millennia on how we should conduct ourselves in our relations with others. Borrowing from Plato, Aristotle described the cardinal virtues of prudence (practical wisdom in making rational choices), temperance (moderation and self-control), courage (fortitude and endurance), and justice (the equitable exchange of goods and the fulfillment of contractual obligations). He observed that achieving virtuous behavior required teaching, experience, and time for developing one's disposition to act appropriately by doing the right thing at the right time for the right reasons.

In his *Metaphysics* (circa 350 BCE), Aristotle discussed abstract topics such as different kinds of causality, types of knowledge, and the nature of time, and advanced his thesis that the nature of reality is knowable only through the senses and through reason. For some 2000 years, Aristotle's ideas on "being" ("what makes a thing what it is") would shape conceptions about the best way to understand the physical world, the arts, and virtue. By rejecting mysticism, Aristotle became the father of the scientific method and established the intellectual foundation for the Italian Renaissance, which we will discuss shortly. Eventually, this spirit of scientific inquiry would form a basis for scientific management (Chapter 7).

Another Greek, Xenophon (circa 430–354 BCE), described the advantages of the division of labor (circa 370 BCE):

> [T]here are places [workshops] even where one man earns a living by only stitching shoes, another cutting them out, another by sewing the uppers together, while there is another who performs none of these operations but only assembles the parts. It follows, therefore, as a matter of course, that he who devotes himself to a very highly specialized line of work is bound to do it in the best possible manner.[27]

In 146 BCE, Greece fell to the Romans, a hardy stock of people from the banks of the Tiber River. Greece destroyed itself by depleting its forests and natural resources, by internal moral decay, by political disorder, and by decimating its leadership through revolts and counter-revolts. Despite its use of enslaved labor and its antibusiness sentiments, ancient Greece sowed the first seeds of democracy and saw the advent of decentralized participatory government, the

[26] Aristotle, *The Politics of Aristotle*, vol. 1, pp. 137–138, 105, 74.

[27] Xenophon, *Cyropaedia*, vol. 2, trans. Walter Miller (London: W. Heinemann, 1914), p. 333. Written circa 370 BCE.

first attempts to establish individual liberties, and the beginnings of the scientific method, as well as early insights into the division of labor, departmentalization, delegation of authority, and leadership.

ROME

According to legend, Rome was founded by the twin brothers Romulus and Remus on April 27, 753 BCE. Rome was born "stoic" and conquered the decaying Hellenic civilization. The Romans developed a quasi-factory system to manufacture armaments for their military legions, produce earthenware for a world market, and, later, make textiles to be sold for export. The famous Roman road system was built to speed the distribution of goods and rapidly move legionnaires to dissident colonies. Roman patricians (from the Latin *patres*, "fathers") inherited the Greek disdain for trade and left business activities in the hands of the nominally inferior class of freedmen and plebeians (from the Latin *plebs*, "the multitude").[28] As a growing external trade in foodstuffs, animal products, and materials for manufacturing and construction required commercial standardization, the Romans established a guaranteed system of measures, weights, and coins. The first resemblance to a corporate organization appeared in the form of joint-stock companies, which were companies owned collectively by their shareholders. These companies were involved in fulfilling government contracts for necessary war supplies and equipment.[29] With few exceptions, a highly specialized labor force worked in small shops owned by independent artisans. Men who shared a common occupation (e.g., sack carriers, grain measurers, bargemen, ship pilots) formed associations called guilds (*collegia*). These, however, did not function as unions to control wages, hours, or conditions of employment, but to screen members and punish any who stole or were otherwise corrupt, so as to protect a guild's reputation.[30] The Roman Republic (and later Empire) governed all aspects of economic life: it levied tariffs on goods, fined monopolists, and regulated guilds. Large-scale organizations could not exist because joint-stock companies were prohibited for any purpose other than the execution of government contracts.

The Roman Army followed the "rule of ten," although its application varied from time to time. The Roman cavalry had *decuriones,* units of 10 horse soldiers, with 3 *decuriones* constituting a *turma*, and 10 *turmae* (300 cavalry) supporting a legion. Centurions commanded *centuries* of some 100 foot soldiers, and these centuries were organized into cohorts, with 10 cohorts making up a legion. Thus, the Roman genius for order and discipline established units to perform certain tasks, as well as a hierarchy of command or authority to ensure performance.[31] Other Roman contributions to our shared heritage came chiefly from law and government, which were manifestations of a concern for order. Roman law became a guide for later civilizations, and the Roman separation of legislative and executive powers provided a model system of checks and balances for later constitutional governments.

THE ROMAN CATHOLIC CHURCH

From its seedbed in the Middle East, Christianity faced theological as well as organizational challenges. As the Christian faith spread, novel sects (each interpreting the Bible differently) multiplied, and the first blush of a youthful theology threatened to become an adolescence of diversity. Early congregations operated independently, each defining its own doctrine and conditions for membership. Bishops became heads of various local churches, and presbyters and deacons began to appear as their assistants. By the third-century CE, an ascending hierarchy

[28] James W. Gilbart, *Lectures on the History and Principles of Ancient Commerce* (London: Smith, Elder and Co., 1847), p. 223.
[29] Peter Temin, *The Roman Market Economy* (Princeton, NJ: Princeton University Press, 2013), p. 188.
[30] *Ibid.*, pp. 109–110.
[31] Barbara Czarniawska, "Organizing in the Roman Empire," in Tuomo Peltonen, Hugo Gaggiotti, and Peter Case, eds., *Origins of Organizing* (Cheltenham, UK: 2018), pp. 91–113.

based on rank was more apparent, with the addition of subdeacons and acolytes, who assisted with personal and secretarial matters, and exorcists and readers, who performed liturgical duties. At the Council of Arles (314 CE), some bishops were made superior to others, giving rise to a chief bishop, the Bishop of Rome. At the Council of Nicaea (325 CE), the Bishop of Rome was given primal authority as "rector of the whole church," and given the title Pope (*papa*). The outcome was centralized doctrine and temporal (earthly) authority in Rome and the Papacy. Conflict between centralized and decentralized authority, however, has reappeared throughout history, not only in early Christianity, but also in other organizations. In modern terms, church leaders of all faiths have perceived a need to institutionalize; that is, to specify policies, procedures, ecclesiastical doctrine, and differences in authority. This is a recurring challenge even today, given the need for unanimity of purpose, yet discretion for local conditions.

FEUDALISM

Feudalism, as a cultural system, prevailed in Europe from about the ninth- to tenth-centuries CE. At the base of the feudalistic system were serfs, who tilled plots of land owned by manorial lords, much like modern sharecroppers, and were given military protection in exchange for a portion of their crops. Feudalism bound serfs to a lord, set rigid class distinctions, and established a landed aristocracy that endured until the Industrial Revolution. By its nature, feudalism stifled improvements in education, making poverty and ignorance the hallmark of the masses. Many of the challenges typically associated with the Industrial Revolution surfaced during this earlier period. People razed the forests for firewood and overgrazed or carelessly tilled open lands. As forests dwindled, coal became a more important source of fuel, thereby creating air pollution. Eleanor of Provence, Queen consort of England, was forced from her castle at Nottingham in 1257 by the coal smoke and fumes from a nearby village. Water pollution resulted from human and animal waste flowing from open sewers into surrounding streams. Conditions grew worse until the English Parliament passed the first known antipollution legislation in 1388, almost four centuries before the Industrial Revolution.[32]

THE REVIVAL OF COMMERCE

Feudalism saw the spread of Christianity (specifically Roman Catholicism) as the nobility funded religious activities in return for divine favor. The spread of Christianity, in turn, gave birth to the Crusades, a series of religious wars in the eleventh to fourteenth centuries between Christians and Muslims. The Crusades were undertaken by European Christians to recover the Holy Land from Muslim control. They stimulated commerce by opening additional trade routes and exposing parochial, feudal Europe to the riches of the Middle East. This increased worldliness weakened the Catholic Church's influence, as returning crusaders questioned the Papacy's political power and wealth. The feudal system was also disrupted, as thousands of young, aristocratic landowners died in the Crusades and many others sold estates, freeing their serfs in the process, to repay money borrowed to finance their crusading. Further, though they embarked on their journeys with invincible religious convictions, the Crusaders often returned home with the realization that Middle Eastern culture was in many ways superior to their own with regard to manners, morals, trade, industry, and warfare.

Another revelation arrived in the form of travelers who in the mid-thirteenth and fourteenth centuries ventured to the Middle and Far East and wrote accounts of their journeys.[33] Perhaps

[32] Charles H. Cooper, *Annals of Cambridge*, vol. 1 (Cambridge, England: Warwick and Co., 1842), p. 133.

[33] For more on these early travelers, see Manuel Komroff, ed., *Contemporaries of Marco Polo, Consisting of the Travel Records to the Eastern Parts of the World of William of Rubruck (1253–1255); the Journey of John of Pian de Carpini (1245–1247); the Journal of Friar Odoric (1318–1330) & the Oriental Travels of Rabbi Benjamin of Tudela (1160–1173)* (New York: Boni & Liveright, 1928).

the most well-known of these intrepid explorers was a Venetian trader, Marco Polo (1254–1324), who returned from 24 years in Tibet, China, Burma, India, and beyond in 1295. Polo told fantastic tales of a hitherto unseen part of the world. In addition, he recounted how the Tartar tribes of Mongolia and Manchuria organized their armies: "When a Tartar lord goes to war, he has with him 100,000 men. He places a chief over every ten, every hundred, every thousand, every ten thousand, so that each officer, even the commander of the hundred thousand, has to deal with only ten persons; for he gives his orders to the chiefs of ten thousand, they to those of one thousand, they to those of a hundred; and thus every man answers to his captain."[34]

The cultural eye-opening of the Crusades led to a more secular life in Europe through a further weakening of religious bonds. Interest arose in exploration, and a growing spirit of trade and commerce undercut feudalism. Expanded markets, fresh ideas, the rise of towns, the first seeds of a middle class, freer circulation of money and credit instruments, and the resurgence of political order created the base for both the Italian Renaissance and the ensuing Protestant Reformation (1517–1648) in Western Europe.

Before the Industrial Revolution, how were goods produced? Many products were made or grown in the home for a family's use. Other products, however, arose from two basic systems of industrial organization: guilds and the domestic system of production. European guilds, as far as we know, existed primarily between 1100 and 1790, and consisted of two types: *merchant guilds*, which included both wholesalers and retailers who were involved in local and long-distance trade, and *craft guilds*, which were comprised of skilled artisans (such as bakers, blacksmiths, candlemakers, carpenters, cobblers, dyers, jewelers, masons, metalworkers, and weavers) representing a single craft. Within craft guilds, there was a hierarchy of authority descending from masters to journeymen to apprentices. Masters owned workshop tools and raw materials; journeymen were paid workers who had finished their apprenticeship but had not yet opened their own shop; and apprentices were those who were learning a craft. Towns and villages typically regulated the number of masters in each craft, the number of apprentices in a workshop, and the *maximum* wages an apprentice could earn. If an apprentice ran away, wanted posters were circulated and law enforcement authorities were sent to retrieve the culprit. Local officials, who forbade the entry of products from outside a village and, in turn, taxed or licensed guilds to pay for such protection, shielded each guild from competition.

Craft guilds regulated quality and acted to control certain types of work: for example, craft-guild rules prohibited shoemakers from tanning hides, which was the job of tanners, and weavers from dyeing cloth, which was the job of dyers. Tanners and dyers, likewise, had to stick to their own work. Thus, craft guilds used the division of labor to gain greater job control. The modern union practices of controlling job access and engaging in jurisdictional disputes over the right to perform certain jobs or duties are a legacy of early craft guilds.[35]

During the seventeenth and eighteenth centuries, merchant guilds were the cornerstone of what was called the domestic, or "putting-out," system of production. They "put out" raw materials to individuals or families who, using their own equipment, produced items in their homes that the merchants would then purchase and sell. Beyond little direct control over quality, the faults of the domestic system lay in simple tools and technology, with little incentive for improvement, and in the inefficiencies of small-scale production with a limited division of labor. As the volume of trade grew, the domestic system of production proved inefficient, and the need for more capital, the benefits of specialized labor, and the economies of scale derived from a centralized workplace led to the factory system.

Growing trade also required improved accounting methods. Although Italian traders and bankers such as Francesco di Marco Datini of Prato and the Medicis of Florence were using the

[34] Marco Polo, *The Travels of Marco Polo*, 2nd ed., ed. Hugh Murray (Edinburgh, Scotland: Oliver & Boyd, 1844), p. 261. Written in 1298.

[35] Sheilagh Ogilvie, *The European Guilds: An Economic Analysis* (Princeton, NJ: Princeton University Press, 2019), pp. 168–171.

essentials of double-entry bookkeeping (*doppia scrittura*) as early as 1340,[36] a Franciscan friar, Luca Pacioli, first described this advance in his *Summa de Arithmetica, geometria, proportioni et proportionalita* in 1494.[37] Pacioli's system was the earliest information system for management: it provided merchants with information on cash and inventory and enabled a check on cash flow, but did not keep track of costs. It would be some 400 years before any advancements were made in double-entry bookkeeping.

As trade expanded, more souls were placed in jeopardy with respect to the prevailing Roman Catholic doctrine against charging interest to earn personal profit on borrowed money as opposed to helping others. Saint Thomas Aquinas, a thirteenth-century Italian Dominican, had addressed the issue of justice in trade matters with the idea of a "just price."[38] Rather than being "dependent on the play of supply and demand," the just price of, for example, a pair of shoes, included "the cost of the raw materials, the amount needed to sustain the worker at his usual standards of life while making the shoes (i.e., cost of labor), and a small item not so much of profit as of wages of management for the seller."[39] For Acquinas, then, the market price is the just price if buyer and seller are honest and not attempting to deceive each other. Dominican Friar Johannes Nider, active in early fifteenth-century Germany, extended this notion by developing certain trade rules (we might call them, as a whole, a code of ethical conduct), which, if followed, would assure merchants that their transactions were just. For example, the rules declared that goods should be "lawful, honorable, and useful"; prices should be just; sellers should beware (*caveat venditor*) and not engage in "trickery" or "intimidation" or sell to "simpletons," who would not be informed buyers; and those who buy "looking for nothing but a rise in prices [i.e., financial speculators], sin most gravely."[40] Nider's trade rules were published at Cologne in about 1468 and, by 1490, had been reprinted ten times. This was the first publication to focus on business ethics, and its early publication and appeal suggest that a concern for ethical trade practices has a long history. As one author summarized Nider's message for the present age:

> Nider's thoughts are surprisingly modern. . . . Through his eyes we see the moral dilemmas of the past and of the present; the moral choices that must be made in everyday life in business and our personal conduct; and the need for guidelines that provide the ropes to keep us from falling. Nider addressed evergreen issues that ethicists faced in the past and encounter in the present—that laws alone cannot deflect human frailties nor chicanery; that ultimate responsibility for one's actions cannot be avoided; and that virtuous conduct is necessary in exchange relationships.[41]

Feudalism was dead, interred by expanding trade, growing urbanization, the creation of a merchant class, and the development of strong central governments. The age of industrialization, however, had not yet arrived. What was needed now was a fresh spirit, an affirmative license for human initiative and self-fulfillment.

CULTURAL REBIRTH

From its beginnings in late fourteenth-century Italy, the intellectual movement known as the Renaissance (from the French word for "rebirth," symbolizing the rebirth of classical antiquity) subsequently spread throughout Western Europe.[42] With the rediscovery of ancient Greek and

[36] Raymond de Roover, "The Development of Accounting Prior to Luca Pacioli According to the Account-books of Medieval Merchants" in Ananias C. Littleton and Basil S. Yamey, eds., *Studies in the History of Accounting* (Homewood, IL: Richard D. Irwin, 1956), pp. 114–174.

[37] Luca Pacioli, *Summa de Arithmetica, geometria, proportioni et proportionalita* [*Summary of Arithmetic, Geometry, Proportions and Proportionality*] (Venice: Paganino Paganini, 1494).

[38] Thomas Aquinas, *The "Summa Theologica" of St. Thomas Aquinas*, trans. Fathers of the English Dominican Province (New York: Benziger Brothers, 1911), vol. 2, part II, second number, pp. 317–320. Written between 1259 and 1272.

[39] C. Crane Brinton, *Ideas & Men: The Story of Western Thought* (New York: Prentice-Hall, 1950), pp. 208, 205.

[40] Johannes Nider, *On the Contracts of Merchants*, trans. Charles H. Reeves and ed. Ronald B. Shuman (Norman, OK: University of Oklahoma Press, 1966), pp. 38–45. Written circa 1430 and published circa 1468.

[41] Daniel A. Wren, "Medieval or Modern? A Scholastic's View of Business Ethics, circa 1430." *Journal of Business Ethics* 28(2) (November 2000), p. 117.

[42] For a discussion about why the Renaissance originated in Italy (specifically Florence), see Renaissance," in *New World Encyclopedia* (2015). Available online at https://www.newworldencyclopedia.org/p/index.php?title=Renaissance&oldid=989270.

Roman manuscripts—some in Catholic convents and monasteries and others in Islamic libraries in the Middle East and North Africa—the Renaissance revitalized all aspects of Western culture, and is seen as marking the transition from medieval to modern times.[43] The roots and course of three ethics, or standards for individual behavior, that subsequently interacted to change prevailing values toward people, work, and profits may be traced to this renewal. The *Protestant ethic*, which flowed from the Protestant Reformation, ended the near millennium-long religious dominance of the Roman Catholic Church in Western Europe. The *liberty ethic* imposed legal limits on political power by promoting representative government. The *market ethic*, first mentioned in Chapter 1, brought forth the notion of a market-directed economy. Together these three ethics established the foundations of an industrial age that brought people from subservience to a newfound freedom in allocating resources, in social relations, and in political institutions. The outcome of the resulting cultural rebirth was the creation of an environmental ethos that would lead to the formal study of management.

THE PROTESTANT ETHIC

During the Middle Ages, the Roman Catholic Church dominated life in Western Europe. It offered the faithful the hope of eternal happiness in Heaven as a consolation for their worldly plight, whereas those found lacking were doomed to eternal punishment in Hell. The Church's warnings against lending money with interest to other Christians (per Exod. 22:25; Lev. 25:35–38; Deut. 23:19–20), against desiring anything from this world other than subsistence, and against materialistic trade cast business activity as inherently evil. As viewed by the Church, trade encouraged sin by diverting people's thoughts from God to personal gain, from obedience to initiative, and from humility to activity. Indeed, the Holy Scripture expressly warns: "As a nail sticketh fast between the joinings of the stones; so doth sin stick close between buying and selling" (Eccles. 27:2).

Johannes Gutenberg's introduction of the first movable-type printing press in mid-fifteenth-century Europe, however, challenged the Catholic Church's monopoly on matters of faith and morals by allowing unmediated access to sacred texts. "Before Gutenberg, one narrative of reality predominated Western society. By democratizing access to the written word, the press overthrew Rome's monopoly on ideas and allowed competing interpretations to proliferate."[44] Previously, the mass of believers only experienced the Bible in fragments, as paraphrased or quoted in sermons. Moreover, with the translation and printing of the Bible into languages other than Latin, lay readers could decide the meaning of scripture for themselves and, thus, challenge the clergy's teachings and power that structured the faithful's lives.[45] Pre-Reformation English church and monarchical authorities were so frightened of laypersons reading and understanding the Bible on their own that possession of English-language scripture was outlawed from 1408 until 1535 for all but the most privileged.[46] Bible translations liberated people to think their own thoughts and worship as they chose. This led to a withering of religious bonds, as Christian orthodoxy, including papal pronouncements on the everyday lives of the devoted, was increasingly questioned, ultimately igniting a revolt against the Church.

Although other individuals had earlier rejected papal authority and Catholic doctrine, 33-year-old Augustinian Friar Martin Luther, a Wittenberg University lecturer, is generally considered the architect of what became known as the Protestant Reformation. Legend holds that on October 31, 1517, he nailed to the door of All Saints' Church in Wittenberg (Saxony) a list of 95

---

[43] Martin L. McLaughlin, "The Rediscovery of Classical Texts," in Angus Mackay with David Ditchburn, eds., *Atlas of Medieval Europe* (London: Routledge, 1997), pp. 239–241.

[44] Orrin Hatch, "Higher Ed and the Fragmentation of America," *Wall Street Journal* (July 24, 2020), p. A17.

[45] Bernard Cottret, *Calvin: A Biography*, trans. M. Wallace McDonald (Grand Rapids, MI: William B. Eerdmans, 2000), pp. 93–94. French edition published in 1995.

[46] Philip Schaff, *History of the Christian Church*, vol. 5 (part 2): *The Middle Ages*, ed. David S. Schaff, (New York: Charles Scribner's Sons, 1910), p. 344; Mary Dove, *The First English Bible: The Text and Context of the Wycliffite Versions* (Cambridge, England: Cambridge University Press, 2007), p. 58.

theses (a list of questions and propositions) challenging the teachings of the Church. The theses are generally believed to have been the catalyst for the Protestant Reformation, which divided the fifteen-hundred-year-old Roman Catholic Church into two churches—one loyal to Pope Leo X in Rome and the other, in protest to the Pope's rule, becoming known as the Protestant Church. The split launched over a century of religious conflict throughout Europe, and led to the creation of dozens of Protestant denominations, Lutheranism, among them. Although Luther protested many of what he considered to be the Church's abuses, especially the selling of indulgences or pardons granted for the remission of sins and guaranteed entry into Heaven, he agreed with the Church on other matters. Like the Church, Luther considered lending money with interest to be the "sin of usury," believing that, rather than exploiting the temporary needs of a borrower, a loan should be an act of compassion; considered trade a "nasty business"; and spoke out vehemently against the Fuggers of Augsburg, the leading banking family in Germany, for engaging in usury. On January 3, 1521, Pope Leo X excommunicated Luther based on purported errors in his 95 theses and other writings. Three months later, he was summoned to defend his beliefs at a meeting of the Diet (i.e., assembly) of the Holy Roman Empire held at Worms, Germany. Declaring that he was bound by the Word of God, Luther refused to recant his offensive views and seek forgiveness.[47] Luther was subsequently declared an outlaw by Holy Roman Emperor Charles V, to be captured and punished as a heretic. The reading, possession, sale, or printing of Luther's writings was henceforth forbidden. Luther spent the following months at Wartburg Castle under the protection of Friedrich III of Saxony. It was here that he began translating the Bible into German.

In Switzerland, Frenchman John Calvin was inspired by Luther and, like Luther, believed in predestination, the New Testament–based doctrine that all events were willed by God. Calvin taught that God predestined some ("the elect") to be saved, whereas others, who God knew would not follow his teachings, were doomed to ever-lasting damnation. By leaving individuals in doubt about their salvation "yet holding out the chance of grace," predestination encouraged the faithful to act as if they were already among the elect—"sober, earnest, hardworking."[48] Eager to confirm that they were among those to be saved, Calvinists maintained that success gained through hard work would verify their elect status.[49] Indeed, success in business was almost seen as "a sign of spiritual grace, for it is proof that a man has labored faithfully in his vocation, and that 'God has blessed his trade.'"[50] Thus, according to Weber, the doctrine of predestination gave a religious fervor to Calvin's followers as they sought evidence for being among the elect destined for eternal salvation.

Did Luther's and Calvin's belief in predestination provide a religious basis for capitalism? German sociologist Max Weber would answer in the affirmative, by arguing that what he termed the *spirit of capitalism* evolved from the Protestant Reformation. Weber made a clear distinction between an irrational, unlimited greed for gain and "rational capitalism," the equivalent of what is referred to today as *free-market-capitalism*:

> The impulse to acquisition, pursuit of gain, of money, of the greatest possible amount of money, has in itself nothing to do with capitalism. This impulse [to acquisition] has been common to all sorts and conditions of men at all times and in all countries of the earth, wherever the objective possibility of it is or has been given. It should be taught in the kindergarten of cultural history that this naïve idea of capitalism must be given up once and for all. Unlimited greed for gain is not in the least identical with capitalism, and is still less its spirit. Capitalism *may* even be identical with the restraint, or at least a

[47] Charles Beard, *Martin Luther and the Reformation in Germany until the Close of the Diet of Worms*, ed. J. Frederick Smith (London: Kegan Paul, Trench & Co., 1889), p. 441. For the apostolic bull excommunicating Luther, see Pope Leo X, "*Decet Romanum Pontificem*: Papal Bull of Excommunication of Martin Luther and His Followers," (Rome: January 3, 1521). Available online at https://www.papalencyclicals.net/leo10/l10decet.htm.

[48] Jacques Barzun, *From Dawn to Decadence: 500 Years of Western Cultural Life, 1500 to the Present* (New York: HarperCollins, 2000), p. 37.

[49] John Calvin, *A Harmonie upon the Three Evangelists, Matthew, Mark and Luke* (London: George Bishop, 1584), pp. 194–196.

[50] Richard H. Tawney, *Religion and the Rise of Capitalism* (London: John Murray, 1923), p. 246.

> rational tempering, of this irrational impulse. But capitalism is identical with the pursuit of profit, and forever *renewed* profit, by means of continuous, rational, capitalistic enterprise. For it must be so: in a wholly capitalistic order of society, an individual capitalistic enterprise which did not take advantage of its opportunities for profit-making would be doomed to extinction.[51]

Weber began his search for an explanation of the capitalistic spirit by noting the overwhelming number of Protestants among merchants, entrepreneurs, highly skilled laborers, and technically and commercially trained professionals. As reasoned by Weber, Luther had developed the idea of an earthly "calling" in the sense of a duty set by God, rather than simply a means of getting rich. Individuals were to accept the calling chosen for them by God and perform their daily duties in accordance with Christian teaching, as this was "the only way to live acceptably to God."[52] All callings, even the humblest, possessed dignity and worth. This was a novel idea originating from the Protestant Reformation and became a central dogma of Protestant denominations. It discarded the Roman Catholic Church's notion of "ascetic self-denial," which renounced material possessions and worldly pleasures in favor of a life devoted to religious pursuits, and replaced it with "ascetic Protestantism," which believed individuals had a moral obligation to fulfill the obligations God imposed on them in this world—that is, their calling (German *Beruf*), and to do so with a clear conscience. Ascetic Protestant groups such as Anglicans, Baptists, Calvinists, Methodists, and Quakers gave the performance of earthly duties a religious significance and, in turn, material success (resulting from hard work) acquired ethical approval.

In the view of these Protestant groups, everyone's occupation was a calling, and all were legitimate in the eyes of God; every occupation has a dignity of its own and no occupation is on a higher plane than any other. The scriptural basis for this is found in Col. 3:23–24: "Whatever you do, work heartily, as working for the Lord, not for men, knowing that from the Lord you will receive [an] inheritance as your reward. You are serving the Lord Christ." This passage sanctifies work when it is done to the glory of God and not merely in response to the dictates of others. As popularly expressed in the literature of the mid-nineteenth century: "All true work is sacred; in all true Work, were it but true hand-labour, there is something of divineness. Labour, as wide as the Earth, has its summit in Heaven."[53] The idea of occupations as callings placed a new interpretation on the purpose of life: instead of waiting for Judgment Day to see if they had lived their lives according to the Bible, believers were to accept the calling laid out for them by God, and do so with diligence and devotion. Stated differently, everyone was to labor in this world for the glorification of God.

"For Weber, the significance of this shift in perspective was that it stressed the equal worth of all worldly activities (including business activities), as long as they were carried out diligently and with devotion. . . . As such, . . . the pursuit of profit and commercial success could be conceived of as divine activity—carried out in order to increase the glory of God."[54] Accumulating wealth was thus seen as a moral duty, a way of justifying one's time on Earth. Weber argued that this gave "both Protestant business owners and Protestant workers . . . a spiritual incentive to work diligently and devoutly to try and maximise the profits of their commercial enterprises."[55] Weber considered this "providential interpretation of profit-making" to be the basis for the economic success of Protestant believers in Western European cities such as London and Amsterdam, as contrasted with the more heavily Catholic populated cities of Paris and Rome.[56]

---

[51] Max Weber, *The Protestant Ethic and the Spirit of Capitalism*, trans. Talcott Parsons (New York: Charles Scribner's Sons, 1958), p. 17. Originally published as a two-part essay for the journal *Archiv für Sozialwissenschaft und Sozialpolitik* 20(1) (1904), pp. 1–54 and 21(1) (1905), pp. 86–121. This translation, however, is based on a revised edition published as the initial volume in the series *Gesammelte Aufsätze zur Religionssoziologie* [*Sociology of Religion*] (Tübingen: J. C. B. Mohr, 1920).
[52] *Ibid.*, p. 81.
[53] Thomas Carlyle, *Past and Present* (New York: William H. Colyer, 1843), p. 141.
[54] Matthew Hollow, "A Wesleyan Work Ethic? Entrepreneurship and Weber's Protestant Work Ethic in the Case of Isaac Holden, c. 1807–1897," *Business History* 64(7) (October 2022), p. 1348.
[55] *Ibid.*
[56] Weber, *The Protestant Ethic*, p. 163.

As a result of this new Protestantism, numerous corollaries developed in practice. Wasting time was the deadliest of sins, because every hour wasted was negating an opportunity to labor for God's glory. A willingness to work was essential: "He who will not work shall not eat" (2 Thess. 3:10 as quoted above). The division of labor (and resulting specialization) was a result of Divine will because it led to a higher degree of skill and improvement in the quality and quantity of production and, hence, served the good of all. Consumption beyond basic needs was wasteful and therefore sinful: "Waste not, want not."[57] According to Weber, each of these ideas helped create the spirit of capitalism.

Intense activity moved people from a contemplative life to one of continuous physical and mental labor. Willingness to work placed the motivational burden on individuals, and their self-directed, self-controlled lives gave them an internal gyroscope. The division of labor assigned each person to a calling and required a person's best. A person without a calling evidenced a lack of grace. Profitability was a sign of grace, and to waste anything and, hence, reduce profits, or to forgo what might be a profitable venture, was against God's will. By not seeking luxury, people created a surplus or profit from their labors. The created wealth was not to be consumed beyond a person's basic needs, and, thus, the surplus was to be reinvested in additional enterprises or in the improvement of present ventures, thereby, aiding the growth of capitalism. Protestantism provided specific guidelines for the creation of a capitalistic spirit. It taught that people had a duty to work, a duty to use their wealth wisely, and a duty to lead self-denying lives. An unequal distribution of possessions was Divine Providence at work, as people had different talents and, therefore, reaped unequal rewards. Wealth was no assurance of Heaven, and the poor had no need to worry if they performed their calling with diligence and devotion. For Weber, the spirit of capitalism evolved from a Protestant ethic, which equated success in one's calling with spiritual salvation. With no room for self-indulgence and with the tenets of self-control and self-direction, a new age of individualism had been born. In consequence, the "Protestant 'work ethic' created the entrepreneur, the economic man as we know him under capitalism."[58]

An Alternative View

In contrast to Weber's argument that the spirit of capitalism evolved from a Protestant ethic, English economist Richard H. Tawney held that the rise of capitalism was the cause of Protestantism, not the result. Tawney noted that Roman Catholic cities were chief commercial centers, that Roman Catholics were leading bankers, and that the capitalistic spirit was present in Italy, southern Germany, and Flanders in the fifteenth century, far in advance of the sixteenth- and seventeenth-century influences that Weber discussed. According to Tawney, "Is it not a little artificial to suggest that capitalist enterprise had to wait, as Weber appears to imply, till religious changes had produced a capitalist spirit? Would it not be equally plausible, and equally one-sided, to argue that the religious changes were themselves merely the result of economic movements?"[59]

In Tawney's view, the rise of capitalism was action and reaction, molding and, in turn, being molded by other significant cultural forces. The Renaissance placed a fresh focus on reason, discovery, exploration, and science; all were challenges to the monolithic authority of the Roman Catholic Church. In doing so, it promised a new social order in which there would be mobility for all; it signaled the mastery of people over their environment, counter to the opposite view that predominated throughout the Middle Ages.[60] A growing economic life posed novel challenges for religious doctrine, and merchants and artisans engaged in profit-making activities regardless of dogma. Though the Protestant Reformation had begun as a religious reform

[57] *Ibid.*, pp. 157–173. The proverb "Waste not, want not" has origins dating back to Richard Edwards, *The Paradise of Dainty Devices* (London: Printed for Robert Triphook and William Sancho, 1810). Written in 1576.
[58] Barzun, *From Dawn to Decadence*, p. 36.
[59] Richard H. Tawney, "Foreword" to Weber's *Protestant Ethic*, p. 8.
[60] *Idem*, *Religion and the Rise of Capitalism*, pp. 66–67.

movement, it was seized by an emerging merchant class and bent to its economic needs, as the class sought a religion that would sanctify, and a sovereign state that would legalize, its capitalistic impulses. As one authority has commented, the Protestant religion and capitalism went "hand in hand like bride and groom."[61]

With two sets of assumptions, two different conclusions may be reached: Weber's notion that religious institutions changed and then the spirit of capitalism abounded; or Tawney's view that economic motivation was steam pushing on the lid of religious authority until the safety valve of a change in dogma (i.e., the Protestant Reformation and its later proliferation into various sects) could sanctify economic efforts. Tawney's doubts aside, he nevertheless considered Weber's thesis to be "one of the most fruitful examinations of the relations between religion and social theory" to have appeared.[62]

Modern Evidence

There is modern evidence that supports Weber's argument that the spirit of capitalism evolved from the Protestant Reformation. In *The Achieving Society,* Harvard University researcher David C. McClelland began a search for the psychological factors that were generally important for economic development. The principal factor he isolated was the "need for achievement," or in the shorthand version, *n ach*. McClelland's search was both historical and cross-cultural, and his findings support Weber's thesis. First, McClelland found that high *n ach* was essential to engaging in entrepreneurial activities; second, high *n ach* in a society was significantly correlated to rapid economic development; and third, certain ethnic, religious, and minority groups showed marked differences in *n ach*. He found that children of Protestants had higher *n ach* than children of Roman Catholics, and children of Jews had an even higher *n ach*. McClelland concluded that individualistic religions, personified by various Protestant denominations, tended to be associated with a high *n ach*, whereas authoritarian religions, such as traditional Roman Catholicism, tended to have a lower need for achievement. He did concede, however, that there were wide variations among various modern Roman Catholic communities.

What was involved in the need for achievement was not so much the need to reach certain goals (such as wealth, status, and respect), but the need to enjoy success. Wealth was a way of keeping score, not a goal. In this regard, McClelland argued that the entrepreneurial personality was characterized by special attitudes toward risk-taking, a willingness to expend energy, an eagerness to innovate, and a readiness to make decisions and accept responsibility. Historically, the concern for achievement appeared in a culture some 50 or so years before a rapid rate of economic growth and prosperity. McClelland found this to be true in ancient Greece (before its Golden Age), in Spain during the Middle Ages (before the Age of Exploration), and in England during two different periods. The first period was from 1500 to 1625 when Protestantism was growing in strength concurrently with a need for achievement. The second period came in the eighteenth century just prior to the Industrial Revolution. The reasoning that McClelland used to support Weber was (1) the Protestant Reformation emphasized self-reliance rather than reliance on others in all facets of life, and (2) Protestant parents changed child-rearing practices to teach self-reliance and independence. McClelland and his associates empirically demonstrated that these practices led to a higher need for achievement in sons, and that a higher need for achievement led to spurts of economic activity such as those characterized by Weber as the spirit of capitalism.[63] McClelland was, therefore, able to draw an empirical relationship between the influence of Protestantism and Weber's spirit of modern capitalism.

---

[61] Max I. Dimont, *Jews, God, and History* (New York: Simon and Schuster, 1962), p. 233.

[62] Tawney, *Religion and the Rise of Capitalism*, p. 319n22.

[63] David C. McClelland, *The Achieving Society* (Princeton, NJ: Van Nostrand, 1961), pp. 47–53. See also John W. Atkinson and Norman T. Feather, eds., *A Theory of Achievement Motivation* (New York: John Wiley & Sons, 1966). For McClleland's reaction on first reading Weber's "seminal" work, see Larry Gross, *Creativity: Process and Personality* (Bethlehem, PA: Media Studies Press, 1964), p. 82. Available at https://www.mediastudies.press/creativity.

Sociologist Gerhard E. Lenski summarized, evaluated, and presented evidence both for and against Weber's belief in a Protestant ethic. On balance, he found the evidence more in Weber's favor than against. To define the relationship between religious affiliation and the ability of people to move upward in their careers, Lenski explored the relationship between vertical mobility and individual characteristics, such as aspirations, ambition, and attitudes toward work. He found that Jews were the most mobile, followed by Protestants, and then Roman Catholics. Lenski believed this variation could be explained by differences in achievement motivation and attitudes toward work. Roman Catholics held neutral attitudes toward work and labored for reasons other than the satisfaction that came from work itself. In Lenski's view, "Catholics continued to regard work primarily as a necessary evil; a consequence of Adam's fall and a penalty for sin. By contrast, Protestants came to view it as an opportunity for serving God, or, in the Deist version, for building character."[64]

The implications of McClelland's and Lenski's findings can be far-reaching for contemporary society. Not only did McClelland and Lenski provide empirical support for Weber's contentions, but their findings also suggest that a need for achievement can be developed in individuals and, in turn, instilled in entire nations. In underdeveloped countries, one major challenge may be underachievement; if so, an inculcation of a need for achievement may be one means for furthering economic growth and prosperity.

THE LIBERTY ETHIC

Given the implications of a need for achievement and the sanctifying of individual rewards for performance, to grow economically, a nation's political system must be conducive to personal liberty. The "divine right of kings," the aristocracy of the manor lord, the exercise of secular authority by the Roman Catholic Church, and a large population of landless serfs precluded the emergence of an industrialized society. Through the seventeenth and nineteenth centuries, however, the European Enlightenment (sometimes called the Age of Reason) superseded the Age of Religion. In a time of unprecedented intellectual ferment, political philosophers championed equality, justice, the rights of citizens, and governance by the consent of those governed, redefining Europe's culture and life. In doing so, the Enlightenment embraced logic, replacing liturgical dogma and tradition with reason, debate, and experimentation. The Enlightenment further threatened the existing order by challenging the prevailing view of the relationship between citizens and their states. In elevating individual liberty, Enlightenment thought "established the principle that labor and capital are private property and not communal assets subject to involuntary sharing, and thus unleased the explosion of knowledge and production that drives human flourishing to this day."[65] By encouraging free inquiry and an anti-hierarchical egalitarian spirit, the Enlightenment nurtured democracy and promoted the ideal of limited government.

The liberty ethic challenged political theory that called for the government and domination of the many by the few, as advocated for by philosophers such as Niccolò di Bernardo dei Machiavelli and Thomas Hobbes. Machiavelli, an out-of-office administrator and diplomat in the city-state of Florence, wrote *The Prince* in 1513.[66] He was an experienced observer of the intrigues and machinations of Florence and the Roman Catholic Church. *The Prince* is a handbook on how to rule successfully—not how to be good or wise. Machiavelli identified three routes to the top: "fortune," "ability," and "villainy." Those who rose through their good fortune had little trouble

[64] Gerhard E. Lenski, *The Religious Factor: A Sociological Study of Religious Impact on Politics, Economics, and Family Life* (Garden City, NJ: Doubleday, 1961), p. 83.

[65] W. Philip Gramm and Michael Solon, "Enemies of the Economic Enlightenment," *Wall Street Journal* (April 16, 2019), p. A17.

[66] Nicollò di Bernardo dei Machiavelli, *Il principe di Niccolo Machiavelli al magnifico Lorenzo di Piero dé Medici* [*The Prince of Niccolo Machiavelli to the magnificent Lorenzo di Piero d Medici*]. (Rome: Antonio Blado d'Asola, 1532). Written in 1513, but not published until after Machiavelli's death because of its controversial nature.

in reaching the top but had difficulty maintaining their position because they depended on the goodwill of others and were indebted entirely to those who elevated them. Those who reached the top through ability encountered many difficulties but maintained their position more easily. Those who employed villainy, an oft-chosen path in Machiavelli's Florence, used methods that would gain power, but not glory; their crown would always rest uneasily as they awaited the next usurper or palace revolt.[67]

Machiavelli's basic assumption about human nature was indicative of his rationale for the type of leadership he advocated: "whoever desires to found a state and give it laws, must start with assuming that all men are bad and ever ready to display their vicious nature, whenever they may find occasion for it."[68] To cope with these brutes, rulers were justified in pursuing any leadership style that suited their purpose. Rulers should be concerned with having a good reputation, but not with being virtuous; should they have to choose between being feared and being loved, it was better to be feared; and above all, rulers must be both like a lion and a fox, employing force and deceit. Machiavelli wrote of rulers, but not of the ruled; of power (how to obtain it, how to keep it, and how to exercise it), but not of rights; and of ends, but not of means. He influenced the later ideas of British historian John Emerich Edward Dalberg-Acton (also known as Lord Acton) about power corrupting, and absolute power corrupting absolutely.[69] "Machiavellian" has come to connote people who are unscrupulous, crafty, and cunning. For his time, and perhaps for ours, Machiavelli personified the command philosophy of governance.

English philosopher Thomas Hobbes's *Leviathan* (1651) was a later argument for strong central authority. In Hobbes's view, humans originated in a "state of nature," without civil government. He further believed that people are basically selfish, antagonistic, and hostile to one another. Having experienced the upheaval of the English Civil War (1642–1651) between King Charles I and his defiant Parliament (climaxing in the king's beheading for treason), Hobbes concluded that some absolutist power, the Leviathan, must exist to bring order from chaos and avert political and social conflict.[70] This power (a sovereign or an independent state) became supreme in either one of two ways: by force or by people voluntarily submitting in the belief that by trading liberty for safety under the power's rule they would be protected from outside threats.[71] It made no difference to Hobbes whether the Leviathan was secular or ecclesiastical, as long as it had total power to regulate all overt conduct and expression and was, thus, able to prevent chaos and ensure peace. The Leviathan ruled all, and individuals were subordinate to its supreme power. Hobbes's absolutism was a forerunner of today's totalitarian states. The notion of "trading liberty for safety" calls to mind Benjamin Franklin's eighteenth-century admonition: "Those who would give up essential Liberty, to purchase a little temporary Safety, deserve neither Liberty nor Safety."[72]

In the history of human liberty, political theorist John Locke's *Two Treatises of Government* (1689), stands as a defining challenge to philosophers such as Machiavelli and Hobbes who

---

[67] Daniel A. Wren and Ronald G. Greenwood, *Management Innovators: The People and Ideas That Have Shaped Modern Business* (New York: Oxford University Press, 1998), pp. 191–194.

[68] Nicollò di Bernardo dei Machiavelli, "Discourses on the First Ten Books of Titus Livius" in *The Historical, Political, and Diplomatic Writings of Niccolo Machiavelli*, vol. 2, trans. Christian E. Detmold (Boston, MA: J. R. Osgood, 1882), p. 104. Written circa 1517.

[69] Letter from John Emerich Edward Dalberg-Acton to Mandell Creighton, April 5, 1887, reprinted in John Emerich Edward Dalberg-Acton, in *Historical Essays and Studies*, eds. John Neville Figgis and Reginald Vere Laurence (London: Macmillan, 1907), p. 504.

[70] Thomas Hobbes, *Leviathan, or, the Matter, Form, and Power of a Common-Wealth Ecclesiastical and Civil* (London: Andrew Crooke', 1651), p. 1. Hobbes's title was purposefully chosen to evoke the mythological Leviathan (a multiheaded sea serpent) of the Bible (Psalms 74:14). See Kim Ian Parker, "That 'Dreadful Name, Leviathan': Biblical Resonances in the Title to Hobbes's Famous Political Work," *Hebraic Political Studies* 2(4) (Fall 2007), pp. 424–447.

[71] *Ibid.*, p. 88.

[72] [Benjamin Franklin], "Pennsylvania General Assembly: Reply to the Governor, 11 November 1755," *Votes and Proceedings of the House of Representatives of the Province of Pennsylvania, met at Philadelphia, on the Fourteenth of October, Anno Domini 1755, and Continued by Adjournments* (Philadelphia, PA: Printed by B. Franklin, 1756), p. 21. Available online at https://founders.archives.gov/documents/Franklin/01-06-02-0107.

called for the government and domination of the many by the few.[73] Locke's work not only articulated the principles of the "Glorious Revolution of 1688," which brought about the overthrow of the quasi-Catholic King James II and his replacement, Protestant King William of Orange, but also inspired the United States *Declaration of Independence* (ratified on July 4, 1776), as well as the French *Declaration of the Rights of Man and of the Citizen* (adopted on August 26, 1789). Perhaps no other person has had such a profound effect on political theory and action. To begin with, Locke challenged the "divine right of kings" doctrine and the practice of royal or hereditary succession. Divine right proponents traced the belief that monarchs were divinely empowered to the Book of Genesis (especially, Gen. 1:28, 3:16, and 4:7) and Adam's God-given right (as the first monarch) to rule his children.[74] As the self-declared descendants of Adam, monarchs could, therefore, only be judged by God. To oppose the will of a king or queen would be to oppose the will of God. Locke rejected this belief. Drawing on Scripture proclaiming that "God created man in his own image" (Gen. 1:27), Locke countered that God made humans with an inherent dignity that included fundamental rights that cannot be taken away, such as the right to govern their own actions as they see fit. Continuing, he set forth a new concept of earthly authority: "[W]ho shall be Judge, whether the Prince, or Legislative, act contrary to their Trust? . . . To this I reply; The People shall be Judge."[75] For Locke, "The People" rather than their rulers were the source of a nation's political power. This concept is embodied in the opening (and what some consider the most famous) words of the United States *Constitution* (1787), "We the People."[76]

Locke's belief in the inherent dignity of all people resonates in the equally memorable first lines of the United States *Declaration of Independence*:

> We hold these truths to be self-evident, that all men are created equal, that they are endowed by their Creator with certain unalienable Rights, that among these are Life, Liberty and the pursuit of Happiness.—That to secure these rights, Governments are instituted among Men, deriving their just powers from the consent of the governed.[77]

Locke was influenced, in particular, by Roman statesman and philosopher Marcus Tullius Cicero (circa 106–43 BCE) and his idea of natural rights. Cicero believed that innate rights came from nature or nature's God rather than governments. Locke argued that the divinely ordained *law of nature* ("natural law") teaches that all people are born free and equal, that no one should (in words that would be subsequently echoed in the *Declaration of Independence* opening sentence above) harm another's "Life, Health, Liberty or Possessions," as we are "all the Workmanship of one Omnipotent, and infinitely wise maker: All the servants of one Sovereign Master."[78] In sentiments that also found voice in the *Declaration of Independence's* introductory paragraph, Locke held that people have a natural right to overthrow a tyrannical government to form a more just union, arguing that governments are morally legitimate only when they are established by

---

[73] For a discussion of Locke's interest in Hobbes's *Leviathan*, see Felix Waldman, "John Locke as a Reader of Thomas Hobbes's *Leviathan*: A New Manuscript," *Journal of Modern History* 93(2) (June 2021), pp. 245–282.

[74] Kim Ian Parker, "A Critical Analysis of Filmer's and Locke's Use of Genesis in the Development of Their Political Philosophies" (Master's thesis, McMaster University, Hamilton, Ontario, Canada, 1982), pp. 40–62.

[75] John Locke, *Two Treatises of Government: In the Former the False Principles & Foundation of Sir Robert Filmer & His Followers, Are Detected & Overthrown; the Latter Is an Essay Concerning the True Original, Extent & End of Civil Government* (London: Awnsham Churchill, 1690), p. 269. Printed in 1689 but dated 1690.

[76] *The Constitution of the United States*. Available online at https://www.archives.gov/founding-docs/constitution-transcript.

[77] Thomas Jefferson, *Declaration of Independence* (Philadelphia, PA: Wildside Press, 1776), p. 1. Miscellaneous Papers of the Continental Congress, 1774–1789; Records of the Continental and Confederation Congresses and the Constitutional Convention, 1774–1789, Record Group 360; National Archives. Available online at https://www.archives.gov/founding-docs/declaration-transcript?_ga=2.92078682.1120096092.1659811616-885506141.1659625735

[78] Locke, *Two Treatises of Government*, pp. 222–223. For Cicero's influence on Locke's thinking, see Timothy W. Caspar, "Cicero and America," *Expositions* 8(1) (2014), pp. 145–167, available online at https://expositions.journals.villanova.edu/index.php/expositions/issue/view/130; Paul Meany, "Cicero, Locke, and the American Founding," *Cato Unbound: A Journal of Debate* (January 15, 2021). Available online at https://www.cato-unbound.org/2021/01/15/paul-meany/cicero-locke-american-founding/#disqus_thread.

the consent of the governed, protect private property, and are comprised of representatives freely chosen by those governed. The British American colonists' declaration of independence, however, was more than a call for political change: it commenced a social revolution that emphasized freedom and equality as natural rights, challenged the notion of a ruling elite, and promoted dignity and respect for ordinary people.

A century later, Locke's writings would influence Adam Smith (discussed below) and were the basis for Jean-Jacques Rousseau's political philosophy that the primary role of a nation's government was to ensure the freedom of its citizens. Rousseau's 1762 book *Du contrat social; ou Principes du droit politique* [*On the Social Contract; or, Principles of Political Right*], with its famous opening line, "Man is born free, but everywhere he is in chains," helped launch the decade-long first French Revolution in 1789, which led to the end of the Bourbon monarchy and the feudal Ancien Régime political and social order.[79] Locke put forth a new civil order in which people were not simply subjugated by a ruler, but possessed natural rights: (1) laws based on reason, not arbitrary dictates; (2) a government deriving its powers from the governed; (3) liberty to pursue personal goals (as long as nothing was taken immorally from others); and (4) private property and its use in the pursuit of happiness . These four ideas led to the downfall of kings (first in the 13 North American colonies that overthrew British King George III's monarchy in 1776 and then with the beheading of French King Louis XVI in 1793) and formed a solid political foundation for economic growth. The new civil order gave sanction to free-market capitalism and the pursuit of individual rewards, protected against the confiscation of private property, guaranteed contract rights, and created a justice system that treated all people equally. In doing so, these thoughts "spawned the Industrial Revolution and gave birth to the modern world."[80]

The road to "freedom for all" has not followed a straight path. The "Founding Fathers" who signed the United States *Declaration of Independence* did not give the same meaning to the words "all men are created equal" as we do now. The pathway to realizing "equality for all" contained many twists and turns. It witnessed a civil war that divided the nation (North against South) over the practice of slavery (1861–1864); a nearly 75-year battle for woman suffrage (1848–1920); and, beginning in the 1950s and 1960s, an ongoing effort to end discrimination between people based on race, gender, age, religion, disability, or sexual orientation, as well as other categories. These (and other) struggles, however, should not distract from the founding generation's achievement in establishing a unique political system that today is dedicated to the enjoyment of liberty by all. Indeed, some 250 years later, the ideas celebrated in the *Declaration of Independence* (and defined in the United States *Constitution*) continue to give inspiration to people worldwide who yearn to exercise their own "unalienable Rights."[81]

THE MARKET ETHIC

Economic thinking was basically static during the Middle Ages because localized, subsistence-level economies required no commercial framework. Economists only focused on two factors of production: land and labor. In most of the world, people primarily produced food on small

[79] Jean-Jacques Rousseau, *Du contrat social; ou Principes du droit politique* [*On the Social Contract, or Principles of Political Right*] (Amsterdam: Chez Marc-Michel Rey, 1762), p. 2.

[80] W. Philip Gramm and Michael Solon, "The "Stakeholder' War on the Enlightenment," *Wall Street Journal* (May 24, 2022), p. A17.

[81] The adjective "unalienable" defines rights that are incapable of being repudiated or transferred to another. Whereas one might exchange (alienate) one's right to property and labor, unalienable rights are inherent to each person as a human being. As the *Declaration of Independence* proclaims, among these unalienable rights are "Life, Liberty and the pursuit of Happiness." The distinction between "alienable" and "unalienable" may be traced to Scottish Enlightenment philosopher Francis Hutcheson and is recognized as influencing the "Founding Fathers'" thinking regarding limited government. As Hutcheson declared, "Unalienable Rights are essential Limitations in all Governments." Thus, by their nature, unalienable rights entail limited government. See Francis Hutcheson, *An Inquiry into the Original of Our Ideas of Beauty and Virtue* (London: J. Darby, 1725), p. 295.

farms for their own consumption. Capital as an input factor was scorned and, as noted, lending money with an interest charge for its use was damned. Any idea of management as a primary input that afforded a comparative advantage was completely lacking. In the sixteenth and seventeenth centuries, however, the reemergence of strong national identities began to reshape economic thought. As new lands heretofore unknown in the West were discovered through exploration, new trade routes and new products created international markets. Following Columbus's encounters with the "New World" in 1492, European powers, such as France, Spain, Great Britain, Portugal, and Holland, attempted to increase their national wealth through trade with other countries and overseas colonies. The ensuing growth in world trade resulted in an economic philosophy known as *mercantilism*, which held that countries should maintain a favorable balance of trade by exporting more goods than they import, so as to acquire as much wealth (in particular, gold and silver) as possible. It was believed that the resulting addition to a country's riches would bring its people "more Plenty of all the conveniences [*sic*] of Life" relative to its trading partners.[82] Mercantilism encouraged governments to play a central role in financing and protecting trade to build strong national economies. In consequence, nations soon intervened in all economic affairs, engaged in federal economic planning, and, to the extent possible, regulated private commercial activity. As explained by historian Robert Leckie, the primary function of colonies "was to produce raw materials required by their mother countries to convert into finished products—clothing, tools, kitchen utensils, naval stores, grains, and so on—and these very articles were then . . . shipped back to the colonies and sold at outrageous prices."[83] As an example, by British restriction, farming tools such as axes, hoes, sickles, and saws could not be made in North American colonies and had to come from England. In effect, mercantilism thus kept manufacturing and money in the hands of the mother country and kept colonies economically dependent.

Mercantilism eventually collapsed under its own weight. It went awry as it prolonged the life of failing enterprises, curbed private initiative, imposed elaborate bureaucratic controls, encouraged many countries' colonists to rebel, and fostered wars and trade rivalries that destroyed the very markets its adherents were trying to gain. Mercantilism contradicted the natural philosophy of the Enlightenment. Mercantilists thought only of a nation's power, whereas the Enlightenment championed individual rights and viewed all human institutions in terms of the contribution they made to overall happiness.

In the eighteenth century, the Physiocratic school of economic thought emerged to challenge mercantilism. The word "Physiocrat" comes from the Greek words *phýsis*, meaning "nature," and *kràtos*, meaning "power." François Quesnay (1694–1774), the founder of the school of thought, maintained that wealth did not lie in gold and silver, but instead only sprang from agricultural production.[84] He advocated free-market capitalism, meaning that governments should leave marketplace mechanisms alone; for Quesnay, a nation's economy had a natural order, and government intervention interfered with both that order and those marketplace mechanisms. Adam Smith (1723–1790), a Scottish political philosopher, was not a Physiocrat per se, but was influenced by the idea that a nation's economy had a natural order. In *The Wealth of Nations,* he laid the groundwork for what is known as the "classical school of economics." Smith thought that mercantilist tariff polices were destructive and, rather than protecting industry, penalized efficiency and, consequently, misallocated a nation's resources. He felt that economic activity should be regulated solely by marketplace competition. The "invisible hand" of the marketplace (the so-called "market effect") would ensure that resources flowed to their most efficient use and yield

[82] John Locke, *Some Considerations of the Consequences of the Lowering of Interest, and Raising the Value of Money* (London: Awnsham and John Churchill, 1692), p. 15.
[83] Robert Leckie, *"A Few Acres of Snow": The Saga of the French and Indian Wars* (Hoboken, NJ: John Wiley & Sons, 1999), pp. 126–127.
[84] François Quesnay, *Tableau oeconomique* [*Economic Table*] (London: Macmillan, 1894). Originally published in 1758.

the greatest return over time.[85] In this way, the separate interests of each person and nation, acting in a competitive market, would create individual and collective prosperity. As Smith stated:

> As every individual, therefore, endeavors as much as he can both to employ his capital in the support of domestik industry, and so to direct that industry that its produce may be of the greatest value; every individual necessarily labours to render the annual revenue of the society as great as he can. He generally, indeed, neither intends to promote the publick interest, nor knows how much he is promoting it. By preferring the support of domestik to that of foreign industry, he intends only his own security; and by directing that industry in such a manner as its produce may be of the greatest value, he intends only his own gain, and he is in this, as in many other cases, led by an invisible hand to promote an end which was no part of his intention. Nor is it always the worse for the society that it was no part of it. By pursuing his own interest he frequently promotes that of the society more effectually than when he really intends to promote it. I have never known much good done by those who affected to trade for the publick good.[86]

In reflecting on Smith's most famous insight, note that he is not endorsing greed, but simply describing a seller's interest in making a profit or a buyer's in securing the best price for a good or service. Smith believed that allowing individuals the liberty to act in their own economic self-interest eliminated the need for government intervention in the marketplace, as an "invisible hand" would maintain equilibrium between the supply and demand of resources and, in turn, automatically adjust price levels, wages, and employment. Thus, in benefiting themselves, market participants promote the wider public interest without the intention or knowledge of doing so. In this way, millions of people of varying skills and temperaments cooperate to build and provide everything from the simplest child's toy to the most complex devices humans have created and do so exercising individual freedom sans government oversight or central planning. Regulatory actions, such as tariffs and minimum-wage restrictions, only hinder market efficiency in allocating resources and inhibit the growth that benefits everyone and makes a country more prosperous.

Adam Smith (from a medallion by James Tassie, 1787)

Adam Smith, *An Inquiry Into the Nature and Causes of the Wealth of Nations*, vol. 1 (New ed; Glasgow: R. Chapman, 1805) frontispiece).

For Smith, the division of labor was a pillar of marketplace competition. He cited the example of pin makers: when each performed a single or limited number of tasks rather than a broad range of duties, they could produce 48,000 pins a day, whereas one worker alone could produce no more than 20 pins per day. He admitted that this was a trifling example, but he found the same principle operating successfully in many industries:

> This great increase of the quantity of work, which, in consequence of the division of labour, the same number of people are capable of performing, is owing to three different circumstances; first, to the increase of dexterity in every particular workman; secondly, to the saving of the time which is commonly lost in passing from one species of work to another; and lastly, to the invention of a great number of machines which facilitate and abridge labour, and enable one man to do the work of many.[87]

[85] The origin of Smith's "invisible hand" imagery has long been debated. See Emma Rothschild, "Adam Smith and the Invisible Hand," *American Economic Review* 84(2) (May 1994), pp. 319–322; Peter Harrison, "Adam Smith and the History of the Invisible Hand," *Journal of the History of Ideas* 72(1) (January 2011), pp. 29–49; and Paul Oslington, "God and the Market: Adam Smith's Invisible Hand," *Journal of Business Ethics* 108(4) (April 2012), pp. 429–438.

[86] Adam Smith, *An Inquiry into the Nature and Causes of the Wealth of Nations* (London: W. Strahan and T. Cadell in the Strand, 1776), vol. 2, bk. IV, ch. 2, p. 350.

[87] Smith, *Wealth of Nations,* vol. 1, bk. I, ch. 1, p. 9. Smith is believed to have taken the pin-maker example from multiple sources. On this point, see Jean-Louis Peaucelle, "Adam Smith's Use of Multiple References for His Pin-Making Example," *European Journal of the History of Economic Thought* 13(4) (December 2006), pp. 489–512.

Although Smith recognized the benefits of the division of labor, he also foresaw its dysfunctional consequences:

> The man whose whole life is spent in performing a few simple operations . . . naturally loses, therefore, the habit of [mental] exertion, and generally becomes stupid and ignorant as it is possible for a human creature to become. . . . His dexterity at his own particular trade seems . . . to be acquired at the expence [*sic*] of his intellectual, social, and martial virtues.[88]

Smith argued that it was the province of governments, through public education, to overcome the division of labor's debilitating effects. In his view, manufacturers, to gain productivity, must rely on the division of labor. He believed that the division of labor benefited all of society and provided an economic rationale for the factory system. As Smith reasoned, when markets were limited, the domestic system of production could meet consumer needs. As a nation's population grew, however, and new markets opened, the benefits of division of labor and economies of scale associated with the factory system would gain momentum.

The first edition of *The Wealth of Nations* was published on March 9, 1776, and was sold out in 6 months. The second edition (1778) incorporated minor changes, but the third edition (1784) introduced substantial revisions, including Smith's concern for joint-stock companies, in which ownership was separated from management and placed in the hands of stockholders who had little sense of responsibility or knew about the financial or operational policies of their companies. During Smith's time, joint-stock companies in England, such as the British East India Company, the Muscovy Company, the French East India Company, the Hudson's Bay Company, and the Dutch East India Company were established by either royal charter or by an act of Parliament. Apparently, investors preferred joint-stock companies over "private copartnery," or partnerships, as only the amount they invested could be lost rather than their entire net worth. Smith, however, had doubts about this arrangement:

> The directors of such [joint-stock] companies, however, being the managers rather of other people's money than of their own, it cannot well be expected, that they should watch over it with the same anxious vigilance with which the partners in a private copartnery frequently watch over their own. . . . Negligence and profusion . . . . must always prevail, more or less, in the management of the affairs of such a company.[89]

At the time, the largest employers were textile firms, and these were not capital intensive. Yet, Smith anticipated that the separation of ownership from day-to-day control and the resulting rise of salaried managers had a potential downside. Those who managed "other people's money" incurred less personal risk (except for, perhaps, the loss of their jobs) and, thus, Smith felt, would be less vigilant and prudent in their duties. Moreover, he reasoned that when "[m]anagment and ownership diverged, so did their economic interests. Management had an interest in inflating their books to reflect well on their stewardship; stockholders wanted honest books that could be compared with those of other companies."[90]

When Smith first began writing during the early stages of the Industrial Revolution, he attracted a large number of vocal supporters and found fertile ground for his ideas. His views were in tune with the philosophy of the Enlightenment and the interest of newly emerging entrepreneurs who wished to sweep away the restrictions of mercantilism and the controlling power of the landed aristocracy. The market ethic provided a rationale for private initiative rather than

---

[88] *Ibid.*, vol. 2, bk. V, ch. 1, pp. 366–367. An appreciation of the division of labor's harmful consequences may be traced to early Greek and Chinese philosophers. See Guang-Zhen Sun, *The Division of Labor in Economics: A History* (New York: Routledge, 2012), p. 121.

[89] Smith, *Wealth of Nations*, 3rd ed. (1784), vol. 2, bk. 5, ch. 1, pp. 123–124. Compare this with the New Testament allegory of the hired shepherd who abandons the flock he is tending when he encounters a wolf. See John 10: 11–13.

[90] John Steele Gordon, "Regulators Take on Silicon Valley, as They Did Earlier Innovators," *Wall Street Journal* (April 4, 2018), p. A15.

mercantilism, competition rather than protectionism, innovation rather than economic stagnancy, and self-interest rather than a nation's power as a motivating force. In brief, the market ethic was another standard for cultural conduct that changed prevailing values toward people, work, and profits and led to a cultural rebirth that created a new environment that would give rise to the formal study of management.

SUMMARY

Early management thought was dominated by cultural values that were antibusiness, anti-achievement, and largely antihuman. Industrialization could not emerge when people were bound to their stations in life, when monarchs ruled by central dictates, and when people were urged to take no thought of individual fulfillment in this world and instead wait for the hereafter. Before the Industrial Revolution, economies and societies were essentially static, and political values involved unilateral decision-making by a central authority. Although some early advancements in management practice appeared, they were largely localized. Organizations could be run on the divine right of kings, an appeal to dogma among the faithful, and on rigorous military discipline. There was little or no need to develop a formal body of management thought under these circumstances.

Three forces were interacting and combining to provide for a new age of industrialization. Characterized as *ethics*, or standards governing human conduct, these forces illustrate how economic, social, and political attitudes were changing and led to a cultural rebirth. The ethics discussed were in reality a struggle between a traditional and a newly emerging society. The Protestant ethic was a challenge to the central authority of the Roman Catholic Church and a response to human needs in the here and now; the liberty ethic reflected the ancient struggle between monolithic and representative forms of government; and the market ethic was a gauntlet flung before the landed gentry, who preferred mercantilism. These are age-old struggles: government control versus individual liberty, human rights and due process versus whimsical autocracy, and centralization versus decentralization. The struggle goes on.

This cultural rebirth would establish the preconditions for industrialization and, subsequently, the need for a rational, formalized, systematic body of knowledge about how to manage. The emergence and refinement of marketplace economies required managers to be more creative and better informed about how to effectively manage an organization. Faced with a competitive, changing environment, managers had to develop a body of knowledge about how best to use resources. People began thinking of individual gain and had to be accommodated in some logical managerial framework. The emergence of modern management had to be based on rational methods of decision-making; no longer could organizations be operated on the whims of a few. This change did not come suddenly; it evolved over a long period as prevailing culture changed. How these changes came about and how they affected the evolution of management thought is an intriguing story.

The Industrial Revolution in Great Britain

CHAPTER 3

The Industrial Revolution heralded a new era for human civilization. The accompanying cultural rebirth spawned social, economic, and political conditions ripe for advances in technology. Subsequent technological inventions and innovations made possible novel combinations of physical and human resources and ushered in the "factory system," wherein standardized goods were mass-produced in large quantities, replacing the "putting-out" system, in which individual workers fabricated goods in small workshops or in their own homes (see Chapter 2). This chapter examines the main features of the Industrial Revolution and the management challenges it created, and puts into perspective the resulting cultural consequences.

FROM A PREINDUSTRIAL TO AN INDUSTRIAL SOCIETY

Industrial progress is always closely tied to innovations in technology. As noted in Chapter 2, in the mid-fifteenth century, Johannes Gutenberg, an inventor in the Franco-German city of Strasbourg, perfected the first movable-type printing press in Europe. In doing so, Gutenberg began an information revolution that allowed the modern economic world to emerge.[1] Before the development of the printing press, readers relied on expensive manuscripts, painstakingly copied by hand with goosequills on parchment made from animal skins. This meant that books were generally available to only the wealthy who, other than the clergy, were the only people likely to be able to read and write. The subsequent diffusion of printing throughout urban Europe and the wider availability of less costly printed material (e.g., books, pamphlets, newspapers, and more) transformed the production and spread of knowledge. It also contributed to a surge in literacy and numeracy, leading to innovations in virtually every area of human endeavor. Indeed, whereas medieval philosophers had attempted to deduce physical laws from the writings of Plato, Aristotle, Euclid, Pythagoras, Saint Augustine, and the Bible, a period of intense critical thinking arose in the late seventeenth and eighteenth centuries, spawning modern advances in science, art, architecture, botany, chemistry, physics, geology, law, medicine, literature, engineering, and economics. The ideas and discoveries that resulted laid the foundation for the modern world and propelled the technological innovations that were to follow.

[1] Jeremiah Dittmar, "Information Technology and Economic Change: The Impact of the Printing Press," *Quarterly Journal of Economics* 126(3) (August 2011), pp. 1133–1172.

From the time that humans first began to develop methods for tilling the soil, crafting weapons, and weaving cloth, there have been innovations in *technology*, defined as the art and applied science of making and using tools and equipment. Technology has evolved and advanced for thousands of years, but a series of technological innovations in mid- to late-eighteenth-century Great Britain marked the beginning of what was to become known as the Industrial Revolution, an era in which technology progressed more rapidly than ever before.[2] The essence of the Industrial Revolution was the substitution of machine power for other natural sources of energy, such as human, animal, wind, and water power. Phyllis M. Deane, in pinpointing the emergence of the Industrial Revolution, illustrated the difference between preindustrialized and industrialized societies. Preindustrial societies are characterized by low per capita income, economic stagnation, dependence on agriculture, little specialization of labor, and limited geographic market integration. Industrial societies, on the other hand, are characterized by high or rising per capita income, economic growth, limited dependence on agriculture, extensive specialization of labor, and widespread geographic market integration.[3] Based on these characteristics, Deane concluded that the shift in Britain from a preindustrial to an industrial society was evident by 1750 and accelerated thereafter. This shift "involved revolutionary changes in the structure and organization of the [British] economy" and "initiated the sustained upward movement of real incomes that the Western world now takes for granted."[4] More immediately, the Industrial Revolution was "the basis for a British world empire, based improbably on a comparatively minor archipelago of Atlantic Islands."[5] Great Britain was soon to become the world's largest imperial power.

THE STEAM ENGINE

In Chapter 2, we considered the two primary methods of preindustrialized production: the putting-out system and medieval craft guilds. In both methods, the scale of production was small, product markets were limited, and work was more labor-intensive than capital-intensive. In the putting-out system, merchants provided raw materials to families who, working from their homes, performed whatever tasks they were assigned. Thus, we find the ancient source of family names for weavers, dyers, tailors, fullers, and so on. In some instances, skilled artisans worked in craft shops, where work was passed from one stage to another. For example, tanners did their work and passed it along to curriers, and, in turn, came shoemakers and saddlers, who converted cured leather into finished products. Labor was specialized; capital investment was low; and humans, animals, wind, and water (rather than machine power) were sources of energy.

In terms of employment, market value, and capital invested, textile manufacturing was Britain's dominant industry during the Industrial Revolution.[6] From its overseas colonies came cotton, wool, and other fibers to be cleaned, combed, and spun into cloth. Mechanical improvements in the textile industry preceded the Industrial Revolution. John Kay's "flying shuttle," introduced in 1733, doubled the speed with which cloth could be woven on a handloom. Spinning, however, remained the chokepoint in production, as it took some 20 spinners to supply a single weaver with thread.[7] In 1765, James Hargreaves built a spinning wheel that changed the

---

[2] On the first use of the term "Industrial Revolution" see Anna Rezanson, "The Early Use of the Term Industrial Revolution," *Quarterly Journal of Economics* 36(2) (February 1922), pp. 343–356.

[3] Phyllis M. Deane, *The First Industrial Revolution* (Cambridge, England: Cambridge University Press, 1965), pp. 5–19.

[4] Phyllis Deane and H. John Habakkuk, "The Take-Off in Britain," in Walt W. Rostow, ed. *The Economics of Take-Off into Sustained Growth* (London: Macmillan, 1963), p. 63. For a discussion of why the Industrial Revolution occurred where and when it did, see Mark Koyama and Jared T. Rubin, *How the World Became Rich: The Historical Origins of Economic Growth* (Cambridge, UK: Polity Press, 2022), pp. 129–148.

[5] Diarmaid MacCulloch, *Christianity: The First Three Thousand Years* (London: Allen Lane, 2009), p. 736.

[6] For a discussion of the origins of the Industrial Revolution in textiles, see John Styles, "Fashion, Textiles and the Origins of Industrial Revolution," *East Asian Journal of British History* 5 (March 2016), pp. 161–190.

[7] Arthur Young, *A Six Months Tour Through the North of England*, vol. 3 (London: W. Strahan, 1770), p. 212.

standard position of spindles from horizontal to vertical, stacked multiple spindles on top of one another, and wove eight threads at once by turning them all with a single pulley and belt. He called his invention the "spinning jenny" (after his daughter) and added more spindles and power until he could weave 128 threads at a time. Yarn that once took days to spin now just took hours. In 1769, Richard Arkwright invented a "water frame" (so-called because most were powered by waterwheels) that stretched cotton fibers into a tighter, harder yarn. Beyond needing a source of power, the water frame was both too expensive to be owned by a family of spinners and too large for cottage use. This made factories inevitable. By 1776 Arkwright employed 5,000 workers in his mills. In 1779, Samuel Crompton introduced the "spinning mule," which integrated aspects of Hargreaves's spinning jenny and Arkwright's water frame.[8]

Despite these mechanical improvements, which at first were powered by falling water pushing on a mill wheel, the coal-fed steam engine was at the heart of the Industrial Revolution. Steam powered devices were not new: Greek mathematician and engineer Hero of Alexandria (10 CE–70 CE) invented the first steam-powered engine, but it remained a novelty. As Diarmaid MacCulloch has noted, "the ancient world failed to make the breakthrough in energy resources which occurred in England seventeen centuries later. Abundant slave labour . . . blunted the need for any major advances in technology."[9] In effect, there was no incentive for labor-saving technological innovations as the use of enslaved men, women, and children was less costly than a machine. In the ensuing years, others had built mock-ups of proposed steam engines but encountered design problems.[10] In 1712, Thomas Newcomen developed a steam-propelled engine that could continuously pump and drain muck that inevitably leaked into coal mines as shafts went below the water table. This time-, labor-, and cost-saving device was soon in use throughout England, Scotland, Sweden, and Central Europe.

Trained as an instrument maker, Scotsman James Watt developed his first workable steam engine in 1765, after being asked to repair the University of Glasgow's model of a Newcomen engine. Recognizing the inefficiency of reheating steam from boiling water to drive a piston back and forth (as Newcomen engines required), Watt added a separate chamber that condensed steam and allowed a piston cylinder to remain at the same temperature as the steam it generated. This new design was four times more powerful than earlier steam engines. Needing financial support to pursue his invention, Watt formed a partnership with an ironmaster, Matthew Boulton, who today would be called a "venture capitalist." In 1776, Watt's first engine was sold to John Wilkinson for use in driving machinery in his Bersham Ironworks. To set a price, an agreement was reached that the steam engine would be rated by the number of horses required to do an equivalent amount of work, hence the derivation of the word *horsepower* for a unit of power. The standard unit of measurement for power, *watt*, is named in honor of James Watt.

George Williamson, *Memorials of the Lineage, Early Life, Education, and Development of the Genius of James Watt* (Edinburgh: Printed for the Watt Club by Thomas Constable, 1856), p. 120.

James Watt

Until 1782, Watt's engines were used only to pump water and to power blowing engines for blast furnaces. In 1781, Watt made his greatest technological breakthrough when he transformed the up-and-down motion of a drive beam into a rotary motion capable of turning a shaft and, thus, powering machinery. This led to a host of new uses for steam power, such as lifting coal and ore

[8] Richard L. Hills, "Hargreaves, Arkwright and Crompton: Why Three Inventors?" *Textile History* 10(1) (1979), pp. 114–126.

[9] MacCulloch, *Christianity: The First Three Thousand Years*, p. 40.

[10] For a history of the steam engine in Great Britain see Alessandro Nuvolari, Bart Verspagen, and Nick von Tunzelmann, "The Early Diffusion of the Steam Engine in Britain, 1700–1800: A Reappraisal," *Cliometrics* 5(3) (October 2011), pp. 291–321. For a similar history pertaining to the United States, see John C. Merriam, "Steam," in *One Hundred Years' Progress of the United States* (Hartford, CN: L. Stebbins, 1870), pp. 226–273.

from mines, supplying power for breweries and oil mills, and, eventually, powering railway locomotives and steamships. In 1788, Watt patented a "fly-ball governor," which allowed steam to flow at a controlled rate. This first cybernetic system operated on the centrifugal force principle: as an engine sped up, arms on a rotating shaft rose and steam intake vents closed, reducing power intake; as an engine slowed, the arms dropped, allowing more power. After about 1830, steam power became more important than waterpower in British manufacturing.[11]

The historian Arnold J. Toynbee believed that two men, Adam Smith (see Chapter 2) and James Watt, were the most responsible for uprooting the old England, building a new one, and propelling the world toward industrialization.[12] Smith brought about a revolution in economic thought, and Watt a revolution in the use of steam power. Harnessed to the wheels of a hundred industries, steam engines provided cheaper and more efficient power for ships, trains, and factories, revolutionizing English commerce and industry. Steam power reduced production costs, lowered prices, expanded product markets, and enabled manufacturers to construct factories away from rivers and other sources of waterpower. A spirit of inquiry led to other inventions; these inventions led to factories, and factories led to a need for sound management. Cost-reducing inventions similarly lowered the price of goods, thereby expanding product markets that required more workers, more machines, and mass production on a recurring and regular basis. Mass production brought quality goods within the financial grasp of the many rather than only the few who had been able to afford them previously. As noted by economist Joseph A. Schumpeter, mass production meant that factory girls as well as queens could afford silk stockings.[13]

Capital was needed to finance larger industrial undertakings, and individuals who could amass the required funds began to bring workers and machines together in a single location. For example, instead of laboring in their homes on handlooms to make threads into cloth, weavers were assembled in a common workplace with a steam engine to power their looms; similarly, combers, bleachers, dyers, and so on found their efforts shifting from their homes to large factories. As these workers came into a shared workplace, there was a greater need for monitoring and coordinating their efforts. The factory system proceeded unevenly in different crafts, but the new age of industrialization was evident. With the introduction of a new power source that required a large capital investment, the need for efficient and effective performance became increasingly apparent. The fledgling factory system soon toddled forth to create an abundance such as the world had never known.

MANAGEMENT: THE FOURTH FACTOR OF PRODUCTION

Before the Industrial Revolution, economic theory focused on two factors of production: land and labor. With the emergence of the factory system, however, the Roman Catholic Church's admonitions against materialistic trade and profits loosened, and capital was soon recognized as a legitimate third factor of production. At the same time, with the growth in the factory system, the importance of a fourth factor of production became increasingly obvious: management. Jean-Baptiste Say (1767–1832), a French economist, was the first to explicitly recognize management as a fourth factor of production. Say noted that some "adventurers" (entrepreneurs) were the sole owners of a business, but more often they owned only a share, having borrowed capital from others or having formed a partnership. The "adventurer" thus became a manager

[11] Nicholas F. R. Crafts, *Forging Ahead, Falling Behind and Fighting Back: British Economic Growth from the Industrial Revolution to the Financial Crisis* (Cambridge, UK: Cambridge University Press, 2018), p. 11.

[12] Arnold J. Toynbee, *Lectures on the Industrial Revolution of the 18th Century in England* (New York: Humboldt Publishing, 1884), p. 189.

[13] Joseph A. Schumpeter, *Capitalism, Socialism, and Democracy* (New York: Harper & Brothers, 1942), p. 67.

for others and assumed additional risk in combining the factors of land, labor, and capital. He surmised that, to be successful, a manager requires many qualities that are rarely possessed by one person:

> [T]his kind of labour requires a combination of moral qualities, that are not often found together. Judgment, perseverance, and a knowledge of the world as well as of business. [The adventurer] is called upon to estimate, with tolerable accuracy, the importance of the specific product, the probable amount of the demand, and the means of its production: at one time he must employ a great number of hands; at another, buy or order the raw material, collect labourers, find consumers, and give at all times a rigid attention to order and economy; in a word, he must possess the art of superintend[e]nce and administration.[14]

For their skill in combining the three traditional factors of production (land, labor, and capital), managers and management constituted, in Say's judgment, an indispensable fourth factor of production.

MANAGEMENT CHALLENGES IN EARLY FACTORIES

As organizations grew larger with the burgeoning factory system, managers in general faced challenges unlike those previously encountered. The Roman Catholic Church could organize and manage its properties because of accepted dogma and the devotion of its faithful; armies and other military organizations could control thousands of conscripts through a rigid hierarchy of discipline and authority; and government-funded bureaucracies could survive without having to face competition or show a profit. Managers in the fledgling factory system could not resort to any of these methods to ensure effective and efficient performance.

The Industrial Revolution spawned many new industries, and the early 1800s were characterized by the growth of large firms operating in increasingly competitive environments. For these firms, pressure to grow came from the need to reduce the average unit costs of production through economies of scale. Some advocated resisting the pressure to grow; for example, the 1806 Committee on the Woollen Manufacture of England argued against large factories, claiming that merchants could save on capital investment and would not need to "submit to the constant trouble and solicitude of watching over a numerous body of Workmen."[15] Notwithstanding such claims, competition demanded a decrease in product prices and, in turn, an increase in product demand to further increase economies of scale. A major factor restraining sustained economic growth was an absence of individuals experienced in meeting the challenges inherent in managing a large factory. Many entrepreneurs, thus, found themselves in a quandary: technology and capital made large-scale production possible, and competitive forces made economies of scale imperative, but at the same time, as factories increased in size, unforeseeable managerial challenges emerged.

THE LABOR CHALLENGE

Once an entrepreneur decided to embark on a venture, capital had to be raised for a power source, machinery, buildings, tools, and so forth. As suggested in the previous section, as an organization grows, it becomes necessary to hire managers and other employees. Workforce development, however, is not an easy task. Broadly conceived, it has three aspects: recruitment, training, and discipline/motivation.

[14] Jean-Baptiste Say, *A Treatise on Political Economy*, vol. 2, trans. Charles R. Prinsep (London: Longman, Hurst, Rees, Orme, and Brown, 1821), p. 104. French edition published in 1803.

[15] "Report from the Committee on the State of the Woollen Manufacture of England," *Journals of the House of Commons* 61 (1806), p. 69.

Recruitment

Setting aside "mathematical practitioners" such as instrument makers who crafted navigating and surveying tools and artisans who made clocks and watches, the labor pool at the onset of the Industrial Revolution consisted largely of unskilled agrarian workers whose education was rudimentary at best.[16] Moving from a family farm to a large factory, often located in a brawling, bustling city, could be perilous. Andrew Ure (see Chapter 4) and others complained that large factories were uncongenial to people who were accustomed to an unfettered domestic or rural life, and who did not easily adapt to the monotony of machine-paced work, regular year-round hours, and impersonal discipline.[17] As a consequence, the typical laborer was thought to be restless, shiftless, and irresponsible. Chemical manufacturer Roebuck and Garbett, for instance, moved its factory from Birmingham, England, to Prestonpans, Scotland, in 1749, "to escape the independence of the local workers for the 'obedient turn of the Scotch'."[18] One observer described early textile weavers as fiercely independent and generally insubordinate. For the most part, these workers were Puritans and were as opposed to the standard factory regime as they were to the Church of England.[19]

The transition from farm to factory was eased for some workers, however, by the prospects of a steadier job and higher wages. Agrarian workers were accustomed to a subsistence living derived from the vagaries of soil and seasons. Studies of labor mobility in England during the early Industrial Revolution show that workers were moving toward the north and west, where factories were primarily located. This demonstrated a "sensitivity of labor to wage incentives," as workers now had an opportunity to improve their material standard of living.[20] Of course, not all workers responded to the prospect of higher wages, preferring agrarian or craft pursuits.

The shortage of skilled labor was particularly vexing to employers. Some high-skilled workers did exist in small, scattered guilds and workshops, but they were generally more resistant to factory life. The Woolcombers Guild, for example, resisted mechanization and factory work, preferring their guild tradition. In the Midlands of England—the center of the British textile industry—wool combers were in such short supply that this advertisement appeared: "To WOOL-COMBERS. Wm. TOPLIS and Co. have opened a Free Shop, at Mansfield, the County Nottingham, for Combers from any Part of the Kingdom. The Prices given are equal to any society [guild] and good steady workmen may make very handsome wages."[21] Employers also had to offer inducements to skilled workers and make major concessions to retain them. The loss of essential workers could shut down an entire factory. James Watt had pressing problems with finding workers who could cut and fit valves and cylinders to the proper tolerances; indeed, many of his early failures were of execution, not design. Richard Arkwright was forced to schedule his skilled workers for extra hours due to a shortage of qualified labor. Many iron mills kept their furnaces going even in slack times to keep from losing trained employees. Employers used every possible medium to advertise for workers, and one authority reported that pauper children were employed as apprentices after other sources of labor were absorbed.[22] In brief, it was difficult to recruit a workforce that had the qualifications necessary to perform skilled factory jobs. Labor mobility was enhanced by higher wages, but traditions bound some to their trades and others to their agrarian lifestyles.

---

[16] Morgan Kelly and Cormac Ó Gráda, "Connecting the Scientific and Industrial Revolutions: The Role of Practical Mathematics," *Journal of Economic History* 82(3) (September 2022), pp. 841–873.

[17] Andrew Ure, *The Philosophy of Manufactures: Or an Exposition of the Scientific, Moral and Commercial Economy of the Factory System of Great Britain* (London: Charles Knight, 1835), p. 15.

[18] Edmond G. Fitzmaurice, *Life of William, Earl of Shelburne*, vol. 1: *1737–1766* (London: MacMillan, 1875), p. 404.

[19] Richard Guest, *A Compendious History of the Cotton-Manufacture: With a Disproval of the Claim of Sir Richard Arkwright to the Invention of Its Ingenious Machinery* (Manchester, England: Joseph Pratt, 1823), pp. 40–43.

[20] Robert M. Hartwell, "Business Management in England during the Period of Early Industrialization: Inducements and Obstacles," *Nebraska Journal of Economics & Business* 8(3) (Summer 1969), p. 66.

[21] "To Wool-Combers," *Northampton Mercury* (Northamptonshire, England), November 17, 1792, p. 2 and November 10, 1792, p. 3.

[22] Stanley D. Chapman, *The Early Factory Masters: The Transition to the Factory System in the Midlands Textile Industry* (Newton Abbot, England: David & Charles, 1967), p. 168.

Training

Training was a second major management challenge faced by the emerging factory system. Once workers were recruited, they often had to be taught the skills necessary for factory life. Literacy was uncommon, and basic schooling was lacking; drawings, instruction sheets, and machine operations demanded an ability to read, figure, and respond in a predictable manner.[23] Training was conducted largely by oral instruction, demonstration, and trial and error. New employees were taught how to operate a machine or process a piece of material by their coworkers. Standardized methods were unheard of, and workers blithely followed the example of others who knew little more than they did. Traditional prejudices against anything new added to the challenge. Further, workers were largely unaccustomed to abiding by the accuracy and tolerances necessary for the manufacture of interchangeable parts that were the basis for mass production.

The haphazard acquisition of knowledge from coworkers or inept supervisors, lack of standardized methods, and worker resistance to new methods posed serious challenges for efficient and effective performance. Employers resorted to developing their own schools to teach elementary arithmetic, geometry, and other necessary skills. Jobs were specialized to ease instruction and to meet the challenge of finding employees willing and able to learn. In short, industrialization required an educated workforce, something sorely lacking in the early days of the Industrial Revolution.

Discipline and Motivation

A third challenge encountered in the emerging factory system was that of discipline and motivation. Accustomed to the independence and self-sufficiency of agrarian life, workers had to develop habits of industry, such as punctuality and regular attendance, as well as accept supervision and the mechanical pacing of their work. Moreover, the factory system demanded a different type of discipline: it required regularity instead of bursts of effort and standardization in place of individual craftsmanship.[24] This new discipline, however, did not come easily. Worker attendance was irregular. Ecclesiastical feasts honoring martyrs and saints, some lasting days, drove high levels of absenteeism, as workers stayed at home to celebrate. In addition, some tended to work in spurts—laboring long hours, collecting their wages, and then disappearing for countless days of dissipation. As one contemporary, Rev. Morgan Powell, commented, "[I]f a person can get sufficient in four Days to support himself for seven Days, he will keep Holiday the other three; that is, he will live in Riot and Debauchery."[25] Some workers took a weekly holiday they called "Saint Monday," which meant either not working or working very slowly at the beginning

---

[23] Edwin G. West, "Literacy and the Industrial Revolution," *Economic History Review* 31(3) (August 1978), pp. 369–383.

[24] Edward P. Thompson, "Time, Work-Discipline, and Industrial Capitalism," *Past & Present* no. 38 (December 1967), pp. 56–97. See also Mark Hailwood, "Time Work in Rural England, 1500–1700," *Past & Present* No. 248 (August 2020), pp. 87–121.

[25] [Morgan Powell], *A View of Real Grievances, with Remedies Proposed for Redressing Them; Humbly Submitted to the Consideration of the Legislature* (London: Privately printed, 1772), p. 143. The authorship of this anonymously published book has long been a subject of historical interest. The present attribution is based on an inscription (replete with tau cross to indicate Powell's status as an Anglican clergyperson) that accompanies the book's review in the *Monthly Review; or, Literary Review* 48 (January 1773), p. 19. The inscription by *Monthly Review* editor Ralph Griffiths reads: "**T** Written by the rev. Mr. Powell of Fakenham." Born in 1705 and educated at what is now St. Catharine's College, Cambridge University, Powell served at St. Mary and All Saints Church of Little Walsingham from 1755 until his death in 1774. For biographical details see: T. Hugh Bryant, *Norfolk Churches: Hundred of North Greenhoe* (Norwich: "Norwich Mercury" Office, 1898), p. 94 and Diana Honeybone and Michael Honeybone, eds., *The Correspondence of the Spalding Gentlemen's Society, 1710–1761* (Lincoln, England: Lincoln Record Society, 2010), p. 235. For details regarding Griffiths's annotated volumes, see Benjamin C. Nangle, *The Monthly Review, First Series, 1749–1789; Indexes of Contributors and Articles* (Oxford: England: Clarendon Press, 1934), p. 34. Nangle identifies (p. 239) the Rev. Jabez Hirons as the author of the anonymous *Monthly Review's* criticism of Powell's book. We are indebted to Antonia M. Forster for authenticating Griffiths's handwriting (Personal email correspondence from Forster to Arthur G. Bedeian, August 18, 2022).

For a collection of similar statements (dating to 1690) on the "deleterious effects of high wages," see Edgar S. Furniss, *The Position of the Laborer in a System of Nationalism: A Study in the Labor Theories of Later English Mercantilists* (Boston: Houghton Mifflin, 1920), p. 125n1.

of a week.[26] To combat the problem of saints' days, some early employers resorted to using traditional holidays (i.e., holy days) for company-sponsored outings to build loyalty, break the monotony of everyday life, and cement relationships with workers. For example, Richard Arkwright held a feast for 500 employees at his Cromford Mill in 1776, and Matthew Boulton hosted 700 at his Soho plant.

Machine smashing, although sporadic, was another disciplinary problem.[27] Most machine destruction, a common tactic of early weavers, however, antedated the perfection of the steam engine and the advent of large factories. In 1753, John Kay's flying shuttle was smashed and his home destroyed by workers protesting his laborsaving machinery. James Hargreaves suffered a similar fate at his Blackburn mill in 1768. Because operators of traditional hand-spinners were convinced that his spinning jenny would put them out of work and endanger not only their material standard of living but also their dignity, they raided Hargreaves's home and wrecked his workshop. Parliament passed the Malicious Injury Act in 1769, making the destruction of machines punishable by death.[28] Nevertheless, resistance to automation continued.

Machine smashers became known as *Luddites*, a term that supposedly originated with Ned Ludham, a Leicester stockinger's apprentice who, in 1811, destroyed two stocking frames in a fit of anger. The Luddite movement never had a unified purpose or a single leader. Scattered groups at different times and in different districts did the smashing, each proclaiming they were following orders from the fictitious "General Ludd." These protests, however, appeared to have been based on more than just opposition to laborsaving technology. At the time, wages were falling, unemployment was rampant, and food prices were rising as a result of a government policy restricting imports. Machine smashing was a convenient way to demonstrate dissatisfaction, although other latent forces—not technology per se—are what caused increased unemployment.[29] Three Luddites who had assassinated a mill owner were hanged at York in 1813. Public fears of further violence led to more Luddites being hanged (in Nottingham, Lancaster, and Chester), and the machine-smashing movement soon died for lack of leadership.

Given the Luddites' concern that the spinning jenny would drive mass unemployment, it is worth noting that the number of weavers employed actually increased, as "the falling price of woven cloth stoked demand."[30] Although it is true that, in the short term, livelihoods may be threatened as it is not always the same people who get the new jobs when technology changes, over the long run, as noted in Chapter 1, innovative technologies that give workers cutting edge tools are the fundamental catalysts for improvements in a nation's living standards, and create expanded opportunities for employment that are often better paying. Examples of relatively well-paid occupations created by the Industrial Revolution include factory owner, professional manager, clerk, machinist, steam mechanic, telegrapher, locomotive engineer, and plumber. Moreover, history shows that countries that have failed to embrace new technologies permitting the production of more with fewer people, or that have imposed restrictions on technological advancements for the sake of unemployed workers, have fallen behind in global competitiveness.[31] In the present age, opposition to laborsaving innovations (derided as "job-killers") has occurred with the demise of elevator attendants, telephone-switchboard operators, gas-station jockeys, bank tellers, and grocery checkers. The technology-driven productivity gains and unequaled material wealth

[26] Hans-Joachim Voth, "Time and Work in Eighteenth-Century London," *Journal of Economic History* 58(1) (March 1998), pp. 29–58; Douglas A. Reid, "The Decline of Saint Monday 1766–1876," *Past & Present* no. 71 (May 1976), pp. 76–101; and *idem*, "Weddings, Weekdays, Work and Leisure in Urban England 1791–1911: The Decline of Saint Monday Revisited," *Past & Present* no. 153 (November 1996), pp. 135–163.

[27] Eric Hobsbawm, "The Machine Breakers," *Past & Present* no. 1 (February 1952), pp. 57–70; Alessandro Nuvolari, "The 'Machine Breakers' and the Industrial Revolution," *Journal of European Economics* 31(2) (Fall 2002), pp. 393–428.

[28] *The Statutes at Large, From the Seventh Year of the Reign of King George the Third, to the Eighteenth Year of the Reign of King George the Third*, vol. 8, ed. Owen Ruffhead (London: Charles Eyre & Andrew Strahan, 1786), pp. 80–81.

[29] Malcolm I. Thomis, *The Luddites: Machine Breaking in Regency England* (Hamden, CT: Archon Books, 1970), pp. 41–73.

[30] John Browne, *Make, Think, Imagine: Engineering the Future of Civilization* (New York: Pegasus Books, 2019), p. 29.

[31] Carl Benedikt Frey, "The High Cost of Impeding Automation," *Wall Street Journal* (October 25, 2019), p. R2.

resulting from innovations associated with each of these occupations (not to mention the jobs created in the manufacture, sale, and service of automated elevators, switchboards, gas pumps, teller machines, barcode scanners and touch-screen cash registers) is one reason why the quality of life today is better than in the past. Most recently, the hysteria over generative artificial intelligence applications such as ChatGPT and DALL-E destroying careers and lives is reminiscent of the Luddities' concerns some two-hundred years ago.

Attempts to motivate worker performance in early nineteenth-century factories fell into three categories: positive inducements (often referred to as "carrots"), negative sanctions (commonly known as "sticks"), and efforts to build a new factory ethos.[32] In general, however, business operators during this time period embraced poet and philosopher Ralph Waldo Emerson's conclusion that "Mankind is as lazy as it dares to be."[33] "Carrots" were opportunities to earn more money through performance incentives; thus, worker pay was based on output. Performance incentives represented a major break with tradition. As noted, economists of the seventeenth- and eighteenth-century mercantilist school believed that income (i.e., wages) and the supply of labor were negatively related; that is, as wages rose, workers would leave to spend their money, returning only after it had been spent and more was needed. This viewpoint is evident in the conclusion of two wool merchants who worked under the putting-out system. The first noted, "It is a fact well known to those who are conversant in the matter, that scarcity, to a certain degree, promotes industry,"[34] to which the second added, "a reduction of wages in the woolen manufactures would be a national blessing and advantage, and no real injury to the poor. By this means we might keep our trade, uphold our rents, and reform the people in the bargain."[35]

The view that the hungriest worker was the best worker justified keeping wages low to ensure a steady workforce. Adam Smith expressed a contrasting view, however:

> The wages of labour are the encouragement of industry, which, like every other human quality, improves in proportion to the encouragement it receives. . . . When wages are high, accordingly, we shall always find the workmen more active, diligent and expeditious, than where they are low. . . . Some workmen, indeed when they can earn in four days what will maintain them through the week, will be idle the other three. This, however, is by no means the case with the greater part. Workmen, on the contrary, when they are liberally paid by the piece, are very apt to overwork themselves, and to ruin their health and constitution in a few years. . . . If masters [employers] would always listen to the dictates of reason and humanity, they have frequently occasion rather to moderate, than to animate the application of many of their workmen.[36]

With an appeal to moderation, Smith disagreed with the tradition that wages must be kept at a subsistence level and that the best workers were the hungriest. Rather, he held that high wages brought out the best in people and that they would work harder to earn more. This break with mercantilist theory offered the opportunity for individual rewards based on initiative.

The emerging factory system largely continued the putting-out system practice of payment based on output. Performance incentives were used more widely in operations that were labor intensive, that is, where the cost of labor was a large part of total cost and where payment could be tied to individual output. For example, by 1833, 31,950 workers at 225 cotton mills in

---

[32] Sidney Pollard, "Factory Discipline in the Industrial Revolution," *Economic History Review* 16(2) (December 1963), p. 260.

[33] Ralph Waldo Emerson quoted in Edward A. Atkinson, *The Margin of Profits* (New York: G. P. Putnam's Sons, 1887), p. 105.

[34] John Arbuthnot (of Mitcham), *An Inquiry into the Connection between the Present Price of Provisions, and the Size of Farms: With Remarks on Population as Affected Thereby. To Which Are Added, Proposals for Preventing Future Scarcity* (London: T. Cadell, 1773), p. 93.

[35] John Smith, *Chronicon Rusticum-commerciale; Or Memoirs of Wool & Being a Collection of History and Argument Concerning the Woolen Manufacture and the Woolen Trade in General*, vol. 2 (London: T. Osborne, 1747), p. 308. See also William Hutton, *The History of Birmingham* (Birmingham, England: Pearson and Rollason, 1783), p. 50.

[36] Adam Smith, *An Inquiry into the Nature and Causes of the Wealth of Nations* (London: W. Strahan and T. Cadell in the Strand, 1776), vol. 1, bk. I, ch. 8, pp. 90–92.

Lancashire, Cheshire, and Derbyshire counties were reported to be on piecework.[37] Performance standards, meanwhile, were based on the average time necessary for completing a job rather than on a careful study of the job itself and the time it should take to complete.

"Sticks," negative sanctions, were practices for which the early factory system was frequently criticized. Corporal punishment, especially of children, was used, though historians disagree on its frequency and severity. The prevailing attitude toward children, even in respectable homes, was (as the medieval saying suggested) that they should "be seen and not heard" and, in the spirit of Proverbs 13:24, that to spare the rod was to spoil the child. As British historian Stanley D. Chapman has observed, although the mistreatment of children cannot be excused, "[c]ruel punishments to children were not unusual in the eighteenth century."[38]

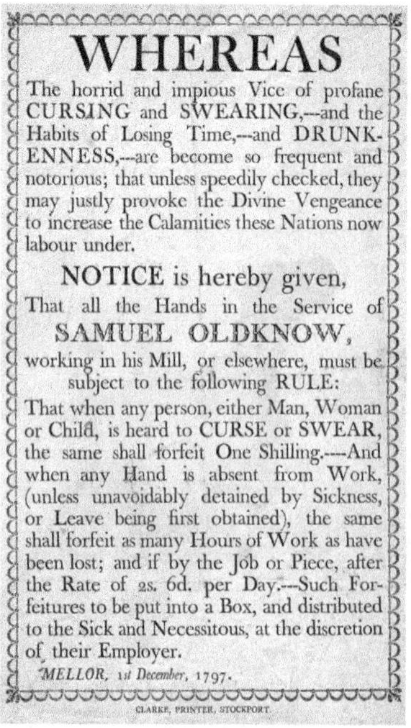

WHEREAS

The horrid and impious Vice of profane CURSING and SWEARING,—and the Habits of Losing Time,—and DRUNKENNESS,—are become so frequent and notorious; that unless speedily checked, they may justly provoke the Divine Vengeance to increase the Calamities these Nations now labour under.

NOTICE is hereby given,

That all the Hands in the Service of

SAMUEL OLDKNOW,

working in his Mill, or elsewhere, must be subject to the following RULE:

That when any person, either Man, Woman or Child, is heard to CURSE or SWEAR, the same shall forfeit One Shilling.---And when any Hand is absent from Work, (unless unavoidably detained by Sickness, or Leave being first obtained), the same shall forfeit as many Hours of Work as have been lost; and if by the Job or Piece, after the Rate of 2s. 6d. per Day.---Such Forfeitures to be put into a Box, and distributed to the Sick and Necessitous, at the discretion of their Employer.

MELLOR, 1st December, 1797.

CLARKE, PRINTER, STOCKPORT.

Box 5, Folder 24, Oldknow Collection, Rare Book & Manuscript Library Butler Library, Columbia University.

FIGURE 3.1 Fines at the Mellor Mill at Derbyshire, England, 1797

Graduated fines were a more common method of discipline: the penalty at one mine for being absent on a Monday morning was 2 shillings and 6 pennies; workers at another mill were fined 5 shillings for "singing, swearing or being drunk."[39] This was a relatively large portion of a worker's pay. On December 1, 1797, Samuel Oldknow, considered one of the most progressive employers of the early factory period, posted the fines shown in Figure 3.1 at his Mellor Mill at Derbyshire, England.[40] To avoid provoking "Divine Vengeance," workers heard swearing were fined one shilling. For being absent, workers forfeited wages for the hours missed. All fines and forfeits went into a box for distribution to the sick and needy. The wording in the Oldknow employee notice mimics that in the Profane Oaths Act passed in 1745. This statute proclaims that after June 1, 1746, anyone convicted of "profanely swearing and cursing" was to be fined proportionate to their social status, with day laborers charged one shilling and gentlemen five shillings.[41] This act was repealed in 1967.

A third method of motivation was oriented toward creating a new factory ethos. The goal was to use religious beliefs and moral values to create "proper" attitudes toward work. To this end, people were encouraged (often on company time) to read the Bible and regularly attend church, and were exhorted to avoid the deadly sins of laziness, sloth, and avarice. A coalition of employers and ministers admonished the populace to guard against these moral depravities, which were not only sinful but also led to a lackadaisical, dissipated workforce. The London Lead Company, for instance, dismissed workers for "tippling [drinking intoxicating liquor], fighting, night rambling, mischief and other disreputable conduct."[42] Doubtless, this moral suasion emanated from

[37] Factories Inquiry Commission, *Supplementary Report of the Central Board of His Majesty's Commissioners Appointed to Collect Information in the Manufacturing Districts, as to the Employment of Children in Factories, and as to the Propriety and Means of Curtailing the Hours of Their Labour*, vol. 1 (London: House of Commons, 1834), p. 136.

[38] Chapman, Early Factory Masters, p. 203.

[39] Pollard, "Factory Discipline in the Industrial Revolution," p. 262.

[40] George Unwin, *Samuel Oldknow and the Arkwrights: The Industrial Revolution at Stockport and Marple* (Manchester, England: The University Press, 1924), p. 198. See also Robert Williams, "Inscribing the Workers: An Experiment in Factory Discipline or the Inculcation of Manners? A Case in Context," *Accounting History* 2(1) (May 1997), pp. 35–60.

[41] Danby Pickering, comp. *Statutes of the United Kingdom of Great Britain and Ireland*, vol. 18: *From the 15th Year to the 20th Year of King George II* (Cambridge, England: J. Bentham, 1765), pp. 444–449.

[42] George H. Mennell, "Discussion," in Arthur Raistrick, "The London Lead Company, 1692–1905," *Transactions of the Newcomen Society* 14(1) (1933), p. 156.

more than a concern for workers' souls. Sidney Pollard presented a succinct statement of these attempts at creating a new factory ethos: "[T]he drive to raise the level of respectability and morality among the working classes was not undertaken for their own sakes but primarily, or even exclusively, as an aspect of building up a new factory discipline."[43]

THE SEARCH FOR MANAGERIAL TALENT

In addition to the challenges of finding, training, and motivating entry-level employees, there was the task of finding qualified managers. As outlined earlier, as organizations grew, the ability of entrepreneurs to directly supervise all their employees diminished, and an intermediate level of supervision became necessary. Judging from period literature, salaried managers (i.e., those in the layer of management below an entrepreneur) were usually workers promoted from the ranks because they evidenced a greater degree of technical skills or had the ability to maintain discipline. Typically, they were paid only a little more than their subordinates and were at times attracted to a managerial position because it gave them the power to hire their spouses and children. Untrained in the intricacies of supervising others, these managers were left on their own to develop a supervisory style. Problems were met and solved on an ad hoc basis. The general view was that success or failure to produce results depended on the character of a manager (i.e., on his personal traits and idiosyncrasies), and not on any generalized concept of leadership. Other potential sources of managerial talent included relatives, hired on the assumption that they were more trustworthy or would act to preserve their potential inheritance.[44] This practice also provided family members with training that would help secure ownership for future generations. Countinghouses were another source of talent; entrepreneurs recruited talented bank clerks and tellers, thinking they probably had both business and financial acumen. On-the-job training (OJT) and apprenticeships were used to develop necessary technical skills.[45]

The transformation of Great Britain from an agrarian to an industrial society occurred at a time when there was no ready supply of either trained or experienced managers, or a common body of knowledge about how to manage. The formal training of managers supplemented OJT with instruction in production techniques, sources and characteristics of materials, machine operations, trade practices, and the legal obligations of firms. This training was oriented toward a specific industry (cotton, woolen, mining, etc.) and did not readily lend itself to wider generalization. Managers, trained in one industry, were bound to that industry; to move to another they would need to learn new skills. Furthermore, there was no universal set of expectations about how a manager should act. Codes of conduct that provided advice about a manager's responsibility for safety, the security of plant and equipment, design standards, and procedures to follow in safeguarding a factory owner's interests were developed for specific industries.

Scotsman James Montgomery (1771–1854) prepared what were most probably the first management texts.[46] Montgomery's managerial advice was largely technical in nature; he offered guidance on how to discern quality and quantity of work, how to adjust and repair machinery, how to keep costs down, and how to "avoid all *unnecessary* severity"[47] in disciplining subordinates. He noted that a manager must be "just and impartial—firm and decisive—always on

[43] Pollard, "Factory Discipline in the Industrial Revolution," p. 270.

[44] *Idem*, "The Genesis of the Managerial Profession: The Experience of the Industrial Revolution in Great Britain," *Studies in Romanticism* 4(2) (Winter 1965), p. 63.

[45] B. Zorina Khan, "Human Capital, Knowledge and Economic Development: Evidence from the British Industrial Revolution," *Cliometrica* 12(2) (May 2018), pp. 313–341.

[46] James Montgomery, *The Carding and Spinning Master's Assistant; Or the Theory and Practice of Cotton Spinning* (Glasgow: J. Niven, Jr., 1832); *idem*, *The Cotton Spinner's Manual; Or a Compendium of the Principles of Cotton Spinning* (Glasgow: J. Niven, Jr., 1835). See also James P. Baughman, ed., "James Montgomery on Factory Management, 1832," *Business History Review* 42(2) (Summer 1968), pp. 219–226.

[47] James Montgomery, *The Theory and Practice of Cotton Spinning; Or, The Carding and Spinning Master's Assistant: Showing the Use of Each Machine Employed* (Glasgow: J. Niven, Jr. 1832), p. 219.

the alert to prevent rather than check faults, after they have taken place."[48] This latter comment indicates an early understanding that the control function is both forward- and backward-looking. Montgomery's advice, however, was written for those in the cotton industry and, like most other early writers, he did not seek to develop any generalized principles of management.

Montgomery was so highly regarded as a manager that he was brought to the United States in 1836 to become superintendent of the York Mills in Saco, Maine. This gave Montgomery the opportunity to conduct what was probably the first comparative study of management through an analysis of different economies. He found that the United States had higher production costs, paid higher wages (including wages for women), but had lower material costs. British firms had lower costs, paid lower wages, but paid more for raw materials. The relative competitive efficiency resided in Great Britain, in Montgomery's opinion, because the British firms were better managed.[49] Montgomery's study was of cotton mills only, but it gives some idea of the differing states of managerial knowledge in the United States and Great Britain in 1840.

First-line supervisors, or overlookers, were (as mentioned) typically paid little more than their subordinates. Salaried managers were often paid based on their social class rather than on the extent of their responsibility. After the 1790s, however, the shortage of managerial talent had forced payment based on the job and not the person. By 1830, the pay of salaried managers had risen rapidly and compressed the differential between their pay and that of entrepreneurs.[50] In 1848, John Stuart Mill observed that those who managed others had to possess a "cultivated intelligence," [51] that is, a "general level of knowledge and skill, something acquired through education, both formal and informal and on the job learning."[52] Mill disagreed with Adam Smith's concern about the separation of ownership and management (see Chapter 2). He believed that the "zeal" of hired managers could be stimulated by connecting "their pecuniary interest with the interest of their employers, by giving them part of their remuneration in the form of a percentage on the profits."[53]

In Great Britain, the status of entrepreneurs was rising by the mid-nineteenth century, inducing many young people to seek their fortunes in commerce, or at least become a junior partner in a large firm. Second- and third-generation offspring of founder-entrepreneurs tended to delegate more authority to and depend more on salaried managers. Perhaps their affluence, built by the success of preceding generations, made them less desirous of becoming personally involved in daily workplace activities; or perhaps their firms had grown to such a size and the fund of managerial talent had reached such a point that finding reliable subordinates was easier than it had been for their predecessors. This stands in contrast to early factories, where the challenges of finding and developing managerial talent were acute. There were no business schools for recruiting, and no systematic programs for developing managers. Managerial skill was judged in a localized, idiosyncratic manner.

PLANNING, ORGANIZING, AND CONTROLLING

In addition to the demands of staffing a factory, early managers faced planning, organizing, and controlling challenges that were similar to those encountered by their counterparts today. In planning operations, early factories required more farsightedness than the putting-out system of production. As the factory system developed, managers became more rational and interested

[48] *Ibid.*, p. 256.

[49] James Montgomery, *The Cotton Manufacture of the United States of America Contrasted and Compared with That of Great Britain* (London: John N. Van, 1840), p. 138.

[50] Pollard, "The Genesis of the Managerial Profession," p. 61.

[51] John Stuart Mill, *Principles of Political Economy with Some of Their Applications to Social Philosophy*, vol. 1 (Boston, MA: C. C. Little & J. Brown, 1848), p. 170.

[52] P. Bruce Buchan, "John Stuart Mill—Contributions to the Principles Management: The Intelligence Factor," *British Journal of Management* 4(2) (June 1993), p. 71.

[53] *Ibid.*, p. 187.

in laying a foundation for long-term growth rather than chasing short-term speculative gains. Mines required long-range planning to develop untapped ore veins and factories required costly equipment. As capital was sunk, managers had to be more aware of the long-term implications of their decisions.

Planning in early factories was largely technically oriented rather than comprehensive in scope and application. Robert Owen and Richard Arkwright led the way in factory layout and design. Their requirements, or principles, emphasized workflow orderliness. New technologies demanded planning power sources and connections, arranging machinery and space for smooth workflow, and reducing confusion through well-placed materials. The Boulton and Watt engine shops developed detailed systems for controlling materials and parts and engaged in rudimentary production planning.[54] The use of standardized, interchangeable parts made production planning necessary, both in product design and execution. Watt's son (James Watt, Jr.) realized that standardized and interchangeable parts would lower manufacturing costs, and that detailed planning and proper execution would ensure that final products meet specifications. Being able to swap out parts also eased product repairs and reduced both company and customer spare-parts stock, thus simplifying inventory control and investment.

Early *departmentalization*, or the grouping of activities, was often based on the number of partners or relatives. With a gesture toward egalitarianism, each partner or relative became a department head with one or two salaried managers to assist in overseeing subordinates. It has been estimated that by 1833, in the 151 Lancashire, Cheshire, and Derbyshire cotton mills mentioned above, there was on average about one "overlooker" for every 28 weavers, one overlooker for every 14 throstle spinners, and one overlooker for every 84 mule spinners.[55] Similar ratios were apparent in mining, shipyards, and construction, suggesting that firms in these industries were also relatively "flat," which means that they had few or no layers of middle management. These firms were typically family owned and managed, and standard wages for "outsiders" were comparatively lower.[56] Firms were rarely vertically integrated manufacturers. For example, although cotton mills might spin wool into fiber, they generally relied on other firms or agents to fabricate and merchandise a final product, such as garments and home textiles.

Within the emerging textile industry, technology played an important role in how activities and relationships were structured.[57] In the beginning, most textile workshops followed a batch-processing system, where a product was made in a limited quantity or batch, followed by another batch of slightly different products, and so on. This description seems to characterize the textile industry until the early 1800s.

As new steam-power applications were developed, another technological innovation further increased efficiency: the arrangement of power-driven machines in the sequence necessary to make a finished product. This "flow technology" resembled a mass-production assembly line, with an output of large quantities of standardized products made at a lower per unit cost, intended for a mass market. With this increase in production, it became more economical to specialize labor even further than before. Unlike the moving assembly line as we know it today, older flow technology saw the movement of products from one stage of production to another by carts, wheelbarrows, chutes, and so on. Departments were established for individual operations. As hinted at above, with more departments came the need for another level of management to

[54] Eric Roll, *An Early Experiment in Industrial Organisation: Being a History of the Firm of Boulton and Watt*, 1775–1805 (London: Longmans Green and Co., 1930). The development of relatively advanced managerial techniques at Boulton and Watt is credited to the founders' sons, Matthew Robinson Boulton and James Watt, Jr. (p. xv).

[55] Sydney Pollard, *The Genesis of Modern Management: A Study of the Industrial Revolution in Great Britain* (Cambridge, MA: Harvard University Press, 1965), p. 135. Pollard's calculations are based on data contained in Factories Inquiry Commission, *Supplementary Report of the Central Board of His Majesty's Commissioners Appointed to Collect Information in the Manufacturing*, vol. 1, Supplement (E.) (General.), p. 125.

[56] *Idem*, "The Genesis of the Managerial Profession," p. 70.

[57] Stanley D. Chapman, "The Textile Factory before Arkwright: A Typology of Factory Development," *Business History Review* 48(4) (Winter 1974), pp. 468–473.

coordinate work as it flowed from one stage to another. Consequently, there was a growth in the chain-of-command that stretched from an organization's lowest to highest level, creating a taller hierarchical structure and the need for more elaborate procedures and systems to integrate a firm's activities. It appears that early textile firms discovered that technology influences an organization's structure. Early batch-production methods, for example, allowed for a relative degree of informality, though the later application of steam-driven power led to new factory technology, which required more formality in organization design.

Entrepreneurs faced numerous challenges in maintaining factory output. With the need for larger factories to accommodate new steam-power applications enabling the production of large quantities of standardized products, they could no longer personally oversee all operations. They thus found it necessary to delegate authority. This was complicated, however, by a lack of trained and trustworthy salaried managers. As Adam Smith observed, salaried managers who would exercise the same vigilance over other people's money as over their own were rare. Accounting had not advanced since Luca Pacioli's time (see Chapter 2), and the use of financial information for making operating decisions was uncommon. Managers kept account books to record earnings, wages, purchases, and sales, but few managers used these accounts to aid decision-making. Josiah Wedgwood, manufacturer of various pottery products, was one of those few. He refined his accounts until he was able to use them in setting prices, fixing potters' piece rates, determining the percentage of selling expenses to sales, and tracing the embezzlement of certain funds by his head clerk.[58] It would be more than a century before better costing techniques were developed.

Through trial-and-error experience, early entrepreneurs attempted to cope with the challenges of managing a factory. The emphasis these entrepreneurs placed on technical rather than managerial challenges was probably due to the available technology and the pressure to keep abreast of competitors. Management was not seen as readily lending itself to wider generalization and success was thought to depend on a manager's personal qualities, not on a grasp of broad principles. Management was an art, not a discipline; pragmatic, not theoretical; and parochial, not universal.

Some individuals, however, were attempting to fill the void in management knowledge. Their efforts are the subject of Chapter 4. Before moving ahead, though, let us attempt to gain a perspective on the cultural impact of the Industrial Revolution.

CULTURAL CONSEQUENCES OF THE INDUSTRIAL REVOLUTION

The consequences of the Industrial Revolution were not only technological; they were also cultural. New machines, new factories, and new cities shook people's tradition-based roots and demanded their participation in a changing era. Agrarian life before industrialization has been often romanticized. Critics of the Industrial Revolution have charged that it ended a golden age of equality and freedom. They allege that industrialization enslaved workers to the owners of capital; turned people into little more than a marketplace commodity; allowed employers to exploit child and female labor; and created poverty, urbanization, and pollution, among other societal ills. Let us examine some of these criticisms and attempt to gain a perspective on the cultural consequences of the Industrial Revolution.

WORKING CONDITIONS

Economics earned its sobriquet, "the dismal science," during the mid-nineteenth century.[59] The Rev. Thomas R. Malthus (1766–1834) set out to disprove the optimism of Adam Smith and

[58] Neil McKendrick, "Josiah Wedgwood and Cost Accounting in the Industrial Revolution," *Economic History Review* 23(1) (April 1970), pp. 45–67.

[59] The name "the dismal science" was coined by Victorian-era Scottish historian Thomas Carlyle after reading Malthus's dire prediction concerning worldwide starvation. See *Fraser's Magazine for Town and Country* 40(240) (December 1849), p. 672.

other classical economists. He contended that as the earth's population increased geometrically (2–4–6–8), its food supply would at best increase only arithmetically (1–2–3–4), with the certain result being worldwide starvation.[60] Thus, Malthus believed that because the world's population is limited by the means of subsistence, and because the masses tend to reproduce beyond this limit, there could be no improvement in their condition. He felt that government relief of the poor only encouraged a population increase, drove food prices up, and left the poor no better off. The only answer for Malthus was to restrict the supply of labor and to encourage "moral restraint" (i.e., delayed marriage and sexual abstinence until then). His was a hopeless view of people as indistinguishable and powerless to overcome the world's natural resource limitations.

David Ricardo (1771–1823), a follower of Malthus, did not appear much more optimistic. He reasoned that wages could not fall below the price-level necessary for workers to subsist because, without the essentials to exist, they would be unable to work. Furthermore, he believed that competition among workers for employment would hold wages at this minimal level.[61] Neither Malthus nor Ricardo foresaw improvements in factory-made implements such as the mechanical reaper and steel plow that would bring about an agricultural revolution in the eighteenth century, or scientific advances such as contraceptives that would slow the birth rate in the nineteenth century. Such innovations allowed both an increase in human populations and living standards.

Utopian socialists, such as Robert Owen (see Chapter 4), saw people as powerless in their environment and wanted to replace marketplace individualism with a communal life. Rather than advocate revolt, the Utopians felt they could achieve change through their writings and example. In contrast, German philosopher Karl Marx (1818–1883) considered violent revolution to be the inevitable "midwife" of history.[62] Marx believed that labor alone creates value; in that, workers' labor adds value to a good or service, and this addition is worth more than the value of their wages. According to Marx, this "surplus value" is appropriated by capitalists (as profit) when a good or service is sold. In Marx's view, because workers (the "proletariat") were thereby exploited by their greedy capitalist factory masters (the "bourgeoisie"), they had to unite to break their chains. The revolt would be bloody but would eliminate economic classes and create an egalitarian workers' paradise. Workers would be free of exploitation and contribute to the production of goods and services according to their abilities and be provided for according to their need. This zero-sum thinking fails to acknowledge that the combination of capital and labor increases the value of each. It fails to understand that market-driven economic growth benefits everyone and reflects the mistaken belief that the only way to become rich is to take from others. If the latter were true, there would have been no economic progress in history. Furthermore, it rejects individual liberty (economic and otherwise) and promotes class warfare in its place. It is of note that Marx's class distinction between property-owning capitalists and wage-earning labor has become increasingly obsolete, as the importance of human capital (e.g., what people know and their ability to efficiently exchange information and ideas with others) eclipses the value of economic capital (e.g., machinery, tools, buildings) in today's digital age.

Although the writings of Marx and his benefactor Friedrich Engels (who incidentally inherited his father's English textile mills) were more political essays than economic analyses, they did reflect a dismal view of a world in which a ruling capitalist class oppresses the toiling masses. Marx and Engels's solution to this social injustice, as expressed in their *Communist Manifesto*,[63] would eventually become the basis for the Union of Soviet Socialist Republic's abolition of private property, state ownership of the means of production, and a planned economy under the "Dictatorship of the Proletariat." Their "solution" would lead to the enslavement, torture, and

[60] Thomas R. Malthus, *An Essay on the Principle of Population; Or, A View of Its Past and Present Effects on Human Happiness*, 3rd ed., vol. 1 (Washington, DC: Roger Chew Weightman, 1809), p. 18.

[61] David Ricardo, *On the Principles of Political Economy, and Taxation* (London: John Murray, 1817), pp. 90–91.

[62] Karl Marx, *Das Kapital: Kritik der politischen Oekonomie* [*Capital: Critique of Political Economy*], vol. 1: *Der Produktionsprocess des Kapitals* [*The Process of Capitalist Production as a Whole*] (Hamburg: Verlag von Otto Meissner, 1867), p. 782.

[63] Karl Marx and Frederick Engels, *Manifest der Kommunistischen Partei* [*Manifesto of the Communist Party*], trans. Samuel Moore (London: Workers' Educational Association, 1848). Written in 1846.

deaths of untold millions when in 1917 Russia replaced the despotism of Czar Nicholas II with the despotism of the Bolshevik Party and the ascent of Vladimir I. Lenin as head of government. The Bolshevik Party changed its name to the "All-Russian Communist Party" in 1918 because Marx favored the word *communism* ("of or for the community") to describe the classless society that he hoped to ultimately create.

Were people powerless and exploited by capitalism? The masses had spent the previous thousand or more years surviving at a subsistence level as serfs tied to feudal landlords.[64] Under mercantilism, the British government regulated wages, keeping them low to maintain a favorable balance of trade, such that exports exceeded imports. Further, as we saw earlier, it was a common belief that low wages provided an incentive to work. The Industrial Revolution did not create poverty; it inherited it. With Adam Smith came a new market-based philosophy that higher wages made people work harder to earn more and this, in turn, fostered additional economic growth. The rise of capitalism released people from drudgery through labor saving machines, making them more productive. It also offered jobs that were better paid for less effort.[65] It is difficult to agree with Marx and Engels that workers were exploited by their factory masters: first, as described, the shortage of labor (especially skilled) diminished the power of factory owners to exploit labor; and second, from 1790 to 1830, workers' real wages steadily rose, improving "well above the level of mere subsistence."[66] For those who were willing to learn the necessary skills, new machines and methods made them more productive and raised their wages, which, in turn, added industrial efficiency, reduced the prices of goods, and increased their real income. Incentive-payment plans held out a promise of economic betterment for the common masses; no longer tied to remitting a tithe to a feudal lord, individuals could enhance their well-being through their own effort.

Eric Hopkins studied a heavily industrialized region of England and concluded: "[T]here was no marked deterioration of working conditions during the classic period of the Industrial Revolution . . . [and] to suggest that . . . the majority of workers . . . were forced to . . . become the slaves of a new time discipline is really a very doubtful proposition, and its unthinking repetition can serve only to perpetuate a historical myth."[67] Claims of worker exploitation should be considered against this: through performance incentives, increased wages, rising real income, steady employment, and regular hours, workers were improving their lot beyond a subsistence level. As Thomas Hobbes famously noted, life in preindustrial England was "solitary, poor, nasty, brutish, and short,"[68] as most people lived a subsistence lifestyle in abject poverty. Additionally, as Jacob Bronowski reminds us, "Mines and workshops had been dank, crowded, and tyrannical long before the Industrial Revolution."[69]

CHILD AND FEMALE LABOR

Child and female labor were likewise not inventions of the Industrial Revolution. For eons, women and children throughout the world had been an essential part of domestic and agricultural economies, doing household chores, growing crops, and caring for animals. Farming, in particular, demanded long hours under a relentless sun and required that everyone in a family—womenfolk

[64] Sheilagh Ogilvie, "Economics and History: Analyzing Serfdom," Working Paper 200, Economic and Social History Working Papers, University of Oxford (Oxford: September 2022), p. 3.

[65] Friedrich A. Hayek, "History and Politics," in *idem*, ed., *Capitalism and the Historians* (Chicago, IL: University of Chicago Press, 1954), pp. 15–16.

[66] Thomas S. Ashton, "The Standard of Life of the Workers in England: 1790–1830," *Journal of Economic History* 9 (Supplement 1949), p. 37.

[67] Eric Hopkins, "Working Hours and Conditions during the Industrial Revolution: A Re-Appraisal," *Economic History Review* 35(1) (February 1982), pp. 63, 66.

[68] Thomas Hobbes, *Leviathan, or, the Matter, Form, and Power of a Common-Wealth Ecclesiastical and Civil* (London: Andrew Crooke, 1651), p. 62.

[69] Jacob Bronowski, *The Ascent of Man* (Boston, MA: Little, Brown and Company, 1973), p. 279.

and children included—shared in the tilling, sowing, cultivating, and harvesting, all of which was done by hand. Women and children worked and child workers, indeed, were expected to work. One authority noted that child labor "was at its worst and greatest height before anybody thought of a factory."[70] Outside the home and farm, child and female workers were found primarily in textile weaving, but also in mines and collieries, where the technology was relatively simple.[71] Employers would have preferred a mature, stable, adult workforce, but such workers were scarce and hard to attract.

Concern in Great Britain over child-labor practices led to two parliamentary investigations: the first in 1819, at the behest of Robert Owen, and chaired by industrialist Sir Robert Peel, himself an employer of children, and the second, in 1832, chaired by Leeds businessman Michael T. Sadler.[72] Extensive and detailed evidence was collected in both inquiries. Children often began working a 12-hour day at age five. This practice was widespread in cotton, wool, flax, and silk mills. In both inquiries, informants described prevailing hours (long), wages (low), working conditions (often extremely poor), and the methods of discipline (often harsh). Overall, however, there is evidence that "not only did the industrial revolution not increase exploitation, it gradually improved the situation of children. . . . Industrialization, far from being the source of the enslavement of children, was the source of their liberation."[73] Industrialization created more jobs and better jobs, allowing children to escape even greater exploitation at home under the putting-out system of production or in agriculture, where working conditions were often worse than in factories and limits on their employment were virtually non-existent. Indeed, it has been observed that in Victorian England, children counted "for little in social life," and that "[r]aising a child often appeared synonymous with breaking its will."[74]

As a result of the Peel investigation, the first British law to regulate child labor, the Cotton Mills and Factory Act, was passed in 1819.[75] Applying to only the cotton industry, the act prohibited the employment of children under age nine, and for those under 16 set 12 hours as the maximum workday and forbade night work. With no effective enforcement mechanism, however, it was widely violated. It was not until the Factory Act of 1833, spurred by the Sadler investigation, that an "inspectorate of factories" was created with the power to impose penalties to ensure compliance. The 1833 act applied to both cotton and woolen mills and set the maximum workday for children aged nine to thirteen at 8 hours and for those thirteen to eighteen at 12 hours. It also marked an important step forward in requiring that children under thirteen receive at least 2 hours of formal schooling each day. Heretofore, until graded education was widely established in England some 60 years later, the only opportunity the children of the industrial working class had to learn basic reading and writing, often using the Bible as their textbook, was in Sunday schools, which became widely established in the early 1780s. Classes were held in teachers' homes. The schools operated on Sundays, as this was the only day the children working in factories six days a week could attend.[76]

Female workers were attracted to factory work to pay off farm debts, to build dowries for enticing a potential groom, or to supplement their family income. Unmarried women and widows

---

[70] Cyrus Redding, *An Illustrated Itinerary of the County of Lancaster* (London: How and Parsons, 1842), p. 39.

[71] For more on the working conditions confronted by children in mines and collieries, see *The Condition and Treatment of the Children Employed in the Mines and Colliers of the United Kingdom* (London: William Strange, 1842).

[72] *Reasons in Favour of Sir Robert Peel's Bill, for Ameliorating the Condition of Children Employed in Cotton Factories; Comprehending a Summary View of the Evidence in Support of the Bill, Taken before the Lords' Committees in the Present Session of Parliament* (London: W. Clowes, 1819); *Report from the Committee on the "Bill to Regulate the Labour of Children in the Mills and Factories of the United Kingdom": with the Minutes of Evidence, Appendix and Index* (London: House of Commons, 1832).

[73] Clark Nardinelli, "Were Children Exploited during the Industrial Revolution?" *Research in Economic History* 11(1988), p. 268.

[74] Ian McEwan, "Five Best: Books on Writing About Children," *Wall Street Journal* (September 24–25, 2022), p. C8.

[75] House of Lords, "Cotton Factories Regulation Bill," *Parliamentary Debates from the Year 1803 to the Present Time* 40 (June 14, 1819) (London: T. C. Hansard, 1819), pp. 1130–1133.

[76] Thomas B. Walters, *Robert Raikes: Founder of Sunday Schools* (London: Epworth Press, 1930), pp. 30–38.

were able to escape dependence on relatives or parish relief.[77] One observer, Paul Mantoux, felt that entrepreneurs were "tyrannical, hard, sometimes cruel: their passions and greeds were those of upstarts. They had the reputation of being heavy drinkers and of having little regard for the honour of their female employees."[78] Mantoux was guilty of overgeneralizing; ample examples can be given, such as Josiah Wedgwood, Jr., Matthew Robinson Boulton, James Watt, Jr., John Wilkinson, Robert Owen, and a host of others, for whom there is no evidence of loose and fancy-free behavior toward female employees.[79] Further, in contrast to the traditional norm of paying what was "suitable" for women's work, Joyce Burnette found that, during the Industrial Revolution, women received market wages, and the assertion their pay was determined instead by custom "needs to be revised."[80] There was also great concern that unemployed females would be forced by circumstances into prostitution, but Bisset Hawkins, a physician, presented evidence from Manchester, England, that of the 50 prostitutes who had been apprehended in the previous 4 years (1829–1833), only 8 had been employed in factories, whereas 29 came from the ranks of former household servants.[81]

Evidence concerning child and female labor is contradictory; most testimony hints at the moral degradation of factory life, but hard statistics are lacking.[82] It appears that emotional and religious overtones were given more credence, isolated instances were ballooned, and no thorough studies compared the past with the conditions at that time. As textile technology advanced and as incomes rose, child labor decreased dramatically before the passage of legislation regarding the employment of children.[83] What critics have overlooked is the fact that capitalism was slowly but surely releasing children from the workforce. As machines were developed to perform simple jobs, it became uneconomical to employ children. Moreover, as Bradley G. Bowden has noted, "[a]s mechanization took hold . . . children were found to be ill-suited to factory work, which increasingly demanded literacy and formal training."[84] It was an economic force—broadening capitalism—not legislative fiat nor a moral rebirth that freed children from loom rooms.[85]

THE GREAT ENRICHMENT

To understand the nineteenth-century critics of the factory system, it is necessary to consider the era's Victorian values. The Victorian period began before Queen Victoria ascended the throne in 1837.[86] Victorian values concerning employing women and children and adherence to strict

---

[77] For the case in the United States, see "Letters from Susan: Letter Fourth," *The Lowell Offering* 4(5) (September 1844), p. 258. Craig Muldrew suggests, however, that during the late seventeenth century the ability to support themselves through spinning may have led some English women to remain single rather than marry; see his "'Th'ancient Distaff' and 'Whirling Spindle': Measuring the Contribution of Spinning to Household Earnings and the National Economy in England, 1550–1770," *Economic History Review* 65(2) (May 2012), p. 520.

[78] Paul J. Mantoux, *The Industrial Revolution in the Eighteenth Century*, trans. Marjorie Vernon (New York: Harcourt, Brace & Co., 1927), p. 397.

[79] For comments on these and other examples, see William O. Henderson, *J. C. Fischer and His Diary of Industrial England 1814–51* (London: Frank Cass & Co., 1966). Individuals such as Mantoux had in mind undoubtedly existed, as they do in all ages, but Fischer maintained that they were not representative of the era.

[80] Joyce Burnette, "An Investigation of the Female-Male Wage Gap during the Industrial Revolution in Britain," *Economic History Review* 50(2) (May 1997), p. 278.

[81] "Medical Reports by Dr. Hawkins," Factories Inquiry Commission, *Second Report of the Central Board of His Majesty's Commissioners Appointed to Collect Information in the Manufacturing Districts, as to the Employment of Children in Factories, and as to the Propriety and Means of Curtailing the Hours of Their Labour,*" *Parliamentary Papers* 21(519) (1833), D3, p. 4.

[82] Hugh Cunningham, "The Employment and Unemployment of Children in England c. 1680–1851," *Past & Present* no. 126 (February 1990), pp. 115–150; Jane Humphries, *Childhood and Child Labour in the British Industrial Revolution* (New York: Cambridge University Press, 2010).

[83] Clark Nardinelli, *Child Labor and the Industrial Revolution* (Bloomington, IN: Indiana University Press, 1990), p. 105.

[84] Bradley G. Bowden, *Work, Wealth, and Postmodernism: The Intellectual Conflict at the Heart of Business Endeavour* (Basingstoke, England: Palgrave Macmillan, 2018), p. 10.

[85] William H. Hutt, "The Factory System of the Early 19th Century," *Economica* no. 16 (March 1926), p. 91n2.

[86] John W. Osbourne, *The Silent Revolution: The Industrial Revolution in England as a Source of Cultural Change* (New York: Charles Scribner's Sons, 1970), pp. ix–xi.

standards of personal and social morality began forming around 1800. Economic and social conditions had been worse before the Industrial Revolution, but the values of Victorian-era writers such as Charles Dickens, evidenced in his serialized novels such as *Oliver Twist* (1838) and *Hard Times* (1854), advanced a basis for criticizing the emerging factory system. In truth, however, "Dickens and many Victorian authors were moved by a mass of poor people, who had been largely invisible in rural Britain but became all too visible as they surged into the cities to work in factories."[87] As ugly as these urban slums were, one group of historians has noted that the neighborhoods in which the working class crowded "sometimes represented a positive improvement over rural slums in which the grandparents of the millhands had lived." These same historians point out that "[t]oo often, whitewashed or vine-covered country cottages concealed behind their picturesque exteriors a contaminated water supply, a total lack of sanitary facilities, and an appalling incidence of infant mortality and tuberculosis."[88] Poverty was not new; it had just been collected in one place—cities—and made more easily visible to legislators, intellectuals, and others. Isolated and scattered, agrarian poverty did not shock the sensibilities, but next door and down the street, it became a bane.

As innovations occurred and output increased, for the first time in history the net standard of living of ordinary people in England and other industrialized nations began to undergo sustained growth. With improvements in medicine and sanitation, the average person was living longer, eating better, and earning higher incomes.[89] The improvement in well-being is, perhaps, most evident when considering "time prices," which represent the length of time a person must work to buy a good or service at different points in time. For example, it took a U.S. factory worker in 1850 2 hours and 50 minutes to earn enough to buy a pound of sugar. His counterpart in 2021 must work only 35 seconds. Multiply that by similar gains in hundreds of commodities and the result is what Marian L. Tupy and Gale L. Pooley call "superabundance."[90] The social costs associated with the Industrial Revolution in England, the United States, and other industrialized nations were immense. Nonetheless, as Steven Kates has commented, "many of those who were living at the time were content that England should exchange its 'green and pleasant land' for a highly productive economic structure that allowed many individuals to move forward in what they could earn and in the range and quantity of the goods and services they could buy."[91] This is, in part, no doubt due to the fact that living conditions in the era's preindustrial societies were characterized by an "equality of poverty" in which large masses of humanity lived at subsistence levels.

In moving to alleviate poverty, the Industrial Revolution set the stage for what Deirdre N. McCloskey aptly termed "The Great Enrichment"—the unparalleled growth in income and wealth that began in the early 1800s and has been responsible for increasing the world's material standard of living beyond anything our ancestors could have imagined.[92] This outcome continues to benefit us all every day. It should also be noted that beyond its material benefits, industrialization brought other gains: it "widened people's horizons, encouraged greater equality within

[87] W. Philip Gramm and Michael Solon, "In Defense of Scrooge, Whose Thrift Blessed the World," *Wall Street Journal* (December 24, 2020), p. A15.
[88] C. Crane Brinton, John B. Christopher, and Robert Lee Wolff, *A History of Civilization*, vol. 2: *1715 to the Present* (New York: Prentice-Hall, 1955), p. 203.
[89] Clark Nardinelli, "The Industrial Revolution and the Standard of Living," *The Concise Encyclopedia of Economics*, 2nd ed., Library of Economics and Liberty (2008). Available online at https://www.econlib.org/library/Enc/IndustrialRevolutionandtheStandardofLiving.html. See also Joyce Burnette and Joel Mokyr, "The Standard of Living Through the Ages," in Julian L. Simon, ed., *The State of Humanity* (Malden, MA: Blackwell Publishers, 1995), pp. 135–148; Robert E. Lucas, *Lectures on Economic Growth* (Cambridge, MA: Harvard University Press, 2002), pp. 109–188.
[90] Marian L. Tupy and Gale L. Pooley, *Superabundance: The Story of Population Growth, Innovation, and Human Flourishing on an Infinitely Bountiful Planet* (Washington, DC: Cato Institute, 2022), Box 5.1, p. 165.
[91] Steven Kates, [Review of the book *New Perspectives on Political Economy and Its History*]. *EH.Net* (March 2021). Available online at https://eh.net/book_reviews/new-perspectives-on-political-economy-and-its-history/.
[92] Deirdre Nansen McCloskey, "The Great Enrichment: A Humanistic and Social Scientific Account," *Social Science History* 40(4) (Winter 2016), pp. 583–598.

family relationships, and fostered . . . commitments to education and the rule of law," thereby broadening and enhancing freedom and democracy.[93] Moreover, as Diarmaid MacCulloch notes, the industrial revolution challenged "aristocracies whose wealth and power were based mainly on land and agriculture." Strikingly, as MacCulloch further observes, the main impulse to overthrow the established order came from "groups outside the landed class: lawyers, journalists, businesspeople, urban workers with specialist skills—what is clumsily but unavoidably called the middle class." Moreover, "middle-class groups sought to legislate into being political institutions to give themselves voices in national affairs appropriate to their wealth and talent, at least to share power with the landed aristocracy. They aimed to create structures designed to reward ability and personal achievement rather than birth, and the right to express their political and religious opinions as they wished."[94] In a word, this represented a "struggle of a new elite against an old" and restructured society in a way that now reverberates worldwide.

SUMMARY

As historian John Steele Gordon has written, "[I]n the 18th century, engineers learned how to turn the heat-energy of fire into work-doing energy via the steam engine—and the Industrial Revolution moved into high gear." In turn, as he has further noted, by the "[l]ate 19th century engineers learned how to turn heat-energy (and falling water) into electricity, which, it turned out, could power all sorts of things, including . . . microprocessors found in smartphones and high-end toothbrushes."[95] The Industrial Revolution thereby created a new age and posed a revised set of managerial challenges. People's needs became more complex as they sought to adjust to city and factory life. Industries were reshaped by the demands for heavy infusions of capital, by the division of labor, and by the need for efficient and predictable performance. Organizations needed to innovate and compete in a free-market economy; this created pressures for growth and the economies of scale obtained from large-scale production and distribution. Economists recognized that entrepreneurs performed a distinct role in successfully combining the traditional three factors of production in the ever-growing factory system. With increased size came the need for salaried managers; the need for a capable, disciplined, trained, and motivated workforce; and the need for rationalizing the planning, organization, and control of operations in early enterprises. By "[m]echanizing production, speeding communication, and transforming a rural, decentralized workforce into a urban, class-organized consumer base, the Industrial Revolution gave us the very idea of modernity, the slippery concept of a world in which humanity, liberated from the constraints imposed by nature, could advance to faster, more interconnected, ever-more quantifiable ways of life than ever before."[96] In the following chapter we examine some early management pioneers who proposed solutions for coping with the challenges presented by the emerging factory system.

[93] Daniel Walker Howe, *What Hath God Wrought: The Transformation of America, 1815–1848* (New York: Oxford University Press, 2007), p. 849.
[94] MacCulloch, *Christianity: The First Three Thousand Years*, p. 40.
[95] John Steele Gordon, [Review of the book *Power Trip: The Story of Energy*], *Wall Street Journal* (June 4, 2019), p. A15.
[96] Heather Souvaine Horn, "A System of Denial," *The New Republic* (April 16, 2018), sp. 1. Available online at https://newrepublic.com/article/147993/system-denial.

Management Pioneers in Early Factories

CHAPTER 4

A prevailing theme in the preceding chapters has been the relationship between the evolution of management thought and prevailing cultural values. The factory system of production posed new challenges for entrepreneurs, salaried managers, and society as a whole. This chapter focuses on four individuals who pioneered solutions to these challenges. History, in general, leaves a notoriously scanty scent; records have been lost, materials intended for one-time or temporary use have been destroyed, and notable ideas may never have been committed to writing. Judgments about the past, thus, must often be made with incomplete and uncertain information. Of the earliest management pioneers, history has provided the best records for four unique individuals: Robert Owen, Charles Babbage, Andrew Ure, and Charles Dupin.

ROBERT OWEN: THE SEARCH FOR A NEW HARMONY

Welshman Robert Owen (1771–1858), introduced in Chapter 3, was a paradox in the turbulent early years of the Industrial Revolution. Although a successful entrepreneur, he attempted to halt the era's growing industrialization. A Utopian socialist, Owen called for a "new moral order" based on drastic "social reorganization."[1] He envisioned a new industrial society that was to be a combination of agricultural and industrial communes. Owen's vision hearkened back to an earlier and more primitive time. Philosophically, he viewed people as powerless in a new age of machinery, held in the grip of revolutionary forces that destroyed moral purpose and social solidarity.

EARLY MANAGERIAL EXPERIENCES

Owen was a self-made man imbued with the confidence that typified the earliest management pioneers. In 1789, at age 18, Owen co-founded his first business, a machine shop for making "mules" to spin cotton. Owen described his introduction to managing: "I looked very wisely at the men in their different departments, although I really knew nothing. But by intensely observing everything, I maintained order and regularity throughout the establishment, which proceeded

[1] The term "utopian socialism" was introduced some 20 years after Owen's death. See Friedrich Engels, *Socialism: Utopian and Scientific*, trans. Edward Aveling (London: Swan Sonnenschein, 1892). Originally published in 1880. Owen's efforts at New Lanark, however, were labeled "utopian" as early as 1816. See William Hazlitt, *Political Essays, With Sketches of Public Characters* (London: William Hone, 1819), p. 99.

under the circumstances far better than I had anticipated."[2] Some three years later, Owen sold his share of the business and was hired as a manager by Peter Drinkwater, owner of Piccadilly Mill, the first cotton mill in Manchester powered by a steam engine. It was understood that Owen would ultimately become Drinkwater's partner. With yet only a modicum of experience, Owen applied himself to his new position:

> I looked grave,—inspected everything very minutely,—. . . I was with the first [workers] in the morning, and I locked up the premises at night, taking the keys with me. I continued this silent inspection and superintendence day by day for six weeks, saying merely yes or no to the questions of what was to be done or otherwise, and during that period I did not give one direct order about anything. But at the end of that time I felt myself so much master of my position, as to be ready to give directions in every department.[3]

Owen, left on his own by Drinkwater, made a success of the mill. He rearranged the equipment, improved the working conditions, and achieved a great deal of influence over his subordinates. He later attributed his success to his "habits of exactness" and knowledge of human nature. Following a disagreement with Drinkwater concerning his pending partnership, Owen left Piccadilly Mill in 1795 to become a partner in the Chorlton Twist Company, noted for its "Chorlton cotton twist." Owen managed the company's four mills near Manchester, and in the process married the former owner's daughter, "the good and kind-hearted" Anne Dale. In 1797, Owen became part owner and sole manager of New Lanark Mills, located in New Lanark, Scotland. At New Lanark, he encountered a labor shortage and noted, "[I]t was then most difficult to induce any sober, well-doing family to leave their home to go into cotton mills as then conducted."[4] This difficulty influenced Owen's labor policies, and he began envisioning a new society. Between 400 and 500 parish apprentices—paupers or deserted children, supplied by the Poor Law Authorities to whomever would take them (see Chapter 3)—were employed at New Lanark. The children worked 13 hours per day, 6 days a week. Owen continued to employ children but tried to improve their living and working conditions by cutting their workday to 10 3/4 hours, setting 10 years as the minimum age for employment, providing meals and rest breaks, and stressing mill safety. In addition, he sought to reshape the whole village of New Lanark, including its streets, houses, sanitation practices, and school.

While at New Lanark, Owen also began to form new ideas about the welfare of society in general. Industrial progress, he felt, was inadequate to support the growing population. In 1821, he prepared a report for the citizens of Lanark Parish stating his belief that "manual labor, properly directed, is the source of all wealth and of national prosperity."[5] In Owen's view, the dominant economic and social challenge was to develop agriculture, using intensive methods of cultivation, to feed more people. He therefore prepared a plan to do the following:

> 1*st*, To cultivate the soil with the spade instead of the plough.
>
> 2*d*, To make such changes as the spade cultivation requires, to render it easy and profitable to individuals, and beneficial to the country.
>
> 3*d*, To adopt a standard of value, by means of which the exchange of the products of labor may proceed without check or limit, until wealth shall become abundant that any further increase to it will be useless and will not be desired.[6]

---

[2] Robert Owen, *The Life of Robert Owen, Written by Himself*, vol. 1 (London: Effingham Wilson, 1857), p. 23.
[3] *Ibid.*, p. 29.
[4] *Ibid.*, p. 58.
[5] *Idem, Report to the County of Lanark of a Plan for Relieving Public Distress and Removing Discontent by Giving Permanent, Productive Employment to the Poor and Working Classes* (Glasgow: Wardlaw & Cunninghame, 1821), p. 1.
[6] *Ibid.*, p. 10.

Owen asserted that this would create additional jobs and enable more people to be employed, thereby increasing their ability to consume Great Britain's industrial output. The notion of creating more arduous, menial jobs flew in the face of the technological progress that was being made at that time. It was a preface, however, to his vision of a communal society.

In managing New Lanark for over a quarter century, Owen sought to avoid disciplinary problems with the mill's employees. Like other manufacturers who had attempted to create a new factory ethos, he relied on moral suasion as a substitute for corporal punishment to maintain factory discipline.[7] He developed one particularly unique device, the "silent monitor," to aid discipline. Using silent monitors (small wooden blocks), Owen awarded four types of marks to his superintendents, and they, in turn, rated their subordinates. These marks were translated into color codes: black, blue, yellow, and white, in ascending order of merit. A silent monitor was mounted on each weaver's loom, the four sides painted to match the color codes. At the end of each day, the marks were recorded, translated, and the matching side of the block turned outward. Owen reported that he "passed daily through all the rooms, and the workers observed me always to look at these telegraphs,—when black I merely looked at the person and then at the colour,—but never said a word to one of them by way of blame."[8] The silent monitor motivated laggards to improve and, supposedly, induced white-block (good) workers to sustain their performance. It was a precursor of modern management's posting of sales and production data to encourage hard work and discipline.

THE CALL FOR REFORM

Predating Elton Mayo, Fritz J. Roethlisberger, Rensis Likert, and others who have urged concern for a firm's human resources (see Chapters 13 and 15), Owen explained his rationale for a new moral order:

> [Y]ou will find that from the commencement of my management I viewed the population [the labor force] . . . as a system composed of many parts, and which it was my duty and interest so to combine, as that every hand, as well as every spring, lever, and wheel, should effectually co-operate to produce the greatest pecuniary gain to the proprietors. . . . Experience has also shown you the difference of the results between working machines which are neat, clean, well arranged, and always in a high state of repair; and that which is allowed to be dirty, in disorder, without the requisite ingredient to prevent unnecessary friction, and which therefore becomes, and works much out of repair. . . . If then due care as to the state of your inanimate machines can produce such beneficial results, what may not be expected if you devote equal attention to your vital machines [employees], which are far more wonderfully constructed?[9]

Owen chided his fellow manufacturers for not appreciating the profound effect of human nature on workers' productivity. He charged that his counterparts would spend thousands on the best machines yet buy the cheapest labor. Further, they would spend time and money improving machines and cutting costs yet make no investment in their human resources. Owen appealed to their pecuniary instincts, claiming that money spent on improving labor "would return you, not five, ten, or fifteen per cent for your capital so expended, but often fifty, and in many cases a hundred per cent."[10] He claimed a 50-percent return at New Lanark and said it would shortly reach

---

[7] For a commentary on early British manufactures influenced by Owen's reform efforts, see Lee D. Parker, "Corporate Social Accountability through Action: Contemporary Insights from British Industrial Pioneers," *Accounting, Organizations and Society* 39(8) (November 2014), pp. 632–659.

[8] *Idem*, *Life of Robert Owen*, pp. 136–137. The electric telegraph had not been invented; Owen used "telegraph" to mean viewing a record of performance from a distance.

[9] *Idem*, *A New View of Society: or, Essays on the Formation of the Human Character, and the Application of the Principle to Practice* (London: Richard Taylor and Co., 1813), third essay, pp. 71–73.

[10] *Ibid*., p. 74.

Portrait of Robert Owen by John Cranch, 1845, by permission of the Indiana Historical Society.

Robert Owen, 1845

100 percent. Owen asserted that, by showing the same concern for people as for machines, his "friends" would add to their "gains, prosperity and happiness" and, in so doing, "prevent an accumulation of human misery."[11]

Accounting records from New Lanark indicate that Owen's estimates of return on investment and profits were only slightly exaggerated. The mill's partners took 5 percent of their investment as a return to capital and then prorated the remaining profits according to each partner's stake in their partnership. During Owen's time at New Lanark (1799–1828), his approximate share of gross profits was £128,500 (British pounds), plus 5 percent of his £130,000 capital (£6,500 per year). His annual return on investment typically exceeded 15 percent and, from 1811 to 1814, some 46 percent.[12]

Owen's partnership in New Lanark was profitable, but there are doubts whether this was due to his labor policies. One biographer noted that profits in the cotton-spinning industry at that time were so great, averaging 20 percent or more on capital invested, that any labor policy could have been profitable. The same biographer concluded: "In fact the margin of profit was so wide that we need scarcely look for any other explanation of Owen's success as a manufacturer."[13] Whatever the reason for Owen's success, he deplored the commercialism of the time. He declared an intellectual war on capitalism and attacked the Church of England because, in his view, it condoned the new industrial age and its accompanying evils. Owen's views were considered radical and made it more difficult for him to persuade others of the need for reform. He felt that the crucial error of all established religions was a belief in the doctrine of human responsibility. Owen held that humans were creatures of their material and moral environments, relatively incapable of escaping their surroundings without a moral rearmament achieved through education. Contrary to the Church of England's view that good character was promoted by the promise of rewards and punishment, especially in relation to the hereafter, Owen felt that a person's character developed only if one's surroundings were conducive. To this end, in about 1813, he became more politically active and, as described in Chapter 3, in 1819 proposed legislation to prohibit children under age 9 from working in cotton mills and set 12 hours as the maximum workday for those under 16.

Failing to achieve his goals in Great Britain, Owen read an ad in the *Morning Chronicle* (London) that offered some 20,000 acres for sale in Posey County, Indiana, on the east bank of the Wabash River in the United States.[14] The sellers were a religious sect, the Harmonists, followers of J. Georg Rapp. In the decade or so that the Harmonists had farmed the land, some 3,000 acres had been cleared for vineyards, orchards, and gardens. Machine shops and a sawmill, as well as flour, grist, hemp, and oil mills, had been erected and numerous brick and log dwellings had been completed. Owen acquired the property, known as New Harmony, in 1825 and set out to create a secular utopian community. His primary goal was to provide for the happiness of the community's members. Like other socialists, Owen believed that "without the distortions of inequality or poverty, people would naturally behave to one another as brothers."[15] A new currency would be created based on labor credits; there would be no division of labor; everyone would receive a general education; and although community members would be trained for jobs, they would be able to work in other jobs as they wished. Freedom of speech was guaranteed, and women were granted the same rights and privileges as men. Owen promised to give New Harmony to the community's members.

---

[11] *Ibid.*, p. 77.

[12] John Butt, "Robert Owen as a Businessman," in *idem*, ed., *Robert Owen, Prince of Cotton Spinners* (Bristol, England: David & Charles, 1971), pp. 199–201, 211–213.

[13] Frank Podmore, *Robert Owen: A Biography* (New York: Appleton, 1924), p. 642.

[14] "Town of Harmony, Posey County, Indiana, North America," *Morning Chronicle* (London) (June 30, 1824), p. 1.

[15] Diarmaid MacCulloch, *Christianity: The First Three Thousand Years* (London: Allen Lane, 2009), p. 815.

News about New Harmony spread quickly. By the time it opened, 800 people were ready to move to the community formerly occupied by 700 Harmonists. Although the sheer number of people that moved to New Harmony was a burden, a more serious challenge arose from the nature of the new arrivals. There were some dedicated people who were aware of Owen's beliefs and took them as their own, but there were also those who had heard that New Harmony was a place where you could work a little, or not at all, and you would still be fed, clothed, and housed. For a few months, the excitement of the new venture kept everyone's morale high, but steadily the exhilaration and novelty began to wear thin. Due to a lack of brewers, the brewery was dark. Because there were no millers, the grain mill was idle. With only a few dozen farmers, the task of feeding a population soon swollen to nearly 1,000 became increasingly difficult. Although New Harmony was by no means ready to collapse, these and other difficulties left many dispirited. Owen assumed the position of governor, but many felt that in reassuming his previous position of complete authority, he was abandoning his promise to turn New Harmony over to the community's members. Owen tried to reorganize the community, but gave up and left in 1827, abandoning New Harmony in less than 2 years.[16]

After New Harmony, Owen found himself both financially and emotionally broken. He had thought that what he had learned and applied in his New Lanark cotton mills could be applied to all society. Owen, however, was unable to persuade others that his new moral order was realistic rather than utopian. As a reformer, Owen devised laws for helping the poor and proposed solutions to decrease unemployment. He proposed Villages of Cooperation, like New Harmony, which would be agriculture-based, with the sharing of any surplus. Owen fought against Thomas R. Malthus's belief that, because the world's population is limited by means of subsistence and the masses tend to reproduce beyond this limit, there can be no improvement in their condition (see Chapter 3). He argued that no one would hunger if all shared. Owen deplored the division of labor's mind-numbing and debilitating effects (see Chapter 2); in his ideal world, each person would do a number of different jobs, switching easily from one to another. For Owen, the twin evils of capitalism and the wage system provided workers with only enough money to live at a subsistence level. In 1833, Owen returned to Britain and helped create the Grand National Consolidated Trades Union. Renamed the British and Foreign Consolidated Association of Industry, Humanity and Knowledge, the association appointed Owen as its Grand Master. By 1834, however, the association had folded. Owen was frustrated in his efforts to reform society and inflexible in his views. A second biographer concluded it was "obvious" that the "shut-up-ness" of Owen's "mind was the cause of his becoming mentally unbalanced in old age."[17] Nevertheless, Robert Owen had sown the first seed of concern for the human side of management.

CHARLES BABBAGE: THE "IRASCIBLE GENIUS"

To call Charles Babbage (1791–1871) an "irascible genius" is to pay him the highest compliment, for he embodied both qualities.[18] Babbage was distinctly ahead of his time. He held the Lucasian chair of mathematics at Cambridge University, a position formerly held by Isaac Newton, although it seems that Babbage never delivered a lecture there. Babbage sought to apply technology to replace human effort and, in doing so, earned a place in history as the patron saint of Operations Research and Management Science (see Chapter 21). He applied a scientific approach to management long before the scientific-management era began in the United States (see Chapter 7). Born in Devonshire, England, the son of a wealthy banker, Babbage

[16] John H. Hoagland, "Management before Frederick Taylor," in Billy Goetz, ed., *Proceedings of the Annual Meeting of the Academy of Management* (1955), pp. 15–24. See also *idem*, "Charles Babbage—His Life and Works in the Historical Evolution of Management Concepts" (Doctoral dissertation, Ohio State University, Columbus, OH, 1954); *idem*, "Historical Antecedents of Organization Research," in William W. Cooper, Harold J. Levitt, and Maynard W. Shelly II, eds., *New Perspectives in Organization Research* (New York: John Wiley & Sons, 1964), pp. 27–38.

[17] George D. H. Cole, *Robert Owen* (Boston, MA: Little, Brown, and Company, 1925), p. 316.

[18] Maboth Moseley, *Irascible Genius: The Life of Charles Babbage, Inventor* (London: Hutchinson & Co., 1964), p. 1.

Obituary, *The Illustrated London News* (59) (November 4, 1871), p. 424.

Charles Babbage, circa 1860

used his inheritance in a lifelong quest to understand "the causes of all those little things and events which astonish the childish mind."[19] He remarked that his first question after receiving a new toy was always, "Mamma, what is inside of it?" and he invariably broke open the toy if her answer was unsatisfactory. The value of Babbage's work was recognized by few of his contemporaries, and his neighbors generally considered him a crackpot. His personal traits were not endearing to those who disturbed his meditations. To retaliate against the ubiquitous English organ-grinders that gathered outside his house, he repeatedly summoned the police, who seemed powerless to stop the "music," even when he was lying on his deathbed. In response to his pleas for quiet so he could continue his work, organ-grinders, fiddlers, brass bands, and other assorted street musicians, accompanied by what Babbage referred to as "ladies of elastic virtue and cosmopolitan tendencies,"[20] responded by playing louder and longer in front of his home. One friend said that Babbage "spoke as if he hated mankind in general, Englishmen in particular, and the English Government and Organ Grinders most of all."[21]

THE FIRST COMPUTER

Babbage's scientific output was phenomenal. He demonstrated a small working model of the world's first automatic calculator, his Difference Engine, in 1822. It returned results to six decimals and provided solutions for second-order difference equations. Despite thousands of pounds sterling of government funding, Babbage was never able to build a full prototype of the Difference Engine. Ninety-one years later, however, its basic principles were being employed in William Seward Burroughs's accounting machines. Babbage had received grants totaling £17,000 from the Chancellor of the Exchequer, Sir Robert Peel II, to develop his Difference Engine. His irascibility, however, cost him similar backing for his Analytical Engine, a versatile general-purpose computer capable of any mathematical operation, which was a successor to his Difference Engine. As early as 1833, Babbage had conceived a calculating machine that could, in effect, scan a stream of instructions and automatically put them into operation. Touring a textile mill in Lyon, France, he saw looms weaving complex patterns, such as brocades, by means of holes punched in cards. A silk weaver, Joseph Marie Jacquard, drawing on earlier inventions by Basile Bouchon (1725), Jean-Baptiste Falcon (1728), and Jacques de Vaucanson (1740), had developed a mechanical loom. In Jacquard's loom, "horizontal steel rods with springs at the end 'sense' the holes punched in a rectangular piece of cardboard. When a rod 'feels' a hole it passes through and activates a mechanism for lifting the appropriate warp thread, which is then skipped in the weaving, while the other threads are regularly woven. The way the holes are punched programs the pattern."[22] In extending Jacquard's innovation, Babbage used punch cards for storing information, as well as for guiding machine operations. Building on Babbage's work, Herman Hollerith created a punched-card tabulating machine half a century later to input data for the 1890 U.S. Census, reducing the time for data analysis from 8 to 6 years.[23]

---

[19] Charles Babbage, *Passages from the Life of a Philosopher* (London: Longman, Green, Longman, Roberts, & Green, 1864), p. 7.

[20] *Ibid.*, p. 314.

[21] Bertram V. Bowden, "A Brief History of Computation," in *idem*, ed., *Faster Than Thought: A Symposium on Digital Computing Machines* (London: Sir Isaac Pitman & Sons, 1953), p. 18.

[22] Molly Gleiser, "The Looms of Lyons," *Datamation* 25(9) (September 1979), p. 220.

[23] George E. Biles, Alfred A. Bolton, and Bernadette M. DiRe, "Herman Hollerith: Inventor, Manager, Entrepreneur—A Centennial Remembrance," *Journal of Management* 15(4) (December 1989), pp. 603–615.

Perhaps even more significantly, Babbage's innovativeness anticipated by some 20 years the binary, or base 2, system (zero/one, off/on, yes/no, true/false) developed by English mathematician George Boole (1815–1864) for comparing mathematical functions. Boole's work later formed the basis for the electrical switches used by modern digital computers to process logical expressions.

Babbage's Analytical Engine, the first digital computer able to perform any calculation, had all the basic elements of today's computers. It had a "store" (or memory device), a "mill" (or arithmetic unit), a punch-card input system, external memory storage, and conditional transfer.[24] In retrospect, Babbage's genius was not in the calculating power of his engine but in his mechanization of the organizing and logical control of mathematical functions.[25] The Analytical Engine was capable of raising numbers to the second and third powers and extracting the root of a quadratic equation. Babbage also conceived an "apparatus for printing on paper, one, or if required, two copies of the results" of a computer program's output—a Victorian version of a modern printer.[26] Babbage encountered so many problems in constructing his Analytical Engine that he was never able to build a full-scale model. He not only had to invent tools and tool shapers, and design lathes to machine the hand-fitted steel and die-cast pewter gear wheels of his Analytical Engine, but he also had to develop his own abstract notation when standard mechanical drawing symbols proved inadequate.[27] Shortly before Babbage's death in 1871, he wrote, "If I survive some few years longer, the Analytical Engine will exist, and its works will afterwards be spread over the world."[28] For more than a century his work would lie dormant, waiting for other times and other people to advance his seminal ideas.

One of the few bright spots in Babbage's life was his friendship with Augusta Ada King (1816–1852), the Countess Lovelace, wife of William King, 1st Earl of Lovelace, and the estranged daughter of the poet Lord Byron. Lovelace was still a teenager when she first met Babbage in 1833. The countess had a gift for mathematics and engineering and was one of the few who really understood Babbage's work. She wrote treatises that expressed his ideas better than he could and wrote programs for his Analytical Engine. Lovelace warned people against becoming dependent on the engine, which "has no pretentions whatever to *originate* anything . . . [and would] do whatever we *know how to order it* to perform."[29] Together with Babbage, Lovelace developed a system for applying the Analytical Engine to mathematically handicap horse races. The system was unsuccessful, and twice the countess had to pawn the Lovelace family jewels to pay her gambling debts.[30] Undaunted by the countess's losses, Babbage continued his work and developed programs for his Analytical Engine that were a forerunner of modern business-gaming techniques. Babbage also developed a program to play the games tic-tac-toe and chess that calculated the best possible combinations of positions as far as three moves in advance. In addition, he was the era's outstanding cryptologist.

---

[24] In computer terminology, conditional transfer refers to the "if" statement: that is, instructing the computer "if such and such occurs, follow this path; if not, proceed in the normal sequence of control."

[25] Daniel A. Wren, "A Calculating Genius," *Knowledge Management* 2(5) (May 1999), p. 104.

[26] Details of Babbage's printing apparatus are provided in Harry W. Buxton, *Memoir of the Life and Labours of the Late Charles Babbage, Esq. F.R.S.*, ed. Anthony Hyman (Cambridge, MA: MIT Press, 1988), p. 182. Written between 1872 and 1880.

[27] Leopold Froehlich, "Babbage Observed," *Datamation* 31(5) (March 1985), p. 122.

[28] Babbage, *Passages from the Life of a Philosopher*, p. 449. In 1991, a team at London's Science Museum succeeded in constructing a full-scale model of the Analytical Machine using Babbage's original drawings. It weighs 3 tons, is 11 feet long, 7 feet high, and 18 inches deep, with 4,000 parts and can calculate numbers up to 31 digits. Doing so, however, requires turning a crank nearly 27,000 times. "Calculator Designed in 1894 Works," *Morning Advocate* (Baton Rouge, LA) December 13, 1991, p. 4A.

[29] A. A. L. [Augusta Ada Lovelace], "Translator's Notes to M. Menabrea's Memoir," *Scientific Memoirs, Selected from the Transactions of Foreign Academies of Science and Learned Societies and from Foreign Journals* 3(12) (1843), p. 722. Correspondence between Lovelace and Babbage is archived at the British Library and available online at https://www.bl.uk/collection-items/letter-from-ada-lovelace-to-charles-babbage.

[30] Margot Strickland, *The Byron Women* (New York: St. Martin's Press, 1974), pp. 209–210.

ANALYZING INDUSTRIAL OPERATIONS

Babbage's inquisitive mind and wide interests inevitably led him to write about management. His most successful book, *On the Economy of Machinery and Manufactures*, was published in 1832. Babbage became interested in management because of difficulties he encountered while constructing his Analytical Engine. Searching for solutions, Babbage visited a wide variety of British and French factories. In the *Economy of Machinery and Manufactures*, he not only described tools and machines and discussed the "economical principles of manufacturing" but also, in the true spirit of inquiry, analyzed operations and their expense, assessed the kinds of skills involved, and suggested improvements.[31]

Babbage was interested in machinery, tools, the efficient use of power, the development of counting machines to check totals, and the economic use of raw materials. He developed a "method of observing manufactories," which was closely akin to a scientific, systematic approach to the study of industrial operations.[32] As part of this method, he prepared a list of questions about capital investment, raw materials, required tools and machinery, necessary labor, waste, wholesale prices, and so on. In essence, it was the same procedure that an operations analyst or a consultant would use today in approaching a method-based analysis. Babbage emphasized the difference between "making" products in small workshops and "manufacturing" or operating on a larger scale, which necessitated carefully arranging the "whole system of [the] factory" to reduce production costs.[33] He recognized that success in a capitalist market economy calls for industry, integrity, and talent.

On the human side, Babbage recalled the destruction of the Luddite movement (see Chapter 3) and pleaded with workers to recognize that a properly designed factory was to their benefit. He explained: "It is of great importance that the more intelligent amongst the class of workmen should examine the correctness of these views; because . . . the whole class may . . . be led by designing persons to pursue a course, which . . . is in reality at variance with their own best interests."[34] Babbage's attempts to show the mutuality of interests between workers and factory owners were somewhat similar to what Frederick W. Taylor would say 75 years later (see Chapter 7). According to Babbage,

> the prosperity and success of the master manufacturer is essential to the welfare of the workman . . . whilst it is perfectly true that workmen, as a class, derive advantage from the prosperity of their employers, I do not think that each individual partakes of that advantage exactly in proportion to the extent to which he contributes towards it. . . . It would be of great importance, if, in every large establishment the mode of payment could be so arranged, that every person employed should derive advantage from the success of the whole; and that the profits of each individual should advance, as the factory itself produced profit, without the necessity of making any change in the wages.[35]

Babbage's profit-sharing plan had two facets: a portion of workers' wages would depend on factory profits, and a worker "should derive more advantage from applying any improvement he might discover . . . than he could by any other course of action."[36] In other words, workers would receive a fixed salary based on the nature of their tasks, plus a share of a firm's profits and a bonus for any suggestions that improved a factory's performance. Babbage saw a number of advantages in his proposal: (1) each worker would have a direct interest in a firm's prosperity, (2) each worker would be stimulated to prevent waste and mismanagement, (3) every department

---

[31] Charles Babbage, *On the Economy of Machinery and Manufactures* (London: Charles Knight, 1832), pp. 94–96. It should be noted that although Babbage's discussion of expenses is somewhat similar to an early form of cost accounting, it differed from modern cost accounting in that it described costs rather than analyzing what costs ought to be, as under a standard cost system.
[32] *Ibid.*, pp. 93–97.
[33] *Ibid.*, p. 99.
[34] *Ibid.*, p. 192.
[35] *Idem*, *On the Economy of Machinery and Manufactures*, 3rd ed. (London: C. Knight, Pall Mall East, 1833), pp. 250–251.
[36] *Ibid.*, p. 254.

would be improved, and (4) "it would be the common interest of all to admit [hire] only the most respectable and skillful [workers]." In effect, work groups, operating under a profit-sharing plan, would act to screen out those who would reduce their share of profits. Finally, Babbage saw his plan as removing the necessity for "combinations amongst workmen" (i.e., trade unions) because their interests would be the same as those of their employers. With a mutuality of interests, neither would oppress the other and all would prosper.

Beyond his scientific contributions, Charles Babbage made significant advancements in understanding the challenges of the emerging factory system. His analytic approach to the study of manufacturing, his recognition of the need for new incentives to enlist labor cooperation, and his emphasis on a mutuality of interests between workers and employers made him a visionary pioneer in the evolution of management thought.

ANDREW URE: PIONEER IN MANAGEMENT EDUCATION

Andrew Ure (1778–1857) provided academic training for fledgling managers in the early days of the factory system. He studied at Edinburgh and Glasgow universities, receiving his MD from the latter in 1801. In 1804, Ure was elected to the Chair of Natural Philosophy at Anderson's Institute in Glasgow, where he remained until 1839. Dr. John Anderson had lectured to large groups of workingmen on science at the University of Glasgow and in his will had proposed that an institution be founded to teach "the whole range of human knowledge to all classes of both sexes." The Institute (which became the University of Strathclyde) was the first technical college to focus on educating members of the "artisan class."[37] Educational pressures for technically trained workers and managers soon shifted the composition of Ure's classes from factory workers to clerks, warehousemen, artisans, and shopkeepers; from these classes, salaried managers for the ever-growing factory system were to be recruited. Ure knew the French engineer and management writer Charles Dupin, and when Dupin visited Great Britain in 1818, Ure escorted him through Glasgow's factories. Dupin commented that many of the factories' managers were Ure's former students. Ure acknowledged this, writing that his onetime students were "spread over the [United] Kingdom as proprietors and managers of factories."[38] Dupin's work was influenced by Ure and, in turn, may have influenced Henri Fayol, another pioneer whose ideas underlie modern management theory (see Chapter 10).

Dr. Andrew Ure . . . : A Slight Sketch. (London: Baines, 1876), frontispiece.

Andrew Ure

PRINCIPLES OF MANUFACTURING

Ure was deeply concerned with industrial education. Writing in his 1835 book, *The Philosophy of Manufactures: Or, An Exposition of the Scientific, Moral, and Commercial Economy of the Factory System of Great Britain*, he provided a systematic account of manufacturing principles and processes. In Ure's judgment, the essential principle in manufacturing was "to substitute mechanical science for hand skill . . . [and to provide] for division or the graduation of labour among artisans."[39] Although Ure devoted a large portion of his 1835 book to the technical challenges of manufacturing cloth from silk, cotton, wool, and flax, he eventually dealt with the challenges of

[37] Wilfred V. Farrar, "Andrew Ure, F.R.S., and the Philosophy of Manufactures," *Notes and Records of the Royal Society of London* 27(2) (February 1973), pp. 300–301. For more about Anderson and the Anderson Institute, see James Muir, *John Anderson: Pioneer of Technical Education and the College He Founded*, ed. James M. Macaulay (Glasgow: John Smith, 1950).

[38] Andrew Ure, *The Philosophy of Manufactures: Or, an Exposition of the Scientific, Moral, and Commercial Economy of the Factory System of Great Britain* (London: Charles Knight, 1835), p. viii.

[39] *Ibid.*, p. 20.

factory management. Ure sought a plan for automatically preventing individual mill-hands from stopping work as they pleased and thereby throwing an entire factory into disorder. He believed that workers had to recognize and not resist the benefits of mechanization. According to Ure's plan for preventing work stoppages, the tasks necessary to manufacture a final product had to be arranged and connected in such a way as to achieve a harmony of the whole. To this end, Ure felt that in every establishment there were "three principles of action, or three organic systems; the mechanical, the moral and the commercial."[40]

Although Ure's explanation of these principles did not entail a clear-cut plan for organizing a factory, he did seek to place them in the framework of a "self-governing agency." "Mechanical" referred to production techniques and processes, "moral" to the "moral constitution" of a factory's operative employees, and "commercial" to the manufacture and sale of a factory's output. Ure treated the mechanical principle of action at length, and the moral aspect reflected a pro-management stance. As the factories of Ure's day were under attack from numerous quarters, he set out to defend his industrial practices. He argued that, as a group, "factory operatives" enjoyed better "personal comforts" than other "labouring classes." They ate better, held jobs that were less physically demanding (due to the nature of the machines they operated), and were better paid. Rebutting investigations into child labor, Ure noted that most of the investigators and their supporters had never visited the factories they found so offensive; he also engaged in character assassination, charging that one investigation witness was an atheist, one a tavern keeper, and one "an assaulter of women." To further counter the investigators' accusations, Ure claimed that children employed in factories lived in well-kept cottages, received both practical and religious education, and were better fed and enjoyed better health than children in general. He also noted that children employed in agriculture were paid half their factory counterparts' wages and received no education or training. Citing Factory Inquiry Commission reports,[41] Ure concluded that the incidence of disease, the dietary habits, and the general state of health of factory workers were better than the general population.

To illustrate workers' inappreciation of employers' concerns for their health, Ure cited an instance in which large ventilating fans had been installed in one factory to reduce the foul air. Instead of thanking the factory owner the workers complained that the freshened air had increased their appetites, and, therefore, they were entitled to a corresponding wage increase. The factory owner reached a compromise with his workers by running the ventilating fans only half the day, thereafter hearing no more complaints about foul air or appetites. Ure defended the factory system, seeing it as more beneficial than disadvantageous to society. Some of his statements in defense of factory working conditions, however, would seem contestable.[42] He contended, for instance, that mill workers suffered no harm from working at temperatures ranging up to 150°F (65.56°C) or that their ill-health was due to eating too much bacon, which was often putrid.[43]

Ure based many of his conclusions on data from the same 1833 survey of Lancashire, Cheshire, and Derbyshire county factories cited in Chapter 3. Focusing on responses collected from 151 cotton mills, Ure countered that the average mill worker labored for 69 hours per week. Of 48,645 "Hands," he calculated that approximately half were female and 41.29 percent

[40] *Ibid.*, p. 55.

[41] Factories Inquiry Commission, "First Report of the Central Board of His Majesty's Commissioners Appointed to Collect Information in the Manufacturing Districts, as to the Employment of Children in Factories, and as to the Propriety and Means of Curtailing the Hours of Their Labour," *Parliamentary Papers* 20(450) (1833); *idem*, "Second Report of the Central Board of His Majesty's Commissioners Appointed to Collect Information in the Manufacturing Districts, as to the Employment of Children in Factories, and as to the Propriety and Means of Curtailing the Hours of Their Labour," *Parliamentary Papers* 21(519) (1833); *idem, Supplementary Report of the Central Board of His Majesty's Commissioners Appointed to Collect Information in the Manufacturing Districts, as to the Employment of Children in Factories, and as to the Propriety and Means of Curtailing the Hours of Their Labour*, 2 vols. (London: House of Commons, 1834).

[42] Farrar, "Andrew Ure, F.R.S., and the Philosophy of Manufactures," pp. 318, 395.

[43] Ure, *The Philosophy of Manufactures*, pp. 385 and 395.

were under the age of 18, with 47.5 percent of this latter group between ages 14 and 18.[44] Using information provided by millowner Henry Houldsworth, Ure also drew a comparison between the wages paid to Manchester cotton spinners in 1804 and 1833. Over this period, the work week for adult male cotton spinners declined from 74 to 68 hours, while their average weekly wage increased from 60 to 65 shillings and 3 pence. Ure further noted that the purchasing power (real wages) of the 65 shillings and 3 pence was greater in 1833 than the 60 shillings in 1804. For example, in 1804, 60 shillings would buy 117 pounds of flour and 62.5 pounds of meat; in 1833, 65 shillings and 3 pence would buy 267 pounds of flour and 85 pounds of meat.[45] Ure concluded that progress in the cotton industry outpaced progress in agriculture where workers were still earning subsistence wages. He did acknowledge that, although child labor and female labor were widely used in cotton mills, this was no different than had been the case in the domestic system in which individual workers fabricated goods in small workshops or in their own homes (see Chapter 2) or in either agriculture or coal mines. For Ure, rising real wages, a trend toward shorter and more regular hours, and advancing mechanization were the hallmarks of English cotton mills. Although Ure's focus on cotton mills precludes a general statement about English management in the mid-nineteenth century, the evidence he marshaled does suggest an increase in mechanization and a growing recognition of the long hours and harsh working conditions endured by men, women, and children.

CHARLES DUPIN: INDUSTRIAL EDUCATION IN FRANCE

A second individual who pioneered in industrial education was a French mathematician, economist, politician, and naval engineer. Baron Pierre Charles François Dupin (1784–1873) was known for his interest in mathematics and mechanics. He was a graduate of the École Polytechnique and the École Spéciale du Génie Maritime. As noted earlier, Dupin had visited Great Britain on various occasions between the years 1816 and 1819 and had observed the results Andrew Ure obtained in educating working-class men and women.[46] In 1819, Dupin was named professor of mathematics and mechanics at the Conservatoire des Arts et Métiers in Paris.[47] He must have immediately initiated his own curriculum, for in 1831 he wrote: "For twelve years I have had the honor of teaching geometry and mechanics applied to the arts, in favor of the industrial class, I have dedicated the first and last sessions of each year to the general consideration of the most important questions affecting the well-being, education, and morality of the workers, to the progress of national industry, and to the development of all means of prosperity that work can produce for the splendor and happiness of our country."[48] Dupin's contribution to the practice of management lies in the influence he had on the course of French industrial education

[44] Andrew Ure, *The Cotton Manufactures of Great Britain Systematically Investigated*, vol. 1 (London: Charles Knight, 1836), pp. 334–342. For the Factory Inquiry Commission source data, see Factories Inquiry Commission, *Supplementary Report of the Central Board of His. Majesty's Commissioners Appointed to Collect Information in the Manufacturing Districts*, vol. 1, Supplement (D.) (General.), p. 124.

[45] Ure, *The Cotton Manufactures of Great Britain Systematically Investigated*, vol. 2, p. 447. For the original Houldsworth wage-book numbers, see "Examination," Henry Houldsworth, June 27, 1833, *Report from the Select Committee on Manufactures, Commerce, and Shipping; With the Minutes of Evidence, and Appendix and Index* (London: House of Commons, 1833), p. 319.

[46] Charles Dupin, *Voyages dans la Grande-Bretagne, entrepris relativement aux services publics de la guerre, de la marine, et des ponts et chaussés, en 1816, 1817, 1818 et 1819* [*Travel in Great Britain undertaken in connection with the public services of war, navy, and bridges and highways, in 1816, 1817, 1818 and 1819*], vol. 3: *Commerciable de LaGrande-Bretagne* [*Commerce of Great Britain*] (Paris: Bachelier, 1824). See also Margaret Bradley and Fernand Perrin, "Charles Dupin's Study Visit to the British Isles. 1816–1824," *Technology and Culture* 32(1) (January 1991), pp. 47–68.

[47] Paul Tannery, "Dupin" in André Brethelot and Camille Drefus, eds., *La Grande Encyclopédie: Inventaire Raisonné des Sciences, des Lettres et des Arts* [*The Great Encyclopedia: Inventory of Science, Letters and the Arts*], vol. 15 (Paris: Lamirault, 1886), p. 81. See also Académié des Sciences, *M. Le Baron Dupin: Discours Prononcés a ses Funérailles le 21 Janvier 1873 et Éloge Historique lu a l'Académie des Sciences le 2 Avril 1883* [*Baron Dupin: Speeches at His Funeral on January 21, 1873 and Eulogies Read at the Academy of Sciences on April 2, 1883*] (Nevers, France: G. Valliére, 1902).

[48] Charles Dupin, *Discours sur le Sort des Ouvriers, Considéré dans ses Rapports avec l'Industrie, la Liberté et l'Ordre Public: Prononcé dans la Séance de Clôture de son Cours, le 19 Juin, au Conservatoire des Arts et Métiers* [*Lecture on the Fate of the Workers, Considered in its Relations with Industry, Freedom and Public Order: Pronounced in the Closing Session of its Course, June 19, at the Conservatory of Arts and Crafts*] (Paris: Bachelier Librairie, 1831), p. 1.

Charles Dupin, 1820

Julien Léopold Boilly, *Recueil de Portraits de Personnages Célèbres Faisant Partie des Quatre Différentes Classes Académiques de l'Institut Lithographiés par Boilly Fils, ed.* Institut Royal de France (Paris: Blaisot, circa 1823) plate 9.

and, as noted, possibly on the later work of Henri Fayol. As will be discussed in Chapter 10, Fayol is widely credited with being the first writer to distinguish between technical and managerial skills and to argue for the necessity of teaching management. Examine this passage from Dupin, however, written over eight decades before Fayol's major published work:

> It is to the director of workshops and factories that it is suitable to make, by means of geometry and applied mechanics, a special study [*étude spéciale*] of all the ways to economize the efforts of workers. . . . [F]or a man to be a director of others, manual work has only a secondary importance; it is his intellectual ability [*force intellectuelle*] that must put him in the top position, and it is in instruction such as that of the Conservatory of Arts and Crafts, that he must develop it.[49]

John H. Hoagland reported that by 1826 Dupin's views on management had been presented in 98 French cities to more than 5,000 workers and supervisors.[50] Because his lectures were published and translated into eight languages, the number of people he influenced was no doubt much larger.[51] Dupin also demonstrated a rudimentary grasp of time study and the need to balance workloads after labor was divided: "When [the] division of work is put into operation the most scrupulous attention must be exercised to calculate the duration of each type of operation, in order to proportion the work to the particular number of workers that are assigned to it."[52] He wrote of the need to provide workers with clear, concise instructions for most efficiently producing desired work and for studying each industry to find and publish the most effective means of accomplishing different tasks.

Dupin's published lectures were not so much an examination of management as they were an exhortation to remove industrial strife. He also recognized worker uneasiness stemming from the increasing mechanization of French industry, discussed the work of James Watt (see Chapter 3), and stressed mechanization's benefits to workers, managers, and society alike. Regarding the dangers of technological displacement, Dupin noted that before Watt's first steam engine was introduced in 1776, British industry employed fewer than one million people; by 1830, this number had grown to over three million and, combined with advances in machinery, equated to the power of seven million workers. Dupin called for widespread industrial training to permit agrarian and unskilled workers to share in the growing industrial prosperity: "He who perfects the machines tends to give them the advantage over the worker; he who perfects the worker, gives him the same fighting chance, and makes the machine serve his well-being, instead of having to suffer from their competition. Let us concern ourselves with man involved with the difficulties of the work and of the industry."[53] These were insights applicable not only to early nineteenth-century France, but also to industrial life in the twentieth and twenty-first centuries.

---

[49] Dupin, *Discours*, pp. 12–13.

[50] John H. Hoagland, "Management before Frederick Taylor," p. 21.

[51] Roberto Romani, *National Character and Public Spirit in Britain and France, 1750–1914* (Cambridge, England: Cambridge University Press, 2002), p. 101.

[52] Charles Dupin, *Géométrie et Méchanique des Arts et Métiers et des Beaux-Arts* [*Geometry and Mechanics of Arts and Crafts and Fine Arts*], vol. 3 (Paris: Bachelier, 1826), p. 128.

[53] Dupin, *Discours*, p. 9.

THE PIONEERS: A FINAL NOTE

The four pioneers discussed in this chapter were instrumental in sowing the seeds of the management discipline. At its best, however, the outgrowth of these seeds was sparse and rudimentary. What prevented the emergence of a formal body of management thought during this early period rather than some three-quarters of a century later? Why would Frederick W. Taylor, and not Charles Babbage, receive credit for founding scientific management? In retrospect, the reasons are manifold.

First, early writings emphasized specific techniques and not managing per se. In an age of expanding technology, it was difficult to separate the role of management from the technical and commercial aspects of running a firm. Managers in this era were more concerned with finance, production processes, selling, and acquiring labor—all of which were indeed critical at the time—rather than with developing principles or generalizations about management. An analogy might be that of young children learning to walk: the motor urge is so great and consumes so much of their energy and attention that the development of speech is slowed. As walking is perfected, speech blooms. At the dawn of the Industrial Revolution, managers were just learning to walk in the new factory system; the technical and human challenges consumed so much of their time that they had little left over for formulating general principles of management.

Second, the figures of the technical genius, the inventor-pioneer, and the founder-entrepreneur dominated the era. Success or failure was more likely to be attributed to their individual intelligence or skill rather than to any generalized ideas about what talents managers needed to be successful. Each industry and its challenges were considered unique and, hence, the lessons learned in one setting were considered inapplicable in another.

Third, the limits of disseminating knowledge must be considered. Many were illiterate, books were relatively expensive, and schools were oriented toward either studying the classics or training artisans. Although scholars read the books of other scholars, it is unlikely that Babbage, Dupin, and Ure were widely read by practicing managers of the day. The lessons taught by Ure and Dupin reached managers in only a comparatively small number of factories.

SUMMARY

The genesis of modern management thought occurred in Great Britain and, to a lesser extent, France. Robert Owen appealed to the heart, as well as to the pocketbook, in his search for a new harmony between humans and machines. Charles Babbage beckoned the mind, became the grandfather of scientific management, and applied science to management before Frederick W. Taylor. Andrew Ure shared his experiences and observations, developing working-class managers for the new factories that heralded the Industrial Revolution. Following Ure's lead, Charles Dupin launched industrial education in France. With the emergence of management thought in Great Britain, our story now moves to the development of "systematic" management in the United States.

CHAPTER 5

The Industrial Revolution in the United States

The nineteenth century in the United States was an era of rapid expansion and growth. Though a British colony with less than three million inhabitants just 24 years earlier and torn by half a decade of internecine strife in mid-century, the fledgling nation was to become the world's leading political and industrial force by 1900. Her total exports were roughly $1,400,000,000 and by 1910 passed the two-billion mark. Indeed, by the early twentieth century, the manufacturing output of the United States surpassed that of Great Britain, Germany, and France combined.[1] This chapter focuses on the Industrial Revolution in the United States, the industries it spawned, and the contributions of various management pioneers from this era to management thought.

THE AMERICAN SYSTEM OF MANUFACTURING

In 1851, the first "Great Exhibition of the Works of Industry of All Nations" was staged at the Crystal Palace in London's Hyde Park. It attracted more than six million visitors to see technological marvels from around the world.[2] The United States won more prizes than any other nation. What amazed visitors the most was the U.S. exhibit featuring Alfred C. Hobbs's unpickable locks, Isaac M. Singer's sewing machine, Samuel Colt's repeating pistol, and Cyrus H. McCormick's mechanical reaper. Not only were these products superior to those crafted in other nations, but they also were all manufactured in a unique fashion—the parts were built to such exacting standards that they were interchangeable, so a person could pick parts at random and assemble a complete product. This unique feature became known as the American System of Manufacturing.

To conclude that the development of interchangeable parts was solely an U.S. innovation, however, would be inaccurate. As early as 1436, the Arsenal of Venice (Italy) was manufacturing warships using standard components. For example, all bows were built to fit any arrow, a single type of rudder fit all sternposts, and deck furnishings and riggings were largely uniform.[3] The

[1] Noam Maggor, *Brahmin Capitalism: Frontiers of Wealth and Populism in America's Gilded Age* (Cambridge, MA: Harvard University Press, 2017), p. ix.

[2] "Exhibition, British Industrial," *American Annual Cyclopædia and Register of Important Events of the Year 1862*, vol. 2 (1863), p. 412.

[3] Frederic Chapin Lane, *Venetian Ships and Shipbuilders of the Renaissance* (Baltimore, MD: Johns Hopkins Press, 1934), pp. 211–212.

arsenal enabled Venice to become the era's supreme maritime power. Frenchman Honoré Blanc introduced the production of interchangeable parts for guns in 1785. Inspired by the earlier success of Jean-Baptiste Vaquette de Gribeauval in boring out identical cannon barrels, he applied a similar standardization to making flintlock muskets.[4] No one, however, had previously used interchangeable parts in private industry on a large-scale basis until Hobbs, Colt, Singer, McCormick, and other U.S. manufacturers. What could have happened in the United States to lead to this new application?

In the United States, the use of interchangeable parts began with Connecticut clockmakers when, in 1809, Eli Terry began to produce "fully interchangeable wooden-movement clocks."[5] It was, however, in manufacturing firearms, one of the era's most sophisticated products, that interchangeability was most notably achieved. Early gunsmiths, such as Simeon North and John H. Hall, had made small batches of firearms using uniform parts, but with limited success. Both men, however, won government contracts to manufacture guns; North in 1799 for 500 horsemen's pistols at the Springfield (Massachusetts) Armory.[6] The armory had been established by Congressional grant in 1794 as a central workshop to bring weaponsmiths together to produce armaments, although it did not begin to apply improved manufacturing and management techniques until Lt. Colonel Roswell Lee became civilian superintendent in 1815. Lee reorganized the armory, centralizing authority and establishing defined areas of responsibility. An early piece-rate accounting system in which workers were paid based on units of output rather than a day-rate was developed and later used to monitor labor and material costs. With a division of labor, specialization also increased: in 1815, there were 34 different occupational specialties; in 1820, 86; and by 1825, 100.[7] Weapons were made by specialists rather than by general metal- and wood-workers. Innovative metalworking machines for channeling barrels, making gunstocks, and milling small parts were introduced. With more accurate measurement devices, parts could be manufactured to closer tolerances, which increased their interchangeability and led to a tripling of output by the 1820s. Colonel Lee also tightened discipline, with a policy that prohibited "playing of Ball or other proceedings that have a tendency to impede the regular advancement and the progress of the work." Fighting and unnecessary noise were forbidden. He further cautioned that any "conduct against the regulations of the Armory" would be grounds for dismissal and declared: "From and after the 15th day of April 1816 no Rum, Gin, Brandy, Whiskey, or ardent Spirits of any kind will be suffered to be carried or drunk in or about the public work shops at this place."[8] Although the Springfield Armory was government-owned, it provides insight into the early development of modern private-sector factories. The armory's division of labor, authority structure, cost controls, plant-wide accounting system, inspection and quality techniques, and advanced metalworking were all crucial to the American System of Manufacturing.

The improvements introduced by Lee at the Springfield Armory were unique in both the governmental and private sectors. A survey commissioned by U.S. Secretary of the Treasury Louis McLane in 1832 provided a partial census of the nation's manufacturers. In the 10 states surveyed, there were 106 manufacturers with $100,000 or more in assets; 88 of these were in textiles, 12 in iron making, and the remaining 6 produced nails and hoops, axes, glass, paper,

---

[4] Simon Winchester, *The Perfectionists: How Precision Engineers Created the Modern World* (New York: HarperCollins, 2018), p. 87.

[5] Donald R. Hoke, "Letters to the Editor: Clocks, Not Muskets, Led 'American System,'" *Wall Street Journal* (May 19–20, 2018), p. A12.

[6] Merritt Roe Smith, "John H. Hall, Simeon North, and the Milling Machine: The Nature of Innovation among Antebellum Arms Makers," *Technology and Culture* 14(4) (October 1973), p. 575n6.

[7] *Idem, Harpers Ferry Armory and the New Technology: The Challenge of Change* (Ithaca, NY: Cornell University Press, 1977), p. 83. See also Robert C. Ford and Kennan D. Yoho, "The Government's Role in Creating an Innovation Ecosystem: The Springfield Armory as Hub in the Connecticut River Valley," *Journal of Management History* (2020) 26(4), pp. 557–579.

[8] Roswell Lee, "Armory Regulations, Superintendents Office, U States Armory 8th March 1816," *Letters Received 1808–1897*, Records of the Springfield Armory, Record Group 156: Records of the Office of the Chief of Ordnance, 1797–1988, Box 1, Folder 5, Entry Number 1362, Identifier 1601077, National Archives, Waltham, MA.

flour, and hydraulic equipment (viz., fire pumps and fire engines). Only 36 of these manufacturers employed 250 or more workers; of these, 31 were textile factories, 3 were iron works, 1 was a nail and hoops work, and another an axe factory.[9] In 1832, the Springfield Armory employed 246 people, so it was among the period's largest manufacturers. Other than textile mills and a few iron works, most nongovernmental organizations were relatively small, employing an average of 10 to 12 workers. The McLane report also indicated that most manufacturers were family-owned and managed as sole proprietorships or partnerships, and there were few corporations. Finally, steam power was rarely used, as the manufacturers primarily relied on hydropower. Recalling Andrew Ure's study of Lancashire cotton mills during this same period (see Chapter 4), there are remarkable similarities in size and how the manufacturers were managed, with the British ahead in using steam power.

In short, U.S. private-sector manufacturers before 1835 were small, family run, and water powered. In the 1840s and 1850s, however, U.S. entrepreneurs unleashed a host of products that would revolutionize industry in both the United States and Great Britain. The management techniques pioneered at the Springfield Armory and elsewhere provided the basis for the later manufacture of shovels, sewing machines, typewriters, steam engines, reapers, and other civilian products for which a mass market existed, thus justifying a large capital investment. What visitors admired at the Crystal Palace was the result of a long chain of developments—beginning at the Springfield Armory and spreading to the private sector. Mass production had not yet been perfected, but its antecedents were present. In commenting on the difference between the American System of Manufacturing and European methods, Joseph A. Litterer noted that European manufacturers were no less knowledgeable and skilled than their American counterparts. The difference, he explained, was in how their knowledge and skill were applied. The European manufacturers used technical knowledge and skills to "make a product." The American manufacturers used them to "make a process for making a product."[10]

NATIONAL INDEPENDENCE AND ECONOMIC FREEDOM

The territory that formed the original boundaries of the United States of America was part of the British Empire beginning with the founding of Jamestown, Virginia, in 1607. For the settlers drawn to the 13 British colonies in North America that later overthrew King George III's monarchy and declared independence in Philadelphia, Pennsylvania, at the Second Continental Congress on July 4, 1776, the lure was manifold: social betterment, economic opportunity, religious freedom, and political separation. The early colonists included aristocrats, apprentices, farmers, felons, tramps, and petty criminals, as well as budding tycoons. Efforts to develop colonial manufacturing were discouraged by Great Britain, as it sought to prevent potential market competition from goods made in its own colonies. The Wool Act (1699), which prohibited colonists from exporting wool, and the Hat Act (1732), which limited the export of colonial-made hats, are but two prominent examples of laws restricting the manufacture, sale, and exportation of colonial goods. Two 1776 documents, however, tolled the end of mercantilist policies intended to favor British traders: the *Declaration of Independence* in the United States and Adam Smith's *The Wealth of Nations* in Great Britain (see Chapter 2). The former was a declaration of national independence, and the latter was a declaration of economic freedom.

Between 1776 and 1787, the ideas of Adam Smith were widely read and discussed in the United States. Political leaders such as Benjamin Franklin, who commented on draft chapters

[9] U.S. Congress, Documents Relative to the Manufactures in the United States, Collected and Transmitted to the House of Representatives, in Compliance with a Resolution of Jan. 19, 1832, by the Secretary of the Treasury [McLane Report], 22nd Congress, 1st Session, H.R. Document 308, 2 vols. (Washington, DC: Printed by Duff Green, 1833). The data in this paragraph were compiled by Alfred D. Chandler III, and reported in Alfred D. Chandler, Jr., "Anthracite Coal and the Beginnings of the Industrial Revolution in the United States," *Business History Review* 46(2) (Summer 1972), p. 143.

[10] Joseph A. Litterer, "Systematic Management: The Search for Order and Integration," *Business History Review* 35(4) (Winter 1961), p. 466.

of *The Wealth of Nations* for Smith, objected to a strong government role in economic matters.[11] Smith's *laissez-faire* philosophy was consistent with the views of the "Founding Fathers," including, Thomas Jefferson, James Madison, Alexander Hamilton and, of course, Franklin.[12] Ratified in 1787, the U.S. Constitution, Article I, Section 8, gave the U.S. Congress the power to impose and collect taxes, borrow money, coin money, fix standards of weights and measures, punish counterfeiters, issue patents, and "regulate commerce with foreign nations and among the several states." Save for the exceptions mentioned above, the U.S. government was to maintain a hands-off approach to private economic affairs and act primarily to ensure uniformity and order among the several states. Among the Founders, Jefferson felt that the United States would be best served by remaining a rural society free from the large cities, factories, and mines he had witnessed in England. He envisioned an agrarian democracy filled with "yeomen farmers," rather than the *métayaers* and *mezzadri*, poor tenant farmers, he had seen in France and Italy. Hamilton, however, understood that industrialization was necessary for the economic independence of the young republic.[13] Political and social conditions in the United States were favorable to free-market enterprise and economic expansion. The nation was rich in natural resources, with a growing labor supply and a largely untapped market for consumer goods. Many merchants made fortunes in trade and other business activities. Two colonial merchants, William Almy and his future father-in-law Moses Brown, of Providence, Rhode Island, provided the capital that brought the Industrial Revolution to the United States.

EARLY INDUSTRIAL DEVELOPMENT

British textile manufacturers were particularly concerned about losing their competitive advantage to lower-priced colonial goods. To protect its mills from imported cloth, Great Britain prohibited both the export of textile machinery and the emigration of skilled mechanics, who knew how to build and repair it.[14] To be allowed to emigrate to the United States in 1789, Samuel Slater (1768–1835), an experienced builder and mechanic who had worked with Richard Arkwright, the British textile pioneer (see Chapter 3), claimed to be a farmer. At the time, cloth in the former colonies was made to sell in hundreds of homes by farm wives and their daughters, using raw materials provided or "put out" by local merchants (see Chapter 2). In 1790, William Almy (1761–1836) and Moses Brown (1738–1836) failed in establishing a textile factory driven by waterpower at Providence, Rhode Island. Brown foresaw tremendous potential in Arkwright's more advanced water frame. Learning of Brown's interest in running his looms with hydropower instead of hand power, Slater offered his services to replicate Arkwright's water frame. The result was the nation's first water-powered textile mill, built at Pawtucket, Rhode Island, in 1790. Striking out on his own in 1798, Slater developed what became known as the "Rhode Island System." Following the practice in Great Britain, the Rhode Island System consisted of a sole proprietorship or mill partnership that produced fine yarn and employed entire families (including children) to do weaving in their homes. Slater supervised mill operations, assisted by his sons, his brother, and other relatives.

[11] John F. Watson, *Annals of Philadelphia, Being a Collection of Memoirs, Anecdotes, & Incidents of the City and Its Inhabitants from the Days of the Pilgrim Founders* (Philadelphia, PA: E. I. Carey & A. Hart, 1830), pp. 514–515. See also Thomas D. Eliot, "The Relations between Adam Smith and Benjamin Franklin before 1776," *Political Science Quarterly* 39(1) (March 1924), pp. 67–96.

[12] Samuel Fleischer, "Adam Smith's Reception among the American Founders," *William and Mary Quarterly* 59(4) (October 2002), pp. 897–924.

[13] For Jefferson's thoughts on "[t]hose who labour in the earth [being] the chosen people of God," see his *Notes on the State of Virginia* (London: John Stockdale, 1787), p. 176. For Hamilton's thoughts on the importance of industry and commerce, see his *Report of the Secretary of the Treasury of the United States on the Subject of Manufactures: Presented to the House of Representatives, December 5, 1791* (Philadelphia, PA: Childs and Swaine, 1791), p. 5.

[14] Theodore F. Marburg, "Aspects of Labor Administration in the Early Nineteenth Century," *Bulletin of the Business Historical Society* 15(1) (February 1941), pp. 1–10.

By 1808, the United States boasted 15 textile mills; over half of them connected with Slater and his various associates. The War of 1812 with Great Britain led to a further surge in U.S. textile manufacturing. Francis Cabot Lowell, a prominent New England merchant, had visited Great Britain and seen textile looms in Manchester and the English Midlands driven by waterwheels. In 1813, along with other investors, he incorporated the Boston Manufacturing Company of Waltham, Massachusetts, to apply this new technology on the Charles River. Rather than emulating Slater's Rhode Island System and putting work out to families in their homes, Lowell employed what was known as the Waltham System.

The Waltham System had become the dominant method of textile manufacturing by 1816. Slow to change, Slater and his associates waited almost a decade before giving up the Rhode Island System.[15] In 1827, Slater became one of the few mill owners to use steam-driven power looms at his Steam Cotton Manufacturing Company in Providence. Whereas other manufacturers depended on hydropower, subject to dry spells and winter freezing, Slater was able to avoid interruptions in production and employment by using steam engines. Use of steam power rather than water also allowed Slater to locate mills closer to customers or suppliers. He also began to integrate spinning and weaving under one factory roof, ending the putting-out of work for families to do in their homes. As Slater's mills became more successful, operating in some 15 separate locations by 1835, he began to hire professional managers. Slater pioneered the use of factory ledgers to determine the cost of producing a yard of cloth, and vertically integrated his business holdings, moving forward to establish a sales office in New York City and backward by employing buyers to locate and purchase raw materials. Slater offers an excellent example of an early U.S. entrepreneur who strategically responded to technological, as well as foreign and domestic, competitive pressures.[16]

The first U.S. textile mills provide insights into early ideas about organization structure and management. As outlined in Chapter 3, as organizations grew in size and number of locations, the ability of founder-entrepreneurs to directly supervise all their employees diminished, and intermediate levels of supervision became necessary. For the first time, there is also evidence of emerging staff positions. For example, a mill manager was often "assisted by a superintendent, a technically trained man, and there were overseers with technical responsibilities that cut across the operations of the mill: overseers of repairs . . . or of belting."[17] Thus, staff began to operate on multiple levels: mechanics, woodworkers, and other skilled workmen were employed as usual, though others were made supervisors and technical overseers. Reflecting Dupin's distinction between technical and managerial skills (see Chapter 4), supervisors did not need both technical and managerial ability, but could rely on specialists in these areas.

Slater's Rhode Island System and Lowell's Waltham System also differed in their labor policies. To attract enough workers for its mills, Slater's Rhode Island System was patterned after the British practice of employing entire families and, consequently, resulted in more child labor. In contrast, the Waltham System was designed to recruit female workers to its mill towns by furnishing boarding houses. These "mill girls" were mainly young women between the ages of 15 and 30. Agents who toured the countryside, "emphasizing the moral and educational advantages of factory work," hired the women from neighboring farms.[18] The mill girls lived in factory-owned boarding houses and "matrons of tried character" carefully monitored their conduct.[19]

[15] Barbara M. Tucker, *Samuel Slater and the Origins of the American Textile Industry, 1790–1860* (Ithaca, NY: Cornell University Press, 1984), pp. 99–124.

[16] For other examples, see Freeman Hunt, *Lives of American Merchants* (New York: Hunt's Merchants' Magazine, 1856).

[17] Steven Lubar, "Managerial Structure and Technological Style: The Lowell Mills, 1821–1880," in Jeremy Atack, ed., *Business and Economic History* 13 (1984), p. 21.

[18] Thomas C. Cochran and William Miller, *The Age of Enterprise: A Social History of Industrial America* (New York: Macmillan, 1942), p. 19. See also Bernard A. Weisberger, "The Working Ladies of Lowell," *American Heritage* 12(2) (February 1961), 43–45, 83–90.

[19] John A. Lowell, "Mercantile Biography: The Late Patrick Tracy Jackson," *Hunt's Merchants' Magazine and Commercial Review* 18(4) (April 18, 1848), p. 360.

Even English novelist Charles Dickens (see Chapter 3), a vocal critic of the British factory system, praised the Waltham System. He reported that the Waltham mill girls were clean, healthy, and well mannered. Dickens felt British mill owners could learn much from the Waltham example.[20] Nonetheless, the American systems, comparatively, had their shortcomings: the Waltham System was less successful in retaining a labor force (Norman Ware estimated that the typical New England cotton mill girl stayed at her job for only a year), and the Rhode Island system used child labor—a practice Dickens opposed.[21] The introduction of steam-powered looms, however, had a dramatic effect on the employment of child labor in Rhode Island: "[W]ith the mechanization of picking and weaving in the early 1820s, Pawtucket's factory system had reached maturity and as a consequence had come to rely increasingly on adult factory labor."[22] Consequently, the evils commonly found in the British factory system were increasingly absent in U.S. textile mills. Employers were paying high wages to attract and retain their workers, child labor was not as prevalent, and abuses were less frequent and less severe.[23]

Overall, U.S. workers were less resistant to the introduction of machinery than their British counterparts. They also took a different stance with respect to organized labor. As a legacy of legislation regulating British guilds, trade or craft unions were viewed as conspiracies that restrained commerce and, therefore, were unlawful in Britain until the Trade Union Act was passed in 1871.[24] By contrast, in a landmark 1842 case (*Commonwealth v. Hunt*), the Massachusetts Supreme Court held that the Boston Journeyman Bootmakers' Society was not a criminal conspiracy, though if it used criminal means to accomplish its goals, its members would be subject to prosecution.[25] The Court's ruling thus established that workers had the right to organize for a legal purpose and to strike or use peaceful coercion to raise wages. In addition, the Court ruled that unions could require what we now call "closed shops," in which all workers are required to be union members. Although these rulings only applied in Massachusetts, they discouraged attempts in other states to prosecute unions on conspiracy grounds. In brief, economic, social, political, and technological forces that encouraged work, thrift, innovation, and competition fostered early U.S. industrial development. The Industrial Revolution in the United States began in textiles but would soon spread throughout other industries.

STEAMBOATS AND RAILROADS: A REVOLUTION IN TRANSPORTATION

Although textile mills represented the largest private enterprises in the United States in the early 1800s, a transportation and communication revolution was on the horizon. In 1807, Robert Fulton's steamboat the *Clermont* made its maiden voyage up the Hudson River to Albany and back, reaching a speed of 5 miles an hour. Within four years, steamboats were operating on the Ohio, Mississippi, and other inland waterways all the way to New Orleans at 12 miles an hour, "taking emigrants to settle on the land and bringing furs, grain, cured meats, and a hundred other products back to market."[26] Built between 1811 and 1837, the paved 620-mile Cumberland

[20] Charles Dickens, *American Notes for General Circulation*, vol. 1 (London: Chapman and Hall, 1842), pp. 156, 163–164. Corroborating evidence for Dickens's observations may be found in William Scoresby, *American Factories and Their Female Operatives* (Boston, MA: W. D. Ticknor Co., 1845).

[21] Norman Ware, *The Industrial Worker: 1840–1860* (Gloucester, MA: Peter Smith Co., 1959), p. 149.

[22] Gary B. Kulik, "The Beginnings of the Industrial Revolution in America: Pawtucket, Rhode Island, 1672–1829" (Doctoral dissertation, Brown University, Providence, RI, 1980), p. 341.

[23] Ross M. Robertson, *History of the American Economy* (New York: Harcourt Brace Jovanovich, 1955), p. 184.

[24] Parliament of the United Kingdom, *An Act to amend the Law relating to Trades Unions* (1871), *34 & 35 Vict c 31*.

[25] *Commonwealth v.* Hunt, 45 Mass. 111 (1842).

[26] Allan Nevins and Henry Steele Commager, *America: The Story of a Free People* (Boston, MA: Little, Brown), p. 161. See also David McCullough, *The Pioneers: The Heroic Story of the Settlers Who Brought the American Ideal West* (New York: Simon & Schuster, 2019), pp. 183–184.

Road, running from Cumberland, Maryland, to Vandalia, Illinois, and connecting the Potomac and Ohio Rivers, was a main throughfare for settlers migrating westward. The Erie Canal, begun in 1817 and completed in 1825, connected the Hudson River and the Atlantic Ocean to the Great Lakes, and the nation's East with the heart of the continent. Upon completion, it helped cement the Midwest's role as a leading industrial region and turned New York City, whose port soon handled more tonnage than any city except London, into a commercial powerhouse. Considered an engineering marvel, the 363-mile canal (40 feet wide and 4 feet deep, with 18 aqueducts and 83 locks) was the longest artificial waterway in the world. It "lowered consumer costs and allowed farmers in places such as Ohio to send their goods cheaply by boat to New York instead of all the way down [the Mississippi River] to New Orleans and then to New York, which itself was far less expensive than dragging the goods across the barely passable roads of early America."[27] Regular transatlantic steamship travel began in 1838.

Development of the iron rail, flanged wheel, and steam locomotive began around 1830. Opposed initially by canal operators who feared both the rate competition and a loss of jobs, the rail industry introduced a new dimension to life in the United States. Railroads were more efficient and faster than canals, which reduced crop spoilage en route to market. Free from the constraint of needing water, they were able to connect rural communities across the western plains. Unlike canals, they did not freeze in winter and, unlike the roads used by horse-drawn wagons, did not become muddy and impassable each spring from rain and melting snow.[28] By 1835, 1,000 miles of railroad track had been laid, and by 1871 this jumped to some 45,000 miles. The rail network in the United States had begun in 1815, when Colonel John Stevens III obtained the nation's first passenger railroad charter from the New Jersey state legislature for the New Jersey Railroad Company.[29] Deemed eccentric, Stevens could not obtain financial backing until 1830, when he and others built the 23-mile-long Camden and Amboy Railroad. After the Camden and Amboy, other lines, such as the Baltimore & Ohio (1830), the New York & Erie (1832), and the Illinois Central (1851), linking Chicago with New Orleans and Mobile, were built and expanded. As one commentator has observed, steam railroads represented "the most spectacular leap in the speed of transport since humankind had first mastered horse-riding."[30] In 1806, a trip from Washington, DC, to Lexington, Kentucky, took 3 weeks by stagecoach. The same trip by rail in 1845 took 4 days.[31] By mid-winter 1855, 58 passenger and 38 freight trains were entering and departing Chicago daily on ten different trunk railroads, making it the principal commercial, financial, and agricultural hub in the upper Mississippi Valley and, in time, the center of a rail network that stretched from the East Coast to the Pacific Ocean.[32] In increasing the speed and lowering the expense of shipping people and goods, these railroads not only created a revolution in transportation, but also reduced the average unit costs of production through economies of scale. This, in turn, decreased product prices and increased product demand. Moreover, as we shall see, railroads emphasized managing in a systematic fashion. First, however, let us examine a concurrent revolution in communication, the electric telegraph.

---

[27] Erik Loomis, *A History of America in Ten Strikes* (New York: New Press, 2018), p. 14. See also Ronald E. Shaw, "Canals in the Early Republic: A Review of Recent Literature," *Journal of the Early Republic* 4(2) (Summer 1984), pp. 117–142.

[28] Robert G. Spinney, *City of Big Shoulders: A History of Chicago* (Northern Illinois University Press, 2000), p. 50.

[29] For an account of John Stevens's various activities, including his anticipation by 3 years of Robert Fulton's steamboat, see Dorothy Gregg, "John Stevens: General Entrepreneur," in William Miller, ed., *Men in Business* (New York: Harper & Row, 1957), pp. 120–152. In England, George Stephenson demonstrated a locomotive and tender able to pull a 36-car train, including 22 passenger carriages and 12 wagon-loads of coal and flour 8 3/4 miles in 65 minutes in 1825; the first intercity line between Manchester and Liverpool opened in 1830. See Samuel Smiles, *The Life of George Stephenson, Railway Engineer* (London: John Murray, 1857), pp. 198–199, 305.

[30] Diarmaid MacCulloch, *Christianity: The First Three Thousand Years* (London: Allen Lane, 2009), p. 813.

[31] Robert W. Merry, *A Country of Vast Designs: James K. Polk, the Mexican War, and the Conquest of the American Continent* (New York: Simon & Schuster, 2009), p. 133.

[32] *Fourth Annual Review of the Commerce, Railroads, and Manufactures of Chicago, for the Year 1855* (Chicago, IL: Democratic Press Steam Printing House, 1856), p. 76.

THE COMMUNICATION REVOLUTION

Tom Standage reminds us that, as humans, we are "chronocentric"; that is, we have

> the egotism that one's own generation is poised on the cusp of history. . . . [W]e are repeatedly told that we are in the midst of a communications revolution. But the electric telegraph was, in many ways, far more disconcerting for the inhabitants of the time than today's advances are for us. . . . Heavier-than-air flying machines were, after all, thought by the Victorians to be totally impossible. But as for the Internet—well, they had one of their own.[33]

The "Victorian Internet" to which Standage refers is the electric telegraph, the invention of Samuel F. B. Morse, who built on a long line of scientific discoveries about electricity and magnetism. The possibilities of "distance signaling" through metal wires were developed by Morse in 1832 but not patented until 1837, the same year William F. Cooke and Charles Wheatstone obtained a British patent and installed 13 miles of telegraph wires on poles along Britain's Great Western Railroad. Morse gained a competitive advantage by developing a code consisting of dots and dashes that could be sent by opening and closing an electrical circuit and, once received, recorded on paper and translated into numbers and letters. The code quickly became the standard format for transmitting telegraphic messages.

The electric telegraph provided the beginnings of a worldwide communication system. An experimental telegraph line was completed between Washington, DC, and Baltimore in 1844, and by 1852, some 23,281 miles of wire and poles crisscrossed the United States, with lines linking New York with commercial centers like New Orleans and Chicago.[34] By 1860, some five-million messages were being sent across the United States per year.[35] On October 24, 1861, the Western Union Telegraph Company completed a transnational telegraph line linking the Atlantic and Pacific oceans. Its impact on long-distance and international communication was dramatic—where it might have taken days, weeks, or months for messages to be sent and received by mail, the telegraph brought instantaneous communication around the world.[36] News items could be sent by the telegraph, enabling daily newspapers to keep their readers informed of global events; stock prices could be sent across the nation to investors from trade exchanges via ticker tape; money could be transferred by wire; and a cable under the Atlantic Ocean connected the United States to Great Britain and the European continent starting in 1858. Credit for the first electronic commerce belongs to Richard W. Sears, who in 1886 was working as a telegrapher and railroad-station agent. He used his position to sell a shipment of gold-filled watches through other station agents along the Minneapolis & Saint Louis Railroad. Sears would partner with Alvah C. Roebuck in 1893 to found Sears, Roebuck and Company, the nation's leading retailer for most of the twentieth century.

Usually built by railroads along their rights-of-way, the telegraph was used to schedule and dispatch trains, as well as to handle commercial and personal messages. Prior to 1883, the United States had no standard time zones; there were hundreds of time zones, as localities ran on solar time, with noon being when the sun was at its apex. This made the cost-effective movement of trains and other on-track railroad equipment impossible, as each rail station ran on a different local time. For instance, there were 27 local times in Illinois, 23 in Indiana, and 38 in Wisconsin.[37] The electric telegraph was indispensable in organizing and coordinating the shipping of passengers and freight. On October 11, 1883, the General Time Convention was held in Chicago, at which time four time zones—each with an hour difference, from Eastern to Central to Mountain to Pacific—were established for the continental United States. The nation's railroads

[33] Tom Standage, *The Victorian Internet: The Remarkable Story of the Telegraph and the Nineteenth Century's On-Line Pioneers* (New York: Walker and Company, 1998), p. 213.

[34] *Report of the Superintendent of the Census for December1, 1852* (Washington, DC: Robert Armstrong, 1853), p. 107.

[35] Richard B. DuBoff, "The Telegraph and the Structure of Markets in the United States, 1845–1890," *Research in Economic History* 8 (1983), p. 255.

[36] John J. McCusker, "The Demise of Distance: The Business Press and the Origin of the Information Revolution in the Early Modern Atlantic World," *American Historical Review* 110(2) (April 2005), pp. 295–321.

[37] Carlton J. Corliss, *The Day of Two Noons* (Washington, DC: Association of American Railroads, 1941), p. 3.

put the time zones into effect at noon on October 18, 1883.[38] Within a few years, this example was followed around the world.

Together the telegraph and railroad enabled goods and ideas to move fast and far across the continental United States. Moreover, by integrating the continent, these technological revolutions in transportation and communication would not only play an important role in the geographic expansion of the United States, but also sweep away local trade barriers, open new lands for settlement, extend product markets and reshape distribution strategies, and provide an inexpensive, rapid, year-round means for travel and commerce.

THE AGE OF RAILS

Railroads were truly the United States' first big business. The textile industry, though growing and dominating the Northeastern states, never developed the scale and scope of the railroads. The railroads grew to such an uncomparable extent and complexity that means had to be developed to cope with massive financial requirements, integrate thousands of miles of rail line, spread fixed costs over more units, and handle a labor force dispersed across an entire continent. These new demands required innovations in managing the first U.S. industry that was national in scope. Unlike manufacturers, railroad operations were spread across an expanding nation, making communication between train crews and dispatchers a significant challenge. Investments in track and rolling stock were immense, and extensive long-range planning was required to prevent large, fixed capital outlays from being invested in unsustainable markets. Passenger safety and preventing damage to or loss of cargo were critical concerns. Roadway maintenance and scheduling eastbound and westbound traffic required coordination, and standing rules and policies had to be developed to guide decentralized operations.[39]

The original 23-mile track of the Camden and Amboy line required little in the way of management. Other lines, however, grew in scale and scope. Whereas railways connected existing cities in Europe, in the United States, the railroads *created* cities as they moved west and increased their range. In 1841, after a series of rail accidents, including a head-on collision between two passenger trains, the Western Railroad (Massachusetts) established defined areas of responsibility and a clear hierarchy of authority to prevent future mishaps.[40] Another large line, the Baltimore & Ohio (B&O), was reorganized in 1847 by Benjamin H. Latrobe II to separate "the working of the road" from "the collection and disbursement of revenue."[41] Although the Western and the B&O lines responded to growth with new organization structures, it was the New York and Erie Railroad that pioneered systematic management in the United States.

DANIEL C. MCCALLUM: SYSTEM AND ORGANIZATION

Daniel C. McCallum was born in Johnstone, Scotland. He came to the United States in 1822,[42] and received his elementary education in Rochester, New York. Rather than learning to be a tailor like his father, McCallum left home (and school) to become an accomplished carpenter and architect. He joined the New York and Erie Railroad Company ("the Erie") in 1848. McCallum showed a talent for management, as well as engineering, and became superintendent of the Susquehanna Division, where he developed an early set of procedures to govern rail operations. Faced with

[38] Stewart H. Holbrook, *The Yankee Exodus: An Account of Migration from New England* (New York: Macmillan, 1950), pp. 311–312.

[39] Alfred D. Chandler, Jr., "A General Introduction to the Readings," in Chandler, ed., *The Railroads: The Nation's First Big Business* (New York: Harcourt, Brace & World, 1965), pp. 9–10.

[40] "Railway Police—Collisions," *American Railroad Journal and Mechanics' Magazine* 7(6) (September 15, 1841), pp. 161–167; George Bliss, *Historical Memoir of the Western Railroad* (Springfield, MA: Samuel Bowles & Company, 1863), p. 156; and Stephen Salsbury, *The State, the Investor, and the Railroad: Boston & Albany, 1825–1867* (Cambridge, MA: Harvard University Press, 1967), pp. 182–190.

[41] *Organization of the Service of the Baltimore & Ohio R. Road Under the New System of Management* (Baltimore, MD: 1847), p. 3.

[42] Personal data on McCallum are from [W. Jerome Arnold], "Big Business Takes the Management Track," *Business Week*, April 30, 1966, pp. 104–106; Charles D. Wrege and Guidon Sorbo, Jr., "A Bridge Builder Changes a Railroad: The Story of Daniel Craig McCallum," *Canal History and Technology Proceedings* 24 (2005), pp. 183–218.

difficulties in rail integration and high accident rates, the Erie's owners appointed McCallum general superintendent in May 1854.

To McCallum, sound management was based on good discipline, specific and detailed job descriptions, frequent and accurate performance reports, pay and promotion based on merit, a clearly defined hierarchy of authority, and personal responsibility and accountability. He laid down the following general principles for assuring the Erie's efficient management:

Daniel C. McCallum, circa 1865

1. A proper division of responsibilities.
2. Sufficient power conferred to enable the same to be fully carried out, so that such responsibilities may be real in their character.
3. The means of knowing whether such responsibilities are faithfully executed.
4. Great promptness in the report of all derelictions of duty, so that evils may be at once corrected.
5. Such information to be obtained through a system of daily reports and checks, which will not embarrass principal officers, nor lessen their influence with their subordinates.
6. The adoption of a system, as a whole, which will not only enable the General Superintendent to detect errors immediately, but will also point out the delinquent.[43]

To enact these principles, McCallum first required all Erie workers to wear a prescribed uniform with insignia indicating their primary duties and rank. He then developed comprehensive rules to limit workers' abilities to do their tasks as they pleased. For instance, Rule 6, "Run Safe First, Fast Afterwards," enjoined engineers to "take all the time necessary to run safe . . . acting under the assumption that every switch was out of place, and a train standing on the main line."[44] Enginemen were told they would be accountable for "running off a switch," even if a switchman were at fault.

Finally, in 1855, McCallum crafted an organization plan that outlined the Erie's lines of authority, its division of labor among operating units, and its communication lines for reporting and control. When depicted as a vine, the Erie's board of directors and president were positioned at the plan's base; its five operating divisions, plus the staff service departments of engine repairs, car, bridge, telegraph, painting, treasurer's, and secretary's offices, were shown as branches; local freight and ticket-forwarding offices were displayed as leaves; subordinate supervisors, crews, and so on to the lowest element, were rendered as smaller leaves. Adherence to formal lines of authority was to be absolute:

> The enforcement of a rigid system of discipline . . . is indispensable to success. All subordinates should be accountable to, and *be directed by their immediate superiors only*; as obedience cannot be enforced where the foreman in immediate charge is interfered with by a superior officer giving orders directly to his subordinates.[45]

---

[43] Daniel C. McCallum, "Superintendent's Report," in *Reports of the President and Superintendent of the New York and Erie Railroad to the Stockholders for the Year Ending September 30, 1855* (New York: Press of the New York and Erie Railroad, 1856), p. 35.

[44] "Engineers' Strike on the New York and Erie Railroad," *The Engineer* 2 (October 31, 1856), p. 589. See also Walter Licht, *Working for the Railroad: The Organization of Work in the Nineteenth Century* (Princeton, NJ: Princeton University Press, 1983), pp. 246–247; Edward Harold Mott, *Between the Ocean and the Lakes: The Story of Erie* (New York: J. S. Collins, 1900), p. 433.

[45] McCallum, "Superintendent's Report," p. 40.

McCallum recognized no exceptions to this "unity of command principle"; to do otherwise would disrupt his control system, which was based on personal accountability.

McCallum also developed an information system that was likely the most advanced of its day. He used the telegraph to make operations safer; coordinate rail traffic by requiring hourly reports showing the position of every train in the Erie system; collect daily passenger and cargo reports; and disseminate monthly planning, ratemaking, and market analysis reports. He designed a clever crosscheck control system by requiring both freight and passenger conductors to report on train movements, loadings, damaged freight, and so on; by comparing the reports, he could readily spot discrepancies and dishonesty.

McCallum's general principles were successful from management's point of view, but trouble was brewing. The Erie's enginemen had never forgiven McCallum for "infamous Rule 6"; 29 engineers had been dismissed for breaking the rule and for violating various other safety standards. A 6-month strike ensued. McCallum was unable to replace the striking engineers and resigned, along with Erie's president, in 1857. He had earned, however, the highest praise of Henry V. Poor, the eminent editor of the *American Railroad Journal* and spokesperson for the industry. Poor later had some doubts about McCallum's approach but agreed that his general principles contributed to efficient management.

All the same, McCallum's managerial days were not over. While on the Erie, he invented and patented (in 1851) an inflexible arched truss bridge. He established the McCallum Bridge Company in 1857 and built bridges throughout the country. In 1862, McCallum was asked by U.S. Secretary of War Edwin M. Stanton to manage the nation's rail traffic and given the power to seize and operate any rail or telegraph lines necessary to meet the needs of the federal government during the War Between the States. By the end of the war, McCallum was a brevet major general. His main feat was supplying General William T. Sherman's 200-day Atlanta Campaign in northwest Georgia. Using principles developed on the Erie, McCallum "was able to transport supplies for 100,000 men and 60,000 animals for 360 miles from [a] supply base on a single-track railroad with turnouts" during Sherman's "March to the Sea."[46] After the war, McCallum served as a consultant for the Atlantic and Great Western and the Union Pacific railroads. Failing health led to his early retirement to Brooklyn, New York, where he wrote poetry. His best-known poem was "The Water-Mill," which advised:

> Possessions, power, and blooming health, must all be lost at last,
>
> "The mill will never grind with water that is past."[47]

McCallum's approach to managing lived on, despite his setbacks at the Erie. Poor widely publicized McCallum's work, and others applied and extended his general principles. For instance, Albert Fink, vice president and general superintendent of the Louisville, Nashville, and Great Southern Railroad Company, developed a cost-accounting system that used information flows, cost classifications, and statistical methods for corporate control. It became a model for modern corporate control.[48] As early as 1847, the B&O Railroad used an internal auditor to check on receipts and disbursements. External auditing by independent public-accounting firms also began as early as 1854, as stockholders sought to verify reports submitted from professional managers.[49]

Dynamic growth, geographical dispersion of once centralized activities, and separation of ownership and management were the driving forces for systematizing railroad management.

---

[46] Wrege and Sorbo, p. 207. For a further account of McCallum's wartime efforts, see Thomas Weber, *The Northern Railroads in the Civil War* (New York: Columbia University Press, 1952).

[47] Daniel C. McCallum, *The Water-Mill; and Other Poems* (Brooklyn, NY: Privately printed, 1870), p. 10.

[48] Albert Fink, "Cost of Railroad Transportation, Railroad Accounts, and Governmental Regulation of Railroad Tariffs," *Annual Report of the Louisville & Nashville Railroad Company for the Year Ending June 30, 1874* (Louisville, KY: Printed by John. P. Morton, 1875), pp. 21–67.

[49] James L. Boockholdt, "A Historical Perspective on the Auditor's Role: The Early Experiences of the American Railroads," *Accounting Historians Journal* 10(1) (Spring 1983), pp. 69–86.

The most complete adoption of McCallum's general principles took place at the Pennsylvania Railroad, which by 1882 had grown to become the largest corporation in the world with an estimated 110,000 employees.[50] J. Edgar Thomson and Thomas A. Scott applied McCallum's ideas on handling a labor force dispersed over a wide geographical area, formal lines of authority, communications, line and staff duties, measuring performance, and cost accounting. As it were, the Pennsy (as it was known) enjoyed the benefits of McCallum's principles, not the Erie, where they had been originally developed. Working on the Pennsy, Andrew Carnegie, a second young Scottish immigrant, learned McCallum's principles from Thomson and Scott. Carnegie will enter our story shortly. As will be noted in Chapter 6, McCallum's approach to managing would later be labeled "systematic management."

HENRY V. POOR: A BROADER VIEW OF MANAGEMENT

Henry V. Poor, through his position as editor of the *American Railroad Journal*, endeavored to become the rail industry's conscience. Whereas McCallum spoke of rail operations, Poor took a broader perspective in appraising the industry's power and vital role in the nation's daily life. Poor, an 1835 graduate of Bowdoin College, was thoroughly imbued with the uniquely American romance and optimism of the nineteenth century.[51] As editor of the *Journal* in the years prior to the War Between the States, Poor made it the leading business periodical of the day and a reliable source of information for rail investors and managers. His editorials not only discussed equipment, facilities, expansion, and legislation, but also the financial status of different rail lines. After the war, Poor's *Manual of Railroads in the United States* continued his efforts to document the finances of rail lines across the nation.[52] Poor's life (1812–1905) paralleled the growth of railroads from their infancy to maturity; from their role in opening the "West," the resource-laden lands between the Appalachians and the Mississippi River, to ultimately binding the plains, mountains, and valleys of the United States with a web of steel.

In its early years, the dismally managed and financed Erie was one of Poor's favorite editorial topics. The advent of McCallum's management reforms soon made Poor its biggest booster. Poor saw a need for professional managers, rather than speculators and promoters, to build the nation's rail network. Drawing on McCallum's general principles, Poor proposed three fundamental principles for a "science of management": organization, communication, and information.[53] *Organization* was basic to all management: There had to be a clear chain command from top to bottom with a clear designation of duties and responsibilities. *Communication* meant devising a method of reporting throughout an organization to give top managers a continuous and accurate accounting of operations. Finally, *information* was "recorded communication"; Poor saw the need for systematically compiled and analyzed operating reports on costs, revenues, and rail rates so as to understand and improve performance. This third principle was an early appearance of a database concept in which information is collected and analyzed to identify patterns in factors essential to a business's success. McCallum's influence on Poor's thinking is readily apparent, and his third principle can be traced to Albert Fink's cost-accounting system that used information flows, cost classifications, and statistical methods for corporate control.

Just as McCallum's general principles were becoming widely known, in large part due to *American Railroad Journal* editorials, Poor began having doubts about whether organization, communication, and information were adequate principles to encompass the entirety of a

[50] Alfred D. Chandler, Jr., *The Visible Hand: The Managerial Revolution in American Business* (Cambridge, MA: Belknap Press of Harvard University Press, 1977), p. 204.

[51] Alfred D. Chandler, Jr., *Henry Varnum Poor: Business Editor, Analyst, and Reformer* (Cambridge, MA: Harvard University Press, 1956), p. 8. As a side note, Poor was Chandler's great-grandfather. See *idem*, "History and Management Practice and Thought," in Arthur G. Bedeian, ed., *Management Laureates: A Collection of Autobiographical Essays*, vol. 1 (Greenwich, CT: JAI Press, 1992), p. 207.

[52] Poor established *Poor's Publishing* in 1860 to provide financial information about other industries; in 1941, a merger with *Standard Statistics* created the *Standard and Poor's Industry Surveys* of today.

[53] Chandler, *Henry Varnum Poor*, pp. 146–147.

manager's job. Poor visited Great Britain in 1858 to survey its more mature rail network. On his return, he wrote about "the grave difficulties of adapting human capabilities and current business practices and institutions to the severe requirements demanded by the efficient operation of large-scale administrative units."[54] Both in Great Britain and on the Erie, Poor saw worker resistance developing in response to "systematic management." The tighter controls required to bring order from chaos, the delimiting of individual discretion in performing tasks, and the rigid hierarchical specifications of a formal organization were all leading to worker protests. Such protests have been a common feature of other periods in which workplace changes were introduced. Poor, however, thought the protests were extreme and defended the need for systematization: "We do not see how a great road like the Erie can be successfully conducted in any other manner,"[55] that is, except through order, system, and discipline.

Accordingly, Poor began to look for broader principles to overcome the risk of "regarding man as a mere machine, out of which all the qualities necessary to a good servant can be enforced by the mere payment of wages." He recognized, however, that "[d]uties cannot be always prescribed, and the most valuable ones are often voluntary ones."[56] In Poor's view, rigid performance criteria and increased bureaucracy reduced individual initiative and inevitably led the railroads to the waste and red tape found in the military and government. His solution was to call for a style of leadership that would overcome dullness and routine by infusing the railroads with an esprit de corps. Top managers should become "the soul of the enterprise, reaching and infusing life, intelligence and obedience into every portion of it. This soul must not be a fragmentary or disjointed one giving one direction to the head, another to the hands, and another to the feet. Wherever there is lack of unity there will be a lack of energy—of intelligence—of life—of accountability and subordination."[57]

In anticipating Fayol's "unity of direction" principle by 60 years (see Chapter 10), Poor felt the primary challenge faced by top managers was assuming and convincing subordinates to assume an overall perspective. He believed that to be leaders, top managers should not only know all aspects of a railroad's operation and administration, but also be able to handle people and prevent interdepartmental conflicts that could destroy unity of purpose. Poor contended that breakdowns in leadership came from two sources: selection on some basis other than ability or training and lack of an information system to pinpoint weak managers. His plea for hiring professional managers ran counter to Adam Smith's downside premonitions voiced nearly a century earlier regarding those who managed "other people's money" (see Chapter 2).

EMERGING GOVERNANCE ISSUES

Early textile mills were largely owned and managed by founding entrepreneurs or a small number of partners. The money was "all in the family," so to speak. Requirements for accounting and financial reporting were consequently reduced. As recounted in Chapter 2, Adam Smith felt there was a danger in joint-stock, limited-liability companies, where ownership and management were typically separated. Smith was deceased by the time this concern was confronted by British railways, as they acquired capital and debt on a scale unknown in any previous human endeavor.

George Hudson, a friend of the British railway pioneer and innovator George Stephenson, envisioned a rail network covering the whole of England, Scotland, and Wales. In 1844, Hudson began promoting assorted ventures to raise capital for new rail lines and for acquiring existing rights-of-way. Under British law, apart from receiving a Royal Charter, each railway company was authorized by a separate Act of Parliament, leading to varying charter requirements.[58] At the

[54] *Ibid.*, p. 151.
[55] Henry V. Poor, "Lease of the Erie Railroad," *American Railroad Journal* 32 (July 2, 1859), p. 424.
[56] *Idem*, "New York and Erie Railroad" *American Railroad Journal* 32 (January 15, 1859), p. 41.
[57] Henry V. Poor, "English Railways and Their Management," *American Railroad Journal* 31 (September 4, 1858), pp. 561–562.
[58] Sean McCartney and Anthony J. Arnold, "George Hudson's Financial Reporting Practices: Putting the Eastern Counties Railway in Context," *Accounting, Business & Financial History* 10(3) (November 2000), p. 296.

time, there were no general rules for accounting and financial reporting, and corporate law was in its infancy. The railways held a romantic fascination for investors, leading to waves of rampant stock speculation. It was said that by 1845, £70.68 million (British pounds) had been invested in railways, and another 620 proposed rail schemes with a value of £563.20 million had been registered, the total being equivalent to almost 80 percent of the British national debt.[59]

Hudson took advantage of these speculative impulses. By 1849, nearly one-third of Britain's 5,007 miles of rail lines were under his management or control. In addition, he had raised money to buy land, build docks, and form canal companies. Hudson was, as all Britain knew, the "King of Railways."[60] His operations extended from Brighton and Southampton in the southeast to Edinburgh in the northeast. Unfortunately, Hudson's machinations offer one of the earliest examples of top-management malfeasance. He wittingly paid dividends out of capital rather than earnings, inflated railway-traffic counts and revenue, and published false financial statements.[61] The British Parliament had passed a Companies Clauses Consolidation Act in 1845 to bring some uniformity to corporate charters, to require "full and true" accounts, and to mandate that three directors and a firm's chief executive sign and verify its annual balance sheet.[62] This legislation, however, did not stop Hudson's chicanery. He was found to have misappropriated a half-million pounds sterling in railway funds for his own personal use.[63] Although Hudson was never criminally prosecuted, destitute and disgraced, he went into exile abroad. Hudson's creditors were never fully satisfied, and thousands of stockholders were ruined.

How does this brief account of George Hudson fit into the history of United States' economic development and Poor's plea for professional managers who were also leaders? Poor kept abreast of railway developments abroad and addressed governance issues in his editorials. For example, he complained that railroads did not separate operating costs from construction expenses, thus hiding such costs from investors. It was common practice to book operating costs as a construction expense, hence leading to higher reported profits and extra dividends.

What was the path to reform? According to Poor, who believed "the germ of all improvement is *knowledge*,"[64]

> the only way to introduce honesty into the management of railroads, is to expose every thing in or about it, to the public gaze. Concealment in either case is certain to breed disease. Instances are very rare in which integrity is preserved unless strict accountability is exacted. Such accountability to the public should be exacted from directors of railroads. . . . For the dishonesty and incapacity in the management of railroads the holders of their securities have in a great measure to thank themselves. They put them in charge of a body of men, responsible to no authority, who soon come to practice concealment, either to escape the consequences of mistake or dishonesty. The perpetuation of their power is an easy matter, so long as they can sustain themselves by the various modes resorted to for *borrowing*.[65]

Poor lashed out against railroad promoters and speculators and endorsed a *laissez-faire* economic philosophy by calling for unrestricted competition. He argued that governments should not

---

[59] "Editorial," *London Times* (November 17, 1845), p. 4; "Projected Railways," *Leeds Mercury* (November 22, 1845), p. 4. For the British national debt (viz., £794,193,645) on January 5, 1845, see "United Kingdom of Great Britain and Ireland," in Henry Vethake, ed., *Encyclopædia Americana*, vol. 14 [Supplement] (Philadelphia, PA: Lea & Blanchard, 1851), p. 593.

[60] [James Richardson], "Biographical Sketch of George Hudson, Esq., M.P., the Railway Napoleon," *The English Gentleman* [London] (September 6, 1845), p. 313. See also *idem*, *The Mysteries of Hudson's Railway Frauds Exposed* (London: C. Mitchell, 1850), p. xvi.

[61] Sean McCartney and Anthony J. Arnold, "'A Vast Aggregate of Avaricious and Flagitious Jobbing'? George Hudson and the Evolution of Early Notions of Directorial Responsibility," *Accounting, Business & Financial History* 11(2) (July 2001), pp. 117–143.

[62] House of Commons, "Companies Clauses Consolidation Act 1845," *Parliamentary Papers* 2 (1845), pp. 173–260.

[63] Edward Cleveland-Stevens, *English Railways: Their Development and Their Relation to the State* (London: George Routledge and Sons, 1915), p. 39.

[64] Henry V. Poor, "Railroad Dishonesty and Remedy," *American Railroad Journal* 29 (April 26, 1856), p. 364.

[65] *Idem*, "How to Improve the Management of Railroads," *American Railroad Journal* 30 (June 20, 1857), p. 392.

regulate rates and the only legislation necessary was the sort that protected "honest rational men" from dishonest promoters. Channeling Adam Smith, Poor insisted that the rapid development of the U.S. railroads was "proof that reliance on the self-interest of individuals operating under conditions of unrestricted competition resulted in the greatest good for the greatest number."[66] Recognizing that the growth in railroads demanded increased financial rigor, he maintained that by giving stockholders and the public full information, by employing professional managers, and by protecting rational from irrational investors, the railroads could fulfill their proper role in the nation's economy.

Henry V. Poor addressed issues that managers still face today and will continue to confront in the future. His belief that the role of government is to protect, not control, illustrates a recurring theme of management rights vis-à-vis government responsibilities. Poor's resolve to bring order from chaos without diminishing individual incentive and dignity still remains a recurring challenge.

SUMMARY

In 1790, New York City was the largest metropolis in the United States, with a population of 33,131; next came Philadelphia, with 28,522 residents; and then Boston, with 8,300. Even the largest city was smaller than the student body at some of today's state universities. In 1790, some 90 percent of the nation's estimated total population of 3,231,533 was engaged in agriculture. From its declaration of independence on July 4, 1776, to 1860, the United States made unmatched progress. Textile mills provided inexpensive clothing to a growing national market; railroads spread further westward from their beginning along the East Coast until they reached the Pacific Ocean, opening new lands and opportunities; telegraph lines delivered messages across vast distances; and mechanical devices such as the sewing machine and the reaper led others to envy the American System of Manufacturing.

The nineteenth century was a defining era in the development of today's modern corporation. In 1809, the U.S. Supreme Court ruled, in *Bank of the United States v. Deveaux*, that corporations have the right to sue in federal courts.[67] A decade later, in *Trustees of Dartmouth College v. Woodward*, a case in which the State of New Hampshire legislature attempted to convert the private college into a public university by amending its corporate charter (originally granted by the British Crown in 1769), the high court concluded that the charter constituted a contract (which had not been nullified by the American Revolution) and that corporations have the same rights as natural persons to enter and enforce contractual obligations.[68] Building from this base, the 1886 Supreme Court case *Santa Clara County v. Southern Railroad Company* established that the Equal Protection Clause of the United States *Constitution's* Fourteenth Amendment guarantees corporations the same legal protections under the law as individuals.[69] In the decades after the War Between the States, "[m]any of the country's major corporations were formed: U.S. Steel, Standard Oil, General Electric. Exports boomed. Food production soared. Railroads 'spidered across the American landscape,' . . . opening the West to settlement, connecting the nation into a single market, and making it possible to haul crops and consumer goods almost anywhere in the United States."[70] This growth created the need for professional managers. Corporations grew to meet mounting consumer demand and life was better as the United States continued its push westward.

---

[66] Chandler, *Henry Varnum Poor*, p. 260.

[67] *Bank of the United States v. Deveaux*, 9 U.S. 5 Cranch 61 (1809).

[68] *Trustees of Dartmouth College v.* Woodward, 17 U.S., 518 (1819).

[69] *Santa Clara County v. Southern Pacific Railroad*, 118 U.S. 394 (1886).

[70] Fergus M. Bordewich, [Review of the book *The Republic for Which It Stands*], *Wall Street Journal* (August 26–27, 2017), p. C5.

Industrial Growth and Systematic Management

CHAPTER 6

When the Industrial Revolution reached the United States in the early nineteenth century, its impact was soon felt in textile manufacturing, mass-produced consumer goods and farm implements, and along the nation's canals and railroads. The War Between the States from 1861 to 1865 was a tragic pause in the United States' march toward global industrial leadership. Eleven Southern states, in response to the nation's sectional divide over states' rights and slavery, formed a Confederacy and seceded from the Union that composed the United States. Accordingly, this chapter describes the continued growth of U.S. industry following the conclusion of the war when the nation was reunited, discusses the accompanying emergence of systematic management, and examines the nation's economic, social, political, and technological environment on the eve of the scientific-management era.

THE GROWTH OF "BIG BUSINESS"

No student of business history had a keener eye for the growth of big business than Alfred D. Chandler, Jr.[1] In his early work, Chandler delineated four phases in the rise of what would become known in the United States as "Big Business": (1) "initial expansion and accumulation of resources"; (2) "rationalization or full use of resources"; (3) "expansion into new markets and lines to help assure the continuing full use of resources"; and (4) "development of a new structure" to enable continued growth. For individual companies, these phases started and ended at different times, depending on technological advances and their ability to react to and capitalize on market opportunities. In the latter part of the nineteenth century, companies that would fit into Chandler's initial expansion and resource-accumulation phase, such as Standard Oil of New Jersey and the American Sugar Refining Company, were forming.

Chandler further noted two periods of industrial growth: one of horizontal growth from 1879 to 1893, and one of vertical growth from 1898 to 1904. *Horizontal growth* occurred through mergers (i.e., two separate companies combining to become one), pools (i.e., companies agreeing to fix prices, production quotas, and allocate markets), or trusts (i.e., combinations of corporations

[1] The subsequent discussion draws on Alfred D. Chandler, Jr., *Strategy and Structure: Chapters in the History of the Industrial Enterprise* (Cambridge, MA: MIT Press, 1962); *idem*, *The Visible Hand: The Managerial Revolution in American Business* (Cambridge, MA: Belknap Press of Harvard University Press, 1977); *idem* and Takashi Hikino, *Scale and Scope: The Dynamics of Industrial Capitalism* (Cambridge, MA: Belknap Press of Harvard University Press, 1990).

whose individual stockholders place their stocks in the hands of trustees who manage the business of all). During the years 1879 to 1893, companies in the oil, beef, sugar, tobacco, rubber, and liquor industries, amongst others, merged, formed pools, and created trusts to reduce competition and achieve economies of scale in production. *Vertical growth* took place when companies entered one or more additional stages in a production-marketing chain. Accordingly, *backward vertical-integration* arose when a company acquired raw material sources or suppliers; *forward vertical-integration* happened when a company established marketing outlets for its own products. For example, a petroleum refiner might integrate backward to explore for oil, drill wells, and build pipelines to its refinery. Conversely, it might integrate forward by acquiring wholesale agents and, perhaps, its own retail gas stations.

In addition, Chandler found a close connection between advances in transportation and communication, like the railroad and the electric telegraph, and the initial expansion and accumulation of resources necessary for a business's growth. When modes of transport were crude and slow, product markets were largely local, so there was little or no need to increase production volume. Thus, the putting-out system of production was entirely appropriate to its time, as it served small markets requiring limited capital investment. With the advent of steam engines in the Industrial Revolution, and their use to power locomotives and steamboats, markets were extended and mechanized, as large-scale production was needed to meet unrivaled demand. Advances in communication encouraged producers, suppliers, and distributors to pursue regional and international markets. Improved transportation and communication also made it possible to produce and market in volume; thus, identical items could be produced in large batches or in a continuous process, and companies could seek mass-market distribution. With these increases in output and distribution came a need for greater capital intensity, and as capital investments in facilities and equipment rose, per-unit production costs were minimized until output could be maintained at the lowest cost possible. In Chandler's terms, capital-intensive industries had to operate at a "minimum efficient scale" (i.e., at a level that resulted in the lowest per-unit costs) to attain a competitive advantage. With a cost advantage, prices could be lowered and markets extended, and the whole cycle of mechanization, greater output, lowered prices, increased distribution volume, and so on would be repeated.

There are limits, of course, to the cost advantages of large-scale production and mass marketing. A company can only profitably gain market share if it can lower its production costs. In Chandler's explanation, the key to profit is not in capacity (the potential to produce or sell in volume), but in how well a company is managed. There must be a smooth flow of inputs (employees, materials, supplies, and so on) through a production process (throughput) such that the value of the resulting output is greater than the cost of additional inputs and production. This residual balance is the necessary profit for replenishing inputs and beginning the input–throughput–output flow once again. Chandler's analysis showed that a company's success (i.e., ability to earn a sufficient profit) over the long term largely depended on how well its inputs–throughputs–outputs were managed. As we view the latter half of the nineteenth century in the United States, we can see how advanced production processes for making steel, refining sugar and corn products, milling grains, canning, packaging, and other advancements led to larger enterprises, but as Chandler's analysis showed, sound management differentiated those that were successful from those that were not. The growth of the Carnegie Steel Company (founded in the mid-1870s) under the direction of Andrew Carnegie offers a prototype example of the four phases Chandler identified in the rise of Big Business in the United States.

CARNEGIE AND THE RISE OF BIG BUSINESS

The name Andrew Carnegie conjures a portrait of a manager who built an empire in steel and left a fortune in the millions. Carnegie, the son of a Scottish handloom-weaver displaced by the advent of the factory system, came to the United States with his family in 1848 as a penniless 12-year-old. His first job, at age 13, was a bobbin boy in a cotton factory, from which he earned $1.20 a week.

He next worked as a telegram messenger and then, hoping to advance his career, as a telegraph operator. In 1853, Thomas A. Scott, superintendent of the Pennsylvania Railroad's Western Division, hired young Carnegie as his personal telegrapher to assist in dispatching trains over the Division's mountainous main line. Carnegie learned fast and made his mark when he untangled a traffic tie-up following a derailment. Scott was absent at the time, and Carnegie sent out orders using Scott's initials. He was rewarded for his initiative, which led to a change in a protocol that had only permitted Scott, as superintendent, the authority to issue dispatch orders. Carnegie learned railroad operations and control from Scott and J. Edgar Thomson, who, as mentioned in Chapter 5, had applied Daniel C. McCallum's general management principles to the Pennsylvania Railroad. At age 24, Carnegie became superintendent of the Western Division, which at the time was the largest sector of the nation's largest railroad. Under his supervision, rail traffic quadrupled, track mileage doubled, and the Division had the lowest ton-per-mile costs of any railroad in the nation. Carnegie was asked to be the Pennsy's General Superintendent in 1865, but he declined because he wanted to strike out on his own.

Andrew Carnegie, *Autobiography of Andrew Carnegie*, ed. by John C. Van Dyke (London: Constable & Co., Ltd., 1920), following p. 214.

Andrew Carnegie, circa 1878

To understand Carnegie and his impact on management thinking, it is necessary to examine the development of the steel industry. Steel is the sinew of any industrial economy. Iron, because of its impurities, caused many problems for early machine designers and factory owners. The race to remove the impurities followed different paths in Great Britain and the United States. In 1847, Kentuckian William Kelly perfected a process for removing impurities from molten metal with a blast of cold air. Kelly, however, did not apply for a patent until 1857, a year after Henry Bessemer had obtained a patent for the same basic process in Britain. At the time, the steel industry in the United States was integrated neither vertically nor horizontally. Some mills owned furnaces that smelted iron ore into pig iron (which is a raw material for making steel); others operated rolling mills and forges that converted pig iron into decarbonized bars or slabs; and still others infused these bars or slabs with extra carbon and rolled them into steel for rails, nails, or wire, amongst other things. Between these independent operations, marketing intermediaries linked producers, each taking a profit for the services they provided. After Carnegie saw the Bessemer process in operation, he realized it could be used for mass-producing steel. He decided to forego railroading to concentrate on steel because, as he explained, "Every dollar of capital or credit, every business thought, should be concentrated upon the one business upon which a man has embarked. He should never scatter his shot. . . . The rule, 'Do not put all your eggs in one basket,' does not apply to a man's life work. Put all your eggs in one basket and then watch that basket, is the true doctrine—the most valuable rule of all."[2]

Using the Bessemer process, Carnegie began to vertically integrate the stages required to produce steel and thereby eliminated the intermediaries' profits. He succeeded in reducing the amount of time it took to produce a ton of steel and, thus, could lower prices and gain market share. He used cost accounting to assist in setting prices to undersell his competitors, many of whom did not know their true expenses. Carnegie integrated backward into iron and coal mines and other steel-related operations to ensure an uninterrupted flow of raw materials to run his furnaces at full capacity and to move from iron ore to finished steel more quickly. By combining the new Bessemer process with McCallum's general principles for assuring efficient management (see Chapter 5), Carnegie had developed a recipe for success that was soon emulated by companies in other industries.[3]

[2] Andrew Carnegie, *The Empire of Business* (Garden City, NJ: Doubleday, Page, 1902), p. 121.

[3] Parallels between McCallum and Carnegie are discussed in Harold C. Livesay, *Andrew Carnegie and the Rise of Big Business* (Boston, MA: Little, Brown, 1975), pp. 38, 95.

On the Pennsylvania Railroad, Carnegie had learned how to measure performance, control costs, and delegate authority. These lessons fueled the success of the Carnegie Steel Company. Until the invention of the open-hearth furnace in 1908, the Bessemer process was the basis for the world's steel industry. In the mid-1870s, iron rails cost $100 per ton; by 1900, 1 ton of steel rails cost $12. Perhaps this was Carnegie's greatest philanthropy; or, as Jonathan Swift expressed it through Lemuel Gulliver's travels: "[W]hoever could make two ears of corn, or two blades of grass to grow upon a spot of ground where only one grew before would deserve better of mankind, and do more essential service to his country than the whole race of politicians put together."[4] To unscramble the metaphor, Carnegie combined technology and efficient management to create more jobs, reduce prices, and expand product markets. In 1868, the United States produced 8,500 tons of steel compared with 110,000 in Britain; in 1879, the countries' outputs were nearly equal; but by 1902, the United States produced 9,138,000 tons and Britain 1,826,000. U.S. industry was showing its mettle. "In 1860 there was not a single industrial corporation listed on the New York Stock Exchange. By 1900 there were dozens, some employing tens of thousands of workers, earning huge profits for stockholders and wielding immense political and economic power."[5]

THE EMERGENCE OF SYSTEMATIC MANAGEMENT

The steel industry illustrates the scale and pace of industrial growth following the War Between the States. Steel was not the only industry, however, to thrust the American System of Manufacturing into world prominence. As further technological advances were made in transportation, communication, machine making, and power sources, old industries were revitalized and new ones emerged. As noted, Chandler saw initial expansion and accumulation of resources as part of the first phase in the development of Big Business in the United States.

As noted in Chapter 5, Daniel C. McCallum introduced what would later be labeled "systematic management" to the Pennsylvania Railroad. His goal was to bring "method" or "system" into railroad operations to promote coordination, eliminate confusion and waste, and re-establish managerial control.[6] Andrew Carnegie learned McCallum's lessons well and created a steel colossus. As other businesses and industries began to grow, they too faced the challenge of managing a large-scale enterprise. They needed to plan ahead to acquire necessary labor, materials, equipment, and capital; to organize by dividing labor, delegating authority, and grouping activities into departments; to lead and motivate by providing wage incentives and building strong interpersonal relationships; and to control by comparing actual to realized plans and taking corrective actions when necessary. With growth also came the need to formalize communications, especially in written memos and reports. JoAnne Yates has shown how, between 1850 and 1920, business communication changed as oral and informal modes of communication gave way to written documents.[7] During this era, however, there was no real appreciation of the skills required to be a successful manager. A great deal of emphasis was placed on technical or financial knowledge, but very little on how to plan, organize, staff, motivate, and control. Faced with ever-larger businesses, how could one learn to manage better?

ENGINEERS AND ECONOMISTS

Engineers played a large role in building canals and railroads and in designing and installing industrial machinery; thus, they frequently became factory managers. Examples we have

[4] Jonathan Swift, *Travels into Several Remote Nations of the World*, vol. 1 (London: Benjamin Motte, 1726), p. 129.
[5] John Steel Gordon, "Regulators Take on Silicon Valley, as They Did Earlier Innovators," *Wall Street Journal* (April 18, 2018), p. A15.
[6] Joseph A. Litterer, "Systematic Management: The Search for Order and Integration," *Business History Review* 35(4) (Winter 1961), pp. 473–474.
[7] JoAnne Yates, *Control through Communication: The Rise of System in American Management* (Baltimore, MD: Johns Hopkins University Press, 1989).

discussed include Samuel Slater and Daniel McCallum. The professionalization of engineering began with the formation of the American Society of Civil Engineers in 1852, followed by the American Institute of Mining Engineers in 1871. Neither of these groups, however, was interested in the challenges confronting the era's factory managers. The first forum for those interested in factory management appears to have been the *American Machinist,* an "illustrated journal of practical mechanics and engineering" that began in 1877. In 1878, James W. See, writing under the pen name Chordal, began submitting a series of letters to the *American Machinist's* editor.[8] See had extensive experience working in and supervising machine shops. He established a successful practice as a consulting engineer and used his *American Machinist* letters to describe machine-shop practices and management. See advocated a work system based on two principles: "a place for everything and everything in its place" and "specific lines of duty for every man."[9] He noted that good workers rarely made good supervisors and that good supervisors should not "bully" their workers but should be tactful and understanding. *Soldiering*, or making only a pretense at working, could be handled best if a supervisor had an "understanding with [the worker] that he is to work for you five days a week for pay, and soldier one day at his own expense. . . . One week day idle in a busy man's life will make him feel glad to get into the shop for five days of occupation."[10] See likewise advocated for paying above-market wages to attract the most qualified workers, standardizing tools, and implementing other techniques for improved factory management. See's writings remained relatively obscure for a century, known only to the *American Machinist's* readership. His experiences and advice, however, may have influenced later writers, even though he was not explicitly cited.

The *American Machinist* also had a hand in another signal event of the period, the formation of the American Society of Mechanical Engineers (ASME) in 1880. The ASME first met at the Stevens Institute of Technology in Hoboken, New Jersey. Its purpose was to address issues of factory management neglected by the other engineering associations. In what is considered a landmark meeting, the ASME convened at Chicago on May 25–28, 1886. On May 26, Henry R. Towne, cofounder of the Yale Lock Company and president of the Yale & Towne Manufacturing Company, presented a paper titled "The Engineer as an Economist." Towne noted that many in his audience were engaged in the "executive duties of organizing and superintending the operations of industrial establishments" and went on to observe that

> There are many good mechanical engineers; there are also many good "businessmen";—but the two are rarely combined in one person. But this combination of qualities . . . is essential to the management of industrial works, and has its highest effectiveness if united in one person . . . the matter of shop management is of equal importance with that of engineering . . . and the *management of works* has become a matter of such great and far-reaching importance as perhaps to justify its classification also as one of the modern arts.[11]

Because no group seemed to be concerned with "the management of works," Towne proposed that the ASME create an Economic Section to act as a clearinghouse and forum for shop management and shop accounting. Shop management would deal with the subjects of organization, responsibility, reports, and all that pertained to the "executive management of works, mills, and factories." Shop accounting would address the questions of time and wage systems, determination and allocation of costs, methods of bookkeeping, and all that pertained to manufacturing accounts.

---

[8] William F. Muhs, Charles Wrege, and Arthur Murtuza, "Extracts from Chordal's Letters: Pre-Taylor Shop Management," in Kae H. Chung, ed., *Proceedings of the Annual Meeting of the Academy of Management* (1981), pp. 96–100.

[9] James W. See, "Extracts from Chordal's Letters," *American Machinist* 2(15) (August 16, 1879), p. 6.

[10] *Idem*, "Extracts from Chordal's Letters," *American Machinist* 3(13) (March 27, 1880), p. 4.

[11] Henry R. Towne, "The Engineer as an Economist," *Transactions of the American Society of Mechanical Engineers* 7 (1886), pp. 428–429. See also Ion Georgiou, "Engineers as Economists: A Study in Gilded Age Sensibilities," *Management & Organizational History* 9(1) (January 2014), pp. 69–91.

Immediately following Towne's presentation, in the same afternoon session, a second significant paper was delivered. It was by Captain Henry Metcalfe, an intellectual heir of the Springfield Armory's Roswell Lee (see Chapter 5). In 1881, at the Frankford Arsenal (near Philadelphia) and the Watervliet Arsenal (Troy, New York), Metcalfe had installed a system for tracking the progress and costs associated with individual work orders as they flowed through the workshop. The system used cards to record the labor and materials each step required to complete an order. Using the cards, direct costs (such as labor and materials) and indirect costs (administrative overhead) could then be determined.[12] In the discussion that followed Metcalfe's presentation, Frederick W. Taylor, an ASME member since 1886, commented that Midvale Steel had been using a similar system for the past 10 years, except that it used a central office and clerks, rather than supervisors, to handle all the associated paperwork. We shall learn more about Taylor in Chapter 7.

Almost all the discussion following the session in which Towne and Metcalfe presented their papers primarily dealt with establishing the true cost of work orders as they are completed. Towne's proposal to create an Economic Section within the ASME received scant notice. Despite evidence that the duties of managers coming from technical schools, such as the Stevens Institute of Technology, were managerial rather than technical,[13] only four other papers on management subjects were presented at ASME meetings from 1887 to 1895.[14] This minimal attention may have been due to a lack of clarity about the skills required to be a successful manager. A manager at the time was part engineer, part business operator, and part accountant. The emphasis was on shop management dealing with the utilization of machinery, and not on general management. Shop management, in particular, focused on machine tools (e.g., lathe machines, drill machines, milling machines) and cutting tools (e.g., threading tools, knurling tools, boring tools), where the trend had been to move from small-batch production to large-scale output based on the American System of Manufacturing. The principal challenges shop managers faced were technical. They were seldom called on to display managerial skills.

One early writer noted that large-scale manufacturing required the "utmost system . . . necessary in every detail [for] the economy and uniformity of production."[15] Thus, "system" in this context referred to developing rules, standards, and procedures to handle increased output. It included topics such as die-setting standards, machine tolerances, job scheduling, quality and quantity of work, coordination of workflow through routing, wage incentives, accounting for costs, assigning responsibility, and handling labor problems such as soldiering.[16]

In contrast to the concerns of the ASME membership, among economists there was a resurging appreciation of the importance of entrepreneurs and professional managers as a factor of production, picking up on Jean-Baptiste Say's earlier work (see Chapter 3). Inventor Edward W. Atkinson, noted that a "difference in management will alter results, in the same place, at the

---

[12] Henry Metcalfe, "The Shop-Order System of Accounts," *Transactions of the American Society of Mechanical Engineers* 7 (1886), pp. 440–468. This paper was a summary of Metcalfe's pioneering cost-accounting book, *The Cost of Manufactures and the Administration of Workshops, Public and Private* (New York: John Wiley and Sons, 1885). See also William H. Reid, "The Development of Henry Metcalfe's Card System of Shop Returns at Frankford Arsenal," *Journal of Management* 12(3) (Fall 1986), pp. 415–423.

[13] The Stevens Institute of Technology had 600 graduates between 1872 and 1896; of these, 230 (38 percent) were in executive positions by 1900. William D. Ennis, "The Engineering Management of Industrial Works," *Engineering Magazine* 22(2) (November 1901), pp. 241–246.

[14] Hirose has noted, however, that whereas some mechanical engineers favored scientific management, it was only in 1920 that the majority of ASME members agree to a separate division of management. See Mikiyoshi Hirose, "The Attitude of the American Society of Mechanical Engineers toward Management: Suggestions for a Revised Interpretation," *Review of Economics and Business* (Kansai University) 25 (September 1996), pp. 125–148. See also *idem*, *The Management Thought of the Engineers: The Emergence of Industrial Management in America, 1880–1920* (Tokyo: Bunshindō, 2005).

[15] Oberlin Smith, "System in Machine Shops," *American Machinist* 8 (October 31, 1885), p. 1.

[16] Joseph A. Litterer, "The Emergence of Systematic Management as Shown by the Literature of Management from 1870 to 1900" (Doctoral dissertation, University of Illinois, Urbana, IL, 1959); released in book form by Garland Press, New York, 1986. See also *idem*, "Systematic Management: The Search for Order and Integration," *Business History Review* 35(4) (Winter 1961), pp. 461–476.

same time, in the use of similar machinery."[17] British economists Alfred and Mary Paley Marshall recognized that, to be successful, the manager of a large business "almost always requires rarer natural abilities and a more expensive training," as he "must look far ahead, and wide around him; and he must be continually on the look out for improved methods of carrying on his business, . . . and [devote] all his energies to planning, and organizing, to forecasting the future and preparing for it."[18]

In acknowledging that managers must devote energy to forecasting, planning, and organizing, the Marshalls hinted at the "functions of management" long before Henri Fayol in France (see Chapter 10). The Marshalls also commented on the division of labor, but advised that it need not lead to monotonous jobs "when the work is light, and the hours of work not excessive."[19] Further, they discussed economies of scale, as well as the internal economies that could be attained by improved management.

These musings were a prelude to Alfred Marshall's fame as the founder of the Cambridge (England) or Neoclassical School of Economic Thought. Like Say, Marshall considered "organization" to be an "agent" of production and recognized the differential advantage that a high-energy manager with exceptional ability could provide. As he explained:

> A manufacturer of exceptional ability and energy will apply better methods, and perhaps better machinery than his rivals: he will organize better the manufacturing and the marketing sides of his business; and he will bring them into better relation to one another. By these means he will extend his business; and therefore he will be able to take greater advantage from the specialization both of labour and of plant. Thus he will obtain increasing return and also increasing profit.[20]

Economists, such as the Marshalls, had less impact than mechanical engineers in the early development of management thought. To mechanical engineers such as Towne, Metcalfe, and Taylor, a manager's primary challenges related to shop management, not managing an overall business. A much broader issue concerned the relationship between labor and capital, which was termed "the labor question."

THE LABOR QUESTION

In Chapter 4, we reviewed criticisms of the factory system of production in Great Britain and the Victorian sense of conscience with respect to subjecting women and children to long hours and harsh working conditions. Similarly, U.S. reformers attacked the American System of Manufacturing. One of the most outspoken critics was Washington Gladden, a Columbus (Ohio) Congregationalist minister, local politician, and social reformer who listed the major problems of the day as labor unrest, intemperance, poverty, slums, and child and female labor.[21] Gladden believed that solutions to labor unrest resided largely in organizing workers into strong workplace unions to resist employer demands, sharing company profits with labor, and using arbitration to settle labor–management disputes. Temperance was essential: the greatest evil was alcohol, because it contributed to an ever-widening circle of ills, including slums, family disintegration, and poverty. As economist Richard T. Ely, one of the early proponents of the Social Gospel movement (see Chapters 9 and 12), put it: "[D]rink [is] the poor man's curse so often, and so often the rich man's shame."[22] Social Gospel advocates held that, above all, society must be Christianized and the Golden Rule applied by both labor and management. They felt a duty to reform social and

---

[17] Edward W. Atkinson, *The Distribution of Products; Or, The Mechanism and the Metaphysics of Exchange* (New York: G. P. Putnam's Sons, 1885), p. 62.
[18] Alfred Marshall and Mary Paley Marshall, *The Economics of Industry* (London: Macmillan, 1879), p. 139.
[19] *Ibid.*, p. 56.
[20] Alfred Marshall, *Principles of Economics: An Introductory Volume*, 6th ed. (London: Macmillan, 1910), p. 614.
[21] Washington Gladden, *Working People and Their Employers* (Boston, MA: Lockwood, Brooks, and Company, 1876). See also Jacob H. Dorn, *Washington Gladden: Prophet of the Social Gospel* (Columbus, OH: Ohio State University Press, 1966).
[22] Richard T. Ely, *The Labor Movement in America* (New York: Thomas Y. Crowell, 1886), p. ix.

economic conditions, both inside and outside of the workplace. Rather than wait for a gradual improvement in the quality of life found in poorer neighborhoods, they argued for immediate action in remaking personnel administration (or, as we know it today, "human-resource management") and industrial-relations policies. They advocated for profit sharing, the right to organize unions, impartial workplace arbitration, and the freedom to establish worker cooperatives, as well as for legislation governing the hiring and firing practices, the employment of women and children, and workplace sanitation.[23] The Social Gospel origins of the American Economic Association are evident: when it was started in 1885 by Gladden, Ely and others, 23 of its 181 founding members were Protestant clergymen.[24]

Whereas Social Gospel reformers defined the labor question broadly, engineers and economists saw workplace issues in a more limited manner. Methods and systems would improve factory efficiency, but there had to be an incentive to ensure worker cooperation and performance. As noted above, some managers, such as See, argued that low employee productivity was due to employees working in spurts and taking it easy when their supervisor was not present. The one thing that engineers and economists felt they could do to address this situation was to only pay for work performed.

Another English economist, David Schloss, reported that workers disliked piecework-pay systems that compensated a set amount for each unit of work completed because "the difficulty of satisfactorily fixing a piece-wage is very great" and often depended upon an employer's idea of how quickly work should be done.[25] Employers were also known to "nibble their piece-wages down," or to gradually increase the amount of work expected for the same pay. In addition, Schloss reported on the mistaken belief that "the amount of remunerative work to be done in the world is a fixed quantity"[26] and, by working more slowly, the available work could be spread more evenly over a workforce so that all would be employed. He attributed this belief, known as the "lump of labor fallacy," to how expected output was determined.[27] In all too many cases, an individual employee's output reflected a trade-off between what an employer could cajole out of them and pressure from other employees to produce less. If employees did too little, they incurred their employers' wrath and risked being dismissed. If an employee did too much, coworker pressure to hold back production would increase. Thus, a day's work was a compromise between contending forces.

Although there were doubts about the wisdom of paying for work performed rather than time worked, there appeared to be a connection between higher pay, lower per-unit costs, and greater productivity. Atkinson observed that "the cheapest labor is the best-paid labor; it is the best-paid labor applied to machinery that assures the largest product in ratio to the capital invested."[28] He reasoned that if an employer paid low wages, output would also be low; but if workers were paid well and provided with the proper tools, output would be high. Another economist, Jacob Schoenhof, compared wages across various countries and found those that paid the highest wages had the lowest labor costs. Thus, nail makers in Pittsburgh were paid 10 times as much as those in Britain, yet the nails they produced were priced at one-half as much.[29] This paradox of high wages and low costs resurfaces in the scientific-management movement as discussed in Chapters 11 and 12.

---

[23] For the views of Social Gospel proponents, see the chapters in William E. Barns, ed., *The Labor Problem: Plain Questions and Practical Answers* (New York: Harper & Brothers, 1886); for an alternative view of the labor question, see Simon Newcomb, *A Plain Man's Talk on the Labor Question* (New York: Harper & Brothers, 1886).

[24] Alfred W. Coats, "The First Decades of the American Economic Association," *American Economic Review* 50(4) (September 1960), p. 562n12.

[25] David F. Schloss, "Why Working-Men Dislike Piece Work," *Economic Review* 1(3) (1891), p. 313.

[26] David A. Wells, *Recent Economic Changes and Their Effect on the Production and Distribution of Wealth and the Well-Being of Society* (New York: D. Appleton, 1891), p. 394.

[27] *Idem*, *Methods of Industrial Remuneration* (London: Williams and Norgate, 1892), p. 38.

[28] Atkinson, *Distribution of Products*, p. 63.

[29] Jacob Schoenhof, *The Economy of High Wages: An Inquiry into the Cause of High Wages and Their Effect on Methods and Cost of Production* (New York: G. P. Putman's Sons, 1892), p. 226.

If high wages led to increased productivity, lowered costs per unit, and the possibility of higher profits, then the obvious solution would be found in linking a business's profits and employee performance. The French economist Anne Robert Jacques Turgot recognized the benefits of a business sharing its profits based on employee performance as early as 1775.[30] Whereas profit sharing had long been commonplace in fishing villages (e.g., "working shares" on whaling vessels) and farming communities (e.g., "sharecropping on halves"), the first industrial application of profit sharing in the United States occurred in 1794 at the New Geneva (Pennsylvania) glassworks of Swiss immigrant Albert Gallatin.[31] Proponents believed that profit sharing would encourage employees to produce more at less cost because they would share in the benefits. The more general purpose behind profit sharing was the expectation that "the loyalty and co-operation of the employees would be increased, that labor turnover would be reduced, and industrial disputes would be avoided."[32] By 1887, over 30 U.S. businesses had adopted some form of profit sharing, including John Wanamaker Dry Goods, Pillsbury Flour, Procter & Gamble, and Yale & Towne Lock Company.[33] Yale & Towne, however, dropped profit sharing when its president, Henry R. Towne, realized that "the interest of each participator in the profit fund is largely affected by the actions of others whom he cannot control or influence, and that what he may earn or save for the common good may be lost by the mismanagement or extravagance of others."[34] Consequently, Towne argued for determining the present cost of a product and sharing any reduction in cost according to each individual worker's increased efficiency or increased economy in the use of materials (or both). Each worker would be guaranteed an annual wage, but, in addition, would receive a pro-rated portion of the resulting cost savings based on his yearly earnings. As Towne explained:

> Supposing, then, that at the end of the year it was found that the cost per unit of product had been reduced from $1 to 95 cents, that the total gain thus resulting was $800; and that the aggregate wages paid during the year had been $10,000. One-half of the gain would be $400, which would equal 4 per cent on earnings during the year. This is equivalent to two weeks' extra wages, no mean addition to any income, and accounting, even in the case of a laborer earning $1.50 per day, to cash a dividend of $18 at the end of the year.[35]

Mechanical engineer Frederick A. Halsey criticized profit sharing and pay-for-work systems.[36] He felt that any profit-sharing system that based its distributions on collective rather than individual efforts was unfair and expressed concern about rate-setting abuses in piece-rate incentive plans. Under the Halsey "premium plan," each day workers were expected to produce a specified minimum output and would receive a premium for any excess, with the "amount of this premium being based on the excess, and being *less per unit of product than the old wages cost*." Halsey offered the following example:

> Taking round numbers for convenience, suppose a workman to be paid three dollars per day of ten hours and to produce one piece of a certain kind per day. The wages cost of the produce per piece is obviously three dollars. Now, under the premium plan the proprietor says to the workman: "If you will reduce the time on that piece I will pay you a premium of ten cents for each hour by which you reduce

---

[30] Anne Robert Jacques Turgot, *Réflexions sur la formation et la distribution des richesses* [*Reflections on the Formation and the Distribution of Riches*] (New York: n.p., 1788), pp. 135–136. (Written in 1766.)

[31] Rudolf A. Clemen, "The Trend in Profit-Sharing," *Factory: The Magazine of Management* 24 (March 15, 1920), p. 810. Gallatin served as Secretary of the U.S. Department of Treasury from 1801–1814. For a history of profit sharing in Britain, see Timothy J. Hatton, "Profit Sharing in British Industry: 1865–1913," *International Journal of Industrial Organization* 6(1) (March 1988), pp. 69–90.

[32] Don D. Lescohier, "Working Conditions," in Lescohier and Elizabeth Brandeis, *History of Labor in the United States, 1896–1932*, vol. 3 (New York: Macmillan, 1935), p. 376.

[33] Mary W. Calkins, *Sharing the Profits* (Boston, MA: Ginn, 1888); Nicholas P. Gilman, *Profit Sharing between Employer and Employee* (Boston, MA: Houghton Mifflin, 1889).

[34] Henry R. Towne, "Gain Sharing," *Transactions of the American Society of Mechanical Engineers* 10 (1889), p. 600.

[35] *Ibid.*, pp. 504–605.

[36] Frederick A. Halsey, "Premium Plan of Paying for Labor," *Transactions of the American Society of Mechanical Engineers* 12 (1891), pp. 755–764.

> the time." If a reduction of one hour is made the first result to the employer is to save the wages of thirty cents for the hour which has been saved, but against this is to be placed the ten cents earned as a premium, leaving a net gain of twenty cents to the employer and net increase of ten cents to the employee.[37]

In 1895, Frederick W. Taylor proposed a rate setting and piece-rate system as a "step toward partial solution of the labor problem."[38] His solution will be compared to the Towne and Halsey plans in Chapter 7. Moving forward, the systematic-management movement was now in firmer hands, with more coherent direction. Its foundations had been prepared: a forum for sharing management practices had been established, a nascent literature was developing, the so-called labor question was being debated, and the need for rationalization or full use of resources had become apparent. Systematic management was a prelude to what came to be known as "scientific management," the topic of the following two chapters.

BIG BUSINESS AND ITS CHANGING ENVIRONMENT

No nation can undergo a transformation on the level of the United States during the last half of the nineteenth century without substantial repercussions. An examination of the U.S. response to its changing environment is necessary to understand the forces that would shape the twentieth century. We have considered what Chandler believed to be the first phase in development of big business (i.e., initial expansion and accumulation of resources) in the United States and the accompanying emergence of systematic management. Let us now look beyond these developments to examine evolving notions of business and society, the beginnings of a national labor movement, the new technologies that transformed how people lived, and the changing relationship between government and business.

BUSINESS AND SOCIETY: BARONS OR BENEFACTORS?

Virtuous conduct seldom makes news. Historians and journalists are awed by the extraordinary, and more frequently than not overemphasize those individuals who are ruthless and unprincipled to the detriment of those quiet, sturdy, responsible people who, unheralded, are true productive builders. As a case in point, criticism of business operators and their methods began to increasingly appear in the late nineteenth century, in what co-authors Mark Twain and Charles Dudley Warner christened the "Gilded Age," a period highlighted (as we have noted) by rapid industrialization, but also political corruption and predatory business practices.[39] By Gilded Age, Twain and Warner meant an era that they saw as seemingly shiny on the surface like fake gold (gild), but rotten underneath. It was a time during which a small number of politicians, industrialists, and financiers became incredibly wealthy. The resulting income inequality was staggering. One early reference described shipping and railroad tycoon Cornelius "Commodore" Vanderbilt as being "[l]ike those old German barons who, from their eyries along the Rhine, swooped down upon the commerce of the noble river, and wrung tribute from every passenger that floated by."[40] In time, this image became so widespread that the public widely assumed all rich and famous business operators had gained their wealth by using monopoly power to exploit the working class. It would be impossible to examine all those deemed to be "robber barons," but a few thumbnail sketches will reveal why Matthew Josephson, who popularized the epithet, felt that some business operators were behaving in socially irresponsible ways.[41]

---

[37] *Idem*, "Experience with the Premium Plan of Paying Labor," *American Machinist* 22(9) (March 9, 1899), pp. 180–118.
[38] Frederick W. Taylor, "A Piece Rate System, Being a Step toward Partial Solution of the Labor Problem," *Transactions of the American Society of Mechanical Engineers* 16 (1895), pp. 856–903.
[39] Mark Twain and Charles Dudley Warner, *The Gilded Age: A Tale of To-Day* (Hartford, CN: American Publishing Company, 1873).
[40] "Your Money or Your Line," *New York Times* (February 9, 1859), p. 4. See also Hal Bridges, "The Robber Baron Concept in American History," *Business History Review* 32(1) (Spring 1958), pp. 1–13.
[41] Matthew Josephson, *The Robber Barons: The Great American Capitalists, 1861–1901* (New York: Harcourt, Brace Jovanovich, 1934), p. vii.

Vanderbilt gained control of the New York and Harlem railroad by manipulating its stock and bribing the New York state legislature. Financier Daniel Drew had the dubious honor of being the first to engage in what came to be called "watering stock." He had purchased a herd of cattle with an enlistment bonus from his army days. In transporting the cattle to market, he fed them salt to make them thirsty, and then, after providing them all the water they could drink, sold some temporarily overhydrated and heavier cattle at a very large profit. Together with Jay Gould and Jim Fisk, Drew turned to railroading and soon gave the Erie line its reputation for mismanagement in the days following Daniel C. McCallum's departure. The "Big Four"—builders of the Central Pacific Railroad, including Collis P. Huntington, A. Leland Stanford, Sr. (a former governor and U.S. senator from California), Mark Hopkins, and Charles Crocker—bribed lawmakers to obtain federal land grants, rail franchises, and favorable legislation. One year Huntington paid $200,000 to get a bill through the U.S. Congress; he later complained to David D. Colton, Central Pacific's Financial Director, that Congress was costing up to a half-million dollars a session and moaned: "I am fearful this Democratic Congress will kill me."[42]

Not all the robber barons were railroad builders. John D. Rockefeller, Sr., combined audacity and cunning in creating the Standard Oil Company trust. By conspiring with railroads, he was able to extract rebates on the cost of transporting his oil, as well as that of his competitors. Andrew Carnegie at one point owned or controlled two-thirds of the nation's steel industry. A strike at the Homestead (Pennsylvania) plant of Carnegie Steel in 1892 earned Carnegie poor press when a force of Pinkerton detectives (hired to protect the plant) were brutally stoned and beaten by striking workers. State militia troops moved in on the order of Governor Robert E. Pattison and secured the plant for nonunionized replacements; in the process, four Pinkerton agents were killed and 300 wounded.[43] Men such as Rockefeller and Carnegie were viewed, at least in Josephson's eyes, as unsavory characters.

What motivated the robber barons? For some historians, the answer was the publication of Charles R. Darwin's 1859 book *On the Origin of Species by Means of Natural Selection, or the Preservation of Favoured Races in the Struggle for Life*.[44] Darwin's book introduced his theory that species evolve across generations through a process of natural, rather than divine, selection. He claimed that there was a continual "struggle for existence" in nature, in which only those members of a species best suited to their environment (the "fit enough") are likely to survive. Some scholars, such as Englishman Hebert Spencer, applied Darwin's theory to society. The result was "Social Darwinism."[45] The phrases "struggle for existence" and "survival of the fittest" (a phrase coined by Spencer) suggested a competition or struggle among individuals for

[42] Letter from Collis P. Huntington to David D. Colton, August 1, 1876, p. 1. Collis Porter Huntington Papers, Box 140, Special Collections Research Center, Syracuse University Libraries, Syracuse, NY. The largest Congressional scandal of this period involved the construction of the transcontinental railroad linking the east and west coasts of the United States. U.S. Representative Oakes Adams (R-MA), working with Union Pacific Railroad executive Thomas C. Durant, sold discounted shares of stock in a Union Pacific railway construction contractor by the name of Crédit Mobilier of America to his congressional colleagues. The contractor was named Crédit Mobilier of America, so that investors would think it was associated with the influential French bank Société Générale du Crédit Mobilier. The contracts the Union Pacific made with Crédit Mobilier to lay track were exorbitantly priced and, given government underwriting, yielded exaggerated profits for Crédit Mobilier. These profits were then divided among Durant and other Crédit Mobilier stockholders (including Adams and his colleagues). As a result, the federal government paid $94,646,288 to Crédit Mobilier via the Union Pacific for building a railroad that cost $50,720,959, leaving $43,929,329 in stocks and bonds for Crédit Mobilier. As the stocks and bonds were heavily discounted, this balance, when reduced to cash, yielded a $23,366,319 profit. For further details, see "The King of Frauds: How the Credit Mobilier Bought its Way Through Congress," *The Sun* (New York) (September 4, 1872), pp. 1–3. The preceding dollar amounts are reported in William A. Piper "The Dangers of Government Subsidies," *Congressional Record: Containing the Proceedings and Debates of the Forty-Fourth Congress, First Session; also, Special Session of the Senate*, vol. 4: Part 3 (Washington, DC: Government Printing Office, 1876), p. 2328.

[43] Joseph F. Wall, *Andrew Carnegie* (New York: Oxford University Press, 1970), p. 559.

[44] Charles R. Darwin, *On the Origin of Species by Means of Natural Selection, or the Preservation of Favoured Races in the Struggle for Life* (London: John Murray, 1859).

[45] Richard Hofstadter, *Social Darwinism in American Thought* (Philadelphia, PA: University of Pennsylvania Press, 1944), p. 6. See also Donald C. Bellonmy, "'Social Darwinism' Revisited," *Perspectives in American History* 1(1984), pp. 1–129.

the resources needed to survive, and that only the most fit would win.[46] Social Darwinists saw Darwin's work as confirming the classical economist's *laissez-faire* philosophy of free-market capitalism. To these late nineteenth-century thinkers, class distinctions and inequities in wealth were the result of natural social and economic forces. They believed that legislation and charity intended to thwart these forces would redound to society's detriment by weakening the human species for, as Darwin was later to explain, "the weak members of civilized societies propagate their kind."[47] For some, the wealth of those who created the world's first large-scale corporations proved that, in a competition for resources, only the most fit would advance up the social and economic ladder of success, whereas the "unfit" would remain on the lower rungs and, eventually, be eliminated through natural selection. For these Social Darwinists, the unrestrained business practices of the robber barons were morally justified, as they carried society forward and favored its "best members."[48] Whether the robber barons were motivated by Social Darwinism, however, was then, as now, open to debate.

As one observer noted, in general, business operators of the late nineteenth and early twentieth centuries were pragmatic doers who did not read Darwin (or Adam Smith's musings on marketplace forces and competition) and cared little for abstract social and economic theories.[49] Another agreed: "[I]t is not true that this commitment [to notions of competition, merited success, and deserved failure] was grounded on Darwinian premises . . . very few businessmen of the 1870's or 1880's knew enough of Darwin . . . to turn biology to the uses of self-justification."[50] What can be concluded about the effect of Social Darwinism on the thinking and practices of those in business? The economics of the "robber-baron era" led to mergers, trusts, and pools rather than to cutthroat competition, as Social Darwinism would predict. As described by Chandler, Rockefeller's efforts to build Standard Oil were an attempt to benefit from economies of scale rather than an effort to monopolize the oil industry. Under Rockefeller, the average cost of producing a gallon of kerosene (lamp oil) went from 1.50 cents before the Standard Oil Trust was formed in 1844 to 0.45 cents by 1885, with profits rising from 0.53 to 1.003 cents per gallon.[51] In 1864, when Standard's market share was marginal, a gallon of kerosene cost 64.75 cents. By 1897, with Standard's market share at 88.5 percent, a gallon cost only 5.91 cents.[52] This was hardly an indication of exclusive control and, in turn, monopoly profits. Before the discovery and refining of oil, animal fat was used for lubricating wheels and gears, and before kerosene, whale oil was used for lighting. Saving the world's whales was not Rockefeller's intention, but the distillation of crude oil into kerosene saved them from extinction. Moreover, whereas oil refining made Rockefeller wealthy, in the process he made oil products less expensive and, thus, available to the masses. As Burton W. Folsom, Jr. writes: "Before 1870, only the rich could afford whale oil and candles. The rest had to go to bed early to save money. By the 1870s, with the drop in the price of kerosene, middle- and working-class people all over the nation could afford the one cent an hour that it cost to light their homes at night. Working and reading became the after-dark activities new to most Americans in the 1870s."[53] Similarly, driving down the price of steel may have been Carnegie's greatest

[46] Darwin introduced the phrase "struggle for existence" as a chapter title in his 1859 book, though the expression "survival of the fittest" was first used by fellow Englishman Herbert Spencer in *Principles of Biology*, vol. 1 (London: William and Norgate, 1864), p. 444. Darwin did, however, make the expression famous by noting in *On the Origin of Species* (5th ed.; 1869, p. 72) that it was "often used by Mr. Herbert Spencer" and acknowledging that "Survival of the Fittest is more accurate, and is sometimes equally convenient."

[47] Charles Darwin, *The Descent of Man, and Selection in Relation to Sex*, vol. 1 (New York: D. Appleton and Company, 1872), p. 162.

[48] William Graham Sumner, "The Challenge of Facts," in *The Challenge of Facts and Other Essays*, ed., Albert Galloway Keller (New Haven, CN: Yale University Press, 1914), p. 25. Written in the 1880s.

[49] Edward C. Kirkland, *Dream and Thought in the Business Community, 1860–1900* (Ithaca, NY: Cornell University Press, 1956), pp. 14, 18. Another who shared this pragmatic view is Peter D'A. Jones, "Introduction," in *The Robber Barons Revisited, idem*, ed., (Boston, MA: D. C. Heath, 1968), pp. v–xi.

[50] Raymond J. Wilson, "Darwinism and Social Ethics" in *Darwinism and the American Intellectual: A Book of Readings, idem*, ed., (Homewood, IL: Dorsey Press, 1967), pp. 93–94.

[51] Alfred D. Chandler, Jr., "The Emergence of Managerial Capitalism," *Business History Review* 58(4) (Winter 1984), p. 484.

[52] Ida M. Tarbell. *A History of the Standard Oil Company* (New York: Macmillan, 1937), p. 23; Appendix 57: pp. 384–385.

[53] Burton W. Folsom, Jr., *Entrepreneurs vs. the State: A New Look at the Rise on Big Business in America, 1840–1920* (Reston, VA: Young America's Foundation, 1987), p. 87.

philanthropic achievement. The Big Four paid bribes when corrupt politicians, willing to sell their votes to the highest bidder, considered payoffs a normal "cost of doing business." Similarly, when Ezra Cornell sought a charter from the New York state legislature to establish a university at Ithaca, he had to strike a "bargain" with the "friends of Genesee College" who, in return for a $25,000 "gift" to the college, assured him the votes necessary for obtaining the charter. Genesee, originally a Methodist seminary, was one of several denominational colleges that initially opposed Cornell University in the belief that, being nonsectarian, it would be hostile to religion. In November 1865, Cornell noted in his ciphering book, "Such is the influence of corrupt legislation."[54]

It is highly doubtful that those in business found much guidance in Social Darwinism. Rather, it appears that in an era of change the robber barons were highly visible targets for Progressive critics:

> Thus the creation of the Robber Baron stereotype seems to have been the product of an impulsive popular attempt to explain the shift in the structure of American society. . . . [M]ost critics appeared to slip into the easy vulgarizations of the "devil-view" of history which ingenuously assumes that all misfortunes can be traced to the machinations of an easily located set of villains—in this case, the big businessmen of America.[55]

In hindsight, what seems remarkable is that, with the rise of Big Business, the robber-baron era was actually a period of expanding societal prosperity. The material well-being of the nation's working class improved faster than any time in history. The decline in the cost of good and services accrued to the benefit of all economic classes as a massive increase in real income. Consider the following measures:

> Between 1870 and 1900, America's inflation adjusted gross national product expanded by an unprecedented 233%. Though the population nearly doubled, real per capita GNP surged by 90%. Real wages of non-farm employees grew by 53%, and life's staples, such as food, clothing and shelter, became more plentiful and cheaper. Food prices plummeted by 63% and the cost of textiles, fuel and home furnishings fell by 70%, 65% and 70%, respectively. The illiteracy rate fell by 46% and life expectancy rose 12.5%. Infant mortality declined by 17%.[56]

The Big Business companies the robber barons and others created, thus, had both a positive and a negative social impact. Progressives were right in targeting those practices that Mark Twain and other critics found objectionable. And, yet, the Gilded Age saw the creation of a middle-class greater than the world had ever known. The so-called robber barons created hundreds of thousands of jobs and, as the preceding measures attest, enriched the lives of millions. They were neither robbers nor barons. They did not need to rob. They became wealthy by providing better and less expensive products that people voluntarily chose to purchase because doing so made them better off. Nonetheless, many of today's anti-business sentiments date to the robber-baron era of the late nineteenth century.

Rising in counterpoint to Social Darwinism was another set of ideas that came closer to grasping the policies and practices of the nineteenth-century business world. These ideas flowed from the Social Gospel movement. People such as Washington Gladden saw the Social Gospel movement as Christianity in action. We will return to the Social Gospel movement in Chapters 9 and 12, and discuss how it led to improved personnel practices.

A separate series of developments also suggests that those in business at the turn of the nineteenth century were far more generous than typically portrayed. Business philanthropy is as ancient as business itself. "Captains of Industry,"[57] a phrase coined by Thomas Carlyle, have been

---

[54] Carl L. Becker, *Cornell University: Founders and the Founding* (Ithaca, NY: Cornell University Press, 1943), pp. 103–107, 154. Genesee College would eventually become Syracuse University, located in Syracuse, New York.

[55] John Tipple, "The Anatomy of Prejudice: Origins of the Robber Baron Legend," *Business History Review* 33(4) (Winter 1959), p. 521.

[56] W. Philip Gramm and Amity R. Shales, "The 'Gilded Age' Myth, Then and Now," *Wall Street Journal* (May 8, 2023), p. A17. *Corrigendum*: (May 10, 2023), p. A16.

[57] Thomas Carlyle, *Past and Present* (New York: William H. Colyer, 1843), p. 149.

patrons of arts and letters, underwriters of community projects, donors to religious groups, and endowers of educational institutions. No one questioned the right of the era's business philanthropists to give away some or all their fortunes; after all, it was their money to do with as they pleased. But what of this new phenomenon, the corporation? Could its managers and directors give a portion of its profits to underwrite nonbusiness endeavors?

The notion of expressed powers as outlined in a corporation's charter and the belief that corporate officers hold property for the benefit of stockholders combined to form the nineteenth-century legal basis for corporate philanthropy. A case in 1881 involved the Old Colony Railroad, whose corporate officers had agreed to underwrite the 1872 World's Peace Jubilee and International Music Festival held in Boston. Despite the fact that the railroad benefitted from increased passenger traffic because of the jubilee, the Massachusetts Supreme Court ruled that the officers' action was *ultra vires* (i.e., outside the railroad's chartered powers).[58] In 1883, in Britain, the West Cork Railroad Company attempted to compensate its employees for the loss of their jobs resulting from its bankruptcy. In ruling against the railroad, Lord Justice Charles S. C. Bowden stated: "Charity has no business to sit at boards of directors *qua* charity . . . [the directors] can only spend money which is not theirs, but the company's, if they are spending it for purposes which are reasonably incidental to the company."[59] What might or might not be "reasonably incidental" would receive some clarification in what is known as the Steinway case. The New York State Supreme Court allowed piano manufacturer Steinway and Sons to buy an adjoining tract of land to be used by its employees for a church, library, and school. The Court reasoned that the employees would benefit, so there was a definite *quid pro quo* accruing to the corporation's well-being through better workplace relations.[60] In short, the law is fairly clear that corporations are chartered to do specific things, that managers and directors are trustees of stockholder-owned property, and that directors can give away assets only if it is to a corporation's measurable benefit to do so. Each of the preceding cases limited the power of directors to engage in corporate philanthropy. This power was extended in 1953 with the *A. P. Smith Manufacturing v. Barlow et al* case.[61] The Smith directors donated $1,500 to Princeton University for general educational purposes. A group of stockholders sued, claiming that the donation was outside the powers granted to the directors under the company's charter. The New Jersey Chancery Court held that the directors had acted within their rights to further corporate (and not personal) ends. It should be mentioned that, on the federal level, the Revenue Act of 1935 included a clause permitting corporations to deduct up to 5 percent of their net income for charitable contributions.[62] It is now accepted that directors, acting on behalf of corporations, may engage in general philanthropy for the public interest.

Although corporate philanthropy might be questioned, it seems unlikely that the hand of individual charity would be nipped. Individual philanthropy would be the vehicle for expressing the social consciences of nineteenth-century business operators. Only a few of the great business philanthropists of this era can be mentioned here.[63] Ezra Cornell's pioneering advancements in telegraphy earned him a fortune as a founder of the Western Union Telegraph Company and, in turn, provided the money to endow Cornell University; William Colgate aided people in following John Wesley's admonition that "Cleanliness is next to godliness"[64] by manufacturing soap, and he and his heirs gave so much to a college that it changed its name in his honor; Moses Brown, Samuel Slater's partner, founded Rhode Island College in Providence (1770),

---

[58] *Davis v. Old Colony Railway Company*, 131 Mass. 258 (1881).

[59] *Hutton v. West Cork Railroad Company*, 23 Chancery Division Reports 654 (1883), pp. 426, 425.

[60] *Steinway v. Steinway and Sons*, 40 N.Y.S. 718 (1896).

[61] *AP Smith Manufacturing Co. v. Barlow*, 98 A.2d 581 (NJ 1953).

[62] *Revenue Act of 1935*, Pub. L. no. 74–407, 49 Stat. 1014, 1016, Section 102(c), (1935).

[63] For an extensive list of business philanthropists, see Daniel A. Wren, "American Business Philanthropy and Higher Education in the Nineteenth Century," *Business History Review* 57(3) (Autumn 1983), pp. 321–346. See also Mark Sharfman, "Changing Institutional Rules: The Evolution of Corporate Philanthropy, 1883–1953," *Business and Society* 33(3) (December 1994), pp. 236–269.

[64] Richard Watson, *The Life of the Rev. John Wesley, A. M.* (New York: S. Hoyt & Co., 1831), p. 180.

which became Brown University in 1804; Johns Hopkins, founder of the Baltimore & Ohio Railroad, founded the Baltimore university that bears his name; and Cornelius Vanderbilt made a nearly $1 million bequest in 1873 that converted a small Methodist seminary in Nashville into a major university.

There were more: Joseph Wharton, whose $100,000 grant to the University of Pennsylvania in 1881 underwrote the Wharton School of Finance and Economy; Edward Tuck, who honored his father with a gift of $300,000 to Dartmouth College to start the Amos Tuck School of Administration and Finance (1899); A. Leland Stanford, Sr., who honored his son's memory with a university (1891); John Stevens, whose will established an institute of technology in Philadelphia (1870); and James B. "Buck" Duke, who created a $40 million trust fund for Trinity College (later renamed for the Duke family). Good fortune did not smile on all colleges who hoped for a philanthropist. In 1867, Daniel Drew signed a $250,000 promissory note to endow a Methodist theological seminary in Madison, New Jersey. The seminary started its work, but Daniel Drew went bankrupt and was unable to deliver the promised money. Nonetheless, the seminary was named Drew University. Other philanthropists are better known. Rockefeller endowed the University of Chicago (1890), gave millions to a general education fund for educating African Americans throughout the South, financed historically black colleges and universities such as Spelman at Atlanta, Georgia, and made key gifts to what is now Rockefeller University. By the time of his death in 1937, he had given half-a-billion dollars to ensure the future of the foundation that bears his family name. During his lifetime, Carnegie gave away over $350 million of his fortune. Libraries, a university, the Carnegie Museum of Natural History (in Pittsburgh), and a foundation are enduring monuments to his expressed "stewardship of wealth philosophy."[65] J. P. Morgan and Marshall Field used their wealth to fund, respectively, the American Museum of Natural History (in New York City) and the Field Museum (in Chicago). Despite such generosity, in February 1915, Frank P. Walsh, chairman of the United States Commission on Industrial Relations (and whom we will read more about in Chapter 11) questioned whether the Rockefeller, Carnegie, and other foundations were potential "menaces to society." In hearings sparked by what became known as the Ludlow Massacre—the seven-month coal-field strike that culminated on April 20, 1914, when twelve miners (some shot in the back) and their families (including 2 women and 11 children) were killed by the state militia at a Rockefeller family–controlled mine outside Ludlow, Colorado—Commission members expressed concern that "improperly administered" foundations might increase rather than lessen the "evil" they sought to remedy were they to fall into "evil hands." Philanthropy by company-sponsored foundations was seen as intruding on the province of government, and reflected a fear that bequests given at the direction of men such as Rockefeller and Carnegie might exercise "a great influence upon the public mind," allowing foundations to increase their control over public institutions, colleges and universities, government, and the masses.[66]

Times have changed: income and inheritance taxes make it difficult to accumulate the wealth of a Rockefeller or a Carnegie, the legal question of corporate philanthropy has been clarified (as we shall see in Chapter 22), and public expectations about the role of business in society have changed. Individually and collectively, however, we remain the beneficiaries of the robber barons' uncommon largess. More recent philanthropists include Nike, Inc. co-founder Phil Knight, who has given more than a half-billion dollars to the Oregon Health Sciences Center and donated more than $100 million to the Stanford University Graduate School of Business;

---

[65] Andrew Carnegie, "Wealth," *North American Review* 148 (391) (June 1889), pp. 653–665; *idem*, "The Best Fields for Philanthropy," *North American Review* 149 (397) (December 1889), pp. 682–698. See also Charles Harvey, Mairi Maclean, Jillian Gordon, and Eleanor Shaw, "Andrew Carnegie and the Foundations of Contemporary Entrepreneurial Philanthropy," *Business History* 53(3) (June 2011), pp. 425–450.

[66] *Industrial Relations, Final Report and Testimony Submitted to Congress by the Commission on Industrial Relations*, vol. 9 (Washington, DC: U.S. Government Printing Office, 1916), pp. 8110–8111, 8159, 8171, 8179, 8298. On the Ludlow Massacre, see Thomas G. Andrews, *Killing for Coal: America's Deadliest Labor War* (Cambridge, MA: Harvard University Press, 2008), p. 2.

former Citigroup CEO Sandy Weil, who has given more than $600 million to Cornell Medical Center; and Melinda and Bill Gates who have saved millions of lives by funding research in HIV (human immunodeficiency virus), malaria, and polio, and underwriting lifesaving vaccines. This list could be extended *ad infinitum*.

BUSINESS AND LABOR: UNEASY RELATIONS

As noted in Chapter 5, in 1842 the Massachusetts Supreme Court ruled in *Commonwealth v. Hunt* that workers had the right to strike or use peaceful coercion to raise wages. At the time, in the United States, labor organizations were found among craft workers, such as those in the building trades, and among so-called brotherhoods of railway employees. Efforts to form general unions across trades or industries were generally less successful. One of the nation's first union federations, the National Labor Union, headed by William H. Sylvis (1828–1869), sought to supplant the employer–employee wage system with cooperative production, in which workers would pool their resources, supply their own labor, and manage their own factories. The Noble Order of the Knights of Labor (organized in 1867) sought an eight-hour workday, establishment of a bureau of labor statistics, protection against child labor, government ownership of railroads and telegraph lines, abolition of national banks, and a graduated federal income tax to raise money for government services and programs.

Labor violence in the 1870s through1890s fueled the public's fear of unions. The Molly Maguires, a secret society of Irish miners seeking to improve working conditions, terrorized the northeast Pennsylvania coalfields with murder and other atrocities during the Long Strike of 1875, which resulted in 20 "Mollies" being hung for committing murder. In 1877, workers in Martinsburg, West Virginia, struck the Baltimore & Ohio Railroad when their wages were cut for the second time in eight months. Over 100 people were killed by the end of the six-week strike. At a rally near Chicago's Haymarket Square in support of McCormick Harvesting Machine Company workers striking for an eight-hour workday, someone hurled a bomb at police attempting to disperse the gathering. Seven policemen were killed by the blast and 60 others were injured. Four labor supporters were also killed. As already referenced, the Homestead Steel Strike occurred in 1892. It saw at least four Pinkerton detectives and eight strikers killed. The Pullman Strike, in 1894, which pitted the American Railway Union against the Pullman Company, a Chicago manufacturer of railroad cars, was sparked by a 25 percent wage cut and an increase in working hours. Some 70 strikers were killed across the country before federal troops were called out and the strike collapsed. In a final example of violence brought about by confrontations between labor and management, in 1897, at the privately owned Lattimer coal mine hear Hazleton, Pennsylvania, 19 unarmed strikers protesting unsafe working conditions were killed by a sheriff's posse called in by the mine's owners. Public fear of radicals and anarchists, who were often equated with legitimate union organizers, kept the union movement at a relative standstill as a percentage of the U.S. labor force. Total union membership grew from 300,000 members in 1870 to 791,000 in 1900; however, only 2.3 percent of the total U.S labor force was organized in 1870, and this percentage declined in the 1880s and 1890s, but recovered and rose to 2.7 percent by 1900.[67]

In contrast to the National Labor Union and the Knights of Labor, the American Federation of Labor (AFL), organized in 1886 as a federation of trade unions, was successful in achieving its goals.[68] The AFL concentrated on immediate economic gains for its members rather than on distant political reforms. Under Samuel Gompers's presidency, AFL membership increased from

[67] Stanley Lebergott, "The American Labor Force," in *American Economic Growth: An Economist's History of the United States*, eds., Lane E. Davis (New York: Harper & Row), 1963), Table 6.16, p. 220.

[68] Trade or craft unions organize workers in a particular industry along trade or craft lines; examples include the carpenters' union, electricians' union, and painters' union. In contrast, industrial unions organize all the workers in a particular industry regardless of craft or trade; examples include automobile workers, steel workers, mineworkers, and shipbuilders.

over 600,000 in 1887 to some 2,865,000 at the time of Gompers's death in 1924.[69] In general, however, workers had to wait for other times and a changing public opinion to legitimize their attempts to unionize.

Immigration provided a steadily growing workforce to meet the labor needs of a rapidly expanding industrial economy: Chinese laborers were brought in to build railroads, and Germans, Irish, and Swiss laborers populated the nation's coalfields and steel mills. After 1880, another flow of Slavic, Polish, and Italian laborers added to a growing workforce. The increased supply of labor, however, did not result in lower wages. Daily wages and annual earnings in manufacturing increased some 50 percent between 1860 and 1890, and real wages (the purchasing power of workers' incomes) increased more than 60 percent from 1860 to 1890.[70] Wage earners benefited from the growth of U.S. industry in terms of both employment and real income.

INVENTIVE AND INNOVATIVE IMPULSES

Railroads influenced the creation of a national market for a growing array of manufacturers. Interest in connecting the east and west coasts of the United States with a transcontinental railroad reached fruition in 1862 when President Abraham Lincoln, in the midst of the War Between the States, signed the Pacific Railway Act, which created the Union Pacific and Central Pacific railroads.[71] This statute (and its various amendments) provided federal land grants totaling some twenty-four million acres and loans eventually amounting to about sixty-five million dollars to the Central Pacific and the Union Pacific to connect Council Bluffs, Iowa, to Sacramento, California. The Union Pacific (building from the West) and the Central Pacific (building from the East) met at Promontory Summit (now in the state of Utah), on May 10, 1869. To link the two railroads and commemorate the symbolic uniting of the country, Central Pacific president A. Leland Stanford, Sr., wielded a silver-plated maul to drive a 17.6 karat gold spike into a polished crosstie to complete the laying of the last rail. In doing so, he fulfilled what journalist John L. O'Sullivan called the country's "manifest destiny" to expand across the North American continent.[72] It was now possible to travel by train from New York to San Francisco within a week's time, a trip that by stagecoach had taken six months. The rail network in the United States would increase from 35,000 miles of track in 1865 to 193,000 by 1900. Technological advancements made rail travel more pleasurable: steel rails replaced iron rails; George Pullman introduced the sleeping car in 1865; George Westinghouse developed the air brake in 1868, making rail travel safer; and meatpacking giant Swift & Company began using refrigerated railcars in 1875 to transport fresh beef carcasses from western processing centers to its Chicago packing plants for sale in eastern markets. The westward-expanding railroads also fostered a retailing revolution, as we shall see, by making it possible to sell products anywhere in the country without a storefront.[73] Aaron Montgomery Ward founded the first mail-order catalog business in 1872. Located in Chicago, he made goods available across the nation. Customers ordered items from the Montgomery Ward Company's catalog (known as the "Wish Book") by mail and picked them up at their local train station. By 1900, the Wish Book was some 1,200 pages long and offered over 70,000 items.[74]

The remarkable spirit of inventive and innovative impulses that shaped the era's technological advances was due to innumerable "prime movers," individuals (such as Montgomery Ward) whose ideas created new wealth. As Edwin A. Locke expressed it, "for wealth to be created,

[69] Philip A. Taft, *The A. F. of L. in the Time of Gompers* (New York: Harper & Brothers, 1957), pp. 52, 362.

[70] Clarence D. Long, *Wages and Earnings in the United States, 1860–1890* (Princeton, NJ: Princeton University Press, 1960), p. 109.

[71] *Act of July 1, 1862 (Pacific Railroad Act), United States Statutes at Large* (12 Stat. 489). Available online at https://www.archives.gov/milestone-documents/pacific-railway-act

[72] John O'Sullivan, "Annexation," *The United States Magazine and Democratic Review* 17(85) (July–August 1845), p. 5.

[73] Carlos A. Schwantes and James P. Ronda, *The West the Railroads Made* (Seattle, WA: University of Washington Press, 2008), p. 106.

[74] Robert G. Spinney, *City of Big Shoulders: A History of Chicago* (DeKalb, IL: Northern Illinois University Press, 2000), p. 64.

individuals must create it . . . *prime movers* . . . moved society forward by the force of their own creative imagination, their own energy, and their own productive capacity."[75] These individuals pushed to advance the nation's capacity to produce more, to create jobs, and to devise means of making, moving, and packaging thousands of consumer products.

The western expansion of the United States, spurred on by the growth of the nation's railroads and the Homestead Act of 1862 (which gave several hundred thousand settlers up to 160 acres of public land provided they live on it for 5 years and improved it), ushered in a period of extensive economic growth.[76] Chandler described this growth in terms of *scale* and *scope*: (1) economies of scale occur when the increased size of a single operating unit producing or distributing a single product reduces the per-unit cost of production or distribution; (2) economies of scope result when processes within a single operating unit are used to produce or distribute more than one product.[77] Carnegie's vertical integration in the steel industry achieved economies of scale by reducing unit costs; economies of scope were realized by manufacturing a variety of different steel products. As scale and scope expanded, an increasing number of managers were needed to plan, coordinate, and monitor a business's activities. With the rail system, telegraph, and Alexander Graham Bell's telephone (patented in 1876), it became possible to produce, transport, and sell to national and global markets leading to further economies of both scale and scope.

Large-scale businesses in the latter half of the nineteenth century were entirely different than the localized, family owned and managed, labor-intensive businesses of the first half of the century. To mention all the "prime movers" of this latter period would require several books. Some, such as Thomas Edison and George Westinghouse, transformed how electricity was transmitted and controlled. Rockefeller's lamp-oil market would be superseded by electricity. The Bell Telephone Company, created in 1877, eventually became the American Telephone and Telegraph Company in 1885. Elisha Gray invented the first facsimile machine for transmitting handwriting via telegraph in 1877. With improvements in communication and transportation came the first mass-marketers, chain-retailers, mail-order houses, and grocery chains such as the Great Atlantic & Pacific Tea Company, which by 1878 operated 70 stores. The American System of Manufacturing enabled mass production of Isaac M. Singer's sewing machines and Cyrus H. McCormick's mechanical reaper. Christopher L. Sholes sold his typewriter patent to E. Remington & Sons in 1873. Andrew Carnegie's stronger, lighter structural steel enabled high-rise buildings, and Elisha Otis's elevator made the trip to the top easier and safer. These were a few of the prime movers whose inventive and innovative impulses accelerated the growth of large-scale businesses in manufacturing, communications, marketing, distilling, refining, transporting, and food processing that created a material abundance unparalleled in human history.

BUSINESS AND GOVERNMENT: SEEDS OF REFORM

The U.S. government was not noted for its progressiveness during the nineteenth century. The patronage system (also known as the "spoils system"), in which the political party in power awarded government positions to friends and relatives, had prevailed since the nation's founding. Calls for government reform went unanswered. In 1883, spurred by the assassination of President James A. Garfield by a disappointed office seeker, the U.S. Congress passed the Civil Service Act—better known as the Pendleton Civil Service Reform Act, after its senatorial sponsor—establishing the permanent nonpartisan Civil Service Commission. By introducing open, competitive exams for civil-service jobs, the act sought to bring qualified employees, rather than political favorites, to government and to provide some stability in public affairs. In this new

[75] Edwin A. Locke, *Prime Movers: Traits of the Great Wealth Creators* (New York: American Management Association, 2000), p. 7.

[76] *Act of May 20, 1862 (Homestead Act)*, Public Law 37–64 (12 STAT 392); 5/20/1862; Enrolled Acts and Resolutions of Congress, 1789–2011; General Records of the United States Government, Record Group 11; National Archives Building, Washington, DC. Available online at https://www.archives.gov/milestone-documents/homestead-act

[77] Chandler and Hikino, *Scale and Scope*, pp. 17–28.

environment, the seeds of government reform found fertile ground in the systematic-management movement emerging in the private sector.

Credit for introducing systematic management to government belongs to Woodrow Wilson, then a young professor at Bryn Mawr College. In 1887, Wilson recognized that civil-service reform must extend beyond the need for qualified public employees to perform the functions of government. To this end, Wilson recommended "administrative study to discover, first, what government can properly and successfully do, and, secondly, how it can do these proper things with the utmost possible efficiency and the least possible cost either of money or of energy."[78] The study of government, according to Wilson, had focused more on politics and not enough on how to manage the public's business. After all, as he reasoned, "the field of administration is a field of business . . . removed from the hurry and strife of politics. . . . The object of administrative study is to rescue executive methods from the confusion and costliness of empirical experiment and set them upon foundations laid deep in stable principle."[79] Later, as the 28th President of the United States (1913–1921), Wilson brought improved systems and methods to government. As will be noted in Chapter 8, Wilson is considered a founder of the "administrative state," and as believing in government by nonpartisan experts who would rationally order public policy. The downside of his belief in the superior wisdom of neutral experts is discussed in Chapter 10. Although Wilson argued in favor of "administration," it is worth pondering whether he would have countenanced the advent of the modern administrative state that has been characterized as comprising an unelected "ruling class."

As the federal government during this era narrowly construed the U.S. Constitution's commerce clause, there were but few efforts made to regulate business practices. The first attempts to do so were aimed at abuses by the railroads. In 1869, Massachusetts passed legislation establishing a railroad commission with authority to set and enforce shipping rates. The Granger laws, passed in the late 1860s and early 1870s by several Midwestern states, regulated the prices charged to farmers by railroads and grain elevator operators; and the Interstate Commerce Act of 1887 became the first federal act to regulate the railroads' monopolistic practices.[80] Beyond the railroads, the Sherman Antitrust Act of 1890 was the first federal act to outlaw all "combinations in restraint of trade" in interstate commerce.[81] Poorly written and narrowly interpreted, it was generally ineffective. Indeed, there is no proof that trusts in industries accused of being monopolistic during the act's debate were restricting output and thereby increasing prices, as their output expanded, on average, by 175 percent from 1880 to 1900—seven times the growth rate of the economy on the whole—and prices, on average, fell three times as fast as the consumer price index.[82] The Wilson–Gorman Tariff Act of 1894 imposed the first peacetime national income tax. It levied a 2 percent personal tax on all incomes above $4,000 and a 2 percent tax on all corporate net income. In 1895, the Supreme Court declared the Wilson–Gorman Tariff Act's income-tax provision unconstitutional. Passed in 1913, the Constitution's Sixteenth Amendment created a federal income tax. The Clayton Antitrust Act of 1914 further strengthened the Sherman Antitrust Act by prohibiting unfair methods of competition such as anticompetitive mergers and acquisitions, price discrimination, and interlocking directorates. In brief, the nineteenth-century economic and political environments remained relatively *laissez-faire*, true to the precepts of Adam Smith; the twentieth century would stand in stark contrast.

---

[78] Woodrow Wilson, "The Study of Administration," *Political Science Quarterly* 2(2) (June 1887), p. 197.

[79] *Ibid.*, pp. 209–210.

[80] *Act of February 4, 1887 (Interstate Commerce Act), Public Law 49–41*, February 4, 1887; Enrolled Acts and Resolutions of Congress, 1789–2011; General Records of the United States Government, 1778–1992; Record Group 11; National Archives. Available online at https://www.archives.gov/milestone-documents/interstate-commerce-act

[81] *Act of July 2, 1890 (Sherman Anti-Trust Act)*, July 2, 1890; Enrolled Acts and Resolutions of Congress, 1789–1992; General Records of the United States Government; Record Group 11; National Archives. Available online at https://www.archives.gov/milestone-documents/sherman-anti-trust-act

[82] Thomas J. DiLorenzo, "The Origin of Antitrust: An Interest-Group Perspective," *International Review of Law and Economics* 5(1) (June 1985), pp. 79–80.

SUMMARY OF PART I

Part I traced developments in management thought up to the scientific-management era in the United States. After a brief introduction to the role of managers in organizations, it reviewed the first attempts at management in early civilizations and discussed how changing cultural values set the stage for the Industrial Revolution. The Industrial Revolution posed new challenges for owner-entrepreneurs, salaried managers, and society at large. The efforts of four individuals—Robert Owen, Charles Babbage, Andrew Ure, and Charles Dupin—who pioneered solutions to these challenges were discussed. Part 1 concluded by examining the

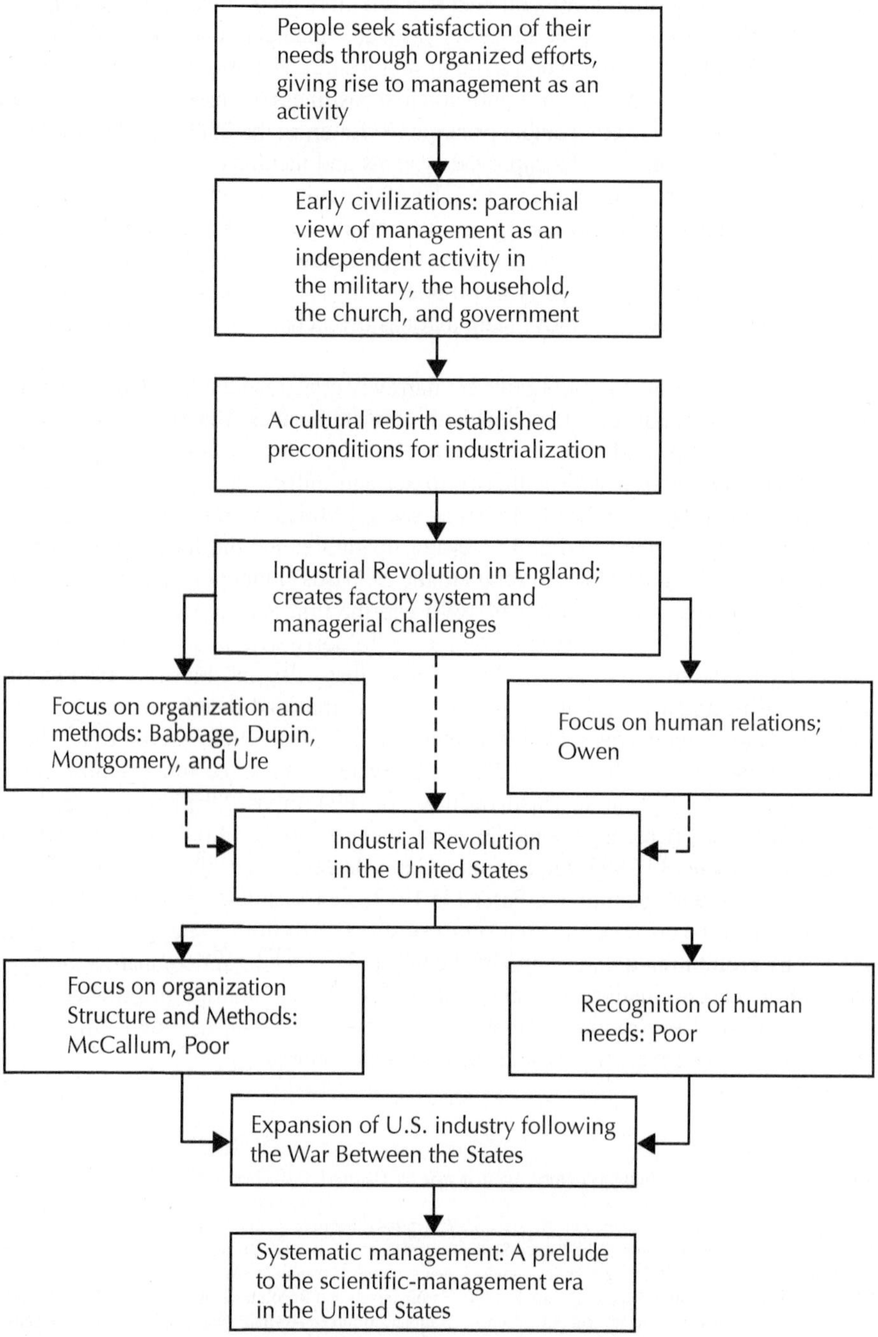

FIGURE 6.1 Synopsis of early management thought

continued growth of U.S. businesses following the War Between the States, the emergence of systematic management, and the nation's economic, social, political, and technological environment on the eve of the scientific-management era.

Figure 6.1 presents a synopsis of early management thought. It opens by noting that people have manifold needs and wants, which they seek to satisfy through organized endeavors. Whereas early civilizations generally placed a low value on economic exchange and held a parochial view of management as an independent activity, a cultural rebirth established preconditions for industrialization. The Industrial Revolution in England beget the factory system, which posed unique managerial challenges. The efforts of Owen, Babbage, Ure, Dupin, and others (such as Daniel McCallum and Henry Poor) in meeting these challenges were noted. Finally, the expansion of U.S. industry following the War Between the States led to systematic management, a prelude to the scientific management-era, our next topic.

The Scientific-Management Era

PART II

Part II begins by reviewing the life of Frederick W. Taylor and the scientific-management movement. Taylor left an indelible mark on management as both an activity and an academic discipline. His work was, and remains, revolutionary. Taylor, however, was not alone in spreading the gospel of efficiency. He was joined by others who would apply, adapt, and refine scientific management. Carl G. Barth, Henry L. Gantt, Frank and Lillian Gilbreth, Harrington Emerson, and Morris L. Cooke were among the most prominent individuals flying the scientific-management banner. Though the work of Taylor and his followers dominated scientific management's early years, social forces were at in play during the same period, and Part II continues by examining how these forces affected industrial psychology, industrial sociology, and industrial relations. Together, these forces set the stage for later developments in labor–management relations, the human-relations school of management, and, eventually, the field of organizational behavior. Part II then considers the ideas of Henri Fayol, a French manager-engineer who was the first writer to advance a formal statement of management elements and principles, and Max Weber, a German economist-sociologist who addressed the more fundamental issue of how organizations should be structured. As the scientific-management movement grew in the United States, it sparked attention in other parts of the world, including Western and Eastern Europe, South America, Japan, China, and Australia. Part II concludes with a retrospective view of the economic, social, technological, and political facets that composed scientific management's cultural environment.

The Advent of Scientific Management

CHAPTER 7

Earlier chapters reviewed the transformation of U.S. industry in the years following the War Between the States. The Industrial Revolution in Great Britain initially spread across the Atlantic Ocean with the mechanization of textile manufacturing. In the United States, with the westward migration of settlers, the Industrial Revolution was most evident in rail transportation. The nation's railroads provided a cost-effective means for transporting manufactured goods, raw materials, and food. The seeds of the modern industrial corporation—the forerunner of today's *Fortune* 500 companies—were sown during this era. As noted in Chapter 5, early railroad pioneers were among the first to feel the need for improved management. Daniel McCallum introduced systematic management on the Erie Railroad, and his ideas influenced other railway operators and Andrew Carnegie in the expanding steel industry. Railroads opened new product markets, and the telegraph connected the nation for financial, production, marketing, and other transactions.

Another stage of the Industrial Revolution began in the latter half of the nineteenth century. It grew out of a complex amalgam of technological advances, changing power sources, evolving labor–management relations, and a desperate need to reconcile these factors through innovations in managing. Given that engineers were vital in developing and installing advances in technology and power, it was natural that they became a prime source of ideas for meeting new management challenges. As recounted in Chapter 6, Henry R. Towne, for example, called for engineers to look beyond the technical side of manufacturing and become involved in increasing the managerial efficiency of industrial operations.[1] One of the engineers who responded to Towne's call was Frederick W. Taylor. He is the focal point of this chapter.

FREDERICK W. TAYLOR: THE EARLY YEARS

Frederick Winslow Taylor (1856–1915) was a son of privilege. He was born in Germantown, Pennsylvania. His father was of Quaker stock, and his mother traced her Puritan roots to a Plymouth, Massachusetts, ancestor who arrived in Colonial America in 1629.[2] Taylor's early

[1] Henry R. Towne, "The General Principles of Organization Applied to an Individual Manufacturing Establishment," *Human Engineering* 2(1) (April 1912), pp. 75–79.

[2] Taylor's life is a popular subject for biographies. A much-cited source is Frank B. Copley's authorized biography, *Frederick W. Taylor: Father of Scientific Management*, 2 vols. (New York: Harper & Brothers, 1923). Other useful sources are Charles D. Wrege and Ronald G. Greenwood, *Frederick W. Taylor, the Father of Scientific Management: Myth and Reality* (Homewood, IL: Business One Irwin, 1991); Daniel M. Nelson, *Frederick W. Taylor and the Rise of Scientific Management* (Madison, WI: University of Wisconsin Press, 1980); and Robert Kanigel, *The One Best Way: Frederick Winslow Taylor and the Enigma of Efficiency* (New York: Viking, 1997).

education was liberally sprinkled with the classics, music, the arts, the study of French and German, and three-and-a-half years' schooling and travel in Europe. His parents originally intended that he follow in his father's footsteps and consider a career in law. Accordingly, in 1872, Taylor (called "Fred" by his friends) entered Phillips Exeter Academy in Exeter, New Hampshire, to prepare for Harvard University. Indicative of the stiff competition among students at Phillips Exeter, one of Taylor's instructor's, George A. Wentworth, used a stopwatch to see which of his students could solve math problems the quickest.[3] Taylor's zeal and restless energy led to late nights and long hours, resulting in vision problems that caused headaches. Due to concerns over his impaired vision, he withdrew from Exeter in March 1874. Despite his failure to graduate, Taylor passed the Harvard University entrance exams 3 months later with honors.[4] Eyeglasses ultimately solved his vision and headache problems. Nonetheless, Taylor decided to turn away from further study. His parents then suggested that he become an engineer. So, at the age of 18, Taylor began an apprenticeship as a machinist and patternmaker for the Enterprise Hydraulic Works (Philadelphia), owned by steam-pump manufacturer Ferrell & Jones.[5] Taylor's decision to become an apprentice was not unusual; upper-class Philadelphians had long been educated in this manner. It was an accepted means of developing elite mechanical engineers. As was customary with apprentices from better-off families, Taylor started his four-year apprenticeship at no wage. During his second and third years, he earned $1.50 a week. By his fourth year he was pocketing the princely sum of $3.00 a week. At Enterprise, Taylor developed empathy for the workers' point of view; he could swear with the best of them and admired the pride they took in their craftsmanship. He noted, however, what he called "bad industrial conditions": worker restriction of output, poor management, and a lack of harmony between labor and management.

TAYLOR AT MIDVALE

Having completed his apprenticeship, Taylor joined the Midvale Steel Company, also located in Philadelphia, in 1878.[6] Midvale specialized in the manufacture of locomotive wheels and railway axles. The economic consequences of the nationwide financial panic of 1873 lingered, and positions were scarce. Taylor consequently took a job as a laborer. Midvale, under the presidency of William Sellers, one of the nineteenth century's most prominent machine-tool inventors, was among the leading steel works of the era.[7] Taylor rose from day laborer to toolroom clerk, to journeyman machinist, to gang boss of machinists, to machine-shop foreman, to master mechanic in charge of all repairs and maintenance, to chief draftsman, and, finally, to chief engineer—all in 6 years.

Taylor's 12 years at Midvale (1878–1890) were a time of experimentation, during which he gained invaluable insights that would be the basis for his later ideas about proper management. Realizing that he lacked a "scientific education," he took a home-study course in mathematics and physics through Harvard University. He then enrolled in a correspondence course offered by the Stevens Institute of Technology (Hoboken, New Jersey). Without ever having been on

[3] Aleksey Tikhomirov, "'The First Case of Scientific Time-Study That I Ever Saw . . .'" *Journal of Management History* 17(4) (2011), pp. 356–378. Wentworth was one of the era's foremost mathematicians and the author of textbooks that sold well over a million copies. He taught at Phillips Exeter for more than 40 years. See "Wentworth, George Albert," in *The National Cyclopædia of American Biography*, vol. 10 (New York: James T. White & Company, 1900), p. 106.

[4] Kanigel, *The One Best Way*, pp. 91,107.

[5] Robert Kanigel, "Frederick Taylor's Apprenticeship," *Wilson Quarterly* 20(3) (Summer 1996), pp. 44–51. See also Andrew W. Dawson, *Lives of the Philadelphia Engineers: Capital, Class, and Revolution, 1830–1890* (Burlington, VT: Ashgate, 2004), pp. 226–246.

[6] Charles D. Wrege and Ronald G. Greenwood, "The Early History of Midvale Steel and the Work of Frederick W. Taylor: 1865–1890," in Lance E. Metz, ed., *Canal History and Technology Proceedings* (1992), pp. 145–176.

[7] Domenic Vitiello, "Engineering the Metropolis: William Sellers, Joseph M. Wilson, and Industrial Philadelphia," *Pennsylvania Magazine of History and Biography* 126(2) (April 2002), pp. 273–303.

campus, except to take his entrance examination and each of his required course examinations, Taylor graduated with a degree in mechanical engineering in 1883. Given that Taylor was able to immediately pass many of his exams in subjects such as French, German, and history due to his experience abroad and to general reading, he was able to graduate in about two-and-a-half years, all the while fulfilling his duties at Midvale.

As Taylor received no formal management training at Midvale, he relied solely on his own experiences in fulfilling his supervisory duties. The company had established a piece-rate pay plan that he knew to be ineffective from his days as a laborer. Midvale's owners believed that laborers would produce more if paid a fixed "piece rate" for each unit produced rather than a flat day rate. When Taylor became gang boss, he learned otherwise. He quickly realized that output was unnecessarily low due to "soldiering" or making only a pretense at working (as described in Chapter 6). Indeed, Taylor estimated that gang output was only one-third of what was possible.

Taylor distinguished between two types of soldiering. "Natural soldiering" proceeded from "the natural instinct and tendency of men to take it easy"; "systematic soldiering" came from the workers' "more intricate second thought and reasoning caused by their relations with other men."[8] Inspiring or forcing workers to come up to the mark could overcome natural soldiering. Systematic soldiering posed a different challenge, and managers had been attempting for years to cope with the tendency of workers to deliberately "underwork." Taylor understood that workers soldiered for several reasons. First, they feared that if they worked faster, they would complete their jobs and be laid off. Second, based on their experience of being paid by the piece, they believed that if they produced more, management would cut the piece rate governing their wages and they would end up doing more work for the same take-home pay. Third, they adhered to rule-of-thumb work methods handed down from generation to generation.[9] Taylor placed the blame on management, not on the workers, for he thought that it was management's responsibility to design jobs properly and offer appropriate performance incentives to overcome worker soldiering.

In no small part, soldiering arose out of a "lump of labor" theory, also discussed in Chapter 6, which held that "the amount of remunerative work to be done in the world is a fixed quantity" and that, by working slowly, the available work could be spread more evenly over a workforce so that all would be employed.[10] A flat daily or hourly wage rate encouraged soldiering, because workers had no incentive to produce more than they had the day before. Pay was based on attendance and position, not on effort. Working harder brought no reward and, thus, workers were encouraged to soldier. Piece-rate systems, in use long before Taylor's time, sought to encourage individual productivity by paying workers based on their output, but such systems had generally been failures; standards were often poorly set, employers cut pay rates as increased output became the norm, and workers hid their shortcut methods to keep management ignorant of how fast work could be performed. Not surprisingly, workers developed a consensus about how much each should produce and earn, not only to protect themselves, but also to avoid sanctions being placed on the less capable. Management was seemingly unaware of the resulting inefficiencies.

---

[8] Frederick W. Taylor, *Shop Management* (New York: Harper & Brothers, 1903), p. 30. Originally published in the *Transactions of the American Society of Mechanical Engineers* 24 (1903), pp. 1337–1456.

[9] Frederick W. Taylor, *The Principles of Scientific Management* (New York: Harper & Brothers, 1911), pp. 15–16. Originally written in 1909 for publication in the *Transactions of the American Society of Mechanical Engineers*, but was withheld because, in part, the meetings committee felt it overstated the "universal applicability" of its claims. Taylor subsequently circulated the book privately in 1911 and arranged for it to be serialized in *American Magazine* 71(5) (March 1911), pp. 570–581; 71(6) (April 1911), pp. 785–793; 72(1) (May 1911), pp. 101–113. For further details, see Carol Carlson Dean, "The Principles of Scientific Management by Frederick W. Taylor: The Private Printing," *Journal of Management History* 3(1) (1997), pp. 18–30.

[10] David F. Schloss, "Why Working-men Dislike Piece-Work," *Economic Review* 1(3) (July 1891), pp. 324–325.

Ida M. Tarbell, one of the era's most noted journalists, offered a glimpse into the working conditions at a typical factory:

> An enormous number of different-sized parts were used in the machines put out by the concern, and is the practice in the average old-fashioned shop these parts, coming from foundry or machine shop, were dumped at any point which was vacant, in the rambling collection of buildings, sheds, and passage-ways. A man never knew exactly where to find any of the parts of the machine he was assembling. Moreover, he never was certain of finding at his machine the tools he had left there the night before.
>
> It was his usual habit to spend the first half hour or more in the morning getting things together and often rowing with his fellows over tools which he believed they had taken from his bench. This is so characteristic a practice that it is no unusual thing for workingmen to hide their tools on leaving the shop at night.[11]

Frederick W. Taylor, circa 1886

Taylor's response to such conditions and his initial experiences as a machine-shop supervisor resulted in a bitter encounter with Midvale's machinists. He told the machinists he knew they could work faster, and he was going to see that they did. Taylor started by showing them how to use metalworking lathes to achieve more output with little additional effort. The machinists refused to follow his instructions. Taylor then turned to training apprentice machinists. Facing entrenched output norms, these machinists promptly disavowed Taylor's methods. Taylor admitted, "I was up against a stone wall. I did not blame . . . these laborers in my heart; my sympathy was with them all of the time."[12] In an effort to force the machinists to work faster to earn the same daily pay, Taylor cut the prevailing piece rate. The machinists retaliated by breaking and jamming their machines and "warned that he had better abandon his practice of going home along a railway track where he could be easily attacked, or else carry arms." Taylor countered by imposing a system of fines (the proceeds going to a worker benefit fund) for damaged equipment and giving notice that "he was going to continue to go on his accustomed way and would go unarmed."[13] After three years, the machinists finally gave in and adopted Taylor's methods. This bitter experience taught Taylor a valuable lesson. He realized a business is a system of human cooperation that will be successful only if everyone involved works toward a common goal. Never again would he impose fines, and he would later establish strict rules against rate cutting. More importantly, Taylor realized a new approach was essential for preventing such bitter labor–management encounters. Taylor set out to develop such an approach.

THE SEARCH FOR SCIENCE IN MANAGEMENT

Taylor thought he could overcome soldiering by determining how each job could be done most efficiently and then establishing performance standards. He believed once workers saw that performance standards had been set "scientifically," rather than on guesswork and tradition, there

[11] Ida M. Tarbell, "The Golden Rule in Business: I. Our New Workshops" *American Magazine* 78(5) (November 1914), p. 14.
[12] *Hearings before Special Committee of the House of Representatives to Investigate the Taylor and Other Systems of Shop Management under Authority of House Resolution 90*, vol. 3 (Washington, DC: U.S. Government Printing Office, 1912), p. 1413.
[13] "The Father of Scientific Management," *The Outlook* 109 (March 31, 1915), p. 755.

could be no appeal and their motivation to soldier would be eliminated. The problem was in defining "a fair day's work" for each job. Taylor set out to determine what the workers *ought* to be able to produce with their equipment and materials. This was the beginning of what was to be called "scientific management"; that is, the application of the scientific method to empirically establish the most efficient way to perform a job. He was not asking workers to produce more with the same effort, but more with improved methods. Taylor had concluded that labor–management conflict was due to ignorance on both sides. Management expected, and workers were ready to provide, "a fair day's work" for "a fair day's pay." Neither side, however, knew what constituted a day's work. Both relied on vague impressions that led to continuing disputes.

Recalling Taylor's Phillips Exeter teacher George A. Wentworth's practice of timing students as they solved math problems, time study became the foundation of Taylor's work. With a stopwatch, weight scale, and tape measure, he literally calculated the distances workers and material traveled. Gradually, he determined that a large share of both effort and materials was needlessly wasted. Some critics would question the originality of Taylor's work. Charles Babbage had previously used a watch to record the labor operations and times necessary for manufacturing pins.[14] In 1912, a subcommittee of the American Society of Mechanical Engineers (ASME) issued a report on time study that made no mention of Taylor's work, but referenced Babbage and Adam Smith (see Chapter 2). Taylor contributed to a discussion of this report to clarify his concept of time study and answer those who doubted the originality of his work.

> Time study was begun in the machine shop of the Midvale Steel Company in 1881. . . . It is true that the form of Tables 1 and 2 [from Babbage's 1835 book *Economy of Machinery and Manufacture*] is similar to that of the blanks recording time study, but here the resemblance ceases. Each line in Table 2, for instance, gives statistics regarding the average of the entire work of an operative who works day in and day out, in running a machine engaged in the manufacture of pins. This table involves no study whatever of the movements of the man, nor of the time in which the movements *should* have been made. Mere statistics as to the time which a man takes to do a given piece of work do not constitute "time study." "Time study," as its name implies, involves a careful study of the time in which work *ought* to be done . . . [rather than] the time in which the work actually was done.[15]

Unlike Babbage, Taylor used time study for inferential rather than descriptive purposes. Rather than simply describe "what is," Taylor used time study to discover "what was possible" in improving job performance. Taylor's time study had two phases: *analysis* and *synthesis*. In analysis, each job was broken into its elementary movements. Nonessential movements were discarded, and the remainder carefully examined to determine the quickest and least wasteful means of performing a job. These elementary motions were then described, recorded, and indexed, along with the amount of time required to cover unavoidable delays, minor accidents, and rest. In the second stage, synthesis, the elementary movements were combined in the correct sequence to determine the time and the exact method for performing a job. This phase also led to improvements in tools, machines, materials, methods, and the ultimate standardization of all elements surrounding and accompanying a job.[16]

More recently, in a further attack on the originality of Taylor's work, it has become fashionable to draw a link between plantation management in the southern United States during the antebellum period (1815–1861) and scientific management. Specifically, some have seen a relationship between the labor and accounting practices used by southern slaveholders and Taylor's methods.[17] This view contrasts with the position of business historian Alfred D. Chandler that

[14] Charles Babbage, *On the Economy of Machinery and Manufacturers* (London: Charles Knight, 1832), pp. 138–152.
[15] *Ibid.*, p. 226.
[16] Taylor, *Shop Management*, pp. 149–176.
[17] Caitlin Rosenthal, "Slavery's Scientific Management: Masters and Managers," in Sven Beckert and Seth E. Rockman, eds., *Slavery's Capitalism: A New History of American Economic Development* (Philadelphia, PA: University of Pennsylvania Press, 2016), pp. 62–86.

the plantations of the antebellum South were "an ancient form of production" and "had little impact on the evolution of the management of modern business enterprise" in the United States.[18] Although Chandler did not specify what he meant by "ancient," by looking back at slavery in the Roman world, it is evident that the labor and accounting practices used by southern slaveholders were, in fact, a remnant of an antiquated form of production. With respect to labor practices, to suggest that there is a connection between the inhumane means used by southern planters to maximize slave output and Taylor's quest for improved performance through scientific investigation is unfounded. As will be recounted, Taylor firmly believed that the concerns of employee and employer should be based on a "mutuality of interests," and sought to develop labor practices that gave both parties satisfaction. Further, the claimed link between how southern planters used accounting to maximize their profit margins and scientific management is equally feeble. The owners of larger southern plantations did keep account books to increase their income. The Romans dating back to Caesar Augustus (63 BCE–14 CE), however, maintained similar financial and inventory registers.[19] How the use of account books on southern plantations ties antebellum slavery to Taylor's use of cost accounting (as discussed below) to classify expenses, distribute overhead costs, and improve material handling and control rather than to ancient Rome, as Chandler suggests, is unexplained. It might also be noted that "[t]he more typical small plantations [in the antebellum South] were one step up from the 19th-century shop that ran on a ledger of credit, or just a box of cash."[20] Records were kept, "but these were in many cases unsystematic and incomplete."[21] This lack of attention to detail would have been profoundly inconsistent with Taylor's methods. In sum, the extent to which antebellum slavery and scientific management are similar belies the fact that all modes of production—slavery, communism/socialism, capitalism—are influenced by common factors and share common features.

THE QUEST FOR IMPROVED PERFORMANCE INCENTIVES

The search for effective performance incentives for increasing output is probably as old as humanity.[22] Piecework, or paying a fixed rate for each unit produced, was the basis of the "putting-out" or domestic system of production, and was used before and during the Industrial Revolution (see Chapter 3). As U.S. industry developed after the War Between the States, numerous pay schemes were proposed. These included Henry Towne's gain sharing and Frederick Halsey's premium plan (see Chapter 6). In a paper presented to the ASME in 1895, Taylor criticized both the Towne and Halsey plans and proposed a new alternative.[23] He felt that a weakness in both the Towne and Halsey plans was that they took present worker output as their performance standard. In contrast, Taylor proposed a new three-part plan: (1) observation and analysis through time study to set output standards and pay rates; (2) a differential piecework system in which a higher rate *per piece* is paid if work is done in less time than specified, and a lower rate is paid if it is done in more time than allowed; and (3) "paying men and not positions." This plan extended an earlier piecework system developed in 1875 by Charles A. Brinley at Midvale Steel.

In Taylor's opinion, profit sharing failed because it discouraged personal ambition by allowing all to share in profits regardless of their contribution, and because of the "remoteness of the

---

[18] Chandler, *The Visible Hand*, p. 66.

[19] Jacob Soll, *The Reckoning: Financial Accountability and the Rise and Fall of Nations* (New York: Basic Books, 2014), pp. 5–8.

[20] Louis R. Hyman, [Review of the book *Accounting for Slavery: Masters and Management*] *ILR Review* 73(1) (January 2020), p. 241.

[21] Alan L. Olmstead and Paul W. Rhode, "Were Antebellum Cotton Plantations Factories in the Field?" in William J. Collins and Robert A. Margo, eds., *Enterprising America: Businesses, Banks, and Credit Markets in Historical Perspective* (Chicago, IL: University of Chicago Press, 2015), p. 272.

[22] E. Brian Peach and Daniel A. Wren, "Pay for Performance from Antiquity to the 1950s," *Journal of Organizational Behavior Management* 12(1) (Spring 1991), pp. 5–26.

[23] Frederick W. Taylor, "A Piece-Rate System, Being a Step Toward Partial Solution of the Labor Problem," *Transactions of the American Society of Mechanical Engineers* 16 (1895), pp. 856–883. See also Wrege and Greenwood, *Frederick W. Taylor, the Father of Scientific Management*, p. 20.

reward." In recognizing this shortcoming, Taylor showed an appreciation of Aristotle's (383–322 BCE) *principle of temporal contiguity*; that is, in conditioning behavior, timing is important in establishing a connection between a stimulus and a response.[24] In Taylor's view, sharing profits at the end of a year gave little incentive for improved daily performance.

In his 1895 ASME paper, Taylor had clearly put the onus on management to establish daily output standards rather than follow the established practice of allowing workers to determine how jobs should be performed. In commenting on the audience remarks that followed his paper presentation, Taylor said he was "much surprised and disappointed that elementary rate-fixing has not received more attention during the discussion."[25] In Taylor's view, those present evidently did not realize that proper performance standards had to be determined before establishing a fair piece-rate. Under Taylor's plan, a special department analyzed each job and then set a performance standard and pay scale instead of relying on guesswork and tradition. Taylor's notion of "paying men rather than positions" partially addressed soldiering but was primarily intended to reward individual initiative. Taylor also understood he was dealing with humans as well as material and machines. He readily acknowledged, "There is another type of scientific investigation . . . which should receive special attention, namely, the accurate study of the motives which influence men."[26]

Taylor's 1895 ASME paper also outlined his initial view of unions, especially with respect to regulating wages and conditions of employment:

> The [author] is far from taking the view held by many manufacturers that labor unions are an almost unmitigated detriment to those who join them, as well as to employers and the general public.
>
> The labor unions . . . have rendered a great service not only to their members, but to the world, in shortening the hours of labor and in modifying the hardships and improving the conditions of wage-workers. . . .
>
> When employers herd their men together in classes, pay all of each class the same wages, and offer them any inducements to work harder or do better than the average, the only remedy for the men lies in combination; and frequently the only possible answer to encroachments on the part of their employers is a strike.
>
> This state of affairs is far from satisfactory and the writer believes the system of regulating wages and conditions of employment of whole classes of men by conference and agreement between the leaders, unions and manufacturers to be vastly inferior . . . to the plan of stimulating each workman's ambition by paying him according to his individual worth, and without limiting him to the rate of work or pay of the average of his class.[27]

Taylor, thus, in his early writing, saw no need for unions under his piece-rate pay plan. Unions, to foster class solidarity, insisted that their members all be treated the same. For Taylor, this prevented union members from fulfilling their personal ambitions. Rather than encouraging workers to better themselves, in Taylor's mind, unions stifled individual initiative. Taylor's view of unions, however, would evolve over time.

Taylor's comments on properly setting performance standards, establishing a fair piece rate, and harmony between labor and management anticipated his assertion that the concerns of employee and employer should be based on a "mutuality of interests." Countering the assumption that if workers earned more, they did so at their employer's expense, Taylor advocated a system that would benefit both employer and employee. In doing so, he addressed the contradiction inherent in the "paradox of high wages and low costs," involving two concepts which, on the

---

[24] Aristotle, *Aristotle's Psychology: A Treatise on the Principle of Life (De Anima* [*On the Soul*] and *Parva Naturalia* [*Short Treatises on Nature*]), trans. William A. Hammond (London: Swan Sonnenschein & Co., 1902), p. 205n2, 208–210. Written circa 350 BCE.

[25] Taylor, "Piece-Rate System," pp. 902–903.

[26] *Idem*, *Principles of Scientific Management*, p. 119.

[27] *Idem*, "Piece-Rate System," p. 882; *idem*, *Shop Management*, pp. 185–186.

surface, appear to be diametrically opposed (see Chapter 6). Rather than encouraging employers to buy the cheapest labor and pay the lowest wages possible in the belief that high wage rates were accompanied by high per-unit costs, Taylor encouraged the opposite: his findings showed that high wages could be associated with low costs. Taylor advocated paying first-class workers a high wage, thereby encouraging them to produce more under standard, efficient conditions with no greater expenditure of effort. The result would be greater productivity and, hence, lower per-unit costs, making higher wages possible. Taylor reasoned that high wages and low costs were possible by using scientific principles to empirically establish the most efficient way to perform each worker's job. Throughout history, it had been taken as self-evident that workers could produce more only by working harder or longer. Taylor showed that the real potential for increased output was not "working harder" but "working smarter." Toward this end, Taylor said that management should strive to ensure that each workman:

> *(a)* . . . be given as far as possible the highest grade of work for which his ability and physique fit him.
>
> *(b)* . . . be called upon to turn out the maximum amount of work which a first-rate man of his class can do and thrive.
>
> *(c)* . . . when he works at the best pace of a first-class man, . . . be paid from 30 percent. to 100 percent. according to the nature of the work which he does, beyond the average of his class.[28]

The notion that workmen should be given the highest grade of work to perform based on their ability indicated that Taylor was aware of the need to match abilities to job requirements. As he explained:

> It becomes the duty of those on the management's side to deliberately study the character, the nature, and the performance of each workman, with a view to finding out his limitations on the one hand, but even more important, his possibilities for development on the other hand; and then, as deliberately and as systematically to train and help and teach this workman, giving him, wherever it is possible, those opportunities for advancement which will finally enable him to do the highest and most interesting and most profitable class of work for which his natural abilities fit him, and which are open to him in the particular company in which he is employed. This scientific selection of the workman and his development is not a single act; it goes on from year to year and is the subject of continual study on the part of the management.[29]

To this, Taylor later added: "Scientific management does not come into existence until the owners of the establishment, all of the managers of the establishment, have the building up of their men, the development of their men, as absolutely the first thought in their minds."[30]

Taylor's use of the term "first-class man," however, caused him much grief, especially when explaining it to others. In testimony before a special committee of the U.S. House of Representatives charged with investigating "the Taylor and other systems of shop management," Taylor defined what it meant to be a "first-class man" by describing a workman who did not meet his definition:

> I believe the only man who does not come under "first class" as I have defined it, is the man who can work and won't work. I have tried to make it clear that for each type of workman some job can be found at which he is "first class," with the exception of those men who are perfectly well able to do the job but won't do it.[31]

---

[28] *Idem*, *Shop Management*, pp. 28–29.

[29] *Hearings before Special Committee of the House of Representatives to Investigate the Taylor and Other Systems of Shop Management*, vol. 3, p. 1456.

[30] Frederick W. Taylor, "Competitive Profit Sharing," *Greater Efficiency: Journal of the Efficiency Society* 3(6) (March 1914), pp. 25–26.

[31] *Hearings to Investigate the Taylor System*, vol. 3, p. 1451.

Under these terms, non-first-class workmen would be those who were physically or mentally unsuited for the work to which they had been assigned (in which case they should be retrained or transferred to another job for which they were suited) or who were unwilling to give it their best. In setting pay rates for each job, Taylor wrote that performance standards should be set at the pace a first-class worker "can keep up for a long term of years without injury to his health. It is a pace under which men become happier and thrive."[32] Taylor anticipated what today is considered sound human-resource management; that is, matching workers' abilities to assigned jobs.

It was management's task to identify the work that employees were best suited to perform and provide them with incentives to give their best. Taylor's views on first-class workers were intertwined with his personal philosophy of "*the will to get there*," the success drive that was the basis of his own life. It was Taylor's observation that individuals "differ not so much in brains as in will, in spirit."[33] First-class workers were people with ambition and who were suited to their work. They were not superhumans, as the term later came to connote.

TASK MANAGEMENT

Taylor's task management extended the systematic-management movement that emerged in the nineteenth century as the scale and scope of businesses grew. It focused on establishing an orderly workflow, determining the quickest and least wasteful means of performing different tasks, training workers in how tasks could be performed more efficiently, and monitoring time, cost, and quality of performance. Time study did not ask workers to do more in the same way, but to use the most appropriate movements and best materials and equipment to meet scientifically determined performance standards. Moreover, Taylor was committed to continued improvement and, as noted above, was open to suggestions from all corners, including workers. As he further explained, he approached workers by saying:

> We do not know the best . . . but what we know is the result of a long series of experiments and careful study of every element connected with shop practice; these standards that lie before you are the results of these studies. We ask you to learn how to use these standards as they are, and after that, the moment any man sees an improved standard, a better way of doing anything than we are doing, come to us with it; your suggestion will not only be welcome but we will join you in making a carefully tried experiment. . . . If that experiment shows that your method is better, your method will become our method and every one of us will adopt that method until somebody gets a better one.[34]

Taylor defined management as "knowing exactly what you want men to do, and then seeing that they do it in the best and cheapest way." He added that no concise definition could fully describe the art of management, but that "the relations between employers and men form without question the most important part of this art."[35] Taylor saw unevenness in traditional shop management and foremen who lacked the special knowledge necessary to plan, teach, and supervise workers. As a remedy, he proposed that workers be instructed by teachers known as "functional foremen," who would bring specialized knowledge to the workplace.[36] As a foreman at Midvale,

---

[32] Taylor, *Shop Management*, p. 25.
[33] *Copley, Taylor*, vol. 1, p. 183.
[34] Frederick W. Taylor, "The Principles of Scientific Management," in *Addresses and Discussion at the Conference on Scientific Management Held October 12, 13, 14, Nineteen Hundred Eleven* (Hanover, NH: Dartmouth Press, 1911), p. 54.
[35] Taylor, *Shop Management*, p. 21.
[36] *Ibid*., p. 138. The term "foreman" dates to the fourteenth century, originating in the trade guilds of Europe. "In those days when the men wanted to talk to management, there was always someone of mature judgment, probably a little older, a well-skilled man, who could talk a little on his feet. When the men got together, they referred to 'John Anderson, fore'; and he became the foreman; he was the man who came to the fore; therefore, he was a foreman." Testimony of Clarence C. Carlton, *Hearings Before the Committee on Military Affairs, U.S. House of Representatives*, 78th Congress, 1st sess. on H. R. 2239, H. R. 1742, H. R. 1728, and H. R. 922, *Full Utilization of Manpower*, March 31, 1943 (Washington, DC: Government Printing Office, 1943), p. 104.

Taylor employed assistants to prepare instruction cards and perform other associated clerical duties. Over time, he gave these assistants more and more responsibility and additional duties. The typical manager of this period was not considered much of a planner, and Taylor sought to overcome this shortcoming by creating a planning department.

In the planning department, an "order of work route clerk" determined workflow and the most efficient assignment of workers and machines, and an "instruction card clerk" furnished written information on necessary tools and materials, the prevailing piece rate, performance premium, and other operating directions. A "time and cost clerk" maintained time tickets and recorded the costs associated with each work order, and a "shop disciplinarian" kept a record of each worker's "virtues and defects"; served as a "peacemaker"; and selected and discharged employees, as necessary. Foremen could no longer hire or fire workers or assign tasks.

Taylor realized that this division of responsibilities required that workers be properly trained. He thus saw "the necessity of systematically teaching workmen how to work to the best advantage."[37] Taylor sought "expert teachers"—chosen for their knowledge, skill, and experience—to become functional foremen. One teacher (the inspector) was responsible for output quality; a second teacher (the gang boss) was in charge of all work up to the time it was machined; a third teacher (the speed boss) took over while work was being machined, and determined the proper tools and cutting operations; and a fourth teacher (the repair boss) was in charge of machinery care and maintenance.[38]

Functional foremen (Figure 7.1) replaced the traditional single foreman with four clerks responsible for planning and four teachers for instructing and monitoring shop performance. Instruction would be individualized: "All workmen engaged in the same kind of work do not require the same amount of individual teaching and attention," depending on aptitude and experience. Taylor added there were opportunities for worker suggestions: "Whenever a workman proposes an improvement, it should be the policy of management to make a careful analysis of the new [proposed] method [and] . . . whenever the new method is markedly superior to the old, it should be adopted [and] . . . the workman should be paid a cash premium for his ingenuity."[39]

Functional foremanship was appropriate for exercising specialized knowledge and instructing workers in new methods and motions. It, however, made coordinating different workshop activities more difficult, as no one person had responsibility for overall workshop performance.

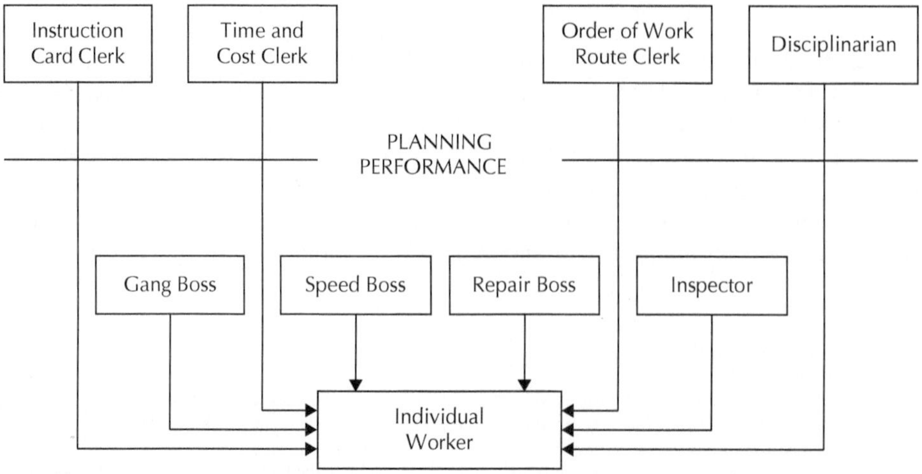

FIGURE 7.1 Taylor's functional foremen

Adapted from Frank B. and Lillian M. Gilbreth, *Applied Motion Study*, New York, NY: Sturgis & Walton Co., 1917, preceding p. 23.

[37] Taylor, *Principles of Scientific Management*, p. 122.
[38] *Ibid.*, pp. 123–124.
[39] *Ibid.*, pp. 125, 128.

This appears to be a violation of the "unity of command" principle—that is, no person should report to more than one superior so as to eliminate the possibility of receiving conflicting orders. Taylor believed that this would not generally occur, as workers were responsible to only one boss/clerk for each activity. In situations where conflicts did arise, Taylor stipulated that an over-foreman be consulted and, if a conflict could not then be settled, an assistant superintendent was to arbitrate any outstanding differences. Where initially this would delay production, Taylor held that over time an "unwritten code of laws by which the shop is governed" would be established.[40] It has been noted that by increasing the number of staff positions in an organization, functional foremanship offered workers additional opportunities for advancement. That said, it has been generally believed that efficiency demands keeping the proportion of employees performing administrative or support roles to a minimum. For Taylor, however, [t]he proper level of staff was whatever number it took to keep capital-intensive machinery running full and fast."[41]

Despite Taylor's endorsement, functional foremanship never became widespread in practice. It offered a limited view of planning, and the unwritten code Taylor believed would develop for shop governance all too often failed to materialize. Functional foremanship, however, has evolved into the present, and specialized knowledge is now exercised through *functional authority* over specialized tasks rather than over individual workers. The value of staff specialists in helping general managers juggle their many demands would be recognized as organizations grew in complexity. This would especially be the case when it came to dealing with either specialized areas (such a legal matters) or significant exceptions from planned performance. In this way, those activities requiring specialized knowledge or immediate attention (the "exceptions") could be promptly and knowledgably addressed. An emphasis on the "exception principle" was one of Taylor's most important contributions:

> Under it the manager should receive only condensed, summarized, and *invariably* comparative reports, covering . . . all of the exceptions to past averages or to the standards . . . both the especially good and especially bad exceptions . . . leaving him free to consider broader lines of policy and to study the character and fitness of the important men under him.[42]

Taylor believed that all authority should be based on knowledge, not position or title, and that the exception principle would improve efficiency by allowing managers time to focus on their most pressing and significant concerns over both the long and short term.

TAYLOR: THE MANAGER AND THE CONSULTANT

Taylor's years at Midvale Steel had been full: increasing responsibilities and numerous promotions; teaming with his boyhood friend and future brother-in-law, Clarence M. Clark, to win the inaugural U.S. National Lawn Tennis Association's amateur doubles championship in 1881 at Newport (RI); earning a mechanical engineering degree from Stevens Institute in 1883; marrying Louise M. Spooner in 1884; experimenting on cutting metals and machine belting; and developing the essentials of task management all made for a busy 12 years. In 1890, he left Midvale to join the Manufacturing Investment Company (MIC), a paper-fiber manufacturer owned by financier J. Pierpont Morgan and other investors.[43] Taylor's experiences as superintendent at MIC's newest mill, in Madison, Maine, were far from satisfactory. He felt that the mill's difficulties were due to a new papermaking process it had installed, whereas its owners believed that Taylor lacked the broad executive experience necessary to make the process operational. In May 1893,

[40] *Idem, Shop Management*, pp. 108–109.
[41] James E. Hoopes, *The False Prophets* (Cambridge, MA: Perseus Books, 2003), p. 47.
[42] *Ibid.*, p. 126.
[43] Daniel M. Nelson, "Scientific Management in Transition: Frederick W. Taylor at Johnstown, 1896," *Pennsylvania Magazine of History and Biography* 99(4) (October 1975), pp. 460–475. See also *idem*, "The Making of a Progressive Engineer: Frederick W. Taylor," *Pennsylvania Magazine of History and Biography* 103(4) (October 1979), pp. 446–466.

Taylor resigned from MIC. The Madison mill closed the following month. In later years, Taylor expressed contempt for financiers who had "absolutely no pride of manufacture" and were interested only in "making money quickly."[44] Taylor's experience at MIC would not be his last encounter with owners who, in Taylor's opinion, were resistant to change and only interested in an immediate return on their investments. MIC filed for bankruptcy in 1899.

Taylor's contempt for financiers aside, he did come away from MIC with a more complete understanding of cost accounting and, in particular, reducing business expenses. During Taylor's tenure at MIC, R. Somers Hayes, a former railroad manager, had revamped the company's accounting system and hired William D. Basley, an experienced railroad accountant, to oversee the system. Basley had worked for the Newark and Hudson Railroad, which was controlled by the Erie Railway, where Daniel C. McCallum had developed accounting and reporting systems in the 1850s (see Chapter 5). Taylor was impressed by Hayes's and Basley's methods, which would later form the basis of his own accounting system.[45] With his newly acquired knowledge of accounting and his engineering background, Taylor decided to become a consulting engineer for management.

One of Taylor's consulting clients was the Johnson Company (Johnstown, Pennsylvania). Asked, in 1896, to increase the efficiency of the Steel Motor Works and the Lorain Steel Railway Company, both subsidiaries of the Johnson Company, Taylor developed a system to track the cost of raw materials. He also devised a routing chart showing how all the parts composing the Steel Motor Works' principal product, electrical streetcar motors, were assembled.[46] Taylor worked closely with Tom L. Johnson, the Johnson Company's founder; Arthur J. Moxham, who worked in the company's comptroller's office; and T. Coleman du Pont, company general manager. Moxham, together with Lorain Steel's Pierre du Pont, later adopted Taylor's cost-accounting system at the E. I. du Pont de Nemours and Company.[47] Alfred D. Chandler has suggested that it is likely that General Electric Company was also influenced by Taylor's cost and routing procedures.[48]

Another of Taylor's clients was Simonds Rolling Machine Company in Fitchburg, Massachusetts, where, in 1897, Taylor conducted experiments in the manufacture of bicycle ball-bearings. In the final stage of the manufacturing process, 120 women inspected ball-bearings for flaws. Over time, Taylor gradually shortened the workday from ten-and-a-half hours to eight-and-a-half, introduced morning and afternoon rest periods, identified the best inspectors, and put the women on a piecework-pay schedule. The interaction of these changes was complex, and it would be difficult to match causes and results. The outcome, however, was that 35 women were able to do the work previously done by 120. Output increased from 5 million to 17 million bearings per month, inspection accuracy improved by two-thirds, wages were averaging 80 to 100 percent higher for fewer hours, and "[e]ach girl was made to feel that she was the object of especial care and interest on the part of the management."[49] While at Simonds, Taylor also introduced his own accounting system to classify expenses, distribute overhead costs, and improve material handling and control.

---

[44] Letter from Frederick W. Taylor to Holden A. Evans, October 23, 1911, p. 3. *Frederick W. Taylor Collection*, SCW.001. Archives and Special Collections; Samuel C. Williams Library, Stevens Institute of Technology, Hoboken, NJ.

[45] Charles D. Wrege, "Nineteenth Century Origins of 'Bookkeeping under the Taylor System,'" in Kae H. Chung, ed., *Proceedings of the Annual Meeting of the Academy of Management* (1983), pp. 106–110. See also Nelson, *Frederick W. Taylor and the Rise of Scientific Management*, pp. 54–55; Rosita S. Chen and Sheng-Der Pan, "Frederick Winslow Taylor's Contributions to Accounting," *Accounting Historians Journal* 7(1) (Spring 1980), pp. 17–35; *idem*, "Frederick Winslow Taylor's Contributions to Cost Accounting, A Reply" *Accounting Historians Journal* 11(1) (Spring 1984), pp. 151–161; and Murray C. Wells, "Taylor's Contributions to Cost Accounting: A Comment," *Accounting Historians Journal* 9(2) (Fall 1982), pp. 69–77.

[46] Michael Massouh, "Technological and Managerial Innovation: The Johnson Company, 1883–1889," *Business History Review* 50(1) (Spring 1976), pp. 66–67.

[47] H. Thomas Johnson, "Management Accounting in an Early Integrated Industrial: E. I. Du Pont de Nemours Powder Company, 1903–1912," *Business History Review* 49(2) (Summer 1975), p. 194.

[48] Alfred D. Chandler, Jr. *The Visible Hand: The Managerial Revolution in American Business* (Cambridge, MA: Belknap Press of Harvard University Press, 1977), p. 430.

[49] Taylor, *Principles of Scientific Management*, p. 95. See also Christopher T. Nyland, "Taylorism and Hours of Work," *Journal of Management History* 1(2) (1995), pp. 8–25.

Taylor's most challenging and controversial consulting assignment was for the Bethlehem Iron Company in South Bethlehem, Pennsylvania.[50] Taylor came to Bethlehem Iron (later Bethlehem Steel Company) in May 1898, at the request of its largest stockholder, Joseph Wharton, who sought Taylor's assistance in decreasing the company's overhead costs and improving its overall efficiency. At the time, Bethlehem's management was under federal investigation for overcharging and price colluding on defense contracts for heavy cannon and armor plate. The Spanish-American War had begun the previous month, following the sinking of the battleship *Maine* in Havana Harbor, Cuba. From Taylor's initial hiring, the company's top managers resented his assertiveness. Taylor felt that many of the top managers were unqualified, having gained their positions due to family connections rather than their ability. After much opposition, Taylor was finally able to convince Bethlehem's owners to reorganize the company, but not without further alienating the company's top managers. These managers, in turn, sought every opportunity to subvert Taylor's efforts.

Taylor organized a tool crib–parts storeroom, established a central planning department, and implemented the cost-accounting system he had developed for Steel Motor Works. As described by one source, the tool crib–parts storeroom itself "became a complex organization. Cutting heads alone, with their different shapes ground to different angles, were too numerous for casual handling, and then there were the drill bits, borers, hammers, gauges, chains, clamps, blocks, bolts, nuts, and washers, all of many different sizes. Taylor arranged these thousands of items in logically ordered bins, trays, drawers, cabinets, and racks, with an elaborate system for checking them in and out, Once returned, each tool was inspected and if necessary reground, rethreaded, or reset to ensure efficient use by the next man." Commenting on the planning department, the same source commented: "For each job, the Planning Department made up a list of tools for a clerk to collect in a wooden box. A 'tool messenger' carried the box to the machinist. So that he had all the tools needed when he turned to the instruction card for his next job." As Taylor reasoned, "if the machinist was to keep his expensive lathe running at the most productive rate, he could not be wasting his time searching for tools. By hiring clerks and couriers to keep track of tools and carry them to the machinists, [it was] possible for an operator to stay at his lathe steadily turning out the highest possible number of pieces across which to spread the machine's cost."[51] To assist in his work, Taylor brought in Sanford E. Thompson, who had probably conducted more time studies than Taylor ever dreamed possible; Henry L. Gantt, who had worked with Taylor at Midvale; Carl G. Barth, a mathematics whiz; Dwight V. Merrick, who became a leading authority on time study; James Gillespie, who had been involved with time studies at Simonds Rolling Machine Company; and J. Maunsell White III, a metallurgist and fellow Stevens Institute graduate, who had earlier helped Taylor with a series of metal-cutting experiments discussed below.

With an increase in the demand for steel spurred on by the continued westward movement of the nation's railroads, the price of pig iron, which is a raw material for making steel, rose sharply in 1899.[52] In response, Bethlehem sold 10,000 tons from its inventory. Shipping the iron by rail required that it be manually loaded onto gondola cars. The iron had been cast as 92-pound ingots, or "pigs," each measuring 32-inches in length, 4-inches in width, and 4.5-inches in height. At the time, Taylor and Thompson were planning to prepare a handbook on the elements of work. The required loading provided an opportunity for them to gather information for the handbook on the time required to perform this type of work. Taylor asked James Gillespie and Hartley C. Wolle to collect the desired information. The workers who loaded the pig iron were known as "pig-iron handlers." They were paid a fixed piece rate for each ton loaded. Gillespie and Wolle selected 10 of the "very best men" and ordered them to work at "maximum speed." During the

[50] Daniel M. Nelson, "Taylorism and the Workers at Bethlehem Steel, 1898–1901," *Pennsylvania Magazine of History and Biography* 101(4) (October 1977), pp. 487–505.

[51] Hoopes, *The False Prophets*, pp. 47, 46.

[52] *Annual Statistical Report of the American Iron and Steel Association* (Philadelphia, PA: American Iron and Steel Association, 1900), p. 20.

first 10-hour day, the workers loaded 75 long tons each (2,240 pounds = a long ton), filling one gondola car. The tons loaded per day had previously averaged about 12.5 long tons per worker. Based on these figures, Gillespie and Wolle, factoring in time for unavoidable delays and rest, set a new output standard at 45 long tons per worker per day. Taylor then set the piece rate at $.0375 per ton, which meant that the first-class worker who met the new 45 long ton–standard would earn $1.85 per day. Because the average flat day rate for a common laborer at Bethlehem was $1.15 per 10-hour day, the new piece rate represented a more than 60 percent increase in pay.

Taylor used the pig iron–handling story to illustrate the savings that could come from carefully examining even menial jobs. On June 4, 1907, a court stenographer was hired to transcribe a talk Taylor gave at his Philadelphia home, which he called Boxly. Taylor described how he selected one of the pig handlers for Gillespie and Wolle to study: "I picked out a Pennsylvania Dutchman . . . and said 'Noll are you a high priced man?'"[53] Henry Knolle (later changed to Noll) became the focal point of Taylor's comments on how to secure higher performance by paying workers on a "piece rate." Noll was then 27 years old, 5 feet 7 in. tall, and weighed 135 pounds. He was singled out because he had been observed trotting "back home for a mile or so after his work in the evening . . . [and was known as someone who placed] a very high value on a dollar."[54]

When *The Principles of Scientific Management* was published, Noll became "Schmidt" in Taylor's account of how the Pennsylvania Dutchman was convinced to load 47.5 tons of pig iron per day. Although the story of Schmidt has entered the management literature as an example of Taylor's scientific study of work, its veracity has been challenged. Charles D. Wrege and Amadeo G. Perroni examined various versions of Taylor's story, as well as a report prepared by Gillespie and Wolle, and noted numerous discrepancies. Among these discrepancies were the reasons for Bethlehem selling pig iron from its inventory, the amount to be loaded, the method of loading, the number of pig-iron handlers, how the workers were selected, and so on. Wrege and Perroni reached the conclusion that the Schmidt story was, to borrow their phrase, a "pig-tale," an embellishment by Taylor of the truth.[55] Over the years, evidence has mounted to suggest that, as judged by Barth, Taylor "greatly exaggerated what had been accomplished at Bethlehem."[56]

Taylor's intent may have been to use pig-iron handling to illustrate the application of scientific management to even menial jobs requiring only physical labor, but he omitted facts that more fully conveyed what occurred. As reported by Gillespie and Wolle, there were three "first-class" workers, not one. Joseph Auer and Simon Conrad joined Noll in this elite group. At times, Conrad loaded more tons than Noll: on June 1, 1899, 70.7 long tons for Conrad, 48 long tons for Noll; on June 2, 1899, 55.7 long tons for Conrad, 68.3 for Noll; and on June 3, 1899, 70.9 long tons for Conrad, 39.7 for Noll, and 30.1 long tons for Auer. The story of Schmidt, as told by Cooke and retold by Taylor, oversimplified what took place at Bethlehem, but made the power of Taylor's methods more memorable. Some may think that Auer, Conrad, and Noll were exploited,

[53] Charles D. Wrege, "F. W. Taylor's Lecture on Management, 4 June 1907, An Introduction," *Journal of Management History* 1(1) (1995), pp. 4–7; the stenographer's transcript follows on pp. 8–32.

[54] Taylor, *Principles of Scientific Management*, pp. 43–44. See also James Gillespie and Herman C. Wolle, "Report on the Establishment of Piecework in Connection with the Loading of Pig Iron, at the Works of the Bethlehem Iron Co., South Bethlehem, PA," June 17, 1899, *Frederick W. Taylor Collection*, SCW.001. Archives and Special Collections; Samuel C. Williams Library, Stevens Institute of Technology, Hoboken, NJ.

[55] Charles D. Wrege and Amadeo G. Perroni, "Taylor's Pig-Tale: A Historical Analysis of Frederick W. Taylor's Pig-Iron Experiment," *Academy of Management Journal* 17 (March 1974), pp. 6–26. Later, Wrege and Greenwood, in *Frederick W. Taylor, the Father of Scientific Management,* p. 102, wrote that the "pig-tale" was "prepared by Taylor's assistant, Morris L. Cooke." The mystery remains, as the penmanship was Cooke's, but were the words Cooke's or Taylor's? See also Charles D. Wrege and Regina A. Greenwood, "Frederick W. Taylor's 'Pig Iron Loading Observations' at Bethlehem, March 10, 1899–May 31, 1899: The Real Story," in Lance E. Metz, ed., *Canal History and Technology Proceedings* (1998), pp. 159–201; Charles D. Wrege and Beulah M. Wrege, "Searching for the Insignificant: Thirty-Eight Years of Successful Historical Research in Bethlehem, Pennsylvania, and Elsewhere: 1957–1995," in Lance E. Metz, ed., *Canal History and Technology Proceedings* (2004), pp. 155–212.

[56] Letter from Carl G. Barth to L. Arthur Sylvester, December 21, 1925, Charles D. Wrege Research Papers, 1925–2013, Series III: Frederick W. Taylor, Collection Number: 6395, Box 6, Folder 65, Kheel Center for Labor-Management Documentation and Archives, Catherwood Library, Cornell University. See also "Conversation at Boxly by Frederick Taylor, 1907," annotated by Carl G. Barth. Papers of Carl G. Barth and his son J. Christian Barth, Carton: 1, Folder: 2 Identifier: Mss:708, Baker Library, Harvard University Business School, Boston, MA.

working day in and day out to achieve the new piece rate. They, however, never worked more than three days without going back to a flat day-rate. Indeed, for the duration of the pig-iron study, March 10 to May 31, 1899, records indicate that Conrad and Noll worked a total of 36 days on the new piece rate and 41 on the flat day-rate.[57]

Although Taylor referred frequently to the pig-iron study as a success, its design was less than ideal, making it difficult to draw firm conclusions regarding the effects of the new piece rate. Gillespie and Wolle arbitrarily set a 40 percent time allowance for rests and delays; Taylor likewise did so for the per-ton piece rate; and Noll and the other pig-iron handlers studied were not randomly selected. Even so, the results were impressive: labor costs fell from $.072 per ton under a flat day-rate to $.033 per ton under a piecework schedule; and the pig-iron handlers averaged a 60 percent increase in wages.

Despite Taylor's success in reducing Bethlehem's labor expenses, its top managers continued to oppose his other efforts, especially his cost-accounting system. Writing on September 23, 1898, to Robert P. Linderman, Bethlehem's president, Taylor described the "method of bookkeeping" he believed to be the "best" as "in general the modern railroad system of accounting adapted and modified to suit the manufacturing business."[58] This was the Hayes–Basley accounting system that Taylor had learned at MIC and adapted and applied in various companies. Taylor abhorred the futility of postmortem accounting that provided annual, semiannual, or monthly reports that were received too late for managerial action. At Bethlehem, he moved the cost-accounting function to the new planning department he had established. The planning department generated cost figures coincident with daily operations reports. Costs then became an integral part of daily planning and control, not a subject for analysis long after they had been incurred. The system was effective, in fact, so much so that Bethlehem's top managers tried to stop its implementation. Apparently, they did not care for an accurate and timely appraisal of their performance. Taylor eventually lost in his struggle to introduce improved managerial methods at Bethlehem, and his consulting contract was terminated on April 16, 1901. Taylor completed his work at Bethlehem Steel in July 1901.[59]

TAYLOR: THE PERIPATETIC PHILOSOPHER

Fred and Louise Taylor were unable to conceive children of their own. In February 1901, 17 years after the Taylors were first married, and when Fred was 45 years old, a tragedy in Savannah (Georgia) left four children of the Aiken family without parents. The Aikens were relatives of Mrs. Taylor's, and she and Fred adopted three of the children: Kempton, Robert, and Elizabeth. A fourth child, Conrad, was older and did not join the Taylor family—he later became a Pulitzer Prize–winning poet and a literary critic.[60] The Taylors and their new family moved from South Bethlehem to Germantown, Pennsylvania, while they awaited the construction of their Chestnut Hill home, where another stage in Taylor's career would begin. It is at this time (late 1901) that Frank B. Copley, Taylor's biographer, explains that Taylor retired from "money making" "partly due to considerations for his health."[61] The exact details of these considerations are unknown, but in 1906 Taylor acknowledged that he had experienced "a bad nervous breakdown several

[57] Charles D. Wrege and Richard M. Hodgetts, "Frederick W. Taylor's 1899 Pig Iron Observations: Examining Fact, Fiction, and Lessons for the New Millennium," *Academy of Management Journal* 43(6) (December 2000), p. 1287.

[58] Letter from Frederick W. Taylor to Robert P. Linderman, September 23, 1898, p. 4. *Frederick W. Taylor Collection*, SCW.001. Archives and Special Collections; Samuel C. Williams Library, Stevens Institute of Technology, Hoboken, NJ.

[59] It has also been noted that Taylor prompted further top-management opposition as his time studies led to a 25-percent reduction in the Bethlehem workforce, thereby depopulating the surrounding community. As a result, Bethlehem's top managers, who owned rental houses and most of the local stores, were upset because "what was gained in the factory" was "lost in the city." See Copley, *Taylor*, vol. 2, p. 46. For details concerning Taylor's dismissal, see W. Ross Yates, *Joseph Wharton: Quaker Industrial Pioneer* (Bethlehem, PA: Lehigh University Press, 1987), pp. 283–303.

[60] John A. Bromer, J. Myron Johnson, and Richard P. Widdicombe, "A Conversation with Robert P. A. Taylor: Interview Conducted in Providence, Rhode Island, October 14 and 15, 1976," Chapter 2, pp. 1–3, typescript dated July 1978, *Frederick W. Taylor Collection*, SCW.001. Archives and Special Collections; Samuel C. Williams Library, Stevens Institute of Technology, Hoboken, NJ. For details on the tragedy, see "Killed Wife and Himself," *New York Times* (February 28, 1901), p. 1.

[61] Copley, *Taylor*, vol. 2, p. 167.

years ago and have been unable to do active business since."[62] Although Taylor attributed the breakdown to the strain of his work resulting from constant squabbling, one might speculate that Taylor's decision to retire was also "partly" due to becoming, at age 45, the instant father of three children aged 6 to 12. Whatever the case, Taylor withdrew from "active business" and, in Copley's words, devoted himself to "the cause of science in management."

At Midvale and Bethlehem, Taylor demonstrated his talents as an inventor and mechanical engineer. At Bethlehem, he developed and patented the world's largest steam hammer (for oversized gun forgings); numerous machine tools such as grinders and boring and turning mills (lathes); and, with J. Maunsell White III, a process for cutting hard-steel forgings that more than doubled the output per machine. The Taylor–White process was first patented in 1900 and revolutionized machine-shop practices for working metals. Taylor and White sold the U.S. patent rights to Bethlehem, retaining the international rights for themselves. Taylor's share of the royalties amounted to some $50,000 before the two principal patents underlying the Taylor–White process were nullified in 1909.[63] Over his lifetime, Taylor held more than 40 patents.[64]

In his spare time, Taylor landscaped and renovated Boxly, developed new mixtures for soils to improve golf greens, and designed golf clubs. He received a patent for a putter with a Y shaft, experimented with lengths and thicknesses of golf-club shafts, and spent a great deal of time on the links, or, more euphemistically, in experimentation. He had taken up golf at age 40 (in 1896), and his skills developed rapidly; he played to an eight handicap and won the men's championship at the Philadelphia Country Club in 1902, 1903, and 1905, and won a fourth place Silver Medal in the 1900 Olympics held at Paris.[65] Taylor was in Paris at the time to attend the 1900 Paris Exposition, where he and Maunsell White received gold medals for their work developing the Taylor–White process for cutting metal. They were similarly honored in 1902 with the Elliott Cresson Gold Medal by the Franklin Institute, the science and technical institute founded in honor of Benjamin Franklin.

In 1906, the year of the San Francisco earthquake, Taylor was elected president of the ASME and awarded an honorary doctorate from the University of Pennsylvania in recognition of his scientific approach and various inventions. His fame was growing, and those who were to spread Taylor's message increased in numbers. Henry-Louis Le Chatelier, H. King Hathaway, James "Jimmie" M. Dodge, Morris L. Cooke, Frank B. Gilbreth, and others we will discuss were joining the earlier followers Gantt, Barth, and Thompson.

Asked to teach a course on task management at what was to become the Harvard University Graduate School of Business Administration, Taylor refused, saying that his methods could be learned only in practice. Professor Edwin Gay, soon to be dean of the school, told Taylor that the

---

[62] Frederick W. Taylor, "Testimony, January 24, 1906" *Bethlehem Steel Co. v. Niles-Bement-Pond Company*, United States Circuit Court of New Jersey, Case 4641 (1906), p. 54.

[63] "The High-Speed Patent Decision," *Electrochemical and Metallurgical Industry* 7(3) (March 1909), pp. 105–107. For a summary of the Taylor–White patent suit, see Thomas J. Misa, *A Nation of Steel: The Making of Modern America* (Baltimore, MD: Johns Hopkins University Press, 1995), pp. 18–205. For White's unsung contribution to the Taylor–White process, see Christopher P. Neck and Arthur G. Bedeian, "Frederick W. Taylor, J. Maunsell White III, and the Matthew Effect: The Rest of the Story," *Journal of Management History* 2(1) (1996), pp. 20–25. See also Charles D. Wrege, Ronald G. Greenwood, and Ti Hsu, "Frederick W. Taylor's Early Work at Bethlehem Steel Company: First Phase; 1898–1899—Some Insights," in Lance E. Metz, ed., *Canal History and Technology Proceedings* (1993), pp. 102–138; *Idem*, "Frederick W. Taylor's Work at Bethlehem Steel, Phase II: The Discovery of High-Speed Tool Steel, 1898: Was It An Accident?," in Lance E. Metz, ed., *Canal History and Technology Proceedings* (1994), pp. 115–161; *Idem*, "Frederick W. Taylor's Work at Bethlehem Steel, Phase III: Sale of the 'Taylor–White' Patent and the Initiation of the High Speed Steel Patent Suit: 1902–1905," in Lance E. Metz, ed., *Canal History and Technology Proceedings* (1995), pp. 105–127; *Idem*, "Frederick W. Taylor at Bethlehem Steel Company, Phase IV: The High-Speed Steel Patent Suit, 1906–1908," in Lance E. Metz, ed., *Canal History and Technology Proceedings* (1993), pp. 125–164; Charles D. Wrege, Ronald G. Greenwood, and Regina A. Greenwood, "A New Method of Discovering Primary Management History: Two Examples Where 'Little Things Mean a Lot'," *Journal of Management History*, 1997, 3(1), pp. 59–92.

[64] J. Myron Johnson, "Fred Taylor '83: Giant of Non-repute," *Stevens Indicator* 97(2) (Spring 1980), p. 4.

[65] Georges Lefèvre, "Les championnats de Golf" ["The Golf Championships"], *La Vie Au Grand Air* 3(109) (October 14, 1900), pp. 726–727. See also Shannon G. Taylor and Arthur G. Bedeian, "From Boardroom to Bunker: How Fred Taylor Changed the Game of Golf Forever," *Management & Organizational History*, 2(3) (2007), pp. 195–218. Taylor was an avid sportsman who also participated in baseball, rowing, skating, gymnastics, cricket, and croquet. See *idem*, "The Fred Taylor Baseball Myth: A Son Goes to Bat for His Father." *Journal of Management History* 14(3) (2008), pp. 294–298.

course would be taught with or without him, period. Taylor succumbed, although he was never entirely happy about teaching his methods in a classroom. Taylor was not against business education but believed that experience was the only way to learn his system. His Harvard lectures began in 1909 and were given each winter through 1914.[66] Taylor never accepted a penny of reimbursement for his lectures, not even for traveling expenses.

THE EASTERN RATE CASE

Taylor also found task management getting some extraordinary free publicity. The Boston attorney Louis D. Brandeis, later an Associate U.S. Supreme Court Justice, was widely known as "the people's lawyer,"[67] and a prominent critic of the power wielded by railroads, banks, and insurance companies. In June 1910, a group of railways operating north of the Ohio and Potomac rivers and east of the Mississippi (known collectively as the "Eastern railroads") asked the Interstate Commerce Commission (ICC) for a 10 percent hike in freight rates to cover investments in permanent improvements such as stations, tunnels, and bridges. The group included the Pennsylvania, Baltimore & Ohio, New York Central, and Erie lines.[68] A 10 percent increase would have yielded an additional $27,000,000 in revenue per year. The last rate hike the railroads had received was in 1887, the year the ICC was created. Brandeis took up the cause of the shippers (which included the American National Livestock Association, the Corn Belt Meat Producers' Association, and the Grain Dealers' Association, as well as the Boston and Philadelphia Chambers of Commerce and the Merchants' Association of New York, banded together as the Commercial Organizations of the Atlantic Seaboard) who would be affected by the proposed increase. In doing so, he brought about an unusual series of hearings, known as the "Eastern Rate Case," which thrust Taylor's task management into the public eye.

Earlier in 1910, Cooke and Taylor had submitted a paper, "The Philosophy of Management," to the ASME Meeting Committee. Cooke recalled Taylor had used the phrase "scientific management" in his Boxly talks and in a paper titled "Shop Management" he delivered at the 1903 ASME meeting, and suggested that Taylor consider changing the title of their paper to "The Principles of Scientific Management."[69] Taylor responded positively: "As to the title our paper . . . 'The Principles of Scientific Management' sounds less bombastic and pretentious. I am afraid the word 'philosophy' in the title will tend to make the thing sound rather high-falutin."[70]

ICC examiners began preliminary public hearings on August 15, 1910, at the United States Custom House in New York City. The hearings attracted such a crowd that by September 7 they were moved to the larger Astor Gallery at the Waldorf-Astoria Hotel. As one of the shippers' attorneys, Brandeis recalled his previous work in 1903 for the W. H. McElwain Company, a Boston shoe manufacturer that professed being guided by Taylor's methods.[71] Brandeis subsequently read Taylor's 1903 ASME paper and "studied the series of articles by Harrington

[66] Frederick W. Taylor, "An Outline of the Organization of a Manufacturing Establishment under Modern Scientific or Task Management," a lecture given at Harvard University, Boston, 1909–1914. Reprinted in Sasaki Tsuneo and Daniel A. Wren, ed., *Intellectual Legacy of Management Theory*, ser. 2, pt. 2, vol. 2 (London: Pickering and Chatto, 2002), pp. 259–303.

[67] The label "the people's lawyer" appears as a picture caption in Ernest Pool, "Brandeis: A Remarkable Record of Unselfish Work Done in the Public Interest," *American Magazine* 71(4) (February 1911), p. 489. For further background, see Oscar Kraines, "Brandeis and Scientific Management," *Publications of the American Jewish Historical Society* 41(1) (September 1951), pp. 41–60; Bernard K. Duffy, "The Rhetoric of Efficiency: Louis D. Brandeis, Scientific Management, and the 'Gospel of Hope,'" *Journal for the Humanities and Technology* 5 (1983), pp. 8–19.

[68] On this point, see Keith D. Revell, *Building Gotham: Civic Culture and Public Policy in New York City, 1898–1938* (Baltimore, MD: Johns Hopkins University Press, 2003), pp. 64–69.

[69] Letter from Morris L. Cooke to Frederick W. Taylor, March 27, 1910. *Frederick W. Taylor Collection*, SCW.001. Archives and Special Collections; Samuel C. Williams Library, Stevens Institute of Technology, Hoboken, NJ.

[70] Letter from Frederick W. Taylor to Morris L. Cooke, March 29, 1910, *Frederick W. Taylor Collection*, SCW.001. Archives and Special Collections; Samuel C. Williams Library, Stevens Institute of Technology, Hoboken, NJ.

[71] Horace B. Drury, *Scientific Management: A History and Criticism* (New York: Columbia University, 1915), p. 17 references Brandeis's retainer with the W. H. McElwain Company. Edward L. Prescott, McElwain Company Treasurer, discussed the manufacturer's experiences with Taylor's methods at the Amos Tuck Conference in 1911. See *Addresses and Discussion at the Conference on Scientific Management*, pp. 204–214.

Emerson in the *American Engineer and Railroad Journal* in 1906 on the application of efficiency methods in the locomotive repair shops of the Atchison, Topeka, and Santa Fe Railroad" in preparing his brief in the Eastern Rate Case.[72]

Following a meeting with Emerson, Brandeis telephoned Taylor from Emerson's office and arranged to visit Taylor at the home of Taylor's mother-in-law in Plymouth, Massachusetts. Brandeis subsequently requested a list of "all the different kinds of businesses into which scientific management had (to a greater or less extent) been introduced."[73] Taylor responded with a list of "the various kinds of work to which the principles of scientific management have been applied."[74] On November 1, Brandeis toured the Link-Belt Company, one of the better-known applications of Taylor's ideas.[75] Brandeis later met with Cooke, who reported to Taylor: "I dined with him [Brandeis] Tuesday [November 8] and explained to him the situation in regard to scientific management in those establishments with which I am familiar. He asked me to testify, and I declined, on the ground of being too busy."[76]

Thus, Brandeis was well acquainted with the term "scientific management" when, on November 20, he met with a group of Taylor followers and prospective Eastern Rate Case witnesses at the Great Northern Hotel in New York City. Henry v. Riper Scheel was present at the meeting and noted that Brandeis "repeatedly used the term 'scientific management' and this established the appellation as standard thereafter."[77] In a later correspondence with Horace B. Drury, Brandeis, however, noted:

> The term "scientific management" was not adopted as synonymous with the Taylor system, but as expressing the fundamental conception of the new movement, to which Mr. Taylor's contribution was of course greater than any other.
>
> It seemed to me important that all differences between the various advocates of efficiency should be eliminated, and some term be adopted to express the new idea which was common to them all; and I asked all who were to be witnesses to agree on this subject. Several names, like "Taylor System", "Functional Management", "Shop Management" and "Efficiency" were proposed. It seemed to me that the only term which would properly describe the movement and also appeal to the imagination, was "Scientific Management", and as I recall it all present were ultimately unanimous in the adoption of that term.[78]

---

[72] Oscar Kraines, "Brandeis' Philosophy of Scientific Management," *Western Political Quarterly*, vol. 13(1) (March 1960), p. 192.

[73] Letter from Louis D. Brandeis to Taylor, October 26, 1910, *Frederick W. Taylor Collection*, SCW.001. Archives and Special Collections; Samuel C. Williams Library, Stevens Institute of Technology, Hoboken, NJ. See also Keith D. Revell, "Professionalism and Public Service: The Brandeis/Taylor Alliance of 1910" (Master's thesis, University of Virginia, Charlottesville, VA, 1989). Available online at https://libraetd.lib.virginia.edu/public_view/5999n347r.

[74] Letter from Taylor to Brandeis, November 4, 1910, *Frederick W. Taylor Collection*, SCW.001. Archives and Special Collections; Samuel C. Williams Library, Stevens Institute of Technology, Hoboken, NJ.

[75] Letter from James Mapes Dodge to Taylor, November 3, 1910, *Frederick W. Taylor Collection*, SCW.001. Archives and Special Collections; Samuel C. Williams Library, Stevens Institute of Technology, Hoboken, NJ.

[76] Letter from Morris L. Cooke to Taylor, November 10, 1910, *Frederick W. Taylor Collection*, SCW.001. Archives and Special Collections; Samuel C. Williams Library, Stevens Institute of Technology, Hoboken, NJ.

[77] Henry van Riper Scheel, "Some Reflections of Henry Laurence Gantt," *Journal of Industrial Engineering*, 12(3) (May–June 1961), p. 221. In addition to Scheel and Brandeis, Gantt, Frank B. Gilbreth, and Robert T. Kent attended the meeting. For Gilbreth's recollections of this meeting, see Frank B. Gilbreth and Lillian M. Gilbreth, "Science in Management for the One Best Way to Do Work," in *Atti della III Conferenza Internazionale di Psicotecnica Applicata all'Orientamento Professionale [Proceedings of the III International Conference on Applied Psychotechnics for Professional Orientation]*, Milano 1922 (Milan: Società Umanitaria, 1923), pp. 145–146. It should be noted that U.S. Navy Commander Holden A. Evans used the term "scientific management" in *American Machinist* 5 months before this November 1910 meeting. In doing so, he suggested that the term was already in general use: "The term 'scientific management' is now generally accepted as referring to the type of management advocated by Fred W. Taylor and those who have been associated with him." See Evans, "Scientific Factory Management," *American Machinist* 33 (June 16, 1910), p. 1108. For more on the Evans-Taylor relationship, see David W. Holden, "Managing Men and Machines: U.S. Military Officers and the Intellectual Origins of Scientific Management in the Early Twentieth Century" (Doctoral dissertation, University of Kansas, Lawrence, KS, 2016), pp. 144-167.

[78] Letter from Brandeis to Horace B. Drury, January 31, 1914, reprinted in Louis D. Brandeis, *Letters of Louis D. Brandeis*, vol. 3: 1913–1915: *Progressive and Zionist*, eds. Melvin I. Urofsky and David W. Levy (Albany, NY: State University of New York, 1973), pp. 240–241.

With the conclusion of the preliminary hearings in late September, the counsel for the shippers and railroads met before the entire ICC in Washington, DC, on October 12, 1910. On November 22, Brandeis began calling his parade of scientific management "experts." H. King Hathaway, the first called, testified that scientific management had increased workers' wages at the Tabor Manufacturing Company, a producer of molding machines. James M. Dodge then attested to the successful introduction of scientific management at the Link-Belt Company, a manufacturer of chain-belt drives. Frank B. Gilbreth vouched that scientific management could be used in a union shop. Charles B. Going (editor of *Engineering Magazine*) described the efficiency methods used in the locomotive repair shops of the Atchison, Topeka, & Santa Fe Railroad. It was Harrington Emerson's testimony, however, that sensationalized the hearings. Emerson had developed "standard unit costs" for the Santa Fe; comparing the costs of other railroads with these standards, he estimated that by adopting Taylor's methods, the railroads could annually eliminate $240 million in labor costs and cut $60 million in materials and maintenance expenses.[79] Emerson's calculations overlooked operational differences among various railroads, never examined the question of whether Taylor's methods could be applied to all types of rail shipments, and subjectively assumed (based on his "general knowledge") that all railroads are, on "an absolutely ideal basis," 5 percent inefficient.[80] Regardless of these obvious shortcomings, Emerson's testimony, which at times was openly flippant, stunned the popular press and was reported in the next morning's papers.[81] When Taylor was asked about Emerson's $300 million annual savings, he replied:

> I believe we can save a million dollars a day, just as he said we can, but the reports of these hearings in Washington were not quite fair enough to say that it can't be done all at once. It would take four or five years.[82]

The phrase "scientific management" caught on with the press, and overnight Taylor gained a worldwide audience. The ICC, with the decision (announced on February 23, 1911) going against the railroads on the basis that investments in permanent improvements could not be considered operating expenses in setting freight rates, concluded that it was too early to judge the merits of scientific management.[83] Nevertheless, the resulting widespread publicity popularized Taylor's ideas. Within 24 hours, scientific management, previously an obscure idea developed by a relatively unknown engineer, became international news. Although Taylor had not testified, most of Brandeis's witnesses identified him as their teacher. Taylor became a national hero overnight. Newspapers and magazines published dozens of articles about his work. This publicity and the

---

[79] *Evidence Taken by the Interstate Commerce Commission in the Matter of Proposal Advances in Freight Rates by Carriers*, Senate Document 725, 61st Cong., 3rd sess., vol. 4 (Washington, DC: U.S. Government Printing Office, 1911), pp. 2829–2830, 2836. See also Louis D. Brandeis, *Scientific Management and Railroads: Being part of a Brief Submitted to the Interstate Commerce Commission* (New York: Engineering Magazine, 1911), pp. 83–86; Harrington Emerson, "The Fundamental Principles of Efficiency," *Official Proceedings Railway Club of Pittsburgh* 9(4) (February 25, 1910), p. 175.

[80] *Ibid.*, p. 2842. For a critique of Emerson's testimony, what an editorial in the *Railway Age Gazette* called the "merest of moonshine," see William J. Cunningham, "Scientific Management in the Operation of Railroads," *Quarterly Journal of Economics* 25(3) (May 1911), pp. 539–562. See also "Railway Rates and Railway Efficiency," *Railway Age Gazette* 49(23) (December 2, 1910), p. 1035.

[81] See, for example, "All Scoff at Brandeis: Officials Say Railroads Are Economically Managed," *New York Times* (November 23, 1910), p. 4; "Invite Brandeis to Manage Their Roads: Westerners Wire Lawyer to Name His Salary if He Can Save $300,000,000," *New York Times* (November 24, 1910), p. 8. See also "Railways Can Save $300,000,000 a Year," *New York Times* (November 16, 1910), p. 10.

[82] Frederick W. Taylor, "The Conservation of Human Effort," *City Club Bulletin* [City Club of Philadelphia] 4(1) (January 18, 1911), pp. 35–36.

[83] Having lost their 1910–1911 bid for a hike in freight rates, the Eastern Railroads filed a new second petition on May 14, 1913, asking for an average 5 percent increase. Rather than representing either the railroads or shippers, Brandeis was retained by the ICC as a special counsel "to undertake the task of seeing all sides and angles of the case are presented of record." Letter from James S. Harlan (ICC Commissioner) to Brandeis, August 15, 1913, reprinted in *Nomination of Louis D. Brandeis: Hearings on the Nomination of Louis D. Brandeis to be an Associate Justice of the Supreme Court of the United States before the Subcommittee of the Senate Commission on the Judiciary*, 64th Congress, 1st Session (1916), p. 158. The railroads' second petition for a rate increase was approved for selected areas with Brandeis's concurrence. See "Willard Cheered by Rate Decision," *New York Times* (December 31, 1914), p. 13.

publication of Taylor's book *The Principles of Scientific Management* in 1911 gave a new impetus to his campaign for efficiency. Within 2 years of publication, his book was translated into French, German, Dutch, Swedish, Russian, Italian, Spanish, and Japanese. Conferences were held and societies formed to study Taylor's work.

On the other hand, labor unions, especially the machinists' union and various railway brotherhoods, opposed all aspects of Taylor's methods, particularly time study. Labor leaders characterized Taylor's piece-rate pay plan as a return to "sweat shop" exploitation. Moreover, they feared that Taylor's methods would lead to laying off unnecessary workers. Organized labor had struggled long and hard to grow its membership, and it instinctively assumed that anything new originating in management was for its own advantage and labor's disadvantage. Taylor tried to counter labor opposition by expressing support for unions:

> We welcome the cooperation of the unions and will pay them for their cooperation; we welcome it and want it. We want their help. . . . I never look for the unions to go out. I am heartily in favor of combinations of men. I do not look for a great modification in the principles of unions as they now exist; they are of necessity largely now fighting organizations; I look for educational institutions, for mutual and helpful institutions; I look for great modifications, but never for the abolition of them. I simply look for a change, that the union shall conform itself to this new idea, the idea of a standard that is over all of us, and a set of laws that will be over all sides.[84]

Picking up on this theme, Taylor called for unions and management to come together in achieving better wages and working conditions. To this end, he stated, "Any company that has any sense at all would be delighted to have the union appoint an expert and the company would be willing to pay the wages." To this, he added:

> If the unions will take up the education of their members, it will be a step in the right direction. They will have to take this step before we can co-operate with them. Instead of preparing for war they must try to promote working conditions which render possible higher wages.
>
> The unions have done an immense amount of good. Unions have made better working conditions. They have stopped great injustices in the trades and for that they deserve commendation. Because a man points out that they are doing a few things that are wrong it does not mean that he does not tolerate anything that they are doing.[85]

Shortly before his death, Taylor again expressed his commitment to improved labor–management relations: "The earnest and honest effort for improved relations between employer and employee, the striving to abolish the antagonism between two factions—to this we must steadfastly hold."[86] Because Taylor firmly believed that his methods were objective, he never fully comprehended organized labor's hostility toward scientific management. Moreover, he pointed out that efficient methods such as those he proposed had historically increased employment, not reduced it. Nevertheless, for a company to introduce scientific management was to invite labor trouble.

WATERTOWN AND THE CONGRESSIONAL INVESTIGATION

The 1910 ICC hearings thrust Fred Taylor and scientific management into the limelight, but there were also unanticipated repercussions. At the time of the hearings, Taylor was introducing his methods at the Brooklyn Navy Yard and at the U.S. Army's Ordnance Department. Despite

---

[84] *Industrial Relations, Final Report and Testimony Submitted to Congress by the Commission on Industrial Relations*, vol. 1 (Washington, DC: U.S. Government Printing Office, 1916), pp. 789, 810.

[85] Frederick W. Taylor, "Scientific Management and Labor Unions," *Bulletin of the Society to Promote the Science of Management* 1(1) (December 1914), p. 3.

[86] Frederick W. Taylor quoted in Adolf O. Wallichs, "What Do the Germans Think of Taylor?" in *Frederick Winslow Taylor: A Memorial Volume* (New York: Taylor Society, 1920), p. 46.

repeated attempts, his efforts at the Navy Yard were largely unsuccessful, as the naval bureaucracy rejected his recommendations.[87] In contrast, Major General William Crozier, Chief of the U.S. Army's Ordnance Department, had read Taylor's work and saw its applicability to military arsenals.[88] In early 1911, Crozier selected the arsenals at Watertown (Massachusetts) and Rock Island (Illinois) as sites to test Taylor's methods. In protest, James O'Connell, president of the International Association of Machinists (IAM), in a circular sent to all IAM lodges, railed against time studies, saying that by "[s]tandardizing the movements of a workman," they made "an automaton of him."[89] The IAM opposed Taylor's methods in both governmental and nongovernmental applications.

Taylor advised Crozier to install scientific management at Watertown despite the resistance at Rock Island, but cautioned him to do so carefully, step-by-step, including first sounding out worker sentiments in each department. Barth, who oversaw the installation, attempted to follow Taylor's advice, but trouble started when Dwight V. Merrick, who was assisting Barth, attempted to use a stopwatch to time the arsenal's molders as they cast molds for making shell casings. One of the molders refused to be timed, citing "the organization" (the IAM) as the reason for his opposition. Lt. Colonel Charles B. Wheeler, the arsenal's commanding officer, explained to the worker why the stopwatch timing was necessary. The worker again objected and was discharged for "refusal to obey orders."[90] In sympathy, the arsenal's other molders likewise resisted. In August 1911, the first strike opposing the installation of scientific management occurred at the Watertown Arsenal. Taylor attributed the strike to a mistake in tactics: the sentiments of the molders had not been examined, nor had they been briefed on the purposes of the time study. Taylor did not fault the molders or the IAM but blamed a premature attempt to time various jobs without following his recommendation to consult workers first before beginning any time studies. Moreover, as was Taylor's practice prior to conducting any time studies, the arsenal had not yet been reorganized following his methods. The molders returned to work after one week and offered no further resistance.

After the strike, however, the IAM petitioned the U.S. Congress to investigate the arsenal workers' complaints alleging inferior working conditions and humiliating treatment.[91] In response, the U.S. House of Representatives appointed a special committee to conduct hearings into what it called "the Taylor system." The committee consisted of three members. William B. Wilson was a former official of the United Mine Workers Union. He had joined the union at the age of 11, and at the time of the hearings was chair of the House Labor Committee. Wilson later served as Secretary of Labor under President Woodrow Wilson. William C. Redfield was a manufacturer who later became Secretary of Commerce under Wilson. The third member, John Q. Tilson, represented the state of Connecticut in the House. He was the only Republican on the committee.

The hearings began in October 1911 and lasted through February 1912. Taylor spent 12 hours, scattered over 4 days, testifying before the committee. In Copley's recounting, "Terrorism was in the air," as organized labor set out to harass Taylor.[92] Hearing transcripts illustrate the hostility and sharpness in both questions and answers. For example, following a series of

[87] John C. Solberg, "The Application of Scientific Management to the Watertown Arsenal" (Graduation thesis, Boston University),1986; Peter B. Petersen, "Fighting for a Better Navy: An Attempt at Scientific Management (1905–1912)," *Journal of Management* 16(1) (March 1990), pp. 151–166.

[88] *Idem*, "The Pioneering Efforts of Major General William Crozier (1855–1942) in the Field of Management," *Journal of Management* 15(3), 1989, pp. 503–516.

[89] James O'Connell, "Official Circular no. 12," Office of the International President, International Association of Machinists, April 26, 1911, Washington, DC, p. 2. *Frederick W. Taylor Collection*, SCW.001. Archives and Special Collections; Samuel C. Williams Library, Stevens Institute of Technology, Hoboken, NJ.

[90] Copley, *Taylor*, vol. 2, p. 344.

[91] Hugh G. J. Aitken, *Scientific Management in Action: Taylorism at Watertown Arsenal, 1908–1915* (Princeton, NJ: Princeton University Press, 1985).

[92] Copley, *Taylor*, vol. 2, p. 347.

questions and discussion about the effect of scientific management on worker displacement, the following clash erupted over Taylor's definition of a "first-class man":

> THE CHAIRMAN [MR. WILSON]. Is it not true that a man who is not a good workman and who may not be responsible for the fact that he is not a good workman, has to live as well as the man who is a good workman?
>
> MR. TAYLOR. Not as well as the other workman; otherwise, that would imply that all those in the world were entitled to live equally well whether they worked or whether they were idle, and that certainly is not the case. Not as well.
>
> THE CHAIRMAN. Under scientific management, then, you propose that because a man is not in the first class as a workman that there is no place in the world for him—if he is not in the first class in some particular line that this must be destroyed and removed?
>
> MR. TAYLOR. Mr. Chairman, would it not be well for me to describe what I mean by a "first-class" workman. I have written a good deal about "first-class" workmen in my books, and I find there is quite a general misapprehension as to the use of that term "first class."
>
> THE CHAIRMAN. Before you come to a definition of what you consider a "first-class" workman I would like to have your concept of how you are going to take care, under your scientific management, of a man who is not a "first-class" workman in some particular line?
>
> MR. TAYLOR. I can not answer that question until I define what I mean by "first class." You and I may have a totally different idea as to the meaning of these words, and therefore I suggest that you allow me to state what I mean.
>
> THE CHAIRMAN. The very fact that you specify "first class" would indicate that in your mind you would have some other class than "first class."
>
> MR. TAYLOR. If you will allow me to define it I think I can make it clear.
>
> THE CHAIRMAN. You said a "first class" workman can be taken care of under normal conditions. That is what you have already said. Now, the other class that is in your mind, other than "first class," how does your system propose to take care of them?
>
> MR. TAYLOR. Mr. Chairman, I can not answer that question. I can not answer any question relating to "first-class" workmen until you know my definition of that term, because I have used these words technically throughout my paper, and I am not willing to answer a question you put about "first-class" workmen with the assumption that my answer applies to all I have said in my book.
>
> THE CHAIRMAN. You yourself injected the term "first class" by saying that you did not know of a condition in normal times when a "first-class" workman could not find employment.
>
> MR. TAYLOR. I do not think I used that term "first class."
>
> MR. REDFIELD. Mr. Chairman, the witness has now four times, I think, said that until he is allowed to define what he means by "first class" no answer can be given, because he means one thing by the words "first-class" and he thinks that you mean another thing.
>
> THE CHAIRMAN. My question has nothing whatever to do with the definition of the words "first class." It has to do with the other class than "first class" not with "first-class." A definition of "first class" will in no manner contribute to a proper reply to my question, because I am not asking about "first class," but the other than "first class" workmen.
>
> MR. TAYLOR. I can not describe the others until I have described what I mean by "first class."
>
> MR. REDFIELD. As I was saying when I was interrupted, the witness had stated that he cannot answer the question for the reason that the language that the chairman uses, namely, the words "first class" do not mean the same thing in the Chairman's mind that they mean in the witness's mind, and

he asks the privilege of defining what they do mean, so that the language shall be mutually intelligible. Now, it seems to me, and I think it is good law and entirely proper, that the witness ought to be permitted to define his meaning; and then if, after his definition is made, there is any misunderstanding, we can proceed.[93]

Then Wilson, Redfield, and Tilson engaged in a spirited discussion of whether or not Taylor should be allowed to define his terms; Redfield and Tilson prevailed, and Taylor proceeded to explain his use of the term "first-class" and concluded:

[A]mong every class of workmen we have some balky workmen—I do not mean men who are unable to work, but men who, physically well able to work, are simply lazy, and who through no amount of teaching and instructing and through no amount of kindly treatment, can be brought into the "first class." That is the man whom I call "second class." They have the physical possibility of being "first class," but they obstinately refuse to do so.

Now, Mr. Chairman, I am ready to answer your question, having clearly in mind that I have these two types of "second-class" men in view; the one which is physically able to do the work, but who refused to do it—and the other who is not physically or mentally fitted to do that particular job. These are the two types of "second-class" men.

THE CHAIRMAN. Then, how does scientific management propose to take care of men who are not "first-class" men in any particular line of work?

MR. TAYLOR. I give it up.

THE CHAIRMAN. Scientific management has no place for such men?

MR. TAYLOR. Scientific management has no use for a bird that can sing and won't sing.

THE CHAIRMAN. I am not speaking about birds at all.

MR. TAYLOR. No man who can work and won't work has any place under scientific management.

THE CHAIRMAN. It is not a question of a man who can work and won't work; it is a question of a man who is not a "first class" man in any one particular line, according to your own definition.

MR. TAYLOR. I do not know of any such line of work. For each man some line can be found in which he is first class.[94]

In another instance, Taylor was being questioned by John R. O'Leary (third vice president of the International Molders' Union of North America) on fines that had been levied against workers at Midvale Steel:

MR. O'LEARY. Did I understand you to say that you had the permission and cooperation of the men in putting in that system?

MR. TAYLOR. Yes . . . they ran it, invested the funds, took care of the sick; they furnished the doctor and the nurse. . . .

MR. O'LEARY. What did they charge the men who were injured, for the doctor?

MR. TAYLOR. Not a cent. The services were all free.

MR. O'LEARY. Are you aware that there have been many suits instituted against the Midvale Steel Company to recover those fines, and that they were recovered?

MR. TAYLOR. No; I am not aware of it.

---

[93] *Hearings to Investigate the Taylor System*, vol. 3, pp. 1452–1453.

[94] *Ibid.*, vol. 3, pp. 1455–1456.

MR. O'LEARY. Are you aware that men are fined a dollar for going to the urinal?

MR. TAYLOR. I have not the slightest idea that is true. Who ever said that told an untruth. Nothing of that kind was done while I was there.[95]

No support for O'Leary's charges ever appeared in any other testimony. As journalist Ida Tarbell declared:

> One of the most sportsmanlike exhibits the country ever saw was Mr. Taylor's willingness to subject himself to the heckling and the badgering of labour leaders, congressmen, and investigators of all degrees of misunderstanding, suspicion and ill will. To a man of his temperament and highly trained intellect, who had given a quarter of a century of the hardest kind of toil to develop useful truths, the kind of questioning to which he was sometimes subjected must have been maddening.[96]

Coming from Tarbell, this was quite a compliment. Baited, insulted, and made to appear a beast, Taylor staggered from the stand at the close of his testimony. Taylor's pride was sorely wounded, his lifework reviled before a congressional committee. At one point, it appeared as if Taylor and his organized-labor opponents would come to blows. The ensuing exchange was so heated that it was removed from the transcript of the day's hearings.[97] There was no victory for anyone in the committee's final report. Phrased in political double-talk, the report said that it was too early "to determine with accuracy their [Taylor's and other scientific management systems'] effect on the health and pay of employees and their effect on wages and labor cost."[98] The committee found no evidence to support abuses of workers or any need for remedial legislation. It did refer to possible abuses, perhaps to appease opponents, but presented no evidence that they had occurred.

Despite the committee's recommendation that no legislation was needed, the representatives from the Watertown and Rock Island congressional districts succeeded in passing a House resolution to prevent the use of time-measuring devices and performance incentives in any military installation.[99] In considering the 1914–1915 military appropriation bill, however, a heated debate occurred in the U.S. Senate. Among the pro-rider anti-Taylor advocates was Senator Henry Cabot Lodge, a descendant of the early Massachusetts textile tycoons, who spoke of ending "the days of slavery" brought about by men such as Taylor who thought it "profitable to work the slaves to the last possible point and let them die."[100] Such demagoguery clearly indicated his ignorance of what Taylor was attempting. The rider failed in the Senate but was restored in conference between the two chambers and attached to an army appropriations bill. Legislation prohibiting the use of federal funds for time study with "a stopwatch or other time-measuring device" stayed in effect from 1916 until 1949.[101] It should be noted that there was never a strike at any company at which Taylor was personally in charge nor had any workers operating under his system found it desirable to unionize.

---

[95] *Ibid.*, vol. 1, pp. 745–746.

[96] Ida M. Tarbell, *New Ideals in Business: An Account of Their Practice and Their Effects upon Men and Profits* (New York: Macmillan, 1916), p. 315.

[97] Copley, *Taylor*, vol. 2, p. 348.

[98] *Hearings to Investigate the Taylor System*, vol. 3, p. 1930.

[99] U.S. House of Representatives, Labor Committee, *Hearings on House Resolution 8662, A Bill to Prevent the Use of the Stop Watch or Other Time-Measuring Device on Government Work and the Payment of Premium or Bonus to Government Employees for Other Purposes* (Washington, DC: Government Printing Office, 1914).

[100] Henry Cabot Lodge, February 23, 1915, *Congressional Record Containing the Proceedings and Publications of the Sixty-Third Congress*, Third Session, vol. 52, pt. 5 (Washington, DC: Government Printing Office, 1915), p. 4352. Mary B. Gilson, an early employment counselor and later lecturer at the University of Chicago, called Lodge an "exhibitionist" who tilted at windmills. See. Gilson, *What's Past Is Prologue: Reflections on My Industrial Experiences* (New York: Harper & Brothers, 1940), p. 55.

[101] Milton J. Nadworny, *Scientific Management and the Unions: 1900–1923* (Cambridge, MA: Harvard University Press, 1955), pp. 82, 103.

THE MENTAL REVOLUTION

Taylor believed that labor and management should strive to find common ground. He wrote that "Scientific management . . . has for its very foundation the firm conviction that the true interests of the two [employers and employees] are one and the same; that prosperity for the employer cannot exist through a long term of years unless it is accompanied by the prosperity for the employé, and *vice versa*; and that it is possible to give the workman what he most wants—high wages—and the employer what he wants—a low cost—for his manufactures."[102] Taylor declared: "The principal object of management should be to secure the maximum prosperity for the employer, coupled with the maximum prosperity for each employee."[103] To make this a reality, he called for a "mental revolution" where "both sides take their eyes off the division of surplus . . . and together turn their attention toward increasing the size of the surplus."[104] Thus, as envisioned by Taylor, the concerns of labor and management should be based on a "mutuality of interest." In brief, he advocated a harmony between the goals of employee and employer such that there would be "justice for all . . . parties through impartial scientific investigation of all elements of the problem."[105] In his words: "It is safe to say no system or scheme of management should be considered which does not in the long run give satisfaction to both employer and employee, which does not make it apparent that their best interests are mutual, and which does not bring about such thorough and hearty cooperation that they can pull together instead of apart."[106] Taylor recognized that self-proclaimed "efficiency experts" were damaging scientific management's reputation. He warned, "the mechanism of management must not be mistaken for its essence, or underlying philosophy."[107] This philosophy, reflecting a mutuality of interests, had four basic principles:

> *First.* The development of a true science.
> *Second.* The scientific selection of the workman.
> *Third.* His scientific education and development.
> *Fourth.* Intimate friendly cooperation between the management and the men.[108]

For Taylor, no single element constituted scientific management. Rather it was a combination of elements, which could be summarized as follows:

Science, not rule of thumb. Harmony, not discord.

Cooperation, not individualism.

Maximum output, in place of restricted output.

The development of each man to his greatest efficiency and prosperity.[109]

Taylor's ideas aroused much interest. Unfortunately, many imitators used his name but short-circuited his methods, promising they could produce the same results in half the time.[110] Taylor deplored these fakers, properly fearing that they promised quick panaceas without grasping the fundamental attitudes that had to be changed and the necessity of gaining workers' acceptance of the new methods. He made a marked distinction between "true" scientific management and the efficiency craze that had suddenly emerged. True scientific management required a "mental revolution" on the part of employers and employees, which came about from mutual

[102] Taylor, *Principles of Scientific Management*, p. 10.
[103] *Ibid.*, p. 9. See also Christopher T. Nyland, "Taylorism and the Mutual-Gains Strategy," *Industrial Relations* 37(4) (October 1998), pp. 519–542.
[104] *Hearings to Investigate the Taylor System*, vol. 3, p. 1387.
[105] Taylor, *Principles of Scientific Management*, p. 139.
[106] Taylor, *Shop Management*, p. 21.
[107] Taylor, *Principles of Scientific Management*, p. 128.
[108] *Ibid.*, p. 130n1.
[109] *Ibid.*, p. 140.
[110] "Inefficient Efficiency Experts." *Bulletin of the Taylor Society* 2(4) (April 1913), pp. 8–9.

respect over time and not from the mechanical adoption of purported efficiency devices. At the congressional hearings following the Watertown Arsenal strike, Taylor tried to clarify first what scientific management was by explaining what it was not:

> Scientific management is not any efficiency device, not a device of any kind for securing efficiency; nor is it any bunch or group of efficiency devices. It is not a new system of figuring costs; it is not a new scheme of paying men; it is not a piecework system; it is not a bonus system; it is not a premium system; it is no scheme for paying men; it is not holding a stop watch on a man and writing things down about him; it is not time study; it is not motion study nor an analysis of the movements of men; it is not the printing and ruling and unloading of a ton or two of blanks on a set of men and saying, "Here's your system; go use it." It is not divided foremanship or functional foremanship; it is not any of the devices which the average man calls to mind when scientific management is spoken of. The average man thinks of one or more of these things when he hears the words "scientific management" mentioned, but scientific management is not any of these devices. I am not sneering at cost-keeping systems, at time study, at functional foremanship, nor at any new and improved scheme of paying men, nor at any efficiency devices, if they are really devices that make for efficiency. I believe in them; but what I am emphasizing is that these devices in whole or in part are not scientific management, they are useful adjuncts to scientific management, so are they also useful adjuncts of other systems of management.
>
> Now, in its essence, scientific management involves a complete mental revolution on the part of the workingman engaged in any particular establishment or industry—a complete mental revolution on the part of these men as to their duties toward their work, toward their fellow men, and toward their employers. And it involves the equally complete mental revolution on the part of those on the management's side—the foreman, the superintendent, the owner of the business, the board of directors—a complete mental revolution on their part as to their duties toward their fellow workers in the management, toward their workmen, and toward all of their daily problems. And without this complete mental revolution on both sides scientific management does not exist.
>
> That is the essence of scientific management, this great mental revolution.[111]

Taylor believed that labor-union leaders were the principal opponents of his methods, not the unions' rank-and-file members. He was convinced that there was a conspiracy among union leaders to oppose scientific management. On April 26, 1914, speaking in Milwaukee at a joint meeting of the Wisconsin State Federation of Labor and Milwaukee Federated Trades Council executive boards, Taylor presented the case for time study, improved work methods, and rewarding workers based on output:

> I want to make it clear that in the work that I have been doing and am doing the last 12 years, that I have just one thing in view; that is to promote the interests of the working people in this country. Now I want to say that any man who thinks he can work in the interest of the working people and not work at the same time in the interest of the manufacturers, is nothing but a fool. It is necessary to work in the interest of both sides in order to get any results. But what I want to make clear is that my personal interest is for the welfare of the working people of this country. And while our methods may be different, my object is the same that you are aiming for. We are all aiming for the same thing—shorter hours, better working conditions, higher wages and more happiness for the working people in this country, and I want to make it clear to you, gentlemen, at the start, that in placing this matter before you, that's what I have in mind and nothing else.[112]

---

[111] *Hearings to Investigate the Taylor System*, vol. 3, p. 1387.

[112] Frederick W. Taylor quoted in Executive Board, Wisconsin State Federation of Labor, *A Report on The Taylor System of Scientific Shop Management* (Milwaukee, WI: 1914), pp. 24–25. For more on the Taylor–Alifas exchange, see "Report of Frank J. Weber," *Proceedings of the Twenty-second Annual Convention of the Wisconsin State Federation of Labor* (Milwaukee, WI: 1914), p. 4.

Nels P. Alifas, president of IAM's District #44 (Navy Yards and Arsenals), was invited to respond to Taylor's comments. Alifas, a Danish immigrant, had been a toolmaker during the 1911 Rock Island Arsenal strike and had testified at the 1911–1912 *Hearings to Investigate the Taylor System*. He stated the IAM's position:

> Some people may wonder why we should object to a time study. In the first place it is humiliating for a man to be suspected of soldiering and loafing. . . . That's not the principal objection. The objection is that in the past one of the means by which an employe has been able to keep his head above water and prevent being oppressed by the employer has been that the employer didn't know just exactly what the employe could do. The only way that the workman has been able to retain time enough in which to do the work with the speed with which he thinks he ought to do the work, has been to keep the employer somewhat in ignorance of exactly the time in which he could do the work. The people of the United States have a right to say we want to work only so fast. We don't want to work as fast as we are able to. We want to work as fast as we think it's comfortable for us to work. We haven't come into existence for the purpose of seeing how great a task we can perform through a lifetime. We are trying to regulate our work so as to make it an auxiliary to our lives and be benefited thereby.[113]

Taylor repeatedly invited Samuel Gompers, president of the American Federation of Labor, to visit plants using his methods and to get the facts for himself; Gompers refused.[114] In Taylor's view, organized labor's philosophy and that of scientific management were in direct opposition. Whereas labor unions stood "for war, for enmity," scientific management encouraged a "mutuality of interests."[115] To Gompers, labor's gains came from employers' pockets. As he explained: "Trade unions strive for more of the product of their labor—more, more, more—and when they have achieved that they will seek more. And then, when that is done, we shall ask still more, more, more."[116] In contrast, for Taylor, "more" came to everyone through improved productivity. True, by searching for technological breakthroughs, scientific management made it possible to get more output for the same amount of input and, thus, higher profits. At the same time, working with better technology and work methods, scientifically selected and trained workers naturally produce more output per hour. In a competitive labor market, the demand for these more productive employees increases, driving up their wages. As Taylor reasoned, both employers and employees have a mutual interest in increasing a company's productive efficiency so it will be able to provide one of them higher wages and the other higher profits. If the company fails, everyone loses. Taylor considered his inability to convince labor to accept scientific management to be his greatest failure.[117]

---

[113] Nels P. Alifas quoted in *Ibid.*, pp. 24-25. Further details regarding Alifas's views on scientific management, or what he considered "merely a name for an ingenious set of oppressive practices," are available at *Hearings to Investigate the Taylor System*, pp. 1860–1863; U.S. House of Representatives, Labor Committee, *Method of Directing the Work of Government Employees: Hearings Before the Committee on Labor, Sixty-fourth Congress, First Session on H.R. 8665, a Bill to Regulate the Method of Directing the Work of Government Employees. March 30, 31, April 1 and 4, 1916* (Washington, DC: Government Printing Office), p. 203 and Nels P. Alifas, "Fight Against Taylor System," *Labor Clarion* 15(14) (May 12, 1916), p. 11.

[114] Copley, *Taylor*, vol. 2, pp. 403–404. In his testimony before the committee to investigate the Taylor System, Gompers categorically denied the existence of soldiering and labor resistance; see *Hearings to Investigate the Taylor System*, p. 27. Gompers's biographer, Philip Taft, has suggested that Gompers was not unalterably opposed to scientific management, but yielded to the influence of IAM president William H. Johnson because the machinists were the largest and most powerful affiliate in the American Federation of Labor. See Philip Taft, *The A.F. of L. in the Time of Gompers* (New York: Harper & Brothers, 1957), pp. 299–300. For Gompers's view, in his own words, of scientific management, see: Gompers, "Editorial: Machinery to Perfect the Living Machine," *American Federationist* 18(2) (February 1911), pp. 116–117; *idem*, "The Miracles of 'Efficiency,'" *American Federationist* 18(4) (April 1911), pp. 273–279; and *idem*, "'Speeding Up,'" *American Federationist* 20(7) (July 1913), pp. 524–525.

[115] Frederick W. Taylor quoted in Copley, *Taylor*, vol. 2, p. 407.

[116] "Talks on Labor: Addresses by President Gompers at Erie, PA.; Providence, R.I., and Poughkeepsie, N.Y.," *American Federationist* 13(7) (July 1906), p. 474.

[117] Kenneth E. Trombley, *The Life and Times of a Happy Liberal: A Biography of Morris Llewellyn Cooke* (New York: Harper & Brothers, 1954), p. 258.

TAYLOR AND THE HUMAN FACTOR

In response to the charges that scientific management was cold, impersonal, and disregarded the human factor, Taylor wrote about systems and people: "No system can do away with the need of real men. Both system and good men are needed, and after introducing the best system, success will be in proportion to the ability, consistency, and respected authority of the management."[118] Taylor well understood he was dealing with human needs as well as materials and machines. Writing in *Shop Management*, he quoted from his 1895 ASME paper "Piece-Rate System":

> No system of management, however good, should be applied in a wooden way. The proper personal relations should always be maintained between the employers and men; and even the prejudices of the workmen should be considered in dealing with them.
>
> The employer who goes through his works with kid gloves on, and is never known to dirty his hands or clothes, and who either talks to his men in a condescending or patronizing way, or else not at all, has no chance whatever of ascertaining their real thoughts or feelings.
>
> Above all it is desirable that men should be talked to on their own level by those who are over them. Each man should be encouraged to discuss any trouble which he may have, either in the works or outside, with those over him. Men would far rather even be blamed by their bosses, especially if the "tearing out" has a touch of human nature and feeling in it, than to be passed by day after day without a word, and with no more notice than if they were part of the machinery.
>
> The opportunity which each man should have of airing his mind freely, and having it out with his employers, is a safety-valve; and if the superintendents are reasonable men, and listen to and treat with respect what their men have to say, there is absolutely no reason for labor unions and strikes.
>
> It is not the large charities (however generous they may be) that are needed or appreciated by workmen so much as small acts of personal kindness and sympathy, which establish a bond of friendly feeling between them and their employers.
>
> The moral effect of this system on the men is marked. The feeling that substantial justice is being done them renders them on the whole much more manly, straightforward, and truthful. They work more cheerfully, and are more obliging to one another and their employers. They are not soured, as under the old system, by brooding over the injustice done them; and their spare minutes are not spent to the same extent in criticising their employers.[119]

On resistance to change, Taylor wrote:

> Through generations of bitter experiences working men as a class have learned to look upon all change as antagonistic to their best interests. They do not ask the object of the change, but oppose it simply as *change*. The first changes, therefore, should be such as to allay the suspicions of the men and convince them by actual contact that the reforms are after all rather harmless and are only such as will ultimately be of benefit to all concerned.[120]

Taylor believed that it took "two to five years at the very least" to fully install his methods.[121] Scientific management was not an overnight panacea. Its implementation required diligence and an understanding of Taylor's philosophy to be successful. Even then, it was not a cure-all:

> Scientific management fundamentally consists of certain broad principles, a certain philosophy, which can be applied in many ways. . . . It is not here claimed that any single panacea exists for all of the troubles of the working people or of employers. . . . No system of management, no single expedient

[118] Taylor, *Shop Management*, p. 148. See also *idem*, "A Piece-Rate System," pp. 880–881.
[119] *Idem, Shop Management*, pp. 184–185.
[120] *Ibid.*, p. 137.
[121] Frederick W. Taylor, "Scientific Management," *Journal of the Efficiency Society* 3(8) (September 1914), p. 23.

> within the control of any man or any set of men can insure continuous prosperity to either workmen or employers.[122]

Perhaps a few words are in order on how Taylor changed the social pattern at Midvale Steel by integrating its workforce. The hiring of African American workers at Midvale was a result of a deliberate initiative by Taylor to break up the ethnic loyalties of different work gangs and prevent soldiering. Beginning in the 1880s, as Midvale's chief engineer, Taylor hired 200 African American laborers and distributed them among the various gangs. In his 1899 book, *The Philadelphia Negro: A Social Study*, sociologist W. E. B. Du Bois wrote: "There came some time since to the Midvale Steel Works a manager whom many dubbed a 'crank'; he had a theory that Negroes and whites could work together as mechanics without friction or trouble. In spite of some protest, he put his theory into practice, and to-day any one can see Negro mechanics working in the same gangs with white mechanics without disturbance."[123] That "crank" was Fred Taylor.[124] Whereas historian Andre W. Dawson suggests that Taylor's primary concern was to increase production, he acknowledges that, "however tangentially," Taylor did alter hiring practices for African American workers in Philadelphia, and made Midvale a conspicuous exception among area manufacturers.[125] In reflecting on Taylor's decision to end African American workplace exclusion, however, one might recall that Taylor's parents were ardent abolitionists, and this may well have influenced his thinking. Within 20 years, more than 4,000 of Midvale's 11,000-strong workforce was African American.

In 1915, three weeks before his death, Taylor spoke to the Cleveland Advertising Club:

> Scientific management at every step has been an evolution, not a theory. In all cases the practice has preceded the theory. . . . All the men that I know of who are connected with scientific management are ready to abandon any scheme, any theory, in favor of anything else that can be found this is better. There is nothing in scientific management that is fixed.[126]

---

[122] *Ibid.*, pp. 28–29. Taylor made a similar statement in his presentation at the first conference on scientific management: Frederick W. Taylor, "The Principles of Scientific Management," in *Scientific Management: First Conference at the Amos Tuck School,* p. 54.

[123] W. E. Burghardt Du Bois with Isabel Eaton, *The Philadelphia Negro: A Social Study* (Philadelphia, PA: University of Pennsylvania Press, 1899), p. 129.

[124] E. Digby Baltzell, "Introduction," in W. E. Burghardt Du Bois with Isabel Eaton, *The Philadelphia Negro: A Social Study* (New York: Schocken Books, 1967), p. xxxvii. The attribution that Taylor was the "crank" to which Du Bois referred has been questioned on the grounds that Taylor departed Midvale Steel on September 30, 1890, and the time period to which Du Bois refers was after this date. The record indicates, however, that African Americans were hired at Midvale as early as 1889 and some 500 were employed by October 1891. As Copley notes, while at Midvale, Taylor was called a "crank" so often, he was driven to strongly protest the idiom's use by one of the company's "chief men." It might also be noted that Taylor was descended from a long line of Quaker abolitionists and sponsored C. Bertrand Thompson's 1912 apprenticeship at Plimpton Press and later recommended him for various consulting assignments. Taylor also spoke to Thompson's Harvard University Business School classes. Thompson was the first African American faculty member at the Harvard Business School. For Taylor's departure date from Midvale, see "Letter from Wm. A. Fannon," in *Frederick Winslow Taylor: A Memorial Volume*, p. 103; for the employment of African Americans at Midvale as early as 1889, see "Interview with John (Jack) Jones," interviewer Charles Hardy, June 1, 1982, in *Goin' North: Tales of the Great Migration*, Louie B. Nunn Center for Oral History, University of Kentucky Libraries, https://goinnorth.org/jack-jones-interview; for the number of African Americans employed at Midvale in October 1891, see "Race Gleanings," *The Freeman* (Indianapolis, IN) (October 31, 1891), p. 6; for Taylor being known as a "crank," see Copley, *Taylor*, vol.1, p. 124; and for details on Taylor and Thompson's interactions, see Daniel A. Wren, Regina A. Greenwood, Julia Kurtz Teahen, and Arthur G. Bedeian, "C. Bertrand Thompson and Management Consulting in Europe, 1917–1934," *Journal of Management History* 21(1) (2015), pp. 19–21. As for African American employment in the North during the period in question, agents were sent South to recruit African American laborers from rural areas. Recruits received a free train ticket North in exchange for their labor. In some instances, African Americans were hired to break labor strikes. "As early as 1878 the steel companies of Pittsburgh systematically recruited African American strikebreakers from southern mills. . . . In fact, [it has been claimed] that nearly all the African American strikebreakers used in the steel industry of Pennsylvania during the 1870s and 1890s had prior training in the South." On this point, see Warren C. Whatley, "African-American Strikebreaking from the Civil War to the New Deal," *Social Science History* 17(4) (Winter 1993), pp. 538–539. For the referenced claim, see Sterling D. Spero and Abram L. Harris, *The Black Worker: The Negro and the Labor Movement* (New York: Columbia University Press, 1931), p. 250.

[125] Sadie Tanner Mossell, "The Standard of Living Among One Hundred Negro Migrant Families in Philadelphia" (Doctoral dissertation, University of Pennsylvania, Philadelphia, PA, 1921), p. 7.

[126] *Idem,* "The Principles of Scientific Management," *Bulletin of the Taylor Society* 2(5) (December 1916), p. 15. Address before the Cleveland Advertising Club, March 3, 1915, published posthumously.

In recognizing that there was never only "one best way," Taylor realized that management should continually strive to improve its methods through scientific investigation. Worried by the declining health of his wife, bedeviled by organized labor's antagonism, and frustrated by imitators who used his name, but short-circuited his methods and disdained his underlying philosophy, Taylor's last days were nigh. In a drafty railcar drawing room, while returning from a speaking trip, he became ill. He died from pneumonia on March 21, 1915, one day after his 59th birthday.[127] His headstone at the West Laurel Hill Cemetery, Philadelphia, bears this inscription: "*Frederick W. Taylor, 1856–1915, Father of Scientific Management.*"

A FINAL NOTE

Frederick W. Taylor was a central figure in the development of management thought. Entering the U.S. industrial scene at a time of transition from owner-entrepreneurs and small- and medium-sized businesses to large-scale, fully integrated corporations run by professional managers, Taylor gave a push and added credibility to the belief that management was an independent science and discipline. The engineers of the day, having opened the door to efficient resource utilization, turned to technical subjects and left it to Taylor and others to promote what would come to be known as *scientific management*. Characterized by advancing technology, market growth, labor unrest, and a lack of managerial knowledge, U.S. companies of all sizes and in all industries were eager to learn better methods to improve their efficiency. To meet this need, Taylor provided a voice, a spirit that captured the public's imagination, including those of the army and navy, business leaders, government reformers, farmers, legal and medical professionals, church workers, clubwomen, home economists, educators, and academics.[128] In an ironic twist, although Taylor's efforts at the Brooklyn Navy Yard were generally unsuccessful, in 1943, the U.S. Maritime Commission recognized his service by naming a World War II Liberty Ship (the 7,176-ton SS *Frederick W. Taylor*) in his honor.[129]

Although Taylor died over 100 years ago, he is still considered to be "the most influential business guru of the twentieth century."[130] In reviewing Taylor's ideas, Edwin A. Locke concluded that "Taylor's track record is remarkable . . . *most of his insights are still valid today*."[131] In the eyes of many, however, Taylor was a divisive person. His biographer wrote that he was not "the possessor of a nature that ordinarily would be called lovable" and acknowledged that "most of the men with whom I talked about Fred Taylor and his work either spoke of him personally with significant reserve or denounced him with bitterness which sometimes was really remarkable in its intensity."[132] Taylor was sometimes dogmatic and expressed himself in terms that made him an easy target for contemporary social critics. He once remarked that the first requirement of a pig-iron handler is that he be so dull that he resembles an ox and that an "intelligent gorilla," if properly trained, would be better suited to the job.[133] Arguably, his point was intended to illustrate that savings could come from carefully examining even menial jobs requiring only physical labor, and

---

[127] Karen Pennar and Christopher Farrell, "Micromanaging from the Grave," *Business Week* (May 15, 1995, p. 34) reported that Frederick W. Taylor was "micromanaging from the grave" with a gift of $10 million to the Stevens Institute of Technology. Rather than coming from Taylor, the gift came from his son, Robert P. A. Taylor, and was given in the name of his father.

[128] Samuel Haber, *Efficiency and Uplift: Scientific Management in the Progressive Era, 1890–1920* (Chicago, IL: University of Chicago Press, 1964), pp. 51–74.

[129] "5 Ships to be Named for Noted Engineers," *New York Times* (December 5, 1943), p. 67.

[130] Geoffrey Colvin, "Managing the End of an Era," *Fortune* (March 6, 2000), p. F-8. See also Arthur G. Bedeian and Daniel A. Wren, "Most Influential Management Books of the 20th Century," *Organizational Dynamics* 29(3) (Winter 2001), pp. 221–225; Daniel A. Wren and Robert D. Hay, "Management Historians and Business Historians: Differing Perceptions of Pioneering Contributions," *Academy of Management Journal* 20(3) (September 1977), pp. 470–475.

[131] Edwin A. Locke, "The Ideas of Frederick W. Taylor: An Evaluation," *Academy of Management Review* 7(1) (January 1982), pp. 22–23.

[132] Frank B. Copley, "Frederick W. Taylor, Revolutionist," *The Outlook* 111 (September 1, 1915), p. 41.

[133] Taylor, *Principles of Scientific Management*, pp. 40, 59. For more on Taylor's coarse language, see Horace B. Drury, "Scientific Management and Progress," *Bulletin of the Taylor Society* 2(4) (November 1916), p. 7.

to emphasize that there was nothing special about the fact that some workers were suited to this kind of job and others were not.[134] His choice of analogies, however, was less than diplomatic, and such references were understandably ill received. Taylor, however, clearly understood that "the working man" had "the same feelings, the same motives, the same ambitions, the same failings, the same virtues" as "men who are not workmen" and that their wants are the same. That is, both want "a high salary and the chance for advancement."[135] Whereas Taylor could be short and sharp with "workingmen," he was, perhaps, even less diplomatic with employers who could not grasp his "mental revolution." "A shoe manufacturer questioned the need of giving workers a bonus of from 35 to 50 per cent for maintaining standards; in his opinion, 20 per cent was plenty. 'Well,' said Taylor, peering at him over his spectacles, 'you are a damn hog.'"[136]

As Daniel M. Nelson has observed, social scientists of every stripe have set up Taylor as a "straw man," emblematic of a hierarchical, authoritarian style of management that caused decades of labor strife, forgetting that scientific management "was a commitment to knowledge, reason and continuous attention to detail that was equally antithetical to old-fashioned empiricism and to new-fashioned panaceas."[137] Responding in his own defense, Taylor explained in a June 10, 1914, letter to Abraham J. Portenar, a special organizer of New York Typographical Union No. 6, that he viewed his efforts as a means for bettering the lives of working people and that

> [i]t ought to be perfectly evident to any man that no other human being would devote the whole of his life and spend every cent of his surplus income for the purpose of producing higher dividends for a lot of manufacturing companies in which he has not the slightest interest and of which he has never heard before. . . . I have devoted nearly all my time and money to furthering the cause of Scientific Management. This is done entirely with the idea of getting better wages for the workmen—of developing the workmen coming under our system so as to make them all higher class men—to better educate them—to help them to live better lives and, above all, to be more happy and contented.[138]

A true appreciation of Taylor's efforts acknowledges that the customs of his time differ from those of today. As Lillian M. Gilbreth recognized, "No one who did not know Taylor's struggle against tradition, opposition and inertia can realize what he did and how great his achievements were."[139] To this she later added, "Although some of those who worked with and knew Taylor personally might question his tact and diplomacy, none would deny his earnestness, his sincerity, and his dedication to his high-principled goal."[140]

SUMMARY

Taylor's ideals, including the belief that the concerns of employee and employer should be based on a "mutuality of interests," were well ahead of his time. The original seed Taylor sowed has spread and multiplied a million-fold. It has spread from the mechanical operations on which he focused at the beginning of his career into workplace activities such as employee selection and training, job design, inventory control, and wage and salary administration. Further, Taylor's methods began an economic revolution that enabled

[134] Lyndall F. Urwick, "The Truth about 'Schmidt': Reflections of Col. Lyndall F. Urwick," *Working Paper Series*, 3, no. 1, Management History Division, Academy of Management, 1978, pp. 8–9, 12. Reprinted in Arthur G. Bedeian, ed., *Evolution of Management Thought*, vol. 1 (London: Routledge, 2012), pp. 252–271.
[135] Frederick W. Taylor, "The Working Man," a lecture given at Harvard University, Boston, 1909–1914. Reprinted in Ernest Dale, ed., *Readings in Management: Landmarks and New Frontiers*, 3rd ed. (New York: McGraw-Hill, 1975), pp. 100, 102.
[136] *Idem* quoted in Copley, *Taylor*, vol. 2, p. 287.
[137] Daniel M. Nelson, "Epilogue," in *idem*, ed., *A Mental Revolution: Scientific Management since Taylor* (Columbus, OH: Ohio State University Press, 1992), p. 239.
[138] Letter from Frederick W. Taylor to Abraham J. Portenar, June 10, 1914. *Frederick W. Taylor Collection*, SCW.001. Archives and Special Collections; Samuel C. Williams Library, Stevens Institute of Technology, Hoboken, NJ. See also "Testimony of Frederick W. Taylor," *Industrial Relations, Final Report and Testimony Submitted to Congress by the Commission on Industrial Relations*, vol. 1, p. 766.
[139] Taylor, *Principle of Scientific Management*, p. 8.
[140] Lillian M. Gilbreth and William J. Jaffe, "Management's Past—A Guide to Its Future," *Journal of Engineering for Industry* 83(3) (August 1961), p. 239.

industrial workers in the developed world to earn middle-income wages and achieve middle-class status. They have lifted countless millions of the developing world's poor out of extreme poverty and turned cities such as Tokyo, Hong Kong, Dubai, and Beijing into financial hubs that rival New York, London, and Paris. Of equal significance, the application of scientific management has assisted many of the world's underdeveloped and poverty-stricken countries to become world-class competitors within a single generation.[141]

Taylor's efforts also produced a change in the way managers regarded themselves. The old "rule-of-thumb" and "seat-of-the-pants" images were replaced by "an attitude of questioning, of research, of careful investigation . . . of seeking exact knowledge and then shaping action on the discovered facts."[142] Scientific management was to be a tool for increased productivity, greater purchasing power, and a higher standard of living. The legacy of scientific management has spread beyond the workplace to all aspects of modern life, including public policy, art, architecture, and literature.[143] In this regard, Taylor would be pleased. He early on expressed the belief that "the same principles can be applied with equal force to all social activities: to the management of our homes the management of our farms; the management of the business of our tradesmen, large and small; of our churches, our philanthropic institutions, our universities, and our governmental departments."[144]

On balance, Taylor left an indelible mark on his age and ours. His emphasis on efficiency remains a prevailing value of contemporary management.[145] He was not alone, but was joined by others who would apply, adapt, and refine. Taylor, however, was the lodestar that guided all those who have since followed in his footsteps to bring professional management to the workplace and replace opinion with fact.

[141] Peter F. Drucker, "The New Productivity Challenge, *Harvard Business Review* 67(6) (November–December), 1991, p. 71; *Idem*, "The Coming Rediscovery of Scientific Management," *Conference Board Record* 13(6) (June 1976), p. 26.

[142] Majority Report of Sub-Committee on Administration, "The Present State of the Art of Industrial Management," *Transactions of the American Society of Mechanical Engineers* 34 (1912), p. 1137.

[143] Richard G. Olson, *Scientism and Technocracy: The Legacy of Scientific Management* (Lanham, MD: Lexington Books, 2016).

[144] Lillian M. Gilbreth, [Review of the book *Frederick W. Taylor: Father of Scientific Management*]. *Journal of Personnel Research* 3(8) (October 1924), p. 226.

[145] Daniel A. Wren, "The Centennial of Frederick W. Taylor's *The Principles of Scientific Management*: A Retrospective Commentary," *Journal of Business and Management* 17(1) (2011), pp. 11–22.

Spreading the Gospel of Efficiency

CHAPTER 8

History rarely provides a full measure of individuals within their own lifetimes. This was true of Frederick W. Taylor and applies to those who joined with him in advocating scientific management. The present chapter focuses on six individuals who were prominent in the embryonic days of the scientific-management movement: Carl G. Barth, Henry L. Gantt, Frank B. and Lillian M. Gilbreth, Harrington Emerson, and Morris L. Cooke. These individuals led the vanguard in spreading the gospel of efficiency.

THE MOST ORTHODOX: CARL G. BARTH

Carl Georg Lange Barth (1860–1939) was born in Christiania (renamed Oslo in 1925), Norway. He received his early education in the Lillehammer public schools. Barth attended the Royal Norwegian Navy's Technical School at Horten, graduating with honors in 1876, at only 16 years old. He then began a civilian apprenticeship as a machinist, first serving as a blacksmith's helper and then as a lathe and slotting machine operator in the boiler shop at the Karljohansvern navy yard. His computational skills were soon recognized, however, and he was appointed an assistant instructor in mathematics and office assistant to the superintendent at the Technical School, earning less than 3 cents an hour. In 1881, Barth immigrated to the United States in the hope of higher pay. His first job was with William Sellers & Company (Philadelphia, Pennsylvania), a leading machine-tool manufacturer, where he began as a draftsman earning $2 a day. Barth's talents quickly became evident, and his salary was soon raised to $20 a week. Barth worked at Sellers for 13 years (1881–1895, except for 1891, spent with Arthur Falkenau Machine Company as engineer and chief draftsman) and rose to the position of chief machine designer. Beginning in 1882, he concurrently taught mechanical drawing in the evening school at the Franklin Institute

Frederick W. Taylor, "The Principles of Scientific Management," *American Magazine* 71(5) (March 1911), p. 574.

Carl G. Barth

and continued to do so for six years.[1] For a time Barth also gave private mathematics lessons, and later, for two years, ran an evening school of his own, teaching mechanical drawing.

Beginning in 1895, Barth worked for 2 years as an engineer and chief draftsman with Rankin & Fritsch Foundry & Machine Company at St. Louis, Missouri. He subsequently worked at the St. Louis Water Commission as a machine designer, and then for a year and a half at the International Correspondence Schools (Scranton, Pennsylvania), revising a paper on machine design for its International Library of Technology and preparing monthly articles such as "Designing of a Pin Joint" and "Cone Pulleys and Back Gearing" for its *Home Study Magazine*. From 1899–1900, Barth taught mathematics at the Ethical Culture School of New York, a private academy now known as Fieldston. In 1884, Wilfred Lewis, a former associate at William Sellers & Company, had suggested that Barth might be of assistance to Fred Taylor, who was searching for someone to handle complex mathematical problems in his metal-cutting experiments at the Bethlehem Iron Works. Barth ultimately joined Taylor at Bethlehem in late 1899. His first assignment was to help Henry L. Gantt calculate machine settings that often took a skilled machinist as much as an hour to configure by trial-and-error. Barth's solution was a circular logarithmic slide rule that gave near instantaneous results for the interrelation of depth of cut, machine speed, and material feed.[2] An ordinary slide rule consisted of a single slide, whereas "Barth's had five slides to accommodate all the variables involved in determining machine settings."[3] Taylor credited Barth's extraordinary analytic ability with eliminating rule-of-thumb procedures in determining the best combination of machine speeds, material feeds, and tools for cutting metals.

During the remainder of his life, Taylor relied on Barth more than anyone in developing new engineering methods. Barth assisted Taylor in the pioneering installations of scientific management at the Tabor Manufacturing Company, the Link-Belt Engineering Company, Fairbanks Scales, Yale & Towne Manufacturing Company, and later at the Watertown Arsenal. He also helped George D. Babcock install scientific management at the Franklin Motor Car Company (1908–1912) and, thus, was a pioneer in rationalizing the automobile industry. Before the advent of the moving assembly line, component parts were brought to stationary work areas for fabrication. Franklin made three models of cars—touring, runabout, and sedan—and relied on a sales forecast to determine which models to produce, when, and in what quantities. One-hundred cars were produced per *month* in lots, or batches. Franklin was unprofitable due to high manufacturing costs and rampant labor turnover (425 percent). After Barth finished installing scientific management, Franklin was producing 45 cars per *day*, wages were up 90 percent, labor turnover was less than 50 percent, and it was profitable.[4] Between 1908 and 1913, the Ford Motor Company would

[1] Biographical data are from "Testimony of Carl G. Barth, of Philadelphia, PA," *Hearings before Special Committee of the House of Representatives to Investigate the Taylor and Other Systems of Shop Management under Authority of House Resolution 90* (Washington, DC: U.S. Government Printing Office, 1912) vol. 3, pp. 1539–1543. See also Florence M. Manning, "Carl G. Barth: A Sketch" (Master's thesis, University of California, Berkeley, CA, 1927); *idem*, "Carl G. Barth, 1860–1930: A Sketch," *Norwegian-American Studies and Records* 13 (1943), pp. 114–132; and Kenneth Bjork, *Saga in Steel and Concrete: Norwegian Engineers in America* (Northfield, MN: Norwegian-American Historical Association, 1947), pp. 278–312.

[2] Carl G. Barth, "Supplement to Frederick W. Taylor's 'On the Art of Cutting Metals'—I–IV," *Industrial Management* 58(3) (September 1919), pp. 169–175; 58(4) (October 1919), pp. 282–287; 58(5) (November 1919), pp. 369–374; and 58(6) (December 1919), pp. 483–487; *idem*, "Slide Rules for the Machine Shop as a Part of the Taylor System of Management," *Transactions of the American Society of Mechanical Engineers* 25 (1904), pp. 49–62.

[3] James E. Hoopes, *The False Prophets* (Cambridge, MA: Perseus Books, 2003), p. 45.

[4] George D. Babcock, *The Taylor System in Franklin Management: Application and Results* (New York: Engineering Magazine, 1917).

perfect the moving assembly line for mass production of automobiles to replace the small-batch assembly methods of the past (see Chapter 9).

Barth lectured on scientific management at the University of Chicago (1914–1916) and Harvard University (1911–1916 and 1919–1922) and was "exceedingly proud of being accused of being Mr. Taylor's most orthodox disciple."[5] He resisted any tampering with Taylor's methods and later maintained that only those who had worked directly with Taylor fully understood the task-management system. Barth's contribution to management thought resided in his faithful execution of Taylor's methods. He was patient and accurate in his experiments and analyses. Although he may not have possessed Taylor's imagination, Barth performed the bulk of the technical work necessary for developing scientific management. In this respect, Taylor and Barth complemented each other in temperament and skills. Barth conducted his later consulting management work in conjunction with his son, J. Christian Barth, under the firm name of Carl G. Barth & Son.

CHARTING OTHER PATHS: HENRY L. GANTT

Henry Laurence Gantt (1861–1919) was born into a Calvert County, Maryland, farm family barely a month after forces from the breakaway Confederate States of America bombarded the U.S. Army garrison at Fort Sumter in Charleston Harbor, South Carolina, igniting the War Between the States. When the war left the family destitute, Gantt learned the meaning of hard work, the demands of frugal living, and the self-discipline required to make one's way in the world.[6] He received his preparatory education at the McDonogh School at Owings Mills, Maryland. McDonogh was founded in 1872 as a "military, boarding, farm school" for "poor boys of good character." Gantt graduated with distinction from Johns Hopkins University in 1880, when he was only 19 years old. In the next 3 years, Gantt taught natural science and mechanics at McDonogh and earned a mechanical engineering degree from the Stevens Institute of Technology. He then became a draftsman for Poole and Hunt, an engineering firm located in Baltimore. In 1886 Barth returned to his teaching post at McDonogh. He joined the Midvale Steel Company in 1887 as an assistant in the engineering department. Here the 26-year-old Gantt met and began to work with a man who would have a significant influence on his future career: Fred Taylor.

Taylor and Gantt were an unusual team. They shared a common interest in science as a means of improving management methods and developed a deep mutual admiration for each other's work. Gantt collaborated with Taylor at Midvale, followed him to the Simonds Rolling Machine Company to become superintendent, and joined him again at Bethlehem Steel. In 1901, Gantt became a "consulting industrial engineer" on his own, and, although he espoused the tenets of scientific management throughout his life, he later expanded his concern to include the nation's economic growth. During his lifetime, he published over 150 papers and three major books; made numerous presentations before the American Society of Mechanical Engineers (becoming vice president in 1914); patented more than a dozen inventions; lectured at universities, including Stevens, Columbia, Harvard, and Yale; and became one of the first successful management consultants.

Courtesy of Peter B. Petersen

Henry L. Gantt as a student at Johns Hopkins University, circa 1880

[5] Carl G. Barth, "Discussion," on "The Present State of the Art of Industrial Management: Majority and Minority Report of Sub-Committee on Administration," *Transactions of the American Society of Mechanical Engineers* 34 (1912), p. 1204.

[6] Biographical data are from Leon P. Alford, *Henry L. Gantt: Leader in Industry* (New York: American Society of Mechanical Engineers, 1934). See also Alex W. Rathe, *Gantt on Management* (New York: American Management Association, 1961); Peter B. Petersen, "A Further Insight into the Life of Henry L. Gantt: The Papers of Duncan Lyle," in Dennis F. Ray, ed., *Proceedings of the Southern Management Association* (1984), pp. 198–200.

THE TASK AND BONUS SYSTEM

Gantt's initial ideas on machines, tools, and methods were a direct outgrowth of his association with Taylor. The influence of Taylor's ideas on the mutual interests of employees and employers, scientifically selecting employees, appropriate performance incentives, detailed task instructions, and more is reflected in Gantt's early work. Gantt recognized that the workingman, "a human unit in a living organization," was the most important component in any successful undertaking. He believed that if business was to reflect society's values and serve social purposes, worker exploitation could not be tolerated. In his words, "the only healthy industrial condition is that in which the employer has the best men obtainable for his work, and the workman feels that his labor is being sold at the highest market price."[7]

On this road to high wages and low costs, Gantt developed a task and bonus system of compensation that was simpler than Taylor's differential piece-rate pay plan. His views on organized labor paralleled Taylor's, but he was more persuasive and philosophical in expressing them:

> If the amount of wealth in the world were fixed, the struggle for the possession of that wealth would necessarily cause antagonism; but, inasmuch as the amount of wealth is not fixed, but constantly increasing, the fact that one man has become wealthy does not necessarily mean that someone else has become poorer, but may mean quite the reverse, especially if the first is a producer of wealth. . . . As long . . . as one party—no matter which—tries to get all it can of the new wealth, regardless of the rights of the other, conflicts will continue.[8]

To Gantt, the "more, more, more" of organized labor was an antagonistic force unless it cooperated in producing more for the mutual benefit of both labor and management. He was not convinced that the differential piece-rate pay plan favored by Taylor would secure worker cooperation.[9] Gantt's "task work with a bonus" system guaranteed a day wage and paid a daily bonus of 50 cents if workers completed their tasks assigned for the day. Gantt later discovered, however, that this arrangement offered little incentive for additional effort beyond the minimum required to receive each day's bonus. To overcome this shortcoming, he modified his task and bonus system to pay workers if a task was completed in less time than expected. Thus, a worker could, for example, receive a full 3 hours' pay for doing a 3-hour job in less time.[10]

In extending his task and bonus system, Gantt adopted a suggestion by the superintendent of the Bethlehem machine shop, Edgar P. Earle, to give first-line supervisors a daily bonus for each of the workers they supervised who completed all their assigned tasks for the day, plus an extra bonus based on the bonuses the workers received. Thus, if 9 of 10 workers in a department completed their assigned tasks for the day, their supervisor would receive 10 cents per worker, or \$0.90; if all 10 did so, the supervisor would receive 15 cents per worker, or \$1.50. Gantt viewed this extra bonus as means to encourage supervisors to teach and otherwise help workers improve their performance. He knew the importance of education from his days as a teacher and felt that "task work with a bonus" would shift first-line supervisors from drivers to leaders.[11] Gantt was convinced that force could not be the basis for leadership and believed that increased productivity could only be achieved through knowledge. Like Taylor, Gantt encountered more resistance from first-line supervisors concerned with protecting their authority than from the workers they supervised. For Gantt, all the elements within a business must come together to achieve efficient performance. Further, he maintained that workplace rewards should be equitably distributed according to each person's individual contributions.

---

[7] Henry L. Gantt, *Work, Wages, and Profits: Their Influence on the Cost of Living* (New York: Engineering Magazine, 1910), p. 27.
[8] *Ibid.*, p. 49.
[9] Alford, *Gantt*, pp. 85–106.
[10] *Ibid.*, p. 165. For a detailed explanation and the computations necessary for implementing Gantt's "task work with a bonus" system, see Charles W. Lytle, *Wage Incentive Methods* (New York: Ronald Press, 1942), pp. 185–200.
[11] Henry L. Gantt, *Industrial Leadership* (New Haven, CT: Yale University Press, 1916), p. 85.

THE HABITS OF INDUSTRY

As a consulting industrial engineer, Gantt would serve some 50 clients, including American Locomotive Company, Robins Conveying Belt Company, and Brighton Mills, before his death in 1919. Sayles Bleachery, a textile dye plant located in Lincoln, Rhode Island, was one of Gantt's early clients. Despite patenting three different machines to aid in finishing cotton cloth, Gantt encountered resistance from both management and labor. Ultimately, the employees in a folding room went out on strike. They objected to Gantt's plant reorganization, asked for a 10-percent increase in wages, and went on strike when it was refused. The strike spread, and Gantt had to hire and train replacements. This experience forced Gantt to rethink how to best train new employees; from then on, he considered intensive employee training to be an essential management responsibility.

Gantt felt that, in training employees, supervisors should do more than improve their skills and knowledge; he added an ingredient to training called the "habits of industry." These habits were *industriousness* and *cooperation*, which would facilitate the acquisition of all other forms of knowledge. Gantt felt that, in doing their jobs to the best of their ability, employees would experience more "pleasure and pride in their work." As an example, he cited a group of women who formed a society of "bonus producers," with membership open only to those who consistently earned a daily bonus.[12] To Gantt, this was the ideal in labor–management relations. Gantt believed, however, that such relations could only occur after management had created a proper atmosphere of cooperation and trust. The result would be a win–win situation: higher wages for employees and increased profit (due to lower costs) for employers.

Speaking at an American Society of Mechanical Engineers convention in 1912, Gantt stressed the importance of sound labor–management relations for successful employee training. He warned, "Until proper relations are established between employer and employee, no system of management or training can be permanently successful." Gantt went on to admonish those who viewed his methods as a means for controlling employees and as "a chance to get something for nothing." In a further rebuke, he concluded, "While the idea of exploiting workmen for some one's benefit is obnoxious to most people engaged directly in industrial pursuits, this is not the case with those farther removed from the workmen."[13]

GRAPHIC AIDS TO MANAGEMENT

Gantt was less inclined to undertake painstaking experiments than either Taylor or Barth. Eventually, he turned to graphs for recording and conveying operating information. One of his earliest graphs involved using horizontal and vertical columns to compare planned and actual output.[14] "Danger lines" on the graph provided performance feedback, with shortfalls ("condemnations") highlighted in red ink for immediate attention. Gantt expanded his graphs to show daily output, production costs, output per machine/worker (in comparison with original estimates), and losses due to idle machinery.[15]

Gantt's breakthrough in charting came, however, when serving as a dollar-a-year consultant to the United States Department of the Army during World War I (1914–1918).[16]

[12] *Idem, Work, Wages, and Profits*, p. 134.

[13] Henry L. Gantt quoted in "Giving Worker His Share: Efficiency Methods Discussed by Mechanical Engineers," *The Evening Post* (New York) (December 6, 1912), p. 2.

[14] Henry L. Gantt, "A Graphical Daily Balance in Manufacture," *Transactions of the American Society of Mechanical Engineers* 24 (1903), pp. 1322–1336.

[15] Peter B. Petersen, "The Evolution of the Gantt Chart and Its Relevance Today," *Journal of Managerial Issues* 3(2) (Summer 1991), pp. 131–155.

[16] For a discussion of Gantt's contributions to the War Industries Board in World War I, see Kyle D. Bruce, "Scientific Management and the American Planning Experience of WWI: The Case of the War Industries Board," *History of Economics Review* 23 (Winter 1995), pp. 37–60.

The conversion of U.S. industry to wartime production did not come quickly or smoothly. The United States had the productive capacity, but the coordination of private industrial efforts with government agencies was haphazard. Plants were scattered all over the nation, shipments were late, warehouses were crowded or disorganized, and the military used its resources poorly. Gantt had had some experience with government work before the war. In 1911, along with Charles Day and Harrington Emerson, he was asked by Secretary of the Navy George von L. Meyer to serve on a civilian board to study inefficiency at the navy yards in New York City, Boston, Philadelphia, Norfolk, Portsmouth, Mare Island, and Puget Sound. The board concluded that costs could be reduced by half if work at the sites visited was "fully standardized and planned."[17] Its efforts went for naught, however, when Secretary Meyer's attempt to introduce scientific management in the navy's shipyards was met with stern resistance from line officers.[18] Just prior to the war, Gantt had also served as a consultant to General William Crozier, head of the U.S. Army's Ordnance Department.[19] Crozier, impressed by Gantt's graphs, developed a series of progress and performance charts to aid in managing army arsenals. When Gantt gave up his consulting work to aid in the war effort, he puzzled over how to track the huge amount of defense work being performed at so many different sites. Scheduling was especially crucial, and the information necessary to plan and coordinate private contractors' efforts with those of government agencies was lacking. Gantt spent 3 months trying to solve this puzzle before realizing, "We have all been wrong in scheduling on a basis of *quantities*. The essential element in the situation is *time*, and this should be the basis in laying out any program."[20]

Gantt's solution was a bar chart that depicts, across time, the activities that compose a project, as shown in Figure 8.1.[21] Activities represented by overlapping bars can be performed

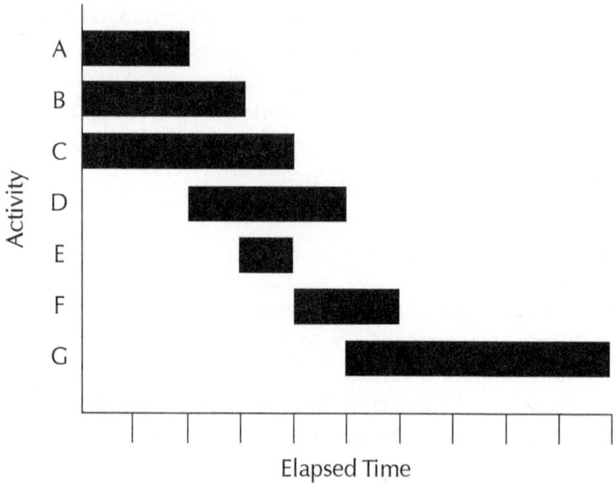

FIGURE 8.1 A simplified Gantt chart

[17] "Navy Yard System Is Declared Faulty," *New York Times* (March 9, 1912), p. 16.

[18] Peter B. Petersen, "Fighting for a Better Navy: An Attempt at Scientific Management (1805–1912)," *Journal of Management* 16(1) (March 1990), p. 159. For background into the politics surrounding Myer's decision, including Fred Taylor's meeting with President William H. Taft at the White House to offer his services to personally train Naval Constructor Holden A. Evans for introducing scientific management in the nation's navy yards, see Evans's *One Man's Fight for a Better Navy* (New York: Dodd, Mead & Company, 1940), pp. 251–259.

[19] Leon P. Alford, "An Industrial Achievement of the War: Widespread Application of Management Principles in the Ordnance Bureau of the Army," *Industrial Management* 55(2) (February 1918), pp. 97–100. See also Peter B. Petersen, "The Pioneering Efforts of Major General William Crozier (1855–1942) in the Field of Management," *Journal of Management* 15(3) (September 1989), pp. 503–516.

[20] Alford, *Gantt*, p. 207.

[21] For a history of the Gantt chart, see James M. Wilson, "Gantt Charts: A Centenary Appreciation," *European Journal of Operational Research* 149 (2) (September 2003), pp. 430–437.

concurrently to the degree they overlap. Activities represented by nonoverlapping bars must be performed in the sequence indicated. For instance, Activity D in Figure 8.1 cannot begin until Activity A is completed. It can, however, be performed concurrently with Activities C and E, at least to the extent of their overlap. Applying his newfound solution at the army's Frankford Arsenal, Gantt developed a means for scheduling and coordinating munitions production and supply between private contractors and army arsenals.

At the height of the war, German submarines were sinking merchant vessels more than twice as rapidly as they could be replaced. Together with fellow consultants Harrington Emerson and Walter N. Polakov, Gantt worked with the U.S. Emergency Fleet Corporation to overcome this shortfall. The results were exceptional. The Fleet Corporation launched more cargo ships in 1918 than were constructed in the entire world throughout 1917: "On the day of the Armistice, the United States had 341 shipyards, 350,000 shipyard workers, and had had 1,284 launchings."[22] Wallace Clark, a member of Gantt's consulting firm who will enter our story shortly, was Director of the U.S. Shipping Board's Scheduling Section. He used Gantt charts to route and monitor some 12,000 ships. Improved scheduling reduced inactive and unavailable ship times from 4 to 2 weeks.[23] World War I took a measurable turn for the better due to Gantt's contributions. The productive might of the United States was brought to fruition as arsenals and shipyards boomed. Surely this must have provided some consolation to the man whose efforts to improve the management of navy shipyards had been spurned so few years before. Gantt's and Emerson's wartime efforts were honored in 1943, when the U.S. Maritime Commission named Liberty Ships in their honor.[24]

Gantt never patented his bar charts or profited from them. He, however, was awarded the Distinguished Civilian Service Medal "for meritorious service to the government of the United States." Wallace Clark popularized the Gantt chart in a book that has been translated into eight languages.[25] Gantt charts were used as part of the Union of Soviet Socialist Republic's first Five-Year Plan, adapted in 1928, to industrialize its largely agrarian economy (see Chapter 11) and were used in the 1930s to build the Hoover Dam on the Colorado River between the U.S. states of Arizona and Nevada.[26] All subsequent graphic project controls drew their inspiration from Gantt's bar-chart concept; the modern variation became the Program Evaluation and Review Technique (PERT), a computerized, more intricate scheme for planning and controlling both time and costs.

THE LATER YEARS

As early as 1916 (the year after Fred Taylor's death), Gantt widened his views on industry and the role of industrial engineers. In particular, he criticized "the business system" for prioritizing profits over community service, which, in his opinion, was caused by career advancement based on favoritism or privilege rather than ability. Gantt argued for a "new" era in which engineers, not financiers or labor activists, would lead an industrial democracy based on equality of opportunity. He believed that only engineers could cope with the complexities of wealth creation and, thus, should lead the United States with a concern not for profits, but for productive efficiency. Gantt asserted: "We have come to the time when there is no choice. We can no longer follow the lead of those who have axes to grind, disregarding economic laws; but must accord leadership to him who knows what to do and how to do it for the benefit of the community. This man is the engineer."[27]

---

[22] *Ibid.*, p. 199.

[23] Daniel A. Wren, "Implementing the Gantt Chart in Europe and Britain: The Contributions of Wallace Clark," *Journal of Management History* 21(3) (2015), pp. 309–327.

[24] "5 Ships to Be Named for Noted Engineers," *New York Times* (December 5, 1943), p. 67.

[25] Wallace Clark, *The Gantt Chart: A Working Tool of Management* (New York: Ronald Press, 1922).

[26] For further information on the worldwide impact of Wallace Clark's work, see Pearl Franklin Clark, *Challenge of the American Know-How* (New York: Hillary House, 1957).

[27] Henry L. Gantt quoted in "Wake up, Engineers!" *Industrial Management: The Engineering Magazine* 57(4) (April 1919), p. 332.

Gantt was influenced by Thorstein B. Veblen's criticism of *laissez-faire* economics and the role of big business in shaping modern society.[28] Veblen saw a conflict between business executives and engineers, with business executives defending the status quo and engineers championing progress. Gantt was also impressed by the views of *North American Review* editorialist Charles Ferguson, who believed that a "democratic aristocracy" should lead society; that is, "a class of persons of superior capacity, who might enjoy the privileges and immunities of an upper class who shall willingly submit to the conditions of life that are imposed upon the lower class."[29]

In late 1916, Gantt formed the New Machine, an organization whose membership comprised of engineers and other sympathetic reformers who sought to acquire "political as well as economic power."[30] Its goal was to restructure industry and society according to scientific management. Gantt served as chairman of the New Machine's executive committee. In addition to Ferguson, other executive committee members were Charles R. Mann (President, American Federation of Teachers of Natural Sciences), Robert B. Wolf (Spanish River Pulp and Paper Mills), Richard A. Feiss (Joseph & Feiss Company), Henry Van Riper Scheel (Brighton Cotton Mills), and Walter Rautenstrauch (Columbia University professor of mechanical engineering). The New Machine operated on the premise that engineers would constitute Ferguson's "aristocracy of the capable" and "put down the rule of the mob."[31] It took its name from the notion that "[a] working community is a big machine," and that, given the state of world affairs, for the community to survive, a new form of democracy was required.[32] In a letter dated February 17, 1917, the New Machine called on President Woodrow Wilson to transfer "control of the huge and delicate apparatus of industry out of the hands of idlers and wastr[e]ls and to deliver it over to those who understand its operations." In a postscript added to this letter the following day, the New Machine's executive committee asked Wilson to support its efforts to establish offices for better placement of employees according to their abilities, to set up "public-service banks," and to organize "commercial organizations to lower the cost of food."[33] There is no record in Wilson's presidential papers that he either acknowledged or replied to the letter.

As outrageous as the New Machine's proposal may sound today, in November 1912, as governor of New Jersey and a candidate for U.S. President in that month's election, Wilson (a determined political reformer) had stressed the importance of specialized knowledge as a basis for government decisions and argued that as "an instrument of civilization and of humanity," government should be made "as efficient as a successful business would be."[34] In the eyes of the New Machine, what better way to make this happen than by turning the levers of power to a cadre of supposed experts who, by dint of their self-professed superior wisdom and judgment, were more

---

[28] Thorstein Veblen, *The Theory of Business Enterprise* (New York: Charles Scribner's Sons, 1904), pp. 374–400. See also Edwin Layton, "Veblen and the Engineers," *American Quarterly* 14(1) (Spring 1962), p. 68. Beyond being an editorial writer for the *North American Review*, Ferguson had previously been a practicing attorney, an Episcopal priest, a Unitarian minister, and a special agent for the U.S. Department of Commerce. On the latter assignment, see Robert D. Cuff, "Woodrow Wilson's Missionary to American Business, 1914–1915: A Note," *Business History Review* 43(4) (Winter 1969), pp. 545–551.

[29] Charles Ferguson, "A Democratic Aristocracy, Or Voluntary Servitude," *North American Review* 166(498) (May 1898), p. 638. See also *idem*, "A Democratic Aristocracy," *The Bookman: A Magazine of Literature and Life* 46(2) (October 1917), pp. 147–148.

[30] Alford, *Gantt*, p. 264. See also Peter B. Petersen, "Henry Gantt and the New Machine (1916–1919)," in John A. Pearce II and Richard B. Robinson, Jr., eds., *Proceedings of the Annual Meeting of the Academy of Management* (1986), pp. 128–132; *idem*, "Correspondence from Henry L. Gantt to an Old Friend Reveals New Information about Gantt," *Journal of Management* 12(3) (Fall 1986), pp. 339–350; and *idem*, "Henry Gantt's Last Hurrah," unpublished paper presented at the annual meeting of the Academy of Management, San Antonio, TX, August 16, 2011, Ronald G. Greenwood Collection, University Archives, Alvin Sherman Library, Nova Southeastern, Fort Lauderdale, FL.

[31] Samuel Haber, *Efficiency and Uplift: Scientific Management in the Progressive Era, 1890–1920* (Chicago, IL: University of Chicago Press, 1964), p. 45.

[32] Henry L. Gantt, "War for Democracy," *The World Court: A Magazine for International Progress* 3(2) (May 1917), p. 221.

[33] Letter from Henry L. Gantt, Charles R. Mann, Robert B. Wolf, Richard A. Feiss, Henry v. Riper Scheel, and Walter Rautenstrauch to Woodrow Wilson, Library of Congress, Woodrow Wilson Papers: Series 2: Family and General Correspondence, 1786–1924; 1917, Feb. 4–Apr. 6, Images 341–350. Available online at https://www.loc.gov/resource/mss46029.mss46029-086_0018_1147/?sp=341.

[34] Woodrow Wilson, "The New Meaning of Government," *Woman's Home Companion* 39(11) (November 1912), pp. 3–4.

knowledgeable than ordinary people? Such thinking highlights the defining belief of "progressives" (as they called themselves)—that government was the solution to society's ills. Years later, Austrian economist Friedrich Hayek would label the notion that committees of "know-better" experts (engineers or otherwise) have the requisite knowledge to shape society according to their wishes the "fatal conceit."[35]

Reform tendencies aside, Wilson, however, seemed capable of molding his campaign oratory to fit his audience. Two months prior to the November 5, 1912, presidential election, in a September 2, 1912, Labor Day address to the United Trades and Labor Council of Buffalo, New York, Wilson ridiculed the idea of expert commissions, saying, "God forbid that in a democratic country we should . . . give the government over to experts," and asking, "What are we for if we are to be scientifically taken care of by a small number of gentlemen who are the only men who understand the job?" Candidate Wilson went on to assure his union audience that he had "never heard more penetrating debate of public questions than [he had] sometimes been privileged to hear in clubs of workingmen."[36]

Wilson won the 1912 presidential election, defeating incumbent William H. Taft and former U.S. President Theodore Roosevelt (a third-party candidate and fellow progressive). He served a second term from 1917 to 1921. Despite his Labor Day comments, in hindsight, Wilson is considered a founder of the "administrative state," and is remembered for believing in government by experts, insofar as he considered the general public incapable of self-government. The downside of Wilson's belief in the superior wisdom of experts in determining public policy is discussed in Chapter 10.

In urging top-down government control and central planning by a credentialed elite, Gantt was calling for a kind of government that neither Thomas Hobbes nor John Locke nor Jean-Jacques Rousseau nor the U.S. Constitution envisioned (see Chapter 2). To a large degree, he was reacting to global events. In March 1917, the Bolshevik faction of the Russian Social Democratic Workers' Party overthrew Czar Nicholas II, and violent bloodshed swept Russia. Two years later, U.S. workers went on strike in the coal, meatpacking, steel, telephone, and textile industries. Anarchists mailed dynamite-filled bombs to prominent government officials such as Associate Justice of the U.S. Supreme Court Oliver Wendell Holmes, Jr., as well as public figures, including industrialists J. P. Morgan and John D. Rockefeller. Eugene V. Debs, a founder of the Industrial Workers of the World (IWW) and five-time Socialist Party of America candidate for U.S. President, had become something of a folk hero among "American Bolsheviks." In the 1920 presidential election, he received 919,799 votes, even though he campaigned from the Atlanta Federal Penitentiary.[37] Between 1918 and 1920, there had been Communist (Bolshevik) riots and uprisings in Bavaria and Hungary. The Wobblies (as IWW members were known) were provoking labor unrest as they sought to unite the workers of the world against capitalist interests. Many people were convinced that Bolshevism would spread revolution throughout the world.[38] In a bid

[35] Friedrich Hayek, *The Fatal Conceit: The Errors of Socialism*, ed. William W. Bartley III (Chicago: University of Chicago Press, 1988), p. 27.

[36] Woodrow Wilson, "A Labor Day Address in Buffalo" (September 2, 1912), *Papers of Woodrow Wilson*, vol. 25: Aug.–Nov. 1912, ed. Arthur S. Link (Princeton, NJ: Princeton University Press, 1978), p. 78.

[37] In a 1918 speech delivered at Canton, Ohio, Debs expressed the Socialist Party's opposition to World War I and declared: "The master class has always declared the war; the subject class has always fought the battles." He was subsequently found guilty under the Espionage Act of 1918 for interfering with military recruitment and enlistment and sentenced to a ten-year prison term. Debs had served over 30 months in prison when President Warren G. Harding commuted his sentence on Christmas Day 1921. Harding welcomed Debs to the White House the next day, and remarked: "Well, I've heard so damned much about you, Mr. Debs, that I am now glad to meet you personally." The Debs quote is taken from *Eugene V. Debs' Canton Speech* (Chicago, IL: Socialist Party of the United States, 1918), p. 18. See also Eugene V. Debs, *Walls and Bars* (Chicago, IL: Socialist Party of the United States, 1927), pp. 30, 218. The Harding quote appears in John W. Dean, *Warren G. Harding* (New York: Times Books, 2004), p. 128, but also see "Debs Holds to Views: Socialist Says He Made Attitude Clear on Visit to Harding," *Washington Post* (December 27, 1921), pp. 1, 5.

[38] Henry C. Emery, "Under Which King, Bezonian?" *Yale Review* 8(4) (July 1919), pp. 685–686; "Red Threats of Revolution Here," *The Literary Digest* 63(6) (November 8, 1919), pp. 15–16, and "Radicalism of American Labor," *The Literary Digest* 66(1) (July 2, 1920), p. 282.

to reduce industrial conflict, in 1919 and 1920, President Woodrow Wilson convened national conferences to develop a plan for resolving labor–management disputes. Among the reasons for labor unrest, the second conference's vice-chairman and future U.S. president Herbert Hoover cited "spectacular instances of excessive profits, excessive accumulation and misuse of wealth, [and] . . . social revolutionary theories imported from Europe."[39]

In the preface to his last book, published in 1919 (shortly before his death), Gantt wrote:

> The attempt which extreme radicals all over the world are making to get control of both the political and business systems on the theory that they would make the industrial and business systems serve the community, is a real danger so long as our present system does not accomplish that end. . . . In order to resume our advance toward the development of an unconquerable democratic civilization, we must purge our economic system of all autocratic practices of whatever kind, and return to the democratic principle of rendering service, which was the basis of its wonderful growth.[40]

Gantt believed that businesses had a social responsibility to incorporate community service in their activities. He argued that "the business system must accept its social responsibility and devote itself primarily to service, or the community will ultimately make the attempt to take it over in order to operate it in [the community's] own interest."[41] To this end, he further contended that "the engineer, who is a man of few opinions and many facts, few words and many deeds, should be accorded the economic leadership which is his proper place in our economic system."[42] In November 1919, Gantt was stricken with a "digestive disturbance" and died at age 58.[43]

With Gantt's death, the New Machine lost its champion and soon disbanded. Gantt did not live to see the direction that management thought would take in the 1920s and afterward. Rather than engineers providing the economic leadership, as advocated by the New Machine, "the business system" would turn to improved human-resource practices, labor–management cooperation, better employee-representation plans, and, overall, an enhanced understanding of the human factor at work. Given his concern for the "workingman," Gantt would have been pleased. In 1929, the Institute of Management and ASME posthumously awarded Gantt the first Henry Laurence Gantt Medal—"For his humanizing influence upon industrial management and for invention of the Gantt chart."

PARTNERS FOR LIFE: THE GILBRETHS

Frank Bunker Gilbreth (1868–1924) and his wife Lillian Moeller Gilbreth (1878–1972) were contemporaries of Fred Taylor and part of the small band of original scientific-management pioneers.[44] Their accomplishments still stand out for their fervor and devotion to a single goal: eliminating waste and discovering the "one best way." It was the Gilbreths' contention that of the various ways of doing a task, only one was the best, and it was their job to find it. This ideal became their credo and religion, and they did everything in their power to end the tragedy, as they

[39] Herbert Hoover, May 14, 1920, *Report of the Industrial Conference*, Hearing before the Committee on Education and Labor, United States Senate, Sixty-Sixth Congress, Second Session (Washington, DC: Government Printing Office, 1920), p. 37. See also Gary Dean Best, "President Wilson's Second Industrial Conference, 1919–20," *Labor History* 16(4) (Fall 1975), pp. 505–520.

[40] Henry L. Gantt, *Organizing for Work* (New York: Harcourt Brace Jovanovich, 1919), pp. iv–v.

[41] *Ibid.*, p. 15.

[42] *Ibid.*, p. 20.

[43] For commemorative comments by Gantt's colleagues Harrington Emerson, Walter N. Polakov, and Wallace Clark, see "Henry Laurence Gantt: In Appreciation," *Industrial Management* 58(6) (December 1919), pp. 488–491. See also Peter B. Petersen, "The Followers of Henry L. Gantt (1861–1919)," in Dorothy P. Moore, ed., *Proceedings of the Annual Meeting of the Academy of Management* (1993), pp. 174–178.

[44] Biographical data are from Edna Yost, *Frank and Lillian Gilbreth: Partners for Life* (New Brunswick, NJ: Rutgers University Press, 1949); Laurel D. Graham, *Managing on Her Own: Dr. Lillian Gilbreth and Women's Work in the Interwar Era* (Norcross, GA: Engineering & Management Press, 1998); Jane L. Lancaster, *Making Time: Lillian Moller Gilbreth—A Life Beyond "Cheaper by the Dozen"* (Boston, MA: Northeastern University Press, 2004); and Julie Des Jardins, *Lillian Gilbreth: Redefining Domesticity* (Boulder, CO: Westview Press, 2013). See also Lillian M. Gilbreth, *As I Remember* (Norcross, GA: Engineering and Management Press, 1998). Written in 1941.

The Gilbreth family at their summer home on Nantucket Island, Massachusetts, October 20, 1923—Left to right: Frank, Sr. (55); Frank, Jr. (12); Bill (11); Fred (7); Dan (6); Jack (4); Bob (3); Jane (14 months); Lill (9); Martha (13); Ernestine (15); Anne (17); and Lillian Gilbreth (45)

saw it, of the enormous waste taking place everywhere—in government, in industry, in homes, and in personal lives. The Gilbreths viewed their quest for the one best way as a means by which individuals could maximize their full potential, benefiting both themselves and society.

Frank, the son of a Fairfield, Maine, hardware merchant, was born in 1868. He learned the virtues of frugality and thrift characteristic of New England Puritanism at an early age. When he was 3 years old, his father died, and his mother relocated Frank and his two sisters to Andover, Massachusetts. In 1878, after the unexplained loss of Frank's father's estate, the family moved to Boston, where Frank was educated at Rice Primary School and English High School, graduating in 1885. Although he had passed the Massachusetts Institute of Technology entrance exam, Frank was unwilling to attend college while his mother ran a boardinghouse to support him and his two sisters. He was urged to take up bricklaying by his Sunday-school teacher, Renton Whidden, who offered Frank the impressive pay of $3 a day. Frank needed the money and took the job. To learn his new job, Frank studied other bricklayers as they went about their work. He found that they performed their task in three ways: they used one set of motions when working deliberately but slowly, a second when working rapidly, and a third when trying to teach an apprentice. It was this simple observation that led to the first precepts of *motion study*. For, as Frank reasoned, if one set of motions was right, then the other two must be wrong.[45]

Frank was determined to learn to lay bricks the "right" way. At first, he was Whidden's slowest apprentice, but he soon began developing his own ideas. Designing his own scaffolds (later patented and improved to be adjustable) and work methods for everything from mortar consistency to trowel usage, he cut the motions required to lay a brick from 18 to 6 and, thereby, tripled output. Within a year, Frank was faster than any of his coworkers. A journeyman was expected to lay 175 bricks an hour. Frank could easily lay 350 bricks. Over the next few years,

[45] Lillian M. Gilbreth, *The Quest for the One Best Way* (New York: Society of Industrial Engineers, 1924), p. 16.

with Whidden's approval, he worked at nearly every task on a construction site and later said that by age 20 he had drawn a journeyman's pay in more than 50 trades. Several years later, in 1910, Frank testified before the Interstate Commerce Commission in the Eastern Rate Case. He explained his new science of bricklaying as follows:

> Bricks have been laid the same way for 4,000 years. The first thing a man does is to bend down and pick up a brick. Taylor pointed out that the average brick weighs ten pounds, the average weight of a man above his waist is 100 pounds. Instead of bending down and raising this double load, the brick-layer could have an adjustable shelf built so that the bricks would be ready to his hand. A boy could keep these shelves at the right height. When the man gets the brick in his hand, he tests it with his trowel. If anything, this is more stupid than stopping to pick up his material. If the brick is bad he discards it, but in the process it has been carried up perhaps six stories, and must be carted down again. Moreover, it consumes the time of a $5-a-day man when a $6-a-week boy could do the testing on the ground. The next thing the bricklayer does is to turn the brick over to get its face. More waste: more work of the $6 boy. Next what does the bricklayer do? He puts his brick down on the mortar and begins to tap it down with his trowel. What does this tapping do? It gives the brick a little additional weight so it will sink into the mortar. If anything this is more stupid than any of the others. For we know the weight of the brick and it would be a simple matter in industrial physics to have the mortar mixed so that just that weight will press it down into the right layer. And the results? Instead of having eighteen motions in the laying of a brick, we have only six. And the men put on the work to try to lay 2,700 with apparently no more effort than they laid a thousand before.[46]

NOTHING SUCCEEDS LIKE . . .

By 1895, Frank had begun his own construction business in Boston with *speed work* as its motto.[47] To assure that cost arrangements would be satisfactory to his customers, Frank designed a "cost-plus-a-fixed-sum" contract. Before long, Frank's construction work spread from Maine to New Mexico. At one time, he employed up to 10,000 men. He maintained offices in London and Berlin to manage his patent rights and consult on building design and labor methods.

To keep track of the work his company was doing, Frank ordered weekly photographs showing the progress of each job. These were supplemented by daily correspondence and an array of supporting forms. Gilbreth's company constructed dams, houses, factories, canals, skyscrapers, and even whole towns (e.g., Woodland, Maine). It helped rebuild San Francisco following the 1906 fire and earthquake that devastated the city. Frank's reputation for record-setting performances drew increasing attention. One of his most famous—and least conventional—practices was to start moving construction materials toward a job site even before a contract was awarded. Then, once the contract was signed, he would startle the public by beginning work within hours. Frank soon became one of the best-known building contractors in the world.[48]

As Frank's ideas gained prominence, they also gained acceptance. Persuaded that a system that was not in writing was unworthy of a name, he set out to put his ideas into book form.[49] Working in conjunction with Lillian, he published *Field System* and *Concrete System* in 1908, and followed with *Bricklaying System* (1909), *Motion Study* (1911), *Fatigue Study* (1916), and

[46] Frank B. Gilbreth quoted in Paul U. Kellogg, "A National Hearing for Scientific Management," *The Survey* 25 (December 3, 1910), pp. 411–412. This testimony does not appear *ad verbum* in the official 10-volume *Evidence Taken by the Interstate Commerce Commission in the Matter of Proposal Advances in Freight Rates by Carriers*, Senate Document 725, 61st Cong., 3rd sess. (Washington, DC: U.S. Government Printing Office, 1911).
[47] Mark J. Steel and David W. Cheetham, "Frank Bunker Gilbreth: Building Contractor, Inventor and Pioneer Industrial Engineer," *Construction History* 9 (1993), pp. 51–69.
[48] James D. Gifford, "Frank B. Gilbreth, General Contractor: Construction Projects 1895–1910," *Construction History* 36(1) (2001), pp. 69–96.
[49] Gilbreth, *Quest for the One Best Way*, p. 22.

Applied Motion Study (1917). The *Field System* was an accounting system without a set of books and contained practical rules for job-site efficiency, such as destroying worn shovels and safe materials management. It was designed to aid construction contractors by showing operating costs, costs related to estimates, and the total cost of a job each Saturday up to the previous Thursday. No bookkeepers were needed, and because original memoranda or receipts were filed, there was no general ledger. Frank developed other facets of the field system and provided detailed instructions for its use, even including a rule about no smoking on the job and an admonition that whistle blasts at starting and quitting time should not be over 4 seconds long. He demonstrated the value of involving employees in making improvements by establishing a suggestion program, including a $10 first prize each month for the best idea on how to increase efficiency, give better service to customers, or secure additional construction work. Included in the field system were provisions for photographing working conditions at the time of any accident for use in lawsuits or other claims. Though Frank's advice was quite detailed and largely only applicable to construction, it was indicative of his desire to rationalize work.

The *Concrete System* contained detailed advice for concrete contractors.[50] Frank wrote here too of motivating employees, including contests between work groups to finish a wall or build concrete pillars. The *Bricklaying System* was also technical but brought forth a facet of study new to Frank. His original concern was with the training of apprentices, and Frank saw the wastefulness of hand-me-down instruction from experienced employees. For example, he proposed first finding the best way of laying bricks through motion study, followed by instruction, and insisted that an emphasis be placed on learning the right way to lay bricks before maximum output was expected of a new bricklayer. At a record pace, some of Frank's employees could individually lay 3,000 bricks per day.[51] This early work was but a prelude to his later in-depth analysis of motion and study of fatigue, which was considered a by-product of inefficient motions. In this connection, Frank devised a system for classifying hand motions into 17 (later 18) basic divisions called *therbligs* (*Gilbreth* spelled backwards with the *th* transposed).[52]

As Frank's contacts grew, his interests broadened. Through membership in ASME, he met Taylor and other leaders of the new scientific-management movement—men like Barth and Gantt.

AND SO, INTO SCIENTIFIC MANAGEMENT

By 1912, Frank had given up the construction business and begun devoting his full attention to management consulting. With the same single-minded focus he had given to bricklaying, Frank now studied the emerging scientific-management field. More and more convinced that "the greatest waste in the world comes from needless, ill-directed, and ineffective motions,"[53] Frank sought new methods of discovering those motions and eliminating them. In 1892, he used motion-picture cameras to analyze a worker's motions. Frank also applied motion study to musicians, oyster-openers, and fencers; put roller skates on messengers in a Montgomery Ward office to reduce their fatigue and increase delivery speed; and, at the suggestion of Jacob M. Dickinson, former Secretary of War, he tried to develop a better method of picking cotton.[54] He observed 150 appendectomies to find the one best way to remove an appendix. In conjunction with Lillian, Frank authored papers such as "The Application of Scientific Management to the Work of the

[50] Jane Morley, "Frank Bunker Gilbreth's Concrete System," *Concrete International: Designed Construction*, 12 (November 1990), pp. 57–62.
[51] Leland W. Peck, "A High Record in Bricklaying Attained by Novel Methods," *Engineering News* 62 (August 5, 1909), pp. 152–154.
[52] Frank B. Gilbreth and Lillian M. Gilbreth, "Classifying the Elements of Work: Methods of Analyzing Work into Seventeen Subdivisions," *Management and Administration* 8(2) (August 1924), pp. 151–154 and 8(3) (September 1924), pp. 295–298.
[53] Frank B. Gilbreth and Lillian M. Gilbreth, "Motion Study and Time Study Instruments of Precision," *Transactions, International Engineering Congress*, 1915, vol. 2 (San Francisco, CA: 1916), p. 473.
[54] "Efficiency Expert Will Lecture on Waste of Effort," *New Orleans Times-Picayune* (April 17, 1916), p. 5.

Nurse," "Motion-Study in Surgery," and "Scientific Management in the Hospital."[55] At one point, he even studied the motions of epileptics.[56] And with the same dedication, working now with Walter Camp, Frank filmed and analyzed the swings of golf champions such as Gil Nichols and James "Long Jim" Barnes. At the invitation of the *New-York Tribune*, in 1913, Frank filmed and analyzed a baseball game between the Phillies and the Giants at the Polo Grounds.[57] Frank's many industrial clients included Eastman Kodak, Lever Brothers, Pierce-Arrow Motor Car Company, and U.S. Rubber.

Frank's use of a motion-picture camera to eliminate unnecessary motions and thus reduce the time to perform a task was a major contribution to the field of scientific management.[58] Initially, he and Lillian filmed a worker going through his work-cycle against a black background with a net of 4-inch squares. Then they would run the film forward and backward to study the worker's motions and even construct wire models depicting the worker's movements. They called this "micromotion study." Subsequently, they conceived the idea of attaching small light bulbs to the worker's hands so that by filming the worker in motion they would be able to obtain a luminous white tracing of the worker's movements in three dimensions and to determine distances and speed of the smallest motions. They called this a *cyclegraph*. They developed a special clock, or *microchronometer*, to place in view of their cameras. It showed correct time to one-thousandth of a minute. To reproduce the time required for each movement, they created a *chronocyclegraph* showing, instead of a continuous white tracing, a series of dashes, with the pattern of dashes—bunched up (where the movement had been slowest) or spread out at greater intervals elsewhere—indicating the time occupied in a worker's separate movements. As a further refinement, they employed a stereoscopic camera to see a worker's movements in three dimensions. They called this a *stereochronocyclegraph*.[59] Despite the connotations of *speed work*, Frank remained something of an idealist. It is said "nothing ever aroused his temper more than a selfish employer who wanted to adopt all the latest things in management in his plant, but wanted to hog all the savings himself and not share with his employees."[60] In contrast to the "blacklists" of the period, Frank instituted a "white list" to keep track of "first class men" for priority hiring on subsequent jobs. In an effort to develop the skills of the men who worked for him, Frank developed "the three-position plan of promotion."[61] Under the plan, each man should perform his own job, as well as train the man below him to be his successor and to learn the next higher position to which he might be promoted. These efforts were part of his goal of developing

[55] For more on the Gilbreths' pioneering work in the medical field, see Charles D. Wrege, "The Efficient Management of Hospitals: Pioneer Work of Ernest Codman, Robert Dickinson, and Frank Gilbreth, 1910–1918" in Richard C. Huseman, ed., *Proceedings of the Annual Meeting of the Academy of Management* (1980), pp. 114–118; *idem,* "Medical Men and Scientific Management: A Forgotten Chapter in Management History," *Review of Business and Economic Research* 18(3) (Spring 1983), pp. 32–47; and Caitjan Gainty, "'Going after the High-Brows': Frank Gilbreth and the Surgical Subject, 1912–1917," *Representations* 118(1) (Spring 2012), pp. 1–27.

[56] Frank B. Gilbreth, "Discussion," on "Job Specification—Job Analysis," *Proceedings, Annual Convention, Industrial Relations Association of America* (1920), pp. 206–207.

[57] "'Movies' to Help Baseball Players Economize Force,'" *New-York Tribune* (June 15, 1913), sports section, p. 3. See also Arthur G. Bedeian, "Frank B. Gilbreth, Walter C. Camp, and the World of Sports," *Management & Organizational History* 7(4) (November 2012), pp. 319–335.

[58] The filming of visual movement in space has a long history predating the Gilbreths' industrial applications. For a review of these historical forerunners, see Siegfried Giedion, *Mechanization Takes Command: A Contribution to Anonymous History* (New York: Oxford University Press, 1948), pp. 24–25, 100–105; Anson Rabinbach, *The Human Motor: Energy, Fatigue, and the Origins of Modernity* (New York: Basic Books, 1990), pp. 84–119, 133–136.

[59] Bruce Kaiper, "The Cyclegraph and Work Motion Model," in Lew Thomas and Peter D'Agostino, eds., *Still Photography: The Problematic Model* (San Francisco, CA: NFS Press, 1981), pp. 57–63. See also Scott Curtis, "Images of Efficiency: The Films of Frank B. Gilbreth," in Vinzenz Hediger and Patrick Vonderau, eds., *Films That Work: Industrial Film and the Productivity of Media* (Amsterdam: Amsterdam University Press, 2009), pp. 83–99.

[60] Frank B. Gilbreth, Jr. *Time Out for Happiness* (New York: Thomas Y. Crowell Company, 1970), p. 140. See also Arthur G. Bedeian, "Finding the 'One Best Way,'" *Conference Board Record* 13(6) (June 1976), pp. 38–39.

[61] Frank B. Gilbreth and Lillian M. Gilbreth, "The Three Position Plan of Promotion," *Iron Age* 96(19) (November 4, 1915), pp. 1057–1059, and *idem*, "The Three Position Plan of Promotion," *Annals of the American Academy of Political and Social Science* 65 (May 1916), pp. 289–296.

employees to their fullest potential. As Frank put it, "We want to find the highest task a man can perform permanently, year after year, and thrive, and be happy. A man wants to do more than get fat; he wants to be happy."[62]

Frank's efforts paralleled what Taylor was attempting, although they differed in terminology. Taylor called his work "time study," and Frank dubbed his "motion study." Although Taylor slowly came to understand that motions needed to be optimal for his time studies to be valid, he primarily focused on "time" regardless of how speed was achieved, whereas Gilbreth was all about efficiency of movement, which would lead to time savings. Unlike Taylor, however, Frank maintained that the stopwatch was not the essence of his system. In one of the many amusing anecdotes about the Gilbreths in *Cheaper by the Dozen*, his son, Frank, Jr., and daughter, Ernestine, wrote that Frank was fascinated with time and was always the efficiency expert at home and on the job. He buttoned his vest from the bottom up, instead of top down, because the former took only 3 seconds, and the latter took 7. He used two shaving brushes (one in each hand) to lather his face and found that he could reduce shaving time by 17 seconds. He similarly tried shaving with two straight razors and found that he could reduce the total shaving time by 44 seconds but gave up this idea because it took 2 minutes to bandage each nick and cut. His children suggested that it was the 2 lost minutes that bothered him and not the nicks and cuts.[63]

SUPPORT FOR THE SCIENTIFIC-MANAGEMENT MOVEMENT

Frank was one of the scientific-management movement's most fervent advocates. Taylor devoted eight pages of *The Principles of Scientific Management* to Frank's motion studies of bricklayers. In 1911, Taylor asked Frank and Lillian to write responses to all the letters he had received after the serialized publication of *The Principles of Scientific Management* in *The American Magazine*. The magazine refused to print the responses; it was fearful that doing so would offend its subscribers. Aware of the publicity Taylor's work was generating, D. Van Nostrand Company agreed to publish the responses in book form, but only if Lillian's name did not appear on the cover, as it did not want it known that Frank's heretofore undisclosed coauthor was his wife. The Gilbreths agreed and, furthermore, declined any royalties so that the book could be sold at a lower price and, thus, have a wider circulation.[64] The Gilbreths' responses became the basis for Frank's *Primer of Scientific Management*, ghostwritten by Lillian. In the 103-page *Primer*, Frank posed common questions about scientific management and provided answers to explain Taylor's workplace philosophy. The following questions and responses are illustrative examples:

> **Does [Scientific Management] not make machines out of men? . . .**
>
> Is a good boxer, or fencer, or golf player a machine? . . . He certainly approaches closely the 100 per cent mark of perfection from the standpoint of the experts in motion study. It is not nearly so important to decide whether or not he is a machine as to decide whether or not it is desirable to have a man trained as near perfection as possible. . . .

---

[62] Frank B. Gilbreth quoted in Milton J. Nadworny, "Frank and Lillian Gilbreth and Industrial Relations," *Journal of Industrial Engineering* 13(2) (March–April 1962), p. 122; Jack F. Jericho, "Time Marches On," in J. Landon Short, ed., *Proceedings of the Thirteenth Annual Conference and Convention of the American Institute of Industrial Engineers* (1962), p. 15; and Gilbreth, *Time Out for Happiness*, p. 93.

[63] Frank B. Gilbreth, Jr., and Ernestine Gilbreth Carey, *Cheaper by the Dozen* (New York: Crowell, 1948), p. 3.

[64] Brian C. Price, "One Best Way: Frank and Lillian Gilbreth's Transformation of Scientific Management, 1885–1940" (Doctoral dissertation, Purdue University, West Lafayette, IN, 1987), p. 141. See also *idem*, "Frank and Lillian Gilbreth and the Motion Study Controversy, 1907–1930," in Daniel Nelson, ed., *A Mental Revolution: Scientific Management since Taylor* (Columbus, OH: Ohio State University Press, 1991), pp. 58–76; Carol Carlson Dean, "*Primer of Scientific Management* by Frank B. Gilbreth: A Response to Publication of Taylor's *Principles* in *The American Magazine*," *Journal of Management History* 3(1) (1997), pp. 31–41.

Does not the monotony of the highly specialized subdivision of work cause the men to become insane?

No, he will not become insane, for if his brain is of such an order that his work does not stimulate it to its highest degree, then he will be promoted, for under Scientific Management each man is specially trained to occupy that place that is the highest that he is capable. . . .

Does not the "speed boss" speed up the men to a point that is injurious to their health?

"Speed boss," like "task," is an unfortunate name . . . the "speed boss" does not tell the men how fast they shall make their motions . . . [but he does] tell the men at what speeds their machines shall run. . . .

If Scientific Management is a good thing for the workers, why do the labor leaders all oppose it?

They do not all oppose it. Some oppose it for the simple reason that they do not understand it; the others have visions that Scientific Management is something that will reduce the value of their jobs,—and all are afraid, because of the bad treatment that workmen as a whole have had in the past, that Scientific Management is simply a new "confidence game," presented in a more attractive manner than ever before . . . they simply cannot imagine Dr. Taylor or any other practical man working for their interests unless there is a "come-back" somewhere.[65]

Frank also observed that Taylor's ideas and scientific management should not be confused with what Henry Ford was doing with assembly-line production. He had toured a Ford assembly plant and was totally without sympathy for how jobs were designed:

> [A]t the Ford plant he [Frank] saw men at benches too low for them, men stretching farther than their normal reach, men in uncomfortable positions as they put on rear wheels, and much other evidence of making workers adjust to the line rather than making the line conform to the best needs of human beings. Management claimed that people adjusted to these things and did not mind, just as contractors kept saying that bricklayers did not mind stooping for bricks.[66]

Frank had been one of Taylor's most devout disciples. Beginning in 1912, however, they became increasingly estranged.[67] This was partially due to Taylor's reluctance to consider motion study separate from time study and doubts Taylor harbored about whether Frank possessed the patience required to spend the minimum 2–5 years Taylor felt necessary to successfully introduce his methods. Taylor was also concerned, given his reservations regarding Frank's qualifications, that Frank was becoming increasingly identified with the Taylor system in the mind of the public.[68] Their final break came in 1914 when Taylor received a complaint from Milton C. Herrmann at Herrmann, Aukam & Company, a New Jersey handkerchief-manufacturing company. Herrmann alleged that Frank had overcharged for his services and that inferior assistants had been assigned in Frank's place while he was in Germany consulting with Berlin-based Auergesellschaft/Deutsche Gasglühlicht AG. Taylor wrote to Gilbreth concerning Herrmann's complaints, ending his letter with "Is there anything that you wish me to do in this matter?"[69] Subsequently, Taylor dined with the Gilbreths at their home, received an autographed copy

[65] Frank B. Gilbreth, *Primer of Scientific Management* (New York: D. Van Nostrand, 1912), pp. 49, 53–54, 65, 87–88.
[66] Yost, *Frank and Lillian Gilbreth*, p. 246.
[67] See Milton J. Nadworny, "Frederick Taylor and Frank Gilbreth—Competition in Scientific Management," *Business History Review* 21(1) (Spring 1957), pp. 23–34; Daniel Nelson, *Frederick W. Taylor and the Rise of Scientific Management* (Madison, WI: University of Wisconsin Press, 1980), pp. 131–136.
[68] Hugo J. Kijne, "Time and Motion Study: Beyond the Taylor-Gilbreth Controversy," in J.-Spender and Hugo J. Kijne, eds., *Scientific Management: Frederick Winslow Taylor's Gift to the World?* (Boston, MA: Kluwer Academic, 1996), p. 69.
[69] Frederick W. Taylor to Frank B. Gilbreth, March 11, 1914, Taylor Collection, file 59A. For more on what some considered the "hucksterism" of Frank Gilbreth, see Bernard Mees, "Mind, Method, and Motion: Frank and Lillian Gilbreth," in Morgen Witzel and Malcolm Warner, eds., *The Oxford Handbook of Management Theorists* (Oxford, England: Oxford University Press, 2013), pp. 39–41.

of Lillian's book *The Psychology of Management*, and the Herrmann, Aukam matter was discussed further. We do not know the course of that evening, but H. King Hathaway took over the consulting work at Herrmann, Aukam. Frank was understandably bitter. In the ensuing years, the Gilbreths went their own way, concentrating their efforts on motion study.

THE FIRST LADY OF MANAGEMENT

In his move away from the Taylor system, Frank was aided by his wife Lillian. She was the daughter of a wealthy Oakland, California, wholesale dealer in hardware and plumbing goods. The oldest of nine siblings, Lillian (called "Lillie" by her family and friends) had attended the University of California, Berkeley, majoring in English and modern languages. In 1900, she was the first woman to give a university's commencement address. After receiving an M.Litt. degree in English literature with a minor in psychology in 1902, she began work toward a Ph.D. degree in psychology. She interrupted her studies in mid-1903 for a trip abroad and, upon arriving in Boston prior to embarking, was introduced to Frank. Shortly after Lillian returned from Europe, Frank proposed marriage and a dozen children, which by his calculation was the most efficient number.[70] Lillian and Frank married in 1904. After their marriage, Lillian changed her academic interests to industrial psychology, for she thought that this field would best complement Frank's work. Combining marriage and an ever-growing family with assisting in Frank's work, Lillian continued to do research on her thesis "The Psychology of Management" and submitted it in 1912. The University of California accepted the thesis but informed her that she would have to return to campus for a year of residency before her Ph.D. degree could be granted. Lillian had been led to believe that this requirement would be waived in her case, but university officials were steadfast. Frank was furious and began looking for a publisher for what was to have been Lillian's thesis, one of the first contributions of its kind. *Industrial Engineering and the Engineering Digest* published the thesis in serial form (May 1912–December 1912), and it was eventually published as a book by Sturgis & Walton, but only after Lillian agreed that her name would appear as L. M. Gilbreth and that no publicity would be given to the fact that the author was a woman.[71] Eventually, the university authorities agreed that Lillian could spend her residency in any college that granted advanced degrees in industrial psychology or management. Such institutions were scarce at the time, but Frank found that Brown University was planning to offer a Ph.D. degree in educational psychology with an emphasis on applied management. At Brown, Lillian wrote a new dissertation, "Some Aspects of Eliminating Waste in Teaching," finally completing her Ph.D. degree requirements in 1915, the same year that the word "flapper" entered the English language.[72]

Courtesy of the Ronald G. Greenwood Collection, University Archives, Alvin Sherman Library, Nova Southeastern, Fort Lauderdale, Fla.

Lillian M. Gilbreth, 1914

[70] For more on Gilbreth family life, see Arthur G. Bedeian and Shannon G. Taylor, "The *Übermensch* Meets the 'One Best Way': Barbara S. Burks, the Gilbreth Family, and the Eugenics Movement," *Journal of Management History* 15(2) (2009), pp. 216–221.

[71] Lillian M. Gilbreth, *The Psychology of Management: The Function of the Mind in Determining, Teaching and Installing Methods of Least Waste* (New York: Sturgis & Walton, 1914). Originally serialized in *Industrial Engineering and The Engineering Digest* 11(5) (May 1912), pp. 343–349; 11(6) (June 1912), pp. 429–438; 12(1) (July 1912), pp. 13–17; 12(2) (August 1912), pp. 65–68; 12(3) (September, 1912), pp. 116–121; 12(4) (October 1912), pp. 155–158; 12(5) (November 1912), pp. 199–204; and 12(6) (December 1912), pp. 248–257.

[72] Ronald G. Greenwood, Charles D. Wrege, and Regina A. Greenwood, "Newly Discovered Gilbreth Manuscript," in Kae H. Chung, ed., *Proceedings of the Annual Meeting of the Academy of Management* (1983), p. 111.

Lillian brought a human element into scientific management through her training, insight, and concern for worker welfare. *The Psychology of Management* was an early bridge between applied psychology and management as an academic discipline. She defined her topic as "the effect of the mind that is directing work upon that work which is directed, and the effect of this undirected and directed work upon the mind of the worker."[73] Heretofore, management had been considered an area in which no one could hope to succeed who had not inherited the "knack"; that is, individuals were leaders either because of heredity (as evidenced by ruling dynasties) or because they possessed some genetic trait. Thus, leadership was thought to be derived from nature: biology alone explained who would and who would not become a leader. Learned behavior was considered irrelevant. In contrast, with the advent of scientific management, it became possible to base management on "laws" and to study it in the classroom. Lillian would observe that successful management "lies on the *man*, not on the *work*."[74] Scientific management provided a means to make the most of peoples' efforts. As Taylor explained:

> In the past the prevailing idea has been well expressed in the saying that "Captains of industry are born, not made"; and the theory has been that if one could get the right man, methods could be safely left to him. In the future it will be appreciated that our leaders must be trained right as well as born right, and that no great man can (with the old system of personal management) hope to compete with a number of ordinary men who have been properly organized so as efficiently to cooperate.[75]

Lillian characterized three historical styles of management: *traditional*, *transitory*, and *scientific*. Traditional management was the driver, or "Marquis of Queensbury," style that followed a chain of command and was typified by successive levels of authority. Lillian adopted the prizefighting term "Marquis of Queensbury" because she felt that it embodied the physical and mental contest waged between employees and their managers "according to the rules of the game." Transitory management referred to all forms in the interim stage between the traditional and the installation of scientific management, the goal toward which all firms should strive.

Lillian compared these three styles of management according to how they affected individuality, functionalization, measurement, analysis and synthesis, standardization, records and programs, teaching, performance incentives, and welfare. On individuality, she noted that psychologists up to that time had been largely concerned with the psychology of crowds. Comparatively little work had been done on the psychology of individuals. Under traditional management, individuality was stifled by the power of a central figure; under scientific management, individuality became a fundamental principle in employee selection, performance incentives, and overall consideration of worker welfare, that is, "general wellbeing, mental, physical, moral and financial."[76] The objective of scientific management was to develop each worker to the fullest potential by strengthening personal traits, special abilities, and skills. Its focus was on how management could develop workers for their mutual benefit, not on employees' use and exploitation, as under the Marquis of Queensbury style of management.

Functionalization promoted worker welfare by improving skills through specialization, enabling greater pride in output and higher wages; measurement ensured that employees received the product of their labors; standardization improved morale and prevented employees from becoming machines; and teaching overcame fear and instilled pride and confidence in employees. Traditional management relied solely on rewards and punishment, whereas scientific management attempted to enlist worker cooperation. The rewards under scientific management differed from those of traditional management because they were predetermined (ensuring against fear of rate cutting); prompt (rather than delayed under profit sharing); and personal (in the sense that employees were rewarded for their efforts and not by their class of work). With scientific

[73] Gilbreth, *The Psychology of Management*, p. 1.
[74] Gilbreth, *The Psychology of Management*, p. 3.
[75] Frederick W. Taylor, *The Principles of Scientific Management* (New York: Harper & Brothers, 1911), pp. 6–7.
[76] Gilbreth, *The Psychology of Management*, p. 30.

management, employees gained "mental poise and security" rather than the anxiety created by traditional management. Concerning employee welfare, scientific management promoted regular work, encouraged good personal habits, and fostered the physical, mental, moral, and financial development of employees.

Lillian fully intended to become a practicing psychologist. She found, however, that she was devoting most of her time to rearing the 12 Gilbreth children (11 of whom survived to adulthood). The scientific management of the Gilbreth family and their Montclair, New Jersey, home was immortalized in the best-selling novels *Cheaper by the Dozen* and *Belles on Their Toes*, as well as in the later *Time Out for Happiness*.[77]

On June 14, 1924, tragedy struck the Gilbreths. Three days before they were to sail to Europe to attend the First World Power Conference (June 30–July 1, 1924) in London and the First International Management Congress in Prague, Czechoslovakia (July 20–24, 1924), Frank died of a heart attack while talking to Lillian from a telephone booth at the Lackawanna Railroad Terminal in Montclair. A family meeting was held, and it was decided that Lillian would fulfill the Gilbreths' European commitments. She sailed for London 5 days later, and, at the World Power Conference, she spoke on Frank's behalf.[78] In Prague, Lillian presided over a session on Education, participated in various activities of the U.S. delegation, attended a memorial service in Frank's honor, and was made a member of the Masaryk Academy of Labor, the highest scientific honor in Czechoslovakia.[79]

Returning to Montclair, Lillian was determined to continue Frank's work. She became president of Frank B. Gilbreth, Inc., and in the fall of 1924 joined the faculty at Purdue University as a lecturer. In 1935, she was made a professor of management in the Purdue School of Mechanical Engineering, the first woman to hold such an appointment. A strong psychological thread ran through all of Lillian's work. To ease access and save time, she designed refrigerators with features to store eggs, milk, and butter. To minimize movement and fatigue, she devised a foot-pedal trashcan.[80] She worked tirelessly to redesign jobs for the handicapped.[81] She advocated for the use of leisure time to create "happiness minutes."[82] She developed and marketed products to meet the specific needs of female consumers.[83] As a result of Frank's service during World War I, he and Lillian had become interested in how to use motion study to design jobs to retrain soldiers, especially amputees, so they could resume a productive life after the war. They developed devices to assist the disabled, such as a typewriter for a one-armed typist, and Lillian worked with the General Electric Company to redesign home appliances for disabled homemakers.[84] The

[77] Frank B. Gilbreth, Jr., and Ernestine Gilbreth Carey, *Cheaper by the Dozen* (New York: Crowell, 1948); Frank B. Gilbreth, Jr. and Ernestine Gilbreth Carey, *Belles on Their Toes* (New York: Crowell, 1950); Frank B. Gilbreth, Jr., *Time Out for Happiness* (New York: Crowell, 1970).

[78] For Lillian's assessment of papers delivered at the conference, see Lillian M. Gilbreth, "A Review of the Papers Presented before the First World Power Conference," *American Machinist* 61(6) (August 7, 1924), p. 222.

[79] International Management Congress, *Report of the Proceedings of the First International Management Congress in Prague (PIMCO)*, July 20–24, 1924 (Prague, Czechoslovakia: Institute for the Technical Management of Industry, Masaryk Academy of Work, 1925), pp. 29, 53–54, 102–103, 110.

[80] Anne M. Perusek, "The First Lady of Management," *SWE* [Society of Women Engineers] *Magazine* 46(1) (January–February 2000), p. 88. For a review of earlier efforts to improve the efficiency of "American housewives," see Giedion, *Mechanization Takes Command*, pp. 520–522.

[81] See J. Michael Gotcher, "Assisting the Handicapped: The Pioneering Efforts of Frank and Lillian Gilbreth," *Journal of Management* 18(1) (March 1992), pp. 5–13; Franz T. Lohrke, "Motion Study for the Blinded: A Review of the Gilbreths' Work with the Visually Handicapped," *International Journal of Public Administration* 16(5) (1993), pp. 667–682.

[82] Mario Krenn, "From Scientific Management to Homemaking: Lillian M. Gilbreth's Contributions to the Development of Management Thought," *Management & Organizational History* 6(2) (May 2011), pp. 145–161.

[83] Laurel D. Graham, "Lillian Gilbreth's Psychologically Enriched Scientific Management of Women Consumers," *Journal of Historical Research in Marketing* 5(3) (2013), pp. 351–369.

[84] Lillian M. Gilbreth, *The Home-Maker and Her Job* (New York: Appleton-Century-Crofts, 1927); *idem*, *Management in the Home: Happier Living through Saving Time and Energy* (New York: Dodd, Mead, 1955). See also Elspeth H. Brown, "The Prosthetics of Management: Motion Study, Photography, and the Industrialized Body in World War I America," in Katherine Ott, David Serlin, and Stephen Mihm, eds., *Artificial Pasts, Practical Lives: Modern Histories of Prosthetics* (New York: NYU Press, 2002), pp. 249–281; Nicholas Sammonds, "Picture This: Lillian Gilbreth's Industrial Cinema for the Home," *Camera Obscura* 21(3, 63) (December 2006), pp. 102–133.

Gilbreths were among those who lobbied Congress to pass the War Risk Insurance Act for disabled veterans. Later, this act served to pioneer legislation for those who were not war casualties but needed vocational rehabilitation.[85]

Lillian also contributed to healing the rift between Frank's motion study and Taylor's time study. In 1921, 6 years after Taylor's death, the Gilbreths issued an "indictment" of time study in the *Bulletin of the Taylor Society*. They attacked Taylor's followers (Carl G. Barth, Dwight V. Merrick, and Sanford E. Thompson) for continuing to promote stopwatch studies to support their interest in selling time devices, forms, and books. Further, they argued that time study was less precise and, therefore, less scientific than motion study, which provided accurate times and the "one best way."[86] The attack was probably unnecessary. After Taylor's death, his followers began to recognize that, to overcome union resistance, they needed to address the widespread belief that time study was synonymous with "speed work." Following Frank's death, Lillian wrote in the *Bulletin of the Taylor Society* that time study and motion study were complementary and that a stopwatch was used by Gilbreth's protégés when it was appropriate, but film studies were more accurate and useful.[87]

Moving from Frank's shadow, Lillian went on to become a pioneer in the field now known as human-resource management. She was keenly interested in the scientific selection, placement, and training of employees. Always progressive in her thinking, she displayed a deep appreciation of the human factor in industry. As early as 1914, she wrote that scientific management is "built on the basic principle of recognition of the individual, not only as an economic unit but also as a personality, with all the idiosyncrasies that distinguish a person."[88] Whereas much of Lillian's work is now taken as self-evident, it was far in advance of its time. More than 90 years ago, she publicly urged an end to discrimination in both the hiring and retention of employees over 40.[89] Convinced that programs to hire and train "older" employees were simply "good business," she called for research to measure comparative job performance by age. In the larger public arena, Lillian served under Presidents Hoover, Franklin D. Roosevelt, Eisenhower, Kennedy, and Johnson on committees dealing with civil defense, war production, aging, and rehabilitation of the physically disabled.

In addition to teaching at Purdue University and lecturing throughout the world, Lillian taught at the University of Wisconsin at Madison; Rutgers University at New Brunswick, New Jersey; Newark College of Engineering (now known as the New Jersey Institute of Technology); and served as a Resident Lecturer at the Massachusetts Institute of Technology. The Gilbreth Medal, named for both Frank and Lillian, was awarded to Lillian in 1931—the only female recipient to date; she was also the only woman to receive the coveted Gantt Gold Medal (1944) and the only woman to be awarded the prestigious Comité Internationale de l'Organisation Scientifique (CIOS) Gold Medal (1954). Being the recipient of 22 honorary degrees, Lillian was the first woman to be named an honorary member of the ASME (1926), as well as the first elected to the National Academy of Engineering (1965). In 1984, she was honored when the U.S. Postal Service issued a stamp to commemorate her achievements as the "First Lady of Engineering."

The Gilbreths were a formidable team. He an engineer and she a psychologist, they pooled their talents in search of the one best way. Their interests ranged widely. They made contributions ranging from material handling and work methods to the study of motion and the detrimental

[85] Daniel A. Wren and Ronald G. Greenwood, *Management Innovators: The People and Ideas That Have Shaped Modern Business* (New York: Oxford University Press, 1998), p. 146. Like Taylor, Gantt, and Emerson, Frank was also honored by the U.S. Maritime Commission in 1943 with a Liberty Ship named in his honor; see "5 Ships to Be Named for Noted Engineers," *New York Times* (December 5, 1943), p. 67.

[86] Frank B. and Lillian M. Gilbreth, "An Indictment of Stop-Watch Time Study," *Bulletin of the Taylor Society* 6(3) (June 1921), pp. 99–108. See also the discussion that followed the Gilbreths' paper (pp. 109–135).

[87] Lillian M. Gilbreth, "The Relations of Time and Motion Study," *Bulletin of the Taylor Society* 13(3) (June 1928), pp. 126–128.

[88] *Idem*, *Psychology of Management*, pp. 18–19.

[89] Lillian M. Gilbreth, "Scrapped at Forty," *The Survey* 62(7) (July 1, 1929), pp. 402–403; *idem*, "Hiring and Firing: Shall the Calendar Measure Length of Service?" *Factory and Industrial Management* 79(2) (February 1930), pp. 310–311.

effects of fatigue, to empowering the disabled, and to modern human-resource management. The impact of their contributions has shaped business, industrial, and everyday life for over a century, from simplicities such as refrigerator door shelves to the modern surgical arena to workplace ergonomics and humane labor relations. Many principles from the Gilbreths' study of fatigue are reflected in U.S. Occupational Safety and Health Administration standards and the configurations for the crew compartment, crew seats, and instrument panel of the National Aeronautical and Space Administration's Apollo command and service modules were designed using techniques pioneered by Frank and Lillian Gilbreth.[90]

Some may assume that in an era when few women pursued business as a profession, Lillian was both quiet and shy. Peter F. Drucker, one of the last century's most influential management thinkers, however, sought to dispel what he called Lillian's "charming deception." Drucker offered this description of a forceful and confident woman: "Believe me, the lady *was* the original tiger—her demure charm was pure facade, put on (a) to disarm those who did not accept a woman as an equal, let alone as a superior, and (b) to better eat you up. Even God knew better than to help those who let themselves be lulled to sleep by Dr. Lillian's charm, warmth and deceptive gentility—and yet she was the most generous of people to those who asked for help, admitted her undeniable superiority and were willing to follow where she led. I have not in my life met an Emperor, but I met an Empress—Lillian Gilbreth."[91]

Is there any doubt about why Lillian Gilbreth has also been called the "First Lady of Management"?

EFFICIENCY THROUGH ORGANIZATION: HARRINGTON EMERSON

Harrington Emerson (1853–1931) was born in Trenton, New Jersey, and educated at private schools in Paris, Munich, Siena, and Athens.[92] His father was a professor of political economy who taught at various European universities, and he was a grandson of Samuel D. Ingraham, Secretary of the Treasury under President Andrew Jackson. He earned an engineering degree from the Royal Polytechnic (Munich) in 1875. Returning to the United States in 1876, he taught modern languages at the University of Nebraska (Lincoln) until 1882, when he was dismissed because he favored allowing students and faculty greater freedom in their personal behavior and advocated removing religion from classroom instruction.[93] After holding a succession of jobs, he established the Emerson Institute (later the Emerson Efficiency Engineers) at New York City in 1901. Emerson was symbolic of the new breed of "efficiency engineers" (a term he coined) who were bringing innovative methods of time and cost savings to U.S. industry. The nation's first big business, the railroads, was showing signs of wear and tear. Locomotive and railcar repair and maintenance shops were a bottleneck that kept rolling stock from rolling. Emerson began as a troubleshooter for the general manager of the Burlington Railroad and in 1904 became a consultant to the Atchison, Topeka & Santa Fe

Bain Collection/ The Library of Congress

Harrington Emerson

[90] Mark Paterson, "Fatigue as a Physiological Problem: Experiments in the Observation and Quantification of Movement and Industrial Labor, 1873–1947," *History and Technology* 39(2) (June 1923), p. 17. Norman J. Ryker, Jr., "Man-Equipment Task System for Apollo," in *The Frank Gilbreth Centennial* (New York: American Society of Mechanical Engineers, 1969), pp. 4–36.

[91] Letter from Peter F. Drucker to Ronald G. Greenwood, April 6, 1979, Ronald G. Greenwood Collection, University Archives, Alvin Sherman Library, Nova Southeastern, Fort Lauderdale, FL.

[92] For further biographical data, see Edward J. Mehren, "Harrington Emerson's Place in Industrial Engineering," *Society of Industrial Engineers Bulletin* 13(7) (June–July 1931), pp. 4–8; Sidney Brooks, "Harrington Emerson: Some Glimpses of His Life," *Society of Industrial Engineers Bulletin* 13(7) (June–July 1931), pp. 9–11. See also Morgen L Witzel, ed., *The Biographical Dictionary of Management*, vol. 1 (Bristol, England: Thoemmes Press, 2001), pp. 276–282.

[93] William F. Muhs, "Harrington Emerson as Professor," unpublished paper presented at the annual meeting of the Academy of Management, Detroit, MI, August 11, 1980, p. 4, William F. Muhs Collection, Harry W. Bass Business History Collection, University of Oklahoma Libraries, Norman, OK.

Railroad. He standardized materials and tools, centralized production scheduling and routing, instituted time study, and introduced a performance-incentive plan. After 2 years, output was up 57 percent, costs were down 36 percent, and the average pay of Santa Fe employees was up 14.5 percent. In spite of conflict with union members (who lost the struggle), Emerson's efforts were praised as an example of what scientific management could do for the nation's railroads.[94] His railroad work and later testimony in the Eastern Rate Case (see Chapter 7) led to consulting engagements with clients such as Aluminum Company of America (Alcoa), Bethlehem Steel, and General Motors.

By 1925, Emerson's reputation had spread to Germany, Japan, Britain, India, Kenya, and Uganda. His innovations enabled railroads (including the London Underground) to reduce costs, minimize operating downtime, and decrease capital requirements by standardizing methods, materials, and equipment.[95] Success on the Santa Fe and other railroads created opportunities for Emerson's firm to apply his ideas to a cross section of companies in multiple industries and to municipalities such as Seattle, Milwaukee, and New York. Though Emerson used many of Taylor's methods, in soliciting clients he "emphasized his flexibility and deviation from Taylor's more rigid prescriptions."[96]

Like the Gilbreths, Emerson saw waste and inefficiency as the twin evils that were pervading the entire U.S. industrial system. His experience had shown that railroad repair shops averaged 50 percent efficiency and that preventable labor and material wastes were costing the railroad industry $300 million annually (hence his well-publicized Eastern Rate Case testimony of savings equaling $1 million a day).[97] Emerson believed that national prosperity was not a function of either an abundance or a lack of natural resources, but rather the "ambition, the desire for success and wealth" of a nation's workers.[98] In Emerson's view, the United States possessed abundant resources and an ambitious workforce, which had led to its rise as a global industrial power, yet it was losing its advantage due to inefficient use of resources. Emerson was convinced that the resulting waste could only be reduced by the proper organization of men, machines, and materials.

LINE AND STAFF ORGANIZATION

Taylor's "functional foremanship" did not appeal to Emerson. He agreed with Taylor that the specialized knowledge of staff members was necessary, but differed from Taylor in how best to use this expertise. Influenced by his European education, Emerson admired Count Helmuth Karl Bernhard Graf von Moltke who, from 1857 to 1888, had modernized the Prussian army's General Staff.[99] The logic behind Moltke's modernization was straightforward. Each subject vital to military efforts was to be studied to perfection by a separate staff specialist who, with other specialists, would form a supreme general staff to advise the nation's field marshals on all matters pertaining to the Prussian army.

---

94 Carl Graves, "Applying Scientific Management Principles to Railroad Repair Shops—The Santa Fe Experience, 1904–1918," in Jeremy Atack, ed., *Business and Economic History* 10 (1981), pp. 124–136.

95 Mark Aldrich, "On the Track of Efficiency: Scientific Management Comes to Railroad Shops, 1900–1930," *Business History Review* 84(3) (Autumn 2010), pp. 501–526.

96 James P. Quigel, Jr., "The Business of Selling Efficiency: Harrington Emerson and the Emerson Efficiency Engineers, 1900–1990" (Doctoral dissertation, Pennsylvania State University, State College, PA, 1992), pp. 301, 421.

97 Harrington Emerson, "Preventable Waste and Losses on Railroads," *Railroad Age* 45 (June 5, 1908), p. 12.

98 Harrington Emerson, *Efficiency as a Basis for Operations and Wages* (New York: Engineering Magazine, 1911), p. 37. Originally serialized in *The Engineering Magazine* 35(4) (July 1908), pp. 529–536; 35(5) (August 1908), pp. 661–672; 35(6) (September 1908), pp. 909–920; 36(1) (October 1908), pp. 33–432; 36(2) (November 1908), 170–178; 36(3) (December 1908), 336–346; 36(4) (January 1909), pp. 676–683; 36(5) (February 1909), pp. 815–824; 36(6) (March 1909), pp. 998–1002.

99 *Ibid.*, pp. 64–66. After the unification of the German Empire in 1871, the Prussian General Staff's title was changed to "Great General Staff." Karl von Clausewitz commented on the Prussian Army's General Staff as early as 1793. See Clausewitz, *Vom Kriege* [*On War*], vol. 2 (Berlin: Ferdinand Dümmlers Verlagsbuchhandlung, 1832), p. 198, Originally written 1816–1830.

Emerson sought to apply Moltke's staff logic to the workplace. His goal was to achieve a "complete parallelism between line and staff, so that every member of the line can at any time have the benefit of staff knowledge and staff assistance."[100] As envisioned by Emerson, each firm was to have a chief-of-staff serving over four major subdivisions. The first would plan, direct, and advise on the well-being of employees; the second, direct and advise on structures, machines, tools, and other equipment; the third, direct and advise on materials, including their purchase, custody, issue, and handling; and the fourth, plan, direct, and advise on methods and conditions, including standards, records, and accounting. Staff knowledge and advice were to be available to every line manager: "It is the business of staff, not to accomplish work, but to set up standards and ideals, so that the line may work more efficiently."[101] The distinction between Emerson's line and staff organization and Taylor's functional foremanship is, thus, apparent: instead of giving one person the responsibility and authority over each workplace function, Emerson left supervision and authority to line managers, who then accessed staff for specialized knowledge and advice. This shift maintained the advantages of specialized knowledge and facilitated coordination without the disadvantages associated with violating the unity of command principle.

TWELVE PRINCIPLES OF EFFICIENCY

Ironically, Emerson's efficiency work was somewhat overshadowed by the press coverage Taylor's task-management system received after the Eastern Rate Case hearings. Following the hearings, Emerson published *Twelve Principles of Efficiency*, which became another landmark in the history of management thought. A chapter was devoted to each of the eponymous principles; broadly conceived, the first five concerned relations with people and the remainder concerned methods, institutions, and systems. The principles were interdependent and a basis for testing the efficiency of any undertaking. In the book's preface, Emerson stated his basic premise: "It is not labor, not capital, not land, which has created modern wealth or is creating it today. It is ideas that create wealth, and what is wanted is more ideas—more uncovering of natural reservoirs, and less labor and capital and land per unit of production."[102]

No modern author could state the contemporary challenges facing today's global organizations more cogently. For Emerson, "ideas" were the dominant force for eliminating waste and assuring national prosperity. He saw his 12 principles as instruments for this purpose and the line-staff form of organization as essential for enabling managers to access specialized knowledge and advice. To Emerson, "defective organization" was "the industrial hookworm disease."[103] Emerson's 12 principles of efficiency sought to combat such deficiencies. The first principle was "clearly defined ideals." This principle made explicit the need for agreement among employees and employers on workplace goals ("ideals") and the importance of everyone pulling in a "straight line." Emerson hoped to reduce conflict, vagueness, uncertainty, and the aimlessness that arose when people did not understand or share a common purpose. The second principle, common sense, exhorted managers to take a larger view of problems and to seek special knowledge and advice wherever they may be found. All employees who had something of value to contribute were encouraged to participate in problem-solving.[104] The third principle,

---

[100] Emerson, *Efficiency as a Basis for Operations and Wages*, p. 69.

[101] *Ibid.*, p. 112.

[102] Harrington Emerson, *The Twelve Principles of Efficiency* (New York: Engineering Magazine, 1913), p. x. Originally serialized in *The Engineering Magazine* 39(3) (June 1910), pp. 321–330; 39(4) (July 1910), pp. 481–493; 39(5) (August 1910), pp. 679–691; 39(6) (September 1910), pp. 841–852; 40(1) (October 1910), pp. 77–82; 40(2) (November 1910), pp. 161–174; 40(3) (December 1910), pp. 413–424; 40(4) (January 1911), pp. 496–506; 40(5) (February 1911), pp. 761–768; 40(6) (March 1911), pp. 943–950; 41(1) April 1911), pp. 27–32; 41(2) (May 1911), pp. 293–300; 42(3) (June 1911), pp. 441–447; 41(4) (July 1911), pp. 632–640; 41(5) (August 1911), pp. 810–818; 41(6) (September 1911), pp. 897–904.

[103] *Ibid.*, p. 29.

[104] William F. Muhs, "Worker Participation in the Progressive Era: An Assessment by Harrington Emerson," *Academy of Management Review* 7(1) (January 1982), pp. 99–102.

competent counsel, was related to the second principle in that it pertained to assembling an experienced and knowledgeable staff. Discipline became the fourth principle and called for obedience and adherence to workplace rules. It was the foundation for the other 11 principles and prevented anarchy. The fifth and final principle pertaining to people was the fair deal. Peace, harmony, and high performance were dependent upon fairness in all employee–employer relations. Rather than being patronizing or altruistic, the employee–employer relationship was to be based on mutual advantage.

The seven principles pertaining to workplace methods were more mechanistic and largely self-explanatory: "reliable, immediate, accurate, and permanent records" (information and accounting systems); "dispatching" (planning and routing of work); "standards and schedules" (methods and time for tasks); "standardized conditions"; "standardized operations"; "written standard practice instructions"; and "efficiency reward" (rewards proportionate to efficiency). Each principle was liberally sprinkled with examples from Emerson's consulting experience and formed a thorough, though often redundant, statement of his workplace philosophy.

THE "HIGH PRIEST OF EFFICIENCY"

Emerson made other contributions in cost accounting, in using Hollerith tabulating machines for accounting records, and in setting standards for judging worker and shop efficiency. In cost accounting, Emerson made a clear distinction between historical cost accounting (descriptive) and "the new cost accounting," which estimated what costs should be after waste was eliminated and before work commenced. Although others had written about cost-accounting standards, Emerson appears to have been the first to develop a system of standardized costs for assessing more accurately relative efficiencies in materials and services.[105] G. Charter Harrison took Emerson's ideas and installed the first full-fledged standard cost-accounting system in the Boss Manufacturing Company, Kewanee, Illinois, in 1911. At that time, Boss Manufacturing was the nation's largest maker of work gloves and boots.[106] As early as 1920, Emerson was using Gantt charts to measure and monitor expenses.

In addition, Emerson devised an incentive plan that paid employees a 20 percent bonus for 100 percent efficiency; above 100 percent efficiency, employees received their standard wages for time saved plus a 20 percent bonus for the time worked. For example, at 100 percent efficiency, the bonus was 20 cents per 1 dollar of wages; at 120 percent efficiency, the bonus was 40 cents per 1 dollar of wages (i.e., 40 cents = 20 cents for bonus and 20 cents for working 20 percent more efficiently).[107] In practice, scheduling and staff specialists had a more lasting effect on productivity than incentive bonuses, which contributed to worker unrest and "tended to favor skilled workers but [were] limited by inaccurate time studies."[108] Emerson's experiences with performance bonuses met similar resistance as encountered by other scientific-management consultants. On the Baltimore & Ohio Railroad, Emerson found 99 percent employee turnover and recognized the waste in hiring, training, and other costs. The B&O's experience was typical in the 1900–1919 period, when annual labor turnover rates in the United States exceeded 100 percent.[109]

Emerson's consulting firm was a seedbed for others who became distinguished consultants and executives. These included Earl K. Wennerlund, later a vice president of production at General Motors; Charles E. Knoeppel, who would form his own consulting firm (C. E. Knoeppel

---

[105] Emerson, *The Twelve Principles of Efficiency*, pp. 167–201; *idem*, "Standardization and Labor Efficiency in Railroad Shops," *Engineering Magazine* 33(5) (August 1907), pp. 783–786.

[106] David Solomons, "Retrospective: Costing Pioneers, Some Links with the Past," *Accounting Historians Journal* 21(2) (December 1994), pp. 135–149.

[107] Emerson, *Efficiency as a Basis for Operations and Wages*, pp. 193–196.

[108] Quigel, "The Business of Selling Efficiency," p. 424; Aldrich, "On the Track of Efficiency," p. 525.

[109] Laura Owen, "History of Labor Turnover in the U.S.," *EH Net Encyclopedia*, ed. Robert Whaples, April 29, 2004. Available online at http://eh.net/encyclopedia/history-of-labor-turnover-in-the-u-s/.

and Company, Industrial Engineers) and develop the "profit graph," a forerunner to the breakeven chart; and Herbert N. Casson, who would take efficiency methods and scientific management to Great Britain.[110] In 1925, following a series of disagreements with his partners, Emerson resigned from the firm he founded. Originally called Emerson Engineers, even though none of the members of the association were engineers, the firm later took the name Emerson Consultants.

Emerson has been called the "high priest of efficiency" for his efforts to eliminate waste in industry.[111] He testified before the Special Committee of the House of Representatives to Investigate the Taylor and Other Efficiency Systems (1911–1912); helped found the Efficiency Society (1912); served on the Federated American Engineering Societies' Committee on the Elimination of Waste in Industry (1921); and was instrumental in the founding of the Association of Management Consulting Firms (1929). His contributions were unique in advocating a line-staff form of organization, developing standards for use in cost accounting, and anticipating the need for employment specialists. His testimony at the Eastern Rate Case hearings brought the scientific-management movement to the world's attention.

THE GOSPEL IN PUBLIC-SECTOR ORGANIZATIONS: MORRIS L. COOKE

While Taylor, Barth, the Gilbreths, Gantt, and Emerson were eliminating waste and inefficiency in industry, Morris Llewellyn Cooke (1872–1960) was extending the gospel of efficiency to public-sector organizations. Cooke attended Lehigh Preparatory School and then Lehigh University in Bethlehem, Pennsylvania, graduating in 1895 with a degree in mechanical engineering. After an apprenticeship at Cramp's Shipyard (Philadelphia), he worked in various companies in the surrounding area. Long before he had met or heard of Fred Taylor, he was applying a "questioning method" to the waste he saw all around him. As scientific management gained notoriety, Cooke became an avid defender of Taylor's methods. Cooke eventually met Taylor and evidently impressed him, as Taylor asked Cooke to join a committee Taylor was forming to apply scientific management to the ASME's offices. Taylor, who was then ASME president, personally financed the study, and paid Cooke's salary.[112] During the year-and-a-half study their friendship grew. Cooke soon became an insider in the scientific-management movement.

Distrustful of the so-called new breed of "efficiency engineers," Taylor only trusted four men, all of whom had worked under his direction, to introduce his methods: Carl G. Barth, Henry L. Gantt, H. King Hathaway, and Morris L. Cooke.[113] Known as a friend of labor, Cooke once saw a sign at a factory gate reading, "Hands Entrance." In response, he asked, "Where do the heads and hearts enter?"—the sign was promptly removed.[114] Perhaps Cooke was being flippant, but he made his point: scientific management called for more than hands.

In 1909, Henry S. Pritchett, president of the Carnegie Foundation for the Advancement of Teaching, asked Taylor to recommend someone to conduct an economic study of higher education to determine if the best use was being made of university faculty and facilities. Taylor recommended Cooke. The resulting report was a bombshell in the academic world.[115] Cooke visited physics departments at nine universities, as they were believed representative of university teaching and research, in general. In his final report, Cooke attempted something that few were eager to attempt: measure the cost of inputs relative to outputs in teaching and research.

[110] William F. Muhs, "The Emerson Engineers: A Look at One of the First Management Consulting Firms in the U.S.," in John A. Pearce II and Richard B. Robinson, Jr., eds., *Proceedings of the Annual Meeting of the Academy of Management* (1986), pp. 123–127. For insights into the life and work of Herbert N. Casson and Charles E. Knoeppel, see Morgen L Witzel, ed., *The Biographical Dictionary of Management*, pp. 137–144 and pp. 539–540, respectively.

[111] [W. Jerome Arnold], "Famous Firsts: High Priest of Efficiency," *Business Week* (June 22, 1963), pp. 100, 104.

[112] Bruce Sinclair with James P. Hull, *A Centennial History of the American Society of Mechanical Engineers 1880–1980* (Toronto: University of Toronto Press, 2018), pp. 86–87.

[113] Frank B. Copley, *Frederick W. Taylor: Father of Scientific Management* (New York: Harper & Brothers, 1923) vol. 2, p. 357.

[114] Kenneth E. Trombley, *The Life and Times of a Happy Liberal: A Biography of Morris Llewellyn Cooke* (New York: Harper & Brothers, 1954), p. 10.

[115] Morris L. Cooke, *Academic and Industrial Efficiency* (New York: Carnegie Foundation for the Advancement of Teaching Bulletin no. 5, 1910).

Harris & Ewing Collection / The Library of Congress

Morris L. Cooke

His findings were quite upsetting. Inbreeding (an institution hiring its own graduates) was widespread; managerial practices were even worse than those in industry; committee management was a curse; departments enjoyed excessive autonomy, which worked against university-wide coordination of course offerings and scheduling; pay was based on seniority rather than merit; and life tenure for professors protected the unfit, who should be retired. Cooke believed that professors should spend more time in teaching and research, leaving administrative tasks to specialists rather than faculty committees. Assistants should be used more widely, allowing higher priced talent to undertake more complex assignments, and the costs of teaching and research should be more closely controlled by a university's central administration. Cooke concluded, "[T]here are very few, if any, of the broader principles of management which obtain generally in the industrial and commercial world which are not more or less applicable to the college field, and so far as [I have] discovered no one of them is now generally observed."[116] Initial reactions to the report were predictable: Richard C. Maclaurin, president of the Massachusetts Institute of Technology, asked how Isaac Newton's 14 years of research on his theory of gravitation would have fared if Cooke's ideas were implemented. He felt a focus on efficiency distracted from a university's fundamental purpose and would lead to higher administrative overhead, and that Cooke's report was "written from the point of view of the man who is used to report[ing] on the efficiency of a glue factory or soap works."[117] Nonetheless, as Robert Kanigel notes, the effects of Cooke's report "are felt today, as any college professor who's ever filled out a state-mandated faculty productivity form can attest."[118]

---

[116] *Idem* quoted in "Scores Management of Our Universities," *New York Times* (December 19, 1910), p. 1.

[117] Richard C. Maclaurin, "Educational and Industrial Efficiency," *Science* 33(838) (January 20, 1911), p. 101.

[118] Robert Kanigel, *The One Best Way: Frederick Winslow Taylor and the Enigma of Efficiency* (New York: Viking, 1997), p. 490.

THE BOXLY TALKS

Throughout this period, Taylor continued to give his famous talks at Boxly, his Philadelphia home. Always interested in improving his presentation, Taylor asked Cooke, who arranged most of the talks, to analyze his standard presentation with the aim of enhancing its flow and content. Taylor had previously suggested that Cooke write a book for a general audience describing the Taylor system. As noted in Chapter 7, a court stenographer was hired to transcribe Taylor's June 4, 1907, talk. In his opening remarks, Taylor assured his audience that "task management" (his preferred term before "scientific management" became popular) was superior to previous ideas: "I want to try to convince you that the task idea, because that is what is back of everything we do, is overwhelmingly better than [ordinary management] in its practical results."[119] Taylor's two-hour talk, plus a question-and-answer period, was strongly worded and included his well-worn pig-iron-handling anecdote. When Taylor read the stenographer's transcription, he was surprised at what he had said and responded, "Did I actually say that!"[120] He vowed to be more careful in the future about what he said and how he spoke about task management.

After acquiring a copy of the Boxly transcript, Cooke told Taylor that he intended to use it, along with other materials he had collected, as the basis for a book titled *Industrial Management*, to be of assistance to those installing Taylor's methods. In the course of events, as interpreted by Charles D. Wrege and Anne Marie Stotka, Cooke's *Industrial Management* became Taylor's *The Principles of Scientific Management*. In Wrege and Stotka's eyes, Taylor "attached his name to someone else's work," and Cooke "created a classic."[121] Was the "Father of Scientific Management" a plagiarist? Or was this a mutual agreement between Taylor and Cooke to promote Taylor's ideas? The story is involved, but merits examination.

The foundation for Cooke's *Industrial Management* was Taylor's Boxly talk, which Cooke had been asked to edit. By late 1909, Taylor and Cooke had agreed to become the book's joint authors. Cooke revised an earlier manuscript he had prepared, rewrote 31 pages of Taylor's 62-page Boxly talk, and added 43 pages from other sources. The resulting manuscript, however, was never published, but 69 pages of *Industrial Management* (which began with a stenographer's transcription of Taylor's talk) were incorporated into Taylor's *The Principles of Scientific Management*.[122] On this basis, Wrege and Stotka concluded that Cooke "created the classic" and that "Taylor's use of Cooke's manuscript is merely an example of [Taylor's] tendency to publish, under his own name, material written by others."[123]

Is there another side to this story? On the *Industrial Management* manuscript Cooke was preparing, he printed this comment:

> [T]his chapter [Chapter 2] is very largely a recital of Mr. Taylor's personal experiences in the development of scientific management, and as such has been written by himself in the first person.[124]

Cooke told Taylor that he would forgo any profits from *Industrial Management*. Taylor responded that all royalties from *The Principles of Scientific Management* would be paid to Cooke. The archives of Harper & Brothers, Taylor's publisher, indicate that royalties were paid to Cooke

---

[119] "Report of a Lecture by and Questions Put to Mr. F. W. Taylor: A Transcript," *Journal of Management History* 1(1) (1995), p. 8. See also Charles D. Wrege, "F. W. Taylor's Lecture on Management, 4th June 1907: An Introduction," *Journal of Management History* 1(1) (1995), pp. 4–7.
[120] Copley, *Taylor*, vol. 2, p. 284.
[121] Charles D. Wrege and Ronald G. Greenwood, *Frederick W. Taylor: The Father of Scientific Management: Myth and Realty* (Homewood, IL: Business One Irwin, 1991), pp. 182, 188.
[122] Wrege and Greenwood, *Taylor*, p. 182.
[123] Wrege and Stotka, p. 749.
[124] *Ibid.*, pp. 746–747. The Cooke manuscript is preserved at the Kheel Center for Labor-Management Documentation and Archives, Catherwood Library, Cornell University, under the title "Morris L. Cooke 'Industrial Management' Monograph on Microfilm," Collection Number: 5930 mf.

from June 1911 (*The Principles of Scientific Management* was published on April 18, 1911) until the last quarter of 1913.[125] According to Carol Carlson Dean:

> [T]he royalty money was likely a minor matter to both Taylor and Cooke. Neither of them needed the royalty money, as suggested by the fact that Cooke was making nearly $50,000 a year through Taylor [from consulting referrals]—a considerable sum considering the time. The royalty payment to Cooke was likely a mere gesture on Taylor's part for Cooke's contribution to Taylor's "principles."[126]

A reasonable conclusion is that Cooke contributed to, but did not write, *The Principles of Scientific Management*. He edited and enriched Taylor's Boxly talk and duly received royalties for his efforts. It was an arrangement agreed upon and fulfilled, indicating the solid relationship that existed between Taylor and Cooke. It should be noted that Harper & Brothers royalty ledgers also indicate that, for an indeterminate period, Taylor's *Shop Management* royalties were also paid to Cooke for an unknown reason.

PUBLIC ADMINISTRATION

In addition to working closely with Taylor and consulting with various businesses, Cooke also became involved in public administration. In 1911, Rudolph Blankenburg, a reform candidate, was elected mayor of Philadelphia. He asked Taylor to become the city's Director of Public Works. Citing his failing health, Taylor recommended Cooke for the job. Cooke had been eager for civic reform ever since, as a poll watcher, he had been bullied by a machine politician. Journalist Lincoln J. Steffens considered Philadelphia "the worst governed city in the country."[127] Cooke found the city's Department of Public Works honeycombed with corruption. He insisted that government be nonpolitical and use science and technology for the public good.

In 4 years, as Public Works Director, Cooke saved the city over $1 million in garbage-collection costs, achieved a $1.25 million reduction in utility rates, fired 1,000 inefficient employees, established pension and benefit funds, opened channels of communication for all employees, and moved municipal administration from smoke-filled rooms into the sunshine. Although he was unable to apply time study or incentive pay, Cooke revamped budgeting procedures, replaced political favorites with qualified officeholders, advocated hiring a professional city manager, and sought to replace committees with individuals who had responsibility and authority. In his book *Our Cities Awake: Notes on Municipal Activities and Administration*, Cooke called for cooperation and full workplace participation by employees from the top of an organization to the bottom:

> Here then is a work in which we can all have a hand, a work which will always be ineffectually done if it is confined to well-educated and highly trained men at the top . . . administrative leadership will in the future more and more consist in getting the largest possible number "into the play"—in having the great body of employees increasingly critical in their judgments about both their own work and the work which is going on around them.[128]

---

[125] *The Archives of Harper and Brothers (1817–1914)*. "Royalty Ledgers" [microfilm reels 44 (vol. 9; 1909–1912, p. 762) and 46 (vol. 11; 1912–1915, p.709)] and "English Royalty Ledgers" [microfilm reels 31 (vol. 2; July 1908–June 1913, p. 590) and 32 (vol. 3; 1913–1919, p. 764)]. (Cambridge, England: Chadwyck-Healey, 1980). It appears that, at some point after the second quarter of 1913, Taylor's royalties from *The Principles of Scientific Management* were paid to the Stevens Institute of Technology. J. Myron Johnson, "Fred Taylor '83: Giant of Non-Repute," *Stevens Indicator* 97(2) (Spring 1980), p. 8. The royalty ledgers showing Taylor's *Shop Management* royalties being paid to Cooke appear on reels 44 (p. 763) and 46 (p. 710).

[126] Carol Carlson Dean, "*The Principles of Scientific Management* by Fred Taylor: Exposures in Print beyond the Private Printing," *Journal of Management History* 3(1) (1997), pp. 11–12.

[127] Lincoln J. Steffens, "Philadelphia: Corrupt and Contended," *McClure's Magazine* 21(3) (July 1903), p. 249.

[128] Morris L. Cooke, *Our Cities Awake: Notes on Municipal Activities and Administration* (Garden City, NJ: Doubleday, Page, 1918), p. 98.

After serving in the Blankenburg administration, Cooke opened his own consulting firm in 1916. Like other scientific-management pioneers, he contributed his knowledge to the War Department during World War I, serving as executive assistant to the United States Shipping Board. Always concerned with gaining the cooperation of labor, he became increasingly interested in the growing postwar national labor movement. He became a friend and advisor to Samuel Gompers, president of the American Federation of Labor. Cooke saw a need to bring labor and management together in a time of mutual antagonism.[129]

In his 1928 Presidential Address to the Taylor Society, Cooke expressed doubts about "company unions" not freely established by their members: "Certainly no grouping of workers where the urge for organization does not originate with the workers themselves would be expected to hold their interest."[130] He believed that insistence on "management prerogatives" and "labor intransigence" must give way to cooperation. Cooke held that labor was just as responsible for production as management and stressed that improved productivity was an effective barrier against unemployment and low wages. In this last book, *Organized Labor and Production: Next Steps in Industrial Democracy*, coauthored with Philip Murray, Cooke advised management to "tap labor's brains," by which he meant actively involving labor in determining workplace procedures and policies for increasing the output and distribution of goods and services.[131] Murray was one of the most important labor leaders of the era: the first president of the Steel Workers Organizing Committee (SWOC), the first president of the United Steelworkers of America (USWA), and the longest-serving president of the Congress of Industrial Organizations (CIO).

During the administration of U.S. President Franklin D. Roosevelt, Cooke held numerous positions, chief among them being Director of the Rural Electrification Administration (1935–1937). In 1950, Roosevelt's successor Harry S. Truman appointed Cooke chair of the President's Water Resources Policy Commission. When Cooke was asked by his biographer to list his lifetime accomplishments, he replied:

1. Rural Electrification
2. Inexpensive electricity in our homes
3. Progress in labor–management relations
4. Conservation of our land and water
5. Scientific management in industry[132]

To this, Cooke's biographer added another accomplishment: "service to government." On balance, "Cooke's interest lay in the broader social and political implications of scientific management."[133] He worked to further cooperation between labor and management and favored increased worker participation in management decision making. If scientific management was

[129] For more on Cooke's involvement with Gompers, see Christopher T. Nyland, "Taylorism and the Mutual-Gains Strategy," *Industrial Relations* 37(4) (October 1998), pp. 519–542.
[130] Morris L. Cooke, "Some Observations on Workers' Organizations," *Bulletin of the Taylor Society* 14(1) (February 1929), p. 7. "Company unions" were outlawed in the United States by the 1935 National Labor Relations Act (the Wagner Act), 29 *U.S.C.*§8(a)(2), p. 7. Cooke's contact with labor leaders was extensive. For details, see Sanford M. Jacoby, "Union-Management Cooperation in the United States: Lessons from the 1920s," *Industrial and Labor Relations Review* 37(1) (October 1983), pp. 20–24.
[131] Morris L. Cooke and Philip Murray, *Organized Labor and Production: Next Steps in Industrial Democracy* (New York: Harper & Brothers, 1940), p. 211. As for the actual authorship of this book, see Jean Christie, *Morris Llewellyn Cooke: Progressive Engineer* (New York: Garland Publishing, 1983), p. 244n2.
[132] Trombley, *Cooke*, p. 249.
[133] Edwin T. Layton, Jr. *The Revolt of the Engineers: Social Responsibility and the American Engineering Profession* (Baltimore, MD: Johns Hopkins University Press, 1986), p. 157.

to make headway in the twentieth century, it required someone like Cooke to open new vistas in public administration and to gain the support of the U.S. labor movement.

SUMMARY

The scientific-management movement's search for a meaningful identity is reflected in the lives of the individuals examined in this chapter. Carl G. Barth was the true believer who remained faithful to Taylor's orthodoxy. Henry L. Gantt began under Taylor's guidance, contributed significantly, and then developed his own unique ideas. The Gilbreths combined motion study with Taylor's time study, investigated fatigue, and emphasized the psychology of management. Harrington Emerson embraced the efficiency movement while rejecting Taylor's "functional foremanship" and differential piece-rate plan. Morris L. Cooke, nurtured by Taylor, introduced scientific management to public administration and sought a rapprochement between management and organized labor. These individuals led the vanguard in spreading the gospel of efficiency in the early days of the scientific-management movement. As we will see, however, changing times would bring new challenges.

The Human Factor: Preparing the Way

CHAPTER 9

Scientific management was born and nurtured in an era that emphasized science as a way of life and living. Throughout the first decade of the twentieth century, President Theodore Roosevelt and others were troubled by the depletion of the United States' natural resources (see Chapter 12). This was part of a larger question about how to increase national efficiency and eliminate waste. One aspect of concern dealt with the efficiency of "industrial and manufacturing establishments," in general, and, in particular, the "men . . . working in these establishments." For Fred Taylor and the band of scientific-management pioneers that had gathered around him, the "blundering" methods used by management were "ill-directed" and responsible for an untold loss in human effort.[1] Their solution to eliminating this waste was carefully selecting and developing "first-class" workers. Simply stated, their goal was to put "The Right Man in the Right Place." This chapter examines how modern personnel management (or, as we know it today, "human-resource management") grew out of "welfare work" on the one hand, and scientific management on the other.[2] More broadly inspired social forces were also afoot during the period, and these are examined as they affected industrial psychology, industrial sociology, and industrial relations. Together, these forces set the stage for later developments in labor–management relations, the human-relations school of management, and, eventually, the field of organizational behavior.

PERSONNEL MANAGEMENT: A DUAL HERITAGE

The first appearance of what today would be termed "employment agencies" in the United States occurred as early as the 1750s, when the so-called "intelligence offices," "statute halls," and "register offices" (modeled after their earlier European counterparts) began to appear in

[1] Frederick W. Taylor, *The Principles of Scientific Management* (New York: Harper & Brothers, 1911), pp. 5–8.
[2] Henry Eilbirt, "The Development of Personnel Management in the United States," *Business History Review* 33(3) (Autumn 1959), pp. 345–364; Guy Alchon, "'The World We Seek as Christians': Mary van Kleeck, Philanthropy, and Early Social Science Initiatives," in Theresa Richardson and Donald Fisher, eds., *The Development of the Social Sciences in the United States and Canada: The Role of Philanthropy* (Stamford, CT: Ablex, 1999), pp. 59–73; Patrick Selmi and Richard Hunter, "Beyond the Rank and File Movement: Mary van Kleeck and Social Work Radicalism in the Great Depression, 1931–1942," *Journal of Sociology and Social Welfare* 38(2) (June 2001), pp. 75–100; and Chris Nyland and Tom Heenan, "Mary van Kleeck, Taylorism and the Control of Management Knowledge," *Management Decision* 43(10) (2005), pp. 1358–1372.

larger cities.[3] Whereas most people found jobs and employers found workers through friends and family, these "special marts," described as "often operating in dimly lit basement offices to evade the surveillance of police officers tasked with enforcing urban licensing requirements," sold information to those offering and those needing services for fifty cents to a dollar. Some employment agents defrauded both groups by gulling "workers out of a fee" and never finding them work and fleecing "employers by charging a fee and supplying them with lazy or fractious employees who would neither do the requisite work nor stay on the job," and as such their general reputation was that of "swindlers and sharpers."[4] Indeed, one contemporary source reports that "there is a great deal of roguery carried on in connection with the business. . . . In some cases these offices have been used to decoy unsuspecting girls to places of shame."[5] Modern personnel management, in contrast, had a separate and dual heritage. This heritage may be traced to the 1880s and the overlapping emergence of the scientific management and Social Gospel movements. Scientific management originated from an engineering philosophy that focused on the need for the "strictest economy in the use of workers."[6] In contrast, the roots of the Social Gospel movement resided in religion and philanthropy and the desire to improve "the general tenor of American living and the standards of the poor and unfortunate."[7]

PERSONNEL ADMINISTRATION AS WELFARE WORK

Paternalism, whether by state, church, or business, is as old as civilization. As described in Chapter 2, the feudal system of the Middle Ages was based on paternalistic ideals, and many nineteenth-century factory owners, such as Robert Owen (see Chapter 4), sought to ameliorate the anguish of working life and to "elevate" their employees by providing recreational activities, dancing lessons, meals, housing, education, sanitation, and so on. Similarly, the Waltham System for textile manufacturing, popular in the early 1800s, had paternalistic overtones as mill owners looked after employees' education, housing, and morals (see Chapter 5). The 1832 McLane Report on *Manufactures in the United States* found the typical firm to be family owned with relatively few employees and owner managed.[8] The nature of the work relationships within these firms was often, by extension, paternalistic. The rapid growth of the U.S. economy in the latter third of the nineteenth century, however, created unsurpassed accumulations of physical and human resources in factories and mills. This rapid growth moved the means of production from small workshops and homes to establishments where it was possible to manufacture items on a grand scale. It also changed the general nature of work relations between owner-managers and their employees. The Social Gospel movement emerged in the 1880s as a counterpoint to the unrestrained business practices of the period and the assertion advanced by Social Darwinists that society's progress depended on the "survival of the fittest." Indeed, Social Gospel proponents felt a duty to reform social and economic conditions (both in the home and workplace) to address the resulting class distinctions and inequities of wealth. Rather than wait for a gradual improvement

---

[3] See, for example, "Publick Register Office," *Philadelphia Gazette* (August 5, 1756), p. 3. See also Benjamin Leigh, "For the Benefit of the Public," *Boston Gazette and Country Journal* (July 25, 1768), p. 3.

[4] Brian P. Luskey, *Men Is Cheap: Exposing the Frauds of Free Labor in Civil War America* (Chapel Hill, NC: University of North Carolina Press, 2020), p. 56. For the history of "intelligence agencies," see Anton Tantner, "Intelligence Offices in the Habsburg Monarchy," in Joad Raymond and Noah Moxham, eds., *News Networks in Early Modern Europe* (Leiden, Netherlands: Koninklijke Nijhoff, 2016), pp. 443–464; David G. Van Arsdale, *The Poverty of Work: Selling Servant, Slave and Temporary Labor on the Free Market* (Leiden, Netherlands: Koninklijke Brill, 2016), pp. 57–84.

[5] "Something About Intelligence Offices," *New York Herald* (August 31, 1859), p. 1.

[6] Ordway Tead and Henry C. Metcalf, *Personnel Administration: Its Principles and Practices* (New York: McGraw-Hill, 1920), p. 27.

[7] Eilbirt, "Development of Personnel Management," p. 348.

[8] U.S. Congress, *Documents Relative to the Manufactures in the United States, Collected and Transmitted to the House of Representatives, in Compliance with a Resolution of Jan. 19, 1832*, by the Secretary of the Treasury [McLane Report], 22nd Congress, 1st Session, H. R. Document 308, 2 vols. (Washington DC: Printed by Duff Green, 1833).

in the quality of life found in poorer neighborhoods, they argued for immediate action in improving personnel administration and industrial relations policies in the belief that doing so would "fundamentally change . . . social conditions in the community."[9] In particular, the responses of the era's owner-managers built on the familial (and paternalistic) traditions of the past, as expressed through "industrial betterment" or "welfare work."[10] John R. Commons coined the latter term, which he defined as "all of those services which an employer may render to his work people over and above the payment of wages."[11]

Drawing on the Social Gospel movement, the first "welfare-work office" was established at the National Cash Register Company in 1897, when Lena H. Tracy was named NCR's first welfare director.[12] Tracy's efforts included an employee suggestion program (with prizes) to encourage workers to submit ideas for workplace improvements, fifteen minute morning and afternoon recesses with "gymnastic exercises," baths where employees could bathe once a week, and cooking lessons intended to improve dietary habits. When female employees were given a hot lunch at the company's expense, an "instant improvement" in their general health was noted, as well as "less delay from sickness, fewer absences, and an ability to work harder and more enthusiastically."[13] The Colorado Fuel and Iron Company hired a welfare secretary in 1901 and the H. J. Heinz Company did so in 1902. The International Harvester Company followed suit in 1903. During the same period, other welfare-work offices were established at Filene's Department Stores, Plymouth Cordage, John B. Stetson Company, and Westinghouse Electric. Clearly, concern for employee welfare was becoming fashionable among large companies.

Although employee-welfare programs were, in part, intended to counter a growing union movement, they were also motivated by the realization that "employees' productivity depended quite as much upon their environment and lives in the fourteen hours away from work as the ten hours while at work."[14] As a consequence, many welfare programs extended beyond the workplace and into employees' homes, including their spouses and children. Thus, "welfare secretaries" were tasked with improving employees' lives, both on and off the job. The secretaries handled employee grievances, operated medical dispensaries, oversaw recreation and educational activities, arranged job transfers, administered dining facilities, prepared nutritious menus, and watched over the moral behavior of employees, especially unmarried females.[15] Many of the era's welfare secretaries were women with backgrounds in vocational guidance and social work. In addition to Lena H. Tracy, other women welfare secretaries included Gertrude B. Beeks at International Harvester, Elizabeth Briscoe at Bancroft & Sons, Florence Hughes at New Jersey

---

[9] Mary van Kleeck quoted in Percy S. Brown, "The Work and Aims of the Taylor Society," *Annals of the American Academy of Political and Social Science* 119(208) (May 1925), p. 136.

[10] Homer J. Hagedorn, "A Note on the Motivation of Personnel Management: Industrial Welfare 1885–1910," *Explorations in Entrepreneurial History* 10(3–4) (April 1958), pp. 134–139; Oscar W. Nestor, "A History of Personnel Administration, 1890–1910" (Doctoral dissertation, University of Pennsylvania, Philadelphia, PA, 1954); released in book form by Garland Press, New York, 1986; and Andrea Tone, *The Business of Benevolence: Industrial Paternalism in Progressive America* (Ithaca, NY: Cornell University Press, 2018).

[11] John R. Commons, "'Welfare Work' in a Great Industrial Plant," *American Monthly Review of Reviews* 28(1) (July 1903), p. 79.

[12] See Lena Harvey Tracy, *How My Heart Sang: The Story of Pioneer Industrial Welfare Work* (New York: R. R. Smith Publisher, 1950); John H. Patterson, "Altruism and Sympathy as Factors in Works Administration," *Engineering Magazine* 20 (January 1901), pp. 577–602; and Samuel Crowther, *John H. Patterson: Pioneer in Industrial Welfare* (Garden City, NY: Doubleday, 1923) pp. 190–207.

[13] Charles R. Richards, "An Industrial Democracy," *Pratt Institute Monthly* 4(8) (April 1896), p. 230. See also Paul Monroe, "Possibilities of the Present Industrial System," *American Journal of Sociology* 3(6) (May 1898), p. 746.

[14] Edwin E. Witte, *The Evolution of Managerial Ideas in Industrial Relations*, Bulletin 27 (Ithaca, NY: New York State School of Industrial and Labor Relations, Cornell University, 1954), p. 8.

[15] For more on the duties of social secretaries, see William H. Tolman, *Social Engineering* (New York: McGraw, 1909), pp. 48–59. See also Stuart D. Brandes, *American Welfare Capitalism: 1880–1940* (Chicago, IL: University of Chicago Press, 1976); Nikki D. Mandell, *The Corporation as Family: The Gendering of Corporate Welfare, 1890–1930* (Chapel Hill, NC: University of North Carolina Press, 2002).

Zinc, Laura Ray at Greenhut-Siegel, Aggie Dunn at H. J. Heinz, Lucy Bannister at Westinghouse, and Diana Hirschler at Filene's.[16]

The role of welfare secretaries, however, was not always clearly defined, as the experience of Henry L. Gantt at Bancroft & Sons illustrates. Bancroft's first welfare secretary, Elizabeth Briscoe, was appointed in 1902. In 1903, the company experienced severe productivity problems, and John Bancroft, superintendent of its mills, employed Gantt as a consultant. Gantt's recommendations soon ran counter to Briscoe's welfare efforts. When Gantt suggested dismissing inefficient employees, Briscoe objected. She insisted that all workers, inefficient or not, should be retained. Gantt argued that poor personnel selection and unstructured work assignments were contributing to the productivity problems that he had been hired to solve. Gantt was able to increase productivity to some extent by improving work methods, upgrading training, and installing a bonus system in one department, but he was unable to fully implement all of his recommendations because of Briscoe's opposition. When Gantt completed his consultancy in 1909, it appeared that welfare work had won out over scientific management.[17] In later years (1911–1927), however, Bancroft & Sons blended "welfarism" with scientific management in a manner consistent with its owner's Quaker beliefs about how employees should be treated while still increasing productivity. Thus, though Gantt may have "lost" initially, in the end, it was shown that welfare work and scientific management could complement each other by enhancing both employee relations and productivity.

By about 1910, use of the phrase "welfare work" began to wane, and it was replaced with the phrase "personnel management." According to Meyer Bloomfield, who was instrumental in forming an early employment managers' association, the personnel movement (with its emphasis on the scientific selection and placement of employees) could do more to enhance employee efficiency than welfare work because "welfare work . . . often lacked analysis, self-criticism and human insight [and] the good which [welfare] work could do was often vitiated by sentimentality, if not self-deception."[18] Moreover, as welfare work reached further into workers' personal lives, it was resented, with workers objecting to being told what they could or could not do on their own time and in their own homes. Although welfare secretaries and welfare-work offices are not found in today's workplace, their legacy survives in the "fringe benefits" and industrial relations policies of contemporary human-resource programs.

SCIENTIFIC MANAGEMENT AND PERSONNEL ADMINISTRATION

At the turn of the twentieth century, unskilled workers would line up each morning at the gates of many factories across the country and wait for a foreman to hire the day's labor. This often amounted to little more than workshop foremen hiring friends or the well connected, or, in some cases, even selling jobs and later demanding kickbacks and personal "treats" (e.g., "cases of beer" and "boxes of cigars") for workers to retain their positions. As foremen had the power to hire, they also had the right to fire. Fred Taylor denounced this practice and argued that the scientific selection of workers required "not just leav[ing] it to the poor overworked foreman to go out

[16] LeeAnne G. Kryder, "Humanizing the Industrial Workplace: The Role of the Early Personnel Manager, 1987–1920," *Henry Ford Museum & Greenfield Village Herald* (1985) 14(1), pp. 14–19; Charles D. Wrege and Bernice M. Lattanzio, "Pioneers in Personnel Management: A Historical Study of the Neglected Accomplishment of Women in Personnel Management," *Working Paper Series*, Management History Division, Academy of Management, 1977.

[17] Daniel Nelson and Stuart Campbell, "Taylorism versus Welfare Work in American Industry: H. L. Gantt and the Bancrofts," *Business History Review* 46(1) (Spring 1972), pp. 1–16. Although Nelson and Campbell concluded that Gantt lost this battle at Bancroft, there is other evidence that Gantt introduced Bancroft's senior management to options they would pursue later. For this latter viewpoint, see Peter B. Petersen, "Henry Gantt's Work at Bancroft: The Option of Scientific Management," in John A. Pearce II and Richard B. Robinson, eds., *Proceedings of the Annual Meeting of the Academy of Management* (1985), pp. 134–138. For more on Briscoe's contributions, see Peter B. Petersen, "A Pioneer in Personnel," *Personnel Administrator* 33(6) (June 1988), pp. 60–64.

[18] Meyer Bloomfield, "Man Management: A New Profession in the Making," *Bulletin of the Taylor Society* 6(4) (August 1921), p. 161.

and say, 'come on, what do you want? If you are cheap enough I will give you a trial.'"[19] As early as 1903, the year of the first cross-country road trip by car across the United States, Taylor proposed that an Employment Bureau should be part of a central planning department, and one of the specialized functions he identified was "shop-disciplinarian." Taylor listed the duties of a shop-disciplinarian, including selecting and discharging employees, keeping performance records, handling disciplinary problems, administering wage payments, and serving as a peacemaker.[20] Several of Taylor's earliest disciples, including Henry P. Kendall at Plimpton Press (Norwood, Massachusetts) and Richard A. Feiss at garment manufacturer Joseph & Feiss Company (Cleveland, Ohio), founded "employment departments."

A History of Opheleum Fraternity: Published Upon the Occasion of the Tenth Anniversary (Pittsburg: F. G. Wetterstein, 1913), p. 99.

Mary Barrett Gilson

Created in 1910, the Employment Department at Plimpton Press was managed by Jane C. Williams.[21] Its purpose was to achieve savings by minimizing human costs. Williams's duties included determining job applicants' suitability, training and orienting workers, maintaining performance records, interviewing employees monthly, reviewing efficiency ratings every 6 months to determine pay increases, hearing grievances, providing a nurse in case of accident or illness, maintaining a library of popular and technical magazines and books, helping families with financial counseling, and operating a lunchroom.

Established in 1913, the Employment and Services Department at Joseph & Feiss was among the first to use psychological tests for selecting and promoting employees. As described by Mary Barnett Gilson, the department's head at that time, employee selection was quite haphazard, following the "old way" that Taylor had denounced:

> On the first Monday morning I saw the accustomed method of hiring. Out in the front vestibule stood men and women, boys and girls, of every age, size, and apparent capacity, foremen were milling around among them. A likely-looking girl would be spotted by a foreman, "Can you run a power machine?" he would ask. "Sure I can," was the response. A little further questioning would perhaps reveal more specific information or perhaps not. It was a case of trial and error, and the errors were of necessity many.[22]

In justifying the cost associated with an employment department, Richard Feiss, son of Julius Feiss (the "Feiss" in Joseph & Feiss), echoed Edward Atkinson's observation from over 30 years earlier (quoted in Chapter 6) that a "difference in management will alter results, in the same place, at the same time, in the use of similar machinery." In reference to what Feiss labeled the "personal problem," meaning the "responsibility for handling men," he explained:

> Given two establishments in the same industry, in the same locality, build for them the same buildings, equip them with the same machinery and establish for them similar methods of handling equipment

---

[19] Frederick W. Taylor, "The Principles of Scientific Management," *Bulletin of the Taylor Society* 2(5) (December 1916), p. 17. Address before the Cleveland Advertising Club, March 3, 1915, published posthumously.

[20] *Idem*, "Shop Management," *Transactions of the American Society of Mechanical Engineers*, 24 (1903), p. 1404.

[21] Jane C. Williams, "The Reduction of Labor Turnover in the Plimpton Press," *Annals of the American Academy of Political and Social Science* 71 (May 1917), pp. 71–81. For a discussion of the role played by other women in the early growth of personnel as an occupation, see Frank B. Miller and Mary Ann Coghill, "Sex and the Personnel Manager," *Industrial and Labor Relations Review* 18(1) (October 1964), pp. 32–44.

[22] Mary B. Gilson, *What's Past Is Prologue* (New York: Harper & Brothers, 1940), p. 61. See also Charles D. Wrege and Ronald G. Greenwood, "Mary B. Gilson—A Historical Study of the Neglected Accomplishments of a Woman Who Pioneered in Personnel Management," in Jeremy Atack, ed., *Business and Economic History* 11 (1982), pp. 35–42. Although the Joseph & Feiss Company is often cited as the first major employer in the United States to use psychological tests for selecting employees, such tests (developed by Walter D. Scott) were used at the Hawthorne Works of Western Electric beginning in 1911. See J. Walter Dietz, *Walter Dietz Speaking* (Summit, NJ: Privately printed,1973), p. 42.

> and materials—and yet, in the course of time, there will be a difference in both the quantity and quality of their output. This difference in result will be caused by the difference between the two in the quality of their personnel. . . .
>
> If one of the above plants were headed by a management of the ordinary or traditional type and the other by a management which fully realized the importance of personnel and had developed an active philosophy tending toward the solution of the personal problem, the difference between the two in practical result would be so great as to be unbelievable by the uninitiated. In fact, this difference would often spell failure in the one case and success in the other.[23]

Ordway Tead dated the appearance of the modern personnel department to "about 1912," when some dozen companies had established distinct functions devoted to personnel work.[24] The first nationwide organization to deal with personnel matters was the National Association of Corporation Schools (NACS), founded in 1913. Recognizing that "it pays in dollars and cents," the goal of the NACS member corporations was to educate their employees "to increase their efficiency."[25] By 1917, the NACS had expanded its reach to include "human relations" (i.e., employee relations). NACS was later renamed the National Association of Corporation Training (NACT). In 1922, the NACT merged with the Industrial Relations Association of America (IRAA, founded in 1918 as the National Association of Employment Managers [NAEM]) to form the National Personnel Association. The NAEM had grown out of a local employment managers' association started in 1911 by Meyer Bloomfield, who was then the director of the Vocational Bureau in Boston. In 1922, the NAEM merged with the IRAA to form the National Personnel Association (NPA), which in 1923 became the American Management Association.

In 1915, the first training program for employment managers was offered at Dartmouth College's Amos Tuck School of Administration and Finance. Under Harlow Person's direction, the program required preparing "a thesis which is the solution of a specific problem of management in a specific plant."[26] Through his role in the Society to Promote the Science of Management, later renamed the Taylor Society, Person was able to promote employment management, or as it was called by the 1920s, "personnel administration," as a means for treating workers with the fairness and dignity to which they were entitled.[27]

Despite rising professionalism, the era's personnel practices continued to reflect earlier welfare programs. For example, in March 1913, Ford Motor Company created a Sociological Department to improve employees' standard of living. It hired 100 "advisers" to visit its employees' homes to ensure that the homes were neat and clean and to verify that the employees did not abuse alcohol, that their sex lives were without tarnish, and that they used their leisure time wisely. Services of the company's legal department were free, and it assisted employees with everything from applying for U.S. citizenship to buying a home. The company's concern for its employees' private lives, however, lasted less than 2 years. It ended in November 1915 when Henry Ford engaged his Episcopalian pastor, the Very Reverend Samuel S. Marquis, to head the Sociological Department. Ford told Marquis, "There is too much of this snooping around in private affairs. We'll change this from a sociology department to an education department."[28] Thereafter, the home visits stopped, and the Ford Motor Company began offering Americanization

---

[23] Richard A. Feiss, "Personal Relationship as a Basis of Scientific Management," *Annals of the American Academy of Political and Social Science* 65 (May 1916), p. 27.

[24] Ordway Tead, "Personnel Administration," in Edwin R. A. Seligman, ed., *Encyclopedia of the Social Sciences*, vol. 12 (New York: Macmillan, 1934), p. 88.

[25] "Training Their Own Employees," *The Outlook* 105(1) (September 6, 1913), p. 10.

[26] Harlow S. Person, "University Schools of Business and the Training of Employment Executives," *Annals of the American Academy of Political and Social Science* 65 (May 1916), p. 126.

[27] Witte, *Evolution of Managerial Ideas*, p. 9.

[28] John R. Commons, "Henry Ford, Miracle Maker," *The Independent* 102 (May 1, 1920), p. 160. Other facets of Ford's employment policies, including hiring the handicapped, those with criminal records, minorities, and "those past middle life" are found in John R. Lee, "The So-Called Profit Sharing System in the Ford Plant," *Annals of the American Academy of Political and Social Science* 65 (May 1916), pp. 297–310.

classes.[29] In the first 5 years, some 16,000 employees attended the classes. In further outreach, the company maintained a staff of 10 physicians and 100 nurses should employees become injured or sick, and pioneered in hiring disabled employees, ex-convicts, and minorities. For example, the Ford Company employed 5,000 African Americans in 1923, and that number would double to 10,000 by 1926.[30]

Faced with a tight Detroit labor market and a 400 percent annual employee turnover in his area factories, on January 5, 1914, Henry Ford announced that he would raise the company's minimum wage from $2.34 per 9-hour day to $5.00 (about $150 in today's dollars) per 8-hour day. This was double the average wage in the Detroit area and not only put pressure on rival employers to do the same, but also provided his workers the wherewithal to purchase the Model-T's they assembled.[31] Ford also announced a plan to share $10,000,000 in profits with 26,000 current employees.[32] Over 15,000 applicants besieged Ford's Highland Park factory seeking some 5,000 available jobs. Fire hoses had to be used to disperse the crowd. Three days later, with the rush of job seekers showing no sign of abating, newspapers around the country were asked to warn workers against coming to Detroit, as the available jobs were only for Detroiters.[33] Ford saw the $5.00-a-day wage as "neither charity nor wages [but] simply profit sharing." He did acknowledge, however, "[i]n a way it is a piece of efficiency engineering, too. We expect to get better work, more efficient work, as one result."[34] Indeed, Ford's groundbreaking move reduced turnover to 23 percent and "the retention of [a] steady labor force resulted in an increase of working efficiency estimated . . . at 44 per cent."[35] In 1922, at a time when the average manufacturing worker put in 47.9 hours a week,[36] the company instituted a 5-day, 40-hour week for 50,000 of its employees. Edsel Ford, Henry's son, explained: "Every man needs more than one day a week for rest and recreation. . . . The Ford Company always has sought to promote [an] ideal home life for its employees. We believe that in order to live properly every man should have more time to spend with his family."[37] Following Ford's lead, the 5-day, 40-hour week soon became standard practice in other companies.

It has been estimated that from 1915 to 1920 at least 200 personnel departments were established in the United States.[38] "Present development," Ordway Tead and Henry C. Metcalf wrote in 1920, "is in the direction of a new science and a newly appreciated art—the science and art of personnel administration."[39] A study by the Bureau of Labor Statistics for the years 1913–1919 determined that modern employment practices reduced labor turnover, thus decreasing training and other costs, while also providing workers with more stable employment, especially in larger firms. The study found that the larger the firm, the lower the turnover rate. This was, in part, because larger firms could pay higher wages, provide better working conditions, and guarantee stable employment. They were also more likely to have a central department devoted

---

[29] Daniel M. G. Raff, "Ford Welfare Capitalism in Its Economic Context," in Sanford M. Jacoby, ed., *Masters to Managers: Historical and Comparative Perspectives on American Employers* (New York: Columbia University Press, 1991), p. 99.
[30] Joe William Trotter, Jr., "African Americans in the Industrial Revolution," *OAH Magazine of History* 15(1) (Fall 2000), p. 21.
[31] Boyd Fisher, "Methods of Reducing the Labor Turnover," *Annals of the American Academy of Political and Social Science* 65 (May 1916), p. 144; Henry Ford with Samuel Crowther, *Today and Tomorrow* (Garden City, NY: Double, Page & Company, 1926), p. 154.
[32] "Gives $10,000,000 to 26,000 Employees," *New York Times* (January 6, 1914), p. 1.
[33] "No Jobs for Outsiders: Ford Co. Warns That 5,000 Places Are Only for Detroiters," *New York Times* (January 9, 1914), p. 1.
[34] Henry Ford quoted in "Ford Gives Reasons for Profit Sharing," *New York Times* (January 9, 1914), p. 1.
[35] Fisher, "Methods of Reducing the Labor Turnover," p. 144.
[36] Ethel B. Jones, "New Estimates of Hours of Work per Week and Hourly Earnings, 1900–1957," *Review of Economics and Statistics* 45(4) (November 1963), Table 1, p. 375.
[37] Edsel Ford quoted in "5-Day, 40-hour Week for Ford Employees," *New York Times* (March 25, 1922), p. 1. Although the Ford Company is often cited as the first major employer in the United States to introduce a 5-day workweek, this innovation was introduced at Joseph & Feiss Company in 1917. See Richard A. Feiss, "Why It Paid Us to Adopt the Five-Day Week," *Factory: The Magazine of Management* 25(4) (August 15, 1920), pp. 523–526.
[38] Daniel Nelson, "'A Newly Appreciated Art': The Development of Personnel Work at Leeds & Northrup, 1915–1923," *Business History Review* 44(4) (Winter 1970), pp. 520–535.
[39] Tead and Metcalf, *Personnel Administration*, p. 1.

to employee welfare.[40] Interest in improved employment practices was not confined to the United States, however. In Great Britain, beginning in the 1920s, B. Seebohm Rowntree, owner of the family-owned Rowntree and Company Cocoa Works at York, a British chocolate-manufacturer, employed an in-house industrial psychologist to assist in employee selection and a sociologist to supervise employee education, health, canteens, housing, and recreation.[41] The Cocoa Works offered various employee benefits, including a suggestion program, a pension plan, a profit-sharing scheme, a central works council, unemployment insurance, and paid holidays. Rowntree has been called the "Father of British Management."[42] Rowntree & Co. is now part of Nestlé S.A.

Interest in the potential of personnel administration to increase employee productivity led to significant changes in assumptions about human behavior. For instance, Tead partially backed away from an earlier "instinct" theory of behavior he had developed as the coauthor of the first collegiate textbook in the area, *Personnel Administration: Its Principles and Practice*.[43] Tead and his coauthor Metcalf (founding director of the Bureau of Personnel Administration in New York City, which convened the nation's first executive development seminars) concluded that instincts (i.e., inborn tendencies) still had a great deal to do with human conduct, but advances in personnel research were opening new vistas that enabled scientific employee selection, placement, and training. Writing alone later, Tead argued that managers should adopt a "psychological point of view" to seek "the cause and effect relations in behavior." He believed that such relations could be studied for guiding human conduct.[44] Moreover, he contended that an understanding of such relations would encourage proper work habits. Tead is remembered as being associated with Robert G. Valentine and Richard Gregg in creating the profession that was first known as "industrial counselor."[45]

In brief, the dual origins of personnel administration led to a common meeting ground in the 1920s. Although the employee-welfare movement realized that productivity depended, in part, on employee attitudes and loyalty, it lacked the rigor and professionalism necessary to sustain the growth of modern organizations. Scientific management provided some of this rigor by being coupled with industrial psychology, by fostering national associations devoted to improving employee relations, and by inspiring the first college-level preparation for employment managers. Welfarism was not dead but would continue in a less emphatic fashion in the years ahead. Scientific management, on the other hand, would find its goals and methods reshaped by the behavioral and social sciences. Together, the scientific management and Social Gospel movements paved the way for modern human-resource management.

PSYCHOLOGY AND THE INDIVIDUAL

The main flow of early economic thought largely addressed how humans attempt to satisfy their wants and desires. Near the middle of the nineteenth century, Irish-born University of Melbourne economist William E. Hearn advanced a then novel theory explaining how these wants and desires are a chief source of human action:

[40] Paul F. Brissenden and Emil Frankel, *Labor Turnover in Industry* (New York: Macmillan, 1922), especially pp. 54–79.

[41] Wendy Hollway, "Efficiency and Welfare: Industrial Psychology at Rowntree's Cocoa Works," *Theory & Psychology* 3(3) (August 1993), p. 304.

[42] Lyndall F. Urwick, "The Father of British Management," *The Manager* 30(2) (February 1962), pp. 42–43. See also Asa Briggs, *A Study of the Work of Seebohm Rowntree: 1871–1954* (London: Longmans, Green, 1961).

[43] Tead and Metcalf, *Personnel Administration*. See also Tead, *Instincts in Industry: A Study of Working-Class Psychology* (London: Constable, 1919). Tead's thinking on instincts "stemmed indirectly" from Thomson J. Hudon's *The Law of Psychic Phenomena: A Systematic Study of Hypnotism, Spiritism, and Mental Therapeutics, Etc.* (Chicago, IL: A. C. McClurg, 1893), among other influences. See Tead, "Ordway Tead," in Louis Finkelstein, ed., *Thirteen Americans: Their Spiritual Autobiographies* (New York: Institute of Religious and Social Studies, 1953), pp. 17–30.

[44] Ordway Tead, *Human Nature and Management: The Applications of Psychology to Executive Leadership* (New York: McGraw-Hill, 1929), p. 9.

[45] Richard Washburn Child, "The Human Audit," *Harper's Weekly* 61 (July 17, 1915), pp. 52–54. See also Henry P. Kendall, "The First Industrial Counselor—Robert G. Valentine, 1871–1916," *The Survey* 37 (November 25, 1916), pp. 189–190; "Labor Problems in Scientific Management," *Iron Age* 94 (December 10, 1914), pp. 1369–1372; and Charles D. Wrege, Ronald G. Greenwoood, and Racquel A. Frederiks, "New Insights into the Contributions of the First Industrial Counselor: The Private Papers of Robert G. Valentine 1912–1916," in Kelly A. Vaverek, ed., *Proceedings of the Southwest Academy of Management* (1992), pp. 69–73.

> Food, drink, air and warmth are the most urgent of [our] necessities [which] . . . man shares with all other animals. . . . The satisfaction, therefore, of his primary appetites is imperative upon man . . . first in the degree of their intensity . . . [and] the first which he attempts to satisfy. . . . [M]an is able not merely to gratify his primary wants, but to devise means for their better and more complete gratification. . . . Thus the comparative range of human wants is rapidly increased . . . [a]s the attempt to satisfy the primary appetites thus gives rise to new desires . . . [and] when they have acquired such comforts they are pained at their loss, but their acquisition does not prevent them from continuing to desire a further increase.[46]

The Business Philosopher: The Magazine of Practical Business Building 6(11) (November 1910), p. 638.

Katherine M. H. Blackford

This anticipation (by some 80 years) of a hierarchy of human needs (see Chapter 15) and the premise that once a lower-level need is satisfied higher-level needs are subsequently pursued was not a result of an empirical investigation, but rather introspection and deductive reasoning. Before the advent of scientific management, pseudo-psychologies such as physiognomy, phrenology, and graphology were commonly used by managers to select employees. Lacking a true scientific foundation, these techniques were based on the simple premise that physical features (such as hand length and head shape) and handwriting (such as whether letters flow in a smooth or erratic manner) could reveal a person's character, intelligence, and personality.[47]

Even reputable consulting firms used such techniques. For example, Emerson Efficiency Engineers employed Katherine M. H. Blackford, M.D., to assist its clients in using "character analysis" to select employees.[48] Blackford based her claims on two "laws":

FIRST, *Human bodies vary in nine ways*: Color, Form, Size, Structure, Texture, Consistency, Proportion, Expression, Condition.

SECOND, Men's characters vary in accordance with the way their bodies vary in these nine particulars.[49]

To illustrate the nature of her beliefs, which at the time were considered by many to be scientific, Blackford maintained, for instance, that "[s]ome work requires positive energy, the driving power to get things done, some requires a slow, enduring pace. If a man has high cheekbones and a nose which is convex when seen in profile, he has this positive energy. If he also has a high forehead and a large head and is a man of fine texture, he can best use his energy in mental work.

---

[46] William E. Hearn, *Plutology; Or, the Theory of the Efforts to Satisfy Human Wants* (Melbourne, Australia: George Robertson and Co., 1863), pp. 12–15. For more on Hearn's theory, see Gregory C. G. Moore, "The Anglo-Irish Context for William Edward Hearn's Economic Beliefs and the Ultimate Failure of *Plutology*," *European Journal of the History of Economic Thought* 18(1) (2011), pp. 19–54.

[47] For a further discussion of these pseudosciences, see Mary H. Booth, *How to Read Character in Handwriting* (Philadelphia, PA: John C. Winston, 1910); Gerald E. Fosbroke, *Character Reading through Analysis of the Features* (New York: G. P. Putnam's Sons, 1914); and Fenneke Sysling, "Phrenology and the Average Person, 1840–1940," *History of the Human Sciences* 34(2) (2021), pp. 27–45.

[48] Blackford has been accused of having a "fictionalized resume." Born in West Mineral, Kansas, in 1875, she held a medical degree awarded by the College of Physicians and Surgeons of Keokuk (Iowa) in 1898 under her maiden name Katharine (note original forename spelling) Huntsinger and completed further training the following year at the Dearborn Medical School (Chicago). Blackford subsequently practiced medicine in Rochester, New York, prior to pursuing a career lecturing on "character analysis," initially in association with phrenologist William Windsor and his Boston College of Vitosophy. See "On March 15th the College of Physicians and Surgeons of Keokuk Graduated a Class of Forty-Five," Iowa Medical Journal 4(4) (April 1898), p. 148; John T. Miller, Applied Character Analysis in Human Conservation (Boston, MA: Richard G. Badger, 1922), p.217; and "Blackford, Katherine M. H., " in Alberta Lawrence, ed., Who's Who among North American Authors, 1929–1930, vol. 4 (Los Angeles, CA: Golden Syndicate Publishing, 1929), pp. 101–102.

[49] Katherine M. H. Blackford, "The Science of Character Analysis—What It Is and What It Will Do for You" quoted in Arturo F. Ratti, "Secrets of the Psyche," *American Mercury* 19(2) (February 1930), p. 140. See also Katherine M. H. Blackford and Arthur Newcomb, *Analyzing Character: The New Science of Judging Men; Misfits in Business, the Home and Social Life* (New York: Blackford, 1916); *idem*, *The Job, The Man, The Boss* (New York: Doubleday, 1916).

If his forehead is low, his shoulders broad, his waist small and his texture coarse, he is best suited for physical work."[50] By the 1920s, Blackford's character analysis had given way to new models of employee selection as successive studies discredited her assertion that there was an association between a person's "external signs" and appropriate occupation.[51]

TOWARD SCIENTIFIC PSYCHOLOGY

Elsewhere, psychology was escaping its pseudoscientific beginnings. When Wilhelm Wundt opened the world's first psychological laboratory in 1879 at the University of Leipzig (Germany), scientific methods took hold of psychology. Wundt did not entirely abandon introspection, but began to examine human behavior through controlled experiments. As the founder of experimental psychology, Wundt opened the way for applied psychology, and later, through the work of his students, the field of industrial psychology, which survives to this day under the name "industrial and organizational psychology." Wundt sought to understand "psychological man" by identifying the constituent parts of human consciousness. His own observations of human behavior, combined with the emergence of the psychoanalytic theories of Sigmund Freud, soon led Wundt to develop an instinct-based explanation for behavior and thought. Concluding that people are not rational, but controlled by innate (i.e., inborn) instinctual drives, Wundt believed that by understanding "instinctive actions," the secrets of the hitherto unexplored mind could be revealed.[52] In the ensuing years, economist Thorstein B. Veblen would identify three positive hereditary instincts (sense of workmanship, parental bent, and idle curiosity), which promote the collective welfare of society, and three negative hereditary instincts (pecuniary interests, emulation, and predation), which negate the collective welfare of society and promote individualism. Others during this period created more encompassing lists of inborn instincts. Ordway Tead, for instance, delineated 10, including sex, self-assertion, pugnacity, and play. William James, the "Father of American Psychology," identified 37 different instincts, including anger, love, curiosity, and sociability.[53]

The disparities and disagreements among these competing lists of instincts soon proved that this approach was futile, and instinct theory was dismissed as an oversimplified basis for explaining behavior. The variability evidenced in attempts to identify a set of universal human instincts, however, suggested that psychological differences existed between individuals. In the same way that Fred Taylor had recognized the importance of employee selection in matching the right man to the right job, psychologists came to understand that a science of human behavior required the study of individual differences and not their innate instincts. It is here that applied psychologists such as Lillian M. Gilbreth, whose contributions were reviewed in Chapter 8, formed an alliance with scientific management.

THE BIRTH OF INDUSTRIAL PSYCHOLOGY

Scientific management gave industrial psychology its scope and direction. Echoing the scientific-management ethos, the earliest objective of industrial psychology was to promote "the maximum

[50] Katherine M. H. Blackford quoted in Floyd Taylor, "What Do Your Hands Tell?" *Popular Mechanics* 47(1) (January 1927), pp. 21–22.

[51] For a full critique of the "Blackford Employment Plan," see Elspeth H. Brown, *The Corporate Eye: Photography and the Rationalization of American Commercial Culture 1884–1929* (Baltimore, MD: Johns Hopkins University Press, 2005), pp. 23–64; Karen Mahar, "'New Race of Businessmen': Scientific Racism, Eugenical Assumptions, and Executive Potential, 1910–1925," unpublished paper presented at the 2023 Business History Conference, Detroit, MI, March 18, 2023. For a history of selection models, see Andrew J. Vinchur, "A History of Psychology Applied to Employee Selection," in Laura Koppes Bryan, ed., *Historical Perspectives in Industrial and Organizational Psychology*, 2nd ed. (New York: Routledge, 2021), pp. 103–123.

[52] The notion that people are not rational but controlled by innate (i.e., inborn) instincts may be traced to Charles Darwin who wrote that "the very essence of an instinct is that it is followed independently of reason." See Charles Darwin, *The Descent of Man, and Selection in Relation to Sex*, vol. 1 (New York: D. Appleton and Company, 1872), pp. 95–96.

[53] Thorstein Veblen, *The Instinct of Workmanship, and the State of the Industrial Arts* (New York: B. W. Huebsch, 1914), pp. 1–37; William James, *The Principles of Psychology*, vol. 2 (New York: Henry Holt, 1890), pp. 383–441; and Tead, *Instincts in Industry*, p. 11. For more on Veblen's notion of "good" and "bad" instincts, see Phillip A. O'Hara, "Thorstein Veblen's Theory of Collective Wealth, Instincts and Property Relations," *History of Economic Ideas* 7(3) (1999), pp. 153–179.

efficiency of the individual in industry" and "his optimum *adjustment* . . . in the industrial situation."[54] Although engineers studied mechanical efficiency and industrial psychologists studied human efficiency, their goal was the same—eliminating waste and inefficiency while maximizing employee satisfaction.

Hugo Münsterberg (1863–1916) is generally credited with the establishment of industrial psychology as an academic discipline. Münsterberg recognized Fred Taylor as "the brilliant originator of the scientific management movement," saying that Taylor had "introduced most valuable suggestions which the industrial world cannot ignore."[55] In promoting industrial psychology, Münsterberg drew on Taylor's work and stressed the importance of using genuine scientific methods to achieve workplace efficiency. Münsterberg, however, did not fail to appreciate the social implications of industrial psychology. As he explained:

> We must not forget that the increase of industrial efficiency by future psychological adaption and the improvement of the psychophysical conditions is not only in the interest of the employers, but still more of the employees; their working time can be reduced, their wages increased, their level of life raised. And above all, still more important than naked commercial profit on both sides, is the cultural gain which will come to the total economic life of the nation, as soon as every one can be brought to the place where his best energies may be unfolded and his greatest personal satisfaction secured. The economic experimental psychology offers no more inspiring idea than this adjustment of work and psyche by which mental dissatisfaction in the work, mental depression and discouragement, may be replaced in our social community by overflowing joy and perfect inner harmony.[56]

Born in Danzig (Germany) and educated in Wundt's University of Leipzig laboratory, Münsterberg was enticed by William James to join the Harvard University faculty in 1892. His interests were far ranging, including the application of psychological principles to crime detection, education, law, morality, industry, art, and philosophy.[57] To lay a broader foundation for scientific management, he met with President Woodrow Wilson, Secretary of Commerce William C. Redfield, and Secretary of Labor William B. Wilson to encourage them to create a government bureau dedicated to applying scientific research to the psychological problems of industry. Interest in scientific management was high, and Münsterberg sought to place the study of workplace behavior in the hands of qualified scientists and at the forefront of the nation's consciousness. According to Münsterberg, "While today the greatest care is devoted to the problems of material and equipment, all questions of the mind . . . like fatigue, monotony, interest, learning . . . joy in work . . . reward . . . and many similar mental states are dealt with by laymen without any scientific understanding."[58]

Even though the government bureau Münsterberg sought never materialized, his applied research interests grew. In attempting to understand "business life," he once again echoed Taylor in seeking answers to three primary questions:

> We ask how we can find the men whose mental qualities make them best fitted for the work which they have to do; secondly, under what psychological conditions we can secure the greatest and most satisfactory output from every man; and finally how we can produce most completely the influences on human minds which are desired in the interests of business. In other words, we ask how to find the best possible work, and how to secure the best possible effects.[59]

---

[54] Morris S. Viteles, *Industrial Psychology* (New York: W. W. Norton, 1932), p. 4.

[55] Hugo Münsterberg, *Psychology and Industrial Efficiency* (Boston, MA: Houghton Mifflin, 1913), pp. 166, 50. German edition published in 1910.

[56] *Ibid.*, pp. 308–309.

[57] Jeremy T. Blatter, "Screening the Psychological Laboratory: Hugo Münsterberg, Psychotechnics, and the Cinema," *Science in Context* 28(1) (2015), pp. 53–76.

[58] Margaret Münsterberg, Hugo Münsterberg*: His Life and Work* (New York: Appleton-Century-Crofts, 1922), p. 250. See also Merle J. Moskowitz, "Hugo Münsterberg: A Study in the History of Applied Psychology," *American Psychologist* 32(10) (October 1977), pp. 824–842; Frank J. Landy, "Hugo Münsterberg: Victim or Visionary?" *Journal of Applied Psychology* 77(6) (December 1992), pp. 787–802; Jutta Spillman and Lothar Spillman, "The Rise and Fall of Hugo Münsterberg," *Journal of the History of the Behavioral Sciences* 29(4) (October 1993), pp. 322–338; and Erik J. Porfeli, "Hugo Münsterberg and the Origins of Vocational Guidance," *Career Development Quarterly* 57(3) (March 2009), pp. 225–236.

[59] Münsterberg, *Psychology and Industrial Efficiency*, pp. 23–24.

The direction of Münsterberg's work was directly linked to Taylor's vision for scientific management and contained three broad parts: (1) "The Best Possible Man"; (2) "The Best Possible Work"; and (3) "The Best Possible Effect." Part 1 was a study of job demands and the necessity of identifying the men whose mental qualities made them best fit to meet those demands. Part 2 sought to determine the psychological conditions under which the greatest and most satisfactory output could be achieved. Part 3 examined how to influence human needs in a manner consistent with the interests of business. For each of these objectives, Münsterberg outlined definite proposals relating to the use of tests in worker selection, the application of research on learning in employee training, and the study of psychological techniques to increase workers' ethical and aesthetic motives. To illustrate his proposals, Münsterberg drew on evidence gathered from studies he had conducted, as early as 1910, on trolley-car motormen, telephone operators, and merchant-marine officers.

Münsterberg answered Taylor's call for studies that would provide insights into the "motives that influence men." The spirit of scientific management was readily apparent in Münsterberg's focus on individuals, his emphasis on efficiency, and his awareness of the social benefits to be derived from applying the scientific method to investigate workplace behavior. Moreover, Münsterberg's notoriety stimulated popular interest in applying psychology to everyday life. This growing interest led to the founding of *The Journal of Applied Psychology* in 1917. Among those in the United States and Great Britain who followed in Münsterberg's footsteps were Charles S. Myers, who pioneered industrial psychology in Great Britain; Walter D. Scott, who devised personnel classification tests for the U.S. Army during World War I; Cecil A. Mace, who performed the first experiments in goal setting as a motivational technique; Walter V. Bingham, whose Division of Applied Psychology at the Carnegie Institute of Technology led to the creation of the Bureau of Personnel Research and the first psychological consulting service for industry; and Morris S. Viteles, whose textbook became the "bible of industrial psychology."[60] In Germany, Georg Schlesinger, William Stern, Otto Lipmann, Walter Moede, and Curt Piorkowski, among others, were early contributors to the *industrielle psychotrechnik* movement.[61] It was Münsterberg, though, who blazed the way by defining the goals and terrain of industrial psychology.

THE SOCIAL-PERSON ERA: THEORY, RESEARCH, AND PRACTICE

Scientific management shaped its times and was shaped by those times in turn. It provided the rationale for personnel administration, industrial psychology, and institutional labor economics. Another set of forces, only related to scientific management in time, would apply Christian ideas to society at large, including the everyday world of work. And so it was the late nineteenth century also marked the dawning of the "social-person era."

[60] See Geoff Bunn, "'A Flair for Organization': Charles Myers and the Establishment of Psychology in Britain," *History & Philosophy of Psychology* 3(1) (2001), pp. 1–13; Edmund C. Lynch, "Walter Dill Scott: Pioneer Industrial Psychologist," *Business History Review* 42(2) (Summer 1968), pp. 147–170; Paula Phillips Carson, Kerry D. Carson, and Ronald B. Heady, "Cecil Alec Mace: The Man Who Discovered Goal-Setting," *International Journal of Public Administration* 17(9) (January 1994), pp. 1679–1708; Michelle P. Kraus, "Walter Van Dyke Bingham and the Bureau of Personnel Research" (Doctoral dissertation, Carnegie Mellon University, Pittsburgh, PA, 1982; released in book form by Garland Press, New York, 1986); Morris S. Viteles, "Morris S. Viteles," in Edwin G. Boring and Gardner Lindzey, eds., *The History of Psychology in Autobiography*, vol. 5 (New York: Appleton-Century-Crofts, 1967), pp. 417–449; *idem*, "Industrial Psychology: Reminiscences of an Academic Moonlighter," in Theophile S. Krawiec, ed., *The Psychologists: Autobiographies of Distinguished Living Psychologists* (New York: Oxford University Press, 1974), pp. 440–500. See also Peter B. Petersen, "Early Beginnings: Occupational Safety Management 1925–1935," *Journal of Managerial Issues* 11(4) (Winter 1990), pp. 382–405; Jesús F. Salgado, "Some Landmarks of 100 Years of Scientific Personnel Selection at the Beginning of the New Century," *International Journal of Selection and Assessment* 9(1–2) (March/June, 2001), pp. 3–8; and Ben Shepherd, "Psychology and the Great War, 1914–1918," *The Psychologist* 28(11) (November 2015), pp. 944–946.

[61] Anson Rabinbach, *The Eclipse of the Utopias of Labor* (New York: Fordham University Press, 2018), pp. 16–17, 100–112. See also Lothar Sprung and Helga Sprung, "History of Modern Psychology in Germany in 19th- and 20th-Century Thought and Society," *International Journal of Psychology* 36(6) (December 2001), pp. 364–376.

ANTECEDENTS OF INDUSTRIAL SOCIOLOGY

As recounted earlier, the Social Gospel movement emerged as a counterpoint to Social Darwinism. Chapter 6 discussed the reforms sought by both Richard T. Ely, founder of the Christian Social Union, and Congregationalist minister Washington Gladden. Social Gospel proponents (predominantly Protestant, but also Roman Catholic and Jewish) felt that they had a duty to reform social and economic conditions in both the home and workplace.

Another proponent of the Social Gospel movement was C. Whiting Williams (1878–1975). Born into a relatively prosperous family, Williams was educated at Oberlin College, graduating in 1899. He held various positions before being named vice president and director of personnel for the Hydraulic Pressed Steel Company (Cleveland, Ohio) in 1918. He resigned from this position after only a year because he felt he did not know enough about workers and their lives to be a personnel director. Inspired by the Social Gospel movement's emphasis on direct involvement in social and political action, Williams shed his white collar and headed out disguised as a worker to study industrial conditions firsthand.[62] He felt the only way to gain an intimacy with workers' daily lives was to participate and observe at the same time. He explained: "[M]en's actions spring rather from their feelings than their thoughts, and people cannot be interviewed for their feelings."[63] His first job was in a steel mill, cleaning out open-hearth furnaces so they could be rebricked and refired. It was hot, dirty work; the daily shifts were 12 hours long; and the pay was 45 cents per hour, with time-and-a-half for work over 8 hours a day. This was Williams's introduction to workers' lives on the job. Over a period of 7 months, he labored in coal mines, a railroad roundhouse, a shipyard, and an oil refinery, as well as in various steel mills.

Whiting Williams, *What's On the Worker's Mind* (New York: Charles Scriber's Sons, 1920), frontispiece.

Whiting Williams, applicant for a job, circa 1920

According to Williams, the workers' prayer was "Give us this day our daily job," because a job meant "bread": the opportunity to provide sustenance for themselves and their families. He discovered that all workers—including managers—measured their individual worth and their value to society in terms of their jobs. Jobs influenced workers' social standing, and how they earned their living determined where and how they and their families lived. Without jobs, people were isolated not only economically but also from their community and society at large: "[the worker's] vision of himself, his friends, his employer, and the whole of this world to come is circumscribed by his job."[64] Work was thus central to workers' lifestyles and friends, and had an impact on where they lived, how they spent their leisure time, and how they felt about themselves: "This vital connection between job status and social status means that the problem of effective relations with the worker inside the factory cannot be successfully separated from the whole problem of general social relations outside [the factory]."[65] Williams appreciated that work is important not only for economic support, but also for social and psychological well-being. He was well ahead of industrial psychologists and others who were just beginning to view the workplace as part of a broader social system in which work provides a sense of fulfillment and

---

[62] Daniel A. Wren, *White Collar Hobo: The Travels of Whiting Williams* (Ames, IA: Iowa State University Press, 1987). For the story of a Whiting contemporary who also disguised himself to study industrial conditions (in the Detroit-area automobile factories), see Myron W. Watkins, "The Labor Situation in Detroit," *Journal of Political Economy* 28(10) (December 1920), pp. 840–852.

[63] Whiting Williams, *What's on the Worker's Mind: By One Who Put on Overalls to Find Out* (New York: Charles Scribner's Sons, 1920), p. vi.

[64] *Idem*, "What the Worker Works For," *Collier's* 66(6) (August 7, 1920), p. 8.

[65] *Idem*, "Theory of Industrial Conduct and Leadership," *Harvard Business Review* 1(3) (April 1923), p. 326.

happiness, as well as a source of identity and self-worth. In his 1918 monograph, Williams was among the first to discuss "what every worker wants" in a job.[66]

Within factories, Williams observed the operations of a job hierarchy that had little or nothing to do with pay, but rather emphasized the nature of an individual's work. While working in a steel mill, he was promoted to millwright's helper. His pay was now 2 cents more per hour, but his former fellow shovelers envied him not because of the pay increase, but because the nature of his job had changed from the dirty, hot work of a shoveler to the cleaner, more pleasant work of an assistant to a skilled worker. This made Williams skeptical about the notion that people would work harder if they were given more money. He recognized that one's occupation or the type of work one performs confers social status:

> We give the dollar altogether too great an importance when we consider it the cause . . . of men's industry. . . . The dollar is merely an especially convenient and simple means for facilitating the measurement of a man's distance from the cipher of insignificance among his fellows. . . . Beyond a certain point . . . the increase of wages is . . . quite likely to lessen as to increase effort.[67]

Williams's perspective was unique in that he viewed earnings as a means of social comparison—the pay a worker received was considered not in absolute terms, but relative to what others received. Using the dollar as a unit of self-evaluation facilitated understanding of a person's "distance from the cipher of insignificance." This did not mean that money was unimportant; instead, it conveyed that money carried social value that might enhance or deflate how people viewed themselves relative to others. Hence, incentive plans that ignored this fact were less than effective as motivators. The mainspring of workers' lives was the "wish to enjoy the feeling of [their] worth as persons among other persons."[68] Togetherness in thinking, feeling, and being part of a group was important to workers because they drew their social status, security, and concept of self-worth from their peers. They chose to get along with one another not because they could not always find another job, but because they could not always move from their respective communities. From their employer, and especially their supervisor, they expected recognition and treatment conducive to preserving self-worth. It was not the paternalistic clubs, cafeterias, and recreation activities that won worker loyalty; it was the successful relations with their supervisors. Williams recommended an Eleventh Commandment, "Thou Shalt Not Take Thy Neighbor for Granted," and urged managers to motivate employees by appealing to "hope and surety of reward" rather than fear. Latent in Williams's study of workers' daily lives was Charles H. Cooley's "looking-glass self," (the idea that the self arises reflectively in reaction to the opinions of others) and the realization that one's self is embedded in one's work group as a primary social unit of importance.[69]

Other findings from Williams's "shirt-sleeve empiricism" included: (1) workers restricted output ("stringing out the job") because they perceived scarce job opportunities and employers tended to hire and lay off indiscriminately; (2) unions arose out of workers' desire for job security, and unions would not have made much progress if employers had evidenced concern for this desire; (3) long factory hours (e.g., 12-hour shifts in steel mills) made both workers and supervisors grouchy and tired, causing interpersonal conflict; and (4) workers listened to radical agitators because employers failed to speak "of the plans and purposes, the aims and ideals—the character—of his employer, the company."[70] Williams made a career of lecturing, consulting, and

---

[66] *Idem*, *Human Relations in Industry* (Washington, DC: U.S. Department of Labor, 1918). See also *idem*, "What Every Worker Wants," in Herbert J. Chruden and Arthur W. Sherman, Jr., eds., *Readings in Personnel Management* (Cincinnati, OH: South-Western Publishing, 1961), pp. 239–250.

[67] *Idem*, *What's on the Worker's Mind*, p. 323. See also, *idem*, "Environment's Power over Our Decisions," *100%: The Efficiency Magazine* 14(5) (May 1920), pp. 80–84.

[68] Idem, Mainsprings of Men (New York: Charles Scribner's Sons, 1925), p. 147. Originally serialized in *Scribner's Magazine* 73(1) (January 1923), pp. 90–96; 73(2) (February 1923), pp. 233–240; 73(3) (March 1923), pp. 346–357; 73(4) (April 1923), pp. 489–496.

[69] Charles H. Cooley, *Human Nature and the Social Order* (New York: Charles Scribner's Sons, 1902), p. 152.

[70] Williams, *What's on the Worker's Mind*, p. 289.

writing of his experiences as a worker. Over the years, he resumed his worker's disguise to study strikers and strikebreakers, unemployment, and labor–management relations in Great Britain and continental Europe.

Despite his pioneering work in the discipline that is known today as industrial sociology, Williams's efforts were not widely recognized. Rather, the roots of industrial sociology are traditionally traced to the Hawthorne studies (see Chapter 13).[71] There are, perhaps, several reasons why Williams's work was largely overlooked. One reason is that it was simply overshadowed by the era's fascination with scientific management. Jeffrey Muldoon notes, however, that it would be incorrect to think that contemporaries were unfamiliar with Williams's findings. Instead, he contends that Williams's work, limited to his own personal encounters, was considered highly subjective and, therefore, unscientific.[72] This may explain why Williams's books were rarely reviewed or cited in the scholarly journals of the period. Moreover, as a relatively new discipline, sociology was striving to become more respected. The prestige enjoyed by sociologists affiliated with leading universities provided a mantle of legitimacy that Williams's work lacked.

SOCIOLOGICAL FOUNDATIONS

The study of sociology began in the late nineteenth century as an outgrowth of its parent discipline, philosophy, rather than as an applied area of study. The ideas of sociologists Max Weber, Émile Durkheim, and Vilfredo Pareto would shape the thoughts of management writers in later years. In Chapter 10, we will discuss how Weber's scholarly efforts contributed to economics, sociology, and a theory of bureaucracy. Durkheim differentiated between two modes for maintaining social order: *mechanical solidarity*, characterized by cohesion and integration, and *organic solidarity*, characterized by a division of labor and societal interdependence that results from a division of labor. These types equate with societies that are either *mechanical* or *organic*. According to Durkheim, in mechanical (i.e., "traditional") societies, individuals interact within a close-knit community that shares common sentiments and values. Within these communities, there is a solidarity built around friendliness, neighborliness, and kinship, which gives individuals (who often perform the same job throughout their lives) a work identity as well as a personal identity in their public life. A lack of such close-knit communities in organic societies, however, leads to a malady he called "anomie," a state or condition that results in some individuals feeling disconnected from society due to a breakdown or absence of social norms.[73] Building on this distinction, Elton Mayo (see Chapter 13) would view work-group cohesion and integration as a prescription for achieving social order in a modern industrial society.

Pareto recognized that society is made up of interdependent parts that comprise what he called a "social system." He understood that the state of a society could be analyzed both at a particular time and with regard to the successive transformations that it underwent over a period of time as it sought equilibrium among its varied parts. As we will see in the coming chapters, Pareto's ideas may have remained gibberish without the work of Lawrence J. Henderson, a Harvard University physiologist, who influenced a number of scholars such as Talcott Parsons, George Homans, Elton Mayo, Fritz Roethlisberger, and Chester Barnard through his seminar known as the "Pareto Circle."[74]

[71] Daniel A. Wren, "Industrial Sociology: A Revised View of Its Antecedents," *Journal of the History of the Behavioral Sciences* 21(4) (October 1985), pp. 311–320. See also Steven R. Cohen, "From Industrial Democracy to Professional Adjustment," *Theory and Society* 12(1) (January 1983), pp. 47–67; Mark Pittenger, "'What's on the Worker's Mind': Class Passing and the Study of the Industrial Workplace in the 1920s," *Journal of the History of the Behavioral Sciences* 39(2) (Spring 2003), pp. 143–161.

[72] Jeffrey Muldoon, "The Hawthorne Legacy: A Reassessment of the Impact of the Hawthorne Studies on Management Scholarship, 1930–1958," *Journal of Management History* 18(1) (2012), pp. 105–119.

[73] Émile Durkheim, *The Division of Labor in Society*, trans. George Simpson (New York: Free Press, 1947). French edition published in 1893.

[74] Barbara S. Heyl, "The Harvard 'Pareto Circle,'" *Journal of the History of the Behavioral Sciences* 4(4) (October 1968), pp. 316–334.

EARLY EMPIRICAL INVESTIGATIONS

Before Whiting Williams undertook his own brand of "shirt-sleeve empiricism," there had been other studies on workers' daily lives. Two of these studies merit a brief mention because of their unique insights and international perspectives. Anticipating Williams by some 25 years, Paul Göehre, a young theology student and later General Secretary of the Evangelical Social Congress, worked for 4 months pretending to be an apprentice in a Chemnitz (Germany) machine-making factory in 1891 to see why workers were attracted to Social Democracy, an ideology that advocated a peaceful transition from capitalism to socialism.[75] Göehre observed that workers took more pride in producing a complete unit of work rather than an unidentifiable fragment, that higher productivity occurred when supervisors instilled a feeling of group interdependence and teamwork, and that there was informal group pressure for adherence to workplace norms. Lower morale and reduced efficiency resulted when workers were isolated and did not feel part of a broader "community of labour." Göehre's findings predated research on the relationship between job design and productivity that first appeared in the 1940s (see Chapter 15).

In an equally prescient effort, in 1924 and 1926, Belgian psychologist Hendrik de Man asked 78 "wage workers and salaried employees of both sexes from various parts of Germany," who were attending lectures he gave at the University of Frankfurt, to complete a detailed questionnaire "concerning their own feelings about their daily work."[76] Based on the completed questionnaires, he concluded that there was a natural impulse in people to find "joy in work." As explained by de Man, this impulse reflected a desire for activity, play, constructiveness, curiosity, self-assertion, and "mastery" (power). Inhibitive factors that contributed to a "distaste for work" derived from job elements such as detail work, monotony, reduction of worker initiative, fatigue, and poor working conditions, and in "social hindrances," like a sense of dependency, unjust wage systems, speedups, insecurity of livelihood, and lack of social solidarity. De Man's main conclusion that a worker's mental attitude toward work is a mix of "pleasurable and unpleasurable elements" is remarkably similar to that of Frederick I. Herzberg's later two-factor theory of job satisfaction (see Chapter 20), published some 30 years later. Much like Herzberg, de Man felt that work itself was a motivator and that management's job was to remove the "hindrances" that prevented employees from finding joy in work. In this regard, de Man believed that "it is psychologically impossible to deprive any kind of work of all its positive emotional elements," and that human beings will find a "certain scope for initiative which can satisfy after a fashion the instinct for play and the creative impulse" in any assigned work.[77]

"DEMOCRATIZATION OF THE WORKPLACE"

Theory and research into various aspects of industrial life steadily advanced during the first two decades of the twentieth century. Inspired by the spirit of democracy enshrined in President Abraham Lincoln's immortal words, "[A] government of the people, by the people, for the people,"[78] employee and employer representatives also made advances in labor–management relations. These were most evident in the trade-union movement and the changing nature of union–management cooperation.

[75] Paul Göehre, *Three Months in a Workshop: A Practical Study*, trans. A. B. Carr [pseudonym of Elizabeth Nelson Fairchild] (London: Swan Sonnenschein, 1895). German edition published in 1891. See also Richard J. Whiting, "Historical Search in Human Relations," *Academy of Management Journal* 7(1) (March 1964), pp. 45–53. For details regarding Fairchild's pseudonymous translation, see letter from Elisabeth Fairchild to Richard T. Ely, March 22, 1895, *Richard T. Ely Papers*, Box 8, Folder 1, Wisconsin Historical Society, Madison, WI.

[76] Hendrik de Man, *Joy in Work*, trans. Eden and Cedar Paul (London: G. Allen & Unwin, 1929), p. 9. German edition published in 1927.

[77] *Idem*, *The Psychology of Socialism*, trans. Eden and Cedar Paul (London: G. Allen & Unwin, 1928), p. 9. Translated from the second German edition published in 1927.

[78] Abraham Lincoln, "Gettysburg Address," delivered November 19, 1863, Gettysburg, PA, p. 2, Library of Congress, Abraham Lincoln papers: Series 3. General Correspondence. 1837–1897: Abraham Lincoln, [November 1863] (Gettysburg Address: Hay Copy). Available online at https://www.loc.gov/resource/mal.4356600/?sp= 2&r=0.204,0.167,0.87,0.534,0.

THE TRADE-UNION MOVEMENT

The year 1886 was marked by several momentous events. While Henry R. Towne was encouraging engineers to think in economic terms, the American Federation of Labor (AFL) was being formed under the presidency of Samuel B. Gompers. The AFL was a federation of craft unions that would succeed where the Knights of Labor and the National Labor Union had failed (see Chapter 6). Also of note, Richard T. Ely's *The Labor Movement in America* was published the same year. As Ely explained, "[t]rade unions and other associations of laborers are designed to protect and advance the interest of the great mass of the working classes."[79]

Although at one time associated with the Social Gospel movement, Ely developed his ideas regarding the role of labor to incorporate both Christian and socialist elements. He advocated independent worker associations and public ownership of the nation's railway, gas, electric, telephone, and telegraph industries. Ely would later reverse his views regarding the conversion of private property to public use and operation but continued to see capitalist employers as a separate social class.[80] He insisted, however, that neither socialism nor communism could advance the cause of labor more than workers forming voluntary associations to negotiate with employers.

Prior to the publicity scientific management received following the 1910 Eastern Rate Case, organized labor had paid scant attention to Fred Taylor and his followers. In 1912, following on the heels of the 1911 House of Representatives investigation into the Taylor system, Congress created a Commission on Industrial Relations to "inquire into the general condition of labor in the principal industries of the United States."[81] One member of the commission, John R. Commons, was Ely's former pupil and University of Wisconsin colleague. Commons was a central figure in institutional labor economics, which emphasized the employment relationship in broad social and legal terms rather than the labor market view of neoclassical economics. As an advocate for social justice, and someone who believed that carefully crafted legislation could create social change, Commons had taken an early position that the "clever devices of compensation"—formulated by Taylor, Gantt, Emerson, and others—divided workers and forced job negotiations between an employer and individual employees.[82] He felt strongly that workers needed to organize and bargain collectively to offset employers' economic strength.

As a member of the Commission on Industrial Relations, Commons had the opportunity to meet with Taylor and "came to realize that improved methods of management and personnel administration were yet another valuable approach to solving labor problems and improving industrial relations."[83] After visiting various factories that had implemented Taylor's methods, Commons concluded that scientific management and labor could cooperate, but only under certain circumstances. Plimpton Press, one of the most scientifically managed companies Commons visited, was unionized, but experienced little labor–management conflict. In contrast, the Joseph & Feiss Company, another model Taylor installation, was not unionized, but was managed so well that Commons felt a union was unnecessary. In Commons's judgment, however, such companies were rare. Indeed, he believed that some 75 to 90 percent of the nation's employers were so backward that "only the big stick of unionism or legislation" could assure worker interests were protected.[84]

---

[79] Richard T. Ely, *The Labor Movement in America* (New York: Thomas Y. Crowell, 1886), p. 92.

[80] *Idem, Social Aspects of Christianity, and Other Essays* (New York: Thomas Y. Crowell, 1889), pp. 72–78; and *idem, Ground under Our Feet: An Autobiography* (New York: Macmillan, 1938), pp. 251–252.

[81] *Final Report of the Commission on Industrial Relations*, Senate Document no. 415, 64th Cong., 1st sess. (Washington, DC: U.S. Government Printing Office, 1916), vol. 1, p. 3.

[82] John R. Commons, "Organized Labor's Attitude toward Industrial Efficiency," *American Economic Review* 1(3) (September 1911), pp. 463–472.

[83] Bruce E. Kaufman, "The Role of Economics and Industrial Relations in the Development of the Field of Personnel/Human Resource Management," *Management Decision* 40(10) (2002), p. 970.

[84] John R. Commons, "The Opportunity of Management," in John R. Commons, Willis Wisler, Alfred P. Haake, Otto F. Carpenter, Jennie McMullin Turner, Ethel B. Dietrich, Jean Davis, Malcolm Sharp, and John A. Commons, *Industrial Government* (New York: Macmillan, 1921), p. 263.

In his book *Industrial Goodwill,* Commons wrote of the need for workers to unionize so that they would have a "voice" in workplace governance. He called on employers to view workers as "human resources," in which parents, taxpayers, and the nation had made a significant investment.[85] Although Commons openly admired Taylor, he felt that scientific management cut across "the solidarity of labor," placed job knowledge in the hands of employers rather than workers, and had the "defects of autocracy."[86] In his autobiography, Commons explained, "I was trying to save Capitalism by making it good. . . . I wanted also to make trade unions as good as the best of them that I knew."[87]

Based on his work with the Commission on Industrial Relations and his contact with Taylor, Commons took a broad view of labor–management relations. He was concerned about the greater strength of employers relative to employees. In response to the imbalance of individual workers bargaining alone, he sought to strengthen labor by advocating "industrial goodwill," sound managerial practices, and government legislation and oversight. In time, Commons would come to be considered the "Father of Industrial Relations."[88] Other prominent economists who also played a role in expanding personnel management to include industrial relations were luminaries such as Senator Paul H. Douglas (Illinois); Harvard University professors Sumner H. Slichter and John T. Dunlop; and Clark Kerr, president of the University of California.[89] The Industrial Relations Research Association (IRRA) was founded in 1947. It became the Labor and Employment Relations Association (LERA) in 2005.[90]

Practitioners and consultants were also influential in reshaping industrial relations, especially in the post–World War I period. The philosophy of the AFL, as represented by Samuel B. Gompers, was to achieve gains for labor through power rather than through cooperation.[91] Organized labor during this period viewed scientific management as autocratic, because it forced employees to depend on employers' conception of fairness. Employees had no voice in setting standards, determining wage rates, or deciding other work-related issues. As Gompers explained in a letter to Robert Hoxie, Special Investigator, U.S. Commission on Industrial Relations: "The main objections which organized labor raises against scientific management are: The 'system' operates not to develop the individual powers and creative faculties of the workers but produces mechanical workers who are treated as part of the machinery. That is to say, the system is dehumanizing—it degrades rather than elevates. The practical results of the operation of experience with scientific management indicate that it is a speeding-up device that increases the profits of the employers but benefits only a few individual workers.[92]

THE CHANGING NATURE OF UNION–MANAGEMENT COOPERATION

To understand the eventual union–management cooperation that was achieved following Fred Taylor's death in 1915, it is necessary to reach back to the Social Gospel movement, which

[85] *Idem, Industrial Goodwill* (New York: McGraw-Hill, 1919), pp. 129–130.
[86] *Ibid.*, pp. 18–19.
[87] John R. Commons, *Myself* (New York: Macmillan, 1934), p. 143.
[88] Bruce E. Kaufman, *The Origins and Evolution of the Field of Industrial Relations in the United States* (Ithaca, NY: ILR Press, 1993); *idem*, "John R. Commons: His Contributions to the Founding and Early Development of the Field of Personnel/HRM," *Proceedings of the 50th Annual Meeting, Industrial Relations Research Association* (Madison, WI: IRRA, 1998), pp. 328–341.
[89] *Idem*, "Personnel/Human Resource Management: Its Roots as Applied Economics," *History of Political Economy* 32(4) (Winter 2000), supplement, pp. 229–256; *idem*, "Human Resources and Industrial Relations: Commonalities and Differences," *Human Resource Management Review* 11(4) (Winter 2001), pp. 339–374; *idem*, "The Theory and Practice of Strategic HRM and Participative Management: Antecedents in Early Industrial Relations," *Human Resource Management Review* 11(4) (Winter 2001), pp. 505–533.
[90] *Idem*, "The Founding of Industrial Relations and LERA," *Perspectives on Work* 24 (2020), pp. 46–53.
[91] Jean Trepp McKelvey, *AFL Attitudes toward Production: 1900–1932* (Ithaca, NY: New York State School of Industrial and Labor Relations, Cornell University, 1952), pp. 6–11.
[92] Letter from Gompers to Robert F. Hoxie, September 17, 1914, reprinted in Samuel Gompers, *The Samuel Gompers Papers*, vol. 9: *The American Federation of Labor at the Height of Progressivism, 1913–17*, eds. Peter J. Albert and Grace Palladino (Urbana, IL: University of Illinois Press, 1986), pp. 187–189.

espoused industrial betterment and sought to resolve labor unrest through associations such as the National Civic Federation (NCF), formed in 1900.[93] The NCF aimed to mediate disputes, educate the public about labor–management relations, and improve industrial relations by demonstrating that labor and management had mutual interests. The era's most prominent call for improved labor–management relations came from President Woodrow Wilson. In his May 20, 1919, Annual Message to Congress, he declared that there "must be the genuine democratization of industry, based upon a full recognition of the right of those who work, in whatever rank, to participate in some organic way in every decision which directly affects their welfare or the part they are to play in industry."[94] During the Great War, President Wilson's National War Labor Board, established in 1918, also furthered many of organized labor's goals. It prohibited employers from engaging in antiunion activities, required time-and-a-half pay for work over 8 hours per day, sanctioned shop committees elected by employees to confer with management regarding grievances, proposed the principle of a "living wage" for all workers (in practice, this became an early minimum wage), acknowledged the right of women to receive equal pay for equal work, and provided mediation and conciliation services to settle unresolved disputes.[95]

The now largely forgotten 1920–1921 economic depression weakened unions, reducing their membership as employment plummeted. During the same period, companies became more benevolent, as they campaigned for "open shops," in which workers were not required to join or financially support a union as a condition of hiring or continued employment. Government and the courts were growing hostile to union organizers' militant tactics. As noted in Chapter 8, there was also a concern that "radicals" and Bolsheviks, who had seized power in Russia during 1917, were gaining a foothold in the union movement. The public reacted with alarm.[96] Union membership suffered, declining from around 5 million in 1921 to 3.5 million in 1929.[97] In response to the resulting loss in bargaining power, unions had little choice but to become less confrontational and more cooperative.

Under the direction of Daniel Willard, president of the Baltimore and Ohio Railroad, and Bert M. Jewell, president of the AFL's Railway Employees' Department, a model plan for labor–management cooperation was developed following what came to be known as the Great Railroad Strike of 1922. The strike prompted an anguished outcry as nationwide rail travel was halted. In the aftermath of the strike, some firms moved to in-house unions, thus ousting the AFL. Recognizing that the momentum of the pro-union Wilson years had been lost, the AFL gave its support to several joint labor–management initiatives to improve productivity and, departing from earlier policies, agreed to the linking of wages to productivity increases.[98]

In the coming years, successful union–management cooperation could be found in the clothing trades and railroads. The clothing unions, under the stewardship of Sidney Hillman (a Lithuanian immigrant), were among the first segments of organized labor to agree to cooperate in implementing scientific management. Hillman was head of the Amalgamated Clothing Workers of America and a key figure in the founding of the Congress of Industrial Organizations. The railroads also developed extensive plans for cooperation, first on the Baltimore and Ohio and then later on the Chesapeake and Ohio, the Chicago and North Western, the Canadian National

[93] Marguerite Green, *The National Civic Federation and the American Labor Movement, 1900–1925* (Washington, DC: Catholic University Press, 1956).
[94] Woodrow Wilson, *The Papers of Woodrow Wilson: May 10–31, 1919*, vol. 59, ed. Andrew S. Link (Princeton, NJ: Princeton University Press, 1988), p. 291. Wilson had been a student of Richard Ely's at Johns Hopkins University. See Ely, *Ground under Our Feet*, pp. 108–119.
[95] Valerie Jean Conner, *The National War Labor Board* (Chapel Hill, NC: University of North Carolina Press, 1983). The seeds planted by the National War Labor Board would bear fruit for more than half a century through legislation such as the Fair Labor Standards Act (FLSA; 1938), the National Labor Relations Act (1947), and the Equal Pay Act (1968), an amendment to FLSA.
[96] Sanford M. Jacoby, "Union-Management Cooperation in the United States: Lessons from the 1920s," *Industrial and Labor Relations Review* 37(1) (October 1983), p. 22.
[97] Melvyn Dubofsky, *Hard Work: The Making of Labor History* (Urbana, IL: University of Illinois Press, 2000), p. 191.
[98] Jacoby, "Union-Management Cooperation in the United States," p. 24.

Railways, and others.[99] In each instance, the railway unions implicitly accepted scientific management and participated through joint union–management shop committees in improving work routing and scheduling, hiring practices, and job analysis.

When William F. Green was elected AFL president in 1924, scientific management gained even greater acceptance. At its 1925 convention, the AFL "declared unreservedly for a policy of cooperation with progressive management in the elimination of industrial waste." Scientific management was to be supported to the extent that it "first, recognizes the right of workers to organize into responsible trade unions; second, is just as much concerned with the welfare of the human being engaged in manufacture as with the increased production of material goods; third, recognizes the potential value of trade unions as a constructive factor in production, and, fourth, is willing to participate in the setting up of joint union–management cooperative machinery directed to increases productivity with these conditions." It soon, thereafter, began articulating a set of what was to grow to be 16 principles of "progressive management." These principles were published in 1930 under the title "Labor's Principles of Scientific Management."[100] In an effort to further labor and management cooperation, the AFL made its engineering service and educational department available to employers.[101] The goal of both units was to demonstrate how union–management cooperation could lead to increased employer profits, as well as to improved worker benefits. This "new unionism," with its recognition of what Fred Taylor had earlier termed a "mutuality of interests," completed a cycle in labor–management relations. Both labor and management now accepted scientific management.

EMPLOYEE REPRESENTATION PLANS

Whereas union–management cooperation plans involved organized labor, the idea of employee representation and participation through shop councils and committees emerged as another approach for achieving industrial cooperation. The roots of the employee representation movement were in part a continuation of earlier welfare programs, in part a hope for a restoration of the prewar open-shop days when unions had little influence, and in part an outgrowth of the old Social Gospel theme that labor and management could coexist peacefully if they recognized their common purpose. In the waning days of his term of office, President Wilson had appointed two industrial commissions to investigate the unusual number of industrial conflicts that had occurred in 1919. One of the commissions, vice-chaired by Herbert Hoover, endorsed the idea of workers being represented through employee-elected shop councils. These councils would give workers a choice to be represented without having to join a union and pay dues. Hoover disagreed with the unionists who felt that shop councils were antiunion. He felt that shop councils provided an alternative for workers who wished to have a voice and a choice in the nation's economic system.[102]

John R. Commons and eight of his University of Wisconsin colleagues studied 30 employee-elected shop councils from July to September 1919, including those at Filene's Department Store, the Dennison Manufacturing Company, the Ford Motor Company, the White Motor Company, and the Joseph & Feiss Company. One colleague praised Joseph & Feiss Company as

---

[99] Otto S. Beyer, Jr., "Experiences with Cooperation between Labor and Management in the Railway Industry," in Otto S. Beyer, Jr., Joseph H. Willits, John P. Frey, William M. Leiserson, John R. Commons, Elton Mayo, and Frank W. Taussig, *Wertheim Lectures on Industrial Relations, 1928* (Cambridge, MA: Harvard University Press, 1929), pp. 3–31.

[100] Geoffrey C. Brown, "Labor's Principles of Scientific Management," *American Federationist* 37(2) (February 1930), pp. 194–195.

[101] *Idem*, "What the Union Offers the South," *American Federationist* 37(9) (September 1930), pp. 1068–1073. See also Rexford G. Tugwell, *Industry's Coming of Age* (New York: Harcourt, Brace, 1927), p. 41; Tom Tippett, *When Southern Labor Stirs* (New York: Jonathan Cape & Harrison Smith, 1931), p. 183.

[102] Robert H. Zieger, "Herbert Hoover, the Wage-Earner, and the 'New Economic System.' 1919–1929," in Ellis W. Hawley, ed., *Herbert Hoover as Secretary of Commerce* (Iowa City, IA: University of Iowa Press, 1981), pp. 84–85, 96–98.

"the greatest experimental laboratory of industrial psychology that we have found in America."[103] Another noted that the White Motor Company required all foremen and executives to spend 1 hour each day exercising in the company's gymnasium. She observed that doing so "gets them acquainted with each other undressed; it keeps them in splendid physique; and it keeps them from indigestion and getting cross and sour with their workmen."[104] The results of this experiment in managerial exercise to improve labor–management relations were not recorded.

The employee representation plan at the Dennison Manufacturing Company in Framingham, Massachusetts, was perhaps more typical of attempts at worker involvement. In 1911, Dennison Manufacturing initiated an Employees' Industrial Partnership Plan to share company profits through a stock-dividend plan. Five years later, it established the country's first company-sponsored unemployment compensation fund to stabilize employment and provide worker security. It formed a workers' council in 1919.[105]

During the same period, the Russell Sage Foundation's Division of Industrial Studies, under the direction of social activists, sponsored numerous studies of employee representation plans that typically reported lower labor turnover, mutual employee and employer prosperity, more effective grievance handling, and a voice for workers.[106] By 1924, some 814 employee representation plans were in existence, covering over 1.5 million workers.[107] Despite union opposition to these so-called "company unions," these plans paved the way for the idea that workers could meaningfully participate in designing the nature of work in addition to doing their jobs. Admittedly, some plans were no doubt used to forestall unionization. For this reason, the National Labor Relations Act (the Wagner Act) outlawed employee representation plans in 1935. Such plans were seen as being a form of company unions, wherein representatives could not bargain as equals (they generally lacked the ability to sign legally enforceable agreements), and the right to strike was not recognized.

When Sumner H. Slichter retrospectively examined labor policies in the 1920s, he wondered why employers did not take advantage of the surplus of labor following World War I to exploit workers. The short, steep 1920–1921 economic depression had created a buyer's market for labor. Employers had an oversupply of workers from whom to choose, yet the era was marked by an increase in employee benefits. Employee turnover was low; employment-stabilization policies had increased job security; real wages rose 11 percent; 300 companies had some form of employee stock-ownership plan; 370 companies provided industrial pension plans; and more

---

[103] Alfred P. Haake, "The Measurement of Motives," in Commons, *Industrial Government*, p. 46. See also Richard A. Feiss, "Personal Relationship as a Basis for Scientific Management," *Annals of the American Academy of Political and Social Science* 65 (May 1916), pp. 27–56.

[104] Jennie McMullin Turner, "Thinking and Planning," in Commons, *Industrial Government*, p. 11.

[105] Charlotte Heath, "History of the Dennison Manufacturing Company—II," *Journal of Economic and Business History* 2(1) (November 1929), pp. 175–178, 182. See also W. Jack Duncan and C. Ray Gullett, "Henry Sturgis Dennison: The Manager and the Social Critic," *Journal of Business Research* 2(2) (April 1974), pp. 133–143; C. Ray Gullett and W. Jack Duncan, "Employee Representation Reappraisal . . . with Special Regard to the Contributions of Henry Dennison," *Conference Board Record* 13(6) (June 1976), pp. 32–36. See also Kim McQuaid, "Henry S. Dennison and the 'Science' of Industrial Reform, 1900–1950," *American Journal of Economics and Sociology* 36(1) (January 1977), pp. 79–98; Kyle D. Bruce, "Activist Manager: The Enduring Contribution of Henry S. Dennison to Management and Organization Studies," *Journal of Management History* 21(2) (2015), pp. 143–171.

[106] See, for example, Ben M. Selekman's study of the Partnership Plan at Dutchess Bleachery Inc. at Wappingers Falls, New York, *Sharing Management with the Worker* (New York: Russell Sage Foundation, 1924). For more on van Kleeck's 40-year career at the Russell Sage Foundation's Division of Industrial Studies, see Guy Alchon, "'The World We Seek as Christians,' Mary van Kleeck, Philanthropy, and Early Social Science Initiatives," in Theresa Richardson and Donald Fisher, eds., *The Development of the Social Sciences in the United States and Canada: The Role of Philanthropy* (Stamford, CT: Ablex, 1999), pp. 59–73; Patrick Selmi and Richard Hunter, "Beyond the Rank and File Movement: Mary van Kleeck and Social Work, Radicalism in the Great Depression, 1931–1942," *Journal of Sociology and Social Welfare* 38(2) (June 2001), pp. 75–100; and Chris Nyland and Tom Heenan, "Mary van Kleeck, Taylorism and the Control of Management Knowledge," *Management Decision* 43(10) (2005), pp. 1358–1372.

[107] Harold B. Butler, *Industrial Relations in the U.S.* (Geneva: International Labor Office, 1927), pp. 84–105.

progress had been made in improving labor–management relations within nonunion than union shops. Indeed, union membership was down 30 percent. Instead, Slichter noted that employers had created "industrial goodwill" with group-insurance plans, loans to purchase homes, and paid vacations.[108] The 1920s was a prosperous decade for employees and employers alike.

SUMMARY

The dual heritage of modern personnel management may be traced to the early 1880s and the near simultaneous emergence of the scientific management and Social Gospel movements. Whereas scientific management originated from an engineering philosophy that focused on the need for the "strictest economy in the use of workers," Social Gospel proponents strived to improve "the general tenor of American living and the standards of the poor and unfortunate." Scientific management inspired psychologists and sociologists to become involved in the study of workplace dynamics. With advances in understanding the relationship between work and workers' lives on and off the job, there were also advances involving labor–management relations. These advances were most evident in the trade-union movement and the changing nature of union–management cooperation. The path ahead was opening for further progress in understanding people at work.

[108] Sumner H. Slichter, "The Current Labor Policies of American Industries," *Quarterly Journal of Economics* 43(3) (May 1929), pp. 393–435. See also Robert F. Foerster and Else H. Dietel, *Employee Stock Ownership in the United States* (Princeton, NJ: Princeton University Press, 1926).

The Emergence of the Management Process and Organization Theory

CHAPTER 10

The two individuals who are the focus of this chapter both lived during the late nineteenth and early twentieth centuries; both wrote during the scientific-management era; both were Europeans; and both made lasting contributions to the evolution of management thought. One was a practicing manager and the other an academician; one was trained in the physical sciences, the other in the social sciences; and neither received wide recognition for his contributions until some decades after his death. Henri Fayol, a French manager-engineer, and Max Weber, a German economist-sociologist, addressed the fundamental issue of how organizations should be structured. They both sought to combine theory with practice. Their ideas have influenced succeeding generations of managers and scholars and, even today, continue to shape managerial thinking.

HENRI FAYOL: THE MAN AND HIS CAREER

Jules Henri Fayol (1841–1925) was born in Constantinople (now Istanbul, Turkey). His father, a noncommissioned artillery officer, was an engineer fulfilling his military-service obligation in a cannon factory under an agreement between the French and Turkish governments.[1] André and Eugénie (née Quentin) Fayol, Henri's parents, returned to France after André completed his military service. The family resided in La Voulte-sur-Rhône, where André headed a workshop at Pouzin. After Henri received his elementary education in La Voulte at the École des Maristes, he attended the Lycée des Lyon (now the Lycée Ampère) at Valence, graduating in 1858. He then entered l'Ecole Nationale Supérieure des Mines de Saint-Étienne (the youngest in his class at age 17) to become a mining engineer. After graduating in 1860, he went to work at the Commentry coalfield in central France. Société Boigues, Rambourg et Cie, a limited partnership (*société en commandité*), owned the coalfield and steel mills at Fourchambault and Torteron, a forge at d'Imphy, foundries at Fourchambault and Montluçon, and an iron mine at Berry. Following the death of several partners, Société Boigues, Rambourg was reorganized in 1874 as Société

[1] For biographical details on Fayol's life, see Henri Fayol, *Notice sur les Travaux Scientifiques et Techniques de M. Henri Fayol* [*Notice on the Scientific Technical Work of Mr. Henri Fayol*] (Paris: Gauthier-Villars et Cie, 1918); Amédée Fayol, "Henri Fayol (1841–1925): Ingénieur, Géologue, Administrateur" ["Engineer, Geologist, Manager"], *La Nature: Revue des Sciences et de Leurs Applications* no. 3144 (September 15, 1947), pp. 303–304; John D. Breeze, "Harvest from the Archives: The Search for Fayol and Carlioz," *Journal of Management* 11(1) (Spring 1985), pp. 43–47; Tsuneo Sasaki, "Henri Fayol's Family Relationships," *Journal of Management History* 1(3) (1995), pp. 13–20; and *idem*, "The Comambault Company Revisited," *Journal of Economics* (College of Economics, Nihon University, Tokyo, Japan) 68 (January 1999), pp. 33–50.

Commentry-Fourchambault (popularly known as Comambault), a joint-stock company (*société ànonyme*). In 1892, it was renamed Société Commentry-Fourchambault et Decazeville.[2]

Henri Fayol, 1900

Henri Fayol, 1900. *La Société de Commentry-Fourchambault et Decazeville, 1854–1954*. Paris: Brodard et Taupin, 1954, p. 160.

From 1860 until 1866, Fayol worked as a mining engineer, conducting geological research, advancing a new theory about the formation of coal-bearing strata, and developing methods for fighting underground mine fires. His efforts were rewarded with a promotion to manager of the Commentry coalfield at age 25; 6 years later, he was placed in charge of several colliers. In 1888, Comambault was in dire financial straits: no dividends had been paid since 1885; its Fourchambault and Montluçon foundries were operating at a loss; and its coal deposits at Commentry and Montvicq were nearing depletion. This same year, Fayol was named Comambault's managing director (chief executive officer) and charged with revitalizing its operations. He closed the foundry at Fourchambault, centralized production at Montlucon to gain economies of scale, and acquired new coal deposits at Brassac and Decazeville and iron reserves at Joudreville. With the assistance of Joseph Carlioz, who was in charge of Comambault's commercial department, Fayol expanded Comambault's operations backward to mine coal and iron ore and forward to smelt the iron into steel and to sell both mined coal and raw steel.[3] Fayol established research facilities to advance Comambault's technical capabilities; entered into alliances with or acquired other firms; opened new mills to broaden Comambault's geographical base; hired staff specialists in research, manufacturing, and sales; and, to gain a competitive advantage, repositioned Comambault as a supplier of specialty steels.

Though his training was in engineering, Fayol realized that managing a geographically dispersed company with 10,000 employees required skills other than those he had studied. He viewed management as more than a tool to devise systems and methods for increasing throughput (as it had been for scientific management). For Fayol, management involved all the activities associated with producing, distributing, and selling a product. A manager needed to be able to formulate plans, organize plants and equipment, deal with people, and much more. Fayol's engineering courses at l'Ecole Nationale Supérieure des Mines de Saint-Étienne had stressed technical knowledge and did not cover these skills.[4]

Drawing on his experiences as a general manager, Fayol began to develop a theory of business management. He "drew his theory from his everyday practice," recognizing that, if true, the "more general the theory, the wider its applications."[5] Beginning in his early days as a mining engineer at the Commentry coalfields, Fayol had kept notes on events that disrupted mine output. For example, as early as 1861, he observed that all work had to be stopped because a draft horse working in the St. Edmund mine fell and broke its leg. A replacement horse could not be secured in the absence of the mine's manager, as the livery stable-keeper had no authority to act on his own.[6] Fayol's resolution of this impasse was not a result of his technical training, but of the

---

[2] Tsuneo Sasaki, "Fayol and Comambault," *Enterprises et Histoire* no. 34 (December 2003), pp. 8–28; *idem*, "The Comambault Company Revisited," *Keizai Shushi: The Nihon University Economic Review* 68(4) (January 1999), pp. 113–128.

[3] John D. Breeze, "Administration and Organization of the Commercial Function by J. Carlioz," in Kae H. Chung, ed., *Proceedings of the Annual Meeting of the Academy of Management* (1982), pp. 112–116.

[4] Norman M. Pearson, "Fayolism as the Necessary Complement to Taylorism," *American Political Science Review* 39(1) (February 1945), p. 73.

[5] Jean-Louis Peaucelle and Cameron Guthrie, *Henri Fayol, the Manager* (London: Pickering & Chatto, 2015). p. 1. See also Daniel A. Wren, "Henri Fayol: Learning from Experience," *Journal of Management History* 1(3) (1995), pp. 5–12.

[6] Henri Fayol, diary entry of July 29, 1898, in Frédéric Blancpain, ed., "Les cahiers inédits d'Henri Fayol" ["Henri Fayol's Unpublished Notebooks"], *Bulletin de l'Institute International d'Administration Publique* 28/29 (1973), p. 23.

managerial insight that responsibility and authority must be co-equal, or delays and disorder will result. Foreshadowing modern thinking on work groups (see Chapter 15), Fayol organized miners into self-selected teams. This increased group cohesiveness and, in turn, reduced employee turnover. Moreover, work-group output increased as the teams refused to accept inferior members. Anticipating the job-redesign movement by some 50 years (see Chapter 15), Fayol also recognized that some jobs could be enlarged to relieve monotony and enhance skill levels. For example, at Commentry he returned responsibility for reinforcing mine tunnels (so that tunnel walls and ceilings would not collapse) to the miners rather than using timbering crews.[7]

Speaking in Saint-Étienne on June 16, 1908, at the 50th anniversary (*Cinquantenaire*) of the Société de l'Industrie Minérale's founding, Fayol expressed the belief that "All the employees in an enterprise . . . participate to a greater or lesser degree in the administrative function . . . [and] all have occasion to exercise their administrative faculties and to be noticed for them . . . . [Those] who are particularly talented, can climb steadily from the lowest rung to the highest levels of the hierarchy in . . . an organization."[8] In this simple statement, Fayol was beginning to distinguish between managerial ability and technical knowledge. He noted that the effect of management on business activities was not fully understood and that technical expertise "can be completely destroyed by defective administrative procedures." Fayol further observed that "a leader who is a good administrator but technically mediocre is generally much more useful to the enterprise than if he were a brilliant technician but a mediocre administrator." Thus, according to Fayol, a firm's performance depended more on its leaders' managerial abilities than on their technical knowledge. In this same address, Fayol also presented an early list of management principles, including unity of command, hierarchical transmission of orders, separation of powers among distinct departments, and centralization/decentralization. In addition to these and other principles, Fayol spoke of *prévoyance* ("foresight"), the act of forecasting, planning, and budgeting. He also stressed the value of organization charts, meetings and reports, and an accurate and rapid accounting system.[9] Although Fayol's Société de l'Industrie Minérale address revealed advances in his thinking, it lacked the depth and conceptual clarity of his yet-to-come *magnum opus*.

Fayol was 75 years old when his masterpiece, *Administration industrielle et générale*, was first published in the *Bulletin de la Société de l'Industrie Minérale* in 1916.[10] Republished in book form the next year by H. Dunod et E. Pinat, Éditeurs, it was known throughout France as "a catechism for the chief executive's education."[11] Fayolism became as firmly entrenched in French management thinking as Taylorism had become in the United States. From 1918 to his death in 1925, Fayol presided over the meetings of the Centre d'Etudes Administratives, a group he formed to promote Fayolism. In 1926, the Centre merged with Henry le Chatelier's Conference de l'Organisation Française to form the still active Le Comité National de l'Organisation Française.[12] This merger brought together France's two main professional management associations.

World War I initially slowed the dissemination of Fayol's ideas beyond France. Although a Russian translation of Fayol's masterpiece appeared in 1923 and a German translation appeared in 1929, it was almost four decades before his originality was appreciated outside a small circle

[7] Donald Reid, "Fayol: From Experience to Theory," *Journal of Management History* 1(3) (1995), p. 23.
[8] Henri Fayol, "L'Exposé des Principes Généraux d'Administration," reproduced and translated in Daniel A. Wren, Arthur G. Bedeian, and John D. Breeze, "The Foundations of Henri Fayol's Administrative Theory," *Management Decision* 40(9) (2002), p. 911.
[9] *Ibid.*, pp. 910, 912–916. For a full treatment of Fayol's contributions to contemporary accounting, see Lee D. Parker and Philip Ritson, "Accounting's Latent Classicism: Revisiting Classical Management Origins," *Abacus* 47(2) 2011, pp. 234–265.
[10] Henri Fayol, "Administration industrielle et générale," ["General and Industrial Administration"] *Bulletin de la Société de l'Industrie Minérale*, 10(3) (1916), pp. 5–162. See also Bennett H. Brough, "The Mining and Metallurgical Congress at St Etienne," *Journal of the Iron and Steel Institute* 76(1) (1908), pp. 203–208.
[11] Charles de Fréminville, "Henri Fayol: A Great Engineer, A Great Scientist, and A Great Management Leader," *Bulletin of the Taylor Society* 12(1) (February 1927), p. 304.
[12] John D. Breeze, "Henri Fayol's Centre for Administrative Studies," *Journal of Management History* 1(3) (1995), pp. 37–62.

of scholars in Europe and Great Britain.[13] Early interpretations contrasted Fayol's and Taylor's work. Whereas Taylor approached the study of management from the workshop or technical level, Fayol approached it from the viewpoint of upper-level administration. Fayol's emphasis on administrative management reflected his more than 50 years' experience as a general manager. He insisted that his work complemented Taylor's thinking, in that both he and Taylor sought to improve managerial practice.

THE NEED FOR MANAGEMENT THEORY

Fayol noted in his earlier writings that managerial ability was essential for an enterprise's success. If managerial ability was important, however, then why did schools and universities neglect managerial training to focus exclusively on teaching technical knowledge? The answer, according to Fayol, was the absence of management theory. Fayol defined theory as "a collection of principles, rules, methods, and procedures tried and checked by general experience."[14] He believed that simply recounting stories told by older managers as a way to educate future managers was ineffective. Managers' experiences were limited to specific situations and not easily generalized to other settings. Fayol recognized that a sound theoretical base was necessary to understand the many contradictions encountered by practicing managers.

Every enterprise required management: "Be it a case of commerce, industry, politics, religion, war, or philanthropy, in every concern there is a management function to be performed."[15] Thus, like Charles Dupin (see Chapter 4), Fayol felt that management required special study apart from technical matters and could be taught in schools and universities as theory was developed and codified.

Managerial ability, according to Fayol, depended on certain qualities and knowledge:

- *Physical qualities:* health, vigor, address [literally, manner of behaving]
- *Mental qualities:* ability to understand and learn, judgment, mental vigor, and adaptability
- *Moral qualities:* energy, firmness, willingness to accept responsibility, initiative, loyalty, tact, dignity
- *General education:* general acquaintance with matters not belonging exclusively to the function performed
- *Special knowledge:* that peculiar to the function, be it technical, commercial, financial, managerial, and so on
- *Experience:* knowledge arising from the work proper; the recollection of lessons a person has derived from things.[16]

Fayol believed that the relative importance of technical and managerial abilities varied according to the nature of a person's job. As he explained, at lower levels, technical ability is most important; but as individuals move up the "scalar chain," the relative importance of managerial ability increases, whereas the need for technical ability decreases. Simply put, managerial ability is imperative at higher levels of an organization. Ability in commercial, financial, security, and accounting matters also diminishes in importance as a manager's authority increases. As for

---

[13] See Henri Fayol, *Общее и промышленное управление,* trans. Borisovich V. Korenva (Moscow: Central Labor Institute, 1923); *idem, Allgemeine und industrielle Verwaltung*, trans. Karl Reineke (Munich: Rudolf Oldenbourg Verlag), 1929; *idem, Industrial and General Administration*, trans. John A. Coubrough (Geneva: International Management Institute, 1930); *idem*, "The Administrative Theory of the State," trans. Sarah Greer, in Luther Gulick and Lyndall Urwick, eds., *Papers on the Science of Administration* (New York: Institute of Public Administration, Columbia University, 1937), pp. 99–114; and *idem, General and Industrial Management*, trans. Constance Storrs (London: Sir Isaac Pitman and Sons, 1949).

[14] *Idem, General and Industrial Management*, trans. Storrs, p. 15. Except where specifically noted, the Storrs translation will be referenced, as it is the most readily available English translation.

[15] *Ibid.*, p. 41.

[16] *Ibid.*, p. 7.

differences in firm size, Fayol contended that managers of small firms need relatively more technical ability than do their counterparts in larger firms, where managerial rather than technical ability is required at upper levels.

In summary, Fayol held that all employees, from supervisors to work superintendents, should receive some managerial training. He believed that schools and universities did not teach management theory because it was thought that practice was the only way to acquire managerial skill. Recognizing that most higher managers have "neither the time nor inclination for writing,"[17] Fayol used his experiences and observations to propose a body of knowledge that included principles as guides to thinking and practice and general elements or functions that compose a manager's job. His goal was to begin a general discussion from which a theory of management might emanate.

THE PRINCIPLES OF MANAGEMENT

Fayol recognized that the term "principles" is often misunderstood. To some observers, it suggests an unquestioned or rigid way of doing things, or the order of laws in the physical sciences. For this reason, Fayol was careful to explain what he meant by "principles":

> For preference I shall adopt the term principles whilst dissociating it from any suggestion of rigidity, for there is nothing rigid or absolute in management affairs, it is all a question of proportion. Seldom do we have to apply the same principle twice in identical conditions; allowance must be made for different and changing circumstances. . . .
>
> Therefore principles are flexible and capable of adaptation to every need; it is a matter of knowing how to make use of them, which is a difficult art requiring intelligence, experience, decision and proportion. Compounded of tact and experience, proportion is one of the foremost attributes of the manager.[18]

Moreover, Fayol stressed that in advancing a list of principles he was not suggesting that the list was exclusive; other principles could be identified. The principles he chose to review were simply those he had found most useful in his own career. The 14 principles on which Fayol concentrated were as follows:

- Division of work
- Authority
- Discipline
- Unity of command
- Unity of direction
- Subordination of individual interests to the general interest
- Remuneration
- Centralization
- Scalar chain (line of authority)
- Order
- Equity
- Stability of tenure of personnel
- Initiative
- *Esprit de corps*.

[17] *Ibid.*, p. 15.
[18] *Ibid.*, p. 19.

Division of work (or, alternatively, division of labor) is the well-known idea of assigning separate tasks to individual specialists with the intent of producing "more and better work with the same effort." Fayol recognized that the division of work leads to heightened expertise, which increases productivity. In addition, he noted that, because of the specialization that derives from dividing work, tasks are not only performed with greater expertise, but also with greater speed because employees do not lose time shifting from one activity to another. Nevertheless, like Adam Smith before him (see Chapter 2), Fayol appreciated that benefits derived from dividing work must be balanced against obvious disadvantages such as boredom and monotony. As he unequivocally stated, "division of work has its limits which experience and a sense of proportion teach us may not be exceeded."[19]

Authority was defined as "the right to give orders and the power to exact obedience." Fayol distinguished between the formal authority managers held by virtue of office or rank and personal authority, which was "compounded of intelligence, experience, moral worth, ability to lead, past services, etc."[20] Well ahead of modern-day scholars, Fayol recognized that savvy managers complement their official authority with personal authority. He further realized that authority and responsibility are corollaries in the sense that wherever authority is exercised, responsibility arises. Fayol stated the classic case for authority being commensurate with responsibility. This principle appears throughout management literature.

Discipline is essentially respect and obedience between a firm and its employees. Fayol felt that discipline was vital for a smoothly functioning and prosperous firm. He viewed "defects in discipline" to be a result of ineptitude on the part of a firm's managers. Discipline came from placing knowledgeable managers at all levels of authority, workplace agreements that were satisfactory to both managers and employees, and the judicious use of employee sanctions.

Unity of command was expressed as follows: "For any action whatsoever an employee should receive orders from one superior only."[21] Just as the Biblical injunction (Matthew 6:24) advises: "No one can serve two masters." To Fayol, dual command was a threat to authority, discipline, and stability.

Unity of direction means "one head and one plan for a group of activities having the same objective."[22] It provides the coordination necessary for focusing a firm's efforts. Unity of direction comes from a sound organization structure and is essential to "unity of action."

Subordination of individual interests to the general interest is a plea to abolish "ignorance, ambition, selfishness, laziness, weakness and all human passions."[23] As viewed by Fayol, the placing of an individual's or group's interests over a firm's general welfare would inevitably lead to conflict among participants. Fayol's observations in this respect represent an early expression of what modern agency theory refers to as "opportunism," meaning a form of self-interested behavior (see Chapter 19). Fayol recognized that individuals or groups who serve only themselves are harmful to the interests of their fellow employees and the interest of a firm in general.

Remuneration deals with day wages, piece rates, bonuses, and profit sharing. Fayol concluded that appropriate employee remuneration depends on many factors. In general, however, a firm's method of payment should be fair, should motivate by rewarding successful performance, and should not lead to excessive overpayment. Fayol also acknowledged nonfinancial incentives (such as housing and food) as a form of remuneration.

Centralization is a principle that Fayol felt was always present to a greater or lesser extent and, thus, belonged to the "natural order." His discussion of centralization as a question of proportion unique to each firm, and his appreciation of the distortion that occurs as information

[19] *Ibid.*, p. 20.
[20] *Ibid.*, p. 21.
[21] *Ibid.*, p. 24.
[22] *Ibid.*, p. 25.
[23] *Ibid.*, p. 26.

is transmitted serially along a scalar chain, continue to offer valuable insights for contemporary managers:

> Centralization is not a system of management good or bad of itself, capable of being adopted or discarded at the whim of managers or of circumstances; it is always present to a greater or less extent. The question of centralization or decentralization is a simple question of proportion, it is a matter of finding the optimum degree for the particular concern. In small firms, where the manager's orders go directly to subordinates, there is absolute centralization; in large concerns, where a long scalar chain is interposed between manager and lower grades, orders and counter-information, too, have to go through a series of intermediaries. Each employee, intentionally or unintentionally, puts something of himself into the transmission and execution of orders and of information received, too. He does not operate merely as a cog in a machine. What appropriate share of initiative may be left to intermediaries depends on the personal character of the manager, on his moral worth, on the reliability of his subordinates, and also on the condition of the business. The degree of centralization must vary according to different cases. The objective to pursue is the optimum utilization of all faculties of the personnel.[24]

Scalar chain refers to "the chain of superiors ranging from the ultimate authority to the lowest ranks."[25] As Fayol explained, this path shows a firm's line of authority and the links through which communications are transmitted from the top to the bottom of a firm and back. To counter possible communication delays caused by the unity-of-command principle, Fayol developed what is referred to as the "gang plank." The gangplank (see Figure 10.1) allows communications to cross lines of authority. Thus, Foreman F desiring to communicate a message to Foreman P could do so directly without reporting upward (F through E to A) and having the message in turn transmitted downward to P. The gangplank permits lateral communication through the shortest path and avoids overburdening a firm's scalar chain.

Citing the same seventeenth-century proverb as James W. See (see Chapter 6), Fayol found that *Order*, with regard to material things, ensures "A place for everything and everything in its place." As Fayol noted, the same may be said for people: "The right man in the right place." The objective of *material order* is to avoid wasting resources. Fayol recognized that *social order* requires good organization and good selection and, by necessity, a need to balance a firm's human requirements with its available resources. Fayol considered ambition, nepotism, favoritism, ignorance resulting in unnecessary positions, or positions filled with incompetent employees, to be the enemies of social order.

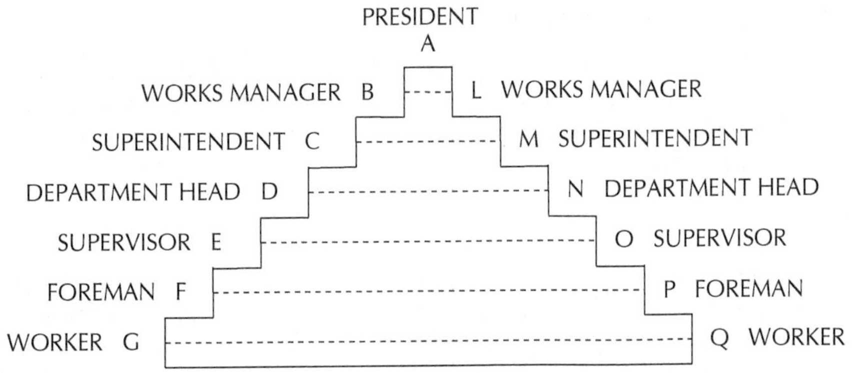

FIGURE 10.1 Fayol's gangplank

[24] *Ibid.*, p. 33.
[25] *Ibid.*, p. 34.

Equity, as envisioned by Fayol, results from a combination of kindliness and justice. As such, equity provides a basis for dealing with employees and instilling devotion and loyalty. Fayol took care to distinguish between equity and equality and, in doing so, anticipated modern equity theory (see Chapter 20). Recognizing the difficulty invoked by instilling a sense of equity at all levels of a firm, Fayol—no doubt reflecting on his personal experience—observed that in dealing with employees' desire for equity, "the head of the business must frequently summon up his highest faculties."[26]

Fayol's 12th principle, *stability of tenure of personnel,* sought to provide for orderly human-resource staffing and establish provisions to assure that a firm's employees possessed the requisite abilities for the work to be performed. Fayol appreciated that it took time to develop the necessary skills to perform at a superior level. He also recognized that it took time for a manager and a group of employees to develop into a high-performing team. Managers must make a concerted effort to know their employees and inspire their confidence. From his own experience, Fayol knew this could be a lengthy undertaking.

Initiative, as a principle, exhorted employees to display zeal and energy in all endeavors. Fayol observed "thinking out a plan and ensuring its success is . . . one of the most powerful stimulants of human endeavour . . . and . . . [this] is what is called initiative." Fayol considered the "freedom to propose and execute" to be key aspects of initiative that were essential to subordinate satisfaction. As Fayol thus realized, "The initiative of all, added to that of the manager, and supplementing it if need be, represents a great source of strength for businesses."[27]

Finally, *esprit de corps* stressed building harmony and unity within a firm. Fayol warned against sowing dissension among subordinates. Calling once again on his years of experience as a general manager, he understood that "real talent is needed to co-ordinate effort, encourage keenness, use each man's abilities, and reward each one's merit without arousing jealousies and disturbing harmonious relations." Quoting the Aesopian proverb "union is strength," Fayol advised: "Dividing enemy forces to weaken them is clever, but dividing one's own team is a grave sin against the business."[28]

As Fayol explained, his principles were intended as guides to theory and practice and were not meant to be exhaustive in scope or rigidly applied. The factory system of production that developed during the Industrial Revolution (see Chapter 3) reflected many of these principles in practice. Fayol, however, was the first person to formulate a set of general management principles.

THE ELEMENTS OF MANAGEMENT

Fayol is also credited with being the first person to identify and describe the elements or functions that compose a manager's job. He labeled the elements Planning, Organizing, Command, Coordination, and Control. Taken together, these five elements represent what is referred to as "the management process."

Planning

Fayol recognized that planning, by defining a firm's objectives, set the stage for the other elements of a manager's job. At various times, he used the French *prévoyance* (anticipation or foresight) instead of *préparer* (to plan) when discussing this function. To Fayol, managing meant looking ahead, and foresight was an essential element of managing. As described by Fayol, a firm's plan of action represented "the result envisaged" and should rest on (1) a firm's resources,

---

[26] *Ibid.*, p. 38.
[27] *Ibid.*, p. 39.
[28] *Ibid.*, p. 40. The moral of Aesop's fable "The Old Man and His Sons" is generally rendered as "Unity is strength." See *Three Hundred and Fifty Aesop's Fables*, trans. George Fyler Townsend (Chicago, IL: Belford, Clarke & Co, 1884), p. 267.

including buildings, tools, materials, employees, sales outlets, and public relations; (2) the nature of work in process; and (3) future trends in a firm's business activities that cannot be predetermined. In modern terms, Fayol was describing a rudimentary strategic audit that assesses a firm's present capabilities and strengths and scans the surrounding environment to anticipate future marketplace opportunities.

Fayol also understood the importance of what modern authorities call "contingency planning." Fayol's 30-year career as managing director was characterized by numerous technological, political, social, and economic changes that required recurring adjustments. While adjusting to these external changes, though, Fayol also kept his eyes on the horizon: "By constantly looking to the future, Henri Fayol promoted the idea of a lasting enterprise, renewing her assets as those on hand eroded. The profits made at the Commentry mine financed investments in the company's future, reinforcing its position in the mining and steel industries that would continue growing for another half century."[29] He observed:

> One cannot anticipate with precision everything which will happen over a longer period but one can minimize uncertainty and carry out one's program as a result . . . any long-term program should be susceptible to being changed according to the variety, complexity and instability of events. Like any living object the industrial enterprise undergoes continuing transformations: the personnel, the tooling, the methods, even the goals of the association change; the program must without ceasing be kept, as far as possible, in harmony with the environment.[30]

In commenting on the advantages and shortcomings of the forecasting system he used at Comambault, Fayol underscored the benefit of involving a firm's managers in anticipating a firm's future. In doing so, he showed an early appreciation of what would become known as "participative management":

> The study of resources, future possibilities, and means to be used for attaining the objective call for contributions from all departmental heads within the framework of their mandate, each one brings to this study the contribution of his experience together with recognition of the responsibility which will fall upon him in executing the plan.[31]

Such participation ensured that no resource was neglected and promoted managers' interest in a firm's future success. Further, Fayol realized that lower-echelon managers would give increased attention to planning because they would be more committed to executing what they themselves had planned. Fayol saw that a good plan of action would facilitate the efficient use of a firm's resources and, in doing so, would possess certain characteristics: unity (formulate one overall plan followed by specific plans for each supporting activity); continuity (incorporate both short- and long-range plans); flexibility (be capable of adjusting to unexpected events); and precision (eliminate as many uncertainties as possible). Considering these characteristics, Fayol advised that firms establish a series of separate plans that would together constitute one overall plan for obtaining their objectives. Thus, he recommended that daily, weekly, monthly, annual, 5-year, and 10-year forecasts (or plans) be prepared and redrafted as time passed or as conditions changed. Fayol's stress on long-range planning was a unique contribution to management thought, and his ideas are as important today as they were for his own time. He also offered innovative insights into planning on a national scale. The French government planned and budgeted on an annual basis with little or no regard for long-term development; the result was an emphasis on day-to-day operations and a lack of future planning on the part of government ministers. Fayol attributed the ministers' failure to develop long-term forecasts to the fact that ministers "come and go" and, thus, "have no time to acquire professional competence, business experience and

[29] Peaucelle and Guthrie, *Henri Fayol, the Manager*, pp. 52–53.
[30] Fayol, "L'Exposé des Principes Généraux d'Administration," p. 915.
[31] *Idem, General and Industrial Management*, p. 48.

managerial capacity indispensable to the drawing up of a plan."[32] For this reason, he argued for an increase in ministerial tenure to hold ministers to their work and to give them a sense of moral responsibility for the future of France.

Organizing

Organizing is the second element or function that Fayol identified as being part of a manager's job. For Fayol, organizing meant providing a firm with everything it needed to achieve its objectives. This included the classical factors of production: land, labor, and materials. Later writers divided Fayol's organizing element into two separate functions: organizing and staffing (human-resource management). According to Fayol, it was the duty of a firm's managers to ensure that its "human and material organization is consistent with [its] objectives, resources, and requirements."[33] In this regard, a firm's managers should provide unity of direction, define duties clearly, encourage initiative and responsibility, harmonize activities and coordinate efforts, and resist "excess of regulation, red tape, and paper control."[34] Fayol appreciated that structure should not be an end in itself and urged that the human factor not be neglected:

> [T]o create a useful organization it is not enough to group people [into departments] and distribute duties; there must be knowledge of how to adapt the organic whole to requirements, how to find essential personnel and put each where he can be of most service. . . . Of two organizations similar in appearance, one may be excellent the other bad, depending on the personal qualities of those who compose them.[35]

Thus, like Edward Atkinson and the Marshalls before him (see Chapter 6), Fayol realized it was people, not structure, that made the difference between the success or failure of two otherwise similar firms. In retrospect, Fayol anticipated today's contingency approach to management (see Chapter 20).

Fayol noted that the tiered layers of authority that compose an organization (the so-called "organizational pyramid") are a product of functional and scalar growth. "Functional growth" relates to the horizontal structure of a firm, in that employees are added to perform functional duties as a firm's workload expands. In contrast, "scalar growth" is vertical, caused by the need to add layers of supervision to coordinate various activities divided among departments. Fayol described what happens to a firm's structure as its workforce increases. As an illustration he considered what occurs relative to functional and scalar growth in a firm where 15 employees report to each first-line supervisor and, in turn, each group of four supervisors is under the direction of a higher-level supervisor or manager. In such a situation, every 60 employees required 4 supervisors, and these 4 supervisors required 1 common manager.

This illustrated how a hierarchy developed, but in practice Fayol "had to adapt to a number of other considerations, including the cooperation between specialized technical functions and a large number of other units in other hierarchies."[36] He realized there is a natural limit to the number of subordinates that a manager can effectively supervise, termed "the span of control," but this number was not formula driven and, in practice, adjustments were sometimes necessary.

On the subject of staff employees, Fayol visualized a group of individuals who had the "strength, knowledge, and time" to assist line managers by acting as an "extension of a manager's personality." Staff employees were to take orders only from a firm's general manager and to "subserve" line managers in dealing with daily obligations such as correspondence, interviews, and

---

[32] *Ibid.*, p. 52.
[33] *Ibid.*, p. 53.
[34] *Ibid.*, p. 54.
[35] *Ibid.*, p. 57.
[36] Peaucelle and Guthrie, *Henri Fayol, the Manager*, p. 63.

conferences, as well as assisting in harmonizing current operations and future plans. Based on his own experience as an executive, Fayol believed that line managers generally had neither time nor energy to focus on long-term strategy. Staff employees, freed of daily pressures associated with running a department, could "search for improvements" in work methods, identify developing changes in immediate business conditions, and consider longer term trends.[37]

Fayol reviewed the differences between his recommendations for utilizing staff employees and Taylor's functional foremanship. Fayol agreed with Taylor's goal, providing specialized assistance, but disagreed with the means. Functional foremanship negated the unity of command principle, and to Fayol this was treading on dangerous ground. Order must be maintained, and for Fayol this was possible only if no subordinate reported to more than one superior: "So . . . let us treasure the old type of organization in which unity of command is honoured. It can, after all, be easily reconciled . . . with [staff] assistance given to superintendents and foremen."[38] In extending his comments, Fayol expressed the opinion that organization charts, showing all the positions in a firm and their relationships to one another, aided in maintaining the unity of command principle throughout a firm. He observed that, compared to lengthy written descriptions, organization charts enabled managers to grasp more easily a firm's "organic whole." Unfortunately, Fayol's thoughts on organizing were not published until recently.[39]

Focusing on what he referred to as the "body corporate," Fayol viewed employee selection and training to be vital for determining a firm's fate. He considered selecting capable employees to be among "the most important and most difficult of business activities." Noting that the consequences of poor selection are "commensurate with the rank of the employee," Fayol advised that the length of time devoted to choosing an employee should increase with the level of the position being filled. On balance, like Taylor, Fayol's treatment of evaluating a firm's employees was limited, reflecting the rudimentary practices of the day. Training, in contrast, was dealt with at length, primarily because Fayol had an ulterior motive. As previously discussed, Fayol called for less technical training of young engineers and more attention to the elements of management. In Fayol's view, contemporary education in French schools was based on two illusions: "[T]hat the value of engineers and industrial leaders comprises technical ability almost exclusively [and] bears a direct relationship to the number of years devoted to the subject of mathematics."[40] Fayol believed that the latter "illusion" was just as "dire" as the former, but would likely prove harder to dispel: "Long personal experience has taught me that the use of *higher* mathematics counts for nothing in managing businesses."[41] Basic mathematics helped train the mind, but further study should be devoted to management rather than more math. Fayol sought balance and advised young engineers to study their employees, "their behaviour, character, abilities, work, and even their personal interests."[42] Indeed, Fayol thought that everyone should study the elements of management, for they were necessary in the workshop as well as in the home.

Command, Coordination, and Control

After it was organized, Fayol reasoned that a firm must be set into motion. He viewed this as the "mission of command," as spread among a firm's managers. Fayol used the French *commander* (to command) as well as *diriger* (to direct) in his writing. Because "command" has a more specific meaning in English, perhaps the most representative translation of this third element of management would be "to direct or to supervise." Fayol felt that it was every manager's duty to

[37] *Ibid.*, p. 63.
[38] *Ibid.*, p. 70.
[39] See Fayol's previously unpublished typescript "Personal Observations and Experiments" in Peaucelle and Guthrie, *Henri Fayol, the Manager*, pp. 183–221.
[40] Fayol, *General and Industrial Management*, pp. 83–84.
[41] *Ibid*, p. 84. By "higher mathematics" Fayol meant "special mathematics," such as differential and integral calculus.
[42] *Ibid.*, p. 91.

"get the optimum return from all employees" and that doing so required certain personal qualities and principles of management. Fayol held that managers should:

- have a thorough knowledge of their employees
- eliminate incompetent employees
- be well versed in the agreements binding a firm and its employees
- set a good example for others
- conduct periodic audits of a firms' performance
- confer with their assistants as a group to provide for unity of direction and the focusing of effort
- avoid becoming engrossed in detail
- strive at making unity, energy, initiative, and loyalty prevail among all employees.[43]

In a diary entry dated July 29, 1898, Fayol wrote: "In business administration, the question of [managing] people represents more than one-half of the problem."[44] As a young manager, Fayol had built effective work teams in the Commentry mines, discontinued paternalistic practices such as monitoring employee church attendance, closed company-owned stores in areas where local merchants were present, and demonstrated other people-management skills that led to his promotions. With his insight that people represent more than one-half the challenge managers face, Fayol learned that communication skills were crucial. He saw conferring with assistants to be important for establishing and maintaining clear communications. His admonition to avoid being engrossed in detail was not antithetical to keeping informed, but rather meant to be a warning not to neglect large problems while lavishing attention on picayune matters. Further reflecting an appreciation of the human element, Fayol believed that to encourage initiative, managers should allow subordinates "the maximum share of activity consistent with their position and capability, even at the cost of some mistakes."[45] Moreover, Fayol felt that authority should be delegated downward to develop employees' abilities and to avoid "drying up initiative and loyalty."

Coordination was Fayol's fourth element or function of management. By coordination, Fayol meant "to harmonize all the activities of a concern so as to facilitate its working, and its success."[46] Later writers stressed the necessity of coordination in all elements of management rather than treating it as a separate element. To Fayol, coordination required balancing expenses with revenues, equipment maintenance with meeting production goals, and sales against production. The functions of planning and organizing facilitated coordination by specifying duties, establishing schedules, and focusing responsibilities on furthering a firm's objectives. Command instilled initiative, and conferences with assistants and subordinates provided a clearinghouse for airing problems, progress, and plans. Fayol recommended that line managers use staff employees to enhance coordination but warned that their use did not replace line managers' direct responsibility for achieving a firm's objectives.

Control, Fayol's final element of management, consisted of "verifying whether everything occurs in conformity with the plan adopted, the instructions issued, and the principles established."[47] Fayol's *contrôler* was a positive view of monitoring plans and performance to gauge and verify a firm's progress toward achieving its goals. Control was to be applied to people, objects, and activities, and its objective was to identify and correct errors and prevent their recurrence. The accounting function played a key role in the information system with regard to collecting and disseminating information for internal decision-making and external reporting. Effective

[43] *Ibid.*, pp. 97–98.
[44] *Idem*, in Blancpain, "Les cahiers inédits d'Henri Fayol," p. 24.
[45] *Idem, General and Industrial Management*, pp. 102–103.
[46] *Ibid.*, p. 103.
[47] *Ibid.*, p. 107. In *Henri Fayol, the Manager*, p. 260, Peaucelle and Guthrie suggest "to verify" is a more accurate translation.

control should be based on prompt action, followed by sanctions, if necessary. Fayol saw control as having an integrative effect on the other elements of management because it could be used to stimulate better planning, simplify and strengthen a firm's organization structure, enhance the directing of employees, and facilitate coordination. In effect, control completed a cycle of activities that could then be improved as the management process continued.

A FINAL NOTE

Fayol's orientation was that of a top-level executive. He believed that "[t]he responsibility of general management is to conduct the enterprise toward its objective by making optimum use of available resources. It is the executive authority, it draws up the plan of action, selects personnel, determines performance, ensures and controls the execution of all activities."[48] Fayol assumed the top management position when Commentry-Fourchambault et Decazeville was headed for bankruptcy and restored it to prosperity in a period characterized by economic, social, political, and technological change. He remained on the Commentry-Fourchambault board until his death in 1925. Essentially, Fayol was a strategist before that term became popular.[49] The familiar ring of Fayol's ideas suggests how thoroughly they have penetrated current managerial thinking. Whereas many of them may seem relatively self-evident today, they were revolutionary when first advanced. They remain important not only because of Fayol's influence on succeeding generations of managers but also because of their continuing validity. As a keen observer of management practice has noted: "Whether they admit it or not, it's obvious most managers today are fundamentally Fayolists."[50] For this reason, Fayol is known as the "Father of Modern Management." By the time of his death in 1925, Fayol had been awarded the Delesse Prize of the French Academy of Sciences, the Gold Medal of the Société d'Encouragement pour l'Industrie Nationale of France, the Gold Medal and Medal of Honor of the Société de l'Industrie Minérale and named a Chevalier (Knight) of the Légion d'honneur and a Commander of the Order of the Crown (Romania).

MAX WEBER: BUREAUCRACY

The life and work of Karl Emil Maximilian "Max" Weber (1864–1920) ran chronologically parallel to those of Henri Fayol and Fred Taylor. Born in Erfurt, Prussia, to a life of affluence in a family with social and political connections, Weber (pronounced *Vay-ber*) was an intellectual of the first order, with far-ranging interests in sociology, religion, economics, and political science. He received an undergraduate degree in 1886 and a doctorate in law in 1889 from the University of Berlin. His dissertation was titled "Zur Geschichte der Handelgesellschaften im Mittelalter" ["On the History of Trading Companies in the Middle Ages"].

While in the final stages of preparing his epochal study, *The Protestant Ethic and the Spirit of Capitalism*,[51] on why capitalism (in the form of free-market enterprise) only flourished in certain parts of seventeenth- and eighteenth-century Europe, Weber had an opportunity to visit the United States, which he considered the most capitalistic of all nations. Weber had been invited by his former University of Freiburg colleague Hugo Münsterberg to attend the International Congress of Arts and Sciences, which was being held in conjunction with the 1904 St. Louis World's Fair. He presented a paper at the congress titled "The Relations of the Rural Community

---

48 Fayol, *General and Industrial Management*, pp. 61–62; see also p. 6.

49 Daniel A. Wren, "Henri Fayol as Strategist: A Nineteenth Century Corporate Turnaround," *Management Decision* 39 (2001), pp. 475–487. See also Lee D. Parker and Philip A. Ritson, "Revisiting Fayol: Anticipating Contemporary Management," *British Journal of Management* 16(3) (September 2005), pp. 175–194; Daniel A. Wren, "The Influence of Henri Fayol on Management Theory and Education in North America," *Entreprises et Histoire no.* 34 (December 2003), pp. 98–107.

50 [W. Jerome Arnold], "Famous Firsts: Discoveries from Looking Inward," *Business Week* (June 6, 1964), p. 152.

51 Max Weber, *The Protestant Ethic and the Spirit of Capitalism*, trans. Talcott Parsons (London: Allen & Unwin, 1930). German edition published in 1904.

Marianne S. Weber, *Max Weber: A Biography*, trans. and ed. Harry Zohn (New Brunswick, NJ: Transaction Publishers, 1988), p. 347. Originally published in 1926.

Max Weber, circa 1896–1897

to Other Branches of Social Sciences."[52] Weber combined attending the congress with a stop in New York City to do some further research at Columbia University and the New York Public Libraries, and a short stay with relatives in Mount Airy (North Carolina). Further, curious to see firsthand how the spirit of capitalism abounded in the United States, Weber also took time to visit several cities, including Philadelphia, Washington (DC), Baltimore, Boston, Chicago, New Orleans, and Tuskegee (Alabama), as well as the Muskogee Indian Territory in Oklahoma.[53]

The economic developments he observed differed from those in Germany. As documented in the McLane Report (Chapter 5), U.S. manufacturing and marketing had grown from small stores and owner-managed businesses to large professionally managed firms that were bound together by an intercontinental network of communication and transportation. In Germany, large-scale firms had been developed only in chemicals, metals, and complex industrial machine-goods.[54] In these industries, cartels had been formed to control prices and ration markets. Antitrust laws limited this practice in the United States, but German cartels could operate without fear of either government intervention or threat of competition. In contrast to Germany, a "spirit of capitalism" in the United States encouraged innovation and competition.

BUREAUCRACY AS THE IDEAL

Primarily prescriptive in nature, Weber's writings strike an interesting contrast with the practitioner-oriented recommendations offered by Taylor and Fayol. Weber's major contribution was an outline of the characteristics of what he termed "bureaucracy," that is, government by bureaus (German *Büro*).[55] In reviewing Weber's work, it is important to emphasize four points:

1. Weber did not use the term *bureaucracy* in the disparaging, emotionally tinged sense of red tape, endless lines, and rule-encumbered inefficiency. Rather, he used it as a noncritical label referring to what he regarded as the most modern and efficient method of organizing yet developed. In Weber's words:

   Experience tends universally to show that the purely bureaucratic type of administrative organization—that is, the monocratic variety of bureaucracy—is, from a purely technical point of view, capable of attaining the highest degree of efficiency and is in this sense formally the most rational known means of carrying out imperative control over human beings. It is superior to any other form in precision, in stability, in the stringency of its discipline, and in its reliability. It thus makes possible a particularly high degree of calculability of results for the heads of the organization and for those acting in relation

[52] *Idem*, "The Relations of the Rural Community to Other Branches of Social Science," trans. Carl W. Seidenadel, in Howard J. Rogers, ed., *Congress of Arts and Science, Universal Exposition, St. Louis*, vol. 7 (Boston, MA: Houghton, Mifflin, 1906), pp. 725–746.

[53] Henry W. Brann, "Max Weber and the United States," *Southwestern Social Science Quarterly* 25(2) (June 1944), pp. 18–30. See also Larry G. Keeter, "Max Weber's Visit to North Carolina," *Journal of the History of Sociology*," 3(2) (Spring 1981), pp. 108–114; Lawrence A. Scaff, "Remnants of Romanticism: Max Weber in Oklahoma and Indian Territory," *Journal of Classical Sociology* 5(1) (2005), pp. 53–72, *idem*, *Max Weber in America* (Princeton, NJ: Princeton University Press, 2011).

[54] Alfred D. Chandler, Jr., "The Emergence of Managerial Capitalism," *Business History Review* 58(4) (Winter 1984), pp. 498–501.

[55] The word "bureaucracy" was coined by Frenchman Vincent de Gournay in 1745. See Fred Riggs, "Shifting Meanings of the Term 'Bureaucracy,'" *International Social Science Journal* 31(4) (November 1979), pp. 563–584. For more on the history of bureaucracy as "critique and theory," see Sebastian Felten and Christine von Oertzen, "Bureaucracy as Knowledge," *Journal for the History of Knowledge* 1(1) (2020), article 8, pp. 1–16.

to it. It is finally superior both in intensive efficiency and in the scope of its operations, and is formally capable of application to all kinds of administrative tasks.[56]

What is not often understood is that bureaucracy developed as a reaction against the personal subjugation and cruelty of earlier administrative systems (such as monarchies and dictatorships) in which the lives and fortunes of all were completely dependent upon the whims of a despot, whose only law was his own wish. For this reason, the benefits Weber attributed to bureaucracy can perhaps best be understood when compared to the alternatives it replaced: "Thus, for example, tax farming, whereby local collectors worked for a percentage of the take, was displaced by bureaucracies staffed with full-time salaried officials; inside contracting, whereby owners of equipment and materials contracted with foremen for labor, gave way to modern hierarchies."[57] Officials no longer sold offices, and commissars no longer worked on commission. Compared to the administrative practices that preceded them, the efficiencies attributed to bureaucracies become understandable. The world observed by Weber was decidedly unjust. It was dominated by class-consciousness and nepotism. To be a military officer or an official in government or industry presupposed an aristocratic birth. In Weber's view, this was a waste of human resources and ran counter to his belief that the working class could produce leaders as well as followers. Bureaucracy, with its emphasis on legal authority (see below), was intended to put an end to the exploitation of the masses and to assure equal opportunity and treatment for all.

2. To Weber, bureaucracy was an ideal or optimal method of organizing that did not actually exist.[58] It was an intellectual construct to be used as a measuring stick to gauge the relative performance of different types of administrative organizations. In this regard, Weber's bureaucratic model is hypothetical rather than factual. It is not meant to correspond completely with concrete or empirical reality.

3. Weber's ideal bureaucracy is based on *legal* authority rather than on either *tradition* (custom) or *charisma* (divine grace).[59] As developed by Weber, legal authority stems from rules and other controls that govern an undertaking in pursuit of specific goals. Managers are given the authority to interpret and enforce these rules and other controls by virtue of their position. Obedience is not owed to a person, but to the impersonal authority inherent in an office or position. Thus, authority adheres to specific positions rather than to individuals. This is necessary if authority is to outlast the tenure of individual managers or officeholders. Familiar examples of legal authority structures are the military, politically elected offices, government bureaus, colleges or universities, and business firms.

4. The need Weber identified for efficient organizing is inherently culture-free. Reliance on rationality and legalism, the idea of equality of citizens, and the vast services offered in a modern state make some form of expert administration inevitable. In addition, the increasing size of firms, advanced technology, and the global marketplace make bureaucracy unavoidable. Thus, bureaucracy in government was followed by an increase in the bureaucracy of business firms, trade unions, churches, service groups, and voluntary associations. Today, *all* undertakings of any size in any culture are bureaucratic to some degree.

---

[56] Max Weber, *The Theory of Social and Economic Organization*, trans. Alexander M. Henderson and ed. and trans. Talcott Parsons (New York: Free Press, 1947), p. 337. German edition published in 1922.

[57] Marshall W. Meyer, "Organizational Structure as Signaling," *Pacific Sociological Review* 22(4) (October 1979), p. 484.

[58] Max Weber, "'Objectivity' in Social Science and Social Policy" in *The Methodology of the Social Sciences*, ed. and trans. Edward A. Shils and Henry H. Finch (Glencoe, IL: Free Press, 1949), pp. 42–43. Adapted from an essay published in *Archiv für Sozialwissenschaft und Sozialpolitik* 19(1) (1904), pp. 22–87.

[59] *Idem*, *The Theory of Social and Economic Organization*, p. 328. See also Max Weber, "The Three Types of Legitimate Rule," trans. Hans Gerth, *Berkeley Journal of Sociology* 4(1) (Summer 1958), pp. 1–11. Adapted from an essay published in *Preußische Jahrbücher* 187(1) (1922), pp. 1–12.

ADVANTAGES OF BUREAUCRACY

Weber identified the essential characteristics of his "ideal" bureaucracy and believed that specific advantages would accrue to undertakings that embodied them. These characteristics and sample advantages include the following:

- *Division of labor.* Labor is divided so that authority and responsibility are clearly defined. Tasks are not only performed with greater expertise, but also with greater speed because employees do not lose time shifting from one activity to another. At lower levels of authority, employees have less to learn on the job, lowering the cost of labor.

  Advantage—Efficiency will increase through specialization.

- *Managerial hierarchy.* Offices or positions are organized in a hierarchy of authority.

  Advantage—A clear chain of command will develop from the highest to the lowest level of an organization (Fayol's scalar-chain principle), defining different levels of authority, and thus individual discretion, as well as enabling better communication.

- *Formal selection.* All employees are selected based on technical qualifications demonstrated by formal examination, education, or training. This applies to both public and non-public employment. As noted in Chapter 6, with the passage of the Pendleton Civil Service Reform Act in 1883, the U.S. government replaced the "spoils system" with a Civil Service Commission that would select and promote civil servants based on merit rather than political connections.

  Advantage—The most qualified employees will be hired and promoted, thus benefiting both them and their employer.

- *Career orientation.* Although in the public sector a measure of flexibility is attained by electing higher level officials who presumably express the will of an electorate (e.g., a body of citizens or a board of directors), both public and private employees are career professionals rather than "politicians." They work for fixed salaries and pursue "careers" within their respective fields.

  Advantage—The hiring of career professionals will assure the performance of assigned duties without regard for extraneous pressures, as well as assure a continuity of operations across election cycles.

- *Formal rules and other controls.* All employees are subject to formal rules and other controls regarding the performance of their duties.

  Advantage—Efficiency will increase as formal rules and other controls relating to employee performance are enforced.

- *Impersonality.* Rules and other controls are impersonal and uniformly applied in all cases.

  Advantage—When rules and other controls are applied impersonally and uniformly, involvement with personalities and personal preferences is avoided. Subordinates are thereby protected from arbitrary actions of their superiors. Moreover, when rules are fixed and announced beforehand, it is possible to foresee how authority (coercive and otherwise) will be used in given circumstances and to plan based on this knowledge.[60]

DISADVANTAGES OF BUREAUCRACY

Although Weber considered bureaucracy to be the most efficient means of organizing, both his own experience and subsequent research have shown that it often results in certain disadvantages. These include the following:

- Bureaucracies, especially those whose funding comes from government coffers rather than repeat business from satisfied customers, are typically bent on self-preservation and the

[60] *Idem*, "Religious Rejections of the World and Their Directions" in *From Max Weber: Essays in Sociology*, ed. and trans. Hans H. Gerth and C. Wright Mills (New York: Oxford University Press, 1946), pp. 333–334. Adapted from an essay published in *Archiv für Sozialwissenschaft und Sozialpolitik* 41(1) (1916), pp. 1–30.

advancement of their members above all else. In general, government programs are kept going long after their usefulness has expired, as their advocates seek to not only justify their continuation, but also their expansion. Furthermore, changes that might, for instance, increase efficiency and innovation, and thereby put jobs at risk, are seldom willingly embraced. Similarly, when government programs fail to produce intended results, in the absence of a profit motive, they are continued with the rationale that all that is needed to gain success is an expanded mandate, larger budget, more regulations, and absolute authority. Indeed, as one political commentator has observed, "When a government entity cannot, or would rather not, adequately perform its primary function, or when it feels that its primary function is insufficiently grand, the agency will expand its mission, thereby distracting attention from its core inadequacy."[61]

In this context, for the individual bureaucrat, whether hiring more people is justified economically may be an afterthought, as an expansion in a program's size and services represents an increase in power and prestige. Consequently, bureaucracies may become bloated and cumbersome, losing the ability to make fast decisions and, thus, becoming more an impediment than a means for achieving desired results. This especially may be the case in government agencies protected from competition, where success in producing results is not constantly monitored, where change-inhibiting agency heads do not have to respond to the economics of supply and demand, and where political appointees do not have to oversee a payroll as if their livelihoods were at stake.

Moreover, public-sector bureaucrats are inherently biased politically in the support of ever-bigger government. Collective bargaining in the private economy is, by its nature, adversarial. Unions, however, face limits on their bargaining demands lest they bankrupt their employers and end up jobless. Public unions, however, sit on both sides of the bargaining table, as their campaign contributions help elect the politicians with whom they negotiate, and taxpayers otherwise pick up the bill. Not surprisingly, "this works to lubricate [civil-service] union support of politicians, who repay with overly generous benefit packages and endless backing of a greater bureaucracy."[62] In such circumstances, as their own best advocates, government bureaus always seem to find new ways to justify their existence, which, in turn, leads to their further growth and additional regulations that expand their authority. Even "temporary" agencies seem to be absorbed into bureaucracy. As U.S. Senator James F. Byrnes famously quipped, "The nearest approach to immorality on earth is a government bureau."[63]

- Rules and other controls may take on a significance of their own and become ends in themselves. Employees, for example, may accuse budget personnel of being more interested in applying rules and regulations than achieving a firm's primary goals. Further, whereas rules fixed and announced beforehand do enhance the predictability of outcomes, they also increase complexity after a certain point, thereby amplifying the likelihood of errors. This highlights that, once introduced, rules tend to become more expansive and seldom more limited.
- Extreme devotion to rules and other controls may lead to situations in which past decisions are blindly repeated without appreciation or concern for changed conditions that produce unintended consequences. Such "bureaucratic rigidity" leads to hidebound managers being compensated for doing what they are told and not for thinking. The result is "rule by rules" rather than common sense. In commenting on the inflexibility of government bureaucracies in applying rules and regulations, a former U.S. Senator has confessed to learning the hard way about the resulting unintentional effects. Upon retiring, the senator had invested his savings in a Connecticut hotel. He quickly realized there was no way to absorb or pass on to his customers the increased costs associated with federal, state, and local rules. The senator consequently

[61] George Will, "Biden Proposes Saddling an Already Struggling Federal Reserve with Two Political Activists," *Washington Post Sunday* (January 30, 2022), p. A17.

[62] Donald O. Henry, "Letter to the Editor: The Bloated Deep State Benefits One Party," *Wall Street Journal* (April 5, 2018), p. A16.

[63] James F. Byrnes, *Speaking Frankly* (New York: Harper & Brothers, 1947), p. 7.

found that the rigid application of "'one-size-fits-all' rules for business ignore the reality of the marketplace. And setting thresholds for regulatory guidelines at artificial levels—for example, 50 employees or more, $500,000 in sales—takes no account of other realities, such as profit margins, labor intensive vs. capital intensive businesses, and local market economics."[64] Within a few years, the hotel was bankrupt. Whereas the intent of bureaucratic rules and other controls may be laudable, their inflexible application does not always ensure good policy. Moreover, as the senator's experience shows, unrestrained bureaucracy can have a suffocating effect on economic growth, as it destroys private wealth.

- As noted, in the absence of profit as an indicator of market success, within government bureaucracies, an expansion in a program's size and services represents an increase in power and prestige. Consequently, bureaucratic empire building and fights over turf are inevitable. Such rivalries can easily lead to the internalization of narrow program goals at the expense of accomplishing an agency's or bureau's overall mission. A typical example can be found in many universities where conflicts over which program is going to offer what courses often result in unnecessary duplication of courses across departments, resulting in the needless expenditure of limited resources.
- Though rules and other controls are intended to counter worker apathy, they may instead contribute to it by defining unacceptable behavior and, thus, specifying a minimum level of acceptable performance. That is, it is possible, once rules have been defined, for employees to remain apathetic, for they now know just how little they can do and remain secure. This is known as "working to the rules," because what is not covered by rules is, by definition, not an employee's responsibility. Within an educational setting, statements such as "all students must attend at least 50 percent of the classes during a term to pass" or "the minimum requirement for graduation is a C average on all course work undertaken" are illustrations of this phenomenon in that they clearly define minimum levels of acceptable behavior. Unfortunately, a typical administrative response in such circumstances is to enact additional rules (such as mandatory class attendance) and, in turn, further aggravate an already poor situation. Unless care is taken, such a situation may result in a "vicious circle of bureaucracy," wherein rules beget more rules. Furthermore, once employees discover the appeasing effect of working to the rules, they may push for even more rules to further restrict management's power and protect their own prerogatives, power, and jobs. Therefore, rules may be functional in one sense, but in another (unintended) sense they permit employee involvement without requiring emotional commitment.
- The nature of bureaucracies leads to a compromise among competing ideas. In searching for improvements in practice and evaluating alternatives, rather than hashing out differences in opinion and identifying an optimum course of action, bureaucracies too often adopt compromises to placate as many special-interest groups as possible (what Follett labeled "sham reconciliation," see Chapter 14). In the instance of politicians, their goal may be to win as many votes for reelection as possible rather than achieve a real and lasting improvement. By stifling true innovation, compromise inhibits achieving an organization's goals in the most efficient and effective manner. This situation is exacerbated further in government agencies where the political views of unelected and unaccountable career bureaucrats (who theoretically are nonpartisan experts faithfully implementing elected officials' policies) impede initiatives they oppose for ideological reasons and promote pet projects they favor. This undermines democracy, as career bureaucrats have no authority to replace the decisions of politically accountable officeholders.

In extreme cases, in what has been labeled the "administrative state," agenda-driven agency regulators who rule by fiat have been thought to intentionally sabotage the policy initiatives of

[64] George S. McGovern, "Manager's Journal: A Politician's Dream Is a Businessman's Nightmare," *Wall Street Journal* (June 1, 1992), p. A12.

elected officials, as well as use their power as an implied threat against companies and industries that depend on their goodwill and spending. It has been argued that to the extent that the Pendleton Civil Service Reform Act (1887) reduced the number of government jobs awarded based on political connections rather than merit, it created "a protected class of civil servants . . . that is as partisan as classes that preceded civil service reform."[65] As if in response, during its 2021–22 term, in *West Virginia v. Environmental Protection Agency*, the U.S. Supreme Court ruled that federal agencies cannot exercise unrestrained power in matters of "vast economic and political significance" without clear authorization from Congress.[66] Thus, Congress can no longer sidestep difficult policy decisions by passing them on to a self-perpetuating unelected "ruling class," and federal agencies are no longer free to interpret statutes for themselves and find entirely new meaning in regulations years after they were written.

Despite these and other criticisms, bureaucracy is a central feature in modern societies. It is thus important to realize that the disadvantages just outlined are not necessarily inherent in bureaucracy per se. As envisioned by Weber, the bureaucratic model is both rational and efficient. Gaining its benefits, however, requires learning enough about its characteristics to avoid being controlled by them.

Though many of us may feel that we live in a bureaucratic world of baffling rules and other controls, we should not forget that bureaucracy also makes it possible for us to get potable water instantly, place an international telephone call in seconds, and have a package delivered a continent away overnight. Indeed, almost all the benefits of modern living that we take for granted—modern medicine, modern science, modern industry—rest upon a bureaucratic foundation. In this respect, Weber's ideas have stood the test of time remarkably well. His pioneering work, like that of Fayol, has stimulated a wealth of research into the management process and remains a landmark in the evolution of management thought. In recognition of his contributions in developing the tenets of bureaucracy, Weber is known as the "Father of Organization Theory." His goal was not perfection, but systematization—moving managerial practice and organizational design toward more logical ways of operating. Weber's work on bureaucracy remained largely unknown to English-speaking audiences until it began to be translated in the late 1920s. Like Fayol, Weber had to wait until cultural conditions created the need to think in theoretical terms. As firms grew larger and more complex, the search for a theory of organizations led researchers and practitioners to Max Weber and his bureaucratic model.

SUMMARY

The emergence of the management process and organization theory took place in two forms: Fayol's identification of the principles and elements of management and Weber's search for an ideal way of organizing. From different backgrounds and perspectives, both Fayol and Weber attempted to develop methods for managing large-scale organizations. Fayol stressed education in management rather than technical training and the importance of planning, organizing, command, coordination, and control. Weber sought to replace authority based on tradition and charisma with legal authority and to prescribe an impersonal merit basis for selecting, hiring, and promoting employees. Both Weber and Fayol had history's misfortune of being overshadowed by others and having to wait until after their deaths to receive proper credit for their roles in the ongoing evolution of management thought.

[65] Mark Adams, "Letter to the Editor: Why Liberals Dominate Federal Bureaucracy," *Wall Street Journal* (June 17, 2021), p. A16.

[66] Supreme Court of the United States, *West Virginia v. Environmental Protection Agency*, no. 20–1530 (2022). Available online at https://www.supremecourt.gov/opinions/21pdf/20-1530_new_l537.pdf.

CHAPTER 11 Scientific Management in Theory and Practice

Although Fred Taylor and his contemporaries provided the early impetus for the scientific-management movement, several other individuals helped shepherd it to maturity. Their efforts involved various developments. First, following the urging of Henry R. Towne and Henri Fayol, there was a growing recognition of the need to establish college curricula to formalize the study of management and to undertake efforts to educate practicing managers in properly applying its principles. Second, as the scientific-management movement grew in the United States, it sparked attention in other parts of the world, including Eastern and Western Europe, Japan, China, Australia, and beyond. Finally, moving past scientific management's emphasis on the shop floor, it became apparent that rather than uniformly applying a traditional military command-and-control style of organizing, firms should be structured based on their individual goals and the unique demands of their specific industries.

THE STUDY AND PRACTICE OF SCIENTIFIC MANAGEMENT

The demand for formal courses in business education in the United States and Europe was a belated outgrowth of the Industrial Revolution and the corresponding workplace transformation in the means of production.[1] The unequaled economic expansion created a burgeoning demand for trained managers. In the United States, the first collegiate course on business practice was offered at William and Mary College in 1779, with Adam Smith's *Inquiry into the Nature and Sources of the Wealth of Nations* as a primary text.[2] Proprietary commercial "colleges" offering

[1] Willis J. Winn, *Business Education in the United States: A Historical Perspective* (New York: Newcomen Society, 1964), p. 7.
[2] Lyon G. Tyler, "Early Courses and Professors at William and Mary College," *William and Mary College Quarterly Historical Magazine* 14(2) (October 1905), p. 76.

business instruction began appearing in the 1830s.[3] Among the most notable was Robert M. Bartlett's Commercial College, opened first in Philadelphia in 1834, then Pittsburgh, and finally Cincinnati. The quality of early commercial colleges should not be underrated. In Pittsburgh, future business luminaries, such as Andrew Carnegie, Henry Clay Frick, Thomas A. Mellon, and George Westinghouse, Jr., attended classes at Peter Duff's Mercantile College. John D. Rockefeller and Harvey Firestone studied accounting, penmanship, business law, and banking at Ezekiel G. Folsom's Commercial College, founded in Cleveland in 1848. Business programs were established at the University of Louisiana (now Tulane University) under the direction of James D. B. DeBow in 1851[4] and at what is now Washington and Lee University in 1868 under the direction of Joseph B. Walker.[5] Both programs were short-lived.

The Wharton School of Finance and Economy was established at the University of Pennsylvania in 1881. It was funded by Joseph Wharton, a Philadelphia philanthropist and industrialist who had built a commercial empire that included the Bethlehem Steel Corporation and the American Nickel Company. A sense of the skepticism surrounding the Wharton School's founding and the opposition of other colleges within the university to it may be gleaned from the recollection of its dean, Edmund J. James:

> The members of the faculty were men whose education had been primarily classical; whose instincts were against the attempt to make university education practical, and who looked upon all such attempts as this proposed by Mr. Wharton as covert attacks upon the very principle of higher education itself. . . .
>
> There were no models which we could follow. There was no experience from which we could profit. The funds themselves were inadequate for the purpose in hand. The other departments in the University and most of the other members of the faculty were bitterly opposed to the whole project. And even if they did not actually interfere to prevent the progress of the work, they stood with watchful, jealous eyes to see that no concession of any sort should be made to these new subjects which, in their opinion, might in any way lower the level of scholarship as the ideal had been accepted by the upholders of the traditional course.[6]

It was not until 17 years later (1898) that the second and third schools of business were begun at the University of Chicago and the University of California at Berkeley, respectively. The Amos Tuck School of Administration and Finance at Dartmouth College, established in 1900,

---

[3] Edgar M. Barber contends that the "first commercial school founded in America" was established at New York City in 1824 by J. Gordon Bennett, Sr. As evidence, he cites an October 1824 "announcement" that Bennett would accept applications from "young gentlemen" for admission to a "permanent commercial school" under his direction. See Barber, "A Contribution to the History of Commercial Education," *Business Educator* 8(9) (May 1903), p. 17. For the announcement, see "Permanent Commercial School," *New York Evening Post* (October 28, 1824), p. 3. Bennett's obituary notes, however, that "not a solitary application was made, and young BENNETT in disgust gave up the idea of being a pedagogue." See "Obituary. James Gordon Bennett," *New York Times* (June 2, 1892), p. 3. Bennett went on to found the *New York Herald* newspaper. For early surveys of "commercial education" around the world, see Eugène Léautey, *L'enseignement commercial et les écoles de commerce en France et dans le monde entire* [*Business Education and Business Schools in France and Around the World*] (Paris: Librairie Comptable et Administrative, 1886); Edmund J. James, *Commercial Education* (Albany, NY: J. B. Lyon Company, 1899); Frederick Hooper and James Graham, *Commercial Education at Home and Abroad* (London: Macmillan, 1901).

[4] Maunsel White, Sr., "The University of Louisiana," *De Bow's Review of the Southern & Western States* 3(3) (March 1847), pp. 260–265.

[5] Mame Warren, "Chronology," in *idem*, ed., *Come Cheer for Washington and Lee* (East Greenwich, RI: Meridian Printing, 1998), p. 305. See also Charles S. Marsh, "General Lee and a School of Commerce," *Journal of Political Economy* 34(5) (October 1926), pp. 857–659.

[6] Edmund J. James, "Origin and Progress of Business Education in the United States," in *Conference on Commercial Education and Business Progress* (Urbana-Champaign, IL: University of Illinois Urbana-Champaign, 1913), pp. 52–53. For more on the early skepticism surrounding a university offering business education, see Gabriel Abend, *The Moral Background: An Inquiry into the History of Business Ethics* (Princeton, NJ: Princeton University Press, 2014), pp. 215–259.

was the first graduate school of business administration; the second graduate school of business was formed in 1908 at Harvard University. Whereas Dartmouth was the first institution to offer an advanced business degree (a Master of Science in commerce), Harvard's Graduate School of Business Administration was the first to establish what is known today as a Master of Business Administration (MBA) degree. The first doctoral program in business was established at the University of Chicago in 1907.

Mention should also be made of two prominent correspondence schools. The International Correspondence Schools (ICS), which was founded in 1890, was launched by Thomas Foster, a newspaper editor and publisher. By the early 1900s, it had enrolled around one million students. It would go on to offer some 370 separate courses, including bookkeeping and foremanship. The Alexander Hamilton Institute was established in 1909 by New York University's School of Commerce, Accounts and Finance dean Joseph F. Johnson. The Institute offered its students the "Modern Business Course and Service," which it described as "a systematic, time-saving method of bringing to any man's office the business knowledge and training that he needs and that he cannot acquire through his own experience."[7] Scientific-management pioneer Harrington Emerson was among its faculty members, as was Dexter Kimball, dean of Cornell University's Sibley College of Engineering. ICS and the Alexander Hamilton Institute were hardly alone, as by 1925–26 some 350 proprietary correspondence schools were in operation throughout the United States.[8] Today's distance learning is anything but new.[9]

The Bureau of Personnel Administration in New York City convened the nation's first executive-development seminars beginning in the 1920s.[10] Prior to World War II, Sears, Roebuck and Company was among the few companies that offered a systematic program for finding, developing, and training its future executives.[11] "Modern executive education" is said to have begun with the launching of the Advanced Management Program at Harvard Business School in 1949. Similar programs were soon initiated at other universities in the United States and abroad.[12] Despite Taylor's belief that aspiring managers had to live their calling and learn through years of shop-floor experience, the benefits of studying general management as an academic discipline were quickly recognized.[13]

EDUCATION FOR INDUSTRIAL MANAGEMENT

Exactly when management first became an academic subject in the United States is impossible to determine.[14] Towne's 1886 paper, "The Engineer as an Economist," in which he proposed that the AMSE create an Economic Section to act as a clearinghouse and forum to discuss the "executive management of works, mills, and factories" is, however, considered a landmark event (see Chapter 6). Towne observed that, at the time, the study of management was unorganized, was without a distinct literature, was bereft of professional associations, and had no medium for

---

[7] Alexander Hamilton Institute, *Forging Ahead in Business* (New York: Alexander Hamilton Institute, 1915), p. 29.

[8] James D. Watkinson, "'Education for Success': The International Correspondence Schools of Scranton, Pennsylvania," *Pennsylvania Magazine of History and Biography* 120(4) (October 1996), p. 362.

[9] Reuven Brenner, "Distance Learning Began in 1890," *Wall Street Journal* (May 13, 2021), p. A17.

[10] J. David Thompson, *Personnel Research Agencies: A Guide to Organized Research in Employment Management, Industrial Relations, Training, and Working Conditions*, Bulletin of the United States Bureau of Labor Statistics, no. 299 (Washington, DC: 1921), pp. 89–90.

[11] Peter F. Drucker, "Executives Are Made . . . Not Born," *Nation's Business* 40(10) (October 1952), p. 34.

[12] Rolv Petter Amdam, "Creating the New Executive: Postwar Executive Education and Socialization into the Managerial Elite," *Management & Organization History* 15(2) (2020), p. 106.

[13] Frederick W. Taylor, "Why Manufacturers Dislike College Students," in Henry S. Munroe, Arthur L. Williston, and Henry H. Norris, eds., *Proceedings of the Seventeenth Annual Meeting of the Society for the Promotion of Engineering Education, June 24–26, 1909* 17 (1910), pp. 79–104.

[14] John F. Mee, "Management Teaching in Historical Perspective," *Southern Journal of Business* 7(2) (May 1972), pp. 21–29. See also Daniel M. Nelson, "Scientific Management and the Transformation of University Business Education," in *idem*, ed., *A Mental Revolution: Scientific Management since Taylor* (Columbus, OH: Ohio State University Press, 1992), pp. 77–101.

exchanging experiences.[15] With a growing appreciation for and emphasis on scientific management among engineers and the public, the ASME experienced an identity crisis: Was its purpose to further mechanical engineering, or was it to become an outlet for ideas about performance incentives, cost accounting, and other facets of sound management? The ASME refused to publish Taylor's book *The Principles of Scientific Management* in its *Transactions* due to a disagreement over its interest to the society's membership. As a result, Taylor had the book privately printed and distributed.[16] By 1919, however, 4 years after Taylor's death, the ASME recognized industrial engineering as a legitimate subject for study and created a management division in 1920.[17] Within 3 years, this was the ASME's largest section.

On the collegiate side, John Richards used his experiences as an inventor and construction engineer as a basis for a series of 10 lectures on "works administration" at Stanford University in 1895–1896.[18] Hugo Diemer offered a course in "factory economics" at the University of Kansas as early 1899, covering topics such as the "organization and management of industrial establishments."[19] Dexter Kimball credited Taylor's 1903 ASME paper on shop management as the inspiration for his own Cornell course on works administration. Offered for the first time in the spring term of the 1904–1905 academic year, the course addressed the economics of "modern" production. Kimball's 1913 textbook *Principles of Industrial Organization* grew out of his course notes.[20] The course applied scientific management to plant location, equipment policies, production control, labor compensation, and much more. Kimball stressed the need for scientific management, noting that "as industrial enterprises have grown in magnitude, as processes have become more refined and competition keener the problems of organization have steadily grown in importance."[21] Two early courses in "scientific shop management" were initiated at the University of Missouri's School of Engineering in 1909–1910. Together, the courses covered topics such as functional foremanship, time studies, "training in the principles of handling men," "the building up and preservation of an organization," and the "selection and training of officers."[22]

Edwin F. Gay, first dean of Harvard's Graduate School of Business Administration, questioned whether anything practical could be learned in a college classroom. He was advised by Wallace Sabine, dean of Harvard's School of Applied Science, to look at Taylor's *Shop Management*. Impressed by what he read, Gay attended one of Taylor's Boxly lectures, toured local plants

---

[15] Henry R. Towne, "The Engineer as an Economist," Transactions of the American Society of Mechanical Engineers 7 (1886), pp. 428–429. See also Ion Georgiou, "Engineers as Economists: A Study in Gilded Age Sensibilities," Management & Organizational History 9(1) (January 2014), pp. 69–91. *The Business Guide; Or, Safe Methods of Business* by James L. Nichols, first published in 1886, is one example of the era's management literature. By 1917 it had sold three-million copies. Among the advice it imparted were "maxims" such as: "Undertake no business without mature reflection, and confine your capital closely to the business you have established," and "Lead a regular life, avoid display, and choose your associates discreetly, and prefer the society of men of your own type." James L. Nichols, *The Business Guide; Or, Safe Methods of Business* (Cleveland, OH: Lauer & Mattill, 1886), p. 7. See also Tana Reff, "Pearls from a Fossil," *Sky* [Delta Airlines] 19(5) (May 1990), pp. 118–120; Darryl W. Miller, "Forgotten Classics: *The Business Guide* by James L. Nichols (1894)," *Journal of Historical Research in Marketing* 8(4) (2016), pp. 564–584.

[16] Carol Carlson Dean, "*The Principles of Scientific Management* by Frederick W. Taylor: The Private Printing," *Journal of Management History* 3(1) (1997), pp. 18–30.

[17] "Foreword," in Charles M. Merrick, ed., *ASME Management Division History, 1886–1980* (New York: American Society of Mechanical Engineers, 1984), p. v. See also Mikiyoshi Hirose, "The Attitude of the American Society of Mechanical Engineers toward Management: Suggestions for a Revised Interpretation," *Kansai University Review of Economics and Business* 25(1–2) (September 1996), pp. 125–148.

[18] Richard J. Whiting, "John Richards—California Pioneer of Management Thought," *California Management Review* 6(2) (Winter 1963), pp. 35–38.

[19] *Thirty-Third Annual Catalogue of the University of Kansas for the Year, 1898–'99* (Lawrence, KS: 1899), p. 163. See also Charles W. Lytle, "Collegiate Courses for Management: A Comparative Study of the Business and Engineering Colleges," *Journal of Engineering Education* 22(10) (June 1932), pp. 806–839.

[20] Dexter S. Kimball, *I Remember: An Autobiography* (New York: McGraw-Hill, 1953), p. 85.

[21] *Idem, Principles of Industrial Organization* (New York: McGraw-Hill, 1913).

[22] H. Wade Hibbard and Herbert S. Philbrick, "Teaching of Scientific Shop Management, with Use of Engineering School Shops as the Laboratory," William G. Raymond, Arthur N. Talbot, and Henry H. Norris, eds., *Proceedings of the Nineteenth Annual Meeting Society for the Promotion of Engineering Education, June 27–29, 1911* 19 (1912), pp. 91–92.

that applied Taylor's principles, and invited Taylor to speak to the Harvard Business School students. Harvard's "industrial management" course began in 1908; Taylor gave two lectures in the spring of 1909 and would lecture annually until 1914. C. Bertrand Thompson, the first African American faculty member at the Harvard Business School, assumed responsibility for "Industrial Management" in 1911, and arranged lectures by Taylor and other scientific-management stalwarts. Thompson compiled the most extensive bibliography of scientific management for that period, served an apprenticeship with Taylor and his disciplines, and did much to further the scientific-management movement in academia and industry.[23] Thompson's Harvard affiliation, and the notion that management was an academic discipline amenable to scientific inquiry, gave credibility to its formal study among those who opposed business education as being too vocational for college students. By 1913, scientific management was being taught either in engineering or business schools at the Carnegie Institute of Technology, Cornell, Dartmouth, Harvard, Northwestern (which began teaching personnel management in 1912), Ohio State University, Pennsylvania State University, University of Pittsburgh, and University of Wisconsin.[24]

Dartmouth's Tuck School led the way for those pursuing graduate-level studies; by 1910, the Dartmouth catalog listed a course in business management. In 1911, as dean of the Tuck School, Harlow S. Person hosted the first conference on scientific management in the United States.[25] Serving as president of the Taylor Society (successor to the Society to Promote the Science of Management) from 1913 to 1918, Person broadened interest in scientific management through his efforts. He extended the society's membership and range of interests and took an expansive view of business education. Person worked to dissipate the notion that scientific management was merely the use of a stopwatch. In Person's view, educators should emphasize the philosophy underlying scientific management and focus on developing creative leadership in industry. Person also recognized the value of involving social scientists in the study of management. He believed that management and labor were so closely entwined in daily activities that they failed to see larger relationships; however, social scientists would be able to take a larger, more objective view of workplace dynamics in charting a future course of action for research and practice.[26]

Management historians have not generally acknowledged the role of Leon P. Alford in management education; nevertheless, his influence as a journal editor, as a member of various professional committees, and as an author was substantial.[27] Alford was trained as an electrical engineer, worked in industry, and became editor-in-chief of the influential journals *American Machinist, Industrial Engineering, Management Engineering,* and *Manufacturing Industries.* He also edited several management handbooks.[28] Among Alford's early work was an attempt to provide an alternative interpretation of science in management. Writing with Englishman

---

[23] Daniel A. Wren, Regina A. Greenwood, Julia Kurtz Teahen, and Arthur G. Bedeian, "C. Bertrand Thompson and Management Consulting in Europe, 1917–1934," *Journal of Management History* 21(1) (2015), pp. 15–39. See also C. Bertrand Thompson, ed., *Scientific Management: A Collection of the More Significant Articles Describing the Taylor System of Management* (Cambridge, MA: Harvard University Press, 1914) and *idem, The Theory and Practice of Scientific Management* (Boston, MA: Houghton Mifflin, 1917).

[24] Nelson, "Scientific Management and the Transformation of University Business Education," in *idem*, ed., *A Mental Revolution*, pp. 77–101. For more on early scientific-management education at Harvard University, and especially the role of Henry H. Farquhar, see Hindy L. Schachter, "Frederick Winslow Taylor, Henry Hallowell Farquhar, and the Dilemma of Relating Management Education to Organizational Practice," *Journal of Management History* 22(2) (2016), pp. 199–213.

[25] *Addresses and Discussions at the Conference on Scientific Management Held October 12, 13, 14, Nineteen Hundred and Eleven* (Hanover, NH: Amos Tuck School of Administration and Finance, Dartmouth College, 1912).

[26] Harlow S. Person, "The Manager, the Workman and the Social Scientist," *Bulletin of the Taylor Society* 3(1) (February 1917), pp. 1–7.

[27] William J. Jaffe, *L. P. Alford and the Evolution of Modern Industrial Management* (New York: New York University Press, 1957).

[28] Leon P. Alford, ed., *Management's Handbook* (New York: Ronald Press, 1924); and later, *idem*, ed., *Cost and Production Handbook* (New York: Ronald Press, 1934), and coedited with John R. Bangs, *Production Handbook* (New York: Ronald Press, 1944). See also Alford, *Laws of Management Applied to Manufacturing* (New York: Ronald Press, 1928) and *Principles of Industrial Management* (New York: Ronald Press, 1940).

A. Hamilton Church, he explained that he deplored the term "scientific management" because it implied that there was "a science rather than an art of management."[29]

The weakness of Taylor's approach, in Alford and Church's view, was that it substituted the art of leadership with an "elaborate mechanism" or system and overlooked the dynamic possibilities of effective leadership. Alford thought that Taylor's so-called "principles" were too mechanical. To remedy this problem, he (and Church) proposed three broad principles: (1) the systematic use of experience; (2) the economic control of effort; and (3) the promotion of personal effectiveness. The first principle emphasized the personal experiences of executives and setting standards of performance; the second was based on the subprinciples of division of labor, coordination, conservation (expending the least effort to achieve a given end), and remuneration; and the third prompted personal effectiveness through adequate leadership and favorable working conditions. As Church would later explain, "the real objective of the new science . . . is not to throw the square pegs out of the round holes, but to gently shepherd the round pegs towards the round holes, and the square pegs towards the square holes."[30] From these three broad principles, Alford and Church believed that a truly scientific basis for the *art* of management could be discovered.

Alford's call for *art plus science* in management reflected his admiration for Gantt, the subject of his comprehensive biography (see Chapter 8). Like Gantt, Alford pleaded for engineers to become involved in community service and foster improved relations between employers and employees. Alford continued to stress these themes as a member of the American Engineering Council and contributed to the better-known reports of this group, including *Waste in Industry* (1921), *The Twelve-Hour Shift in Industry* (1922), and *Safety and Production* (1928).[31]

The above discussion focuses on the United States. The history and spread of business education around the world is more complex, reflecting different cultural influences and pedagogical models.[32] Several papers detailing this history have appeared and are referenced below.[33]

THE INTERNATIONAL SCIENTIFIC-MANAGEMENT MOVEMENT

France and Britain

Whereas the Industrial Revolution began in Great Britain and spread to the United States, the scientific-management movement began in the United States and spread to other countries, like Great Britain. Worldwide interest in scientific management was largely determined by a nation or region's level of industrialization and shaped by context and culture. As early as 1907, Taylor was in touch with Henry Le Chatelier, professor at the University of Paris (the Sorbonne),

---

[29] A. Hamilton Church and Leon P. Alford, "The Principles of Management," *American Machinist* 36(22) (May 30, 1912), pp. 857–861.

[30] A. Hamilton Church, *The Science and Practice of Management* (New York: Engineering Magazine, 1914), p. 227. See also A. Hamilton Church, "Has 'Scientific Management' Science?" *American Machinist* 35(3) (July 20, 1911), pp. 108–112.

[31] American Engineering Council, *Waste in Industry* (Washington, DCV: Federated American Engineering Societies, 1921); *idem, The Twelve-Hour Shift in Industry* (New York: E. P. Dutton, 1922); *idem, Safety and Production* (New York: Harper & Brothers, 1928).

[32] Andreas Kaplan, "European Management and European Business Schools: Insights from the History of Business Schools," *European Management Journal* 32(4) (August 2014), p. 529.

[33] See, for example, Lúcia Lima Rodrigues, Delfina Gomes, and Russell Craig, "The Portuguese School of Commerce, 1759–1844: A Reflection of the 'Enlightenment,'" *Accounting History* 9(3) (November 2009), pp. 53–71; Alain Burland, "Brève histoire de l'enseignement et de la recherche en gestion en France" ["Brief History of Teaching and Research in Management in France"], (November 2, 2020), available online at https://hal.inria.fr/halshs-02985745/; Eric Godelier, "From the 'Science' of Practice to Management Science: Milestones for a History of Management Education in France (1900s–2000s)," *Management & Organizational History* 15(3) (2020), pp. 219–251; Alistair Mutch, "Business Education in the U.K. Polytechnic Tradition: Uncovering Alternative Approaches through Historical Investigation," *Academy of Management Learning & Education* 20(3) (September 2021), pp. 407–422; and André Spicer, Zahira Jaser, and Caroline Wiertz, "The Future of the Business School: Finding Hope in Alternative Pasts," *Academy of Management Learning & Education* 20(3) (September 2021), pp. 459–466; Mairi Maclean, Charles Harvey, Tom McGovern, and Gareth Shaw, "Elite Solidarity, Social Responsibility, and the Contested Origins of Britain's First Business Schools," *Academy of Management Learning & Education*, in press. For a general review, see Lars Engwall, Matthias Kipping, and Behlül Üsdiken, *Defining Management: Business Schools, Consultants, Media* (New York: Routledge, 2016), pp. 41–58.

regarding metal cutting, time study, and Le Chatelier's efforts to introduce scientific management in France.[34] Taylor's American Society of Mechanical Engineers presential address "On the Art of Cutting Metals" was translated by Leon Descroix and serialized in Le Chatelier's *Revue de Métallurgie* in 1907.[35] A translation of *The Principles of Scientific Management* (including a forward by Le Chatelier) was published in 1911.[36] When Fred and Louise Taylor visited Europe in 1912, and again in 1913, Le Chatelier introduced Taylor to industrialists Louis Renault, a founder of the automobile company Société Renault Frères, and Edouard and André Michelin, founders of the Michelin Tire Company (Compagnie Générale des Établissements Michelin). The Michelin brothers stopped short of applying Taylor's principles before World War I, but afterward applied scientific management in their workshops and formed the Comité Michelin to promote Taylorism in France.[37]

Renault had visited Taylor at Boxly in 1911 and was told to expect 3 to 5 years to successfully implement Taylor's ideas.[38] Under competitive pressure from the Ford Motor Company and German automobile manufacturers, Renault sought a "quick-fix" and employed an untrained engineer, Georges de Ram, to conduct time studies at his Billancourt plant.[39] Piece rates were subsequently cut, and a strike ensued in December 1912. Renault compromised by reducing expected output by 20 percent, but another strike occurred in February 1913. The strike turned into a lockout and, after 6 weeks, a Renault victory.[40] Following the 1913 strike, Taylor wrote Le Chatelier: "If a man [Renault] deliberately goes against the experience of men who know what they are talking about and refuses to follow advice given in a kind but unmistakable way, it seems to me that he deserves to get into trouble."[41]

Charles de Fréminville, a former chief engineer of the Paris-Orléans railroad, learned of scientific management through Le Chatelier's translations of Taylor's writings and became a second leading French proponent of *Taylorisme*.[42] He attempted to apply scientific management to the French manufacturer Panhard et Levassor, a pioneer in the automobile industry. Panhard and Levassor's managers either resisted de Fréminville's efforts or simply took those parts of scientific management they felt would lead to quick returns at little cost. de Fréminville did not lose interest, however; as noted in Chapter 10, he and Le Chatelier helped merge Fayol's Centre d'Etudes Administratives with the Conference de l'Organisation Française to form the still active Comité National de l'Organisation Française.

During World War I, scientific management in France made greater headway when Prime Minister Georges Clemenceau, also serving as Minister of War, ordered that all military plants adopt Taylor's principles.[43] In response, C. Bertrand Thompson (see Chapter 7) and

---

[34] Ralph E. Oesper, "The Scientific Career of Henry Louis Le Chatelier," *Journal of Chemical Education* 8(3) (March 1931), p. 456.

[35] Frederick W. Taylor, "La taille des métaux," trans. Leon Descroix, *La Revue de Métallurgie* 4(1) (January 1907), pp. 108–184; 4(2) (February 1907), pp. 233–336; 4(3) (March 1907), pp. 401–466. See also George G. Humphreys, *Taylorism in France, 1904–1920: The Impact of Scientific Management on Factory Relations and Society* (New York: Garland, 1986), p. 59.

[36] Frederick W. Taylor, *Principes d'organisation scientifique des usines* [*Principles of Scientific Organization of Factories*], trans. Jean Royer (Paris: H. Dunod and R. Pinat, 1911).

[37] Francesca Tesi, "Michelin et le Taylorisme" ["Michelin and Taylorism"], *Histoire, Économie, et Société* 27(3) (September 2008), pp. 111–126; *idem*, "The Application of Taylorism in France: The Role of the Michelin Family in the Rationalization of French Work," *Business and Economic History On-line* 7, 2009, pp. 1–22.

[38] Patrick Fridenson, "Un tournant taylorien de la société française (1904–1918)" ["A Taylorian Turning Point in French Society"], *Annales, Histoire, Sciences Sociales* 42(5) (September–October 1987), p. 1042.

[39] Georges de Ram, "Sur Essai D'Application du Système Taylor: Dans un Grand Atelier de Mécanique Français" ["A Test of the Taylor System in a Large French Works"], *Revue de Métallurgie* 6(9) (September 1909), pp. 929–930.

[40] Gary S. Cross, *A Quest for Time: The Reduction of Work in Britain and France, 1840–1940* (Berkeley, CA: University of California Press, 1989), p. 107.

[41] Frederick W. Taylor to Henry Le Chatelier, March 20, 1913. *Frederick W. Taylor Collection*, SCW.001. Archives and Special Collections, Samuel C. Williams Library, Stevens Institute of Technology, Hoboken, NJ.

[42] Lyndall Urwick and Edward F. L. Brech, *The Making of Scientific Management: Thirteen Pioneers*, vol. 1 (London: Sir Isaac Pitman & Sons, 1951), pp. 105–111.

[43] Clemenceau's February 26, 1918, order is reprinted at "Taylor Methods in French Industries," *Bulletin of the Taylor Society* 4(3) (June 1919), pp. 29–35.

de Fréminville implemented Taylor's methods in the marine engineering facilities at Châlons-sur-Marne, Guérigny, and Clermont-Ferrand. The French Minister of Marine, Georges Leygues, issued instructions that the same methods be adopted in the Arsenal at Touls.[44] The initial French experience with scientific management, however, was less than positive: managers seized the methods and forgot the "mental revolution." In general, as had happened to Taylor's disgust in the United States, managers perverted what Taylor had described as scientific management.[45] Although the French used the term *Taylorisme* to refer to *l'organisation scientifique du travail*, the application of Taylor's principles fell far short of ideal. At the time of Taylor's death in 1915, Le Chatelier reported knowing of only half-a-dozen "partial applications" of scientific management in France.[46]

"Taylorism" was first applied in England at Joseph Hopkinson & Company, a valve manufacturer, in 1905.[47] As reported by Lyndall F. Urwick and Edward F. L. Brech, "the Taylor doctrine" was not well received by the British. Taylor had aroused bitter feelings among British manufacturers over patent rights for the processing of high-speed steel, and organized labor opposed his methods.[48] Kevin Whitson, however, found that British engineering journals cited Taylor's work frequently and, often, positively.[49] In counterpoint, a 1911 editorial appeared in the trade journal *The Engineer*: "We do not hesitate to say that Taylorism is inhuman. As far as possible it dehumanizes the man, for it endeavours to remove the only distinction that makes him better than a machine—his intelligence."[50]

Manufacturers also held conflicting views. Hans Renold Co., a chain-making firm, implemented scientific management in 1908.[51] Hans Renold met with Taylor in the United States on three occasions and was impressed with the application of Taylor's methods at the Link-Belt Company. Renold and his son, Charles, were able to implement scientific management successfully, but one source has suggested that their example "did not appear to make scientific management any more widely accepted [in Britain]."[52] Edward Cadbury, managing director of the Cadbury Brothers chocolate firm, was critical of scientific management's methods and its treatment of workers, but Michael C. Rowlinson concluded Cadbury was out of touch with the firm's shop-level practices that already incorporated the essential elements of "scientific management."[53]

---

[44] Devinat, *Scientific Management in Europe*, p. 237.

[45] Humphreys, *Taylorism in France*, p. 105.

[46] Henri Le Chatelier, "How I Have Known Frederick W. Taylor: Why I Have Endeavored to Popularize Scientific Management," in *Frederick W. Taylor: A Memorial Volume* (New York: Taylor Society, 1920), pp. 20–21.

[47] Angelo Pichierri, "Diffusion and Crisis of Scientific Management in European Industry," in Salvador Giner and Margaret Scotford Archer, eds., *Contemporary Europe: Social Structures and Cultural Patterns* (London: Routledge & Kegan Paul, 1978), p. 58.

[48] Urwick and Brech, *The Making of Scientific Management*, p. 111. See also Urwick, "The Development of Scientific Management in Great Britain," *British Management Review* 3(4) (October–December 1938), pp. 18–96; Steven Kreis, "The Diffusion of an Idea: A History of Scientific Management in Britain, 1890–1945" (Doctoral dissertation, University of Missouri, Columbia, MO, 1990); and Ian Smith and Trevor Boyns,"Scientific Management and the Pursuit of Control in Britain to c. 1960," *Accounting, Business & Financial History* 15(2) (2005), pp. 187–216.

[49] Kevin Whitson, "The Reception of Scientific Management by British Engineers, 1890–1914," *Business History Review* 71(2) (Summer 1997), pp. 207–229. See also *idem*, "Scientific Management and Production Management Practice in Britain between the Wars," *Historical Studies in Industrial Relations*, no. 1 (March 1996), pp. 47–75, and *idem*, "Worker Resistance and Taylorism in Britain," *International Review of Social History* 42(1) (April 1997), pp. 1–24.

[50] "Taylorism," *The Engineer* 111 (May 19, 1911), p. 520. See also "Taylorism Again," *The Engineer* 113 (April 12, 1912), p. 382.

[51] Trevor Boyns, "Hans and Charles Renold: Entrepreneurs in the Introduction of Scientific Management Techniques in Britain," *Management Decision* 39(9) (2001), pp. 719–728.

[52] Edward F. L. Brech, *The Evolution of Modern Management*, vol. 2: *Productivity in Perspective, 1914–1974* (Bristol, U.K.: Thoemmes Press, 2002), p. 30.

[53] Michael C. Rowlinson, "The Early Application of Scientific Management by Cadbury," *Business History* 30(4) (October 1988), pp. 384, 391; Charles Dellheim, "The Creation of a Company Culture: *Cadburys*, 1861–1931," *American Historical Review* 92(1) (February 1987), pp. 13–44.

Germany, Austria, Poland, Hungary, and Russia

A strong engineering tradition, combined with an early interest in commercial education, provided favorable conditions for the introduction of Taylorism in Imperial Germany.[54] Taylor's work was translated into German as early as 1907. A German edition of *Shop Management* was published in 1912, followed by *The Principles of Scientific Management* in 1913, at which time Germany dominated the European continent economically.[55] Numerous German consultants claimed to apply Taylor's principles. Time study was used at Friedrich Krupp AG as early as 1910, with a 25 percent reduction in labor costs.[56] Henry L. Gantt accompanied a group of touring ASME members to Germany in 1913. During 1914–1915, Frank B. Gilbreth had a consulting contract in Berlin to reorganize Auergesellschaft/Deutsche Gasglühlicht AG using his chronocyclegraphs.[57]

In what was called the *rationalization movement*, other firms such as Siemens, Borsig, Orsam, Daimler-Benz, and Bosch attempted to apply Taylor's principles. The response of German trade unions was largely negative, as evidenced by strikes at Bosch in 1912 and 1913. After World War I, Germany took a nationalistic approach to scientific management by creating the Reichskuratorium für Wirtschaftlichkeit (RKW; National Board for Economy and Efficiency). The RKW, a joint initiative of the Ministry of Economics and the Federation of Technical and Scientific Associations, was a clearinghouse for German academic and industry specialists to study and promote industrial efficiency during the interwar years of the Weimar Republic.[58] When Adolf Hitler's National Socialist Workers Party came to power, labor unions were disbanded and the RKW was used to control industrial practices. Thereafter, the combination of deteriorating economic conditions, World War II, and the rise of fascism shaped the course of scientific management in Germany.

In Austria, Taylorism was first publicly discussed in 1914 at the Österreichischer Ingenieurund Architektenverein (Organization of Austrian Engineers and Architects). Discussions of Taylorism in both Germany and Austria were soon interrupted with the beginning of World War I in August 1914.[59] Following the war, however, these discussions resumed as *Taylor–Zeitschrift*, a journal devoted to Taylorism, was published in Austria from 1920 to 1929.[60]

Taylorism found a home in Poland as early as 1913 with the translation of *The Principles of Scientific Management* by economist and engineer Henryk Mierzejewski.[61] An interest among Polish engineers in work methods may be traced to the late-nineteenth century. In 1896, the Russian-educated Polish engineer, Karol Adamiecki, developed a form of graphical analysis known as a "harmonogram" to solve production bottlenecks. Harmonograms charted the flow of work across a production process to minimize delays. Adamiecki's harmonograms had elements of Gantt's charts but were also similar to a Program Evaluation and Review Technique (PERT)

---

[54] The first German school of business, Handelshochschule Leipzig, was opened in 1898. It is now known as HHL Leipzig Graduate School of Management.

[55] Frederick W. Taylor, *Die Betriebsleitung insbesondere der Werkstätten* [*Shop Management*], trans. Adolf Wallichs (Berlin: Julius Springer, 1912); *idem, Die Grundsätze wissenschaftlicher Betriebsführung* [*The Principles of Scientific Management*], trans. Rudolf Roesler (München: R. Oldenbourg, 1913).

[56] Bruce Kogut and David Parkinson, "The Diffusion of American Organizing Principles to Europe," in Bruce Kogut, ed., *Country Competitiveness: Technology and the Organizing of Work* (New York: Oxford University Press, 1993), pp. 184–187.

[57] Florian Hoof, *Angels of Efficiency: A Media History of Consulting*, trans. Daniel Fairfax (New York: Oxford University Press, 2020), pp. 240–294.

[58] J. Ronald Shearer, "*The Reichskuratorium für Wirtschaftlichkeit*: Fordism and Organized Capitalism in Germany, 1918–1945," *Business History Review* 71(4) (Winter 1971), pp. 569–602. See also Robert A. Brady, *The Rationalization Movement in German Industry: A Study in the Evolution of Economic Planning* (Berkeley: University of California Press, 1933).

[59] Mary Nolan, *Visions of Modernity: American Business and the Modernization of Germany* (New York: Oxford University Press, 1994), pp. 41–44.

[60] André Pfoertner, "The Americanization of Austrian Business," in Günter Bischof and Anton Pelinka, eds., *The Americanization/Westernization of Austria* (New Brunswick, NJ: Transaction Publishers, 2004), p. 63.

[61] Frederick W. Taylor, *Zasady organizacji naukowej zakładów przemysłowych* [*Principles of Scientific Organization of Industrial Plants*], trans. Henryk Mierzejewski (Warsaw: Wydawnictwo Przeglądu Technicznego), 1913.

workflow network.[62] Harmonograms were used in some Polish and Russian rolling mills, but their widespread adoption was hindered by the political ideology of Russia's anticapitalistic Communist regime. Adamiecki's work was not translated into English during his lifetime. He became a leading figure in the European scientific-management movement by establishing the Polish Institute of Scientific Management at Warsaw in 1923, presenting a paper at the First International Management Congress in Prague, and being actively involved in the International Labor Organization (ILO) and the Comité Internationale de l'Organisation Scientifique (CIOS).

Hungarian engineers expressed an early interest in scientific management as a means of increasing employee productivity. Taylor's differential piece-rate plan and thoughts on shop management were the subject of a series of four debates sponsored by the Magyar Mérnök-és Építész-Egylet (MMÉE; Hungarian Association of Engineers and Architects) in 1912. Kálmán Méhely, managing director of the National Association of Hungarian Ironworks and Machine Shops, began the debate with a two-hour presentation that was later printed in the MMÉE *Bulletin*, together with the comments of various discussants, including Emil Sóváry, who reported on the introduction of Taylor's ideas at the Ganz Electrical Works (Budapest) as early as 1903.[63] The *Bulletin* was distributed to MMÉE's 2,000-plus members. The losses of World War I and the ensuing economic crisis slowed the dissemination of Taylorism throughout Hungarian industry.[64]

On November 6–7, 1917 [October 25–26 O.S.], Bolshevik (Communist) revolutionaries overthrew Russia's Provisional Government. The provisional government had been formed eight months earlier by members of the *Gosudarstvennaya Duma* (State Assembly) following the abdication of Czar Nicholas II. The collapse of the 304-year-old Romanov Dynasty was triggered by workers' strikes over long hours, low wages, and poor housing, as well as food riots caused by shortages and rising prices in the capital city of Petrograd (now Saint Petersburg). The protests lasted for 8 days with over a thousand people injured or killed by police and loyal government troops. Drawing inspiration from the works of Karl Marx and Friedrich Engels (see Chapter 3), Communist Party founder Vladimir Ilyich Ulyanov, better known as Lenin, wanted to use Taylor's methods to show how society would benefit if workers controlled the means of production. Believing scientific management to be the most advanced means for achieving economic growth, he advocated its use to systematize Russian industry, which lagged far behind Western Europe and the United States.[65]

---

[62] Theodore Limperg and Lyndall F. Urwick, "Charles Adamiecki (1866–1933)," *Bulletin of the International Management Institute* 3(1) (January 1929), pp. 102–103; Edward R. Marsh, "The Harmonogram of Karol Adamiecki," *Academy of Management Journal* 18(2) (June 1975), pp. 358–364; Zdzislaw P. Weslolowski, "The Polish Contribution to the Development of Scientific management," in Jeffrey C. Susbauber, ed., *Proceedings of the Annual Meeting of the Academy of Management* (1978), pp. 12–16, and Bart J. Debicki, "Forgotten Contributions to Scientific Management: Work and Ideas of Karol Adamiecki," *Journal of Management History* 21(1) (2015), pp. 40–67.

[63] Méhely Kálmán, "A munkabérfizetési rendszerek és a Taylor-féle üzemvezetés I–II" ["Wage Systems and Taylor's Plant Management I–II"], *A Magyar Mérnök és Építész-Egylet közlönye* 47(1) (January 5, 1913), pp. 1–16; 47(2) (January 12, 1913), pp. 21–30. "Discussion," 47(3) (January 19, 1913), pp. 41–53; 47(4) (January 26, 1913), pp. 62–69; 47(5) (February 2, 1913), pp. 82–88. Sóváry's comments appear in 47(3) (January 19, 1913), pp. 41–53.

[64] Péter Strausz, "'A gyári üzemnek évszázados fejlődésből leszűrt breviáriuma'—A magyar vezetés- és szervezéstudomány kezdetei: Vitasorozat a Taylor-rendszerről 1912-ben" ["'Summary of the Centuries' Development of the Plant Concept'—Beginnings of Hungarian Management and Organizational Thinking: A Series of Discussions on the Taylor System in 1912"], in Miklós Dobák, ed., *Tanulmányok a magyar menedzsmenttudomány 20. századi történetéből* [*Studies on the History of Hungarian Management Science in the 20th Century*] (Budapest: L'Harmattan Kiadó, 2013), pp. 9–10. See also Béla Krisztián and Zsolt Nemeskéri, "A Taylori Elvek a Magyar Gazdasacran" ["The Taylor Principles in the Hungarian Economy"] *Journal of Management and Organizational Sciences* 6(1–2) (2014), pp. 498–508; Péter Nagy, "Taylor követői Magyarországon: *A tudományos munkaszervezés kezdetei*" ["Taylor's Followers in Hungary: The Beginnings of Scientific Management"], *Korall-Társadalomtörténeti folyóirat* no. 85 (2021), pp. 72–92.

[65] Vladimir I. Lenin, "Ocherednye zadachi Sovetskoj vlasti" ["The Immediate Tasks of the Soviet Government"], *Pravda* (Moscow) no. 83 (April 28, 1918), p. 4. Lenin's 1918 sentiments regarding scientific management stand in contrast to his earlier views: see *idem*, "'Nauchnaya' sistema vyzhimanija pota" ["'Scientific' System of Sweating"], *Pravda* (Moscow) no. 60 (March 13, 1913), p. 2; *idem*, "Sistema Teilora—poraboshenie cheloveka mashinoj" ["The Taylor System—Man's Enslavement by the Machine"], *Put' Pravdy* no. 35 (March 13, 1914), p. 1. See also Judith A. Merkle, *Management and Ideology: The Legacy of the International Management Movement* (Berkeley: University of California Press, 1980), pp. 103–135; Christopher T. Nyland, "Scientific Management and Planning," *Capital & Class* 11(3) (Winter 1987), pp. 55–83; Andrey A. Semenov, "The Origin of Scientific Management Systems in Russia," Working Paper 854, Graduate School of Management, Saint Petersburg State University (Saint Petersburg, Russia: 2010), and Mikhail Grachev and Boris Rakitsky, "Historic Horizons of Frederick Taylor's Scientific Management," *Journal of Management History* 19(4) (2013), pp. 512–527.

In 1920, Alexsei K. Gastev, a leading proponent of scientific management, founded and became director of the Institute of Labor in Moscow.[66] The Institute of Labor merged with the People's Commissariat of Labor's Laboratory of Industrial Psychotechnics to form the Central Institute of Labor in 1921.[67] It has been said that Gastev considered humans inferior to machines and that his goal was to turn workers into robots, "incapable of individual thought" and "so devoid of personality that there would not even be a need to give them names. They would be classified instead by ciphers such as 'A, B, C, or 325, 075, 0, and so on.'"[68] Gastev's vision of a world populated by robot-like workers clashed with, among others, Platon M. Kerzhentsev's belief that this would lead to labor exploitation no different than under capitalism. A founder of the Time League (established in 1923 as a section within the Scientific Organization of Labor), Kerzhentsev charged that Gastev (like Taylor) wanted to deny workers the opportunity to participate in improving workplace methods and, instead, encourage them to blindly obey orders.[69]

Although conferences were held, institutes established, and attempts made to implement "the Taylor System," few improvements were made because of the Communist Party's distrust of capitalism.[70] Ideology prevailed when the Union of Soviet Socialist Republics, successor to the Russian Empire, was formed in 1922. Labor productivity remained low and the idea of "super-workmen" arose. Alexei Grigoryevich Stakhanov became nationally known for his extraordinary performance in mining coal. Working at the Tsentralnaya-Irmino mine, located at Kadiyevsk (Donbas region) in Ukraine (then a constituent republic within the Soviet Union), Stakhanov and his crew mined an impressive 102 tons of coal in 5 hours and 45 minutes on the night of August 30–31, 1935. The output was extraordinary—more than 14 times its daily 7 ton quota—and Stakhanov was hailed as an example for others, receiving the title "Hero of Socialist Labor" in 1970.[71] True or not, this achievement was so remarkable that Stakhanov's photo appeared in the United States on the December 16, 1935, cover of *Time* magazine.[72] Higher productivity was expected to come from the selflessness of hard work and devotion to the Soviet Union rather than from job analysis and improved work methods. Although, by one account, this "new worker" soon "began to receive special privileges (from high wages to new housing, as well as educational opportunities for themselves and their children),"[73] by another, "Stakhanovites" were "ostracized

---

[66] Vadim I. Marshev, "Formation of Management Thought in Russia and the Early USSR from the 1800s to the 1920s," *Journal of Management History* (2019), pp. 285–303. For more on the development of management thought in Russia and the U.S.S.R. see *idem*, *History of Management Thought*, trans. Oleg Geraschenko (Cham, Switzerland: Springer, 2021). Russian edition published in 2005.

[67] Evgeniĭ A. Dobrenko, *Political Economy of Socialist Realism* (New Haven, CT: Yale University Press, 2007), p. 155.

[68] Orlando G. Figes, *A People's Tragedy: A History of the Russian Revolution, 1891–1924* (London: Jonathan Cape, 1996), p. 744. See also Sigmund Slonim, "Russian Scientists in Quest of American Efficiency," *Bulletin of the Taylor Society* 7(5) (October 1922), pp. 194–197; Vladimir V. Mouravieff, "Central Labor Institute: A Russian Contribution to the Success of Work and Workers' Education," *Bulletin of the Taylor Society* 14(4) (August 1929), pp. 168–172.

[69] Platon M. Kerzhentsev, "Dve plaformy po Not: v diskussionnom porjadke," ["Two Approaches to the Scientific Organization of Work: A Discussion], *Trud* (Moscow) no. 41 (Februrary 20, 1924), p. 2. See also Samuel Lieberstein, "Technology, Work, and Sociology in the USSR: The NOT Movement," *Technology and Culture* 16(1) (January 1975), pp. 48–66; Kendall E. Bailes, "Alexei Gastev and the Soviet Controversy Over Taylorism, 1918–1924," *Soviet Studies* 29(3) (July 1977), p. 390; and Ulf Brunnbauer, "'League of Time' (Liga Vremia): Problems of Making a Soviet Working Class in the 1920s," *Russian History* 27(4) (Winter 2000), p. 463.

[70] Daniel A. Wren and Arthur G. Bedeian, "The Taylorization of Lenin: Rhetoric or Reality?" *International Journal of Social Economics* 31(3) (2004), pp. 287–299. See also Zenovia A. Sochor, "Soviet Taylorism Revisited," *Soviet Studies* 38(2) (April 1981), pp. 246–264.

[71] Arthur G. Bedeian and Carl R. Phillips, "Scientific Management and Stakhanovism in the Soviet Union: A Historical Perspective," *International Journal of Social Economics* 17(10) (1990), pp. 28–35.

[72] The accompanying story is titled "Heroes of Labor," *Time* 26(25) (December 16, 1935), pp. 25, 28.

[73] Bogdan Costea and Peter Watt, "How a Soviet Miner from the 1930s Helped Create Today's Intense Corporate Workplace Culture," *The Conversation* (June 29, 2021). Available at https://theconversation.com/how-a-soviet-miner-from-the-1930s-helped-create-todays-intense-corporate-workplace-culture-155814.

by their fellow workers for raising output quotas."[74] It would seem that "rate-busters" may not have been any more welcome in the Donbas than in the Bank-Wiring Department at the Hawthorne Works of the Western Electric Company in Cicero, Illinois (see Chapter 13).

After Lenin's death in 1924, the General Secretary of the Communist Party, Iosif Vissarionovich Dzhugashvili, better known as Stalin, emerged as the leader of the Soviet Union. He viewed scientific management as a way to achieve economic growth equal to that of the United States. Writing in the Bolshevik newspaper *Pravda* (*Truth*), Stalin even claimed, "The combination of Russian revolutionary sweep with American efficiency is the essence of Leninism."[75] To assist in developing a national plan to increase the Soviet Union's economic capacity, Stalin hired one of Gantt's disciples, Walter N. Polakov, as a consultant. Polakov was born at Luga, Russia, in 1879. He earned a degree in mechanical engineering at Dresden's Royal Institute of Technology in 1902 and did graduate work at the University of Moscow in psychology and industrial hygiene. After working for the Tula Locomotive Works and as Chief Engineer and Naval Instructor in the Russian Department of Navigation and Harbors, he immigrated with his wife to the United States in 1906. He was a well-known expert in power-plant management and was active in both the Taylor Society and Association of Russian Engineers. Polakov prepared an appendix titled "The Measurement of Human Work" for Wallace Clark's book *The Gantt Chart: A Working Tool of Management*.[76] He subsequently worked as an independent consultant in Russia from December 1929 to May 1931, using Gantt charts to implement the Soviet Union's First Five-Year Plan to industrialize its largely agrarian economy.[77]

"Walter N. Polakov, Student of Industrial Relations," *Popular Science Monthly* 98(1) (January 1921), p. 22.

Walter N. Polakov

Other European Nations

Taylorism was also imported into other European nations. Its acceptance (and success) varied from one setting to another.[78] The leaders of the scientific-management movement in Czechoslovakia were Tomáš G. Masaryk and Edvard Beneš, both of whom would serve as their country's president.[79] *The Principles of Scientific Management*, however, was not translated into Czech

[74] Victor Kravchenko, *I Choose Freedom: The Personal and Political Life of a Soviet Official* (New York: Charles Scribner's Sons, 1946), pp. 187–205, 298–302. For more on the Stakhanovites' purported accomplishments, see Goronwy Rees, "Stakhanovism and Its Significance," *The Spectator* 136(5611) (January 10, 1936), pp. 10–11; Lewis H. Siegelbaum, *Stakhanovism and the Politics of Productivity in the USSR, 1935–1941* (Cambridge, England: Oxford University Press, 1988); Stephen Kotkin, *Magnetic Mountain: Stalinism as a Civilization* (Berkeley, CA: University of California Press, 1995), pp. 198–207; and Robert W. Davies and Oleg Khlevnyuk, "Stakhanovism and the Soviet Economy," *Europe-Asia Studies* 54(6) (September 2002), pp. 867–903.

[75] Joseph V. Stalin, "Ob osnovakh leninizma—IX: Stiĺ" ["On the Foundations of Leninism—IX: Style"], *Pravda* (Moscow) no. 96 (May 18, 1924), p. 4. For Stalin's thoughts on Stakhanovism, see Stalin, *The Stakhanov Movement in the Soviet Union* [Speech Delivered at the First Conference of Stakhanovites of Industry and Transport, November 17, 1935] (New York: Workers Library Publishers, 1935).

[76] Walter N. Polakov, "The Measurement of Human Work," in Wallace Clark, *The Gantt Chart: A Working Tool of Management* (New York: Ronald Press, 1922), pp. 150–157.

[77] Walter N. Polakov, "The Gantt Chart in Russia," *American Machinist* 75 (August 13, 1931), pp. 261–264. See also Daniel A. Wren, "Scientific Management in the U.S.S.R., with Particular Reference to the Contribution of Walter N. Polakov," *Academy of Management Review* 5(1) (January 1980), pp. 1–11; Diana J. Kelly, *The Red Taylorist: The Life and Works of Walter Nicholas Polakov* (Bingley, England: Emerald Publishing, 2020).

[78] Frank B. Gilbreth and Lillian M. Gilbreth, "Scientific Management in Other Countries than the United States," *Bulletin of the Taylor Society* 9(3) (June 1924), pp. 132–142.

[79] John Mihalasky, "Scientific Management in Central Eastern Europe—Czechoslovakia, Hungary, and Poland," in John-Christopher Spender and Hugo J. Kijne, eds., *Scientific Management: Frederick Winslow Taylor's Gift to the World?* (Boston, MA: Kluwer, 1996), pp. 133–162.

until 1931.[80] In Italy, where most factories possessed outdated technology, the abysmal conditions of the late 1920s and 1930s economy mediated against the wide introduction of scientific management in all but the largest firms such as Olivetti (a typewriter manufacturer), Fiat (an automotive company), and Magneti Marelli (an equipment company).[81] *The Principles of Scientific Management*, however, was first translated into Italian in 1915.[82] The cofounder of the Italian Communist Party, Antonio Gramsci, was critical of scientific management for destroying worker autonomy.[83] The Ente Nazionale Italiano per l'Organizzazione Scientifica del Lavoro (Italian National Organization of Scientific Work), founded in 1926, actively published information on scientific management.[84]

Taylorism was introduced into Sweden in 1912 by Gustav Axel Jæderholm. *The Principles of Scientific Management* was translated into Swedish in 1913 and included a foreword by Erik August Forsberg, who taught at the Royal Institute of Technology in Stockholm.[85] Forsberg had previously embraced Taylor's methods as Technical Director at AB Separator, a company now known as Alfa Laval.[86] *The Principles of Scientific Management* was translated into Finnish in 1914,[87] and, according to Jacob de Julin, it quickly became "the gospel of practically every progressive plant in Finland."[88] The 3-month Bolshevik uprising in 1918, with its accompanying looting and destruction of industrial plants, however, slowed the country's introduction of Taylor's principles. After meeting with Taylor in Philadelphia, Jakob J. Sederholm (director of the Geological Survey of Finland) returned to Espoo and wrote a widely read paper and a book praising scientific management.[89]

Norwegian industrialist Joakim Lehmkuhl brought scientific management to his home country in 1920 with the publication of his book *Rationel arbeidsledelse: En oversigt* (*Rational Labor Management: An Overview*).[90] It, however, did not gain a foothold in Norway until the 1950s.[91] Scientific management came to Denmark in 1905, with an introduction at NKT's cable factory in Middelfart.[92] It reached a wider Danish audience in 1917 with an article by Carl V. Bramsnæs titled "The Taylor System: A Study of the American Theories of Rational Factory

80 Frederick W. Taylor, *Poselství Taylorovo o zásadách vědeckého řízení* [*Taylor's Message on the Principles of Scientific Management*], trans. Emil Zimmler and Alois A. Hoch (Prague: Orbis Nakladatelství, 1931).

81 Perry R. Willson, *The Clockwork Factory: Women and Work in Fascist Italy* (Oxford, England: Clarendon Press, 1993), p. 41.

82 Frederick W. Taylor, *L'organizzazione scientifica del lavoro* [*The Scientific Organization of Work*], trans. Francesco Giannini and Enrico A. Masino (Rome; Athenaeum, 1915).

83 Antoinette S. Phillips and Arthur G. Bedeian, "Understanding Antonio Gramsci's Ambiguous Legacy," *International Journal of Social Economics* 17(10) (1990), pp. 36–41. Gramsci was imprisoned for 11 years (1926–1937) by Italy's fascist government under the direction of Prime Minister Benito A. A. Mussolini. His health had deteriorated in prison to such an extent that he died shortly after being released.

84 See, for example, Francesco Mauro, *L'Organizzazione scientifica del lavoro nei suoi aspetti italiani ed internazionali* [*The Scientific Organization of Work in its Italian and International Aspects*] (Rome: Ente Nazionale italiano per l'Organizzazione Scientifica del Lavoro, 1917).

85 Frederick W. Taylor, *Rationell arbetsledning: Taylor-systemet* [*Rational Management: The Taylor System*], trans. Karl G. Wetterlund (Stockholm: Swedish Confederation of Industry, 1913).

86 Esbjörn Segelod and Leif Carlsson, "The Emergence of Uniform Principles of Cost Accounting in Sweden 1900–1936," *Accounting, Business & Financial History* 20(3) (November 2010), pp. 327–363. See also Nils Runeby, "Americanism, Taylorism and Social Integration," *Scandinavian Journal of History* 3(1–4) (1978), pp. 21–46.

87 Frederick W. Taylor, *Tieteellisen liikkeenhoidon periaatteet* [*Principles of Scientific Management*], trans. Jalmari Kekkonen (Hämeenlinna: Arvi A. Karisto, 1914).

88 Jacob de Julin, "American Industrial Methods in Finland," *Industrial Management* 58(1) (July 1919), p. 51.

89 Jakob J. Sederholm, "Om den amerikanska effektivitetsrörelsen, med särskilt hansyn till den s.k. Scientific Management," ["On the American Efficiency Movement, with Special Attention to the Scientific Management Movement"] *Ekonomiska Samfundets Tidskrift* 2(1) (February 1914), pp. 118–152; *idem*, *Työn tiede* [*The Science of Labor*] (Porvoo, Finland: Werner Söderström Osakeyhtiö, 1915).

90 Joakim Lehmkuhl, *Rationel arbeidsledelse: En oversigt* [*Rational Work Management: An Overview*] (Bergen: Jphn Griegs boktrykkeri, 1920).

91 Francis Sejersted, *The Age of Social Democracy: Norway and Sweden in the Twentieth Century* (Princeton, NJ: Princeton University Press, 2011), p. 45.

92 Jørgen Burchardt, "Introduktion af nye ledelsesformer—da Scientific Management kom til Danmark 1905–1920," ["Introduction of New Forms of Leadership—When Scientific Management Came to Denmark 1905–1920"] *Tidsskrit for Arbejdsliv* 3(2) (2001), pp. 69–90. See also *idem*, "Introduction of New Management Concepts: When Scientific Management Came to Europe," unpublished paper presented at the 2009 Business History Conference, Milan, Italy, June 13, 2009.

Management," published in the journal *Nationaløkonomisk Tidsskrift*.[93] As the economy was primarily comprised of small- and medium-sized firms, scientific management spread slowly in the Netherlands. Huib J. Hendrikse translated *Shop Management* [*Over arbeidspraestatie en loonregeling; het Taylor beheersysteem*] into Dutch in 1909 and *The Principles of Scientific Management* [*De beginselen der wetenschappelijke bedrijfsleiding*] in 1913. Taylorism, however, did not reach its "heyday" in the Netherlands until after World War II.[94] Meanwhile, a Spanish translation of Taylor's *Shop Management* appeared in 1914.[95] Although initially received with enthusiasm, scientific management was seen by Spanish intellectuals as coercive and as detrimental to employee initiative. Others simply questioned if Taylorism could fulfill its claims.[96]

Formalizing Scientific Management in Europe

European interest widened scientific management's frontiers along separate, yet related, paths. In 1924, the First International Congress on Scientific Management was held in Prague; among those attending from the United States were Harlow Person, representing the Taylor Society, and Lillian M. Gilbreth, representing her husband Frank (see Chapter 8). The International Committee of Scientific Management (Le Comité International de l'Organisation Scientifique, known as CIOS) was formed in 1925 to continue exchanging ideas about management. Subsequent CIOS meetings were held in Brussels (1925), Rome (1927), Paris (1929), Amsterdam (1932), London (1935), and Washington, DC (1938). The 1941 meeting, to be held in Berlin, was cancelled due to World War II. CIOS would not resume its work until after the war.[97] It launched the International Academy of Management (IAM) in 1958. The Institute of Industrial Administration was formed at London in 1919 and merged with the British Institute of Management (BIM; founded 1947) in 1957. BIM's academic counterpart, the British Academy of Management (BAM) was established in 1986. The European Group for Organizational Studies (EGOS) was created in 1973.

Beginning in the 1920s, the Twentieth Century Fund, which had been endowed by the Boston department-store owner Edward A. Filene and the Rockefeller Foundation, sought to promote improved management, particularly scientific management, in European industry, which was rebuilding following World War I. With the Fund's backing, the International Management Institute (IMI), a spin-off of the Geneva-based ILO, was formed in 1927 to gather research about better management practices. Frenchman Paul Devinat, former chief of the IMI Employers' Organization Service, was appointed as IMI's first director.[98] Englishman Lt. Colonel Lyndall F. Urwick, whom we will discuss shortly, succeeded Devinat in 1928. The IMI experienced difficulties contending with national employer groups, the threat of war, the rise of fascism in Europe, and a subsequent worldwide economic depression that undercut its funding. The IMI ceased its activities in January 1934, when the Twentieth Century Fund withdrew its financial support.[99]

---

[93] Carl V. Bramsnæs, "Taylor-systemet en undersøgelse af de amerikanske Teorier om rationel Fabrikledelse" ["The Taylor System: A Study of the American Theories of Rational Factory Management"], *Nationaløkonomisk Tidsskrift* 55 (1917), pp. 37–58.

[94] Frederick W. Taylor, *Over arbeidspraestatie en loonregeling: het Taylor beheersysteem* [*About Work Performance and Pay Regulation: The Taylor Management System*], trans. Huib J. Hendrikse (Amsterdam: Van Mantgem & De Does, 1909); *idem*, *De beginselen der wetenschappelijke bedrijfsleiding* [*The Principles of Scientific Management*], trans. *idem* (Eindhoven: Lecturis, 1913). See also Erik S. A. Bloemen, *Scientific Management in Nederland 1900–1930* (Amsterdam: Nederlandsch Economisch-Historisch Archief, 1988).

[95] *La Dirección de los Talleres: Estudio Sobre la Organización del Trabajo* [*The Direction of Workshops: Study of the Organization of Work*], trans. Eduardo Lozano (Barcelona: Libreria de Feliu y Susana, 1914).

[96] Mauro F.Guillén, *Models of Management* (Chicago, IL: University of Chicago Press, 1994), pp. 158–159.

[97] Erik Bloeman, "The Movement for Scientific Management in Europe between the Wars," in John-Christopher Spender and Hugo J. Kijne, eds., *Scientific Management: Frederick Winslow Taylor's Gift to the World?* (Boston, MA: Kluwer, 1996), pp. 111–131.

[98] Charles D. Wrege, Ronald G. Greenwood, and Sakae Hata, "The International Management Institute and Political Opposition to its Efforts in Europe, 1925–1934," *Business and Economic History* 16 (1987), pp. 249–265.

[99] Trevor Boyns, "Lyndall Urwick at the International Management Institute, Geneva, 1928–1934: Right Job, Wrong Man?" Paper presented at the European Business History Association, 11th Annual Conference, Geneva, 13–15 September 2007.

As in the United States, the recognition of scientific management as an academic subject was hindered in Europe by the belief that Taylor's methods could only be learned by experience. In Germany, Taylor had followers among certain industrialists and in technical societies, but he had little impact on institutions of higher education. Alfred Kieser noted the study of business economics (*Betriebswirtschaftslehre*), law, foreign languages, bookkeeping, and business letter writing were taught, but these efforts offered "nothing like a theory of management."[100] In France, scientific management took hold in its oldest technical university, the Conservatoire National des Arts et Métiers (CNAM), founded in 1794. CNAM's director, Jules Amar, applied Taylor's methods to explore aspects of work physiology related to energy and fatigue and organized three lectures on scientific management by C. Bertrand Thompson.[101] CNAM's faculty discussed formal courses on "*Taylorisme*," but did not reach a consensus until 1929, when a chair for *l'organisation scientifique du travail* was given to Louis Danty-Lafrance. Danty-Lafrance became a leading authority on scientific management, and CNAM "became the main body in French higher education for the spread of Taylor's thinking and practice, to be joined by the Institut d'Études Supérieures des Techniques de l'Organisation (IESTO) in 1955."[102]

Japan, China, and Australia

The Meiji Restoration in 1868 marked the transition of Japan from a feudal society to a capitalist economy. Industrialization came slowly, however; in 1870, more than 80 percent of the Japanese population was employed in agriculture and less than 5 percent in manufacturing. Industry, dominated by family firms with a small number of employees, was technologically backward and lacked modern-management methods.[103] Japan's first introduction to Taylorism appears to have occurred in late 1911 with the publication of a series of articles by journalist Ikeda Tōshirō in the Osaka newspaper *Sakigake*.[104] Ikeda had become interested in Taylorism while in the United States at the time of the 1910–1911 Eastern Rate Case (see Chapter 7). Given the popularity of his articles, Ikeda elaborated on Taylor's ideas in a privately printed booklet, *Mueki no tesuu habuku hiketsu* [*The Secrets of Eliminating Useless Labor*], in 1913, which is said to have sold some 1.5 million copies. In a similar coincidence, Hoshino Yukinori, director of Japan's Kajima Bank, was in the United States when Taylor's book *The Principles of Scientific Management* was published in 1911. Hoshino obtained permission to translate the book, which was distributed throughout Japan in 1913 as *Gakuriteki jigyō kanrihō* [*Scientific Business Management*].[105]

Landing in fertile soil, the scientific-management movement grew rapidly in Japan. Earlier, in 1912, Yōichi Ueno, a leading Japanese teacher, author, and consultant, had published a paper titled "On Efficiency," which described the work of Taylor, Frank B. Gilbreth, and C. Bertrand Thompson. Ueno translated many of Taylor's articles, attended international conferences and, in 1922, was the founding president of the Sangyo Noritsu Kenkyusho [Institute of Industrial Efficiency]. He helped form a Japanese branch of the Taylor Society in 1924 and the Nihon

[100] Alfred Kieser, "The Americanization of Academic Management Education in Germany," *Journal of Management Inquiry* 13(2) (June 2004), p. 92.

[101] Jules Amar, *The Human Motor, or, the Scientific Foundations of Labour and Industry*, trans. Elise P. Butterworth and George E. Wright (London: G. Routledge, 1920). French edition published in 1914. See also C. Bertrand Thompson, *Le système Taylor* [*Scientific Management*] (Paris: Payot, 1920).

[102] Jean-Louis Peaucelle and Cameron Guthrie, "The Private Life of Henri Fayol and His Motivation to Build a Management Science," *Journal of Management History* 18(4) (2012), p. 481.

[103] Koji Taira, "Factory Legislation and Management Modernization during Japan's Industrialization, 1886–1916," *Business History Review* 44(1) (Spring 1970), pp. 84–109.

[104] William M. Tsutsui, *Manufacturing Ideology: Scientific Management in Twentieth-Century Japan* (Princeton, NJ: Princeton University Press, 1998), pp. 18–19.

[105] Frederick W. Taylor, *Gakuriteki jigyō kanrihō* [*Scientific Business Management*], ed. Yukinori Hoshino (Tokyo: Sūbunkan Shoten), 1913. See also Toshikazu Nakase, "The Introduction of Scientific Management in Japan and Its Characteristics—Case Studies of Companies in the Sumitomo Zaibatsu," in Keiichiro Nakagawa, ed., *Labor and Management* (Toronto: University of Toronto Press, 1979), pp. 171–202. See also "The Development of Scientific Management in Japan," *Bulletin of the International Management Institute* 3(10) (October 1929), pp. 192–193.

Noritsu Rengokai [Japanese Federation of Management Associations] in 1927. In 1942, the Nihon Noritsu Rengokai and the Nihon Kogyo Kyokai (Japanese Industrial Association) combined to form the Nihon Noritsu Kyokai (Japanese Management Association). Ueno is known as the "Father of Japanese Administrative Science."[106]

In Japanese industry, the most advanced scientific-management application occurred at the Hyōgo Factory of the Kanegafuchi (Kanebō) Cotton Textile Company. Kanebō manager Sanji Mutō had studied in the United States. He saw no inherent conflict between a firm paying above-average wages and earning high profits.[107] Like Taylor and Gantt, Mutō not only began paying more to attract better employees, but also began to train employees and improve factory supervision and organization. Mutō eventually became president of Kanebō, one of Japan's leading textile firms. Together with other scientific-management advocates, he understood that productivity is the link between high wages and high profits, and that productivity is achieved through technology, capital, and improved work methods. What many popular writers call "Japanese-style management" is not a recent phenomenon, but a direct result of scientific management's introduction into Japan during the late Meiji period.[108] Under the influence of scholars such as Ueno and practitioners such as Mutō, scientific management provided the basis for modernizing Japanese industry.

Isaac F. Marcosson, "The Changing East: The Industrialization of China," *The Saturday Evening Post* 195(19) (November 4, 1922), p. 18.

Mu Xiangyue

Interest in scientific management among Chinese engineers, industrialists, government officials, and academics was rapid and widespread. As noted in Chapter 7, Taylor's *The Principles of Scientific Management* first appeared as a serial in the 1911 March, April, and May issues of the *American Magazine*. One month later, the series was the subject of an article in the June 1911 issue of the Chinese monthly magazine *Dong fang za zhi*.[109] Interest in scientific management was further spurred through the efforts of Xiangyue Mu.[110] He earned a BS degree in agriculture from the University of Illinois in 1913, and an MS degree in cotton planting and manufacturing from Texas A&M University in 1914. While at A&M, he wrote to Taylor requesting permission to translate *The Principles of Scientific Management* (which he had read in his coursework) into Chinese.[111] Mu's translation appeared in 1916.[112] Three earlier Chinese-language papers also deserve mention. Taylor's metal-cutting experiments were detailed in a 1912 article by Fang

[106] Ronald G. Greenwood and Robert H. Ross, "Early American Influence on Japanese Management Philosophy: The Scientific Management Movement in Japan," in Sang M. Lee and Gary Schwendiman, eds., *Management by Japanese Systems* (New York: Praeger, 1982), pp. 43–54. See also William M. Tsutsui, "The Way of Efficiency: Ueno Yōichi and Scientific Management in Twentieth-Century Japan," *Modern Asian Studies* 35(2) (April 2001), pp. 441–467, and Tamotsu Nishizawa, "Business Studies and Management Education in Japan's Economic Development," in Rolv Petter Amdam, ed., *Management, Education and Competitiveness: Europe, Japan and the United States* (Oxford, England: Routledge, 1996), pp. 96–110.

[107] Taira, "Factory Legislation," pp. 103–105. See also Mohammed T. Vaziri, Joe Won Lee, and Joseph L. Krieger, "Onda Moku: The True Pioneer of Management through Respect for Humanity," *Leadership and Organization Development Journal* 9(1) (1988), pp. 3–7.

[108] Balázs Vaszkun and William M. Tsutsui, "A Modern History of Japanese Management Thought," *Journal of Management History* 18(4) (2012), pp. 368–385.

[109] Gan Yonglong, "*Shangye zhong zhi kexue jinglifa*" ["*Scientific Management in Commercial Enterprises*"], *Dong fang za zhi* 8(4) (June 1911), pp. 7–12.

[110] Mu's career is profiled in Isaac F. Marcosson, "The Changing East: The Industrialization of China," *Saturday Evening Post* 195 (November 4, 1922), pp. 18–19, 116–118, 121–122.

[111] Hsiang Y. Moh to Frederick W. Taylor, April 23, 1914; Taylor to Moh, May 4, 1914; Moh to Taylor. May 15, 1914. *Frederick W. Taylor Collection*, SCW.001. Archives and Special Collections; Samuel C. Williams Library, Stevens Institute of Technology, Hoboken, NJ.

[112] Frederick W. Taylor, *Gong chang shiyong xueli guanli fa* [*The Industrial Applications of the Scientific Theory of Management*], trans. Xiangyue Mu (Shanghai: Zhonghua Book Company, 1916). Serialized in *Zhonghua Shi Ye Jie* 2(11) (November 1915), pp. 1–17; 2(12) (December 1915), pp. 17–32; 3(1) (January 1916), pp. 33–48; 3(2) (February 1916), pp. 49–63.

Zhuo in the journal *Jinbu*; Taylor's differential piece-rate plan was first described in a 1914 paper by Dingxin Yi in the journal *Zhonghua Shi Ye Jie*; and, in 1915, Xingfo Yang discussed Taylor's methods in a paper titled "Employee Efficiency" in the journal *Ke xue*.[113] By the 1920s, various Chinese firms were experimenting with Taylor's methods. It was not until 1930, however, that the Chinese Management Association (Zhongguo gongshang guanli xiehui) was formed.[114]

The first applications of Taylor's principles in Australia occurred in the early 1920s with Pearson Law and Company (later Pelaco), a clothing manufacturer, and the New South Wales Railways as examples.[115] Later in the decade, scientific management was implemented in Australia by the subsidiaries of multinational corporations such as General Motors Corporation, Goodyear Tire & Rubber Co., and Standard Telephones & Cables. Lucy Taksa has documented how scientific management spread to Australian educational practices, "resulting in the dissemination of a [single] managerial culture which is still relevant today."[116] Based on a wider analysis of scientific management's adoption, Taksa has concluded that "the diffusion of scientific management in different national contexts depended on two interrelated preconditions: a relatively fluid class structure, which gave professionals opportunities for social mobility and an integrated educational system, which provided the credentials to support such mobility" and "these were precisely the conditions that existed in Australia during the early decades of the twentieth century, where leading Australian professionals, public administrators and educators were increasingly drawn to American ideas on industrial reform."[117] According to Richard Dunford, however, evidence for the extent to which scientific management was truly applied in Australia as claimed is sparse.[118] Take the New South Wales railway workers as a case in point. The workers struck to protest the introduction of a "card system" that was considered an application of scientific management. The card system involved recording on a piece of stiff paper how long it took each worker to perform individual jobs. Neither Taylor nor any of his followers would have considered this an example of Taylor's methods.

And Beyond

Records in the Taylor Collection at the Stevens Institute of Technology detailing the early dissemination and translation of Taylor's *Shop Management* and *The Principles of Scientific Management* are at best incomplete. Both volumes appeared in various formats and venues throughout the world. Translated by Ramón Alvarez Martinez in 1911 with the title *Principios del Manejo Científico*, *The Principles of Scientific Management* was published in Mexico in a private edition by Adolfo Prieto for use by the Compañía Fundidora de Fierro y Acero de Monterrey. Henrijs Simsons, the Latvian government's representative in London, contacted Taylor in 1912 for permission to translate *The Principles of Scientific Management* into Lettish.[119] Similarly, William L. Church, president of the Ambursen Hydraulic Construction Company, wrote to Taylor in 1911 on behalf of the New England Esperanto Association to inquire about the possibility of translating

---

[113] Fang Zhuo, "*Kēxué de gōngyè guǎnlǐfǎ*" ["Scientific Industrial Management"], *Jin bu* 1(6) (April 1912), section 4, pp. 1–6; Dingxin Yi, "Gōngzī jìsuàn fǎ" ["Payroll Calculation Methods"], *Zhonghua Shi Ye Jie* 1(3) (March 1914), pp. 1–6; Quan Yang, "Rénshì zhī xiàolǜ" ["Human Efficiency"], *Ke xue* 1(11) (November 1915), pp. 1209–1221. Yang was also known as Xingfo Yang.

[114] Stephen L. Morgan, "Transfer of Taylorist Ideas to China, 1910–1930s," *Journal of Management History* 12(4) (2006), pp. 408–424.

[115] Chris Wright. "Taylorism Reconsidered: The Impact of Scientific Management within the Australian Workplace," *Labour History* no. 64 (May 1993), p. 39.

[116] Lucy Taksa, "The Cultural Diffusion of Scientific Management: The United States and New South Wales," *Journal of Industrial Relations* 37(3) (September 1995), pp. 427–461.

[117] *Idem*, "Uniting Management and Education in Pursuit of Efficiency: F. W. Taylor's Training Reform Legacy," *Economic and Labour Relations Review* 17(2) (April 2007), p. 133.

[118] Dunford, "Scientific Management in Australia: A Discussion Paper," p. 506.

[119] Frederick W. Taylor, *Zinātniskās rīcības principi* [*Principles of Scientific Action*], trans. Henrijs Simsons (Rigâ, Latvia: Apgahdajis A. Gulbis, 1912).

The Principles of Scientific Management into Esperanto, "the universal language."[120] Whether the Church translation ever appeared in print is unknown. Alejandro López promoted Taylor's work to Colombian engineers, translating two articles from the U.S. journal *Railways and Locomotive Engineering* in 1912. The articles "El pago de trabajo por unidades" ("Unit Work Payment") and "Manejo científico" ("Scientific Management") appeared in the Medellín newspaper *La Organización*, nos. 755 and 762, January 12 and February 14, 1912.[121]

In reviewing the spread of scientific management in both the United States and throughout the world, a key point should be kept in mind. As Richard Dunford explains, "It is important not to confuse the existence of scientific management as a form of rhetoric with its existence as a concrete practice."[122] From years of consulting in Europe, C. Bertrand Thompson would have agreed with Dunford's assessment in noting that there was "a large group of shameless fakers, mostly unemployed bookkeepers, who solicited clients from house to house and got quite a number of them at bargain rates."[123] Thompson stated that he had even "seen the installation of an adding machine, or even of a telephone, referred to as 'Taylorization.'"[124] In instances such as the New South Wales railway strike, it seems that worker "hostility to Taylorism was based more on the fear of what could be done with [Taylor's] techniques than what had actually been done."[125]

SCIENTIFIC MANAGEMENT IN INDUSTRIAL PRACTICE

The international practice of scientific management is evident in the work of C. Bertrand Thompson's and Wallace Clark's consulting firms throughout Europe. Thompson's "Taylor-Thompson System" adapted Taylor's ideas to fit the situations he faced, particularly in working with labor unions. For example, Thompson joined with union representatives in a successful installation of Taylor's methods at General Electric's plant at Nancy, France. He declined, however, to do the same at its German plant, as its labor contract prohibited employee bonus payments. Thompson's firm was a model for others, and he left behind a cadre of trained consultants, including Suzanne Garcin-Guynet, the first female management consultant in France.[126]

Wallace Clark worked for Henry L. Gantt's consulting firm and, after Gantt's death, became the foremost promoter of his ideas. Clark demonstrated the versatility of Gantt charts in sales, personnel, production, finance, and budgeting. His work was successful in all but a few instances, such as in the Soviet Union where he refused to follow Polakov's work, believing that "political conditions" would prevail over thorough study and implementation.[127] Trained by Taylor and Gantt, Thompson and Clark provided a better understanding of the practice of scientific management in an international setting.

In the United States, companies such as Plimpton Press, Link-Belt, Tabor Manufacturing, and Joseph & Feiss were considered model scientific-management installations.

[120] William L. Church to Frederick W. Taylor, June 19, 1911; Taylor to Church, June 22, 1911; Church to Taylor, June 26, 1911. Frederick W. Taylor Collection, SCW.001. Archives and Special Collections; Samuel C. Williams Library, Stevens Institute of Technology, Hoboken, NJ.

[121] Personal (email) correspondence from Alberto Mayor Mora to Arthur G. Bedeian, August 12, 2019. See also Alberto Mayor Mora, *Técnica y utopía: biografía intelectual y política de Alejandro López, 1876–1940* [*Technique and Utopia: Intellectual and Political Biography of Alejandro López, 1876–1940*] (Medellín, Colombia: Fondo Editorial Universidad Escuela de Administración, Finanzas e Instituto Tecnológico, 2001); Luis Antonio Orozco and Olga Lucía Anzola-Morales, "A Colombian Classic Management Thinker: Alejandro López Restrepo," *Journal of Management History* 25(2) (2019), pp. 221–236.

[122] Richard Dunford, "Scientific Management in Australia: A Discussion Paper," *Labour & Industry* 1(3) (October 1988), pp. 505–515.

[123] C. Bertrand Thompson, "The Taylor System in Europe," *Advanced Management: Quarterly Journal* 5(4) (October–December 1940), p. 173.

[124] *Ibid.*, p. 172.

[125] Dunford, "*Scientific Management in Australia: A Discussion Paper*," p. 507.

[126] Wren, Greenwood, Teahen, and Bedeian, "C. Bertrand Thompson and Management Consulting in Europe, 1917–1934," pp. 15–39.

[127] Daniel A. Wren, "Implementing the Gantt Chart in Europe and Britain: The Contributions of Wallace Clark," *Journal of Management History* 21(3) (2015), pp. 309–327.

Henry P. Kendall, manager of the Plimpton Press (Norwood, Massachusetts), was an early promoter of scientific management in the printing industry. He thought that industrial plants could become efficient by viewing themselves as systems comprised of interacting parts, but that a greater long-run effect could be achieved only if the scientific-management philosophy was fully accepted by all parties.[128] Plimpton Press also developed an advanced employment department, with centralized hiring, disciplining, and discharging (see Chapter 9). Plimpton Press's employment manager, Jane C. Williams, credited scientific management with reducing labor turnover from 186 percent in 1912 to 13 percent in 1916.[129] James M. Dodge's Link-Belt Company (Philadelphia, Pennsylvania) was a showcase installation for Taylor's methods.[130]

Wilfred Lewis, president of the Tabor Manufacturing Company (Philadelphia, Pennsylvania), a machine-tool producer, was an authority on gearing and an advocate of metric reform. At Tabor, Taylor's principles were credited with increasing output by 250 percent.[131] King Hathaway, general manager of Tabor Manufacturing, advocated careful planning before installing Taylor's methods, including an extensive program of educating workers and supervisors on the principles and purposes of scientific management. At Joseph & Feiss Company (Cleveland, Ohio), Richard A. Feiss recognized the merits of scientific management in the labor-intensive clothing industry. Feiss implemented time-and-motion study, provided bonuses for performance and attendance, installed a planning department to smooth workflow, and employed an orthopedic surgeon to design chairs and tables for worker comfort, reduced fatigue, and increased efficiency. Mary B. Gilson, who headed the Joseph & Feiss Employment and Services Department (see Chapter 9), championed employment testing, proper selection and placement, promoting women to supervisory positions, and other advanced practices that made her the era's best known and most influential personnel manager.[132] At Joseph & Feiss, Taylor's methods were combined with the best innovative ideas in the emerging personnel-management movement.

C. Bertrand Thompson noted that an increase in the "stability of payroll" was one of the many benefits of scientific management in practice.[133] He was referring to employment stabilization through improved production planning, employee selection and placement, and job training. Scientific management sought to reduce costs, and labor turnover was a major expense. General Electric's Magnus Alexander conducted the first reported statistical analysis of labor.[134] He found that, in 1912, for 12 GE factories, 22,031 employees were new, unnecessary hires, amounting to a turnover rate greater than 55 percent. The attrition was estimated to cost $831,030, which included the expense of hiring and training, as well as reduced production while new hires were learning their jobs. Joseph Willits, an instructor at the renamed Wharton School of Finance and Commerce, replicated Alexander's study in a group of Philadelphia textile mills. He found turnover rates ranging from 50 to 100 percent, and, occasionally, rates that even reached 500 percent.[135] Willits recommended improvements in employee selection and placement, employee training, and wage incentives to bolster employee retention. In brief, Taylor's search for "first-class

[128] Henry P. Kendall, "Unsystematized, Systematized, and Scientific Management," in Thompson, ed., *Scientific Management*, pp. 103–131.

[129] Jane C. Williams, "The Reduction of Labor Turnover in the Plimpton Press," *Annals of the American Academy of Political and Social Science* 71 (May 1917), pp. 71–81.

[130] See George P. Torrence, *James Mapes Dodge* (New York: Newcomen Society of North America, 1950); James M. Dodge, "A History of the Introduction of a System of Shop Management," in Thompson, ed., *Scientific Management*, pp. 226–231.

[131] Wilfred Lewis, "An Object Lesson in Efficiency," in Thompson, ed., *Scientific Management*, pp. 232–241. See also H. King Hathaway, "Wilfred Lewis," *Bulletin of the Taylor Society* 15(1) (February 1930), pp. 45–46.

[132] David J. Goldberg, "Richard A. Feiss, Mary Barnett Gilson, and Scientific Management at Joseph & Feiss, 1909–1925," in Nelson, ed., *A Mental Revolution*, pp. 40–57.

[133] C. Bertrand Thompson, *The Taylor System of Scientific Management* (New York: A. W. Shaw, 1917), p. 27.

[134] Magnus W. Alexander, "Hiring and Firing: Its Economic Waste and How to Avoid It," *Annals of the American Academy of Political and Social Science* 65 (May 1916), pp. 128–144. See also Kyle D. Bruce, "Magnus Alexander, the Economists and Labour Turnover," *Business History* 47(4) (October 2005), pp. 493–510.

[135] Joseph H. Willits, "The Labor Turn-Over and the Humanizing of Industry," *Annals of the American Academy of Political and Social Science* 61 (September 1915), pp. 127–137.

workers" and Münsterberg's search for the "best possible worker for the best possible effect" both contributed to lower labor turnover and stabilized employment. Labor turnover carried a high cost, both for employees and employers, and scientific management sought to eliminate such wastefulness.

THE HOXIE REPORT

Organized labor's opposition to scientific management found further voice in an investigation conducted under the auspices of the U.S. Commission on Industrial Relations.[136] The investigation's purpose was to examine the competing claims of organized labor and scientific-management advocates regarding working conditions under the Taylor system.[137] Robert F. Hoxie, an associate professor of political economy at the University of Chicago, directed the investigation. He was assisted by Robert G. Valentine, chairman of the Massachusetts Minimum Wage Commission (see Chapter 9), representing "employing management in general," and John Frey, editor of the *International Molders' Journal*, representing organized labor. Over the period from January to April 1915, some or all of the investigators inspected 30 industrial plants that had, in whole or part, adopted scientific management.[138]

An early inkling of the controversy that was to follow occurred when Hoxie insisted on making no distinction (as suggested by Dunford above) between scientific management as "a form of rhetoric and its existence as a concrete practice." To Hoxie, scientific management was what was practiced by any firm if that firm called it "scientific"; to Taylor, scientific management ceased to exist if the principles and philosophy he had established were violated in practice. Hoxie's logic did not impress Taylor, and this undoubtedly led to Taylor's unfavorable opinion of a report Hoxie prepared detailing the investigators' findings. Taylor's numerous objections to Hoxie's claims are detailed in an appendix attached to the report.[139]

The Hoxie report described a high degree of diversity among the 30 plants inspected. The investigators found that the precepts of scientific management were often violated in practice. They disclosed that many so-called "efficiency experts" who promised quick returns did not have "the ability or the willingness to install scientific management in accordance with the Taylor formula and ideals."[140] Functional foremanship was discovered to have few adherents in practice. Some plants tried using functional foremen but soon returned to the old style, line type of organization. In a third area of inquiry, the investigators established that little or no progress was being made with respect to scientifically selecting workers. "Labor heads," an early designation for employment or personnel managers, were poorly trained and of "doubtful experience and capacity."[141]

[136] This section draws on Christopher T. Nyland, "Taylorism, John R. Commons, and the Hoxie Report," *Journal of Economic Issues* 30(4) (December 1996), pp. 985–1016.

[137] Although the Hoxie Report is the most widely cited investigation on the workplace impact of scientific management, it should be noted that an earlier study into the earnings and expenditures of working women in New York City highlighted the positive impact of scientific management, with wages having increased in one instance "from $6 to between $8 and $10" a week. See Sue Ainslie Clark and Edith Wyatt, *Making Both Ends Meet: The Income and Outlay of New York Working Girls* (New York: Macmillan, 1911), pp. 223–270, and Wyatt's testimony in *Hearings before Special Committee of the House of Representatives to Investigate the Taylor and Other Systems of Shop Management under Authority of House Resolution 90*, vol. 1 (Washington, DC: U.S. Government Printing Office, 1912), p. 595.

[138] Robert F. Hoxie, *Scientific Management and Labor* (New York: Appleton-Century-Crofts, 1915), p. 4. See also *idem*, "Scientific Management and Social Welfare," *The Survey* 35(23) (March 4, 1916), pp. 673–680, 685–686; *idem*, "Scientific Management and Labor Welfare," *Journal of Political Economy* 24(9) (November 1916), pp. 833–854; and *idem*, "Why Organized Labor Opposes Scientific Management," *Quarterly Journal of Economics* 31(1) (November 1916), pp. 62–85.

[139] *Ibid.*, "Appendix II: The Labor Claims of Scientific Management According to Mr. Frederick W. Taylor," pp. 140–149. Gantt in Appendix III (pp. 150–151) and Emerson in Appendix IV (pp. 152–168) also filed statements taking exception to Hoxie's claims. The three statements do not present a unified theory of the scientific-management movement, but do agree on its fundamental aims.

[140] *Ibid.*, p. 29.

[141] *Ibid.*, p. 32.

Instruction and training of workers was another area in which practice fell far short of theory. Learning was by trial-and-error, as trained instructors were scarce, and instruction often focused on attaining a level of output rather than teaching employees how to do quality work. Despite these shortfalls, the Hoxie report concluded that training practices in scientific-management plants were generally better than those that could be found elsewhere in industry. A fifth area of concern, and of greater criticism, was the use of time study and task setting. Standards and performance incentives were often established after only a cursory inquiry. This led to inaccuracies and injustices. In general, time-study men were poorly trained and inexperienced, and often set rates based on management's desires rather than true scientific inquiry and observation. Piece-rate pay plans also came under scrutiny. The investigators found no pure adoptions of the Taylor, Gantt, or Emerson piece-rate pay plans. The Midvale differential piece-rate plan, used briefly by Taylor, was infrequently encountered, and most plans were modifications of the Gantt and Emerson plans.

On a broader plane, the Hoxie report tried to reconcile Taylor's position with that of unions regarding industrial democracy. Taylor maintained that scientific management was the essence of industrial democracy. His argument hinged upon harmony and a mutuality of interest between labor and management. Employees were rewarded based on their effort; workplace discipline fell under scientifically derived laws and not under autocratic, driving management; and protests were to be handled by reliance upon scientific inquiry and mutual resolution. In the union view, however, scientific management monopolized knowledge and power in the hands of management by denying workers a voice in setting work standards, determining wage rates, and establishing conditions of employment. Moreover, it created a spirit of mutual suspicion among employees and destroyed the solidarity and cooperative spirit of labor by emphasizing individual performance. Furthermore, it weakened the protection that unions gave employees and, in turn, stymied the labor movement.

Siding with labor, the Hoxie investigators concluded that industrial democracy could come only through the collective-bargaining process. They saw no possibility for an enlightened management and seemed dedicated to the proposition that the interests of labor and management were inalterably opposed for all times and in all places. In addition, they found no evidence of union officials or union members resisting workplace improvements. On this count, their examination was less than equitable. They, however, accused management of seeking shortcuts to efficiency, faulted Taylor for trying to generalize his machine-shop experience to all types and sizes of firms, and denounced "efficiency experts" that were guilty of selling patent-medicine panaceas to employers who were eager to improve employee performance.

Those who criticize are also open to criticism. What can be said about the methods the investigators used to reach their conclusions? Hoxie, as well as Frey and Valentine, attempted to be fair to Taylor by acknowledging that the rhetoric associated with purported applications of Taylor's methods fell far short of reality. Their predilections toward organized labor, however, resulted in a demonstrable bias. In this regard, there is evidence that their methods were less than meticulous. Mary B. Gilson, at Joseph & Feiss Company, one of the plants included in the study, wrote that when Hoxie and Frey visited, they held a brief interview with Richard A. Feiss and some of his managers, took a few notes, but never visited the plant's work floor. They promised to return to see working conditions in the plant, but never did.[142] If this encounter was characteristic of the investigators' conduct at the other plants they visited, one must conclude that the investigators were less than forthright. It is unfortunate that those charged with conducting a thorough study of scientific management in its early days did so with closed minds and hasty feet.

Christopher T. Nyland noted that the Hoxie report was "heavily skewed" toward organized labor's position and, consequently, "the Taylorists were charged publicly with a great many

[142] Mary B. Gilson, *What's Past Is Prologue: Reflections on My Industrial Experiences* (New York: Harper & Brothers, 1940), p. 93.

crimes, found innocent of none and guilty of many."[143] A pro-labor bias was also evident in the selection of Robert Valentine to represent "employing management in general." Although Valentine considered himself an impartial labor expert who could bring workers and management together, he also believed that government should be used to protect workers from the negative effects of industrialization.[144] Taylor objected to Valentine's appointment given Valentine's lack of business experience and unfamiliarity with scientific management. In previous testimony before the U.S. Commission on Industrial Relations, Valentine had admitted his only experience with scientific management was, "I have run into it on the slant in a number of places . . . a half dozen cases." When asked whether employees should participate if "any efficiency system" was undertaken, he responded, "I not only think the individual should participate, but I think he should participate as a part of a union."[145] In effect, scientific management was without a representative in the Hoxie-Valentine-Frey investigation.

When John Frey reminisced for a Columbia University oral history project, he admitted that "when he and Hoxie came across evidence that did not support the claims of the AFL [American Federation of Labor], he reworked the data until it confirmed his preconceived ideas."[146] Frey also had unfavorable memories of both Valentine, who "didn't care to come" to plant visits or their meetings, and Hoxie, who Frey viewed as someone who "knew little of practical matters" and "even less about work, workers, and industry."[147]

John R. Commons, a member of the Commission on Industrial Relations, recalled two other events that shaped the Commission's overall work. Charles McCarthy, the Commission's director of research and a Taylor supporter, was charged with overseeing the Hoxie-led investigation. The Commission's chair, Frank P. Walsh, a labor attorney from Kansas City, Missouri, soon found reasons to disagree with McCarthy and dismissed him. Similarly, Walsh reassigned or discharged all the individuals Commons selected as his assistants; he had previously refused to approve vouchers to pay anyone Commons hired.[148] Ultimately, Walsh also fired Hoxie. This explains why the Hoxie report was never released by the Commission but was independently published in 1915. Upon its publication, both the academic community and scientific-management advocates harshly reviewed the Hoxie Report. British economist Charles W. Mixter commented that "irrespective of its intent the effect of [Hoxie's] book as a whole will be to multiply misconceptions and misunderstandings with regard to the scientific management practice."[149] Hoxie and his colleagues had botched an exceptional opportunity to examine the relations between organized labor and scientific management and purposefully misled generations of scholars about their findings.

THE THOMPSON AND NELSON STUDIES

The findings of two other inquiries—one conducted during the height of the scientific-management movement and another conducted more recently—of organizations employing

[143] Nyland, "Taylorism, John R. Commons, and the Hoxie Report," p. 1007.

[144] Brad Snyder, *The House of Truth: A Washington Political Salon and the Foundations of American Liberalism* (New York: Oxford University Press, 2017), pp. 63–64. See also Ordway Tead, "Industrial Counselor, A New Profession," *The Independent* 88 (3548) (December 4, 1916), pp. 393–395.

[145] *Industrial Relations: Final Report and Testimony Submitted to Congress by the Commission on Industrial Relations*, vol. 1 (Washington, DC: U.S. Government Printing Office, 1916), p. 853.

[146] John P. Frey, *Reminiscences of John Phillip Frey*. Interview conducted December 22, 1954, Washington, D.C. (New York: Columbia University Oral History Collection, Columbia University, 1953), p. 290. For Frey's contemporaneous account of the Hoxie-Valentine-Frey investigation, see *idem, Scientific Management and Labor* (New York: Efficiency Society, 1916) or "Scientific Management and Labor," *American Federationist* 23(4) (April 1916), pp. 257–268 and (May 1916), pp. 358–368.

[147] *Ibid.*, pp. 287–288. Frey's 1954 assessment of Hoxie contrasts with his laudatory comments following Hoxie's death on June 22, 1916. See John P. Frey, "Robert F. Hoxie: Investigator and Interpreter," *Journal of Political Economy* 24(9) (November 1916), pp. 884–893.

[148] John R. Commons, *Myself* (New York: Macmillan, 1934), pp. 176–177.

[149] Charles W. Mixter, [Review of the book *Scientific Management and Labor*], *American Economic Review* 6 (June 1916), p. 376.

"the Taylor system of scientific management" contrast with the manner and method of the Hoxie report. C. Bertrand Thompson studied 172 "definitely known" applications of scientific management in 80 types of organizations, including factories, municipal governments, department stores, and publishing houses. Of the applications, 149 were in factories. In 113 factories, the applications had progressed far enough to permit a summary analysis. Of these, 59 were judged complete successes, 20 partially successful, and 34 failures. Thompson attributed the failures to "the personality of the consulting engineers and . . . the personality of the managements."[150] Failures by consulting engineers were due largely to their "inexperience and incompetence," whereas management failures were attributed to hasty installations, impatience with the initial pace of results, dissension within a factory's management group, and factors completely outside the control of management (e.g., the prevailing business cycle). With one exception, no failure was attributed to difficulties with workmen.[151]

Thompson was aware of the Hoxie report and commented on the inclusion of plants that were not truly scientifically managed:

> If the system in the plant was developed by Mr. Taylor personally, or by any of his assistants or co-workers while associated with him, then the Taylor system may be held responsible for the results; otherwise not.
>
> When this qualification is kept in mind, an impartial investigator must admit that, from the view-point of the employer, the employee or the public, the Taylor system is a demonstrated success.[152]

In a second study, Daniel M. Nelson investigated 29 applications of scientific management, each directed by one of Taylor's closest followers. Although variations occurred, Nelson found a pattern of "general adherence to Taylor's ideas."[153] The two ideas that were least likely to have been instituted were the differential piece-rate (even Taylor had embraced the Gantt plan) and functional foremanship. Nelson also noted a "strong positive correlation" between scientific management and industrial efficiency. Except for heat-using industries such as beverages, petroleum refining, and chemicals, scientific management was "associated with growth, not stagnation."[154] Scientific management was used mostly in batch-assembly (job shop) and labor-intensive non-assembly operations. In more capital-intensive industries (such as smelting primary metals), scientific management was less likely to be applied. In the automobile industry, scientific management was practiced before the acceptance of Henry Ford's assembly line, but not afterward (see Chapter 12). Barth and George Babcock were successful at the Franklin Motor Car Company, for example, but once the moving assembly-line and mass-production techniques came to the auto industry, scientific-management methods were less useful.[155]

Nelson noted that scientific management was seen as a "partial solution to the labor problem," meaning a partial solution to finding a "scientific" basis for performance incentives.[156] It was organized labor's view that scientific management "tends to eliminate skilled crafts . . . degrades the skilled worker . . . [and] displaces skilled workers and forces them into competition with the less skilled."[157] The belief that skilled labor would be displaced by workplace

---

[150] Thompson, *The Taylor System of Scientific Management*, p. 13.
[151] C. Bertrand Thompson, *The Theory and Practice of Management* (Boston, MA: Houghton Mifflin, 1917), pp. 100–101.
[152] Thompson, *The Taylor System of Scientific Management*, pp. 13, 25.
[153] Daniel M. Nelson, "Scientific Management, Systematic Management, and Labor, 1880–1915," *Business History Review* 48(4) (Winter 1974), p. 500. See also *idem*, "Industrial Engineering and the Industrial Enterprise, 1890–1940," in Naomi R. Lamoreaux and Daniel M. G. Raff, eds., *Coordination and Information: Historical Perspectives on the Organization of Enterprise* (Chicago, IL: University of Chicago Press, 1995), pp. 35–50.
[154] *Idem*, "Taylorism," *Proceedings of the International Colloquium on Taylorism* (Paris: Éditions la Découverte, 1984), pp. 55–57.
[155] Charles B. Gordy, "Scientific Management in the Automobile Industry" (Doctoral dissertation, University of Michigan, Ann Arbor, MI, 1929), pp. 5–7.
[156] Nelson, "Scientific Management, Systematic Management, and Labor, 1880–1915," p. 479.
[157] Hoxie, *Scientific Management and Labor*, p. 16.

improvements is as old as the Luddites who protested the introduction of waterpower to replace handloom weavers (see Chapter 3). In the case of scientific management, however, improved work processes rather than machinery threatened organized labor. Later writers have perpetuated the notion that scientific management "deskilled" or dumbed-down jobs as a means of decreasing management's dependence on skilled labor.[158]

What is the evidence for such claims? If scientific management deskilled jobs, we would expect a decline in the number of craft workers and an increase in the number of unskilled laborers in the United States from 1900 to 1930. U.S. Census Bureau data indicate, however, that the number of "craftsmen and kindred workers," excluding foremen, increased 72 percent from 1900 to 1920 (2,900,000 to 4,997,000) and 96 percent from 1900 to 1930 (2,900,000 to 5,695,000). Similarly, the number of "operative and kindred workers" (semiskilled) increased 77 percent from 1900 to 1920 (3,720,000 to 6,587,000) and 107 percent from 1900 to 1930 (3,720,000 to 7,691,000). The number of unskilled laborers, excluding farmers and miners, increased at a lesser pace: 35 percent from 1900 to 1920 (3,620,000 to 4,905,000), and 47 percent from 1900 to 1930 (3,620,000 to 5,321,400).[159]

Sociologist Douglas M. Eichar took a different tack, examining blue-collar workers by skill level as a percentage of the total U.S. labor force. Craft workers were 10.5 percent of the labor force in 1900, 13 percent in 1920; semiskilled operatives increased from 12.8 percent in 1900 to 15.6 percent in 1920; and unskilled nonfarm laborers decreased from 12.5 percent in 1900 to 11.6 percent in 1920.[160] Both in absolute numbers and as a percentage of the U.S. work force, the number of skilled craft and semiskilled operatives increased while the number of unskilled laborers grew at a far slower pace. The claim that scientific management deskilled the general labor force is a myth that should be put to rest.[161]

In summary, scientific management became an international movement in the first two decades of the twentieth century. In his assessment of organizations applying scientific management, C. Bertrand Thompson cautioned that a key distinction between the "Taylor system" and the "Taylor spirit" must be kept in mind. Thompson observed that, "the System has served and should continue to be made to serve as a symbol, or if you like, an ideal and a model without which principles tend to dissipate into an ever less intense influence and 'spirit,' as has to a large extent already occurred."[162] Thompson's observation continues to be true today as the "spirit" of Taylor's principles still influences modern industry throughout the world.

EMERGING GENERAL MANAGEMENT

Although scientific management as a way of thinking dominated the industrial landscape during the last part of the nineteenth century and the early part of the twentieth century, there were indications that a broader conception of management was emerging. This broadening was grounded in the challenge of managing the increasing number of large-scale enterprises and the resulting need to further examine and refine managerial practices. Before turning to this emergence, however, we will first consider how scientific management inspired other academic disciplines, such

[158] See, for example, C. Wright Mills, *White Collar: The American Middle Classes* (New York: Oxford University Press, 1951), pp. 224–225; David Montgomery, *The Fall of the House of Labor: The Workplace, the State and American Labor Activism, 1865–1925* (Cambridge, England: Cambridge University Press, 1987), pp. 214–256; Harry Braverman, *Labor and Monopoly Capitalism* (New York: Monthly Review Press, 1974), pp. 85–168; Daniel C. Clawson, *Bureaucracy and the Labor Process: The Transformation of U.S. Industry, 1860–1920* (New York: Monthly Review Press, 1980), p. 231; and Donald R. Stabile, *Prophets of Order: The Rise of the New Class, Technocracy and Socialism in America* (Boston, MA: South End Press, 1984), pp. 42–45.
[159] U.S. Department of Commerce, Bureau of the Census, *Historical Statistics of the United States: Colonial Times to 1970*, pt. 1 (Washington, DC: Bureau of the Census, 1975), pp. 139–142.
[160] Douglas M. Eichar, *Occupation and Class Consciousness in America* (New York: Greenwood, 1989), Table 4.1, p. 47.
[161] For a further analysis of data from 1920 to 1935 that reaches a similar conclusion, see Daniel M. Nelson, "Scientific Management and the Workplace, 1920–1935," in Sanford M. Jacoby, ed., *Masters to Managers: Historical and Comparative Perspectives on American Employers* (New York: Columbia University Press, 1991), pp. 74–89.
[162] Thompson, "The Taylor System in Europe," p. 172.

as public administration, office management, marketing, and accounting, to search for improved methods; encouraged an interest in the theory and practice of organization design; provided a basis for the study of business policy; and spawned a philosophy of management.

THE IMPACT OF SCIENTIFIC MANAGEMENT ON OTHER DISCIPLINES

Stimulated by scientific management, other academic disciplines began to search for efficiency through science. William H. Leffingwell applied the principles of scientific management to office management.[163] Leonard D. White picked up where Morris L. Cooke left off and contributed to public administration. White was the first to teach public administration in the classroom and pioneered in personnel management for government agencies.[164] Ralph Starr Butler, Louis D. H. Weld, Paul T. Cherington, Paul D. Converse, and others expanded scientific management to marketing goods and services.[165]

Accounting saw the development of standard costing in Emerson's and Taylor's use of the railroad system of accounts. Through a combination of ideas associated with economic analysis in engineering and accounting, managers were first exposed to contingencies in financial planning and control. The relationships among the volume of production, fixed costs, variable costs, sales, and profits had long been a vexing managerial conundrum. An engineer, Henry Hess, developed a "crossover" chart in 1903, which showed the relationship among these variables.[166] In the chart, the "crossover point" is the point where total costs equaled total revenues; that is, the point where losses turned to profits. Walter Rautenstrauch, a professor at Columbia University, coined the phrase "break-even point" in 1922 to describe the same set of relationships.[167] In the same year, John H. Williams, an accountant, popularized the idea of a "flexible budget," showing how management could plan and control at various levels of output.[168] Taken together, these advances enabled managers to better forecast, control, and account for unforeseen marketplace developments.

James O. McKinsey pioneered in using budgets as planning and controlling aids. McKinsey, like Taylor, deplored traditional postmortem uses of accounting. Rather than treating accounting as an end unto itself, he viewed budgets as an aid in making operational decisions. For McKinsey, a budget was not a set of figures, but a way of assigning responsibility and measuring performance.[169] As a former professor at the University of Chicago, and later as a senior partner of McKinsey and Co., McKinsey was also influential in the early days of the American Management Association (AMA). The AMA was formed in 1923 (see Chapter 9) to be somewhat of a continuing education program for practicing managers. Its objective was to broaden the study of management to encompass not only production control and personnel administration, but to include sales, financial, and other facets of management. Slowly, but undeniably, management

[163] William Henry Leffingwell, *Scientific Office Management* (Chicago, IL: A. W. Shaw, 1917). See also, Frank B. Copley, "Exactly Why Some Are Promoted—and Others Are Not," *American Magazine* 89(1) (January 1920), pp. 18–19, 241, 245.
[164] Leonard D. White, *Introduction to the Study of Public Administration* (New York: Macmillan, 1926); *idem, The City Manager* (Chicago, IL: University of Chicago Press, 1927).
[165] For the extent of scientific management's influence on these and other pioneers, see Joseph C. Seibert, "Marketing's Role in Scientific Management," in Robert L. Clewett, ed., *Marketing's Role in Scientific Management* (Chicago, IL: American Marketing Association, 1957), pp. 1–3; Robert Bartels, *The Development of Marketing Thought* (Homewood, IL: Richard D. Irwin, 1962); and Paul D. Converse, *The Beginnings of Marketing Thought in the United States* (Austin, TX: Bureau of Business Research, University of Texas, 1959).
[166] Henry Hess, "Manufacturing: Capital, Costs, Profits, and Dividends," *Engineering Magazine* 26 (December 1903), pp. 367–379.
[167] Walter Rautenstrauch, "The Budget as a Means of Industrial Control," *Chemical & Metallurgical Engineering* 27(9) (August 30, 1922), pp. 411–416.
[168] John Howell Williams, *The Flexible Budget* (New York: McGraw-Hill, 1934).
[169] James O. McKinsey, *Budgeting* (New York: Ronald Press, 1922); *Organization* (New York: Ronald Press, 1922); *Budgetary Control* (New York: Ronald Press, 1922); and *Managerial Accounting* (Chicago, IL: University of Chicago Press, 1924). See also William B. Wolf, *Management and Consulting: An Introduction to James O. McKinsey* (Ithaca, NY: Cornell University Press, 1978).

education was beginning to shift from an emphasis on shop-floor routines toward a wider perspective that covered all areas of business.

EARLY ORGANIZATION THEORY

During the 1920s, the study of organizations primarily focused on designing relationships among individuals and departments. The early factory system, based on the division of labor, required the coordination of effort, and the grouping of activities into departments that satisfied this requirement. As we have noted, most firms were family owned and managed, with few employees. They relied on personal supervision to coordinate a firm's activities. In 1896, Englishman J. Slater Lewis authored a "handbook for the use of manufacturers who wish to adopt modern methods of organization." As Slater explained, the book was "written throughout from the point of view of an organizer and manager."[170] The text has been referred to as the "first significant book on management in English."[171] With each of these developments, there was a growing recognition that new organization forms were necessary to coordinate the activities of industrial undertakings that were unprecedented in size and scope.

In 1909, Russell Robb, an executive with Stone & Webster engineering firm, gave a series of four lectures in the Industrial Organization course at the newly formed Harvard Graduate School of Business Administration.[172] In the lectures, Robb argued that rather than uniformly applying a traditional military command-and-control style of organizing, firms should be structured based on their individual goals and the unique demands of their specific industries. Robb anticipated modern contingency theorists (see Chapter 20) when he noted: "[A]ll organizations will differ somewhat from each other, because the objects, the results that are sought, and the way these results must be attained, are different . . . there is no 'royal road,' no formula that, once learned, may be applied in all cases with the assurance that the result will be perfect harmony, efficiency, and economy, and a sure path to the main purpose in view."[173] Thus, the goals pursued differed, as did the means (today we might say "strategy") to attain those goals, resulting in diverse patterns of organization. Based on this premise, Robb believed that because business objectives differed from those of the military, distinct styles of organizing were required. Much could be learned from the military as regards responsibility and authority, clearly defining duties and channels of communication, and providing for order and workplace discipline. The military, however, stressed a degree of control unnecessary in business. Robb maintained that because large-scale businesses demanded an extensive division of labor, they required greater coordination among their constituent elements than did their military counterparts. Business success was not based on obedience, but on economy of effort; therefore, the manner of organizing had to be different. More emphasis had to be placed on employee selection and training, workplace processes had to be arranged to achieve maximum efficiency, and managers had to be aware that a "great factor in organization is 'system,' the mechanism of the whole."[174] In taking a systems perspective, Robb's lectures were truly remarkable for the time, predating what became known in the early 1950s as "general systems theory" (see Chapter 21).

---

[170] J. Slater Lewis, *The Commercial Organisation of Factories: A Handbook for the Use of Manufacturers, Directors, Auditors, Engineers, Managers, Secretaries, Accountants, Cashiers, Estimate Clerks, Prime Cost Clerks, Bookkeepers, Draughtsmen, Students, Pupils, etc.* (London: E. & F. N. Spon Books, 1896), p. xxv. See also John S. Raworth, "Obituary Notices: Joseph Slater Lewis," *Journal of the Institution of Electrical Engineers* 31(158) (1901–2), pp. 1367–1368.

[171] Joseph A. Litterer, "The Emergence of Systematic Management as Shown by the Literature of Management from 1870 to 1900" (Doctoral dissertation, University of Illinois, Urbana, IL, 1959), p. 248; released in book form by Garland Press, New York, 1986.

[172] "Course for Business Men," *Harvard Crimson* (February 18, 1909), p. 1.

[173] Russell Robb, *Lectures on Organization* (Privately printed, 1910), pp. 3, 14. Serialized in *Stone & Webster Public Service Journal* 4(4) (April 1909), pp. 220–233; 4(5) (May 1909), pp. 301–313; 4(6) (June 1909), pp. 394–406. For further insights into Robb's thinking, see Edmund R. Gray and Hyler J. Bracey, "Russell Robb: Management Pioneer," *SAM Advanced Management Journal* 35(2) (April 1970), pp. 71–76.

[174] Robb, *Lectures on Organization*, p. 173.

SCIENTIFIC MANAGEMENT AT DUPONT AND GENERAL MOTORS

No story is more fascinating to management historians than the emergence of large-scale enterprises. Scientific management played a part in the development of two industrial giants—DuPont and General Motors. As noted in Chapter 7, in 1896 Taylor had worked closely with Johnson Company's founder Tom L. Johnson; Arthur J. Moxham, who worked in the company's comptroller office; and T. Coleman du Pont, the company's general manager, in developing a system to monitor the cost of raw materials. In 1902, cousins Pierre, Coleman, and Alfred I. du Pont purchased E. I. du Pont de Nemours and Company, after the demise of its president Eugene I. du Pont, to keep the powder company in family hands. Being familiar with Taylor's work at the Johnson Company and at its Steel Motor Works and Lorain Steel Railway subsidiaries, the du Ponts, and especially Pierre as president, sought to broaden Taylor's cost-accounting system to include a measure of overall company performance. Toward this end, as early as 1903, the DuPont Company used "return on investment" (ROI; the ratio between net profit and total capital investment) to not only measure the relative efficiency of its operating departments and the financial performance of the overall company, but to allocate funds across product lines.[175] Pierre is credited with implementing the financial, operational, and managerial techniques necessary to turn the DuPont Company into one of the world's largest multidivisional enterprises. In doing so, he emulated the cost-accounting system Taylor developed at the Johnson Company and its subsidiaries.[176] The influence of Harrington Emerson is similarly evident in the DuPont Company's early development. The company's general manager, Hamilton M. Barksdale, created a line and staff structure that closely followed Emerson's recommendations. Reflecting the systems perspective advocated by Russell Robb, Barksdale also developed uniform objectives and policies for DuPont's divisions and decentralized authority to the division level.[177]

Donaldson Brown, Barksdale's cousin, was another key figure in the DuPont Company's early years. Brown developed a formula to measure the performance of each department within the company. The formula $R = T \times P$ (where R is the rate of return on capital invested, T the rate of turnover on invested capital, and P the percentage of profit on sales) provided a means of comparing performance across departments.[178] Brown also created the famous DuPont Chart System, which was used for corporate decision-making for over half a century before new information technologies emerged for the presentation of financial data.[179]

The General Motors Corporation, founded in 1908, adapted the multidivisional structure developed at DuPont. William C. Durant created General Motors (GM) from a collection of motorcar and parts producers. The combination was unwieldy, and, in 1920, General Motors was saved from financial ruin by an infusion of du Pont family money. Durant resigned, and Pierre du Pont came out of semiretirement to become GM's president. Pierre made at least two key staffing decisions: he brought Donaldson Brown to General Motors as chief financial officer, and he handpicked Alfred P. Sloan, Jr., to be his successor. Sloan took over the GM reins in 1923.

---

[175] H. Thomas Johnson, "Management Accounting in an Early Integrated Industry: E. I. Du Pont de Nemours Powder Company, 1903–1912," *Business History Review* 49(2) (Summer 1975), p. 189; Robert S. Kaplan, "The Evolution of Management Accounting," *Accounting Review* 59(3) (July 1964), p. 397.

[176] Alfred D. Chandler, Jr., and Stephen Salisbury, *Pierre S. du Pont and the Making of the Modern Corporation* (New York: Harper & Row, 1971), p. xxi.

[177] Ernest Dale, *The Great Organizers* (New York: McGraw-Hill, 1960). See also Dale and Charles Meloy, "Hamilton McFarland Barksdale and the Du Pont Contributions to Scientific Management," *Business History Review* 36(2) (Summer 1962), pp. 127–152.

[178] F. Donaldson Brown, *Some Reminiscences of an Industrialist* (unpublished manuscript, Hagley Museum and Library, Wilmington, DE, 1957), pp. 26–28. See also Ernest Dale, Regina S. Greenwood, and Ronald G. Greenwood, "Donaldson Brown: GM's Pioneer Management Theorist and Practitioner," in Richard C. Huseman, ed., *Proceedings of the Annual Meeting of the Academy of Management* (August 1980), pp. 119–123.

[179] American Management Association, *How the Du Pont Organization Appraises Its Performance: A Chart System for Forecasting, Measuring and Reporting the Financial Results of Operations*, Financial Management Series no. 94 (New York: American Management Association, 1950). See also JoAnne Yates, "Graphs as a Managerial Tool: A Case Study of Du Pont's Use of Graphs in the Early Twentieth Century," *Journal of Business Communication* 22(1) (Winter 1985), pp. 5–33.

He centralized administration and decentralized operations, grouping together those that had a common relationship. By decentralizing operations and centrally coordinating control, GM's various product divisions (e.g., Chevrolet, Buick, Pontiac, and Cadillac) could more quickly respond to their market-sector competition. This multidivisional ("M-form") structure enabled GM to more efficiently integrate an increasing number of specialized skills by grouping together all the employees necessary to produce an individual product.[180] With an M-form structure, each major product division was administered through a separate and semiautonomous division. Each division operated as a minicompany, with its own departments for production, marketing, finance, and so on. This structure was reflected in the GM slogan "a car for every purse and purpose."[181] Whereas Henry Ford famously said customers could have a Ford in any color, "so long as it is black,"[182] Sloan created what is today called "market segmentation," dividing the car market into price tiers, with Chevrolet at the low end, Cadillac at the high end, and Buick and Pontiac slotted in-between. Because "the price levels within each tier touched but did not overlap adjoining tiers, the price plan would tempt buyers to spend just a few additional dollars on their car payment that enabled them to afford the next product up in the GM lineup."[183] Decentralizing into product divisions made it possible to also use Brown's $R = T \times P$ formula for measuring and comparing performance across divisions.

Drawing on his knowledge of Taylor's cost-accounting system, Pierre du Pont developed a measure of overall company performance. He went on to build both DuPont and General Motors into two of the world's largest and most successful companies. Taylor and, in turn, scientific management thus played a role in creating what is today known as the "modern corporation."

BUSINESS POLICY

As the notion of general management was emerging during the 1920s, the idea of collegiate schools of business began to spread rapidly. Economics, once called Moral Philosophy and later Political Economy, was the womb that nurtured emerging business subjects. Thus, Towne's call for the "engineer as an economist" found fulfillment not in the ASME, but in nascent schools of business. Their rapid growth resulted in the formation of the Association of Collegiate Schools of Business (ACSB; the present-day American Assembly of Collegiate Schools of Business) in 1916. By 1926–1927, the ACSB had 38 members offering courses in accounting, economics, finance, marketing, commercial law, transportation, statistics, physical environment, social control and ethics, production, personnel, and labor.[184]

Although education for business grew rapidly in the first quarter of the twentieth century, there were few efforts among educators to integrate course offerings to provide a general overview of a manager's job. Arch W. Shaw, publisher of *System* (now *Bloomberg Businessweek*), a magazine devoted to "output and profit increasing methods put to use in leading factories," was a notable exception. In 1908, Shaw lectured at Northwestern University's new School of Commerce, and in 1910 he spoke at Harvard University's Graduate School of Business Administration. While at Harvard, he became familiar with the problem, or case, method of instruction, which had grown out of the interrogative Socratic Method of teaching law developed in the 1870s by Christopher C. Langdell at the Harvard Law School. Using this method, learning takes

[180] The development General Motors is examined by, among others, Alfred D. Chandler, Jr., ed., *Giant Enterprise: Ford, General Motors, and the Automobile Industry* (New York: Harcourt Brace & World, 1964); Peter F. Drucker, *The Concept of the Corporation* (New York: John Day Company, 1946).

[181] Alfred P. Sloan, Jr., *My Years with General Motors*, ed. John McDonald with Catharine Stevens (New York: Doubleday, 1963), pp. 438, 441.

[182] Henry Ford with Samuel Crowther, *My Life and Work* (Garden City, NY: Doubleday, Page, 1922), p. 72.

[183] Thomas L. Powers and Jocelyn I. Steward, "Alfred P. Sloan's 1921 Repositioning Strategy," *Journal of Human Resource Management* 2(4) (2010), p. 430.

[184] Frances Ruml, "The Formative Period of Higher Commercial Education in American Universities," *Journal of Business of the University of Chicago* 1(2) (April 1928), pp. 253–254.

place through an instructor's questions and students' answers rather than lectures. During the 1911–1912 academic year, Shaw taught a business-policy course at Harvard based on the case method. The course was "to deal with top-management problems, and it also aimed at integrating subjects that the students had studied in their first year."[185] Shaw invited business executives to attend his classes and describe a challenge confronting their companies; his students were each required to prepare a report with policy recommendations on how to address the challenge. The students then orally presented their reports to the executives. Despite Shaw's unique approach, only two universities (Harvard and the University of Michigan) required the study of business policy in 1925, and it was not until 1959 that a capstone course (now generally known as "Business Strategy") became a requirement in AACSB (Association to Advance Collegiate Schools of Business) accredited programs.

A. Hamilton Church, discussed earlier in connection with his mentor Leon P. Alford, was in the mainstream of management thought during the scientific-management era. Church began his career in Great Britain, became a consultant on cost-accounting systems, and moved to the United States in 1910. Tutored by J. Slater Lewis (mentioned above), Church sought a more general approach to the study of management than that offered by Taylor.[186] He became interested in a broadened view of management after studying the allocation of overhead costs, that is, those costs (such as management salaries) that are difficult to attribute to any one product or activity. For Church, every industrial undertaking consisted of two elements: (1) the *determinative* element, which fixed a firm's manufacturing and distribution policies; and (2) the *administrative* element, which took a firm's policies as determined and gave them practical expression through buying, manufacturing, and selling.[187] In modern parlance, Church was describing *policy formulation* (the determinative element) and *implementation* (the administrative element).[188] As Church explained, in making these two elements operational, managers used two fundamental "instruments": *analysis*, consisting of cost accounting, time-and-motion study, routing, machine layout, and planning; and *synthesis*, combining workers, functions, machines, and all activities effectively to achieve some useful result. In brief, managers *analyzed* to find better ways to accomplish a desired result and then *coordinated* (synthesized) the activities necessary to attain that result.

In Church's view, Taylor's work only focused on a limited aspect of a manager's job. Church believed that managers should be concerned with a firm's overall efficiency. He incorporated a general-management viewpoint in his books and articles and emphasized the challenge of managing a firm's departments in relation to one another and to the firm as a whole. Writing in *The Making of an Executive*, Church stopped short of formulating a general-management process as Fayol had, but provided early insights into policy formulation and implementation.[189]

Though the work of Taylor and his contemporaries reflected a set of values or beliefs, an Englishman, Oliver Sheldon, was the first to lay claim to developing an explicit philosophy of management. Sheldon began and ended his business career with Rowntree and Company Cocoa Works at York, headed by B. Seebohm Rowntree, noted for his enlightened business practices

---

[185] Melvin T. Copeland, "The Genesis of the Case Method in Business Instruction," in Malcolm P. McNair, ed., *The Case Method at the Harvard Business School* (New York: McGraw-Hill, 1954), p. 26.

[186] Joseph A. Litterer, "Alexander Hamilton Church and the Development of Modern Management," *Business History Review* 35(2) (Summer 1961), p. 214. See also Michael E. Scorgie, "Alexander Hamilton Church: His Family and Early Life," *Abacus* 29(1) (1993), pp. 52–74. Hamilton was a grandnephew of Alexander Hamilton, first U.S. Secretary of the Treasury. Scorgie speculates (p. 66) that Church used the name form "A. Hamilton Church" to avoid the "inevitable question, 'Are you a descendant of Alexander Hamilton?'" As a further aside, the extent of Lewis's mentoring may be called into question: while Church was in Lewis's employ as a "clerk" at the National Telegraph Works Company in Birmingham (England), Lewis filed for bankruptcy with no assets. See "The Affairs of Joseph Slater Lewis," *Birmingham Daily Post* (July 26, 1892), p. 6.

[187] A. Hamilton Church, *The Science and Practice of Management* (New York: Engineering Magazine, 1914), pp. 1–2.

[188] Mariann Jelinek, "Toward Systematic Management: Alexander Hamilton Church," *Business History Review* 54(1) (Spring 1980), p. 72. See also Trevor Boyns, "In Memoriam: Alexander Hamilton Church's System of 'Scientific Machine Rates' at Hans Renold Ltd., c. 1901–1920," *Accounting Historians Journal* 30(1) (June 2003), pp. 3–44.

[189] A. Hamilton Church, *The Making of an Executive* (Scranton, PA: International Textbook Company, 1923).

(see Chapter 9). Sheldon was undoubtedly familiar with Gantt's opinion that businesses had a social responsibility to incorporate community service in their activities. Sheldon held that managers "should devise a philosophy of management, a code of principles, scientifically determined and generally accepted, to act as a guide, by reason of its foundation upon ultimate things, for the daily practice of the[ir] profession."[190]

Sheldon encouraged managers to develop common motives, common ends, a common creed, and a common fund of knowledge. The basic premise of his philosophy of management, like that of Gantt, was community service:

> Industry exists to provide the commodities and services which are necessary for the good life of the community, in whatever volume they are required. These commodities and services must be furnished at the lowest prices compatible with an adequate standard of quality, and distributed in such a way as directly or indirectly to promote the highest ends of the community.[191]

In Sheldon's thinking, combining scientific management's emphasis on efficiency with community service was the responsibility of all managers. Toward this end, Sheldon held that managers must adopt three principles: (1) "the policies, conditions, and methods of industry shall conduce to communal well-being"; (2) "management shall endeavor to interpret the highest moral sanction of the community as a whole" in applying social justice to industrial practice; and (3) "management . . . [shall] take the initiative . . . in raising the general ethical standard and conception of social justice."[192] It was Sheldon's belief that, in applying these principle, managers must consider both human *and* technical efficiency. He endorsed scientific methods of work analysis, but with due consideration being given to developing human potential to the greatest extent possible. Per Sheldon's philosophy, the economic basis of service, the dual emphasis on human and technical efficiency, and the responsibility of managers to provide social justice would all lead to a mutually beneficial "science of industrial management."

SUMMARY

Scientific management was a significant force influencing: (1) the formal study of management; (2) the practice of management in the United States, Europe, Japan, China, Australia, and beyond; (3) early organization theory; (4) applications in other academic disciplines; (5) the creation of a general business-policy course; and (6) an explicit philosophy of management. The original seed planted by Taylor provided the crucial impetus, but it took the efforts of many to spread the scientific-management message. In practice, scientific management did not always run true to its founder's ideals: organized labor resisted it as a threat to its autonomy; its methods were adapted in different countries but frequently without preserving its spirit; and, much too often, firms of all types grasped its techniques but forgot its philosophy. Yet scientific management was not a failure. Growing out of the need to systematize business practices, it gave a voice to efficiency, purpose to practice, and content to theory. Its youth was robust, its maturity was fruitful, and it spawned intellectual descendants throughout the world who still write about, study, and practice its teachings. Scientific management reflected the spirit of the time and prepared the way for subsequent developments in the evolution of management thought.

---

[190] Oliver Sheldon, *The Philosophy of Management* (London: Sir Isaac Pitman and Sons, 1923), p. 284.

[191] *Ibid.*, p. 285. For a further discussion of "business as service" during the British interwar years (1918–1939), see Mairi Maclean, Gareth Shaw, and Charles Harvey, "Business as Service? Human Relations and the British Interwar Management Movement," *Human Relations*, in press.

[192] *Ibid.*, pp. 285–286.

CHAPTER 12

Scientific Management in Retrospect

The scientific-management movement—so obvious today, so original then—can only be fully understood in the context of the world within which it was created. Following Fred Taylor's death in 1915, a web of economic, technological, social, and political facets transformed scientific management as it became a global phenomenon. Though considered separately here, these facets were inextricably intertwined. With the unfolding of the twentieth century, each facet was perpetuated and reinforced by aspects of both the broader cultural landscape in general, and the developing field of management in particular.

Alfred D. Chandler noted that the "initial expansion and accumulation of resources" that marked the growth of "Big Business" in the United States was complete by the beginning of World War I in 1914 (see Chapter 6). In the ensuing years, large-scale enterprises faced two basic challenges: (1) how to improve production techniques and processes to achieve economies of scale to reduce the per-unit cost of production or distribution, and (2) how to improve planning, coordination, and performance tracking.[1] The emergence of these twin challenges marked what Chandler identified as a second phase in the growth of Big Business: "rationalization or full use of resources." The scientific-management movement hit its initial stride as this phase was gaining wider attention. The opening line in Taylor's *The Principles of Scientific Management* quotes President Theodore Roosevelt's 1908 call for "the conservation of our natural resources" as a means of increasing "national efficiency."[2] Roosevelt considered the application of scientific management to the conservation of the nation's natural resources as an act of patriotism.[3] In response to Roosevelt's call, Taylor gave three reasons for writing his most famous book:

> *First.* To point out, through a series of simple illustrations, the great loss which the whole country is suffering through inefficiency in almost all of our daily acts.
>
> *Second.* To try to convince the reader that the remedy for this inefficiency lies in systematic management, rather than in searching for some unusual or extraordinary man.

[1] Alfred D. Chandler, Jr., *Strategy and Structure: Chapters in the History of the Industrial Enterprise* (Cambridge, MA: MIT Press, 1962), pp. 386–390.

[2] Theodore Roosevelt, "Address by the President," in *Proceedings of a Conference of the Governors in the White House*, Washington, DC, May 13–15, 1908, ed. William J. McGee (Washington, DC: Government Printing Office, 1909), p. 12.

[3] Henry Beach Needham, "Roosevelt on Efficiency in Business: 'Scientific Management is the application of the Conversation Principle to Production' [An Interview with Theodore Roosevelt]," *System: The Magazine of Business* 19(6) (June 1911), p. 586.

> *Third.* To prove that the best management is a true science resting upon clearly defined laws, rules, and principles, as a foundation. And further to show that the fundamental principles of scientific management are applicable to all kinds of human activities, from our simplest individual acts to the work of our great corporations, which call for the most elaborate cooperation. And, briefly, through a series of illustrations, to convince the reader that whenever these principles are correctly applied, results must follow which are truly astounding.[4]

As the twentieth century unfolded, people became intrigued with the promise of a better and more efficient world. In the United States, readers of *Harper's Weekly* were told, "Big things are happening in the development of this country. . . . [W]ith the movement toward greater efficiency, a new and highly improved era in national life has begun."[5] This chapter considers the economic, technological, social, and political facets that transformed the scientific-management movement as it sought to eliminate waste and preserve the world's natural resources.

THE ECONOMIC ENVIRONMENT: FROM THE FARM TO THE FACTORY

Industrial growth impacted the world's economic environment and was the initial facet that transformed scientific management as it emerged as a global phenomenon. As the United States became an industrialized nation, millions of jobs were created. Thousands of people left their farms in search of a new life. In 1800, agriculture was the primary livelihood of 74 percent of the population in the United States; by 1900, 40 percent were engaged in farming; and by 1930, 22 percent.[6] The United States was the world's leading manufacturing economy by 1900.[7] The transformation of the United States from a rural, agricultural nation into an industrialized power represents one of the most dramatic changes in world history. The typical citizen who awoke on the morning of January 1, 1901, saw little change between the old and the new centuries, yet the change was there. The United States had moved into a new economic era.

Between 1880 and 1910, more than 23 million immigrants arrived in the United States, a majority from southern and eastern Europe. In contrast with the populations of other industrialized nations such as Britain, France, Germany, Italy, and Japan, the population of the United States in the late nineteenth and early twentieth centuries was very diverse and growing more so. Immigrants or their children composed more than 80 percent of the population in New York City, Chicago, Milwaukee, and Detroit. By 1900, there were more Italian-Americans in New York City than in any city in Italy except Rome; more residents of Polish descent in Chicago than in Warsaw; and, by 1920, more people of Irish ancestry had immigrated to the United States than the total remaining on the Emerald Isle.[8] These individuals and many, many more were responding to Emma Lazarus's famous words, inscribed on the Statute of Liberty in New York harbor: "'Give me your tired, your poor, / Your huddled masses yearning to breathe free . . . / I lift my lamp beside the golden door!'"[9]

---

[4] Frederick W. Taylor, *The Principles of Scientific Management* (New York: Harper & Brothers, 1911), p. 7.

[5] J. George Frederick, "The Efficiency Movement I.—What It Means and What It Is Accomplishing," *Harper's Weekly* 54(2915) (November 2, 1912), p. 11.

[6] Stanley Lebergott, *Manpower in Economic Growth: The American Record Since 1800* (New York: McGraw-Hill Company, 1962), Table A-1, p. 510.

[7] Jeremy Atack, Robert A. Margo, and Paul W. Rhode, "Industrialization and Urbanization in Nineteenth Century America," *Regional Science and Urban Economics* 94(4) (May 2022), article 103678.

[8] Thomas K. McCraw, "American Capitalism," in *idem*, ed., *Creating Modern Capitalism* (Cambridge, MA: Harvard University Press, 1997), p. 307.

[9] Emma Lazarus, "The New Colossus," November 2, 1883. Available online at http://www.mcny.org/story/new-colossus. See also "In Memory of Emma Lazarus," *New York Times* (May 6, 1903), p. 9.

By 1910, 48 percent of the workers employed in mining, 31.9 percent in manufacturing, and 26.3 percent in transportation were born outside the United States.[10] In 1913, Ford Motor's Highland Park (Michigan) plant had a workforce of 71 percent foreign-born workers from 22 different national groups. The nationalities represented came from all across the world, including Armenians, Austro-Hungarians, Canadians, Croatians, Danes, English, French, Germans, Hollanders, Irish, Italians, Japanese, Lithuanians, Poles, Russians, Romanians, Sicilians, Scotch, Serbians, and Turks.[11] Safety bulletins were issued in 42 different languages.[12] Given that such a large percentage of its workers could not speak English, the company started the Ford English School in 1914 under the direction of Peter Roberts, a Young Men's Christian Association educator.[13] In addition to English, students were taught civics, mathematics, and history, and educated in virtues such as thriftiness, cleanliness, good manners, and timeliness. From 1915 to 1916, some 16,000 workers passed through the school.[14]

Contrary to what might be expected, the large influx of immigrant labor from the 1880s to 1920s did not result in lower wages. Rather, as technology and production processes improved, the resulting increase in productivity required a larger workforce. The economic growth resulting from an increase in investment capital and labor productivity opened a path out of poverty for workers everywhere. Daily wages and annual earnings in manufacturing increased some 50 percent between 1860 and 1890, and real wages (the purchasing power of workers' incomes) increased more than 60 percent from 1860 to 1890.[15] In addition, the average number of hours worked per week started to decrease; in 1890, the average industrial workweek was 60 hours; in 1910, 55 hours; and in 1920, 50 hours.[16] At roughly the same time, the number of worker hours input per unit of output dropped from an index number of 74 in 1919 to 42 in 1929 (for comparison, 1899 = 100), for a gain in efficiency of 43 percent.[17]

The economies of scope and scale associated with Big Business demanded an even sharper focus on managerial talent. Large accumulations of resources were needed to meet the demands of mass markets and mass distribution. As firms grew, a new breed of professional managers was replacing the owner-entrepreneurs who built the first wave of the modern corporation. The personalized, informal structures of the family business inevitably yielded to the logic of growth. No longer could owner–entrepreneurs personally supervise all of a firm's activities. Technology demanded specialized knowledge, and staff departments were added to handle personnel, engineering, production, purchasing, legal affairs, and other ancillary activities. Seymour Melman found that between 1899 and 1929, the percent of employees in management relative to those in production almost doubled (9.9 percent in 1899 to 18.5 percent in 1929), and between 1929 and 1947 increased from 18.5 to 22.2 percent.[18]

---

[10] Sumner H. Slichter, "The Current Labor Policies of American Industries," *Quarterly Journal of Economics* 43(3) (May 1929), p. 394.

[11] "Automobile Trade Notes," *New York Times* (November 15, 1914), p. 6. See also Allan Nevins with the collaboration of Frank Ernest Hill, *Ford: The Times, the Man, the Company* (New York: Charles Scribner's Sons, 1954), p. 648; Joyce Shaw Peterson. *American Automobile Workers*, 1900–1933 (Albany, NY: State University of New York Press, 1987), p. 17.

[12] Robert A. Shaw, "Discussion," in *Proceedings of the National Safety Council, Sixth Annual Safety Congress*, New York City, September 12, 1917 (Chicago, IL: The Council, 1917), pp. 236–237. See also Horace Lucien Arnold and Fay Leone Faurote, *Ford Methods and the Ford Shops* (New York: Engineering Magazine, 1915), pp. 56, 59.

[13] Stephen Meyer, "Adapting the Immigrant to the Line: Americanization in the Ford Factory, 1914–1921," *Journal of Social History* 14(1) (Fall 1980), p. 74. See also Clinton DeWitt, "Industrial Teachers," in U.S. Department of the Interior, Bureau of Education, *Proceedings Americanization Conference* (Washington, DC: Government Printing Office, 1919), pp. 114–119.

[14] Clarence Hooker, "Ford's Sociology Department and the Americanization Campaign and the Manufacture of Popular Culture Among Assembly Line Workers c. 1910–1917," *Journal of American Culture* 20(1) (Spring 1977), p. 49.

[15] Clarence D. Long, *Wages and Earnings in the United States, 1860–1890* (Princeton, NJ: Princeton University Press, 1960), p. 109.

[16] Edgar W. Martin, *The Standard of Living in 1860* (Chicago, IL: University of Chicago Press, 1942), p. 220.

[17] U.S. Dept. of Commerce, Bureau of the Census, *Historical Statistics of the United States: Colonial Times to 1970*, pt. 1 (Washington, DC: U.S. Government Printing Office, 1974), p. 162.

[18] Seymour Melman, "The Rise of Administrative Overhead in the Manufacturing Industries of the United States, 1899–1947," *Oxford Economic Papers* 3(1) (February 1951), pp. 66–68, 91. Melman used the U.S. Census of Manufactures' definition of management as salaried employees (i.e., line and staff) and others as wage earners.

THE TECHNOLOGICAL ENVIRONMENT: OPENING NEW HORIZONS

Technology, a second facet that transformed scientific management as it became a global phenomenon, opened new horizons in business. U.S. President Calvin Coolidge, who took office in 1923 upon Warren G. Harding's sudden death from a heart attack, captured the spirit of the era in a January 17, 1925, address to the American Society of Newspaper Editors:

> After all, the chief business of the American people is business. They are profoundly concerned with producing, buying, selling, investing, and prospering in the world. . . . Wealth is a product of industry, ambition, character, and untiring effort. . . . So long as wealth is made the means and not the end, we need not greatly fear it.[19]

The U.S. economy came of age in this period as remarkable inventions improved the nation's standard of living. In Chapter 6, we saw how developments in transportation and communication spurred industrial growth as the nation expanded in the years following the War Between the States. As the twentieth century dawned, a whole series of technological breakthroughs spurred further growth. Open-hearth steelmaking superseded the Bessemer process by 1900. Orville and Wilbur Wright, two bicycle makers from Dayton, Ohio, piloted the first successful flight of their famous "Flyer" at Kitty Hawk (North Carolina) in 1903, traveling 120 feet in 12 seconds. By 1913, at then Standard Oil of Indiana, developments in "cracking" oil molecules during refining yielded richer fuels for automobiles and aircraft. In 1923, U.S. Army pilots Lt. John A. Macready and Lt. Oakley G. Kelly completed the first non-stop transcontinental flight from Long Island (New York) to San Diego (California), covering some 2,440 miles in 26 hours and 50 minutes. Lee de Forest pioneered the vacuum tube in 1908, making radio broadcasting possible in 1910. The Panama Canal (1914) connected the Atlantic and Pacific Oceans. Sunkist marketed a new product called "orange juice" in 1916. The Chillicothe Baking Company in Missouri produced the first packaged sliced bread in 1928. Research at E. I. du Pont de Nemours & Co. led to the first successful synthetic rubber (neoprene) in 1931 and first synthetic textile fiber (nylon) in 1939. The technological breakthroughs of this period were as astounding to our ancestors as those of today are to our generation. Never had the human condition been transformed so completely. Adult stature and lifespan drastically improved due to better sanitation and more effective vaccines and medicines. The spread of mechanical refrigeration put an end to the "spring sickness" that typically followed winters in which people did not have green vegetables to consume. By 1930, overall life expectancy in the United States had increased to 59.7 years from 41.8 years in 1860.[20]

Developments in power generation also deserve mention. Heretofore, water wheels, horses, and coal had been the primary energy sources for the engines of industry. Although coal continued to dominate, newfound oil deposits were soon to reshape the U.S. energy base. Of even greater impact, on October 10, 1879, Thomas A. Edison created a cotton filament for the incandescent light bulb. He built the nation's first central power plant at New York City in 1882. By 1920, one-third of the country's industrial power came from electricity and nearly half (47.4 percent) of urban homes were electrified. In rural areas, 98.4 percent of the homes still relied on kerosene lamps and candles, but not for long.[21] With the spread of electricity, appliances such as electric irons, electric washing machines, and electric kitchen ranges, as well as central heating and hot-water heaters, soon followed.[22]

---

[19] Calvin Coolidge, "The Press under a Free Government," address before the American Society of Newspaper Editors, Washington, DC, January 17, 1925; reprinted in Coolidge, *Foundations of the Republic: Speeches and Addresses* (New York: Charles Scribner's Sons, 1926), pp. 187–188.

[20] Michael R. Haines, "Estimated Life Tables for the United States, 1850–1900," Historical Working Papers 0059 (Washington, DC: National Bureau of Economic Research, 1994), Table 1, p. 11; Elizabeth Arias, "United States Life Tables, 2004," *National Vital Statistics Reports* 65(9) (December 28, 2007), Table 12, p. 35; Susan B. Carter, Scott Sigmund Gartner, Michael R. Haines, Alan L. Olmstead, Richard Sutch, and Gavin Wright, eds., *Historical Statistics of the United States: Earliest Times to the Present, vol. 1: Population,* Millennial ed. (New York: Cambridge University Press, 2006), p. 440.

[21] U.S. Department of Commerce, Bureau of the Census, *Historical Statistics of the United States: Colonial Times to 1970*, pt. 3 (Washington, DC: U.S. Government Printing Office, 1974), p. 827.

[22] Jeremy Greenwood, Ananth Seshadri, and Mehmet Yorkukoglu, "Engines of Liberation," *Review of Economic Studies* 72(1) (January 2005), pp. 109–133; Ruth Schwartz Cowan, "The 'Industrial Revolution' in the Home: Household Technology and Social Change in the 20th Century," *Technology and Culture* 17(1) (January 1976), pp. 1–23.

The automobile was another technological advancement that brought about substantial economic and social change during this period. The automobile gave people a new mobility—a freedom of movement that led to the growth of satellite communities. Following World War II, the automobile made mass-produced suburbs such as Levittown, New York, possible. In 1900, there were 8,000 registered automobiles in the United States. By 1930, there were 26.8 million cars on the road. As noted in Chapter 8, between 1908 and 1913, the Ford Motor Company perfected the moving assembly line to mass produce automobiles. The results were impressive: in 1910 (pre–assembly line), 2,773 workers produced 18,664 autos (6.73 per worker); in 1914 (post–assembly line), 248,307 autos were produced by 12,880 workers (19.28 per worker).[23] Prices were driven downward as productivity increased: in 1908 and 1910, a fully equipped Model T cost \$950; in 1914, \$490; and in 1916, \$360.[24] By 1919, Henry Ford had acquired all minority stock in Ford Motor Company and had assumed operational control. He transformed autos from "toys for the rich" to everyday necessities for the average family. In the process, he sparked the nation's love affair with the open highway. By 1921, "Tin Lizzies," as the Model T came to be known, were made and sold on every continent (except Australia) and accounted for over half the world's motorcar production.

It should be noted that despite the claim that "Fordism" was an extension of Taylor's methods,[25] Taylor's closest associates were adamant that Taylor's ideas should not be confused with Ford's assembly lines (inspired by the "disassembly" lines of Chicago's Union Stock Yard). In addition to Frank Gilbreth's comments regarding the distinction between scientific management and assembly-line conditions at Ford (reported in Chapter 8), according to Harlow S. Person (managing director of the Taylor Society), Taylor was "never sympathetic" to mass production with its "unregulated development." In further comments, Person made it clear that scientific management differed from "efficiency engineering," a term Taylor hated and which his "apostles" considered a "bastard perversion" of Taylor's methods.[26] Although it has been suggested that Ford's engineers "had doubtlessly caught some of Taylor's ideas . . . [and] kept in touch with the ideas of men like Taylor,"[27] Charles E. Sorensen, who spent 40 years with Henry Ford, made it emphatically clear that Taylor's ideas had no influence at Ford Motor Company. He explained: "No one at Ford—not Mr. Ford, Couzens, Flanders, Wills, Pete Martin, nor I—was acquainted with the theories of the 'father of scientific management,' Frederick W. Taylor."[28] For Sorensen, the notion that "Taylor's ideas had any influence at Ford" was a "myth." Moreover, there is no record of either Taylor or the four engineers authorized to implement his methods (Carl G. Barth, Henry L. Gantt, H. King Hathaway, and Morris L. Cooke)[29] ever advising Henry Ford or the Ford Motor Company. Beyond this, when asked directly, Henry Ford denied "any dependence upon scientific management," claiming to have acted wholly on his own inspiration.[30]

Information technology, in the spirit of Henry V. Poor's definition of information as "recorded communication" (see Chapter 5), was also evolving. Smaller firms could rely on informal communications, account books, and face-to-face exchanges to track business affairs. As firms grew, however, adding levels of authority, the transmission of communications from the top to the bottom of a firm and back could be disastrously lengthy. Though Fayol's gangplank

[23] Nevins, *Ford: The Times, the Man, the Company*, pp. 644, 648.
[24] Karel Williams, Colin Haslam, and John Williams, "Ford versus 'Fordism': The Beginning of Mass Production?" *Work, Employment & Society* 6(4) (December 1992), p. 519.
[25] For a discussion that considers "Fordism" to be an outgrowth of Taylor's methods, see Ed Andrew, *Closing the Iron Cage: The Scientific Management of Work and Leisure* (Montréal: Black Rose Books, 1981), p. 98.
[26] Mark Sullivan, *Our Times: The United States 1900–1925, vol. 4: The War Begins, 1909–1914* (New York: Charles Scribner's Sons, 1932), p. 76n1.
[27] Daniel M. Nelson, "Scientific Management, Systematic Management, and Labor, 1880–1915," *Business History Review* 48(4) (Winter 1974), pp. 489–490.
[28] Charles E. Sorensen, with Samuel T. Williamson, *My Forty Years with Ford* (New York: W. W. Norton, 1956), p. 41.
[29] Frank B. Copley, *Frederick W. Taylor: Father of Scientific Management*, vol. 2 (New York: Harper & Brothers, 1923), p. 357.
[30] Arnold and Faurote, *Ford Methods and the Ford Shops*, p. 20. For more on how Ford viewed his approach as differing from Taylorism, see Henry Ford, "Mass Production," *Encyclopædia Britannica*, 13th ed., vol. 30, p. 821.

allowed communications to cross lines of authority (see Chapter 10), more formal systems of gathering, recording, and maintaining information were developed. As mentioned in Chapter 6, Christopher L. Sholes sold his typewriter patent to E. Remington & Sons in 1873. Demand for the typewriter, however, languished until the late nineteenth century when expanding businesses created a need for prompt and legible correspondence. Vertical file cabinets facilitated arranging correspondence and records. The A. B. Dick Company licensed the rights to Thomas A. Edison's "multiplying letters" device for making duplicate copies of letters and introduced it across the world, calling it a "mimeograph" machine. Patented in 1896, the Addressograph made it possible to print thousands of mailing labels an hour and bombard the public with everything from Sears and Montgomery Ward mail-order catalogues to political flyers and unsolicited advertising. Pneumatic tubes were installed in factories and retail stores to send money, receipts, and other papers from floor to floor and between departments.[31] Long before Nike running shoes, the first "swoosh" was the sound of information transmitted via a pneumatic tube.

Beyond quickening the tempo of business, the revolution in information technology had an unintended effect: it shifted clerical work from men to women and created office jobs as an alternative to factory labor for women. In 1880, less than 5 percent of clerical workers in the United States were women. By 1900, women comprised over 30 percent. Male clerks who wrote letters and other documents by hand using pen and ink were largely replaced by female typists and stenographers. At the same time, other women entered formerly all-male offices as cashiers, bookkeepers, and secretaries using new devices such as the mimeograph, Dictaphone, cash register, adding machine, and stenotype.[32] In brief, advancing technology was reshaping the nature of work by increasing the number of skilled and semiskilled jobs, creating alternative employment opportunities for women, and substituting capital (i.e., plants and equipment) for labor.

THE SOCIAL ENVIRONMENT: FROM ACHIEVEMENT TO AFFILIATION

A third facet that transformed scientific management as it became a global phenomenon was most evident in the changing values and cultural fabric of the era's social environment. Between 1868 and 1900, Horatio Alger, Jr., wrote more than 100 dime novels for boys with piquant titles such as *Bound to Rise; or, Fighting His Way to Success*; *Dick Merriwell's Mascot; or, By Luck or Pluck?*; *Sink or Swim; or, Pluck Aways Succeeds*; and *Tom, the Bootblack; or, The Road to Success*. At least 20 million copies were sold, and "Horatio Alger" became synonymous with "rags-to-riches" success. The typical plot involved a poor, young man who overcame poverty and hardship to achieve economic standing by diligence, honesty, perseverance, and thrift. Quite often, a benefactor who recognized his latent talents befriended and assisted him in reaching the pinnacle of the business world. The heroes in Alger's books were a personification of David C. McClelland's "high achiever," who exhibited the self-control, hard work, and orderly life associated with Max Weber's Protestant ethic (see Chapter 2).[33] They learned in the school of hard knocks; no formal schooling could prepare them for success in business. Charles M. Schwab, a protégé of steel magnate Andrew Carnegie (see Chapter 6), stated the case:

> [I]f the college man thinks that his education gives him a higher social status, he is riding for a fall. Some college men . . . have pride in their mental attainments that is almost arrogance. Employers find it difficult to control, guide, and train such men. Their spirit of superiority bars the path of progress.[34]

[31] For more on these and other similar developments during this era, see JoAnne Yates, *Control through Communication: The Rise of System in American Management* (Baltimore, MD: Johns Hopkins University Press, 1989).

[32] Elyce J. Rotella, "The Transformation of the American Office: Changes in Employment and Technology," *Journal of Economic History* 41(1) (March 1981), pp. 51–57. See also Sara Alpern, "In the Beginning: A History of Women in Management," in Ellen A. Fagenson, ed., *Women in Management: Trends, Issues, and Challenges in Managerial Diversity* (Newbury Park: CA Sage Publishing, 1993), pp. 19-51; Angel Kwolek-Folland, *Engendering Business: Men and Women in the Corporate Office, 1870–1930* (Baltimore, MD: Johns Hopkins University Press, 1994), pp. 4–6.

[33] David C. McClelland, *The Achieving Society* (Princeton, NJ: Van Nostrand, 1961).

[34] Charles M. Schwab, "The College Man in Business," in Alta Gwinn Saunders and Hubert LeSourd Creek, eds., *The Literature of Business* (New York: Harper & Brothers, 1920), p. 5.

Early scientific-management theory rested on the tradition of individual initiative, as well as the classical virtue of enlightened self-interest. Utilitarianism, also in vogue during this era, held that all behavior stemmed from the pursuit of personal pleasure and avoidance of pain.[35] It assumed that individuals, acting in their own self-interest, made rational decisions about what pleasures or pains to seek or avoid. The notion that workers, like all other human beings, act in their own self-interest, gave rise to the imaginary of the wealth-seeking and -consuming "economic man," or *homo economicus*, who always acts rationally to maximize his welfare.[36] In the period leading up to the scientific-management era, *homo economicus* was generally assumed to be motivated solely by money. Before Taylor, however, piece-rate incentive plans had largely failed because management had all too often either failed to set performance standards properly or engaged in rate cutting when earnings were judged too high. Neither practice was to management's benefit because it only encouraged workers to engage in systematic soldiering. As envisioned by Taylor, the principal object of management was to secure the maximum prosperity for both employers and employees. The "mental revolution" that Taylor called for recognized a congruency between the goals of employee and employer. There would be justice for all based on the impartial scientific determination of a "fair day's work." In brief, the ideals of scientific management were compatible with the tradition of individual initiative and the classical virtue of enlightened self-interest.

THE COLLISION EFFECT

Changes in cultural thought are always difficult to pinpoint. As the twentieth century progressed, however, new dimensions became apparent that would affect the course of management thought that began to shape the scientific-management movement. Two disparate yet strangely congenial dimensions were coming together to mark a new era in U.S. cultural thinking: (1) the U.S. Census Bureau's declaration that, by 1890, a year after the Oklahoma Land Rush, there was no longer a Western frontier, as "a solid band of states stretched across the continent" to the Pacific Ocean,[37] and (2) the Social Gospel movement's drive to reform social and economic conditions in the nation's workplaces and beyond.

With regard to the passing of the Western frontier, historian Frederick Jackson Turner identified four forces that reshaped economic, social, and political ideals in the United States during this period: (1) "the exhaustion of the supply of free land and the closing of the movement of Western advance as an effective factor in American development"; (2) "the concentration of capital in the control of fundamental industries as to make a new epoch in the economic development of the United States"; (3) "expansion of the United States politically and commercially into lands beyond the seas"; and (4) the division of political parties on "issues that involve the question of Socialism."[38] He believed that the Western frontier virtues of courage, determination, ingenuity, and honor shaped the character of the American people: "Turner proposed that it was America's generations-long encounter with the wilderness of its Western borderlands that forged American institutions and the special capacities in its citizens for resourcefulness and self-reliance."[39] In his analysis, whenever labor-market outcomes or social conditions in the industrial cities of the East

[35] Jeremy Bentham, *An Introduction to the Principles of Morals and Legislation* (London: T. Payne and Son, 1789), p. 7. Written in 1780.

[36] For the origins of the term "*homo economicus*, or dollar-hunting animal," see Michele Bee and Maxime Desmarais-Tremblay, "The Birth of *Homo Œconomicus*: The Methodological Debate on the Economic Agent from J. S. Mill to V. Pareto," *Journal of the History of Economic Thought* (2022), pp. 1–26.

[37] Robert P. Porter, Henry Gannett, and William C. Hunt, "Progress of the Nation: 1790 to 1890," in *Report on Population of the United States at the Eleventh Census: 1890*, pt. 1 (Washington, DC: Government Printing Office, 1895), p. xxxiv; quote from Allan Nevins and Henry Steele Commager, *America: The Story of a Free People* (Boston, MA: Little, Brown and Company, 1942), p. 336.

[38] Frederick Jackson Turner, *The Frontier in American History* (New York: H. Holt and Company, 1920), pp. 244–247.

[39] Richard Adams Carey, [Review of the book *Mothertrucker*], *Wall Street Journal* (January 7, 2022), p. A13.

became too oppressive, the Great West provided an avenue of escape and an opportunity for a new beginning. As Turner explained:

> Americans had a safety valve for social danger, a bank account on which they might continually draw to meet losses. This was the vast unoccupied domain that stretched from the borders of the settled area to the Pacific [O]cean. Endowed with such untold natural resources with a continental sweep of fertile lands, forests, pasture grounds and mines, democracy could make mistakes and never be aware of its errors. . . . No grave social problem could exist while the wilderness at the edge of civilizations opened wide its portals to all who were oppressed, to all who with strong arms and stout heart desired to hew out a home and a career for themselves. Here was an opportunity for social development continually to begin over again, wherever society gave signs of breaking unto classes. Here was a magic fountain of youth in which America continually bathed and was rejuvenated. Out of this freedom of opportunity came the self-made man.[40]

Although "the frontier no longer existed in the physical world," Turner believed that "it lived on as the dominant force shaping the institutions of American society and the character of the American people."[41] What the Mediterranean Sea had been to the ancient Greeks, the receding frontier has been to the American soul.

William G. Scott labeled this era in U.S. history the "period of collision."[42] He held that, unless tempered, the inevitable clash of the events Turner identified as reshaping U.S. ideals would have eventually led to the nation's cultural degeneration, as people were drawn into inescapable proximity and interdependency. He dubbed this decline the "collision effect." Rather than leading to chaos, however, Scott argued that, with the closing of the Western frontier, its ideals were replaced by a new value system he called the "social ethic." This ethic substituted human collaboration for human competition and took "groups," as distinct from their individual members, as its primary focus. This had a profound effect on management thought. By stressing the mutuality of employee–employer interests coupled with the belief that everyone should be given the highest and most interesting work for which they were fit, scientific management bridged the gap between the social ethic's emphasis on human collaboration and the rugged individualism on which the United States had been founded and the West personified. Though neither known nor regarded as a social philosopher, Fred Taylor and other scientific-management advocates fully appreciated the changes occurring in the U.S. social environment and saw scientific management as a means for securing the maximum prosperity for both employers and employees.

THE SOCIAL GOSPEL MOVEMENT

The Social Gospel movement was a second dimension that marked a new era in U.S. cultural thought. As noted in Chapter 6, and discussed further in Chapter 9, the Social Gospel movement emerged in the late nineteenth century as a counterpoint to Social Darwinism. It emphasized a vision that Quaker activist Rufus M. Jones called, in 1902, "one of the most impressive undertakings of the twentieth century—the conquest of unnecessary disease, the banishment of unnecessary poverty, the transformation of environments which breed and foster disease and sin, the spiritualizing of both capital and labor and the recovery of faith in the actual coming of the Kingdom of God in the world."[43] Social Gospel proponents (predominantly Protestant, but also

---

[40] Frederick Jackson Turner quoted in "New Year Dedication: Interesting Ceremonies at the New High School Building," *Portage (Wisconsin) Weekly Democrat* 19(45) (January 3, 1896), p. 1.

[41] Todd Zywicki, [Review of the book *The Western: Four Classic Novels of the 1940s and 50s*], *Modern Age* 63(2) (Spring 2021), p. 53.

[42] William G. Scott, *The Social Ethic in Management Literature* (Atlanta, GA: Bureau of Business and Economic Research, Georgia State College of Business Administration, 1959), p. 9. See also *idem*, "The Early Record of a Modern Administrative Dilemma," *Journal of the Academy of Management* 2(2) (August 1959), pp. 97–110.

[43] Rufus M. Jones quoted in Society of Friends, *Minutes and Proceedings of the Five Years Meeting of the American Yearly Meetings 1902* (Philadelphia, PA: John C. Winston Co., 1902), p. 147.

Roman Catholic and Jewish) felt a duty to reform social and economic conditions, both in and out of the workplace. As noted in Chapter 9, rather than wait for a gradual improvement in the quality of life found in poorer neighborhoods, they argued for immediate action in improving personnel-administration and industrial-relations policies. They appealed for profit sharing, the right to organize unions, workplace arbitration, worker cooperatives, legislation governing the hiring and firing of employees, the employment of women and children, and workplace sanitation. The Social Gospel movement was an antecedent of industrial sociology and was a forerunner of Progressivism.

For Social Gospel proponents, labor unions (in particular) were instruments of social and economic reform. Robert G. Valentine, discussed in Chapter 11 in connection with the Hoxie Report, envisioned the eventual replacement of labor unions and labor–management conflict by enlightened "industrial counselors" who were not advocates of either side, but would put their own ideas forward in the interest of employers, employees, *and* the public.[44] Some of the era's "share in the management" plans involved union consent and cooperation, whereas others gave employees a voice and a choice through various types of employee-representation plans. Valentine viewed such plans as part of an evolution toward true industrial democracy that began with the first welfare-work offices established in the late 1890s by forward-thinking companies such as the National Cash Register Company and Joseph Bancroft and Sons (see Chapter 9). In retrospect, these early efforts were an uneven mixture of philanthropy, humanitarianism, and business acumen.

Scientific management complemented the work of Social Gospel proponents by linking efficiency and morality. For Taylor, hard work led to morality and well-being; for Social Gospel proponents, morality and well-being yielded hard work. This reciprocity between hard work and morality was the core of the romance linking later progressives and scientific management (as discussed below). Uplift through efficiency was in vogue among Social Gospel advocates, who pursued efficiency in virtually all aspects of U.S. society. Popular books and manuals on efficiency in the home, in education, in the conservation of natural resources, in religion, and in industry abounded.[45] Taylor even penned a foreword to Mary Pattison's *Principles of Domestic Engineering: Or, The What, Why and How of a Home*, a book he believed to be "the first work in the field of household or domestic engineering."[46] Members of this new field such as Christine Frederick predicted that scientific management would revolutionize the "*home* of the future," releasing women from the drudgery of housework and freeing them to assume an equal role in society.[47] Taylor's principles held an unprecedented grip on the U.S. psyche.

---

[44] Robert G. Valentine, "Scientific Management and Organized Labor," *Bulletin of the Society to Promote the Science of Management* 1(2) (January 1915), pp. 3–9. See also *idem*, "The Progressive Relation between Efficiency and Consent," *Bulletin of the Society to Promote the Science of Management* 2(1) (January 1916), pp. 7–20.

[45] Among others, see Joseph M. Rice, *Scientific Management in Education* (New York: Hinds, Noble and Eldredge, 1914); Ernest J. Dennen, *The Sunday School under Scientific Management* (Milwaukee, WI: Young Churchman Co., 1914); Eugene M. Camp, *Christ's Economy: Scientific Management of Men and Things in Relation to God and His Cause* (New York: Seabury Society, 1916); Samuel P. Hays, *Conservation and the Gospel of Efficiency* (Cambridge, MA: Harvard University Press, 1959); Samuel Haber, *Efficiency and Uplift: Scientific Management in the Progressive Era, 1890–1920* (Chicago, IL: University of Chicago Press, 1964); and Raymond E. Callahan, *Education and the Cult of Efficiency: A Study of the Social Forces That Have Shaped the Administration of the Public School* (Chicago, IL: University of Chicago Press, 1962).

[46] Frederick W. Taylor, "Foreword," in Mary Pattison, *Principles of Domestic Engineering: Or, The What, Why and How of a Home* (New York: Trow Press, 1915), p. 17.

[47] Mary Pattison, *Principles of Domestic Engineering*, p. 149. Pattison, who conducted motion studies of housekeeping chores at her Experimental Housekeeping Station at Colonia, New Jersey, was also influenced by, and, in turn, influenced, the work of the Gilbreths. See Charles D. Wrege, "Untold Gilbreth Stories," *The Quest* [Newsletter of the Gilbreth Network] 2(2) (Summer 1998), p. 1. See also *idem*, "Achieving Social Change Through Scientific Management: Mary Pattison and 'Domestic Engineering': 1909–1916," Charles D. Wrege Papers, Collection Number: 6012, Box 24, Folder 77, Kheel Center for Labor-Management Documentation and Archives, Catherwood Library, Cornell University. For a review of Christine Frederick's application of scientific management to the home, see Janice Williams Rutherford, *Selling Mrs. Consumer: Christine Frederick and the Rise of Household Efficiency* (Athens: University of Georgia Press, 2003). For commentary on the work of Catharine Esther Beecher, the founder of home economics as a field, and her initial efficiency-oriented push in the second half of the nineteenth century, see Ivan Paris, "Between Efficiency and Comfort: The Organization of Domestic Work and Space from Home Economics to Scientific Management, 1841–1913," *History and Technology* 35(1) (2019), pp. 81–104.

This cultural fascination with efficiency, however, was soon to wane. By the 1920s, the gospel of uplift through efficiency was ebbing as U.S. factories poured forth an abundance of goods. Prosperity reigned, and a new gospel of consumption emerged, with a heavy emphasis on the importance of everyone being part of the "middle class." Whiting Williams, Elton Mayo, Mary P. Follett, and others we have discussed (or will discuss) were beginning to stress the benefits of an egalitarian workplace in which human progress is best achieved through groups that interact, participate, and communicate. Personnel departments advocated welfare programs and worker happiness as both social and business assets (see Chapter 9). The need for affiliation was rising: there was security in group membership, and people were becoming more conscious of social relations and less concerned with maximizing individual gain. The Western frontier was closed, Horatio Alger's self-made man was increasingly seen as a myth, and new social values were replacing the promise of individual freedom on which the nation was founded. The seeds were sown for the next topic in our study of the evolution of management thought.

THE POLITICAL ENVIRONMENT: THE ADVENT OF PROGRESSIVISM

Changes in the U.S. political environment represent a fourth facet that transformed scientific management as it became a global phenomenon. The most evident change occurred in the role of government in business. The task of government and political institutions throughout time has primarily revolved around two basic themes: (1) the need to balance protecting one person's rights against violating another person's rights, and (2) the need to limit the power of government in order to protect individual rights. Political theorists, such as Niccolò di Bernardo dei Machiavelli and Thomas Hobbes, saw a central role for government in connection with the first theme; as for the second theme, Jean-Jacques Rousseau and John Locke sought a system of balances through which individuals could check excesses of government power (see Chapter 2). Constitutional, or representative, government—the philosophy of Rousseau and Locke made manifest in the United States' founding documents—makes consent of the governed the source of all legitimate authority. In the late nineteenth century, the United States was seeking to perfect democracy. In striving to do so, the United States encountered the "collision effect" and the capitalistic excesses of an industrializing nation. Both prompted an outpouring of legislation to change the relationship between individuals and government, as well as between business and government. Founded on a belief in a government with limited powers, the right to own private property, human liberty, and business operation without excessive regulation, the United States encountered imbalances among the ideals and reality of a growing nation.

SCIENTIFIC MANAGEMENT AND THE PROGRESSIVES

The Social Gospel movement's efforts to reform social and economic conditions found a political voice in its successor, progressivism, which expanded the size and reach of government. The roots of the Social Gospel movement, as expressed in its call for "industrial betterment" and "industrial welfare" programs, lie in religion and philanthropy. By contrast, the so-called progressive movement—with origins in the Populist Party of the 1890s—sought to mitigate the perils of the "collision effect" and the rigors of an industrial age by using government power to mandate greater economic equality. The progressive charter was diffuse: it included women's suffrage, direct election of U.S. senators, establishing a minimum wage, limiting working hours for women and children, enacting laws to pay the expenses of employees who incur work-related injuries, federally managing public health, encouraging trade unions, and enacting a federal income tax.[48] It is a strange quirk of history that modern critics have never

[48] Don S. Kirschner, "The Ambiguous Legacy: Social Justice and Social Control in the Progressive Era," *Historical Reflections* 2(1) (Summer 1975), pp. 69–88.

considered Taylor "progressive," yet his work and philosophy eventually became embedded in progressive thought.[49]

Scientific management attracted the progressive movement's attention at the 1910 Eastern Rate Case hearings. As noted in Chapter 7, Boston attorney Louis D. Brandeis took up the cause of a group of shippers who would be affected by a proposed 10 percent hike in freight rail rates. Brandeis had argued that the shippers could be spared a rate increase, and the public a hike in retail prices, if the principles of scientific management were applied to the nation's railroads. By introducing the term "scientific management" to the public, Brandeis, a prominent progressive reformer,[50] made efficiency synonymous with morality and social order. In the mind of progressives, everyone would benefit, as lower costs would also allow higher wages; all that was needed was for business to embrace Taylor's methods. It was here that the progressives' romance with scientific management was consummated. Whereas some of the era's reformers, like Socialist Eugene Debs, wanted to replace the whole free-market system, moderate progressives such as Brandeis and journalist Walter Lippmann thought that efficiency through science, together with leadership by a credentialed elite (who presumably knew what was best for society), would bring social order and harmony. Lippmann envisioned a new era that would remove commerce from the "cesspool of commercialism" and turn business executives into "industrial statesmen."[51] The appeal of scientific management was that it offered leadership by expertise and science and, hence, would rise above class prejudice and overcome rule by drive and whim. High wages for employees and low costs for employers were possible by applying Taylor's principles. Scientific management made the interests of employers and employees congruent. Labor–management conflict was, thus, unnecessary.

BUSINESS AND THE PROGRESSIVES

The era's biggest change in the relations between government and business in the United States came in 1901 following the September assassination of President William McKinley by an insane anarchist and the succession of Theodore Roosevelt to the presidency. Roosevelt's progressive inclinations initially gave business leaders and financial markets little reason for concern. His first annual message to Congress (delivered in December 1901) balanced his progressive beliefs with a pro-business stance.[52] In August 1902, however, he gave a speech in which he warned about the dangers "of the very great increase in private, and especially corporate fortunes."[53] The previous February, the U.S. Justice Department (under Roosevelt's direction) had sued the Northern Securities Company for restraint of trade and called for its dissolution. Northern Securities was a holding formed by J. Pierpont Morgan, Edward H. Harriman, and their associates. It controlled virtually all the railroads from Chicago through the Plains states to the Pacific Ocean, including the Northern Pacific Railway; the Great Northern Railway; and the Chicago, Burlington and Quincy Railroad. The suit opened a new chapter in government–business relations. Roosevelt was elected to a second presidential term in 1904. His election campaign slogan, a "Square Deal," promised fair play to every American: rich or poor, young or old, employee or employer.[54]

---

[49] G. Alan Tarr, "Laboratories of Democracy? Brandeis, Federalism, and Scientific Management," *Publius* 31(1) (Winter 2001), p. 44; Thomas C. Leonard, *Illiberal Reformers: Race, Eugenics, and American Economics in the Progressive Era* (Princeton, NJ: Princeton University Press, 2016), p. 63.

[50] Philip Cullis, "The Limits of Progressivism: Louis Brandeis, Democracy and the Corporation," *Journal of American Studies* 30(3) (December 1996), p. 382. See also David Savino, "Louis D. Brandeis and His Role Promoting Scientific Management as a Progressive Movement," *Journal of Management History* 15(1) (2009), p. 39.

[51] Walter Lippmann, *Drift and Mastery: An Attempt to Diagnose the Current Unrest* (New York: Mitchell Kennerley, 1914), pp. 8, 328.

[52] Theodore Roosevelt, "First Annual Message to Congress," December 3, 1901, Theodore Roosevelt Papers: Series 5: Speeches and Executive Orders, 1899–1918; Subseries 5C: Published Speeches, 1901–1917; 1901, Dec. 3–1905, Dec. 5. Available online at Library of Congress, https://www.loc.gov/resource/mss38299.mss38299-426_0545_1090/?sp=3.

[53] *Idem*, "At Providence, R.I., August 23, 1902," *A Compilation of the Messages and Speeches of Theodore Roosevelt: 1901–1905*, vol. 1, ed. Alfred Henry Lewis (Washington, DC: Bureau of National Literature and Art, 1906), p. 63.

[54] *Idem*, *A Square Deal* (Allendale, NJ: Allendale Press, 1906), p. 7.

In addition to advocating improved consumer protection statutes and the conservation of natural resources, Roosevelt's Square Deal called for the regulation of corporations to address the power imbalance between industrial trusts and the public's wellbeing. Speaking to the Union League Club in Philadelphia less than a week before his second inauguration, Roosevelt explained that "the great development of industrialism means that there must be an increase in the supervision exercised by the government over business enterprises."[55] The Justice Department subsequently filed restraint of trade suits against the Beef Trust (1905), the Standard Oil Company trust (1906), and the American Tobacco Company trust (1907) for limiting competition among the companies they controlled. Roosevelt also initiated new legislation regulating railroads (Elkins Act, 1903, and Hepburn Act, 1906). The 1910 Mann-Elkins Act (signed into law by Roosevelt's successor and fellow progressive William H. Taft) expanded the Interstate Commerce Commission's jurisdiction to include the telephone, telegraph, and wireless industries.

In the tradition of the British Factory Acts (see Chapter 3), other federal legislation in the ensuing years sought to limit working hours and regulate female and child labor. Under the Woodrow Wilson administration, the Clayton Antitrust Act (1914) and the Federal Trade Commission Act (1914) strengthened the Sherman Antitrust Act (1890). The Federal Reserve Act (1913) created a more elastic currency and weakened the hold of New York City banks over money markets. In 1913, the U.S. Congress passed the Underwood–Simmons Tariff Act, which imposed a 1 percent tax on personal incomes over $3,000 and a surtax up to 6 percent on incomes exceeding $500,000. Federal economic regulations proliferated even more rapidly following World War I, leaving "no aspect of modern American life untouched or the same."[56]

Changes in the U.S. political environment during the early twentieth century introduced a new balance in the powers of business and government. Though Taylor's forays into the political arena, especially his experience with the Interstate Commerce Commission (1910) and Commission on Industrial Relations (1915), were less than satisfactory, he persisted in seeking to replace management by privilege with management by science. Joined by Theodore Roosevelt and other like-minded conservationists, he also sought to eliminate waste and preserve the world's natural resources.

SUMMARY OF PART II

Figure 12.1 provides a synopsis of the scientific-management era. Scientific management was not an invention; it was a synthesis, a stage in the evolution of management thought. Charles Babbage could lay a valid claim to devising a rational, systematic approach to management, but Frederick W. Taylor gave systematic management a voice. Taylor was the *deus ex machina*, the unexpected power who suddenly became the focal point for an idea.

Scientific management was more than time and motion study; it was a much deeper philosophy of managing human and physical resources in a technologically advanced world where people were achieving unprecedented domain over their environment. The Industrial Revolution had provided the impetus; Taylor provided the synthesis. As people gained greater control over their lives and experienced a heretofore unimaginable standard of living, they pursued a vision of human prosperity to its fullest. Taylor had an idea, a great idea, on how that might be done—by a mental revolution on the part of all parties, founded on science and not whim, leading to harmony and cooperation. Perhaps he was idealistic, even utopian, but it would be wrong to fault Taylor for seeking the promise of industrial harmony, individual betterment, and greater national productivity.

Those who followed in Taylor's footsteps diverged from his orthodoxy as an interacting web of economic, technological, social, and political facets transformed scientific management into a global phenomenon. Some left large footprints, whereas others only paused long enough to leave small blurred tracks.

[55] *Idem*, "At the Forty-Second Anniversary Banquet of the Union League Club, Philadelphia, January 30, 1905," *A Compilation of the Messages and Speeches of Theodore Roosevelt: 1901–1905*, vol. 1, p. 551.

[56] William J. Novak, "Institutional Economics and the Progressive Movement for the Social Control of American Business," *Business History Review* 93(4) (Winter 2019), p. 668.

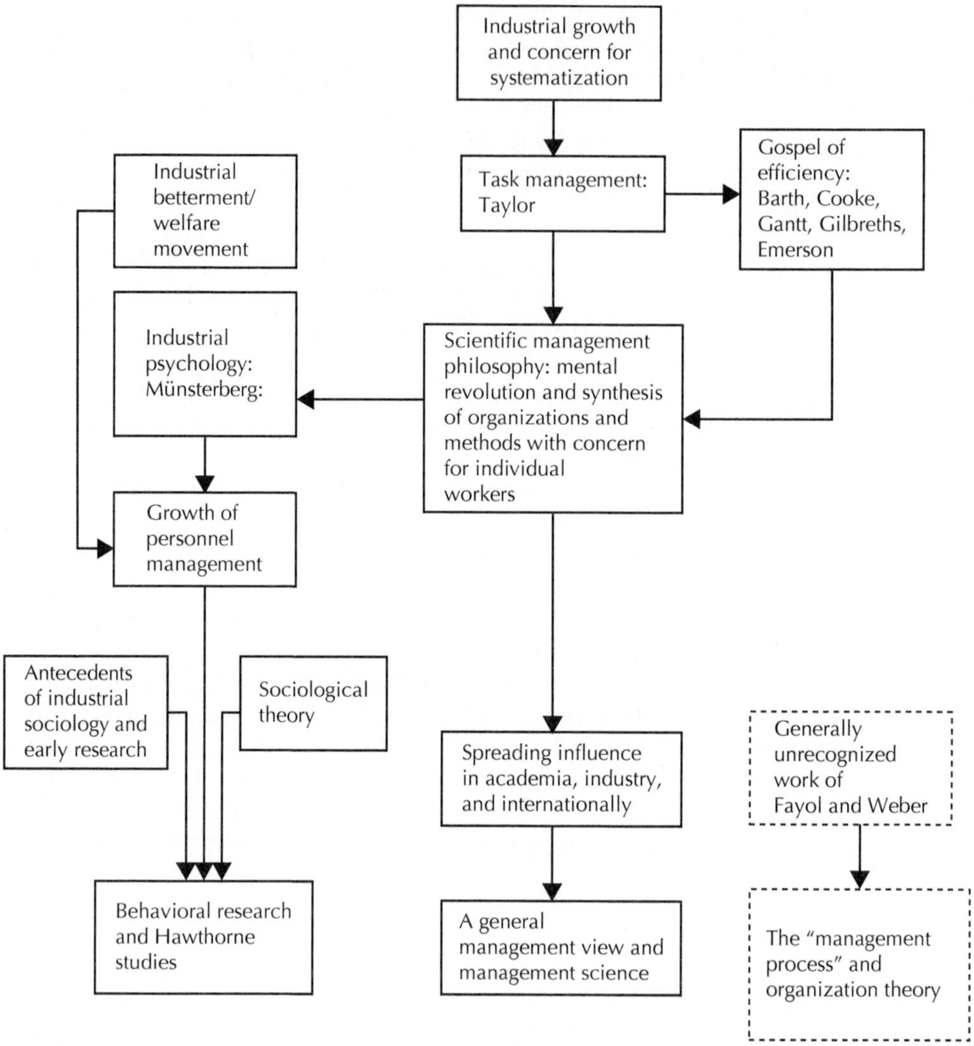

FIGURE 12.1 Synopsis of the scientific-management era

All reflected, however, the imprint of Taylor's search for rationality in a changing and more industrialized world. Two of Taylor's contemporaries, Fayol and Weber, were to achieve acclaim in the future.

The question to what extent "the person makes the times" or "the times make the person" has been debated throughout history. Taylor and his disciples were the products of an era that, in economic terms, sought the rationalization, or full use, of the world's natural resources; in social terms, sanctioned individual initiative; and in political terms, encouraged uplift through efficiency. In turn, they were instrumental in giving voice to a movement that sought greater material prosperity and industrial harmony. Scientific management was the offspring of its culture and, in turn, sired a new era of economic, technological, social, and political vigor. The efforts of Taylor and his disciples still shape our lives today.

The Social-Person Era

PART III

Eras in management thought never begin and end neatly in any particular year. Just as in a musical performance, there is a blending of movements as themes shift among major and minor keys. Reflecting more of an emerging philosophy than a call for managerial action, the "social-person era"—ranging from the advent of the Hawthorne studies in 1924 to the early 1950s—signaled a transformation in the nation's traditional values and beliefs. The movement, however, did not receive any large degree of recognition until the 1930s. This era was dominated by the belief that employee satisfaction and productivity were dependent on favorable social interactions among employees and between employees and their supervisors; therefore, the key to efficiency and workplace harmony was supportive human relations. Part III begins by examining the Hawthorne studies, which served to give academic credence to what became known as the "human-relations movement." The lives and thoughts of two individuals—Mary P. Follett and Chester I. Barnard—who significantly contributed to our understanding of authority and responsibility, the need to coordinate effort, conflict resolution, and how to structure and design organizations for maximum effectiveness and efficiency, are discussed. Next, the growth and refinement of the human-relations movement as it progressed through micro and macro phases, from roughly 1930 into the early 1950s, are reviewed. This is followed by a complementary stream of management thought focused on the structure and design of organizations. Part III concludes with a look at human relations in theory and in practice, and a consideration of the economic, social, technological, and political environments of the social-person era.

The Hawthorne Studies

CHAPTER 13

No studies in the history of management thought have received so much publicity, so many different interpretations, so much praise, and yet so much criticism, as those begun in 1924 at the former Hawthorne Works of the Western Electric Company located at Cicero, Illinois, 7 miles west of downtown Chicago.[1] Colloquially referred to by residents simply as "Western," the Hawthorne Works manufactured telephones and switchboards used by Bell Telephone Company, today's AT&T. The studies spanned an 8-year period and dramatically revealed previously unappreciated patterns of employee behavior. Perhaps the most significant feature of the studies was that, for the first time, resources comparable to those commonly committed to research in the physical sciences were devoted to exploring human behavior in the workplace, thereby counterbalancing the shop-floor focus of the scientific-management era. What are known collectively as the "Hawthorne studies" are widely regarded as "the inaugural step in the creation of the field of human relations in industry."[2]

At the time of the studies, and with over two-million square feet of workspace, the 200-plus acre Hawthorne Works employed some 43,000 people 5½ days a week in nearly every trade and profession.[3] One of the largest manufacturing plants in the world, it had an annual payroll of $58 million dollars. Many employees were either first- or second-generation Cicero residents of Czech, Hungarian, Italian, Lithuanian, Polish, or Scandinavian origin, and the principal breadwinners for their immigrant families. A majority lived no more than 2 miles from the Hawthorne

[1] A 1941 *Reader's Digest* article exposed millions of readers to the studies. See Stuart Chase, "What Makes the Worker Like to Work?" *Readers Digest* 38(226) (February 1941), pp. 15–20. The Western Electric Manufacturing Company was incorporated at Chicago in 1872. At the time, Chicago was still considered "western." The company was purchased by Bell Telephone Company in 1881.

[2] Henry A. Landsberger, *Hawthorne Revisited: Management and the Worker, Its Critics, and Developments in Human Relations in Industry* (Ithaca, NY: New York State School of Industrial and Labor Relations, Cornell University, 1958), p. 8. Although the "Hawthorne studies" are variously referred to as the "Hawthorne experiments," we prefer the former designation, as an "experiment" refers to a specific kind of study design in which participants are randomly selected and randomly assigned. Despite Mayo's claim to the contrary (see Elton Mayo, "The Human Effect of Mechanization," *American Economic Review* 20 [Supplement] [March 1930], p. 157), neither method was applied in any of the Hawthorne studies.

[3] For more on the particular "context" in which the Hawthorne studies were conducted, see John S. Hassard, "Rethinking the Hawthorne Studies: The Western Electric Research in Its Social, Political and Historical Context," *Human Relations* 65(11) (2012), pp. 1431–1461. For visual images of the Hawthorne Works, see Dennis Schlagheck and Catherine Lantz, *Images of America: Hawthorne Works* (Charleston, SC: Arcadia Publishing, 2014). The Hawthorne Works closed after 81 years in 1983 and has since been replaced with a shopping center.

main gate at the corner of Cicero Avenue and what is now Carmack Road and walked to work. The Western Electric Company had long been noted for its enlightened human-resource policies and generous employee benefits.[4] In what Stephen B. Adams and Orville R. Butler have called the "apex of welfare capitalism at Western,"[5] it sponsored athletic, recreational, and social programs; operated a variety store offering merchandise at discounted prices; and sponsored an evening school. It maintained an employee building and loan association, a noncontributory benefit plan, a savings plan, and offered auto insurance at a reduced rate and an employee stock-purchase program. It also operated a company restaurant, several cafeterias, and numerous lunch counters, all where employees could purchase meals at cost. With its own hospital, railroad, power plant, fire department, and water-treatment facility, it was a city within a city. Employee morale was thought to be high, and there had been no labor unrest. As Hawthorne was virtually Bell's sole supplier of telephone apparatuses, there was intense pressure to meet production schedules and, thus, avoid any form of work stoppage.[6]

HUMAN RELATIONS IN INDUSTRY: AN INAUGURAL STEP

ILLUMINATION STUDY (1924–1927)

Initiated in collaboration with the National Research Council's Committee on Industrial Lighting, what became known as the Illumination Study (funded by the General Electric Company) was conducted under the direction of Dugald C. Jackson, a professor of electrical engineering at the Massachusetts Institute of Technology (MIT), who was assisted by his faculty colleagues Joseph W. Barker and Vannevar Bush.[7] The General Electric (GE) Company funded the Illumination Study because it was interested in research that would convince its customers to use artificial illumination in conjunction with natural illumination and, thereby, increase sales of lamps, fixtures, and wiring. GE co-founder Thomas A. Edison, inventor of the incandescent light bulb, was the Committee's honorary chairman. The study's original intent was to investigate the relationship between variations in workplace lighting and employee productivity. Based on prior research, it had been hypothesized that as the total artificial and natural lighting (i.e., illumination) in a workroom increased, employee productivity would increase as well.[8] In the winter of 1924, the MIT researchers investigated existing lighting conditions and performance in Western's punch-press, coil-winding, and relay-assembly departments to establish an initial baseline from which potential changes in employee productivity (i.e., output) could be measured over time. The illumination was then varied in each department, with the result that "output bobbed up and down without direct relation to illumination."[9]

---

[4] In his 1903 ASME paper, "Shop Management," Fred Taylor singled out the Western Electric's employment bureau for special commendation. See Frederick W. Taylor, "Shop Management," *Transactions of the American Society of Mechanical Engineers* 24 (1903), p. 1455.

[5] Stephen B. Adams and Orville R. Butler, *Manufacturing the Future: A History of Western Electric* (New York: Cambridge University Press, 1999), p. 122.

[6] Joseph M. Juran, "Early SQC: A Historical Supplement," *Quality Progress* 30(9) (September 1997), p. 74.

[7] Dugald C. Jackson, "Lighting in Industry," *Journal of the Franklin Institute* 205(3) (March 1928), pp. 285–303; Joseph W. Barker, "Technique of Economic Studies of Lighting in Industry," *Transactions of the Illuminating Engineering Society* 23 (1928), pp. 174–188. See also Charles D. Wrege and Ronald G. Greenwood, "Dugald C. Jackson: The Forgotten First Director of the Hawthorne Studies," unpublished manuscript, Charles D. Wrege Research Papers, 1925–2013, Series I: Western Electric and the Hawthorne Studies, Collection Number: 6395, Box 3, Folder 31, Kheel Center for Labor–Management Documentation and Archives, Catherwood Library, Cornell University, and on Vannevar Bush, the cover story "Yankee Scientist," *Time* 43(14) (April 3, 1944), pp. 52–57. As director of the U.S. Office of Scientific Research and Development during World War II, Bush was a central figure in organizing scientific and engineering talent to develop the atomic bomb, microwave radar, mass produced antibiotics, and other technologies crucial to the Allied victory. Barker went on to become the Dean of Engineering at Columbia University from 1930 to 1946. During World War II, he served as chief of the Division of Training Liaison Coordination for the U.S. Navy.

[8] Charles D. Wrege and Ronald G. Greenwood, "From New York City to Columbus, Ohio: How Illumination Tests Conducted from 1914 to 1923 Influenced the Hawthorne Studies," in Nanette Weiner and Richard J. Klimoski, eds., *Proceedings of the Midwest Academy of Management* (1982), pp. 55–64.

[9] Charles E. Snow, "Research on Industrial Illumination: A Discussion of the Relation of Illumination Intensity to Productive Efficiency," *Tech Engineering News* 8(7) (November 1927), p. 272.

In the summer of 1925, the researchers selected two groups of coil-winding operators, who were equal in experience and performance, for further study. Coil winding consists of turning a fine wire evenly in layers around a piece of iron. When an electric current is sent through the wire, the iron becomes an electromagnet that attracts iron and steel. The wire-wound magnet is called a "coil." One set of coil winders was designated the variable group (i.e., the group for which the level of lighting was to be varied) and the other the control group (the group to experience no changes in lighting). The groups were placed in two different buildings that were away from their regular department. The researchers systematically modified the illumination in the building housing the variable group. This time, however, regardless of whether the lighting was brighter, dimmer, or constant, output generally increased. Other modifications in the illumination also yielded unanticipated and seemingly contradictory results. In one instance, Homer Hibarger, a Western employee, studied two operators and gradually reduced the lighting to the equivalent of ordinary moonlight (0.06 footcandles), and output still increased. Ladialas "Wanda" Beilfus, one of the operators, recalled:

> Geri [Geraldine Sirchio] . . . was with me. We were taken to a small room. Mr. Hibarger was there with us, but it wasn't that bad. The lighting was a little darker but we could see what we were doing. . . . They found out even with the bad lighting we did just as well.[10]

In April 1927, the Illumination Study was abandoned. Two conclusions seemed obvious: (1) illumination was only one of many factors affecting employee output, and (2) no simple cause-and-effect relationship existed between illumination and employee productivity. It was thus recognized that other factors would have to be investigated and that other variables would have to be controlled in future studies. In preparing a report on the study's findings, Charles E. Snow, an MIT graduate student Jackson selected as the field engineer to run the Illumination Study, concluded that there were too many factors at play to establish that illumination was directly related to employee productivity. Snow acknowledged that, whereas many of these factors could be controlled or eliminated, the "one great stumbling block remaining is the problem of the psychology of the human individual."[11] At this juncture, it would have been easy to move on to other pursuits. Hibarger, however, intrigued by the unanticipated and seemingly contradictory results, felt the study should be continued. George A. Pennock, Superintendent of Inspection, and Clarence G. Stoll, Works Manager, agreed. With their support, Hibarger designed and conducted a second study.

RELAY-ASSEMBLY TEST-ROOM STUDY (1927–1932)

In early 1927, under Hibarger's direction, a second study was begun to further investigate the puzzling results of the Illumination Study, with the goal of determining the influence of working conditions (e.g., rest breaks, workday length, company-provided mid-morning lunches, and method of payment) on employee productivity. This phase of the Hawthorne studies, known as the Relay-Assembly Test-Room Study, lasted 5 years. The original study participants were five relay assemblers (Adeline Bogotowicz; Irene Rybacki; Theresa Layman; Wanda Beilfus, who had participated in the Illumination Study; and Anna Haug); one layout operator (Bea Stedry), who supplied the assemblers with parts; and Hibarger, who served as the test room's initial observer. All were between the ages of 18 and 30. Their work involved repetitively assembling telephone relays, which are electromagnetic switches used to amplify an electric current (a signal). The four-inch-long relays weighed a few ounces, consisting of a coil, armature, contact springs, and insulators held in position by four machine screws. A single relay required approximately 1 minute to assemble. In the adjacent photograph of the relay assemblers at their workbench, the trays opposite each assembler contain parts for assembly. In front of each assembler is a jig used

[10] Wanda Beilfus quoted in Alfred A. Bolton, "Relay Assembly Test Room Participants Remember: Hawthorne a Half Century Later," *International Journal of Public Administration* 17(2) (1994), p. 377.
[11] Snow, "Research on Industrial Illumination," p. 282.

Relay-assembly test-room participants, circa 1928: (left to right) Beatrice Stedry (layout operator), Anna Haug (operator #5), Wanda Beilfus (operator #4), Theresa Layman (operator #3), Geraldine Sirchio (operator #2), and Mary Volango (operator #1)

in assembling the relays. Stedry, the layout operator, is on the far left. Hibarger is seated facing the assemblers on the left, out of the picture.[12]

The number of assemblers participating in the study was limited by the capability of the recording device to punch a hole in a telegraph tape each time an assembler dropped a completed relay down a collection chute. The telegraph tape had only five channels, thus limiting the number of assemblers that could be included in the study. Hibarger's role as observer was to record the principal events in the room hour by hour and to create and maintain a friendly atmosphere. How the study participants were selected offers a glimpse of work life in the late 1920s. Frank Platenka, the regular relay-assembly department supervisor, told Wanda Beilfus that there was going to be a study and asked her to "pick out girls who I felt would not be married soon" and who would like to work in a special room and participate in a study.[13] The assemblers were invited to Pennock's office "where the plan and objectives of the study were explained . . . [and] they readily consented to take part in the study."[14] Richard Gillespie has noted that beyond the assemblers agreeing to participate in the study, the work itself "required manual dexterity, along with a willingness to repeat the same task every minute or so for almost nine hours per day, five and a half days per week."[15]

The assemblers were observed in their regular department (without their knowledge) for 2 weeks prior to moving to the special test room, where work conditions could be more closely

---

[12] T. North Whitehead, "Social Relationships in the Factory: A Study of an Industrial Group," *The Human Factor* 9(11) (November 1935), p. 383.

[13] Wanda Beilfus quoted in Bolton, "Relay Assembly Test Room Participants Remember," p. 361.

[14] Claire E. Turner, "Test Room Studies in Employee Effectiveness," *American Journal of Public Health* 23(6) (June 1933), pp. 577–584.

[15] Richard Gillespie, *Manufacturing Knowledge: A History of the Hawthorne Experiments* (Cambridge, England: Cambridge University Press, 1991), p. 51.

controlled.[16] Additionally, measurements were made of factors such as pulse rate, blood pressure, blood condition ratings, and vascular skin reactions, as well as general weather conditions and test-room temperature and humidity. Every 6 weeks the assemblers were given a complete medical examination to track their health and menstrual cycles. Records were kept of the amount of sleep each assembler had had the previous night, what food she had eaten, recreations, home conditions, and other outside influences. Unlike in their regular department, in the study, the assemblers were allowed to talk and to leave their workbenches whenever they wished. The assemblers had no supervisor, as would be customary. At most, Hibarger exercised a quasi-supervisory function. After 5 weeks, the assemblers were placed on a new piece-rate plan that tied their pay to their test-room performance. The new plan was implemented for the benefit of the workers: "[it] was done in order that the entire earnings resulting from their efforts would be returned directly to them and not distributed over a large number of people," as would be the case in the regular relay-assembly department. The assemblers were assured that they would not suffer financially and would have the opportunity to earn more money than they had in their regular department. Thus, the researchers reported "we were able to easily convince the operators that any gains in output would be returned entirely to them and we were thus reasonably assured of their full cooperation."[17]

During the first seven periods of the study (April 25, 1927, to January 21, 1928), various working conditions were changed to determine the effect, if any, on productivity. Two 5-minute rest periods were introduced, followed by two 10-minute rests, then six 5-minute rests, and later a lunch was provided in one of Western's employee restaurants. Whenever a change was planned, its purpose was explained to the assemblers and their comments solicited. Changes that did not meet their approval were abandoned. The most surprising finding during this time was that the assemblers' productivity "tended in general to increase no matter what changes in working conditions were introduced."[18] There was an emerging concern, however, about the behavior and production of Adeline Bogotowicz and Irene Rybacki. Hibarger had evidence that Bogotowicz was restricting output (she and Rybacki were consistently the lowest producers), and Theresa Layman, who sat at a workbench closest to Bogotowicz, said that Bogotowicz and Rybacki talked only to each other and refused to talk with others. Rybacki and Bogotowicz were dismissed from the test room and returned to the regular relay-assembly department. The reasons offered for their dismissal were "lack of co-operation," "poor output," and a "talking problem."[19] A June 1928 Hawthorne report noted that Rybacki had been cooperative when the study began and became antagonistic only after her health declined. Medical tests revealed that Irene was severely anemic; she received medical treatment and was given a 2-week paid leave. She was able to recover her health and return to work in the regular relay-assembly department.[20]

---

[16] Much of the following section is based on the seminal research of Charles D. Wrege, "Facts and Fallacies of Hawthorne: A Historical Study of the Origins, Procedures, and Results of the Hawthorne Illumination Tests and Their Influence on the Hawthorne Studies," 3 vols. (Doctoral dissertation, New York University, New York, NY, 1961); released in book form (2 vols.) by Garland Press, New York, 1986. See also Ronald G. Greenwood, Alfred A. Bolton, and Regina A. Greenwood, "Hawthorne a Half Century Later: Relay Assembly Participants Remember," *Journal of Management* 9(2) (Fall/Winter 1983), pp. 217–231.

[17] [Richard H. Frazier], "An Investigation of Rest Pauses, Working Conditions, and Industrial Efficiency," Progress Report no. 4 (Supplementary Program Report as of May 11, 1929). Reproduced on Reel 1, Box 1, Folder 6, p. 144, *Microfilmed Records of the Industrial Relations Experiment Carried Out by the Western Electric Company at the Hawthorne Works, Hawthorne, IL.* Hawthorne Studies Collection, Baker Library, Harvard University Business School, Boston, MA. Available online at https://digital.libraries.ou.edu/utils/getfile/collection/Hawthorne/id/135/filename/136.pdf.

[18] George A. Pennock, "Industrial Research at Hawthorne: An Experimental Investigation of Rest Periods, Working Conditions and Other Influences," *Personnel Journal* 8(5) (February 1930), p. 297.

[19] T. North Whitehead, *The Industrial Worker: A Statistical Study of Human Relations in a Group of Manual Workers*, vol. 1 (Cambridge, MA: Harvard University Press, 1938), p. 117; Fritz J. Roethlisberger and William J. Dickson (with the collaboration of Harold A. Wright), *Management and the Worker: An Account of a Research Program Conducted by the Western Electric Company, Hawthorne Works, Chicago* (Cambridge, MA: Harvard University Press, 1939), p. 53.

[20] "Case Study of a Relay Assembly Test Room Operator Who Was Removed from the Test for Health and Attitudinal Reasons Possibly Related to Her Work in the Study," June 28, 1928. Rybacki is identified in this report as Operator 2A. Reproduced on Reel 3, Box 5, Folder 2, p. 2, *Microfilmed Records of the Industrial Relations Experiment Carried Out by the Western Electric Company at the Hawthorne Works, Hawthorne, IL.* Hawthorne Studies Collection, Baker Library, Harvard University Business School, Boston, MA. Available online at https://digital.libraries.ou.edu/cdm/singleitem/collection/Hawthorne/id/169/rec/7.

Bogotowicz's and Rybacki's positions in the test room were assigned to Mary Volango and Geraldine "Geri" Sirchio (who also participated in the Illumination Study), two experienced relay assemblers. Output in period eight went up as soon as Sirchio and Volango arrived, exceeding any previous level achieved by the original five assemblers. Sirchio became the work group's informal leader, and although output would vary from one period to the next, the trend continued upward, exceeding previous peak levels. Then, in period 12, over a year after the study started, rest periods were removed, the workday and workweek were returned to their original length, and the assemblers again had to furnish their own lunches. Total output went up as the workweek increased to 5½ days (48 hours), but hourly output declined. Rest periods were reinstated in period 13, and weekly and hourly output reached an all-time high.

It was clear to Pennock, Hibarger, and others that something unusual was happening. Pennock visited MIT, his alma mater, in the winter of 1927 to seek professional advice. MIT's President Julius A. Stratton recommended that Pennock seek out Clair E. Turner, an MIT professor of biology and public health. Turner soon joined the study as a consultant. At Turner's suggestion, fatigue, health habits, and mental attitudes were explored as potential explanations for the assemblers' enhanced productivity.[21] Turner was able to establish that reduced fatigue as a result of rest periods was not the cause of the assemblers' increased output. The rest periods, however, gave the assemblers more opportunities for social interaction. Mental attitudes, more than anything else, seemed to explain the increase. In order of importance, Turner attributed the assemblers' increased output to (1) working in a small group; (2) a less restrictive and friendlier supervisory style; (3) increased earnings; (4) the novelty of being a study participant; and (5) the attention given to the assemblers by company officials and the researchers.[22]

Pennock was the first to note the influence of supervisory style on the assemblers' productivity. The assemblers were aware they were producing more in the test room than they did in the regular relay-assembly department, and they said the increase had occurred without any conscious effort on their part. They offered two explanations. First, "it was fun" working in the test room. They enjoyed being the center of attention. Second, the new supervisory style, or, more accurately, the "absence of supervision," contributed, in Mayo's words, to a "freer and happier environment."[23] For example, in the test room, as noted, the women were allowed to talk with one another, whereas in their regular department conversation was forbidden. Hibarger's efforts to create a friendly atmosphere in the test room resulted in the women receiving a great deal of considerate and personal attention. In short, the test-room supervision was more thoughtful and less authoritarian than the supervision style the assemblers had previously experienced, and the atmosphere was freer and less anxiety provoking. As Donald Chipman, who succeeded Hibarger as the test room's observer, explained in a 1979 interview, the supervisory style changed from "I'm the boss and you'd better know it" to "Let's get along and work together."[24] This was in dramatic contrast to the atmosphere created by the regular relay-assembly room supervisor, Frank Platenka. As one of the operators, Theresa Layman, explained: "[W]e were more relaxed. We didn't see the boss [Platenka], didn't hear him . . . he was mean. He died; I didn't even go to see him." Another operator, Wanda Beilfus added, "It [the test room] was just family, you know, real friendly."[25] Turner summed up the results: "[There was] a fundamental change in supervision . . .

[21] Claire E. Turner, *I Remember* (New York: Vantage Press, 1974), pp. 83–87; Charles D. Wrege, "Solving Mayo's Mystery: The First Complete Account of the Origin of the Hawthorne Studies—The Forgotten Contributions of C. E. Snow and H. Hibarger," in Robert L. Taylor, Michael J. O'Donnell, Robert A. Zawacki, and Donald D. Warwick, eds., *Proceedings of the Annual Meeting of the Academy of Management* (1976), pp. 12–16.
[22] Turner, "Test Room Studies," p. 583.
[23] Elton Mayo, "The Blind Spot in Scientific Management," in *Proceedings, Sixth International Congress for Scientific Management, vol.3: Development Section* (London: P. S. King & Son, 1935), p. 215. See also George C. Homans, "Report of the Committee," in Committee on Work in Industry, National Research Council, *Fatigue of Workers: Its Relation to Industrial Production* (New York: Reinhold Publishing, 1941), p. 63.
[24] Donald Chipman quoted in Jeffrey Sonnenfeld, "Clarifying Critical Confusion in the Hawthorne Hysteria," *American Psychologist* 37(12) (December 1982), p. 1398. See also Donald Chipman, "Remembrances of Hawthorne Studies," *The* [Hawthorne] *Microphone* 6(4) (June–July 1985), pp. 20–23.
[25] Greenwood, Bolton, and Greenwood, "Hawthorne," pp. 222, 224.

no group chief . . . but instead a 'friendly observer.' . . . Discipline was secured through leadership and understanding. . . . An *esprit de corps* grew up within the group."[26]

At this point, style of supervision and the assemblers' *esprit de corps*, or group spirit (which we noted as one of Fayol's 14 principles of management; see Chapter 10), were believed to explain the increases in productivity. One other factor, the assemblers' performance-incentive plan, was believed to contribute, but had not yet been examined empirically. Because the assemblers were paid on the output of 5 rather than 100 or more assemblers, their pay was tied more closely to their own individual effort. The average wage of the assemblers before going into the test room was $16 per week; in the test room, their average weekly earnings ranged from $28 to $50. Could this boost in wages possibly explain the increase in output?

To test this possibility, two new study groups were formed: a group of five relay assemblers and a group of five operators splitting mica, which was used as an insulator (Figure 13.1).

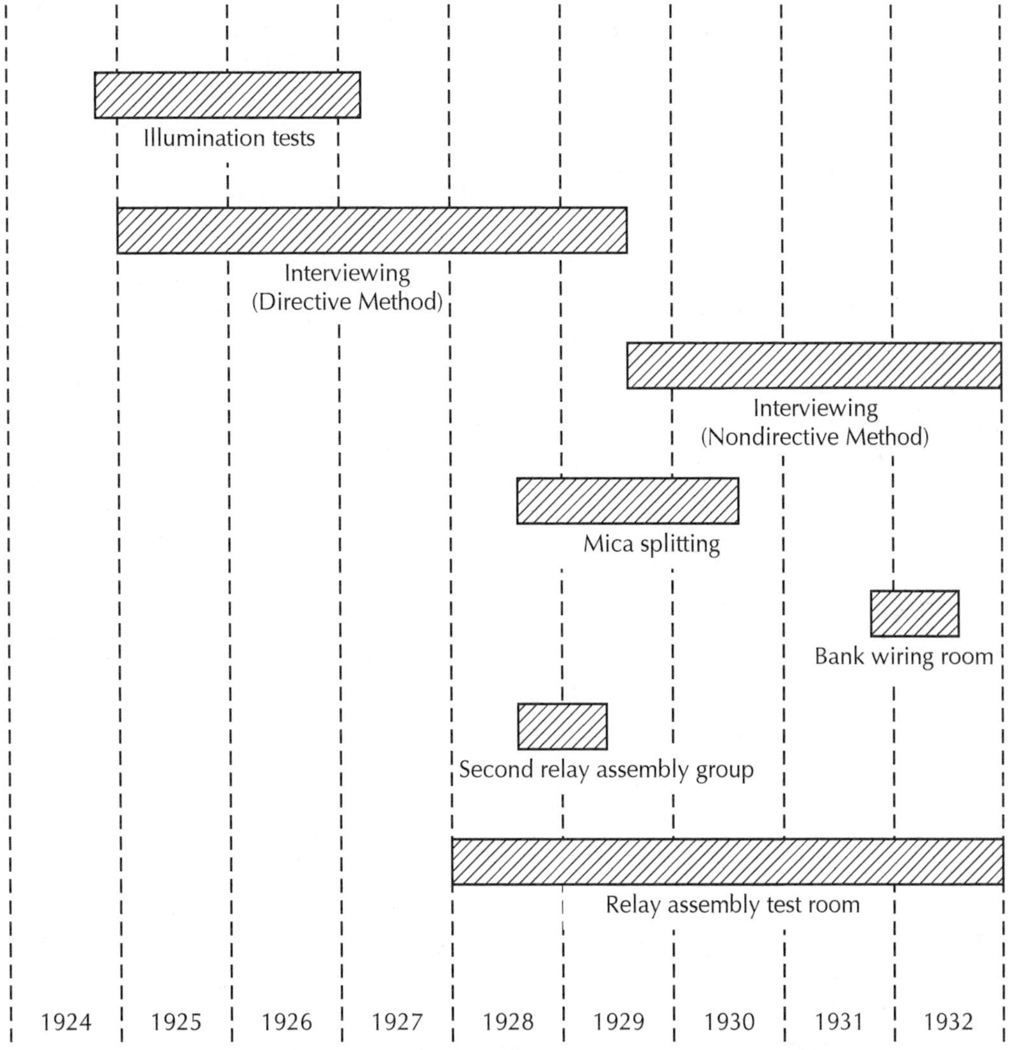

FIGURE 13.1 An overview of the Hawthorne studies

Source: Adapted from Appendix A of Greenwood, Bolton, and Greenwood, "Hawthorne," pp. 229–230. One study involving a typewriting group has been omitted because no report was issued.

[26] Turner, "Test Room Studies," p. 579.

For their first 9 weeks together, the relay assemblers were placed on a performance-incentive plan (the same as that used previously in the relay-assembly test room) that tied their pay to the performance of their small group. Initially, total output went up, leveled off (for all but one assembler whose output decreased), and then remained constant at a new higher level (112.6 percent over an established output base of 100 percent). After returning to the performance-incentive plan used in the regular relay-assembly department for a period of 7 weeks, the assemblers' performance dropped to 96.2 percent of the established output base. The mica splitters had always been on an individual piece-rate plan. After being moved to a special observation room, the mica splitters' rest periods and length of workday were varied, as had been done earlier in the relay-assembly test room. Changes in the mica splitters' output were similarly recorded. The mica splitters were studied for 14 months, and their average hourly output rose 15 percent.

Although the relay assemblers' output had gone up in both studies, except when they were returned to the group performance-incentive plan used in the regular relay-assembly department, Turner was hesitant to solely attribute the increase to the different pay schemes: "[The] changed pay incentive may have been one factor in increasing output but it certainly was not the only factor."[27] A 1929 interim report summarized the results of all three studies: (1) output of the assemblers was up from 35 to 50 percent; (2) fatigue reduction was not a factor in this increased output; (3) pay "was a factor of the appreciable importance in increasing output"; and (4) the workers were more "content" owing to the "pleasanter, freer, and happier working conditions" caused by the "considerate supervision."[28]

INTERVIEWING PROGRAM (1925–1932)

During the Illumination Study, Charles Snow and Homer Hibarger had begun interviewing Western employees to gain insights into employee–supervisor relations.[29] In the interviews, they asked questions such as: "How is your general health?" "Are you happy on the job?" "Are you influenced by any pressure from your working associates?" Because these items could be answered "yes" or "no," they were limited in the information they elicited. Another approach was needed if they were to gain any meaningful insights.

In October 1927, T. Kennedy Stevenson, Western's personnel director, had heard Harvard University professor Elton Mayo speak on "What Psychology Can Do for Industry in the Next Ten Years." Stevenson spoke with Mayo after the speech about the relay-assembly test-room study results and suggested that he visit the Hawthorne Works.[30] An Australian who earned a Bachelor of Arts degree in logic and philosophy from the University of Adelaide, Mayo had made unsuccessful attempts to study medicine at the Universities of Adelaide and Edinburgh. In 1911, he became a lecturer teaching moral philosophy at the University of Queensland.[31] While in Scotland, he participated as a research associate in a study of psychopathology, the scientific investigation of mental disorders; this experience served as an early basis for his work as an industrial researcher.

---

[27] *Ibid*, p. 582.

[28] [Frazier], "An Investigation of Rest Pauses, Working Conditions, and Industrial Efficiency," pp. 126–128.

[29] William J. Dickson, "The Hawthorne Plan of Personnel Counseling," *American Journal of Orthopsychiatry* 15(2) (April 1945), pp. 343–347; *idem*, "An Approach to the Human Factor in Human Relations," in Louis M. Hacker, ed., *The New Industrial Relations* (Ithaca, NY: Cornell University Press, 1948), pp. 95–122; Scott Highhouse, "The Brief History of Personnel Counseling in Industrial-Organizational Psychology," *Journal of Vocational Behavior* 55(3) (December 1999), pp. 318–336.

[30] Gillespie, *Manufacturing Knowledge*, p. 70. See also Richard C. S. Trahair and Kyle D. Bruce, "Human Relations and Management Consulting: Elton Mayo and Eric Trist," in Matthias Kipping and Timothy Clark, eds., *Oxford Handbook of Management Consulting* (Oxford, England: Oxford University Press), p. 57.

[31] For a biography of Mayo's life, see Richard C. S. Trahair, *The Humanist Temper: The Life and Work of Elton Mayo* (New Brunswick, NJ: Transaction Books, 1984). See also Lyndall F. Urwick, "Elton Mayo—His Life and Work," in *Papers and Proceedings Twelfth International Congress of Scientific Management* (Melbourne: CIOS, 1960), n. p. Reprinted in Arthur G. Bedeian, ed., *Evolution of Management Thought*, vol. 3 (London: Routledge, 2012), pp. 113–136.

George Elton Mayo (Elton as he would be called) had immigrated to the United States in 1922. Soon after arriving, he became a research associate at the University of Pennsylvania's Wharton School of Finance and Commerce and, subsequently, received a Laura Spelman Rockefeller Memorial Fund Fellowship to study "Individual Industrial Efficiency." In his research on industrial unrest in Australia, Mayo had found that personal difficulties experienced in the workplace could not be explained by any one factor but must be dealt with in what he called "the psychology of the total situation."[32] This was a Gestalt concept that formed the basis for Mayo's view of organizations as social systems and recognized that knowing the parts is not equivalent to knowing the whole. Moreover, this concept highlighted how, in addition to knowing how each part of a social system functions, it is necessary to foresee how their interactions could produce unanticipated consequences. In a study remarkably similar to the original goal of the Hawthorne researchers, Mayo followed the conventional wisdom of the time and sought a relationship between working conditions and employee output at Continental Mills, a wool textile mill near Philadelphia (Pennsylvania).[33] By introducing rest periods, Mayo was able to reduce employee turnover in the mill's mule-spinning department from 250 to 5 percent, and to improve man-hour efficiency. The rest periods, in Mayo's terms, reduced employees' "pessimistic reveries," thus improving their morale and productivity. By "pessimistic reveries," Mayo meant situations in which employees became lost in negative thoughts about their personal lives'. Mayo considered employee reveries to be a form of mild mental illness or psychopathology encouraged by industrial society.[34] Mayo's research at Continental Mills attracted the attention of Wallace B. Donham, dean of Harvard's Graduate School of Business, to which, in 1926, Mayo was appointed an associate professor of industrial research.

Mayo first visited the Hawthorne Works for two days in April 1928, more than a year after the relay-assembly room study had begun.[35] It has been suggested that if Mayo had not "come on the scene" when he did, the Hawthorne research may have been discontinued given the failure to reach any firm conclusions. Consequently, the Hawthorne studies would have probably remained unknown to anyone outside the Western Electric Company. As one of his former students noted, however, "Mayo had a flare for dramatizing research findings," and "[i]t was Mayo who excited the imaginations of company executives and persuaded them of the importance of continuing exploration in this new field."[36] Mayo visited Western Electric for four days in April 1929 and became more deeply involved in 1930. The 1929 visit was critical for the interviewing program. Mayo felt that "a remarkable change of mental attitude in the group" was the key factor in explaining the Hawthorne puzzle. In his opinion, the relay assemblers had become a social unit, had liked the increased attention they received, and had developed a great deal of pride in being associated with the different studies. According to Mayo, "[t]he most significant change that the Western Electric Company introduced into its 'test room' bore only a casual relation to the experimental changes. What the Company actually did for the group was to reconstruct entirely its whole industrial situation."[37]

To understand a group's "total situation," Mayo felt that a conversational, or nondirective, approach should be used in the Hawthorne interview program. The basic premise of this approach

[32] Elton Mayo, "The Basis of Industrial Psychology: The Psychology of the Total Situation Is Basic to a Psychology of Management," *Bulletin of the Taylor Society* 9(6) (December 1924), pp. 249–259. See also Mayo, "The Irrational Factor in Human Behavior: The 'Night-Mind' in Industry," *Annals of the American Academy of Political and Social Science* 110 (November 1923), pp. 117–130. For more on Mayo's research on industrial unrest in Australia, see Helen Bourke, "Industrial Unrest as Social Pathology: The Australian Writings of Elton Mayo," *Australian Historical Studies* 20(79) (1982), pp. 217–233.

[33] Elton Mayo, "Revery and Industrial Fatigue," *Personnel Journal* 8 (December 1924), pp. 273–281. See also Robert L. Duffus, "Satisfactory Rest Periods Solve Labor Turnover," *New York Times*, November 16, 1924, p. X8.

[34] Mark A. Griffin, Frank J. Landy, and Lisa Mayocchi, "Australian Influences on Elton Mayo: The Construct of Revery in Industrial Society," *History of Psychology* 5(4) (November 2002), pp. 356–375.

[35] For a record of Mayo's Hawthorne visits, see John H. Smith, "Elton Mayo and the Hidden Hawthorne," *Work, Employment & Society* 1(1) (March 1987), pp. 107–120.

[36] William Foote Whyte, [Review of the book *The Elusive Phenomena*], *Human Organization* 37(4) (Winter 1978), p. 414.

[37] Elton Mayo, *The Human Problems of an Industrial Civilization* (New York: Macmillan, 1933), p. 73.

was that a "new" supervisory role was necessary. This role would be one of openness, concern, and willingness to listen. For instance, the Hawthorne researchers had noted that the relay assemblers were "apprehensive of authority," but once the researchers had shown more concern with the assemblers' personal needs, the assemblers lost their shyness and fear, and talked more freely to company officials and observers. Moreover, the assemblers developed a greater zest for work and formed personal friendships, both on and off the job. They began seeing one another socially, attending parties in one another's homes, and going to the theater together. In sum, the assemblers became a cohesive group that stressed loyalty and cooperation. This seemed to improve their *esprit de corps* and to be closely associated with a friendlier supervisory style, both of which were associated with increased productivity. This presumed link between supervision, group spirit, and productivity became the foundation of the so-called "human-relations movement."

Using the nondirective technique Mayo recommended, the Hawthorne interview program allowed employees to express their feelings more freely: "As [t]he interviewers just let the interviewees talk . . . out came stories of personality conflicts, troubles at home, etc., or conversely, stories of satisfied employees, interested in their jobs and comfortable in their outlook toward life."[38] An interviewer's job was to keep employees talking, and the average length of employee interviews increased from 30 to 90 minutes. In later follow-up interviews, employees expressed the opinion that working conditions had improved (although they had not changed) and that their wages had increased (even though the wage scale was no different). In brief, it seemed that the opportunity to be heard made the employees feel better, even though their jobs remained the same.

The complaints gathered in 21,126 interviews between 1928 and 1930 were analyzed and, in general, found to concern personal feelings rather than reliable facts, one example being that "[s]ome complained that the company paid off only for seniority, not merit; others complained that the old-timers weren't getting just reward."[39] This was one of the earliest uses in an industrial setting of the research technique that is now known as "content analysis."[40] The separation of fact and sentiment led the researchers to distinguish between the *manifest* (material) and *latent* (psychological) content of a complaint. For example, one employee interviewed was preoccupied with the noise, temperature, and fumes in his department. Further examination revealed that his latent concern was the fact that his brother had recently died of pneumonia, and the interviewee feared that his own health might be impaired. In another case, complaints about a low piece-rate were traced to an employee's concern for medical bills arising from his wife's illness. In essence, "*Certain complaints were no longer treated as facts in themselves but as symptoms or indicators of personal or social situations which needed to be explored.*"[41] From the researchers' viewpoint, a worker's preoccupation with personal concerns inhibited their performance, a conclusion that, as noted, Mayo had called "pessimistic reveries" in his early research. The outcome of the interviewing program was supervisory training in the need to listen and provide a means of emotional release for employees'. Supervisors were trained to be interviewers, to listen rather than to talk, and "to exclude from their personal contacts with employees any moral admonition, advice, or emotion."[42] In addition, it was found that "[t]he mere fact that the company was asking the questions appeared to improve [employee] morale."[43] Use of this nondirective interviewing technique enabled supervisors to handle employees' personal concerns more intelligently, locate factors adversely affecting employee performance, and remove the events or factors in employees' social or physical environment that were adversely influencing their lives. The "new" supervisor was to be more people-oriented, less aloof, and better skilled in handling social and personal situations.

---

38 Bob Boardman, "The Relay Room Known Round the World," *WE* [*Western Electric News*] 16(2) (March–April 1964), p. 43.
39 *Ibid.*
40 Landsberger, *Hawthorne Revisited*, p. 83.
41 Roethlisberger and Dickson, *Management and the Worker*, p. 269.
42 *Ibid.*, p. 323.
43 Boardman, "The Relay Room Known Round the World," p. 42.

The product of this human-relations style of management was better employee morale, fewer pessimistic reveries, and improved output.

BANK-WIRING OBSERVATION ROOM STUDY (1931–1932)

In late 1930, Clair Turner wrote Mark L. Putnam, chief of Western's Industrial Research Division, stating that, in his opinion, the mica-splitting study was not yielding any useful information and suggested that "[they] would do well to substitute a test room study group of men" to gain additional insights into what factors influence group output.[44] It was subsequently decided that the entire Bank-Wiring Department would be studied as a "group." The plan for the proposed study, however, took a different turn because of objections by the department's supervisor, Henry S. Wolff, and his fellow supervisors in other departments. The supervisors were concerned that the purpose of the proposed study was to increase output, as had happened in the relay-assembly test room, and this would reflect unfavorably on their own job performance. William J. Dickson, chief of Hawthorne's employee-relations research department, summarized the supervisors' sentiments:

> They felt that those girls [in the relay-assembly test room] had been given special inducements in the form of a special gang rate, that ordinary production difficulties had been carefully eliminated, and that the operators had been petted and babied along from the start. "Of course," they said, "anybody could get production that way, only we [bank-wiring supervisors] can't get away with things like that."[45]

To overcome the supervisors' concerns, a number of changes were made in the plan for the proposed study: (1) a group of bank-wiring room operators would be segregated in a special area for observation, but visitors would not be allowed; (2) the operators' earnings would be based on their output as a group, factored into the output of the operators remaining in the regular bank-wiring department; (3) the operators' supervisor would remain the same, and an observer working with the researchers would be kept in the background rather than being "friendly and supportive," as Hibarger had been with the relay assemblers; and (4) workplace layout and procedures would remain constant. In effect, the only similarities to the relay test room would be placing the operators in a separate area and the presence of an observer. The operators selected for the study were a group of 14 men—9 wiremen, 3 soldermen, and 2 inspectors—engaged in assembling terminal banks for use in telephone exchanges.

It was clear from early findings that the operators constituted a complex social group with well-established norms and a common body of sentiments beyond that formally required by their job. They had their own conception of a "fair day's work" and prevailed as a group upon one another not to exceed this level of output.[46] Operators who exceeded the agreed-upon rate were known as "rate-busters." The operators feared that those who could not keep up with the pace of "rate-busters" would be "bawled out." They also were worried that if the rate-busters' output

---

[44] Claire E. Turner to Mark L. Putnam, October 13, 1930. Reproduced on Reel 7, Box 17, Folder 3, p. 12. *Microfilmed Records of the Industrial Relations Experiment Carried Out by the Western Electric Company at the Hawthorne Works, Hawthorne, IL. Hawthorne Studies Collection*, Baker Library, Harvard University Business School, Boston, MA. Available online at https://digital.libraries.ou.edu/cdm/singleitem/collection/Hawthorne/id/243/rec/50. Although Turner planned these studies, the primary investigator was W. Lloyd Warner, a Harvard University anthropologist who moved to the University of Chicago in 1935. See Roethlisberger and Dickson, Management and the Worker, p. 389n1.

[45] William J. Dickson, "Procedures in Establishing Bank Wiring Test Room," circa mid-July 1931. Reproduced on Reel 3, Box 7, Folder 1, p. 4, *Microfilmed Records of the Industrial Relations Experiment Carried Out by the Western Electric Company at the Hawthorne Works, Hawthorne, IL.* Hawthorne Studies Collection, Baker Library, Harvard University Business School, Boston, MA. Available online at https://digital.libraries.ou.edu/cdm/singleitem/collection/Hawthorne/id/174/rec/75.

[46] For more on the use of performance incentives at Hawthorne, see Stanley S. Homes, *Extra Incentive Wage Plans Used by the Hawthorne Works of the Western Electric Company, Inc.*, Production Executives' Series, no. 17 (New York: American Management Association, 1925).

was adopted as a daily output standard, the *bogey,* or "the level of performance which could be sustained by an expert operator at maximum efficiency," would be increased, and they would find themselves having to work harder for the same amount of pay.[47] At the same time, the men strongly believed that an operator's output should not fall too far below the group norm. If it did, an operator was known as a "rate-chiseler." Additionally, the operators held that no one should ever say or do anything that would injure a fellow operator. If he did, he was a "squealer." The operators engaged in several practices that violated company policies. For instance, although it was forbidden, the operators frequently traded jobs. There also was a great deal of informal helping among operators, which was also against company policy. Thus, it was important that no one squeal on a fellow operator. Finally, the operators felt that a person should not attempt to maintain social distance. For example, if someone was an inspector, he should not act like one.[48]

The bank-wiring room operators had developed various methods for enforcing their norms. Pressure was applied through subtle forms of ridicule, sarcasm, and *binging*, a practice whereby one operator expressed displeasure with the actions of another by hitting him as hard as possible on the upper arm. Exceeding the accepted output norm would elicit such chastisement, along with taunts of "Speed King" or "The Slave." The virtue of these practices did not lie in the resulting physical pain experienced by an operator, but rather in the mental hurt that came from knowing that one's coworkers disapproved of his behavior.

Discovery of the bank-wiring room operators' "informal organization" and their restriction of output when incentive pay was available for higher productivity surprised the Hawthorne researchers. Fred Taylor was keenly aware of systematic soldiering and work group pressures; Whiting Williams had recounted his own experiences concerning informal workplace relationships and attitudes; and Stanley B. Mathewson had made an extensive study of pressures leading to employee restriction of output.[49] Despite the experiences of others, the researchers found it noteworthy that "attention had been called to the fact that social groups in shop departments were capable of exercising very strong control over the work behavior of their individual members."[50] Output restriction was news to the researchers because they claimed to have been "unaware of its implications for management practice and employee satisfaction."[51] Knowledge builds on knowledge, and the failure of the researchers to learn from prior writings on informal-group behavior is a fault that was roundly criticized,[52] although it should not detract from the significance of their findings.

What explained the difference in output between the relay assemblers and the bank-wiring room operators? In the former case, employee output had increased, but in the latter, output restriction was the norm. Both groups included observers working with researchers, but their roles were different. In the relay-assembly study, the observer took the assemblers into his confidence, asked for their suggestions, and encouraged them to participate in decisions affecting their welfare. In the bank-wiring room, however, the observer merely watched while the operators engaged in the same informal behavior they had practiced in the past. The Hawthorne researchers' eventual explanation for the output differences would bolster their arguments for a new style of supervision. In explaining the bank-wiring operators' behavior, additional insights for understanding organizations as social systems would be forthcoming.

The Hawthorne researchers found that informal work groups perform two functions: (1) they protect group members from coworker behavior that may be regarded as inappropriate, such as rate busting and chiseling; and (2) they protect employees from employers who would

---

[47] William F. Hosford, "Wage Incentive Applications in the Western Electric Company," *N. A. C. A. Bulletin* 12(21) (July 1, 1931), p. 1769.

[48] Roethlisberger and Dickson, *Management and the Worker*, p. 522.

[49] Stanley B. Mathewson, *Restriction of Output among Unorganized Workers* (New York: Viking Press, 1931).

[50] Roethlisberger and Dickson, *Management and the Worker,* p. 379.

[51] *Ibid.*, p. 380.

[52] Mary B. Gilson, [Review of the book *Management and the Worker*]. *American Journal of Sociology* 46(1) (July 1940), pp. 98–101.

attempt to raise output standards, cut pay rates, or challenge a work group's norms. Informal groups are, in effect, instruments used by employees to control one another's activities and sentiments, as well as to provide protection from the actions of their employers. As discovered in the Hawthorne interview program, in studying group behavior, facts had to be separated from personal feelings. To this end, the Hawthorne researchers began to explore the "facts" as perceived by employees, in contrast to company practices as seen by upper management. With regard to output restriction, the researchers concluded that fears of an economic depression and layoffs were not reasons for evading work, because employees restricted output in both good and bad economic times. Restriction was detrimental to employees because it increased unit costs and, therefore, could lead to a decrease in pay rates, an increase in required output, or the introduction of new technology to offset higher costs. Because Western had a long record of enlightened workplace polices and generous employee benefits, the researchers (reflecting the Paretian ideas discussed below) considered the employees' belief that restricting output was in their best interests to be an example of a "non-logical action," meaning a behavior that does not correspond with its intended purpose.[53]

Having concluded that mismanagement or general economic conditions were unrelated to the informal group's norms, the researchers sought an explanation by viewing the bank-wiring room as part of a larger organization-wide social system, influenced by group sentiments and activities. The researchers reasoned that most employees found interactions with efficiency experts and other staff members to be disturbing, as their actions could impinge on employee welfare. These staff members tended to follow the "logic of efficiency," according to which maximizing goods and minimizing costs is the ultimate argument for doing things. Not surprisingly, employees perceived the study as interfering with their autonomy. Further, supervisors (as a class) represented authority and, thus, possessed power to discipline employees to enhance output. Recognizing that employees were apprehensive of such authority, the researchers reckoned that employees resisted supervisory attempts to force their behavior into an efficiency mold. Again, the researchers concluded that this was non-logical behavior on the employees' part but stressed that supervisors and other managers must recognize this phenomenon and consider employee sentiments when workplace changes were introduced. The Hawthorne researchers thus admonished managers to view every organization as a social system. As they understood, a strict logic of efficiency in administering a technical system would inevitably fail because it omitted the non-logical sentiments of an organization's social system.

ORGANIZATIONS AS SOCIAL SYSTEMS

Mayo's views on organizations as social systems were influenced by the work of his Harvard colleague Lawrence J. Henderson and the Italian economist Vilfredo Pareto. Although Mayo was never a full-fledged Paretian, he did accept many of Pareto's ideas.[54] By contrast, one of Mayo's students, Fritz J. Roethlisberger, was closer in his general philosophy to Paretian thinking, especially about the structure of social systems. Roethlisberger received a B.A. degree from Columbia University in 1921 and a B.S. from MIT in 1922. From 1922 to 1924, he was engaged in industrial practice as a chemical engineer; he then returned to Harvard in 1925 to pursue an M.A. degree. He later joined Harvard's industrial research department and soon became involved in the Hawthorne research.[55]

[53] For more on Pareto's distinction between logical and non-logical actions, see Andrew Bongiorno, "A Study of Pareto's Treatise on General Sociology," *American Journal of Sociology* 36(3) (November 1930), pp. 349–370.

[54] See, especially, Vilfredo Pareto, *The Mind and Society, vol. 4: The General Form of Society*, trans. Arthur Livingston (New York: Harcourt, Brace and Company, 1935). Originally published in 1916.

[55] Fritz. J. Roethlisberger, *The Elusive Phenomena*, ed. George F. F. Lombard (Cambridge, MA: Harvard University Press, 1977). See also Lombard, ed., *The Contributions of F. J. Roethlisberger to Management Theory and Practice* (Cambridge, MA: Graduate School of Business, Harvard University, 1976).

Roethlisberger and William J. Dickson prepared the most widely read report of the Hawthorne studies, *Management and the Worker*. In this report, Pareto's thinking on the structure of social systems is fully evident. According to Roethlisberger and Dickson, the technical needs for efficiency and economic rate of return should be viewed as interrelated with a concern for the human element found in every organization. Employees have physical needs, but they also have personal needs. These needs arise from early social conditioning and persist in relations with coworkers and other workplace participants. Roethlisberger and Dickson recognized that events and objects in a work environment "cannot be treated as things in themselves. Instead, they have to be interpreted as carriers of social value."[56] For example, a physical desk has no innate significance, but if individuals who have desks supervise others, then a desk becomes a status symbol and a carrier of social value. Other items, such as type of clothing, age, gender, and seniority, can also take on social significance. Roethlisberger and Dickson concluded that because individuals are not governed by facts and logic, sentiments about events and objects in a work environment must be considered when dealing with employees and people in general.

Roethlisberger and Dickson recognized that when an organization's formal structure (i.e., its rules, policies, and procedures) clashes with the norms of its members' informal groups, there will invariably be trade-offs and conflict. They stressed, however, that informal groups should not be viewed as "bad," but as an inevitable aspect of the social system within a formal organization. Viewing an organization as a social system enables managers to balance the "logic of efficiency" demanded by formal rules, policies, and procedures and the "logic of sentiments" that is the basis for informal groups.[57] Thus, Roethlisberger and Dickson held that managers must strive to achieve equilibrium between an organization's technical and human requirements. It follows that, to survive, an organization must secure its economic goals in such a way that "individuals through contributing services to this common purpose obtain personal satisfaction that makes them willing to cooperate."[58]

In short, the outcome of the Hawthorne studies was a call for an additional set of managerial skills. Technical skills alone were insufficient to cope with the employee sentiments and behavior discovered at Hawthorne. A second set of skills was required: first, diagnostic skills in understanding human behavior; and second, interpersonal skills in counseling, motivating, leading, and communicating with employees. The economic logic of efficiency must be balanced with an appreciation for the full range of employee sentiments.

COLLABORATION, LEADERSHIP, AND MOTIVATION

Over the intervening years, interpreting what happened at Hawthorne has become part of an evolving story. A phenomenon known as the *Hawthorne Effect* has long been part of social-science folklore. As noted above, one of the early explanations offered for the relay assemblers' increased output was the heightened attention they received. The researchers removed the assemblers from their regular department, placed them in a test room, and adopted a new supervisory style. The use of less stringent controls created a new social situation for the relay assemblers. The assemblers were advised and consulted about changes, their views were listened to sympathetically, and their physical and mental health became matters of great concern to the researchers and company officials. As they progressed, the Hawthorne Studies became less of a preplanned study and more a series of exercises in creating a social environment that encouraged employees to freely air their concerns and establish new interpersonal bonds with each other and with their supervisors. The relay assemblers felt they were part of something special and showed a great deal of pride in being associated with the different studies.

---

[56] Roethlisberger and Dickson, *Management and the Worker*, p. 557.

[57] *Ibid.*, pp. 556–564. "Logic of sentiments" is actually a contradiction because Roethlisberger and Dickson concluded that sentiments were "non-logical."

[58] *Ibid.*, p. 569. Roethlisberger and Dickson acknowledged their indebtedness to Chester I. Barnard (who is discussed in the next chapter) for this distinction.

These changes have prompted the charge that the researchers' actions—indeed, their very presence—altered the situation they hoped to investigate and, thus, tainted their findings. Reminiscent of Taylor's experience at the Simonds Rolling Machine Company (see Chapter 7), it has been suggested that the increase in the assemblers' productivity was a result of being singled out and made to feel important. Variously defined, the central idea behind the "Hawthorne effect," a term coined by Harvard-trained psychologist John R. P. French, is that changes in participants' behavior during the course of a study may be "related only to the special social position and social treatment they received" rather than a hypothesized cause or influence.[59] As a consequence, this "specialness" becomes "confounded with the independent variable under study, with a subsequent facilitating effect on the dependent variable, thus leading to ambiguous results."[60] Mayo recognized this phenomenon early on, writing: "Apparently the greater personal interest, together with the release from dominating supervision, was far more important than wage incentive, length of working day, rest periods, and similar factors" in explaining the assemblers' behavior.[61] As Roethlisberger further acknowledged, "If a human being is being experimented upon, he is likely to know it. Therefore, his attitudes toward the experiment and the experimenters become very important factors in determining his responses to the situation."[62]

Was there a Hawthorne Effect that biased the studies' results? Did the rise in the relay assemblers' output occur because they were being observed and had gained near-celebrity status? Theresa Layman, one of the relay assemblers, recalled, "No, we kept working. It didn't matter who watched us or who talked with us." Donald Chipman, the test room observer, concurred, "I agree . . . early in the study it had some bearing but . . . that just wore off."[63] Clair Turner stated, "We at first thought that the novelty of test room conditions might be partly responsible for increased output but the continuing increase in production over a four-year period suggests it was not of great importance."[64] A survey of industrial-organizational behavior textbooks has concluded: "[M]ythical beliefs among students about the Hawthorne Studies . . . [and] the Hawthorne Effect [are] probably an unfortunate tradition."[65] Although the Hawthorne Effect is widely referenced, there remains considerable doubt that being observed had any continuing impact on participants' performance.[66]

COLLABORATION IN WORK

As the economic depression that followed the October 1929 Wall Street stock-market crash (see Chapter 18) deepened, hours of work at Hawthorne were reduced and the original relay-assembly test-room study was discontinued. With the passage of time, Mayo changed his interpretation of what happened at Hawthorne.[67] As early as October 1931, he began to emphasize the need for "effective human collaboration" and a restoration of "social solidarity" in a changing world that left people without stability, purpose, or norms. When Mayo began to elaborate on his social philosophy, he gained a wider audience. Both academics and business leaders were attracted to

---

[59] John. R. P. French, Jr., "Field Experiments: Changing Group Productivity," in James G. Miller, ed., *Experiments in Social Process: A Symposium on Social Psychology* (New York: McGraw-Hill, 1950), p. 82.

[60] Desmond L. Cook, "The Hawthorne Effect in Educational Research," *Phi Delta Kappan* 44(3) (December 1962), p. 118. Italics omitted.

[61] Elton Mayo, "Psychology and Industry: The Problem of Working Together," in Walter V. Bingham, ed., *Psychology Today: Lectures and Study Manual* (Chicago, IL: University of Chicago Press, 1932), Appendix, p. 23.

[62] Fritz J. Roethlisberger, *Management and Morale* (Cambridge, MA: Harvard University Press, 1942), p. 14.

[63] Greenwood, Bolton, and Greenwood, "Hawthorne," p. 223.

[64] Turner, "Test Room Studies," p. 584.

[65] Ryan Olson, Jessica Verley, Lindsey Santos, and Coresta Salas, "What We Teach Students about the Hawthorne Studies: A Review of Content within a Sample of Introductory I-O and OB Textbooks," *The Industrial-Organizational Psychologist* 41(3) (January 2004), pp. 34–35. See also Charles D. Wrege and Arthur G. Bedeian, ". . . thumbs down for the Hawthorne effect," *The Psychologist* 21(11) (November 2008), p. 990.

[66] Stephen R. G. Jones, "Was There a Hawthorne Effect?" *American Journal of Sociology* 98(3) (November 1992), pp. 451–468.

[67] Trahair, *Humanist Temper*, p. 254.

his view that employee unrest and political dissidence were symptoms of an inherent psychopathology caused by an unsuitable work environment. By contrast, the views of Clair Turner, who had been more involved at Hawthorne on a day-to-day basis, became less influential in explaining the studies' results. Thus, MIT's star waned, and Harvard's waxed. As Roethlisberger recalled, "Mayo was an adventurer in the realm of ideas . . . the [Hawthorne] data were not his; the results were not his; but the interpretations of what the results meant and the new questions and hypotheses that emerged from them were his."[68]

Mayo's education and experiences suggest the basis for his emerging interpretation of human behavior. As noted, for a short time, Mayo studied medicine, and though he never received a medical degree, he developed an interest in psychopathology. At the time, individuals such as Jean-Martin Charcot, a French neurologist; Carl G. Jung, a Swiss psychiatrist; Pierre M. F. Janet, a French psychologist; and Sigmund Freud, the Austrian originator of psychoanalysis, were at the vanguard of psychopathological thought analysis. The works of Janet particularly intrigued Mayo. His last book was devoted to a critique of Janet's theories of obsessive thinking.[69] Janet believed that obsessive thinking was the primary mental disorder among trauma patients. Freudians called this "compulsion." Mayo considered Janet's theories of obsessive thinking and Freud's views on compulsive disorders to be complementary.[70] The essence of Mayo's obsession-compulsion interpretation was that individuals were incapacitated by their obsessions to such a degree that they were inflexible in their responses to life, including their personal, social, and workplace behavior. With respect to work, Mayo maintained that obsessions reduced an individual's general life satisfaction, which then led to decreased productivity and increased turnover and absenteeism. Although Mayo never concluded that any large number of Hawthorne employees suffered from severe trauma, he did think that its interview program had demonstrated that minimal levels of obsession (or preoccupation) existed in the sense that "conditions of work tended in some way to prevent rather than facilitate a satisfactory personal adaptation."[71] In Mayo's view, some employees are unable to find satisfactory work-related outlets for problems in their home, family, or social life. He believed that this blockage resulted in "pessimistic reveries," in which (as noted earlier) the employees became lost in negative thoughts about their personal lives. This discontent manifested as an apprehension of authority, output restriction, and other behaviors that reduced their morale and productivity. With employees unaware of the causes for their discontent Mayo believed that managers must serve as workplace therapists. Mayo further contended that the technical requirements necessary for people to work together cause a sense of personal futility, which leads to social maladjustment and, eventually, to obsessive, irrational behavior. As he explained:

> Human collaboration in work, in primitive and developed societies, has always depended for its perpetuation upon the evolution of a non-logical social code which regulates the relations between persons and their attitudes to one another. Insistence upon a merely economic logic of production . . . interferes with the development of such a code and consequently gives rise in the group to a sense of human defeat. This human defeat results in the formation of a social code at a lower level and in opposition to the economic logic. One of its symptoms is "restriction."[72]

Based on the belief that the technical requirements necessary for people to work together cause a sense of personal futility, which leads to social maladjustment and, eventually, to obsessive, irrational behavior, Mayo and Roethlisberger formed the philosophical rationale for the

---

[68] Roethlisberger, *Elusive Phenomena*, pp. 50–51.

[69] Elton Mayo, *Some Notes on the Psychology of Pierre Janet* (Cambridge, MA: Harvard University Press, 1948). See also Yeh Hsueh, "The Hawthorne Experiments and the Introduction of Jean Piaget in American Industrial Psychology, 1929–1932," *History of Psychology* 5(2) (May 2002), pp. 163–189.

[70] Mayo, *Human Problems of an Industrial Civilization*, pp. 107–110.

[71] *Ibid.*, p. 114.

[72] *Ibid.*, pp. 120–121.

human-relations movement. The movement's goal was to facilitate effective human collaboration in both work and life by balancing an organization's economic goals and its employees' personal needs.

ANOMIE AND SOCIAL DISORGANIZATION

Mayo borrowed Émile Durkheim's term *anomie* as a basis for his thinking about effective workplace collaboration.[73] As noted in Chapter 9, Durkheim used this term to refer to a breakdown or absence of social norms or values that leads some individuals to feel disconnected from society.[74] He held that in mechanical (meaning traditional) societies, individuals interact within a close-knit community that shares common sentiments and values. There is a solidarity, built around friendliness, neighborliness, and kinship, which gives individuals (who often perform the same job throughout their lives) a work identity as well as a personal identity in their public life. Durkheim believed that the onset of the Industrial Revolution destroyed this solidarity as it led to a greater division of labor, increased social and physical mobility, and the growth of large-scale organizations in which interpersonal relations shifted from a personal to an impersonal base. The result was endemic anomie in which individual identities were lost along with the social bonds that gave continuity and purpose to human existence. This led to personal and social disorganization and a general overall sense of futility, defeat, and disillusionment. Durkheim maintained that social inventions to cope with industrial changes had not kept pace with technological developments. Thus, the rapid economic growth experienced by the United States both before and after the turn of the century had disturbed "communal harmony."

Mayo argued that an increasingly technical society placed undue emphasis on engineering and yielded a technological interpretation of the meaning of work, in which achievement was based on a logic of efficiency. The social needs of individuals were pushed into the background, thereby reducing their "capacity for collaboration in work."[75] An emphasis on a logic of efficiency stifled individuals' yearning for group approval, social satisfaction, and social purpose gained through communal life. Drawing on Pareto's concept of an economic *élite*, composed of property owners and entrepreneurs, Mayo championed the creation of an administrative or managerial *élite* that was not only technically oriented but also understood human nature.[76] He hoped that this *élite* would restore a social code that facilitated effective human collaboration in both work and life by balancing an organization's economic goals and its employees' personal needs. As envisioned by Mayo, managers could aid in this restoration by receiving training in the human and social aspects of workplace behavior, developing listening and counseling skills, and recognizing and understanding the non-logical social code that regulates the relation between people and their attitudes to one another. The difficulty, as Mayo perceived it, was that managers thought the answer to effective human collaboration resided solely in technical efficiency, when in fact the challenges they faced were also social and human.

THE NEW LEADERSHIP: DISTINGUISHING FACT FROM SENTIMENT

Elton Mayo and Fred Taylor espoused the same goal: collaboration and cooperation in industry. Although the means they advocated differed, they both believed the employee–employer relationship should be mutually beneficial. Mayo, however, went further in arguing that the notion

[73] *Ibid.*, p. 129. For Mayo's earliest thoughts on anomie and social organization, see *idem*, *Democracy and Freedom: An Essay in Social Logic* (Melbourne: Macmillan, 1917), pp. 1–14.
[74] Émile Durkheim, *Le suicide: étude de sociologie* [*Suicide: A Sociological Study*] (Paris: F. Alcan, 1897), pp. 264–311. For a further discussion of anomie, see David Courpasson, Dima Younces, and Michael Reed, "Durkheim in the Neoliberal Organization: Taking Resistance and Solidarity Seriously," *Organization Theory* 2(1) (January–March 2021), pp. 1–24.
[75] Mayo, *Human Problems of an Industrial Civilization*, p. 166.
[76] *Ibid.*, p. 177.

of unitary authority from a central source (be it government, church, or industry leaders) should be abandoned. Drawing heavily from Chester I. Barnard (see Chapter 14), Mayo concluded that authority used in securing cooperation should be based on human-relations skills rather than on technical skill or expertise. The human relations–oriented manager would act as an investigator of employee sentiments with the intention of furthering collaborative efforts for achieving mutual goals. Because people spent so much time in groups and derived much of their satisfaction from working together, Mayo felt that managers should focus on maintaining group integrity and social solidarity. Groups were the universal solvent, and it was a manager's task to find the universal container.

First-line supervisors, management's most immediate contact with operative employees, played a particularly crucial role in maintaining group integrity and social solidarity. In the bank-wiring observation room, for example, the work-group supervisor did not try to force operators to wire 7,312 terminals a day (the "bogey") but accepted the average of 6,000–6,600. The supervisor's dilemma was explained in a 1932 report:

> In such circumstances the first line supervisor finds himself in a conflict situation. He can do either of two things; uphold the system of ideas common to management and attempt by driving or other methods to enforce them, or take the side of the workmen and conceal the true situation from his superiors. In the test room the Group Chief has seen fit to side with the workmen, and perhaps rightly. It is quite likely that by opposing them he would only aggravate the situation.[77]

Roethlisberger described first-line supervisors ("foremen") as standing in the middle of "two contrasting worlds," subject to conflicting pressures from other managers above and operative employees below.[78] As such, they were necessarily disadvantaged in securing the employee–employer collaboration that Mayo envisioned. The situation, as Mayo perceived it, was worse when supervisors believed in a strict logic of efficiency, failing to recognize that the challenges they face are also social and human. Mayo believed that the answer to preparing managers (at all levels) for their new human-relations role was twofold: train them (1) to understand their subordinates' nonlogical sentiments; and (2) how to maintain an equilibrium between an organization's economic goals and its employees' personal needs. For Mayo, achieving this equilibrium was the key to workplace effectiveness. This was the new leadership, a balancing of the logic of efficiency with an appreciation for the full range of employee sentiments. Later research conducted at the University of Michigan and at Ohio State University would confirm that effective leadership combines a concern for both production and people (see Chapter 15).

HUMAN RELATIONS AND MOTIVATION

As we will see in Chapter 17, how the human relations–oriented manager motivated people became a controversial subject. Early reports of the Hawthorne studies gave some credence to the conclusion that changing to a small-group incentive payment plan was one factor in explaining the relay-assembly test room's increased output. Mark L. Putnam, chief of Western's Industrial Research Division, told *Business Week* magazine that pay was the number one concern expressed by Hawthorne employees during interviews in 1930.[79] When the assemblers were asked what they liked in the relay-assembly test room, one responded, "*We made more money in the Test Room*."[80]

---

[77] [Arthur C. Moore and William J. Dickson], "Supplement to Report on Bank Wiring Test Group for the Period Nov. 9, 1931, to Mar. 18, 1932," March 21, 1932. Reproduced on Reel 3, Box 7, Folder 3, p. 13. *Microfilmed Records of the Industrial Relations Experiment Carried Out by the Western Electric Company at the Hawthorne Works*, Hawthorne, IL. Hawthorne Studies Collection, Baker Library, Harvard University Business School, Boston, MA. Available online at https://digital.libraries.ou.edu/cdm/singleitem/collection/Hawthorne/id/177/rec/102.

[78] Fritz J. Roethlisberger, "The Foreman: Master and Victim of Double Talk," *Harvard Business Review* 23(3) (Spring 1945), p. 290.

[79] "Human Factor in Production Subject of Unique Research," *Business Week*, January 21, 1931, p. 16.

[80] Greenwood, Bolton, and Greenwood, "Hawthorne," p. 220.

This is understandable given that the Great Depression had begun the prior August and that the assemblers' income was important to their families' wellbeing. A November 12, 1930, memo to Mayo from his Harvard assistant, Richard S. Meriam, underscores this point: "Economic and financial factors are of considerable importance in the test room. The employees are anxious for high earnings. The test room has apparently removed the doubt in the employees' minds that the company would permit them to make very high earnings."[81] The evidence regarding economic incentives and output at Hawthorne was available, but the published results presented an alternative interpretation.

There is evidence that Mayo's writings and, in turn, his influence on Roethlisberger and Dickson in preparing the most widely read report on the Hawthorne studies were the basis of this alternative interpretation. An early indication of Mayo's view is revealed in a letter written by Roethlisberger in which he reported that a statistical analysis of the relay-assembly room data had begun to "look interesting," in that, "it looked as if the organization of the girls in the test room was more conditioned by biological factors rather than anything as naive as economic incentive. As this fits in with what Mayo has been saying for the last five years we were very pleased."[82]

In *Management and the Worker*, Roethlisberger and Dickson state that the "efficacy of the wage incentive was so dependent on its relation to other factors that it was impossible to consider it as in itself having an independent effect on the individual."[83] That is, pay for performance was only one factor that could not be addressed separately. As time went on, Roethlisberger mentioned other factors that explained human motivation:

> Whether or not a person is going to give his services whole-heartedly to a group depends, in good part, on the way he feels about his job, his fellow workers, and supervisors . . . [a person wants] . . . social recognition . . . tangible evidence of . . . social importance . . . the feeling of security that comes not so much from the amount of money we have in the bank as from being an accepted member of a group.[84]

Still later, it appears that the notion of the "economic man" was discarded:

> Far from being the prime and sole mover of human activity in business, economic interest has run far behind in the list of incentives that make men willing to work . . . man at work is a social creature as well as an "economic man." He has personal and social as well as economic needs. Work provides him with a way of life as well as a means of livelihood . . . As we discarded the notion of "economic man," we began to question the concept of business organization as merely a logical organization of operations for the efficient production of goods.[85]

What was the human relationists' view of motivation? In early reports, employees were quoted as saying, in effect, that they worked harder because "they made more money" or that pay was their "number one" concern. As Roethlisberger and Mayo examined the Hawthorne data, however, the importance of financial incentives faded. In brief, the Hawthorne studies have been subjected to so much manipulation and misinterpretation that their actual results are clouded in myth and advocacy.[86] Mayo wanted to promote employee–employer collaboration, not pay for performance, and it would require a later generation of scholars to iterate that the social person supplemented, but did not supplant, the economic man.

---

[81] Memorandum from Richard S. Meriam to Elton Mayo, November 12, 1930, p. 1, Charles D. Wrege Research Papers, 1925–2013, Series I: Western Electric and the Hawthorne Studies, Box 2, Folder 24, Kheel Center for Labor–Management Documentation and Archives, Cornell University.

[82] Fritz J. Roethlisberger to Emily Osborne, April 5, 1932, Fritz Jules Roethlisberger Papers, Carton 2, Folder 57, Baker Library, Harvard University Business School, Boston, MA.

[83] Roethlisberger and Dickson, *Management and the Worker*, p. 160.

[84] Roethlisberger, *Management and Morale*, pp. 15, 24–25.

[85] Fritz J. Roethlisberger, "A 'New Look' for Management," *Worker Morale and Productivity*, General Management Series, no. 141 (New York: American Management Association, 1948), pp. 12–13, 16.

[86] Lyle Yorks and David A. Whitsett, "Hawthorne, Topeka, and the Issue of Science versus Advocacy in Organizational Behavior," *Academy of Management Review* 10(1) (January 1985), pp. 21–30.

SUMMARY

In addition to challenging many prevailing assumptions of the day, the Hawthorne studies immeasurably increased our knowledge.[87] As a result of the Hawthorne studies . . .

- . . . it was realized that workplaces are not only technical systems, but also social systems replete with informal structures and with ceremonials, rituals, and non-logical sentiments that regulate relations between people and their attitudes toward one another;
- . . . it became clear that employees are not motivated solely by money;
- . . . the influence of personal and social factors, as well as physical conditions and physiological parameters on workplace motivation and employee attitudes was revealed, highlighting that work behavior is determined by a complex set of interacting forces;
- . . . it was again confirmed that work groups develop and maintain their own accepted standards of behavior;
- . . . it was learned that employee participation in making work-related decisions can reduce resistance to new ways of doing things;
- . . . the importance of effective supervision in maintaining employee job satisfaction and productivity was reaffirmed.

The Hawthorne studies are an intellectual gold mine, forever altering our understanding of the human element in the workplace. Their contribution to the growth and development of the human-relations approach can hardly be overstated. As though responding to Taylor's plea for a "study of the motives which influence men" (see Chapter 7), the Hawthorne researchers systematically explored the nature and content of the human element found in every organization. By testing hypothetical assertions about the basis of work rather than allowing their unquestioned acceptance, the Hawthorne researchers pioneered a course of investigation that is still being pursued today. However, critics note that, by current standards, the Hawthorne studies were unscientific; that is, many of the Hawthorne researchers' conclusions did not necessarily follow from the available evidence. These and other criticisms will be considered in Chapter 17.

[87] Daniel Bell, "Adjusting Men to Machines: Social Scientists Explore the World of the Factory," *Commentary* 3(1) (January 1947), p. 83; William J. Dickson, "Hawthorne Experiments," in Carl Heyel, ed., *The Encyclopedia of Management* (New York: Reinhold Publishing, 1963), p. 279; Sonnenfeld, "Clarifying Critical Confusion in the Hawthorne Hysteria," p. 1399.

The Search for Organizational Integration

CHAPTER 14

Interest in organizations as social systems was stimulated by the Hawthorne Studies and would continue to grow as the social-person era unfolded. This chapter discusses the lives and thoughts of two individuals who, though separated in time, significantly contributed to our understanding of authority and responsibility, the need to coordinate effort, conflict resolution, and how to design organizations for maximum effectiveness and efficiency. One was a political philosopher turned business sage, who never met a payroll in her life; the other, a telephone-company executive whose hobbies were playing classical piano and listening to the music of Johann Sebastian Bach. Their intellectual breadth ranged across multiple specialties and bridged the scientific-management and the social-person eras.

MARY P. FOLLETT: THE POLITICAL PHILOSOPHER

Born in Quincy, Massachusetts, in 1868, Mary Parker Follett had a difficult early life. Her father, an alcoholic, died young; her mother was inclined to social rather than practical matters.[1] A respectable inheritance from her maternal grandfather provided sustenance, while Follett found intellectual uplift in reading and education. She attended Thayer Academy, a preparatory school for college-bound students located in Braintree, Massachusetts. At Thayer, she found a mentor in Anna Boynton Thompson, her history teacher. Thompson introduced Follett to the German Idealist school of philosophy, including the works of Johann G. Fichte and Georg W. F. Hegel. Idealist philosophers believed that an understanding of reality is only possible through human reasoning. Building on this background, Follett would later tell classical scholar F. Melian Stawell:

> One of these [businessmen] gave me in a nutshell the threads of a tangle he had with his employees. He wanted me to straighten it out. I answered him straight out of Fichte: he didn't know that of course, but I did, and it seemed to meet the case.[2]

[1] The definitive biography of Follett is Joan C. Tonn, *Mary P. Follett: Creating Democracy, Transforming Management* (New Haven, CT: Yale University Press, 2003).
[2] Mary P. Follett quoted in F. Melian Stawell, "Mary Parker Follett," *Newnham College Roll Letter* (Cambridge University) (1935), p. 43.

Mary Parker Follett, 1917. Vice President, National Community Center Association

John Collier, "The Crisis of Democracy," *The Community Center: The Magazine of the National Community Center Association* 1(5) (June 1917), p. 1.

After graduating from Thayer Academy in 1884, at the age of 15, Follett continued her studies in 1888 at the Society for the Collegiate Instruction of Women by Professors and Other Instructors of Harvard College (known as "the Annex"; it was renamed Radcliffe College in 1894), where she expanded her interests in philosophy and history to include psychology, especially the emerging Gestalt movement, which led her to think in patterns or wholes. Thompson encouraged Follett to interrupt her studies at the Annex to attend classes at Newnham College, Cambridge University, in England, where Follett's interests extended into law, political science, and government. While at Cambridge, she continued to do research for her first book, *The Speaker of the House of Representatives*. Still considered one of the most insightful analyses of the speaker's role, the book established her reputation as a political philosopher and drew her into Boston's intellectual life.[3] Two years after the book's publication in 1896, Follett received her A. B. degree (*summa cum laude*), from Radcliffe.

With academic opportunities limited for women, Follett spent most of her early years working with various community-service groups that provided vocational and educational guidance, recreation opportunities, and job-placement assistance to less fortunate youth in Boston's Roxbury district. In these largely volunteer organizations, operating with little or no formal warrant, she realized that there was a need to rethink prevailing views on authority and responsibility, organization, leadership, and conflict resolution. By observing and working with different groups, she gained an understanding of group dynamics and the importance of teamwork. Through her involvement with the Boston Placement Bureau, she met and worked with an array of business and community leaders, including progressives such as Louis D. Brandeis, Henry S. Dennison, and Meyer Bloomfield. Follett became active in the Taylor Society in the period following Taylor's death. Chronologically, Follett belonged to the scientific-management era; philosophically and intellectually, she was a member of the social-person era. Her work served as a link between these eras by building on the principles of scientific management while anticipating many of the ideas that would become associated with the later human-relations movement.

THE GROUP PRINCIPLE

Reflecting the influence of Gestalt theory, the basis of Follett's thinking was the "whole man" and, in particular, the relation between "whole men" within groups. From her readings in philosophy, psychology, political science, and law—and her understanding of Fichte, about whom her mentor, Anna Thompson, had written a book[4]—Follett developed what she dubbed "the group principle." Fichte espoused a nationalism in which the freedom of individuals was subordinated to group interests. He believed that individuals could not escape the influence of their social world and that, by extension, their ego belonged to a wider plurality or community of egos.[5] Follett's writings reflected this worldview.

In her second book, *The New State: Group Organization the Solution of Popular Government*, published in 1918, Follett explained that the essence of what she termed the "group

[3] Mary P. Follett, *The Speaker of the House of Representatives* (New York: Longmans, Green & Co., 1896).
[4] Anna Boynton Thompson, *The Unity of Fichte's Doctrine of Knowledge* (Boston, MA: Ginn, 1895).
[5] Henry D. Aiken, *The Age of Ideology: The Nineteenth Century Philosophers* (Boston, MA: Houghton Mifflin, 1957), pp. 54–60. Fichte was a disciple of Immanuel Kant and in his early years followed the Kantian notions of rationalism and freedom. In his later years, Fichte broke with Kant, turned to nationalism and statism, and became part of the Romantic revolt against reason.

principle" was to bring out individual differences and integrate them into a single whole. She quoted the sixth-century BCE Greek philosopher Heraclitus of Ephesus, who said, "Nature desires eagerly opposites and out of them it completes its harmony, not out of similars."[6] This philosophy found expression in what is known as Hegel's *dialectical process,* or three stages of discussion and reasoning: "thesis, antithesis, and synthesis," in which opposing views are compared and contrasted to find a new view that incorporates whatever is true in the originals to form a better way forward and enlarge freedom.[7] Follett was never a full Hegelian. For Hegel, individuals can only find happiness and fulfillment by sacrifcing their independence to the state or greater community. In doing so, Hegel reasoned both the individual and the collective whole would benefit. Follett felt those who interpreted Hegel's ideas to mean that the state is "above and beyond" the individual misunderstood his logic. As she further explained:

> When we say that there is the One which comes *from* the Many, this does not mean that the One is *above* the Many. The deepest truth of life is that the interrelating by which both are at the same time a-making is constant.[8]

This vague jargon of "interrelating" and "a-making" would form Follett's notion of "circular response," in which "the One" and "the Many" are constantly interrelating to create each other. Building on these and other ideas, Follett challenged the prevailing political assumptions of the period. She believed that "[w]e find the true man only through group organization. The potentialities of the individual remain potentialities until they are released by group life. Man discovers his true nature, gains his true freedom only through the group."[9]

Follett's "group principle" was to be the "new" psychology and renounced the established belief that individuals thought, felt, and acted independently. She held that groups and individuals come into existence simultaneously and believed that with "group-man appear group-rights."[10] This view demonstrated Follett's acceptance of the Gestalt movement's recognition that "the whole of anything is greater than its parts." It also reflects an appreciation for Charles H. Cooley's "looking-glass self" (the idea that the self arises reflectively in reaction to the opinions of others) and the realization that one's self is embedded in one's work group as a primary social unit of importance.[11] Using phrases such as "togetherness," "group thinking," and "the collective will," Follett sought a new society based on groups and not individuals.

Follett's underlying premise was that only through group membership could individuals find their "true self." Based on her group principle, Follett concluded that an individual's "true self is the group-self" and that "man can have no rights apart from society or independent of society or against society."[12] In opposing the notion that the purpose of government is to protect individual rights, she proposed a new concept of democracy: "Democracy then is a great spiritual force evolving itself from men, utilizing each, completing his incompleteness by weaving together all in the many-membered community life which is the true Theophany"[13] (the word "theophany" being used here to mean "a divine manifestation").

Follett felt that "the theory of government based on individual rights no longer has a place in modern political theory."[14] In its stead, a collectivistic democracy was to be built; moving in succession from small neighborhood groups to community groups, to state groups, to a national group, and, eventually, to a common international-group will. Setting aside the issue of potential group conflicts, Follett had faith that society could grow a new "social consciousness" and that individuals

---

[6] Mary P. Follett, *The New State: Group Organization the Solution of Popular Government* (London: Longmans, Green & Co., 1918), p. 34n2.
[7] Georg W. F. Hegel, *Lectures on the Philosophy of History*, trans. John Sibree (London: Henry G. Bohn, 1857), p. 66. Originally published in 1837.
[8] Follett, *The New State*, p. 284.
[9] *Ibid.*, p. 6.
[10] *Ibid.*, p. 137.
[11] Charles H. Cooley, *Human Nature and the Social Order* (New York: Charles Scribner's Sons, 1902), p. 152.
[12] Follett, *The New State*, p. 137.
[13] *Ibid.*, p. 161.
[14] *Ibid.*, p. 172.

could live together peaceably in what she dubbed "The World State."[15] She had little confidence in "ballot-box democracy," believing that it reflected crowd psychology and defined "right" by the sheer weight of numbers. *The New State* brought Follett national and international recognition.[16]

CONFLICT RESOLUTION

In her third book, *Creative Experience*, Follett developed the idea that through conferences, discussions, and cooperation, individuals could evoke each other's latent ideas and make manifest their unity in pursuit of common goals. Relying again on Gestalt theory, which holds that every psychological situation has a specific character apart from the absolute nature of its component parts, Follett felt that through group experiences, individuals could achieve a greater unleashing of their creative powers.[17] As viewed by Follett, the goal of group effort was an integrative unity that transcended its component parts. In essence, she was beginning to examine the issue of potential group conflicts that she had not addressed in *The New State*. Follett believed that confronting conflicts would result in one of the following four outcomes: "(1) voluntary submission of one side; (2) struggle and the victory of one side over the other; (3) compromise; or (4) integration."[18] The first and second outcomes were unacceptable because the use of force or power led to strife. Compromise, which she called "sham reconciliation," was considered futile because it postponed rather than resolved an issue and because the "truth does not lie between the two sides."[19] Integration (reflecting Follett's Hegelian thinking) involved finding a solution that satisfied both sides without compromise or domination. One illustration of what Follett meant by integration came from a friend who was involved in the paper industry:

> At a meeting of our manufacturing committee recently the following question came up. Our paper had been six cents, and the competing firm reduced their price to five and three-quarters. We then cut to five and a half and they replied with a price of five and a quarter. The question before us then was whether or not we should make a further reduction. Part were in favor; part, against. The solution came when something quite different was suggested: that we should stand for a higher quality of paper and make an appropriate price for it.[20]

Although Follett realized integration was not an option in all instances, she felt it was a viable alternative more often than might be assumed. As Elliott M. Fox explains:

> She . . . insisted that although integration is not possible in every case, it *is* possible in more cases than we realize. And perhaps if it is not possible now, it will be later. . . . The important thing is to work for something better. . . . We need not be afraid of difference, but rather should welcome it as the opportunity for new social creation. She gave us a theory of human interaction that shows how the same factors that cause change also provide the means for solving the problems presented by change, a theory that tells us that the possibilities for the healthy resolution of conflict is part of the natural process of human intercourse.[21]

Follett recognized that conflict could not always be avoided but felt "we should . . . use it instead of condemning it, we should set it to work for us."[22]

Follett's single-minded search for integrative unity, commonality of will, and human cooperation established her reputation as a political philosopher. By 1924, however, her interest in

---

[15] *Ibid.*, pp. 344–360.
[16] Richard C. Cabot, "Mary Parker Follett: An Appreciation," *The Radcliffe Quarterly* 16(3) (April 1934), p. 81.
[17] Mary P. Follett, *Creative Experience* (London: Longmans, Green & Co., 1924), pp. 91–116.
[18] *Ibid.*, p. 156.
[19] *Ibid.*
[20] *Ibid.*, p. 158.
[21] Elliot M. Fox, "Mary Parker Follett: The Enduring Contribution," *Public Administration Review* 28(6) (November–December 1968), p. 528.
[22] Mary P. Follett, "The Psychological Foundations: Constructive Conflict," in Henry C. Metcalf, ed., *Scientific Foundations of Business Administration* (Baltimore, MD: Williams & Wilkins, 1926), p. 114.

political science had waned, replaced by a growing fascination with the result-oriented world of business. In explaining why she wished to study the role of management in industry, she stated, "industry is the most important field of human activity, and management is the fundamental element in industry."[23] In January 1925, Follett gave the first of a series of four lectures in New York City under the auspices of the Bureau of Personnel Administration, an agency dedicated to advancing sound employer–employee relations. Beginning with these lectures, Follett made the transition from being a political scientist to a business philosopher. In turning to the business world and business executives, Follet was inspired: as she explained in a 1933 lecture at the London School of Economics, "There I found hope for the future. There men were not theorising or dogmatising, they were thinking of what they had actually done and they were willing to try new ways."[24]

A BUSINESS PHILOSOPHER

Viewing management as a universal activity, Follett understood how the principles that apply in the political sphere necessarily apply to business as well. The same challenges of achieving unity of effort, defining authority and responsibility, resolving conflict, exhibiting leadership, and so on, exist in both politics and business. Drawing on this understanding, Follett pushed ahead into the business world. First, from her book *Creative Experience*, she extended her thinking on "constructive conflict" and achieving unity of effort. Because domination and compromise, as methods of conflict resolution, led to strife, Follett held that integration, as a means for confronting contrasting interests, should be paramount in all business affairs. In dealing with labor, she deplored the notion of collective bargaining because it rested on a relative balance of power and inevitably ended in compromise. Bargaining meant that there were competing interests, and in their effort to gain at each other's expense, the confronting sides would likely lose sight of what they held in common. In labor–management negotiations, for example, when pro-labor or pro-management positions solidified, Follett noted that the confronting parties often failed to appreciate that they were partners in a common endeavor, for which they had joint responsibilities. She felt that collective responsibility should begin with group responsibility, wherein employees are involved as partners in shaping workplace policies. Speaking to executives at the Bureau of Personnel Administration, Follett explained:

> When you have made your employees feel that they are in some sense partners in the business, they do not improve the quality of their work, save waste in time and material, because of the Golden Rule, but because their interests are the same as yours.[25]

This was not to be a reciprocal back-scratching arrangement, but a true feeling on the part of both labor and management that they serve a common purpose. Follett believed that in the past an artificial line had been drawn between those who managed and those who were managed. She felt that all members of an organization who accepted responsibility for work at any level should contribute to a "functional whole or integrative unity":

> [L]abor and capital can never be reconciled as long as labor persists in thinking that there is a capitalist point of view and capitalists that there is a labor point of view. There is not. These are imaginary wholes which must be broken up before capital and labor can co-operate.[26]

Follett's "principle of integrative unity" involves finding solutions that satisfy all parties, without domination, surrender, or compromise. It calls for confronting sides to rethink their relationship

[23] *Idem*, "Some Methods of Executive Efficiency," in *Proceedings of the Twenty-third Lecture Conference for Works Directors, Managers, Foremen and Forewomen* (York, England: Yorkshire Printing Works, 1926), p. 15.

[24] *Idem*, "The Giving of Orders," in Lyndall F. Urwick, ed., *Freedom and Coordination: Lectures in Business Organization* (London: Management Publications Trust, 1949), p. 32.

[25] *Idem*, "The Psychological Foundations: Business as an Integrative Unity," p. 160.

[26] *Idem*, *Creative Experience*, pp. 167–168.

and share information to avoid win–lose quick fixes, be creative in examining differences from multiple angles, and see difficulties as "ours" and not "yours." To Follett, for conflict to be constructive, it required respect, understanding, talking things through, and creating win-win solutions.

Beyond viewing a business as a working unit, Follett felt that both labor and management should recognize their interrelationships with creditors, stockholders, customers, competitors, suppliers, and society in general. This wider perspective would encourage seeing society and the larger economy as working together rather than as "congeries of separate pieces."[27] For Follett, integration was a principle applicable to all aspects of life.

AUTHORITY, RESPONSIBILITY, AND POWER

Follett reasoned that integration, as a principle of conduct, would be less than fully effective unless people rethought their concepts of authority, responsibility, and power. In this third area, Follett sought to develop "power-with" instead of "power-over," and "co-action" to replace consent and coercion. She realized that with both an "order giver" and an "order taker," integration would be difficult to achieve, as the notions of "boss" and "subordinate" created barriers to recognizing common interests. To overcome this difficulty, Follett proposed depersonalizing orders and shifting obedience to the "law of the situation, referring to the necessity of acting in accord with the unique requirements inherent in any situation": "One *person* should not give orders to another *person*, but both should agree to take their orders from the situation."[28] She noted that situational requirements are in constant flux, therefore demanding a continual effort to maintain effective work relationships. Thus, she observed, "different situations require different kinds of knowledge, and the man possessing the knowledge demanded by a certain situation tends to be in the best managed business, and other things being equal, to become the leader of the moment."[29] In this sense, Follett's thinking paralleled Elton Mayo's notion (see Chapter 13) that personal difficulties experienced in the workplace cannot be explained by any one factor but must be dealt with in what he called "the psychology of the total situation."

In the same way that Fred Taylor sought obedience to facts determined by study rather than flawed rules of thumb, the rationale for Follett's "law of the situation" was based on facts and not title or position. In a paper for the Taylor Society, Follett put it this way: "If, then, authority is derived from function, it has little to do with hierarchy of position as such. . . . We find authority with the head of a department, with an expert . . . the dispatch clerk has more authority in dispatching work than the President . . . authority should go with knowledge and experience."[30]

Follett understood that by shifting authority to knowledge, personal confrontation could be minimized. She admired this facet of scientific management because it divorced person and situation. To Follett, the essence of good human relations was creating the feeling of working *with* someone rather than working *under* someone. In practice, this became "power-with" versus "power-over." She held that management should not exercise power over workers, nor should workers, through unions, exercise power over management. Jointly exercised power was "coactive," not coercive. Displaying a rare insight into the psychology of power, Follett rejected both the authoritarians striving for power and Mohandas K. Gandhi's policy of peaceful noncooperation as insidious uses of power. She felt that Gandhi's noncooperation movement was still a desire for power-over because it sought to defy the British Colonial Authority to secure Indian independence. Follett maintained that constructive conflict through integration could not be achieved when one or both sides of a conflict were attempting to dominate the other.

[27] *Idem*, "The Psychological Foundations: Business as an Integrative Unity," p. 150.

[28] *Idem*, "The Giving of Orders," in Metcalf, ed., *Scientific Foundations of Business Administration*, p. 139. See also *idem*, *Creative Experience* (New York: Longmans, Green & Co., 1924), p. 152.

[29] *Idem*, "Some Discrepancies in Leadership Theory and Practice," in Henry C. Metcalf, ed., *Business Leadership* (London: Pitman & Sons, 1930), p. 213.

[30] *Idem*, "The Illusion of Final Authority," *Bulletin of the Taylor Society* 2(6) (December 1926), p. 243.

Follett believed that in all human interactions, from interpersonal conflicts to international disputes, power-over had to be reduced and obedience had to be shifted to the law of the situation. The basis for this shift would be what Follett called "circular response": a continuous reciprocal process based on the opportunity for confronting parties to influence each other, such that, through open interactions, over time, "power-with" could be obtained. For labor and management, power-with would come through full disclosure of costs, prices, and profits. Follett was an advocate of employee representation plans that were popular in the 1920s (see Chapter 9). Under these plans, employees elected representatives to shop or work councils; these representatives then gave workers a voice in dealing with management. Follett found great promise in such plans because "management has seen that an enterprise can be more successfully run by securing the cooperation of the workers. . . . [Further] the aim of employee representation . . . should not be to share power, but to increase power . . . in all."[31] As envisioned by Follett, employee representation plans should not be a struggle over who decided what and how profits were to be divided, but a step toward achieving integration. The National Labor Relations Act (the Wagner Act), however, outlawed such plans in 1935. Employee representation plans were seen as a form of company unions, wherein representatives could not bargain as equals (they generally lacked the ability to sign legally enforceable agreements), and the right to strike was not recognized.

Follett thought final authority was an illusion based on a false premise of power and that authority instead accrued to the prevailing situation, not to individuals or their positions. Likewise, she held that final responsibility was also an illusion. Responsibility was inherent in each job or workplace function and was cumulative in the sense that it was the sum of all individual and group responsibilities in a system of cross-relationships. At the individual level, a person was responsible for their work, not responsible to someone. At the departmental level, all those who contributed jointly shared responsibility for getting their jobs done. The role of a department manager was merely to interweave individual and group responsibilities. In turn, an organization's chief executive had cumulative responsibility for interweaving interdepartmental work.

Follett's thoughts on authority and responsibility were clearly iconoclastic. Traditional thinking associated with the military or other organizations held that authority was power-over and rejected the idea that responsibility accrued to a final authority. Follett was nonetheless adamant: authority resided in the situation, not a person or position. Logically then, responsibility was inherent in the work being performed and accumulated in interweaving workplace functions. This was heady material for the executives attending Follett's Bureau of Personnel Administration presentations in the 1920s.

THE TASK OF LEADERSHIP

Two facets of Follett's philosophy have been explored: (1) reducing conflict through an integration of interests and the necessary corollary, and (2) obeying the law of the situation. A third facet concerns building the underlying psychological processes necessary to achieve goals through coordinating and controlling effort. Follett's view of control drew on her "principle of integrative unity." She held that control was impossible to achieve unless there was unity and cooperation among all elements (material and people) in each situation. In this sense, a situation was out of control when contrasting interests were not reconciled. For Follett, the basis for control resided in self-regulating and self-directing individuals and groups who recognized common interests and controlled their actions to meet agreed-upon goals.

Follett recognized that managers did not control single elements, but complex interrelationships; not persons, but situations, with the desired outcome being unity and cooperation.

[31] *Idem*, "How Is the Employee Representation Movement Remolding the Accepted Type of Business Manager?" in Henry C. Metcalf, ed., *Business Management as a Profession* (Chicago, IL: A. W. Shaw, 1927), pp. 344, 353.

How was this unity and cooperation to be achieved? Follett called for a new philosophy of control that was "fact-control rather than man-control" and "correlated control" rather than "superimposed control." She argued that each situation generated its own control because the facts of the situation and the interweaving of the many groups in the situation were what determined appropriate behavior. As most situations were too complex for centralized top-down control to function effectively, controls were to be gathered, or correlated, at many points in an organization. This interweaving and correlation were to be based on four fundamental principles of organization:

1. Co-ordination as the reciprocal relationship of all the factors in a situation.
2. Co-ordination by direct contact of all the responsible people concerned.
3. Co-ordination in the early stages.
4. Co-ordination as a continuing process.[32]

Follett concluded that organization *was* control, because the purpose of organizing and coordinating was to ensure controlled performance; coordination achieved unity, and unity was control. As an illustration, Follett cited a conflict between a purchasing agent and a production manager. The purchasing agent suggested acquiring somewhat inferior material that he said would serve its purpose and could be obtained at a lower price. The production manager, however, maintained that he could not obtain satisfactory results with this material. According to Follett, if the purchasing agent and production manager had followed the principles of early and continuous coordination, they would have known each other's thinking and turned their attention to finding quality materials at a lower cost. An integration of their interests could have been achieved to their mutual satisfaction. This synthesis of interests was self-regulation through coordination to achieve integration.[33]

Follett held that leadership should not be based on power, but on the reciprocal influence of leader on follower and follower on leader in the context of the prevailing situation. A leader's primary task was defining the *purpose* of an organization; the leader "should make his co-workers see that it is not *his* purpose which is to be achieved, but a common purpose, born of the desires and the activities of the group. The best leader does not ask people to serve him, but the common end. The best leader has not followers, but men and women working with him."[34] Further, Follett maintained:

> The leader then is one who can organise the experience of the group . . . and thus get the full power of the group. The leader makes the team. This is pre-eminently the leadership quality—the ability to organise all the forces there are in an enterprise and make them serve a common purpose. Men with this ability create a group power rather than a personal power. . . . When leadership rises to genius it has the power of transforming . . . experience into power. And that is what experience is for, to be made into power. The great leader creates as well as directs power. . . . Leaders and followers are both following the invisible leader—the common purpose. The best executives put this common purpose clearly before their group.[35]

Follett reasoned that an organization's goals should be integrated with individual and group purposes, and this integration called for the highest-caliber leaders. Although she noted that some believed that leadership was an "intangible capacity" that is "beyond human calculation," she

---

[32] *Idem*, "The Process of Control," in Luther H. Gulick and Lyndall F. Urwick, eds., *Papers on the Science of Administration* (New York: Institute of Public Administration, Columbia University, 1937), p. 161.

[33] *Ibid*., p. 167. See also Mary P. Follett, "The Psychology of Control," in Henry C. Metcalf, ed., *Psychological Foundations of Management* (Chicago, IL: A. W. Shaw, 1927), p. 172.

[34] *Idem*, "Leader and Expert," in Metcalf, ed., *Psychological Foundations of Management*, p. 235.

[35] *Idem*, "The Essentials of Leadership," in Urwick, ed., *Freedom and Coordination*, pp. 52, 55.

argued that "it can, in part, be learned," and to think of it as chiefly a matter of personality was a mistake.[36] Follett held that leaders did not depend on commands and obedience, but on skills in coordinating, defining purposes, and evoking responses to the law of the situation. Recognizing that mere exhortation would not bring about such leadership, Follett called for the training of executives in what she called the "capacity for organized thinking." Such thinking eschews dominating or manipulating others and recognizes a broader range of obligations leading to a profession of management that enlists knowledge for the service of others. To those who aspired to be managers, she advised:

> [M]en must prepare themselves as seriously for this profession as for any other. They must realize that they, as all professional men, are assuming grave responsibilities, that they are to take a creative part in one of the large functions of society, a part which, I believe, only trained and disciplined men can in the future hope to take with success.[37]

Follett felt that the notion of substituting a service motive for a profit motive was an oversimplification. Instead, she argued that these motives should be integrated into a larger professional motive:

> We work for profit, for service, for our own development, for the love of creating something. At any one moment, indeed, most of us are not working directly or immediately for any of these things, but to put through the job in hand in the best possible manner. . . . To come back to the professions: can we not learn a lesson from them on this very point? The professions have not given up the money motive. I do not care how often you see it stated that they have. Professional men are eager enough for large incomes; but they have other motives as well, and they are often willing to sacrifice a good slice of income for the sake of these other things. We all want the richness of life in the terms of our deepest desire. We can purify and elevate our desires, we can add to them, but there is no individual or social progress in curtailment of desires.[38]

A FINAL NOTE

Follett passed away on December 18, 1933. Joan C. Tonn has remarked of her legacy: "Although Mary Follett's name may be obscure, her ideas are not."[39] In appreciation of Follett's many contributions to management thought, Sir Peter Parker has declared, "People often puzzle about who is the father of management. I don't know who the father was, but I have no doubt about who was the mother."[40] Follett uncannily presaged many of today's management thinkers in advocating participative management, appreciating the benefits of teams (i.e., groups), endorsing cooperative conflict resolution, and recognizing that authority should go with knowledge.

Critics might maintain, however, that elements of Follett's business philosophy are idyllic notions of a political philosopher. The simplicity of people living and working together without coercion and compromise is nonetheless appealing. Integration, moving to a broader plane for problem solutions, would result in more creativity and imagination than are commonly witnessed in daily life. Depersonalization of authority and obedience to the law of the situation would end tyranny and autocracy. Control based on a perceived unity of purposes would improve labor–management relations.

Follett's call for leaders dedicated to improving business practices through science and service has been a refrain since the earliest days of the Industrial Revolution. Her ideas on reducing conflict, obeying the law of the situation, and building the underlying psychological processes

---

[36] *Idem*, "What Type of Central Administrative Leadership Is Essential to Business Management as Defined in This Course?" in Metcalf, ed., *Business Management as a Profession* (Chicago, IL: A. W. Shaw, 1927), p. 355.
[37] *Idem*, "How Must Business Management Develop in Order to Possess the Essentials of a Profession?" p. 87.
[38] *Idem*, "How Must Business Develop in Order to Become a Profession?" pp. 101–102.
[39] Tonn, *Mary P. Follett*, p. 492.
[40] Sir Peter Parker quoted in Dana Wechsler Linden, "The Mother of Them All," *Forbes* (January 16, 1995), p. 76.

necessary to achieve goals through coordinating and controlling effort, however, were unique for their time and continue to have present-day relevance. As one of her contemporaries recalled, "Mary Follett was a gentle person, not an impressive or aggressive spellbinder, but of all the pioneers she, more than others, approached management through human values, psychology and the laboratory of collaborative work experience. The significance and originality of her contribution cannot be overrated."[41]

CHESTER I. BARNARD: THE ERUDITE EXECUTIVE

Chester Irving Barnard was born in Malden, Massachusetts, in 1886, and educated at the Mount Hermon School for Boys. A Christian school located in Northfield, Massachusetts, Mount Harmon was an "opportunity school," where boys of limited means could toil in fields, orchards, and workshops to pay their tuition.[42] Barnard personified the Horatio Alger ideal of the farm boy who made good. As a student at Harvard University, he supplemented his income by tuning pianos, typing theses and dissertations for fellow students, and conducting a dance orchestra. Barnard studied economics at Harvard, completing all but one degree requirement in 3 years (1906–1909). Lacking a laboratory science credit, he was not allowed to graduate. Even without a bachelor's degree, he did well enough to earn seven honorary doctorates for his lifelong effort to understand the nature and purpose of organizations.

Barnard joined the Boston office of the Statistical Department of the American Telephone and Telegraph (AT&T) system in 1909 as a translator, a job made possible by his natural aptitude for languages. Early on, he became an expert in telephone rates. Barnard later served as vice president of operations for the Bell Telephone Company of Pennsylvania. In 1927, he was named president of the New Jersey Bell Telephone Company (now Verizon). Barnard's commitment to making a difference in the lives of others was reflected in his public service and volunteer work. He assisted David E. Lilienthal in developing operational policies for the U.S. Atomic Energy Commission and was a special assistant to Henry Morgenthau, Jr., Secretary of the U.S. Treasury.[43] Barnard served as president of the Rockefeller Foundation, chairman of the National Science Foundation, and president of the Bach Society of New Jersey, and founded the Newark Art Theatre (now the Paper Mill Playhouse). For his service as president of the United Service Organizations (USO), Barnard was awarded the Presidential Medal of Merit.[44] He also received the U.S. Navy's Meritorious Civilian Award. Barnard was a self-made scholar who applied the theories of the Italian economist Vilfredo Pareto (whom he read in French), Mary P. Follett, Kurt Lewin (see Chapter 15), Max Weber (whom he read in German), and the philosophy of Alfred North Whitehead to create the first

Courtesy of William B. Wolf

Chester I. Barnard as he entered Harvard University, 1906

[41] Luther H. Gulick, "Looking Backward to 1915" (pp. 5–6, unpublished paper presented at the Eastern Academy of Management, Hartford, CT, May 13, 1977), Harry W. Bass Business History Collection, University of Oklahoma Libraries, Norman, OK.

[42] Biographical data and an excellent discussion of Barnard's ideas are found in William B. Wolf, *How to Understand Barnard: An Introduction to Chester I. Barnard* (Los Angeles, CA: Lucas Brothers Publishing, 1968); *idem*, *Conversations with Chester I. Barnard* (Ithaca, NY: New York State School of Industrial and Labor Relations, Cornell University 1973); *idem*, *The Basic Barnard: An Introduction to Chester I. Barnard and His Theories of Organization and Management* (Ithaca, NY: New York State School of Industrial and Labor Relations, Cornell University, 1974). See also *idem*, "Understanding Chester I. Barnard," *International Journal of Public Administration* 17(6) (1994), pp. 1035–1069; *idem* and Haruki Ilino, *Philosophy for Managers: Selected Papers of Chester I. Barnard* (Tokyo: Bunshindo Publishing, 1986).

[43] William B. Wolf, "Chester I. Barnard's Reflections on His Nine Weeks in the United States Treasury Department," *International Journal of Public Administration* (1996) 19(4), pp. 449–458.

[44] George E. Biles and Alfred A. Bolton, "Chester I. Barnard: President of the USO, 1942–1945," *International Journal of Public Administration* 17(6) (1994), pp. 1107–1124.

in-depth analysis of organizations as cooperative systems. He was a Fellow of the American Association for the Advancement of Science and the American Academy of Arts and Sciences, as well as a director of the National Bureau of Economic Research. By the time of his death in 1961, this Harvard dropout had earned a place in history as a management scholar.

THE NATURE OF COOPERATIVE SYSTEMS

Barnard's best-known work, *The Functions of the Executive*, is an expansion of eight lectures sponsored by the Lowell Institute (Boston) in November and December of 1937. At the time, Barnard was president of New Jersey Bell Telephone. His purpose in presenting the lectures was to develop a theory of organizations and to stimulate others to examine the nature of cooperative systems. To Barnard, the search for universals in organizations had been hampered by an overemphasis on religious and government institutions, and their differing views on the origin and character of authority. He complained that most research on cooperative systems had focused on social unrest and reform and had included "practically no reference to formal organization as the concrete social process by which social action is largely accomplished." In Barnard's opinion, social failures throughout history were due to a lack of formal organization. He explained to his readers: "Formal organization is that kind of coöperation among men that is conscious, deliberate, purposeful."[45]

Barnard believed that by developing a theory of organizations, it would be possible to enhance the effectiveness and efficiency of cooperative systems. He sought to understand how to (1) adjust an organization's internal processes so as to ensure its survival; (2) examine the external forces to which an organization must readjust to maintain an equilibrium in a "continuously fluctuating environment of physical, biological, and social materials, elements, and forces"; and (3) analyze the functions performed by executives at all levels in an organization.[46] Barnard's focus on maintaining equilibrium in an organization's internal processes while confronting external environmental forces was seen as novel. He rejected the traditional view of organizations as having fixed boundaries and as being comprised of a defined set of employees. In considering the larger environment in which an organization was situated, Barnard's analyses went beyond earlier thinking to also include investors, suppliers, customers, and others whose actions contributed to an organization although they were not its employees.[47] Barnard's view of organizations as cooperative systems began with his view of individuals as discrete beings; reminiscent of Follett's "group principle," Barnard noted that humans did not interact with one another except in social relationships. As individuals, people could choose whether to enter or join an organization. They made this choice based on their motives (meaning purposes, desires, and impulses of the moment) or other available alternatives. As described by Barnard, organizations, through their executive function, seek to modify individuals' motives and alternatives through influence and control. He recognized that attempts at influence and control were not always successful in attaining the goals sought by organizations and their members. The disparity between personal motives and organizational motives led Barnard to distinguish between "effectiveness" and "efficiency." A formal system of cooperation required an objective or purpose, and, if cooperation is successful and the objective is attained, the system is effective. Barnard saw the matter of efficiency differently. He felt cooperative efficiency is the result of individual efficiencies, because individuals cooperate only to satisfy "individual motives." The efficiency of a cooperative system, then, is the degree to which an individual's motives are satisfied, and only the individual can determine whether this condition has been met.[48]

---

[45] Chester I. Barnard, *The Functions of the Executive* (Cambridge, MA: Harvard University Press, 1938), p. 4.
[46] *Ibid.*, p. 6.
[47] *Idem*, "Comments on the Job of the Executive," *Harvard Business Review* 18(4) (Spring 1940), pp. 295–308.
[48] *Idem*, *Functions of the Executive*, p. 44.

As viewed by Barnard, cooperation within formal organizations affords possibilities for expanding the power of groups beyond what individuals can accomplish alone; for example, moving a large stone, manufacturing an automobile, or constructing a bridge. Individuals cooperate to do what they cannot do individually, and, when their purpose for cooperating is attained, their efforts are deemed effective. Individuals, however, also have personal motives, and the degree to which individuals continue to contribute to a formal organization is a function of the satisfaction or dissatisfaction they personally derive from their membership in an organization. If members' motives are not satisfied by a formal organization, they withhold effort or participation, and from their point of view, the organization is inefficient. Barnard contended that, in the final analysis, "the only measure of the efficiency of a coöperative system is its capacity to survive."[49] For Barnard, this meant that an organization must offer inducements necessary to satisfy individual motives in pursuit of group purposes to assure its continued survival. Viewed in modern systems theory terms, a formal organization must import negative entropy (i.e., energy) by offering net satisfactions to contributing members. An inefficient organization cannot be effective and, therefore, cannot survive beyond its store of energy. For Barnard, efficiency and effectiveness were irrevocable and universal requirements for an organization to survive.

FORMAL ORGANIZATIONS: THEORY AND STRUCTURE

Barnard defined an *organization* as "a system of consciously coordinated activities or forces of two or more persons."[50] He intended for this definition to encompass all such systems, including military, fraternal, religious, academic, and business organizations, amongst others, irrespective of variations in physical or social environments, number and kinds of members, or the nature of members' activities. Barnard treated such systems "as a whole because each part is related to every other part included in it in a significant way."[51] He noted that different levels of systems existed, ranging from departments (subsystems) in a commercial firm to systems forming society as a whole. Regardless of level, Barnard held that to survive, all systems must possess three elements: (1) members who are willing to cooperate; (2) a common purpose; and (3) a method of communication.[52]

As for the first of these elements, Barnard reasoned that an organization, as a system, could not exist without members. Further, a willingness of a system's members to cooperate in accomplishing a common purpose was likewise indispensable. He recognized that the intensity and timing of this willingness would naturally fluctuate, because it is based on the satisfaction or dissatisfaction experienced or anticipated by each individual member. An organization, thus, must provide adequate inducements, both physical and social, to offset the sacrifices individuals make in forgoing membership in other organizations. Barnard further reasoned that the willingness of a system's members to cooperate is the joint effect of "personal desires and reluctances"; for an organization, it is the joint effect of "objective inducements offered and burdens imposed."[53] For Barnard, inducing individuals to cooperate involved an "economy of incentives," consisting of two parts: (1) offering objective incentives; and (2) changing subjective attitudes through persuasion. Objective incentives are material (e.g., money), nonmaterial (e.g., prestige and power), and associational (e.g., social compatibility and participation in decision-making). Persuasion involves changing attitudes by precept, example, and appeal to individual motives.

A common purpose, the second element that Barnard believed all systems must possess to survive, naturally follows from the first required element he identified—a willingness of members to cooperate. This requires that an organization inculcate in its members a common purpose

[49] *Ibid.*, p. 44.
[50] *Ibid.*, p. 73.
[51] *Ibid.*, p. 77.
[52] *Ibid.*, p. 82.
[53] *Ibid.*, pp. 85–86.

or objective. To this end, a sense of unity and a set of common ideals are essential. As noted, Barnard recognized that the motives of an organization and those of its members logically differ, and members cooperate not because their personal motives are the same as the organization's, but because of the personal (non-materialistic) satisfaction they experience (or anticipate) by contributing to a shared purpose.

Barnard considered communication, the third element required by all systems to survive, to be the process by which common purpose and willingness to cooperate become dynamic. He felt that all interpersonal activities are based on communication. He stated: (1) "channels of communication should be definitely known"; (2) "objective authority requires a definite formal channel of communication to every member of an organization"—that is, everyone must report to or be subordinate to someone; and (3) "line[s] of communication must be as direct or short as possible" to speed dissemination and reduce distortions caused by transmission through multiple channels.[54]

Having identified elements essential for a formal organization to survive, Barnard sought to do the same for informal organizations. By informal organization, he meant "the aggregate of the personal contacts and interactions and the associated groupings of people" that are not a part of nor governed by a formal organization.[55] Without structure, and often without consciously recognizing a joint purpose, informal groupings arise out of job-related contacts and, in turn, establish shared attitudes, customs, and norms. Barnard noted that informal organizations often create conditions that lead to the creation of formal organizations and vice versa. He believed that informal organizations serve three necessary functions: (1) they are a means of communication; (2) they promote cohesiveness among an organization's members; and (3) they protect informal group members' personal integrity.

THE ACCEPTANCE THEORY OF AUTHORITY

One of Barnard's most unusual ideas related to his theory of authority. He defined authority as "the character of a communication (order) in a formal organization by virtue of which it is *accepted* by a contributor to or 'member' of the organization as governing the action he contributes." As suggested by this definition, authority has two aspects: (1) "the subjective, personal *accepting* of a communication as being authoritative"; and (2) "the character in [a] communication by virtue of which it is accepted."[56] According to Barnard, authority does not reside in those who give orders, but in the acceptance or consent of individuals. In essence, Barnard held that the real "source of authority lies in the members of an organization, that they confer authority upon their superiors by deigning to accept and act upon commands, that they may, if they wish, decide to accept orders seriatim [one after another], and that they may withdraw conferred authority at any time by refusing to obey the commands of their superiors."[57]

Barnard's thinking in this regard was contrary to all previous concepts of authority, which held that authority resides in "persons of authority" or "those who issue orders."[58] Whereas Follett argued for depersonalizing authority and obeying the law of the situation, Barnard believed authority originated at the bottom of an organization and flowed upward. In this sense, formal authority is real only if it is accepted as legitimate by subordinates. According to Barnard, subordinates will accept a communication as legitimate if four conditions are met: (1) they understand the communication; (2) they believe the communication is consistent with an organization's purpose; (3) they believe the communication is compatible with their personal interests; and (4) they are mentally and physically able to comply with the communication.

---

[54] *Ibid.*, pp. 175–177.
[55] *Ibid.*, p. 115.
[56] *Ibid.*, p. 163.
[57] Cyril J. O'Donnell, "The Source of Managerial Authority," *Political Science Quarterly* 67(4) (December 1952), p. 575.
[58] Barnard, *Functions of the Executive*, p. 163.

To explain how an organization could function according to this view, Barnard contended that there is a "zone of indifference" within which subordinates will rarely challenge a communication from their superiors. This zone of indifference might be narrow or wide, depending on the degree to which inducements outweigh the burdens and sacrifices of complying with the communication. If a subordinate, for instance, feels that a communication runs counter to a personal conviction, the rewards for complying will be weighed against the possibilities of discharge or other sanctions for not conforming. Some communications are accepted without deliberation, but others may require considerable thought. Such discretion would pertain to what Barnard identified as the first, or subjective, aspect of authority.

The second, or objective, aspect of authority that Barnard identified was more closely akin to traditional conceptions of authority. It rests on the presumption that communications are authoritative and have a "potentiality of assent" when they come from individuals in superordinate positions. In one case, a communication from a higher-up might be accepted because it comes from a "person of authority"; this is formal authority, or the "authority of position." In another instance, a communication might be accepted because a subordinate respects and has confidence in a superior's personal ability irrespective of the superiors rank or position; Barnard called this the "authority of leadership."

When authority of leadership is combined with authority of position, the zone of indifference is exceedingly broad. Nevertheless, Barnard stressed that "the determination of authority remains with the individual."[59] In a free society, individuals always have discretion in defining what constitutes an acceptable communication. What is perhaps the most striking insight of Barnard's theory of authority is that all organizations depend on managers (as leaders) that can develop the capacity and willingness of others to follow.

THE FUNCTIONS OF THE EXECUTIVE

Viewed more broadly, Barnard portrayed an executive's job as securing and maintaining the coordination essential to achieve cooperative effort. Such coordination requires a system of communication that can only function if staffed by executives (meaning managers at all levels). To quote Barnard, "It might be said, then, that the function of executives is to serve as channels of communication so far as communications must pass through central positions."[60] Communication was a central value in all Barnard's writings and, undoubtedly, his views were influenced by his own experience in the AT&T system. To Barnard, executive work "is not *of* the organization, but the specialized work of *maintaining* the organization in operation. . . . The executive functions serve to maintain a system of cooperative effort. They are impersonal. The functions are not, as so frequently stated, to manage a group of persons."[61] For Barnard, the role of the executive functions in an organization is analogous to that of the human nervous system in relation to the rest of the body: "It exists to maintain the bodily system by directing those actions which are necessary more effectively to adjust to the environment, but it can hardly be said to manage the body, a large part of whose functions are independent of it and upon which it in turn depends."[62]

Barnard identified three essential executive functions that correspond with the three elements necessary for a system to survive: (1) to create a system of communication; (2) to secure essential services from individuals; and (3) to formulate and define an organization's purpose.[63] In creating a system of communication, Barnard believed that executives had to define individual duties, clarify lines of authority and responsibility, and consider both formal and informal means of communication. Informal communication assists in maintaining internal communication by

[59] *Ibid.*, pp. 173–174.
[60] *Ibid.*, pp. 214–215.
[61] *Ibid.*, p. 216.
[62] *Ibid.*, p. 217.
[63] *Ibid.*, pp. 217–234.

allowing issues to be raised and discussed without forcing decisions and overloading executive positions. By "secur[ing] essential services from individuals," the second executive function, Barnard was referring to the role executives play in establishing cooperative relationships among people and eliciting their individual contributions to an organization's goals. This includes recruiting employees who could work together compatibly, as well as (1) preserving morale; (2) providing positive inducements such as wages and removing negative inducements such as reducing hours or work requirements; and (3) maintaining deterrents such as supervision and control, inspection, education, and training to ensure a cooperative system's viability.

The third executive function, formulating and defining an organization's purpose, was examined above in our comments on Barnard's thoughts relating to the nature of cooperative systems. What was not previously mentioned is that Barnard viewed the delegation of authority and assignment of responsibility to be critical aspects of this function. For Barnard, delegation involved making decisions about the placement of various responsibilities and authority within a cooperative system so that individuals would know how they contributed to the ends being sought, and the means to those ends. Decision-making has two facets: analysis, or the search for the "strategic factors" that create a set or system of conditions necessary to accomplish an organization's purposes; and synthesis, or the recognition of interrelationships among elements or parts that compose a whole system.

Barnard borrowed the term "strategic factor" as used by labor economist John R. Commons to refer to those factors that limit executives in making decisions. According to Barnard, "[t]he strategic factor is, then, the center of the environment of decision. It is the point at which choice applies. To *do* or not to do *this*, that is the question."[64] Like Fayol, Barnard saw organizations as purposeful wholes functioning in a changing environment. Barnard's insights were used in developing the business strategy course at Harvard University, and much of his terminology is still used in the strategic-management literature.[65]

Barnard's ruminations on the decision-making process were also a notable contribution to general management theory. He recognized that individuals are limited in their "power of choice" by "the combined effect of physical, biological, and social factors."[66] In "Mind in Everyday Affairs," an appendix to his *The Functions of the Executive,* Barnard noted (channeling Vilfredo Pareto; see Chapter 13) there were two categories of mental processes: "logical" and "non-logical." Logical processes involve "conscious thinking which could be expressed in words or other symbols, that is, reasoning," whereas non-logical processes are those "not capable of being expressed in words or as reasoning" and "are only made known by a judgment, decision, or action." Non-logical processes may "lie in physiological conditions or factors, or in the physical and social environment," and may not require conscious effort.[67] Barnard concluded, "both kinds [of mental processes] together are much better than either alone if the conditions permit."[68]

Barnard was clear in stating that the three essential executive functions that he had identified had no separate existence but were "aspects of a process of organization as a whole." He labeled and defined the nature of this "executive process" as "the sensing of the organization as a whole and the total situation relevant to it."[69] This is the art of managing and involves integrating the whole with respect to an organization's internal equilibrium as well as its adjustment to external conditions. Working from the micro to the macro level, Barnard viewed all aspects of society as one large, cooperative system. Every organization must secure members, money, and

---

[64] *Ibid.*, p. 205.
[65] Dave McMahon and Jon C. Carr, "The Contributions of Chester Barnard to Strategic Management Theory," *Journal of Management History* 5(5) (1999), pp. 228–240; Kenneth R. Andrews, "Introduction to the 30th Anniversary Edition," in Chester I. Barnard, *The Functions of the Executive* (Cambridge, MA: Harvard University Press, 1968), pp. xix–xx.
[66] Barnard, *Functions of the Executive,* p. 14.
[67] *Ibid.*, p. 302. See also Milorad M. Novicevic, Thomas J. Hench, and Daniel A. Wren, "Playing by Ear . . . in an Incessant Din of Reasons: Chester Barnard and the History of Intuition in Management Thought," *Management Decision* 40(10) (2002), pp. 992–1002.
[68] *Ibid.*, p. 306.
[69] *Ibid.*, p. 235.

materials from its environment and can "survive only as it secures by exchange, transformation, and creation, a surplus of utilities in its own economy."[70]

MORAL LEADERSHIP

Barnard stressed that moral leadership is essential to an organization's long-lasting success. By this he was referring to executive behavior "governed by beliefs or feelings of what is right or wrong, regardless of self-interest or immediate consequences of a decision to do or not to do specific things under particular conditions."[71] This included behavior related to personal responsibility (an individual's character development); official responsibility (when acting "on behalf" of an organization); and corporate responsibility (internal to the interests of stockholders, creditors, and employees, and external to one's community and society in general). Barnard believed that executives should adhere to a code of right and wrong behavior and strive to create a moral faculty in others. He observed, "[T]he endurance of organization depends upon the quality of leadership; and that quality derives from the breadth of the morality upon which it rests . . . . A low morality will not sustain leadership long, its influence quickly vanishes, it cannot produce its own succession."[72]

A FINAL NOTE

Chester I. Barnard was an erudite executive who drew on his own experiences and sociological insights to build a theory of cooperative systems. As Fritz J. Roethlisberger recalled, "[Barnard was] the one and only executive in captivity who could not only run a successful organization but could also talk intelligently about what he was up to in the process."[73] Barnard impressed not only Roethlisberger but also Elton Mayo (Roethlisberger's Harvard mentor), who moved away from viewing organizations as biological organisms and toward seeing organizations as cooperative social systems.[74] Barnard's thoughts on maintaining an equilibrium within cooperative systems also influenced other Hawthorne researchers (see Chapter 13), and later inspired Herbert A. Simon's work on decision-making in organizations (see Chapter 15).[75] Barnard's theory of authority, his call for moral leadership, and his identification of universal elements in both formal and informal organizations remain significant contributions to management thought.

SUMMARY

Mary P. Follett and Chester I. Barnard were bridges between the scientific-management and the social-person eras. Follett ushered in a view of society based on groups while living and working. Barnard was a student of formal organization yet stressed the role of informal groupings in achieving an equilibrium within a cooperative system. Both endeavored to create a spirit of cooperation and collaboration within organizations and society; sought to reshape previous theories of authority; and concluded that moral leadership would enhance the effectiveness of organizations and societal well-being.

---

[70] *Ibid.*, p. 245.

[71] Chester I. Barnard, "Elementary Conditions of Business Morals," *California Management Review* 1(1) (Fall 1958), p. 4.

[72] Barnard, *Functions of the Executive*, pp. 282–283.

[73] Fritz J. Roethlisberger, *The Elusive Phenomena: An Autobiographical Account of My Work in the Field of Organizational Behavior at the Harvard Business School*, ed. George F. F. Lombard (Boston, MA: Division of Research, Graduate School of Business, Harvard University, 1977), p. 67.

[74] Robert T. Keller, "The Harvard 'Pareto Circle' and the Historical Development of Organization Theory," *Journal of Management* 10(2) (1984), p. 199.

[75] See Herbert A. Simon, "Forward: Papers in Honor of Chester I. Barnard," *International Journal of Public Administration* (1994) 17(6), pp. 1021–1031. See also Chester I. Barnard, "Foreword," in Herbert A. Simon, *Administrative Behavior: A Study of Decision-Making Processes in Administrative Organization* (New York: Macmillan, 1947), pp. ix–xii; William B. Wolf, "The Barnard-Simon Connection," *Journal of Management History* 1(4) (1995), pp. 88–99; and Ellen S. O'Connor, "New Contributions from Old Sources: Recovering Barnard's Science and Revitalizing the Carnegie School," *European Management Journal* 31(1) (February 2013), pp. 93–103.

People and Organizations

CHAPTER 15

This and the following chapter examine twin streams of management thought that developed from about 1930 to the early 1950s. The current chapter focuses on the growth and refinement of the human-relations movement as it passed through micro and macro phases. The micro phase saw an outpouring of behavioral research on topics such as group dynamics, participative decision-making, leadership, and workplace motivation. On the macro side, there were groundbreaking attempts to understand the interaction of the social and technical systems operating within organizations. The title of the present chapter, "People and Organizations," conveys the human orientation of both phases, with the structural aspects of organizations being a secondary theme. In contrast, Chapter 16, "Organizations and People," examines the structure and design of organizations, with the human element placed in a relatively subordinate role.

PEOPLE AT WORK: THE MICRO VIEW

Although social scientists had studied workplace dynamics in the first three decades of the twentieth century, the 1930s and 1940s saw a vast outpouring of research into "human relations at work."[1] In contrast to the scientific-management movement that was largely dominated by engineers, the human-relations era was decidedly interdisciplinary in its emphasis, involving sociologists, psychologists, psychiatrists, and anthropologists. A common premise underlying the era's social-science research was the Gestalt notion that all social behavior involves a "multiplier effect." That is, the behavior of individuals within groups is more than the simple sum of their individual actions. Individuals are unique due to their distinctive genetic makeup and life experiences. When placed in interactions with other one-of-a-kind individuals, predicting the resulting outcomes is more difficult, if not impossible. Thus, as recognized by both Mary P. Follett and Chester I. Barnard (see Chapter 14), because of the multiplier effect, individuals within groups cannot be studied in isolation, but must be analyzed as parts of a dynamic social system.

[1] Examples of forerunner studies include Richard Lang and Willy Hellpach, *Gruppenfabrikation* [*Group Manufacturing*] (Berlin: Julius Springer, 1922) and Ralph E. Flanders, "Design, Manufacture and Production Control of a Standard Machine," *Transactions of the American Society of Mechanical Engineers* 46 (1924), pp. 691–738.

DEVELOPING CONSTRUCTS FOR GROUP ANALYSIS

Interest in the study of groups was partially a product of the Social Gospel movement and its emphasis on industrial betterment. In 1922, the Federal Council of the Churches of Christ in America passed a resolution creating the National Conference on the Christian Way of Life. The resolution called for an inquiry into "The Meaning of Christianity for Human Relationships, with special attention to industry, citizenship and race relations in the United States and the function of the church in social and civic affairs."[2] The conference, referred to as "The Inquiry," led to several seminal studies of group behavior.[3] Eduard C. Lindeman joined with other educators (including John Dewey and Robert M. MacIver) to develop methods to observe and to categorize group interactions, to measure the extent of group-member participation, and to classify the personal beliefs and attitudes of a groups members. In Lindeman's view, individuals without membership in a "functioning group" play a diminished role in modern life. He claimed, "Modern life is group life. . . . The group is one of the means wherewith the individual expresses and strives toward his dominant interests. The task of social scientists is to discover the nature of these groupings and their functional attributes."[4] Lindeman held that the traditional methods for studying groups were inadequate and believed that new methods for understanding group phenomena were needed. He coined the phrase "*participant observer*" to describe someone who is a participant in a study, but who has also been trained to be an observer—what he termed a "cöoperating observer"—rather than a researcher disguised as a study participant.[5] Lindeman maintained that the "interpretation of an event can only be approximately correct when it is a composite of two points of view, the *outside* and the *inside*. Thus the view of the person who is a participant in the event, whose wishes and interests were in some way involved, and the view of the person who was not a participant but only an observer, or analyst, coalesce in one final synthesis."[6] The role of participant observers has changed over the years—from that of a covert observer (such as Whiting Williams; see Chapter 9) to what is today generally referred to as a "key informant." It is regrettable that Lindeman's pioneering work seems to have been largely forgotten.

In contrast, the work of psychiatrist Jacob L. Moreno continues to be referenced. Moreno developed a therapeutic technique, *sociometry*, which had as its purpose "a process of classification, which is calculated, among other things, to bring individuals together who are capable of harmonious inter-personal relationships, and so creating a social group which can function at the maximum efficiency and with the minimum of disruptive tendencies and processes."[7] Moreno felt the "socio-psychopathology" of a group's structure was not entirely due to chance. He thus believed that group structures could be studied using quantitative methods to ascertain the evolution and pattern of attitudes and interactions among a group's members. Moreno classified this pattern based on three emotions: *attraction*, *repulsion*, and *indifference*. He assessed these

[2] Charles D. Wrege and Sakae Hata, "Before Bales: Pioneer Studies in Analyzing Group Behavior: 1921–1930," unpublished paper presented at the annual meeting of the Academy of Management, Boston, MA, August 14, 1984, p. 2, Ronald G. Greenwood Collection, University Archives, Alvin Sherman Library, Nova Southeastern University, Fort Lauderdale, FL. See also Gisela Konopka, *Eduard C. Lindeman and Social Work Philosophy* (Minneapolis, MN: University of Minnesota Press, 1958), pp. 33–34; Charles D. Wrege, Ti Hsu, and Ronald G. Greenwood, "The Origins of Small Group Research: Some New Perspectives," unpublished paper presented at the annual meeting of the Southern Management Association, New Orleans, LA, November 13–17, 1984, Ronald G. Greenwood Collection, University Archives, Alvin Sherman Library, Nova Southeastern University, Fort Lauderdale, FL.

[3] For a description of these studies, see Eduard C. Lindeman, *Social Education: An Interpretation of the Principles and Methods Developed by the Inquiry during the Years 1923–1933* (New York: New Republic, 1933).

[4] Eduard C. Lindeman, *Social Discovery: An Approach to the Study of Functional Groups* (New York: Republic Publishing Company, 1924), pp. 111–112.

[5] *Ibid.*, p. 191.

[6] John J. Hader and Eduard C. Lindeman, *Dynamic Social Research* (London: K. Paul, Trench, Trubner & Co., 1933), p. 148.

[7] William A. White, "Foreword," in Jacob L. Moreno, *Who Shall Survive? A New Approach to Human Interrelations* (Washington, DC: Nervous and Mental Disease Publishing, 1934), p. xii. See also Jacob L. Moreno, "The Autobiography of J. L. Moreno, MD," ed. Jonathan D. Moreno, *Journal of Group Psychotherapy Psychodrama & Sociometry* 42(1–2) (Spring 1989), pp. 59–126.

emotions by asking group members to indicate with whom they would (and would not) prefer to associate with within a group. Moreno then paired and ranked group members' feelings for one another using a chart he called a *sociogram*. He recognized that group-member preferences are dynamic and vary as group membership and the challenges facing a group change. For example, in a study of "leadership structures" at the New York Training School for Girls, different pairing preferences were expressed depending on whether respondents were choosing a roommate or a workmate. Other early similar research sought to increase work-team output by sociometrically selecting team members.[8]

Moreno also developed what is known as *psychodrama* and *sociodrama*. Both techniques involve dramatic enactments of real-life situations or conflicts. Together these techniques form a basis for remedying difficulties in individual or group relationships. Psychodrama consists of placing individuals "on stage" to act out their personal problems with the aid of other "actors" and a facilitator.[9] Once an individual's manner of dealing with others is revealed, therapy or treatment is then recommended to resolve any difficulties that may have been disclosed. Psychodrama is intended to be a cathartic experience, enabling individuals to release and relieve their innermost doubts and anxieties.

Sociodrama, an outgrowth of psychodrama, focuses on understanding relationships within groups. It assumes that groups are organized according to social and cultural roles. Group therapy is used to understand these roles and might include role-playing exercises dealing with superior–subordinate relationships, interpersonal and team relationships, gender and race issues, and so forth. Role reversal, or enacting the roles of opposite social or cultural group members—for example, a white supervisor playing the role of an African American worker—might be used to broaden role flexibility and create an understanding of others' views. In effect, sociodrama is group psychotherapy designed to reduce resentments, frustrations, and misunderstandings. Moreno's work supplemented the counseling and interpersonal-relations aspects of the human-relations movement by providing techniques for studying and changing an individual's or group's behavior vis-à-vis other individuals or groups. Heretofore, psychology and psychoanalysis, both essentially concerned with the study of mental processes, had been inadequate for analyzing individual or group workplace behavior.

Group dynamics, as developed by Kurt Lewin, is another concept that developed during the same period in which Moreno was popularizing his sociometric methods. Indeed, there is evidence that Moreno substantially influenced Lewin's work.[10] Lewin studied at the University of Berlin under Max Wertheimer and Wolfgang Kohler, two founders of the Gestalt movement. His own thinking falls under the heading of *field theory*, which holds that a group's behavior is the result of an intricate set of symbolic interactions and forces that not only affect its structure, but also modify its members' behavior. From a field-theory perspective, a group is never at a steady state, but is in a continuous process of mutual adaptation that Lewin labeled "quasi-stationary equilibrium." An analogy might be that of a river flowing within its banks; it appears relatively stationary, but there is continual movement and change. The idea that a group's behavior is maintained in a state of "quasi-stationary equilibrium" parallels Follett's notion of "circular response," in which the One and the Many are constantly interrelating to create each other (see Chapter 14). This is another example of Gestalt theory's influence across the social sciences.

Lewin maintained that a person's behavior at any given time is determined by the continuous interplay between the qualities or characteristics that make individuals unique (e.g., age, gender, education, physical health, experience, integrity, self-awareness, personality, needs, and desires)

---

[8] Raymond H. Van Zelst, "Sociometrically Selected Work Teams Increase Production," *Personnel Psychology* 5(3) (September 1952), pp. 175–185.

[9] Jacob L. Moreno, *Psychodrama*, vol. 1 (Boston, MA: Beacon Press, 1946), pp. 177–222.

[10] Barbara A. Wech, "The Lewin/Moreno Controversy," in Dennis F. Ray, ed., *Proceedings of the Southern Management Association* (1996), pp. 421–423. See also Pitirim Sorokin, *Fads and Foibles in Modern Sociology and Related Sciences* (Chicago, IL: Henry Regnery, 1956), pp. 5–6.

and their psychological environment. This is expressed in his famous formula $B = f(P, E)$, where behavior (B) is a function (f) of the interaction between person (P) and environment (E).[11] "Environment" here refers to a person's psychological environment, meaning the external world as it is subjectively perceived. Taking a person's qualities and characteristics as a constant or given, Lewin's formula offers the possibility that behavior can be changed by altering a person's physical and social surroundings. In one early study, Lewin and his University of Iowa graduate students studied groups of 10- and 11-year-old boys to determine how the environment created by the democratic or authoritarian actions of the groups' adult leaders influenced the behavior of group members. They concluded that authoritarianism bred apathetic submissiveness and aggression among the boys, including scapegoating. By contrast, two leadership patterns that they labeled "democratic" and "laissez-faire" were more effective in maintaining a friendly atmosphere and a positive attitude toward group activities. It is unfortunate that this study has been misrepresented as a study of leadership and its influence on productivity rather than a study of how different leadership philosophies influence a group's social interactions. Ralph K. White, one of the group leaders, was quite shy and had little experience with young boys. White was supposed to be a democratic leader, but when the results for his group were discussed, Ronald Lippitt (another group leader) remarked, "This isn't democratic leadership. That is *laissez-faire*." Rather than discard the observations from White's group, Lewin declared, "Okay, we'll make a third group. A *laissez-faire* group." Over the years, the notion has been erroneously passed down that laissez-faire was intended as a style of leadership when in fact it was recognized as a lack of leadership.[12]

In research on changing family food habits conducted during World War II, Lewin found that changes were more easily induced through group decision-making than through lectures and individual appeals.[13] This was a new insight into introducing change and suggested that changes are more readily accepted when people feel they have been involved in a decision to change rather than simply being asked or told to change. Lewin felt successful change included three aspects: "unfreezing," or recognizing the need for change; "moving," or modifying old ways so that new behavior patterns can be introduced; and "freezing," or establishing new behavior patterns.[14] Lewin's three phases provided a foundation for future "action research" (the purpose of which was to collaborate with group members to study their behavior) and modern organizational change and development techniques that focus on the behavior of groups as groups rather than on how groups influence the behavior of individuals.

Lewin introduced new perspectives for understanding the effects of group processes on individual behavior. His studies showed that an understanding of group dynamics had the potential to modify the behavior of both individuals and groups. In 1945, Lewin founded the Research Center for Group Dynamics at the Massachusetts Institute of Technology.[15] Following his death in 1947, the center was moved to the University of Michigan's Institute for Social Research, where Rensis Likert (pronounced *lick-urt*) and others would further the study of employee participation in decision-making and the use of group interventions to achieve changes in workplace behavior.[16] Likert's studies to determine what principles and methods of leadership work best will be discussed shortly. In 1947, another of Lewin's disciples, Leland P. Bradford, established the first sensitivity training (or human relations) laboratory, the National Training Laboratory for Group Development,

[11] Kurt Lewin, *Principles of Topological Psychology*, trans. Fritz Heider and Grace M. Heider (New York: McGraw-Hill Book Company, 1936), p. 12.

[12] Comments made by Gertrud (Mrs. Kurt) W. Lewin after the presentation of the following paper by her daughter: Miriam Lewin Papanek, "Kurt Lewin and His Contributions to Modern Management Theory," in Thad B. Green and Dennis F. Ray, eds., *Proceedings of the Annual Meeting of the Academy of Management* (1973), pp. 317–322. See also Gertrud W. Lewin quoted in William B. Wolf, "Reflections on the History of Management Thought," *Journal of Management History* 2(2) (1996), p. 8.

[13] Kurt Lewin, "The Dynamics of Group Action," *Educational Leadership* 1(4) (January 1944), pp. 195–200.

[14] *Idem*, "Group Decision and Social Change," in Theodore M. Newcomb and Eugene L. Hartley, eds., *Readings in Social Psychology* (New York: Henry Holt, 1947), p. 344.

[15] *Idem*, "The Research Center for Group Dynamics at Massachusetts Institute of Technology," *Sociometry* 8(2) (May 1945), pp. 126–136.

[16] "The Career of Rensis Likert: Using Science for Man—A Gentle Revolution," *ISR Newsletter* 1(9) (Winter 1971), pp. 1–7.

at Bethel, Maine.[17] "By way of emotionally intensive group experiences—often including body-oriented, practical exercises such as lying on the floor, touching others, or engaging in role-play—[laboratory] participants were supposed to become better aware of their own and others' emotions, thoughts, and behaviors and how to communicate them authentically and spontaneously." Despite its laudable intent, sensitivity training soon gained a reputation for involving "soft, mushy, touch-feely" encounters that often damaged rather than improved work relationships.[18]

By focusing on group interactions rather than isolated individuals and, thus, recognizing that the behavior of group members is more than the simple sum of their individual actions, Lindeman, Moreno, and Lewin introduced novel perspectives for understanding workplace behavior. This focus, reflecting the Gestalt notion that individuals within groups cannot be studied in isolation, led to further studies on introducing change, conflict resolution, and the effects of group processes on individual behavior. Overall, these studies emphasized the dynamic nature of individual interactions within a group setting. In Lewin's view, an understanding of group dynamics had the potential to modify the behavior of not only individuals and groups but also whole societies.

THE GROWTH OF HUMAN-RELATIONS RESEARCH AND TRAINING

The 1930s witnessed the emergence of a more favorable political climate for organized labor. The passage of the National Labor Relations Act (the Wagner Act) and the formation of the Congress of Industrial Organizations (CIO), both in 1935, brought a new emphasis on collective bargaining. Morris L. Cooke (see Chapter 8) and CIO president Philip Murray called for management to "tap labor's brains" for ideas on how to increase workplace productivity.[19] *Industrial democracy*, meaning in essence the workplace application of a human-relations philosophy with organized labor's support, was a common theme.[20] Accordingly, several university-based programs began to appear that would pave the way for the further growth of human-relations research. Of particular note, the Committee on Human Relations in Industry was formed at the University of Chicago in 1943. Drawing its members from the disciplines of business (Burleigh Gardner), sociology (William Foote Whyte), and anthropology (W. Lloyd Warner), the committee characterized a new style of interdisciplinary social-science research.[21] In 1946, Gardner and Warner, along with William Henry, created the consulting firm Social Research, Incorporated (SRI), which specialized in commercial applications of social-science research. Industrial relations centers also came into vogue. The first such center, the New York State School of Industrial and Labor Relations, was established at Cornell University (1945); others followed, such as the Labor-Management Center at Yale University (1945) and the Institute of Labor and Industrial Relations at the University of Illinois (1946).

Human-relations training also gained popularity during the late 1940s. Oriented toward overcoming barriers to communication and enhancing interpersonal skills, this training typically emphasized group-performance incentives, ways to meet employees' social needs, and strategies to encourage workplace collaboration. It often featured techniques such as role-playing, nondirective counseling, group-discussion methods, and, eventually, sensitivity training.

---

[17] Leland P. Bradford, *National Training Laboratories: Its History, 1947–1970* (Bethel, ME: Privately printed, 1974).

[18] Linnea Tillema, "The Crying Boss: Activating 'Human Resources' Through Sensitivity Training in 1970s Sweden," *Journal of the History of the Behavioral Sciences* 59(3) (July 2023), p. 302. See also Scott Highhouse, "A History of the T-Group and Its Early Applications in Management Development," *Group Dynamics: Theory, Research, and Practice* 6(4) (December 2002), p. 278.

[19] Philip Murray and Morris L. Cooke, *Organized Labor and Production: Next Steps in Industrial Democracy* (New York: Harper & Brothers, 1940), p. 211.

[20] For example, see Clinton S. Golden and Harold J. Ruttenberg, *The Dynamics of Industrial Democracy* (New York: Harper & Brothers, 1942).

[21] Burleigh B. Gardner and William Foote Whyte, "Methods for the Study of Human Relations in Industry," *American Sociological Review* 11(5) (October 1946), pp. 506–512. See also David G. Moore, "The Committee in Human Relations in Industry at the University of Chicago, 1943–1948," in Daniel A. Wren and John A. Pearce II, eds., *Papers Dedicated to the Development of Modern Management: Celebrating 100 Years of Modern Management and 50th Anniversary of the Academy of Management* (Briarcliff Manor, NY: Academy of Management, 1986), pp. 45–51, and Jean-Michel Chapoulie, *Chicago Sociology*, trans. Caroline Wazer (New York: Columbia University Press, 2020), pp. 176–178. Originally published in 2001.

CHANGING ASSUMPTIONS ABOUT PEOPLE AT WORK

As noted, whereas engineers largely dominated the scientific-management movement, the human-relations era was decidedly interdisciplinary in its focus. A different perspective on the nature of employee motivation, the role of managers in eliciting employee collaboration, and the importance of employee sentiments and informal work-group activities emerged as a result. This new perspective challenged prevailing assumptions about people at work. Investigations in the post-Hawthorne era led to (1) a deeper understanding of workplace motivation; (2) questions about benefits from division of labor; and (3) an interest in obtaining greater employee commitment to an organization's goals through employee participation in decision-making.

PEOPLE AND MOTIVATION

It has been suggested that we are motivated to behave as we do because we all have needs that we strive to satisfy. *Need theory* is one of the oldest explanations for why individuals engage in specific behaviors (see Chapter 9). Writing in 1938, Henry A. Murray identified 27 basic personality needs individuals attempt to satisfy by their actions.[22] Three of these needs—the needs for power, affiliation, and achievement—have been the focus of continuing research, including that by David C. McClelland, as discussed in Chapter 2. Building on Murray's work, in the early 1940s, Abraham H. Maslow developed one of the most widely recognized need theories of motivation. According to Maslow, individuals are motivated to satisfy five categories of inborn needs: physiological, safety, love, esteem, and self-actualization. Maslow held that these needs form a hierarchy of ascending importance, from low to high. He contended that a "lower" need must be relatively satisfied before the "next higher" need can motivate behavior. For example, an individual's safety needs would have to be generally satisfied before the next level of need (social) could motivate behavior. Thus, the strength of any need is determined not only by its position in the hierarchy, but also by the degree to which it and all lower needs have been satisfied. Relative satisfaction of a need, however, triggers dissatisfaction at the next highest level. This sequence of "increased satisfaction, decreased importance, increased importance of the next higher need" repeats itself until the highest level of the hierarchy (self-actualization) is reached. Maslow suggested that an individual could progress down as well as up the various levels of need. If a satisfied lower level need (safety, for instance) were threatened at some later point in time, it again would become dominant and assume an important position in an individual's overall motivation.

Maslow borrowed the term "self-actualization" from Kurt Goldstein, a well-known "holistic" psychologist. Goldstein saw self-actualization as the master motive from which all other motives sprang.[23] Maslow, however, treated self-actualization in a more limited fashion—it emerged only after all lower level needs were relatively satisfied. For Maslow, self-actualization meant that "[a] musician must make music, an artist must paint, a poet must write, if he is to be ultimately happy. What a man *can* be, he must be . . . to become more and more what one is, to become everything that one is capable of becoming."[24] Maslow believed that self-actualization was not something to be achieved, but one's natural state. He held that people who were not self-actualized had been thwarted by society or ill-fated circumstances. As described by Maslow, "[s]elf-actualizing people were marked by an openness to experience and perception; a trust in their own judgment, even if it meant departure from societal norms; an autonomy and independence from other people's approval or opinions; a capacity for love, enjoyment, humor, and

---

[22] Henry A. Murray, *Explorations in Personality: A Clinical and Experimental Study of Fifty Men of College Age* (New York: Oxford University Press, 1938), p. 145.

[23] Kurt Goldstein, *The Organism: A Holistic Approach to Biology, Derived from Pathological Data in Man* (New York: American Book Company, 1939), p. 160. Originally published in 1936.

[24] Abraham H. Maslow, "A Theory of Human Motivation," *Psychological Review* 50(4) (July 1943), p. 380. For a history of Maslow's hierarchy of needs, see Todd N. Bridgman, Stephen Cummings, and John Ballard, "Who Built Maslow's Pyramid? A History of the Creation of Management Studies' Most Famous Symbol and Its Implications for Management Education," *Academy of Management Learning & Education* 18(1) (March 2019), pp. 81–98.

sympathy; and an ability to sacralize whatever they did, whether this was writing a poem or driving a bus, making a scientific discovery or caring for a child." For Maslow, "[s]elf-actualizers showed what the human species could be at its best."[25] As will be discussed, later management scholars would draw on Maslow's hierarchy and other need theories of motivation to develop new methods of participation to give employees greater autonomy in their work.

Behaviorism and psychoanalysis were two other widely accepted motivation theories in the mid-1950s. As Maslow moved through his career, he became disenchanted with the behaviorist view that all human behavior is determined by responses to environmental stimuli. Similarly, Maslow questioned the views of Sigmund Freud, the dominant figure in psychoanalysis. Freud's thinking largely drew on the study of neurotics or psychotics. Maslow felt that there were shortcomings in basing our understanding of human motivation on the behavior of the emotionally disturbed. He believed that psychology should emphasize the study of the whole person, including those values that make individuals good, honorable, creative, heroic, and so on. Maslow's response, "humanistic psychology," was a revolt against behaviorism and psychoanalysis, creating what became known as the "Third Force" in psychology.[26] The Third Force gathered momentum as other prominent psychologists agreed that previous research and thinking had largely overlooked most well-adjusted individuals leading productive lives.

Maslow's later findings brought rich insights into what motivates managers. In the summer of 1962, he was named a visiting fellow at Non-Linear Systems (Del Mar, California). Non-Linear Systems president Andrew Kay arranged the appointment. This was Maslow's first exposure to a large business. He kept journals that summer that were later published as a book titled *Eupsychian Management*. Drawing on the Greek word for happiness (*eudaimonia*), "eupsychian" is a neologism (a new word) that means "good psychological management," or management by competent, mentally healthy, self-actualizing individuals. Maslow felt that one way to improve mental health in general would be to begin with the workplace, because most people are employed. He further believed that individuals who are psychologically healthy are the best managers.[27]

Whereas Maslow focused on the satisfaction of higher level needs (as noted above), human-relations training typically emphasized group-performance incentives, meeting employees' social needs, and encouraging workplace collaboration. The most widely cited and enduring plan for combining these ideas was developed by Joseph N. Scanlon, an erstwhile seaman, prizefighter, cost accountant, open-hearth steel worker, and union officer.[28] Scanlon worked at the Empire Sheet and Tin Plate Company in Mansfield, Ohio. Faced with the economic pressures brought on by the Great Depression, Scanlon joined with Empire Steel's managers and United Steel Workers of America officials to broker a plan to save the company from bankruptcy and prevent job cuts. The plan featured a joint labor–management committee that met monthly to hear worker suggestions on eliminating waste and improving productivity and, thereby, company profit. The worker suggestions helped the company survive.

Courtesy of Daniel A. Wren

Joseph N. Scanlon, 1955

During World War II, Scanlon developed successful labor–management production committees for the War Production Board. Following the war, he joined the

[25] Nadine Weidman, "Abraham Maslow, Utopian Realist," *Journal of Humanistic Psychology*, in press.

[26] *Idem*, "Toward a Humanistic Biology," *American Psychologist* 24(8) (August 1967), p. 724.

[27] *Idem*, *Eupsychian Management: A Journal* (Homewood, IL: Richard D. Irwin, 1965), p. 75. See also Kira Lussier, "Of Maslow, Motives, and Managers: The Hierarchy of Needs in American Business, 1960–1985," *Journal of the History of the Behavioral Sciences* 55(4) (Autumn 2019), pp. 319–341.

[28] Daniel A. Wren, "Joseph N. Scanlon: The Man and the Plan," *Journal of Management History* 15(1) (2009), pp. 20–37.

Massachusetts Institute of Technology (MIT) faculty, where he became a colleague of Douglas McGregor. McGregor's *The Human Side of Enterprise* devoted a chapter to "the Scanlon plan" as an example of "management by integration and self-control."[29] The Scanlon plan evolved in the years following its introduction at Empire Steel. The plan involves: (1) a suggestion system that seeks methods and means to reduce labor costs; (2) joint labor–management committees that seek to solve production difficulties; and (3) the sharing cost savings (75 percent to labor and 25 percent to management). There are no individual awards, cooperation and collaboration are stressed over competition, and everyone benefits from the cost-saving suggestions of others. Before his death in 1956, Scanlon successfully introduced his plan in small- to medium-sized firms, including various manufacturing and nonmanufacturing industries and union and non-union shops. Frederick Lesieur, an MIT colleague, installed the Scanlon plan in over 200 firms before his retirement in 1986.[30] Others continued this work, and Scanlon's plan achieved high standing among labor-relations scholars as "an organizationwide gain sharing plan that seeks to provide all employees with incentives to search for ways to reduce the overall costs of goods sold."[31] Rather than becoming a management fad, Scanlon's ideas have proven their worth in combining employee participation and financial incentives.

Although the Scanlon plan, when first introduced, was a typical product of the era's emphasis on workplace collaboration, individual incentives did not pass entirely from the industrial scene. Writing in his book *Incentive Management: A New Approach to Human Relationships in Industry and Business*, James F. Lincoln appealed to employee ambition. Lincoln believed that people were trading freedom for security; they were relying on someone else (i.e., the federal government) for their well-being while pride in work, self-reliance, and other time-tested virtues were declining. In Lincoln's view, the remedy to this decline was a return to an "intelligent selfishness," in which people are rewarded based on their individual performance. As president of Lincoln Electric Company (Cleveland, Ohio), the world's largest producer of welding equipment, he pioneered a pay-for-performance incentive plan that is still used today. Designed to motivate employees by rewarding them only for what they produce, the plan also ensures that all employees receive an annual bonus based on their individual output, dependability, degree of cooperativeness with other employees, and company profitability. In 1951, shortly before he stepped down as president, Lincoln reported that in his company, work stoppages were nonexistent, labor turnover was negligible, employee productivity was five times that of other U.S. manufacturers, dividends per share were continually rising, and product prices were steadily declining.[32]

JOB ENLARGEMENT AND JOB ENRICHMENT

Adam Smith warned in 1776 that, despite its economic benefits, the advantages associated with the division of labor seem "to be acquired at the expence [*sic*] of [a person's] intellectual, social, and martial virtues"[33] (see Chapter 2). Almost 175 years later, social scientists and innovative companies had begun to take Smith's warning seriously. In 1944, at its Endicott (New York) plant, the International Business Machines Corporation (IBM) began to combine the work of

[29] Douglas McGregor, *The Human Side of Enterprise* (New York: McGraw-Hill, 1960), p. 110.

[30] Frederick G. Lesieur, ed., *The Scanlon Plan: A Frontier in Labor-Management Cooperation* (Cambridge, MA: Technology Press of Massachusetts Institute of Technology, 1958).

[31] Thomas A. Kochan and Paul Osterman, *The Mutual Gains Enterprise: Forging a Winning Partnership among Labor, Management, and Government* (Boston, MA: Harvard Business School Press, 1994), p. 54. For doubts about employee participation in general, see George Strauss, "Worker Participation: Some Under-Considered Issues," *Industrial Relations* 45(4) (October 2006), pp. 778–803.

[32] James F. Lincoln, *Incentive Management: A New Approach to Human Relationships in Industry and Business* (Cleveland, OH: Lincoln Electric Company, 1951), pp. 251–289. For a history of the Lincoln Electric bonus plan, see Virginia P. Dawson, *Lincoln Electric: A History* (Cleveland, OH: Lincoln Electric Company, 1999).

[33] Adam Smith, *An Inquiry into the Nature and Causes of the Wealth of Nations* (London: W. Strahan and T. Cadell in the Strand, 1776), vol. 2, bk. V, ch. 1, pp. 366–367. For a prescient discussion of the need for job enrichment, see Harry Tipper, "The Labor Problem," *American Machinist* 52(11) (March 11, 1920), pp. 549–556.

two or more machine operators into one job in an effort to relieve the monotony associated with "highly simplified repetitive operations." The intent was to "enrich" the new job's "variety, interest, and significance." IBM called this *job enlargement* and found that doing so led to higher product quality as well as less idle time for employees and machines.[34] Soon afterward, Charles R. Walker and Robert H. Guest found that employees at a General Motors assembly plant rebelled against the "anonymity" and monotony of their work, even though they were satisfied with their pay and employment security.[35] Having met these more basic needs, the employees bridled at the repetitiveness and mechanical pacing of their conveyor-line jobs. With a growing body of similar findings, job enlargement (and later *job enrichment*) assumed a new prominence in studies of workplace behavior. Job enlargement served to increase morale, relieve monotony, and enhance skill levels among employees. Job enrichment went further by also encouraging employers to give as much responsibility to their employees as possible.

PARTICIPATION IN DECISION-MAKING

A third area in which prevailing workplace assumptions were challenged during the 1940s and 1950s concerned the nature of power relations within organizations. There was a growing appeal to give employees a greater voice in workplace decisions. Operating on the premise that employee involvement would yield a greater commitment to organizational goals and further individual and group satisfaction, researchers sought to involve employees in deciding work-related issues. James C. Worthy, drawing on his experiences with Sears, Roebuck and Company, argued for "flatter," less complex organization structures that would decentralize power and authority and, thereby, lead to improved employee attitudes, encourage individual responsibility and initiative, and provide outlets for individual self-expression and creativity.[36] Sears, Roebuck and Company also collaborated with the University of Chicago's Committee on Human Relations in a comprehensive study of organization structure and employee morale. Worthy's analysis of "tall" versus "flat" structures, their impact on employee behavior, and the influence of managers' assumptions on workplace attitudes remains a landmark in advancing our understanding of workplace dynamics.[37]

Courtesy of Arthur G. Bedeian

James C. Worthy

William B. Given, Jr., and Charles P. McCormick were two other executives who challenged prevailing workplace practices. Using the catchphrase "bottom-up management," Given, as president of the American Brake Shoe Company (Mahwah, New York), sought to develop a program "to release the thinking and encourage the initiative of all those down the line, so that ideas and impetus flow from the bottom up."[38] Bottom-up management involves widespread delegation of authority, considerable latitude in decision-making, a free interchange of ideas across hierarchical levels, and the

[34] Charles R. Walker, "The Problem of the Repetitive Job," *Harvard Business Review* 28(3) (May 1950), pp. 54–58. See also Robert H. Guest, "Job Enlargement—A Revolution in Job Design," *Personnel Administration* 20(2) (March–April 1957), pp. 9–16.

[35] Charles R. Walker and Robert H. Guest, "The Man on the Assembly Line," *Harvard Business Review* 30(3) (May–June 1952), pp. 71–83. See also *idem*, *The Man on the Assembly Line* (Cambridge, MA: Harvard University Press, 1952), and *idem* and Arthur N. Turner, *The Foreman on the Assembly Line* (Cambridge, MA: Harvard University Press, 1956).

[36] James C. Worthy, "Organizational Structure and Employee Morale," *American Sociological Review* 15(2) (April 1950), pp. 169–179.

[37] *Idem*, *Big Business and Free Men* (New York: Harper & Brothers, 1959), pp. 104–107. See also *idem*, *Brushes with History: Recollections of a Many Favored Life* (Evanston, IL: Thomson-Shore, 1998), pp. 84–101.

[38] William B. Given, Jr., *Bottom-Up Management: People Working Together* (New York: Harper & Brothers, 1949), pp. 3–4.

corollary acceptance of the fact that managers grow by having the freedom to fail. Recognizing that a "push from the top" was occasionally needed, Given tried to confine top-down management to setting policy, clarifying goals, and providing employee training.

McCormick, president of McCormick & Company (Baltimore, Maryland), introduced a unique model of employee participation that involved establishing a Junior Board of Directors. Part of what became known as the "Multiple Management Plan," the Junior Board was a means of training and motivating younger managers. Junior board directors were given free access to financial and other company records, encouraged to elect their own officers, and told "every recommendation they made for the advancement of the business would have the serious consideration of the company."[39] The Junior Board met with the McCormick & Company "senior board" once a month to submit its recommendations, which were generally accepted and acted on to a greater extent than McCormick himself had originally expected. In fact, McCormick attributed his company's success during the lean years of the Great Depression to the Junior Board's efforts. One example of a Junior Board recommendation involved the redesign of the company's traditional bottle for specialty extracts, which McCormick expected his older executives would wish to retain. The Junior Board conducted a market investigation, considered homemakers' ideas, and developed a new design that was immediately accepted by the company's senior board and the marketplace. The success of the Junior Board led to the creation of a Factory Board and a Sales Board. These boards, which operated essentially as the Junior Board for the company's production and sales departments, were established in 1933 and 1935, respectively. In McCormick's opinion, The Multiple Management Plan offered a number of advantages: It (1) opened communication channels for junior managers; (2) involved young managers in decision-making; (3) provided a means for identifying and developing future executives; (4) relieved senior board members of a great deal of detailed planning and research; and (5) provided for interlocking arrangements between various departments to coordinate and follow through on company activities.

During the 1930s and 1940s, employee participation in decision-making received greater and greater acclaim. It was viewed as democracy in action, opening communication channels, diffusing authority, and motivating employees by encouraging greater commitment to shared organizational goals.[40] Moreover, it was seen as challenging an employer's unilateral authority and as equalizing bargaining power between employees and employers.

LEADERSHIP: COMBINING PEOPLE AND PRODUCTION

Kurt Lewin's experiences as a Jew who fled Germany after Adolph Hitler's National Socialist Workers' Party came to power in January 1933 undoubtedly influenced his thinking about leadership, resistance to change, and the social climate within groups. Lewin's work exemplified the emergence of a pro-participation and anti-authoritarian literature during the 1930s and 1940s. Contributors to this literature included Theodor W. Adorno and his associates, who made a significant impact on the leadership literature in 1950 with their book *The Authoritarian Personality*.[41] Influenced by the Nazism and fascism witnessed in World War II, Adorno and his colleagues tried to relate personality structure to leadership, followership, morals, prejudices, and politics. The "F scale" (Fascist Scale), developed as a part of the book, became an accepted instrument for analyzing leadership styles as well as followers' leader preferences.

Research growing out of military experiences in World War II, however, was beginning to challenge the idea that one leadership style was good and another bad. As early as 1945, the

---

[39] Charles P. McCormick, *Multiple Management* (New York: Harper & Brothers, 1938), p. 5. See also McCormick's sequel, *The Power of People: Multiple Management Up to Date* (New York: Harper & Brothers, 1949).

[40] Gordon W. Allport, "The Psychology of Participation," *Psychological Review* 53(3) (May 1945), pp. 117–132.

[41] Theodor W. Adorno, Else Frenkel-Brunswick, David J. Levinson, and R. Nevitt Sanford in collaboration with Betty Aron, Maria Hertz Levinson, and William Morrow, *The Authoritarian Personality* (New York: Harper & Brothers, 1950).

University of Michigan's Institute for Social Research, under the direction of Rensis Likert, began a series of studies to determine what principles and methods of leadership resulted in the highest employee productivity, least absenteeism, lowest turnover, and greatest job satisfaction. The studies focused on the operation of small work groups. As a result of this effort, two relatively distinct styles of leadership were identified: (1) *job-centered*—leader behaviors oriented toward close supervision, pressure for better performance, meeting deadlines, and evaluating output; and (2) *employee-centered*—leader behaviors oriented toward human aspects of subordinate relations and developing effective work groups with high performance goals. Employee-centered leaders are concerned with employee needs, welfare, advancement, and personal growth, whereas job-centered leaders are concerned with ensuring employees meet performance standards.[42] The Michigan researchers emphasized that a hard-and-fast line could not be drawn between the two styles of leadership they had identified. Both were important to productivity. They explained their results as a matter of emphasis. Managers of high-producing groups were seen as emphasizing high productivity as *one* aspect of their jobs, but not the *only* aspect. In contrast, managers of low-producing groups were viewed as emphasizing high productivity to the exclusion of other important aspects of their job. Likert identified four profiles of organizational characteristics: System 1—"exploitative authoritative"; System 2—"benevolent authoritative"; System 3—"consultative"; and System 4—"participative group."[43]

Likert regarded System 4 to be the "ideal" state for an organization to maximize performance, employee satisfaction and morale, with System 1 being the least effective. System 2 was more effective than System 1, but less effective than System 3, and so on. System 4 involved three basic concepts: (1) the "principle of supportive relationships"; (2) group decision-making and group methods of supervision; and (3) high performance goals. Likert considered the *principle of supportive relationships* to be a guide for applying System 4. Simply stated: "*The leadership and other processes of the organization must be such as to ensure a maximum probability that in all interactions and all relationships with the organization each member will, in the light of his background, values, and expectations, view the experience as supportive and one which builds his sense of personal worth and importance.*"[44] Likert felt that this principle incorporated essential elements for the success of every organization and provided a "fundamental formula" for tapping an employee's full potential.

In his final book, *New Ways of Managing Conflict*, Likert referred to a "System 5" as "an even more sophisticated, complex, and effective system" that would emerge as the social sciences advanced.[45] In System 5, "authority of hierarchy" would be replaced with a pattern of authority relationships spread throughout an organization. In case of conflict, groups would work together through overlapping memberships until a consensus was achieved. Employees would be called "associates"; there would be no position titles. Leadership would involve a "shared sense of purpose." If these ideas sound familiar, it may be because Likert was a great admirer of Mary Follett (see Chapter 14), sharing her belief that labor and management are partners in a common endeavor for which they have joint responsibilities.[46]

At about the same time that the Michigan research was beginning, the Personnel Research Board of the Ohio State University initiated a series of studies that developed a "situational approach to leadership."[47] Conducted under the primary direction of Ralph M. Stogdill and Carroll L. Shartle, the purpose of the studies was to determine the impact of leader

---

[42] See, for example, Rensis Likert, *New Patterns of Management* (New York: McGraw-Hill, 1961), pp. 23–44.
[43] *Ibid.*, p. 223.
[44] *Ibid.* p. 103.
[45] Rensis Likert and Jane Gibson Likert, *New Ways of Managing Conflict* (New York: McGraw-Hill, 1976), p. 41.
[46] *Idem*, "From Production- and Employee-Centeredness to Systems 1–5," *Journal of Management* 5(2) (Fall 1976), p. 151.
[47] Carroll L. Shartle, "The Early Years of the Ohio State University Leadership Studies," *Journal of Management* 5 (Fall 1979), pp. 127–134; Chester A. Schriesheim and Barbara J. Bird, "Contributions of the Ohio State Studies to the Field of Leadership," *Journal of Management* 5(3) (Fall 1979), pp. 135–145.

Ralph M. Stogdill

behavior on job performance and employee satisfaction. The studies revealed that followers perceived their leaders' behaviors to be composed of two principal dimensions: (1) *consideration*—leader behaviors oriented toward developing mutual trust, two-way communication, respect for followers ideas, and concern for their feelings; and (2) *initiating structure*—leader behaviors oriented toward structuring followers activities for the purpose of goal attainment. Because consideration and initiating structure are independent dimensions, it is possible for a leader to be high in initiating structure and low in consideration, low in initiating structure and high in consideration, or high or low in both. Consideration is similar to the Michigan dimension of employee-centeredness and initiating structure is analogous to the Michigan dimension of job-centeredness.

Although one might assume that the most effective leaders would be those high in both consideration and initiating structure, the Ohio State researchers found this is not always the case. Both dimensions are necessary for effective leadership, but it is more important for a leader to strike a balance appropriate for a particular situation than to always exhibit a high degree of both types of behavior. Simply stated, a leader needs to be flexible, because the proper balance of leader behaviors varies from situation to situation.

In retrospect, the Michigan and Ohio State studies added immensely to our knowledge about effective leadership. Perhaps most significantly, they showed that no single leadership style is universally effective. Moreover, the systematic methodology they introduced and the increased awareness they generated concerning effective leaders served as a springboard for the leadership research that followed. In contrast to earlier trait theories of leadership (see Chapter 8), both the Michigan and Ohio State studies showed that leaders may be best characterized by how they behave rather than by their personal traits.

PEOPLE AT WORK: THE MACRO VIEW

On the macro side of the human-relations movement, a search was underway for analytical tools and conceptual models to explain the interactions between the formal and informal processes operating within organizations. In particular, there were a number of attempts to understand the social and technical systems occurring in organizations. The results of these efforts laid the groundwork for later developments in organization theory.

ORGANIZATIONS AS SOCIOTECHNICAL SYSTEMS

One of the earliest and most perceptive attempts to understand the interaction of the social and technical systems operating within organizations was an analysis of human relations in the restaurant industry by William Foote Whyte. A key concept in his analysis was job status, or the relative prestige of a job in a jobholder's eyes or in the regard of others. Restaurants are characterized by varying levels of job status, ranging from the low status of bussers, who clear dirty dishes from tables, to the relatively high status of cooks. Whyte found that a restaurant's workflow—taking customer orders, preparing the orders, and serving the orders—posed a number of human-relations challenges. For example, waiting tables was considered a low-status job. Waitresses, however, when placing customer orders, originated work for higher status cooks. Because those who initiate work for others are of higher status (managers initiate work for subordinates), Whyte discovered that conflicts were inevitable when someone in a lower status job (e.g., a waitress) initiated work for someone of higher status (e.g., a cook). Whyte reported that restaurants avoided conflict between waitresses and cooks by placing a spindle on their order counters. The spindles are wheels on a shaft. The wheel has clips on it so that the lower status waitresses can put

customer orders on the wheel rather than call them out to higher status cooks. In this way, the cooks can remove and prepare customer orders under the pretext that they had not come from a lower status waitress, but from the spindle.[48] The spindles, thus, served to depersonalize authority and required all to obey the "law of the situation." Mary Follett would have been quite pleased.

The Tavistock Institute of Human Relations (London) was also responsible for a number of studies concerning organizations both as social systems and as a part of their broader community. Elliott Jaques (pronounced *jacks*) conducted an extensive case study of the Glacier Metal Company (London) based on Lewin's field theory. His two objectives were to investigate the "psychological and social forces" influencing "group life morale and productivity in a single industrial community" and to develop "more effective ways of resolving tension within and between groups, and of overcoming resistance and hence facilitating agreed and desired social change."[49] As part of the study, Jacques developed a theory of equitable payment and a technique for determining the time span of discretion for different jobs. Such longitudinal research into ongoing firms was (and is) rare.

Jacques's findings underscored the importance of studying organizations as interacting sociotechnical systems and were consistent with Barnard's ideas about all aspects of society being one large, cooperative system. Two of Jacques's Tavistock colleagues, Eric L. Trist and Kenneth W. Bamforth, reported a classic example of how changes in technology disrupt an organization's social relationships. They studied the social and technical consequences of the mechanized longwall method of mining coal as introduced in Great Britain following World War II.[50] (Bamforth had some experience with mining, having previously been a miner in a Yorkshire colliery.) The longwall method required breaking up small, established, highly cohesive work groups and substituting them with larger specialized groups working in shifts. Under the traditional shortwall method, miners had organized relatively autonomous work groups that rotated job assignments and shifts among themselves with minimum supervision. By contrast, with the longwall method, each miner was responsible for a single specialized task. The introduction of the longwall method resulted in a de-skilling of the work performed by the miners and a loss of autonomy. This led to decreased commitment, lower productivity, and an increased sense of personal alienation among the miners. Trist and Bamforth documented how the longwall method so disrupted the miners' social structure that its advantages were essentially negated. The lesson: Technological changes will not be effective unless due consideration is given to integrating the technical and social aspects of an organization. To wit, Trist and Bamforth's research demonstrated that "where workers can self-organise into groups that offer each worker a degree of self-leadership or autonomy in their work, both human morale and economic productivity will be raised." Moreover, "when people are given some responsibility *for* their work, they will be more responsible *in* their work."[51] Trist and Bamforth's findings anticipated later research on strategic change and the responsiveness of organizations to environmental threats.

NEW TOOLS FOR MACRO ANALYSIS

A review of the macro side of the human-relations movement would be incomplete without discussing the contributions of Carnegie Mellon University professor and Nobel laureate Herbert A. Simon. As noted in Chapter 14, Simon was greatly influenced by Chester I. Barnard's thoughts

[48] William Foote Whyte, *Human Relations in the Restaurant Industry* (New York: McGraw-Hill, 1948), pp. 69–76. See also *idem*, "The Social Structure of the Restaurant," *American Journal of Sociology* 54(4) (January 1949), pp. 302–308.

[49] Elliott Jaques, "Studies in the Social Development of an Industrial Community (The Glacier Project)," *Human Relations* 3(3) (August 1950), p. 223.

[50] Eric L. Trist and Kenneth W. Bamforth, "Some Social and Technical Consequences of the Longwall Method of Coal-Getting: An Examination of the Psychological Situation and Defences of a Work Group in Relation to the Social Structure and Technological Content of the Work System," *Human Relations* 4(1) (February 1951), pp. 3–38.

[51] Elizabeth Cory-Pearce and Juliet Scott, "The Vocational Potential of Anthropology: Teaching Organizational Research Through Practitioner Archives," *Teaching Anthropology* 9(1) (2020), p. 17.

on decision-making in organizations, especially on authority, inducements, and communications. Building on Barnard's analysis of how decisions are made in organizations, Simon questioned the validity of the rational model of decision-making grounded in traditional economic theory.[52] Rather than portraying managers as completely rational decision-makers who invariably seek to maximize expected benefits (or minimize costs), Simon advanced the view that all decision-makers are subject to cognitive limitations and emotions, as well as uncontrollable environmental factors. He labeled this "bounded rationality" to reflect the limited capability of humans to grasp not only the full complexity of decisions, but also the uncertainty of future events with which they must cope.[53] Given that organizations exist in highly complex environments, in which many possible alternatives and their consequences may remain unknown, all intended rational behavior is inherently bounded. As this suggests, *optimum decisions* (meaning "best possible" decisions) are almost never made—except perhaps by chance. Even if it were possible to acquire perfect knowledge of all alternatives and their consequences (assumptions of classical economic theory), it is doubtful that, given the constraints of human-information processing, an adequate evaluation could be made. In response to this dilemma, Simon believed that humans typically reduce the complexity they confront by constructing a simplified model that encompasses only the information they feel equipped to handle. Thus, only a limited number of alternatives and a limited range of consequences are considered.

Simon further believed that once managers have identified a limited set of alternatives, they typically deviate from the demands of rationality by selecting the first alternative deemed "satisfactory" or "good enough," rather than searching for the optimum choice. That is, rather than examine all possible alternatives and attempt to rank them according to a well-ordered and stable set of preferences (as described by classical economic theory), they conduct a sequential search and settle for the first that satisfies some predetermined "aspiration level"—a subjectively defined performance goal that is a product of past organization goals, past organization performance, and past performance of comparable organizations. Thus, choices are influenced more by the order in which alternatives are examined than by the preexistence of clear guidelines for ensuring that the optimum choice is selected.

As a shorthand label for this process, Simon coined the word *satisfice* (a blend of satisfy and suffice).[54] Examples of satisficing criteria include "share of market" versus "total market," "adequate profit" versus "maximum profit," and "fair price" versus "best price." Thus, satisficing is evident in a business whose managers are willing to hold to a decision alternative that results in a 25 percent rate of return on investment even if they are aware there *may* be other alternatives that *might* raise profits still higher. For practical purposes (e.g., selecting a source of raw materials), Simon stressed that it is important that satisficing not be seen as irrational. Given the constraints of human-information processing, the cost of searching for alternatives, and the uncertainty of future events, satisficing is sensible.

On balance, Simon rejected the basic traditional economic notion that managers are completely rational decision-makers. Whereas economists have typically focused on how managers *should* behave, Simon focused on how they *do* behave. He posited that managers do not merely seek to maximize expected benefits and that they are not completely rational. Simon's work on bounded rationality replaced the idea of the so-called "economic decision-maker" with the more realistic "managerial decision-maker."

---

[52] Herbert A. Simon, *Administrative Behavior: A Study of Decision-Making Processes in Administrative Organization* (New York: Macmillan, 1947).

[53] Matteo Cristofaro, "Herbert Simon's Bounded Rationality—Its Historical Evolution in Management and Cross-fertilizing Contribution," *Journal of Management History* 23(2) 2017, pp. 170–190.

[54] For Simon's personal statement in this regard, see Larry Gross, *Creativity: Process and Personality* (Bethlehem, PA: Media Studies Press, 1964), p. 25. Available at https://www.mediastudies.press/creativity. See also Reva Brown, "Consideration of the Origin of Herbert Simon's Theory of Satisficing (1935–1947)," *Management Decision* 42(10) (2004), pp. 1240–1256.

The work of George C. Homans represented another step forward on the macro side of the human-relations movement. Homans attended Lawrence J. Henderson's Pareto seminar (the Pareto Circle) at Harvard University (see Chapter 13) and coauthored (with Boston attorney and member of the Harvard Corporation Charles P. Curtis, Jr.) an early book on Vilfredo Pareto's 1916 tract *Trattato di Sociologia Generale* [*Treatise on General Sociology*] that formed the basis for his later view of organizations as social systems.[55] In *The Human Group*, Homans viewed groups as social systems that are comprised of an external system and an internal system.[56] Homans described a group's external system consisting of forces that are determined by the nature of its particular environment. Conversely, he considered a group's internal system to be "the elaboration of group behavior that simultaneously arises out of the external system and reacts upon it," resulting in an interaction between both systems.[57] Carrying this reasoning further, Homans identified and discussed various mutually dependent elements that interact across a group's internal and external systems: (1) activities, or behavior formally required of group members or that informally emerge; (2) interactions, or organizationally prescribed or informally originated transactions between group members; and (3) sentiments, or emotions having positive and negative values (such as like or dislike). Although Homans's treatment of groups as social systems was exceedingly broad, it provided a building block for further developments in organization theory.

Talcott Parsons, another member of Henderson's Pareto Circle, also played a major role in the early years of the human-relations movement on the macro side. Parsons received his doctorate in 1927 from the University of Heidelberg in sociology and economics, wrote his dissertation ("The Concept of Capitalism in the Recent German Literature") on Max Weber and Werner Sombart, and introduced Chester I. Barnard to Weber's views on bureaucracy. In an early work, Parsons drew together the ideas of Weber, Pareto, Alfred Marshall, and Émile Durkheim to develop a "voluntaristic theory of social action."[58] His ideas influenced Barnard's search for a theory of "cooperative systems." Parsons is especially remembered for producing a general theoretical system for the analysis of society known as "structural-functionalism."[59]

SUMMARY

This is the first of two chapters examining the twin streams of management thought that developed from about 1930 to the early 1950s. The current chapter focuses on the growth and refinement of the human-relations movement as it passed through micro and macro phases. The micro phase saw an outpouring of behavioral research into topics such as group dynamics, participative decision-making, leadership, and workplace motivation. The macro phase witnessed a number of attempts to understand the interaction of the social and technical systems operating within organizations. The title of this chapter, "People and Organizations," conveys the human orientation of both phases, with the structural aspects of organizations being a secondary subject of inquiry. In contrast, Chapter 16, "Organizations and People," focuses on the structure and design of organizations, with the human element placed in a relatively subordinate role.

[55] George C. Homans and Charles P. Curtis, Jr., *An Introduction to Pareto: His Sociology* (New York: Alfred A. Knopf, 1934).

[56] George C. Homans, *The Human Group* (New York: Harcourt, Brace & World, 1950).

[57] *Ibid.*, p. 109.

[58] Talcott E. F. Parsons, *The Structure of Social Action: A Study in Social Theory with Special Reference to a Group of Recent European Writers* (New York: McGraw-Hill, 1937), p. 11.

[59] *Idem*, *The Social System* (Glencoe, IL: Free Press, 1951), pp. 19–20.

CHAPTER 16 Organizations and People

Contemporaneous with the writings of Mary P. Follett and Chester I. Barnard; the advent of the Western Electric studies; and the outpouring of behavioral research into topics such as group dynamics, participative decision-making, leadership, and workplace motivation reviewed in Chapter 15, a complementary stream of management thought focusing on the structure and design of organizations began to take shape. Compared to the first stream, this second stream has been accused of ignoring the importance of the human factor to an organization's success.[1] The second stream, however, intentionally distinguished between "the structure of positions and the behavior of persons temporarily occupying them." In doing so, it held that "the only way in which to study organization fruitfully is to isolate it from the personalities and 'politics' of particular undertakings at a particular moment."[2] Thus, the human element was not entirely ignored in this second stream of management thought, though it was intentionally set aside for a specific purpose: to provide an analysis independent of idiosyncratic personalities and politics. This chapter, covering the period from roughly 1930 into the early 1950s, focuses on three aspects of the structure and design of organizations: (1) authority, coordination, span of control, and related issues; (2) the primary responsibilities of top management; and (3) the separation of ownership and control and the transfer of property rights.

ORGANIZATIONS: STRUCTURE AND DESIGN

Before proceeding, it would be best to first comment on the extensive criticism that has been directed at classical organization theory and the so-called "classicists." The work of the classicists has been attacked as being too simplistic, as advancing "principles" which are nothing more than "proverbs," and as reflecting a pro-management bias.[3] Though these criticisms are, to a degree, true, it should be realized that much of what we take for granted today was considered

[1] See, for example, Venkateswarier Subramaniam, "The Classical Organization Theory and Its Critics," *Public Administration* 44(4) (Winter 1966), pp. 435–446; Thomas E. Stephenson, "The Longevity of Classical Theory," *Management International Review* 8(6) (1968), pp. 77–93.

[2] Lyndall F. Urwick, "Why the So-Called 'Classicists' Endure," *Management International Review* 11(1) (1971), p. 6.

[3] Herbert A. Simon, "The Proverbs of Administration," *Public Administration Review* 6(1) (Winter 1946), pp. 53–67. See also Thomas H. Hammond, "In Defence of Luther Gulick's 'Notes on the Theory of Organization,'" *Public Administration* 68(2) (Summer 1990), pp. 143–173.

forward-thinking 70 to 80 years ago. In hindsight, it is easy to be critical. Organization research as we know it today was nonexistent, and classical theorists had very little choice but to rely upon their experience and observations for their recommendations. Evaluated from this perspective, the views of these early contributors were remarkably valid. The influence of classicists such as Henri Fayol, Max Weber, and Lyndall F. Urwick continues to be felt today. For this reason, their insights should not be minimized. Indeed, many management consulting firms continue to make a handsome living by pointing out the "simple" proverbs first formulated by the classicists.

JAMES D. MOONEY: ORGANIZATION THEORY AND PRACTICE

James D. Mooney attended the Case School of Applied Sciences (today's Case Western Reserve University), where he majored in mining engineering but did not graduate. He spent 2 years searching for gold in Mexico and California, and was later employed as an engineer at B. F. Goodrich Company, Westinghouse Electric Corporation, and Hyatt Roller Bearing Company. He served as an artillery captain during the Great War, and at its conclusion returned to Hyatt, which had been acquired by the General Motors Corporation (GM) in 1916. Some 6 years later, Mooney was appointed president of GM's fledgling Export Company.[4] As the Export Company expanded in scope, distributing an increasing variety of different automotive products, Mooney was soon faced with how to best structure its growing international operations. Responding to its overall growth as a company, in 1923, GM adopted an organizing plan originally developed at the Du Pont Company. Following this plan, each of GM's major product lines (Chevrolet, Buick, Pontiac, Oldsmobile, Cadillac, and so on) was administered through a separate and semiautonomous division (see Chapter 11). The divisions operated as mini companies, each with their own departments for production, marketing, and finance, amongst others. Such a multidivisional ("M-form") structure was, however, impractical for GM's overseas operations, which spanned 15 assembly plants serving some 70 different markets with distinct economic, political, and cultural environments. To allow units in different regions to better sense changes in market needs and adapt to varying government regulations across countries, Mooney structured the Export Company's activities geographically (based on natural, legal, political, and cultural considerations), establishing six regions with local managers empowered to act in individual markets and supported by staff headquartered in New York City.

Intrigued by the success of this new arrangement and recognizing that "[o]rganization is as old as human society itself,"[5] Mooney subsequently joined with Alan C. Reiley, a retired Remington Typewriter Company advertising manager, to trace the evolution of organized activities "down through the ages." Their intent was "to expose the *principles of organization*, as they reveal themselves in various forms of human group movement, and to help industry to protect its own growth through a greater knowledge and more conscious use of these principles."[6] Their collaboration resulted in the book *Onward Industry!* Although both men were credited as authors, Mooney was responsible for the book's underlying theme and subject matter, with Reiley primarily contributing examples that trace the history of organization in military, government, and religious institutions from antiquity to the contemporary Soviet Union. Reiley's work as a historian and cartographer extended back to preparing the maps for both Josephus N. Larned's seven-volume *History for Ready Reference* (1895–1910) and John F. Hurst's two-volume *History of the*

[4] For further biographical information on Mooney and his work at GM, see Daniel A. Wren, "James D. Mooney and General Motors' Multinational Operations, 1922–1940," *Business History Review* 87(3) (Autumn 2013), pp. 515–543; [W. Jerome Arnold], "Drawing the Rules from History," *Business Week* (August 3, 1963), pp. 46, 51; and Jacob Anbinder, "Selling the World: Public Relations and the Global Expansion of General Motors, 1922–1940," *Business History Review* 92(3) (Autumn 2018), pp. 483–507.

[5] James D. Mooney and Alan C. Reiley, *Onward Industry! The Principles of Organization and Their Significance to Modern Industry* (New York: Harper & Brothers, 1931), p. xiii. This book was later published in a more concise form under the title *The Principles of Organization* (New York: Harper & Brothers: 1939).

[6] *Ibid.*

Christian Church (1897–1900). Mooney's interest in the structure of organizations may be traced to his graduate studies at Case. Indeed, *Onward Industry!* may be viewed as an expansion of his 1929 master's thesis, "The Science of Industrial Organization."

In the foreword to *Onward Industry!*, Mooney stated that industrial objectives could be justified only by the worthiness of their purpose. He observed that the purpose of industrial enterprises is usually defined as "profit through service." This involved justifying a service and both creating and equitably dividing profits. For Mooney, however, the "true and worthy" purpose of industrial effort was "the alleviation of human want and misery."[7] Though necessary, mere productive efficiency in providing a service was insufficient; throughout an organization, equal efficiency must be realized in supplying the material wants of those who, due to poverty, were unable to purchase them. To this end, Mooney (much like Gantt before him; see Chapter 8) felt that by applying the principles of organization the challenges of modern civilization could be solved.

As Mooney observed, true efficiency requires "the efficient coordination of all relationships"[8] based on principles of organization. Mooney viewed organization as a process and defined it as "*the form of every human association for the attainment of a common purpose*."[9] Mooney's notion of organization was distinct from that of management and was explained using a mind–body analogy:

> Management is the vital spark which actuates, directs, and controls the plans and procedure of organization. With management enters the personal factor, without which no body could be a living being with any directive toward a given purpose. The relation of management to organization is analogous to the relation of the psychic complex to the physical body. Our bodies are simply the means and the instrument through which the psychic force moves toward the attainment of its aims and desires.[10]

The conceptual model of organization Mooney developed consisted of three basic principles: (1) the coordinative principle; (2) the scalar principle; and (3) the functional principle. The first principle, coordination, meant "*the orderly arrangement of group effort, to provide unity of action in the pursuit of a common purpose*."[11] The foundation for coordination was authority, "the supreme coordinating power." Authority in this sense did not imply autocracy; as Mooney explained, "In a democracy like our own, this authority rests with the people, who exercise it through the leaders of their choice."[12] Because coordination implies working together effectively, Mooney felt every member of an organization had to understand its purpose and the "procedure" necessary to attain it, which he called its *doctrine*. Mooney explained that in a religious sense "doctrine" is based on faith, but for industry, it meant the attainment of "*surplus through service*," which (as noted above) should be the purpose of industrial enterprises. Mooney reasoned that the more an organization's doctrine guided its members' actions, the more their level of teamwork would increase, as would the accomplishment of its objectives. The second basic principle of Mooney's conceptual model, the scalar principle, pertained to the "formal process through which [the supreme] coordinating authority operates from the top throughout the entire organized body."[13] This principle had its foundation in leadership, which was how authority entered the scalar chain. Delegation of authority allowed a superior to confer authority on a subordinate. Delegation always meant the conferring of authority, whether authority over people or authority for task performance. Conversely, authority always carried with it responsibility for accomplishing what was authorized.

The final principle of Mooney's conceptual model, the functional principle, pertained to the "*distinction between different kinds of duties*." Functional differentiation exists in every organization to the extent that people perform different kinds of duties, such as production, sales,

---

[7] *Ibid.*
[8] *Ibid.*, p. xv.
[9] *Ibid.*, p. 10.
[10] *Ibid.*, p. 13.
[11] Mooney and Reiley, *Principles of Organization*, p. 5.
[12] *Ibid.*, p. 7.
[13] *Ibid.*, p. 14.

accounting, and security, to name a few. This principle can be seen in the division of labor, which creates a need for coordination. Another example of functional differentiation is the distinction between line and staff. According to Mooney, there should never be any confusion about line and staff because line represented "the authority of *man*; the staff, the authority of *ideas*."[14] Line commanded, staff advised, and Mooney envisioned no potential conflict in line-staff relations as long as this dichotomy was kept in mind.

Following Mooney's section on the principles of organization, Reiley made his major contribution to *Onward Industry!* by showing how these principles evolved from military and church organizations. He used historical examples from Greece, Rome, and other civilizations to illustrate applications of Mooney's three basic principles. With respect to the Roman Catholic Church, the principle of coordination found its authority in God, who delegated it to the Pope (the Bishop of Rome) as the supreme coordinating authority. The scalar principle operated via the Pope, through cardinals (who were often both line and staff), to bishops and priests, and involved conferring authority on subordinates occupying an organization's lower echelons. In developing staff, the Church operated on a *compulsory staff service* principle. Under this principle, a superior had to consult elder monks even on minor matters. On matters of major importance, everyone had to be consulted. This principle did not abridge line authority, but instead compelled the superior to consult with others before rendering a decision. The superior could not refuse to listen. In a business, the compulsory staff principle would not protect managers from errors in judgment, but would serve to reduce errors of knowledge.

In retrospect, Mooney and Reiley's principles resembled Weber's notion of "legal authority" and his call for a clear "managerial hierarchy" and "formal rules and other controls" (see Chapter 10). Mooney and Reiley did not refer to Weber, and because Weber's work had not yet been translated into English, it may be assumed that they independently developed their conceptual model and principles of organization. Mooney's belief that a business could only achieve its true purpose if it was structured following the fundamental principles of organization was reinforced by his experiences as president of GM's Export Company and Reiley's historical examples from the aforementioned civilizations. Mooney and Reiley's major contribution to organization theory was showing the interplay among principles assumed fundamental to any activity with an identified objective. In addition, their belief that the more an organization's "doctrine" guided its members' actions, the more their accomplishments and level of teamwork would increase, was far ahead of the importance placed on socially responsible mission statements in today's corporate world.

TEXTS, TEACHERS, AND TRENDS

Until the publication of Mooney and Reiley's *Onward Industry!* in 1931, most books on management had reflected the shop-floor orientation common to the earlier scientific-management era. For the most part, these books emphasized production layout, scheduling, material handling, shop organization, production control, and other largely technique-oriented subjects. A growing interest in organization structure and design, however, was emerging. This interest was evident in Henry Dennison's book *Organization Engineering*, also published in 1931. Dennison had been a pioneer in the installation of the Taylor system in his South Framingham (Massachusetts) paper-products firm, Dennison Manufacturing Company (today's Avery Dennison Corporation). He advocated an approach to organization design that was diametrically opposed to that proposed by Mooney and Reiley. Dennison began with the idea that the purpose of "organization engineering" was "making a success of group life." He built on the belief that "all the strength of an organization comes from its members."[15] For Dennison, the first task was to form people into groups to

[14] *Ibid.* p. 34.

[15] Henry S. Dennison, *Organization Engineering* (New York: McGraw-Hill, 1931), p. 1.

build teamwork. Recognizing a diversity of motives, Dennison acknowledged that leadership would be required to resolve frictions among individuals. Instead of designing an organization's structure first, Dennison argued for finding like-minded people, grouping them into teams, and then developing a total organization structure. In this sense, Dennison anticipated by a decade or more the work of Jacob L. Moreno and others who advocated sociometrically selected work teams (see Chapter 15).

Dennison's view of motivation was also unique:

> Four general groups of tendencies which may actuate a member of any organization are: (1) regard for his own and his family's welfare and standing; (2) liking for the work itself; (3) regard for one or more members of the organization and for their good opinion, and pleasure in working with them; and (4) respect and regard for the main purposes of the organization.[16]

Dennison believed that a person could be "actuated" by any of these four tendencies, but "only when impelled by the four combined can all of man's power be brought into steady and permanent play."[17] To this end, he anticipated the job-enlargement movement of the late 1940s by advocating modifying jobs so that they would provide greater employee satisfaction. He recognized the nature of informal groups and their influence on output norms and proposed nonfinancial incentives (such as social gatherings and company-sponsored family outings) that, when properly mixed with economic methods, built loyalty. Moreover, he realized that principles of organization were not "sacred in and of themselves," and an organization's structure should be flexible to "strengthen its group[s], not ossify them."[18] Dennison also recognized limits to and variations in the number of persons to whom a manager could give attention without either restricting his "field of influence" or being spread too thin. The span of control, in his view, "seldom runs beyond six to twelve people."[19]

Dennison was a progressive employer who introduced an employee profit-sharing plan, low-interest loans for employees to purchase homes, an employee representation plan, and unemployment insurance to stabilize employees' incomes.[20] Dennison quoted Mary Follett on coordination and the law of the situation, and she appears to have colored his view of labor–management relations as well.[21] Follett's influence on Dennison's thinking is evident in his following remark: "The principal managerial job in any concern is the coordination, the composition, the integration of the impulses, energies, and interests of the three principal groups of human beings—the investors, the customers, the workers—keeping effective powers at a maximum, wasteful resistances at a minimum."[22] This remark underscores Dennison's (and Follett's) belief that an organization does not function based on a straight line of authority that flows from top to bottom, but rather every member has a sphere of influence given, as Follett wrote, "the necessity of acting in accord with the unique requirements inherent in any situation."[23]

Management textbooks popular during the 1930s largely continued to follow the shop-floor orientation that had developed during the earlier scientific-management era and, thus, contributed little to the evolution of general management thought. Writing in *Management of an Enterprise*, C. Canby Balderston, Victor S. Karabasz, and Robert P. Brecht (all at the University of

[16] *Ibid.*, pp. 63–64.
[17] *Ibid.*, p. 64.
[18] *Ibid.*, pp. 124, 126.
[19] *Ibid.*, p. 138.
[20] W. Jack Duncan, "Henry Sturgis Dennison," in Morgen L. Witzel, ed., *Biographical Dictionary of Management*, vol. 1 (Bristol, UK: Thoemmes Press, 2001), pp. 233–236. See also Kim McQuaid, "Henry S. Dennison and the 'Science' of Industrial Reform, 1900–1950," *American Journal of Economics and Sociology* 36(1) (January 1977), pp. 79–98; Kyle D. Bruce, "Activist Management: Henry S. Dennison's Institutionalist Economics," *Journal of Economic Issues* 40(4) (December 2006), pp. 1113–1136; *idem*, "Activist Manager: The Enduring Contribution of Henry S. Dennison to Management and Organization Studies," *Journal of Management History* 21(2) (2015), pp. 143–171.
[21] Dennison, *Organization Engineering*, pp. 100, 166.
[22] *Idem*, "Who Can Hire Management?" *Bulletin of the Taylor Society* 9(3) (June 1924), p. 110.
[23] Mary P. Follett, "The Giving of Orders," in Henry C. Metcalf, ed., *Scientific Foundations of Business Administration* (Baltimore, MD: Williams & Wilkins, 1926), p. 139.

Pennsylvania) defined management as "the art and science of organizing, preparing and directing human effort applied to control the forces and to utilize the materials of nature for the benefit of man."[24] They identified the "principal elements" with which all managers must deal, regardless of an enterprise's purpose, as men, money, machines, and material. They applied these elements to topics such as product design; provision of physical facilities; power, heat, light, and ventilation; controlling inventories; and planning and control of production, clerical, and sales operations. Organization was treated as a means of direction and control *a la* Mooney and Reiley. Together with personnel management, it was one of the few topics outside the bounds of the traditional shop-floor orientation that Balderston, Karabasz, and Brecht addressed.

In a textbook with a similar tone, but different purpose, Edward H. "Andy" Anderson (University of Alabama) and Gustav T. "Gus" Schwenning (University of North Carolina) outlined and described "the fundamentals underlying the process of organization for effective production."[25] The text reflects Anderson's interest in history as a means of studying management and economics, and much like Mooney and Reiley's *Onward Industry!*, contains examples from military history that illustrate the importance of organization and management strategies. After "[a] careful study of the subject," Anderson and Schwenning conclude that "there is a science of organization, and that the science is the product of evolution rather than a single theory."[26] Though they introduce few new ideas, Anderson and Schwenning's analysis and synthesis, together with an extensive bibliography, make an original contribution to the evolution of management thought.

On December 28, 1936, Charles L. Jamison and William N. Mitchell invited a small group of management professors to the University of Chicago's Quadrangle Club to discuss the formation of a society to "advance the philosophy of management."[27] Enough interest was evidenced for C. Canby Balderston to invite the group to meet at Philadelphia's Lenape Club in 1937. After similar informal meetings in 1938, 1939, and 1940, Ralph C. Davis of Ohio State University prepared a constitution, helped select the name "Academy of Management," and aided in electing officers; the Academy began formal operations in 1941. The objectives of the Academy were stated as follows:

> The Academy is founded to foster the search for truth and the general advancement of learning through free discussion and research in the field of management. The interest of the Academy lies in the theory and practice of management . . . as it relates to the work of planning, organizing, and controlling the execution of business projects. It is also concerned with activities having to do with the forming, directing, and co-ordinating of departments and groups which are characteristic of administrative management. . . .
>
> The general objectives of the Academy shall be therefore to foster: (a) A philosophy of management that will make possible an accomplishment of the economic and social objectives of an industrial society with increasing economy and effectiveness. The public's interest must be paramount in any such philosophy, but adequate consideration must be given to the legitimate interests of Capital and Labor. (b) Greater understanding by Executive leadership of the requirements for a sound application of the scientific method to the solution of managerial problems, based on such a philosophy. (c) Wider acquaintance and closer co-operation among such persons as are interested in the development of a philosophy and science of management.[28]

---

[24] C. Canby Balderston, Victor S. Karabasz, and Robert P. Brecht, *Management of an Enterprise* (New York: Prentice-Hall, 1935), p. 4.

[25] Edward H. Anderson and Gustav T. Schwenning, *The Science of Production Organization* (New York: John Wiley & Sons, 1938), p. v.

[26] *Ibid.*

[27] Preston P. LeBreton, "A Brief History of the Academy of Management," in Paul M. Dauten, Jr., ed., *Current Issues and Emerging Concepts in Management* (Boston, MA: Houghton Mifflin, 1962), pp. 329–331.

[28] *Ibid.*, p. 330. See also Charles D. Wrege, "The Inception, Early Struggles, and Growth of the Academy of Management," in Daniel A. Wren and John A. Pearce II, eds., *Papers Dedicated to the Development of Modern Management: Celebrating 100 Years of Modern Management and 50th Anniversary of the Academy of Management* (Briarcliff Manor, NY: Academy of Management, 1986), pp. 78–88.

Although inactive from 1942 to 1946 due to World War II, annual Academy meetings were resumed in 1947. Jamison served as the Academy's founding president from 1936 to 1940; Brecht was president from 1941 to 1947, and Davis became president in 1948. The Academy reflected an increasing awareness of the need for management education. It continues to influence the evolution of management thought worldwide through the teaching and writing of its over 18,000 members from more than 100 countries.

A final notable textbook from this time period, *Industrial Engineering and Factory Management*, was written by Arthur G. Anderson (University of Illinois) and published in 1928.[29] Like other contemporary management textbooks, it was largely devoted to traditional shop-floor management. An indication of a growing trend in management thought is evident in the 1942 revision of Anderson's book. retitled *Industrial Management*. Joined by his Illinois colleague Merten J. Mandeville and his son John M. Anderson as coauthors, Anderson, in the 1942 edition, introduced a broader view of management's role.[30] As its authors explained, managers have a responsibility to promote both economic and social progress through productive and distributive efficiency, as well as through an emphasis on human relations in business. The authors discussed the various groups—customers, stockholders, the public at large, and employees—that play a vital role in an organization's success. In doing so, they showed an awareness of a typical organization's major stakeholders and of the fact that a manager's performance is dependent upon knowing how an organization influences and is influenced by its environment.

BUILDING BLOCKS FOR ADMINISTRATIVE THEORY

In 1936, Luther H. Gulick, director of Columbia University's Institute of Public Administration, compiled a set of papers for the President's Committee on Administrative Management—a three-member panel that, in addition to Gulick, included Louis Brownlow and Robert Merriam. The committee had been commissioned to redesign the sprawling executive branch of the federal government.[31] Gulick "discovered that he and the research staff 'all had different vocabularies.' No one knew of Fayol or Follett or the Hawthorne studies; nobody was then teaching about management in general."[32] To address this predicament, Gulick, with the assistance of Sarah Greer, assembled a set of papers on organization design for the staff to read. Greer then suggested that the papers be printed for wider distribution. Discovering that Lyndall F. Urwick held rights to two papers he had authored, as well as a paper by Follett, Greer suggested adding Urwick as a co-editor. The collection of papers was published in 1937 under the title *Papers on the Science of Administration*.[33] It not only offered the first U.S. rendition of Henri Fayol's work, but also introduced the Follett and the Hawthorne studies to their first mass audiences.[34] Other papers in the collection were written by James D. Mooney, Henry S. Dennison, Lawrence J. Henderson, Elton Mayo, Thomas North Whitehead, John Lee, and Vytautas A. Graičiūnas.

In his one contribution to the *Papers*, titled "Science, Values and Public Administration," Gulick divided the work of chief executives into seven functional elements. He used the acronym

[29] Arthur G. Anderson, *Industrial Engineering and Factory Management* (New York: Ronald Press, 1928).

[30] *Idem*, Merten J. Mandeville, and John M. Anderson, *Industrial Management* (New York: Ronald Press, 1942), p. iii.

[31] *Report of the President's Committee on Administrative Management* (Washington, DC: U.S. Government Printing Office, 1935).

[32] Luther H. Gulick quoted in Paul P. Van Riper, "Luther Gulick, Public Administration and Classical Management," *International Journal of Public Administration* 21(2–4) (1998), p. 207.

[33] Luther H. Gulick and Lyndall F. Urwick, eds., *Papers on the Science of Administration* (New York: Institute of Public Administration, Columbia University, 1937). See also Urwick, "Papers in the Science of Administration," *Academy of Management Journal* 13(1) (March 1970), pp. 361–371.

[34] Van Riper, "Luther Gulick, Public Administration and Classical Management," p. 208.

POSDCORB (pronounced *poz-dee-korb*), representing the initials of the following activities, as shorthand for the elements:

> Planning, that is working out in broad outline the things that need to be done and the methods for doing them to accomplish the purpose set for the enterprise;
>
> Organizing, that is the establishment of the formal structure of authority through which work subdivisions are arranged, defined, and co-ordinated for the defined objective;
>
> Staffing, that is the whole personnel function of bringing in and training the staff and maintaining favorable conditions of work;
>
> Directing, that is the continuous task of making decisions and embodying them in specific and general orders and instructions and serving as the leader of the enterprise;
>
> Co-ordinating, that is the all important duty of interrelating the various parts of the work;
>
> Reporting, that is keeping those to whom the executive is responsible informed as to what is going on, which thus includes keeping himself and his subordinates informed through records, research, and inspection;
>
> Budgeting, with all that goes with budgeting in the form of fiscal planning, accounting, and control.[35]

Although Gulick visualized management as a universal activity, his description of the preceding elements of a chief executive's job chiefly pertained to public administration. Gulick went on to identify four basic forms of grouping activities together, what is known as *departmentalization*: purpose, process, person or things, and place. In Gulick's scheme, there is no one most effective basis for grouping activities. If an organization is first divided at its primary level by place (i.e., geographically), the secondary level of work might be grouped by purpose, process, clientele, or, again, place. The same would be true for the third level, and so on. Any decision about how to manage group activities had to (1) follow the "principle of homogeneity," meaning the activities to be grouped must be compatible; (2) assure coordination; and (3) allow flexibility as an organization grew or as its objectives changed.

Urwick's paper "The Function of Administration" provided a detailed demonstration of the logical relationship between Fayol's "functions of administration" and Mooney and Reiley's principles of organization. Educated at Oxford University, Urwick served in Great Britain's army and government in World Wars I and II, was organizing secretary of Rowntree and Company Cocoa Works (1920–1928), served as director of the International Management Institute in Geneva (1928–1933), and was chairman of Urwick, Orr and Partners, Ltd., management consultants, until his retirement in 1951.[36] Greatly influenced in his thinking by B. Seebohm

Courtesy of Arthur G. Bedeian

Lyndall F. Urwick

[35] Luther H. Gulick, "Notes on the Theory of Organization," in Gulick and Urwick, eds., *Papers on the Science of Administration*, p. 13.

[36] Henry S. Dennison, "The International Management Institute and Its Work," *Mechanical Engineering* 51(9) (July 1929), pp. 534–535; Charles D. Wrege, Ronald G. Greenwood, and Sakae Hata, "The International Management Institute and Political Opposition to Its Efforts in Europe, 1925–1934," in Jeremy Atack, ed., *Business and Economic History* 16 (1987), pp. 249–65; Edward F. L. Brech, Andrew Thomson, and John F. Wilson, *Lyndall Urwick, Management Pioneer: A Biography* (Oxford, England: Oxford University Press, 2010).

Rowntree and Oliver Sheldon, Urwick wrote on a wide range of subjects.[37] He collaborated with Edward F. L. Brech in editing biographical sketches of scientific-management pioneers; with Henry C. Metcalf on editing Follett's papers; with Ernest Dale on line-staff relations; and with many others, too plentiful to mention.[38]

Although Urwick wrote on many topics over the course of six decades, his early work was heavily oriented toward developing principles of organization. In 1952, he identified ten principles applicable to all organizations: (1) the "principle of the objective," that all organizations should be an expression of a purpose; (2) the "principle of correspondence," that authority and responsibility should be coequal; (3) the "principle of responsibility," that the responsibility of higher authorities for the work of subordinates is absolute; (4) "the principle of authority," that a clear line of authority should extend from the highest to the lowest level of an organization; (5) the "principle of the span of control," that no superior should supervise more than five or six direct subordinates whose work interlocks; (6) "the principle of specialization," that one's work should be limited to a single function; (7) "the principle of coordination," that the various parts of an organization should be interrelated for unity of effort; (8) "the principle of definition," that the content of each position should be clearly defined; (9) "the principle of balance," that the parts of an organization should be kept in balance; and (10) "the principle of continuity," that reorganization is a continuous process.[39] As it is said that "[a] prophet is not without honor save in his own country" (Mark 6:4), although Urwick "gained an international reputation[,] . . . his achievements received greater recognition overseas than they did in [Great Britain]."[40]

SPAN OF CONTROL

Although Vytautas A. Graičiūnas's contribution to management thought was less grandiose than Gulick and Urwick's development of a general theory or science of organization, it was nonetheless quite meaningful. His essay in *Papers on the Science of Administration* was a mathematical proof of the logic inherent in limiting a manager's span of control to around three to seven subordinates. It had originally been published in the *Bulletin of the International Management Institute* (Geneva) in 1933, when Urwick was the Institute's director. Graičiūnas, born in Chicago in 1898, was at various times an engineer with firms in the United States and throughout Europe, as well as an associate in Hrant Pasdermadjian's Department Store Management Research Group (later the International Association of Department Stores) in Paris. He cofounded the Lithuanian Scientific Management Society at Kaunas in 1928, serving as its first chairman. In Moscow on a business trip in 1947, Graičiūnas was arrested by the MGB (Ministry for State Security; the name of the Soviet Union's secret police from 1946 to 1953) as he left the United States

Courtesy of Arthur G. Bedeian

Vytautas A. Graičiūnas

[37] On Rowntree's influence, see Lyndall F. Urwick, "The Father of British Management," *The Manager* 30(2) (February 1962), pp. 42–43.

[38] For further details, see Arthur G. Bedeian, "Kismet! A Tale of Management," in Vance F. Mitchell, Richard T. Barth, and Francis H. Mitchell, eds., *Proceedings of the Annual Meeting of the Academy of Management* (1972), pp. 134–137; Lee D. Parker and Philip Ritson, "Rage, Rage against the Dying of the Light: Lyndall Urwick's Scientific Management," *Journal of Management History* 17(4) (2011), pp. 379–396.

[39] Lyndall F. Urwick, *Notes on the Theory of Organization* (New York: American Management Association, 1952), pp. 19–20, 22–23, 51, 57–58. By 1966, Urwick's principles of organization had expanded to 12. See *idem*, *Organization* (The Hague, Netherlands: Nederlands Institut voor Efficiency, 1966), pp. 91–96.

[40] Trevor Boyns, [Review of the book *Lyndall Urwick, Management Pioneer: A Biography*], *Economic History Review* 64(4) (November 2011), p. 1401.

Embassy and subsequently died in prison.[41] Graičiūnas's ideas on the span of control were largely influenced by Urwick's "principle of the span of control." As noted, this principle held that no superior should supervise more than five or six direct subordinates whose work interlocks.

Graičiūnas had observed instances where managers were hampered while trying to supervise too many subordinates; he realized that this was, in part, due to their desire "to enhance their prestige and influence" by adding sections and departments to their responsibilities. Such ego bolstering could be costly from the standpoint of delays and confusion as a manager tried to simultaneously coordinate the activities of an excessive number of direct reports. Graičiūnas noted that according to what psychologists term the "the span of attention," the number of separate factors the mind can grasp simultaneously is limited. In a majority of cases, this limit is six factors or digits. He recognized that the span of attention has an administrative counterpart—the span of control. Building on this reasoning, Graičiūnas demonstrated that a manager with five direct reports, who then adds a sixth, increases the number of his direct single relationships by 20 percent. There are, however, direct group relationships and cross relationships that must also be considered. Rather than increasing arithmetically, these relationships increase exponentially, so that the manager adds approximately 100 percent to the coordination required among relationships. Graičiūnas described the situation this way:

> In almost every case the supervisor measures the burden of his responsibility by the number of direct single relationships between himself and those he supervises. But in addition there are direct group relationships and cross relationships. Thus, if Tom supervises two persons, Dick and Harry, he can speak to them as a pair. The behaviour of Dick in the presence of Harry or of Harry in the presence of Dick will vary from their behaviour when with Tom alone. Further, what Dick thinks of Harry and what Harry thinks of Dick constitute two cross relationships which Tom must keep in mind in arranging any work over which they must collaborate in his absence. . . . Thus, even in this extremely simple unit of organization, Tom must hold four to six relationships within his span of attention.[42]

According to what is known as Graičiūnas's theorem, where n represents the number of subordinates, the total number of direct plus cross relationships equals:

$$F = n\left(\frac{2^n}{2} + n - 1\right)$$

n	1	2	3	4	5	6	7	8	9	10	11	12
F	1	6	18	44	100	222	490	1,080	2,376	5,210	11,374	24,708

The sharp increase beyond four subordinates denotes a rapid rise in the complexity of relationships. Accordingly, in line with the psychological span of attention concept and in full agreement with Urwick's span of control principle, Graičiūnas concluded that the number of a manager's direct reports should be limited to a maximum of five. He conceded, however, that wider spans of control were permissible in the case of routine work at lower echelons where subordinates worked relatively independently, had little or no contact with others, or where supervisory responsibilities were less complex. At the same time, he advised that at upper levels, where responsibility was greater and often overlapped, a manager's span of control should be narrower. Graičiūnas also noted, "[I]t is not possible to assign comparable weights to these different varieties of relationship," indicating that he was aware that not all relationships are always in effect.

[41] For an account of Graičiūnas's life, career, and demise, see Arthur G. Bedeian, "Vytautas Andrius Graicunas: A Biographical Note," *Academy of Management Journal* 17(2) (June 1974), pp. 347–349; Lyndall F. Urwick, "V. A. Graicunas and the Span of Control," *Academy of Management Journal* 17(2) (June 1974), pp. 349–354.

[42] Vytautas A. Graičiūnas, "Relationship in Organization," *Bulletin of the International Management Institute* 7(3) (March 1933), p. 40.

If Dick's work did not interlock with Harry's or if their jobs were routine, then the number of operative relationships would be less, and their manager's permissible span would be wider. Graičiūnas's formula is based on the maximum number of possible direct and cross relationships, not the number that might exist at a given point in time.

TOWARD A TOP-MANAGEMENT VIEWPOINT

A second aspect of the focus on the structure and design of organizations beginning in the late 1930s involved a shift away from a shop-floor orientation to a larger view of executive leadership. The search for universal principles of organization was still ongoing. It was, however, joined by an interest in the primary responsibilities of top management.

RALPH C. DAVIS: *PATER FAMILIAE ET MAGISTER*

Ralph C. Davis received his mechanical engineering degree in 1916 from Cornell University. He was exposed to Dexter S. Kimball's *Principles of Industrial Organization* (1913) when he took the course for which this book was developed in the 1914–1915 semester. Kimball was dean of Cornell's Sibley College of Engineering (see Chapter 11).[43] As a result of the interest that Kimball aroused in many of his students, Davis "took what amounted to a 'minor' in business administration."[44] Intrigued by the shop terms his engineering professors used, Davis went on to work in either a machine shop or tool crib during every summer vacation until he graduated.[45] After passing the necessary licensure exam in 1916, Davis went on to work as a Registered Industrial Engineer for the Winchester Repeating Arms Company, where, as he put it, "I quickly discovered that I knew practically nothing about management."[46] He soon learned, however, by observing the company's president John E. Otterson, who was famous for applying scientific management at the Charlestown Navy Yard in Boston, and watching Carl G. Barth, Dwight V. Merrick, and staff members from A. Hamilton Church's consulting firm, who were all on assignment at Winchester. In 1923, following a stint conducting labor-relations studies for the Cleveland Chamber of Commerce, Davis was invited to Ohio State University to develop courses in management for the College of Commerce and Administration. He wrote his first book, *The Principles of Factory Organization and Management*, in 1928, for use by his students. It followed the traditional, shop-floor orientation of similar books published around this time. Davis stated that the fundamental functions and principles of factory management were universal in their application and that certain considerations underlie good organization. As he explained:

Courtesy of Arthur G. Bedeian

Ralph C. Davis

> In developing the organization, consideration should be given to (1) the fundamental functions to be performed and their relation to one another, (2) the proper division of responsibility, (3) the definite location of responsibility, (4) the proper functioning of the system, (5) the flexibility of the organization, (6) provision for future growth, (7) personal characteristics and abilities, (8) the creation of an ideal, and (9) the quality of the leadership.[47]

[43] Biographical information is based on a letter from Ralph C. Davis to Arthur G. Bedeian, May 18, 1969, and on an article by John F. Mee, "*Pater Familiae et Magister*" ["The Father of the Family and Teacher"], *Academy of Management Journal* 8(1) (March 1965), pp. 14–23.

[44] Letter from Ralph C. Davis to Arthur G. Bedeian, August 14, 1976.

[45] Letter from Ralph C. Davis to William M. Fox, September 19, 1958. See also William M. Fox, "The Contributions of Ralph C. Davis to the Analysis of Management Activity," unpublished paper presented at the Academy of Management Annual Meeting, August 1988, Anaheim, CA.

[46] Letter from Ralph C. Davis to Daniel A. Wren, May 18, 1969.

[47] Ralph C. Davis, *The Principles of Factory Organization and Management* (New York: Harper & Brothers, 1928), p. 41.

In 1927, Davis was asked by General Motors to establish a department of management at the General Motors Institute (GMI; Flint, Michigan). It was at GMI (now Kettering University), from 1928 to 1930, that he was exposed to the thinking of GM executives Donaldson Brown and Alfred P. Sloan, Jr., on what was to become the modern corporation (see Chapter 11). This exposure led Davis to move away from his previous shop-floor orientation and focus on the role of top management. In 1932, his focus was further influenced by John A. Coubrough's translation of Henri Fayol's *Industrial and General Administration*, a book he discovered in the Library of Congress while on a 6-month leave from Ohio State.

Davis's life and work illustrate the evolution of management thought over a span of more than four decades. His first book in 1928 followed a traditional shop-floor approach. By 1934, Davis had concluded that the executive role could be broken down into three "organic functions"—"planning," "organizing," and "controlling."[48] *Planning* was the "specification of the factors, forces, effects, and relationships that enter into and are required for the solution of a business problem" and provided "a basis for economical and effective action in the achievement of business objectives."[49] *Organizing* involved "bringing functions, physical factors, and personnel into proper relationships with one another" and was based on authority, which was "the right to plan, organize, and control the organization's activities."[50] Davis defined *control* as "the function of constraining and regulating activities that enter into the accomplishment of an objective."[51] He broke control into eight sub-functions: routine planning, scheduling, preparation, dispatching, direction, supervision, comparison, and corrective action. In turn, Davis grouped these sub-functions into three phases of control: (1) *preliminary control*, which included routine planning, scheduling, preparation, and dispatching; (2) *concurrent control*, which included direction, supervision, and comparison; and (3) *corrective action*, which involved correcting variations from planned performance. Preliminary control attempts to establish advanced constraints and regulations that ensure proper execution of plans; concurrent control, on the other hand, operates while performance is in progress. Corrective action completes the control cycle and begins the preliminary phase again by identifying deviations from planned performance and by replanning or taking other actions to prevent recurrence of performance shortfalls. Although many of his predecessors had written about control, Davis presented a much more insightful and comprehensive view of this function than had been previously rendered.

In 1940, reflecting a growing interest in the primary responsibilities of top management, Davis identified and then related the basic factors of business to the three "organic" functions of an executive's role that he had identified.[52] This interest was refined in Davis's 1951 classic, *The Fundamentals of Top Management*. His purpose in writing this book was to "present a fundamental statement of business objectives, policies, and general methods that govern the solution of basic business problems" from a top-management viewpoint.[53] Davis's original shop-floor orientation had completely given way to an interest in the primary responsibilities of top management.

In *The Fundamentals of Top Management,* Davis declared that management is "the function of executive leadership"; he used the terms "management" and "executive leadership" synonymously. He stressed the need for professional managers who had a sound philosophy of management with respect to the public's interest. Because business organizations are economic institutions, Davis stated that their primary mission "is to supply the public with whatever goods or services it desires at the proper time and place, in the required amounts having the desired qualities, and at a price that it is willing to pay."[54] Davis added that, in pursuing their missions, businesses must necessarily adhere to accepted standards of conduct for both political and moral

[48] *Idem, The Principles of Business Organization and Operation* (Columbus, OH: H. L. Hedrick, 1934), pp. 12–13.
[49] *Idem, The Fundamentals of Top Management* (New York: Harper & Brothers, 1951), p. 43.
[50] *Ibid.*, pp. 238, 281.
[51] *Ibid.*, p. 663.
[52] *Idem, Industrial Organization and Management* (New York: Harper & Brothers, 1940).
[53] *Idem, The Fundamentals of Top Management*, p. xix.
[54] *Ibid.*, p. 10.

reasons. He believed that executive leadership was the principal force that motivated, stimulated, and coordinated an organization to accomplish its objectives.

HARRY A. HOPF: TOWARD THE OPTIMUM

Harry Hopf was another of this era's notable contributors to our understanding of how to structure and design organizations. Like Davis, Hopf began with the precepts of Fred Taylor and concluded with a broader view of top management's role. Born at London in 1882, Hopf immigrated as a penniless youth to the United States in 1898. He would become a widely respected consultant, author, and executive.[55] Hopf began his career as a foreign-language stenographer in the office of a life insurance company, where he became acquainted with Taylor's views on eliminating workplace inefficiencies. In applying the principles of scientific management to office work, Hopf became interested in efficiency in general, and, more specifically, in applying Taylor's principles to all types of work. He studied compensation programs for office workers and wondered why so little attention had been given to typical executive-payment schemes, such as profit sharing, stock options, and deferred compensation plans. Hopf (like Taylor) felt that such schemes inadequately tied performance to pay. The conventional answer of Hopf's generation was that executives did a different kind of work, which was intangible and not subject to measurement. Not satisfied with this answer, Hopf proposed principles and standards for measuring executive work that linked performance with pay.[56] He believed that all managers should be judged (and rewarded) based on the results they produced.

In discussing organization structure and design, Hopf adopted the architectural notion that "form follows function;" thus, structure had to follow the objectives to be sought.[57] Otherwise, "[if] form dominates over function in organizational structure, we are bound to discover conditions of fixity and rigidity which exercise a baneful influence over accomplishment."[58] In this analogy, Hopf anticipated the dictum that "structure follows strategy," which became a guiding rule for organization theorists and business strategists in the modern era (see Chapter 19).

Hopf wrote on many other management topics: span of control, coordination, and executive control, to name a few. None of his ideas were as far-reaching, however, as his concept of "optimology." It was this concept that would take Hopf beyond Taylor's shop management to a discussion of top-management responsibilities. Hopf defined the *optimum* as "that state of development of a business enterprise which tends to perpetuate an equilibrium between the factors of size, cost, and human capacity and thus to promote in the highest degree regular realization of the business objectives."[59] Much like Mooney, Hopf felt that the typical business reversed the order of priority in fulfilling its societal role: maximize earnings and thereby serve society. In contrast, he believed that a business should serve society and thereby maximize earnings. He also felt that the goal of increased size was a *faux ami* (a false friend) because it caused problems of coordination: growth in size as a goal more often than not sacrificed one part to the whole, benefiting one part at the expense of another. Instead, the optimum would balance all parts and could be achieved through carefully establishing the point (or points) of equilibrium among size, cost, and human

---

[55] See Harold F. Smiddy and Lionel Naum, "Evolution of a 'Science of Managing' in America," *Management Science* 1(1) (October 1954), pp. 20–23; Homer J. Hagedorn, "White Collar Management: Harry Arthur Hopf and the Rationalization of Business" (Doctoral dissertation, Harvard University, Cambridge, MA, 1955); Richard J. Vahl, "A Study of the Contributions of Harry Arthur Hopf to the Field of Management" (Master's thesis, Louisiana State University, Baton Rouge, LA, 1968); and Edmund R. Gray and Richard J. Vahl, "Harry Hopf: Management's Unheralded Giant," *Southern Journal of Business* 6(2) (April 1971), pp. 69–78.

[56] Harry A. Hopf, *Executive Compensation and Accomplishment*, Financial Management Series, no. 78 (New York: American Management Association, 1945).

[57] The phrase "form ever follows function" was coined by architect Louis H. Sullivan, a pioneer in constructing modern skyscrapers. See Louis H. Sullivan, "The Tall Office Building Artistically Considered," *Lippincott's Monthly Magazine* 57(339) (March 1896), p. 409.

[58] *Idem*, "Organization, Executive Capacity and Progress," *Advanced Management: Quarterly Journal* 11(2) (June 1946), p. 38.

[59] *Idem*, *Management and the Optimum* (Ossining, NY: H. A. Hopf and Company, 1935), p. 5.

capacity. Perhaps Hopf's most significant contribution was the notion that a scientific approach could be applied in determining the proper structure and design of organizations. In doing so, he provided another step forward in developing a view of top-management responsibilities.

ANALYZING TOP MANAGEMENT

Whereas the Great Depression of the 1930s dampened economic activity worldwide, World War II mobilized vast productive capabilities, and the postwar period found managers challenged by new demands. With an unparalleled increase in international trade, executives were faced with the challenge of managing operations on a scale larger than ever before. Management scholars turned their attention to research and writing to meet this challenge.

Searching for corporate excellence is not a new idea. One prewar study that was a model for future similar investigations attempted to find practical answers to dilemmas of organization and control faced by top management. In this study, top management included three groups of executives: (1) boards of directors; (2) general managers responsible for a business as a whole; and (3) divisional managers responsible for major departments, divisions, or subsidiaries. The study's authors found that only about half their sample of 31 industrial corporations prepared detailed plans for periods up to a year in advance. Further, few had developed a system of integrated plans or developed long-range objectives. The authors reported that "one of the greatest needs observed during the course of this study is for more adequate planning and clarification of future objectives, both near-term and long-range." They traced this failing to inadequate structural arrangements in which jurisdictions, responsibilities, and relationships were ill defined; staff departments were poorly conceived and coordinated; and committees, the bane of all executive work, were poorly designed and used for the wrong tasks. In staffing, the authors found that "many companies" left provisions for the development and succession of key management personnel "largely to providence."[60] Control practices brought little solace; only half of the corporations used budgets as a means of planning and, subsequently, measuring "overall results of efforts." This pioneering study contributed to the evolution of management thought by empirically confirming the elements or functions (viz., planning, organizing, and controlling) that earlier writers (such a Fayol and Davis) had identified as components of a manager's job.

Jackson Martindell was perhaps the first to devise a system for analyzing the quality of a company's top management. Martindell was a security analyst who had successfully managed an investment-counseling firm in the 1920s. When the Wall Street stock market crashed in 1929 (see Chapter 18) and the Great Depression ensued, Martindell looked back on the investment criteria he had used as a security analyst to see if any had correctly predicted which companies were better able to weather the economic downturn. He found one answer for why some companies prevailed and others failed: "excellent management."[61] From that point forward, Martindell began a search for the factors that typified "excellently managed companies." The result was a management audit that evaluated the performance of companies across 10 criteria:

1. The economic function of a company
2. The organizational structure of a company
3. The health of a company's earnings growth

[60] Paul E. Holden, Lounsbury S. Fish, and Hubert L. Smith, *Top Management Organization and Control: A Research Study of the Management Policies and Practices of Thirty-One Leading Industrial Corporations* (Stanford, CA: Stanford University Press, 1941), pp. 4–8. In a follow-up study of 15 leading corporations, many improvements in managerial practices were noted, especially with respect to long-range planning, executive development, and management information systems. See Paul Holden, Carlton A. Pederson, and Gayton E. Germane, *Top Management: A Research Study of the Management Policies and Practices of Fifteen Leading Industrial Corporations* (New York: McGraw-Hill, 1968).

[61] Jackson Martindell, *The Scientific Appraisal of Management: A Study of the Business Practices of Well-Managed Companies* (New York: Harper & Brothers, 1950).

4. The fairness of a company's practices to stockholders
5. A company's research and development practices
6. The value contributed by a company's board of directors
7. A company's fiscal policies
8. A company's productive efficiency
9. A company's sales organization
10. The abilities of a company's executives.

Martindell's method of evaluation consisted of awarding points on each of the 10 criteria, summing these points for an overall performance rating, and then comparing the excellence of any company with the scores obtained from companies in similar industries. Although Martindell's approach to conducting a management audit is of doubtful validity, it contributed to the evolution of management thought by identifying criteria that could be used to judge a company's overall performance and, by implication, the quality of its top management in comparison to its competition.

OWNERSHIP AND CONTROL

A third aspect of the emerging focus on the structure and design of organizations concerned the separation of ownership and control and the transfer of property rights. At the outset of the Great Depression, Adolf A. Berle, Jr., an adviser to Franklin D. Roosevelt in the early days of the New Deal (see Chapter 18), and Gardiner C. Means, an economist, criticized the executives of large corporations for losing sight of whose interests they served: the corporations' stockholders. Citing Adam Smith's warning about those who managed "other people's money" being less vigilant than if they were managing their own funds (see Chapter 2), Berle and Means, noting the concentration of capital and economic power in large corporations, argued that the owners of corporate stock (stockholders) only nominally controlled the use of their property. That is, because stock was so widely dispersed among minority stockholders, corporate executives and directors could pursue their own interests rather than maximize stockholder wealth. Whereas Smith felt that ownership and control should be combined, resulting in joint risk, Berle and Means found that corporate executives and directors rarely held an appreciable amount of stock in the companies they managed. They characterized corporate executives and directors as "economic autocrats" who formed "a controlling group" that "may hold the power to divert profit into their pockets."[62] As a result, Berle and Means believed that, in most instances, stockholders had surrendered control over the corporations they owned. Although Berle and Means offered no clear solution to this separation of ownership from control, they revived Smith's earlier concerns and prepared the way for later work in corporate governance and agency issues (see Chapter 19).

Berle and Means's criticism found further expression in a study of 155 corporations conducted by economist Robert A. Gordon.[63] Focusing on the direction and coordination of large corporations in the United States, Gordon also noted the separation of ownership and management and, further, that many industries were dominated by a small number of competitors or, in some instances, by a single corporation. Consequently, he stressed the need for the "professionalization of management." In Gordon's view, the era of profiting by managing one's own investments had passed and had been succeeded by a new period in which salaried or so-called

[62] Adolf A. Berle, Jr., and Gardiner C. Means, *The Modern Corporation and Private Property* (New York: Commerce Clearing House, 1932), pp. 124, 333.

[63] Robert A. Gordon, *Business Leadership in the Large Corporation* (Washington, DC: Brookings Institution, 1945), pp. 317–352.

"professional" managers were hired by corporate boards of directors. He argued that the hiring of professional managers led to a decline in the profit motive, greater inflexibility, and increased bureaucracy. Gordon saw dangers in this increased insulation of managers from owners, especially with respect to the possibility that a self-perpetuating oligarchy of executives might place its own interests above those of a corporation's shareholders. His answer to this dilemma was a call for professional managers who were responsive to the needs of all a corporation's constituents.

TRANSACTION COST ECONOMICS

In Chapters 3 and 6, we noted that economists Jean-Baptiste Say, Edward Atkinson, and Alfred and Mary P. Marshall considered management to be a fourth factor of production. The Marshalls observed that the earnings of management were different from profits returned to owners. In doing so, they recognized the role of managers in efficiently allocating a firm's resources. In contrast, other economists have focused on what occurs in the broader environment or marketplace surrounding a firm, largely ignoring what happens between the acquisition of inputs (factors of production) and the sale of outputs (goods and services subsequently produced or provided). Two separate yet compatible developments in the 1930s would have a substantial impact on the evolution of management thought. Modern scholars, however, would only come to fully appreciate these developments years later.

Writing in 1934, John R. Commons noted that *transactions* were the smallest unit of analysis in the transfer of property rights. In Commons's view, transactions were not the exchange of commodities, but were instead the transfer of future ownership that must be negotiated "before labor can produce, or consumers can consume, or commodities be physically delivered to other persons."[64] He identified three types of ownership transfers: "bargaining," "managerial," and "rationing." *Bargaining transactions* derive from a market of willing buyers and sellers who negotiate the transfer not of commodities, but of ownership rights. *Managerial transactions* occur between an employer and employee, in which authority is used to give orders and direct the work of others. Managerial and bargaining transactions resemble one another because employees are free to negotiate regarding wages and hours of work. *Rationing transactions* involve a "collective superior," including legislatures, criminal courts, or commercial arbitrators, all of which apportion outcomes such as wealth or justice to subordinate others without bargaining and without managing.[65] For whatever reason, Commons's views on the ownership and transfer of property rights lay relatively dormant until scholars discovered their inherent power some two decades later.

English born and educated, Ronald H. Coase approached the question of transactions and the ownership and transfer of property rights from a different perspective. Coase had been introduced to Adam Smith's view that the "invisible hand" of the marketplace would ensure the efficient allocation of available resources. A trip to the United States in 1931–1932 to discover why its industries were structured in so many ways led Coase to pose a follow-up question: If markets are so efficient in allocating resources, why do business firms exist? Coase recalled Smith's observation that barter transactions are only possible when two people coincidentally wish to exchange commodities that are mutually needed by one another.[66] Simply stated, the butcher does not always desire the baker's bread or the brewer's beer. Because money or currency is tradable and can be stored for future use, it eliminated not only the "double coincidence of wants," but

[64] John R. Commons, *Institutional Economics: Its Place in Political Economy* (New York: Macmillan, 1934), p. 58.
[65] *Ibid.*, pp. 55–74.
[66] Ronald H. Coase, "The Institutional Structure of Production," *American Economic Review* 82(4) (September 1992), pp. 713–719.

also the costs associated with searching for a willing barter partner, and the "disutility" of having to wait for such a partner to be found. In a similar effort to reduce costs, as Coase went on to explain, at some point, someone (an entrepreneur) will create a business to engage in all or most of the transactions necessary to secure the resources required to produce a desired product. As Coase reasoned, "the operation of a market costs something and by forming an organisation and allowing some authority (an 'entrepreneur') to direct the resources, certain marketing costs are saved."[67] In this sense, to the extent that costs associated with marketplace transactions can be reduced, a business firm is an alternative method of coordinating production. Costs associated with marketplace transactions might include locating dependable raw-material suppliers, negotiating contracts, transportation charges, legal fees, and broker commissions. Firms thus come into existence when the cost of securing the resources necessary to produce a desired output is less than the cost of securing those resources on the open market.

While still a 21-year-old undergraduate student at the University of London, Coase wrote a paper in 1931 that would be published in 1937 titled "The Nature of the Firm." Rediscovered in the 1970s, the paper would become a classic contribution to understanding the workings of business firms vis-à-vis the marketplace and would be cited by the Royal Swedish Academy of Sciences in awarding Coase the 1991 Alfred Nobel Memorial Prize in Economic Sciences. In the paper, Coase asked:

> [I]n view of the fact that it is usually argued that co-ordination will be done by the price mechanism, why is such organization necessary? . . . Outside the firm, price movements direct production, which is co-ordinated through a series of exchange transactions on the market. Within a firm, these market transactions are eliminated and in place of the complicated market structure with exchange transactions is substituted the entrepreneur-co-ordinator, who directs production. It is clear that these are alternative methods of co-ordinating production.[68]

Coase thus realized that firms exist because hiring employees, negotiating prices, and enforcing contracts are time-consuming marketplace activities that incur heavy transaction costs that would be reduced if a firm could coordinate its exchange transactions. With few exceptions, economists had engaged in "blackboard calculations" that failed to view firms as agents that sought to engage in transactions at a cost lower than that associated with market forces. Simply stated, firms exist because they are a means for entrepreneurs to lower their transaction costs. The young Coase did not pursue this line of thinking until years later. In accepting his Nobel Prize, he commented: "[I]t is a strange experience to be praised in my eighties for work I did in my twenties."[69] In Chapter 19, we will see how Coase's ideas reentered management theory and were used to explain how the "visible hand" of management is typically more efficient in allocating resources than the "invisible hand" of the marketplace. Finally, we should note that though Coase's theory of "the firm" is framed as a theory of a single firm, it is meant to be a theory of all firms.[70]

SUMMARY

Whereas human-relations theorists sought greater productivity and satisfaction based on social solidarity and collaboration, the contributors to the evolution of management thought discussed in this chapter were more concerned with the structure and design of organizations to reach essentially the same ends. Contributors to this complementary stream of management thought have been accused of ignoring the importance of the human factor in achieving an organization's success when in fact they intentionally distinguished

[67] *Idem*, "The Nature of the Firm," *Economica* 4(16) (November 1937), p. 392.

[68] Ronald H. Coase, "The Nature of the Firm," *Economica* 4(16) (November 1937), p. 388.

[69] *Idem*, "1991 Nobel Lecture: The Institutional Structure of Production," in Oliver E. Williamson and Sidney G. Winter, eds., *The Nature of the Firm: Origins, Evolution, and Development* (New York: Oxford University Press, 1993), p. 231.

[70] For a review of the transaction-cost economics literature, see Ilya R. P. Cuypers, Jean-François Hennart, Brian S. Silverman, and Gokhan Ertug, "Transaction Cost Theory: Past Progress, Current Challenges, and Suggestions for the Future," *Academy of Management Annals* 16(1) (January 2022), pp. 111–150.

between “the structure of positions and the behavior of persons temporarily occupying them.” In doing so, they held that “the only way in which to study organization fruitfully is to isolate it from the personalities and ‘politics’ of particular undertakings at a particular moment.” Thus, although the human element was not entirely omitted from this second stream of management thought, it was intentionally set to one side for a specific purpose: to provide an analysis independent of idiosyncratic personalities and politics. Covering the period from the roughly 1930 into the early 1950s, the present chapter focused on three aspects of the structure and design of organizations: (1) authority, coordination, span of control, and related issues; (2) the primary responsibilities of top management; and (3) the separation of ownership and control and the transfer of property rights.

CHAPTER 17

Human Relations in Theory and Practice

What began as an investigation of the relationship between variations in workplace lighting and employee productivity at the Hawthorne Works of the Western Electric Company forever altered the landscape of management theory and practice. Though the Hawthorne studies had historical precedents, for some it represented a novel approach to improving employer–employee relations. In addition to examining the impact of the human-relations movement, including its extensions and applications, this chapter critically reviews the premises, research methods, and results of the Hawthorne studies.

THE IMPACT OF HUMAN RELATIONS ON THEORY AND PRACTICE

Like scientific management, the human-relations movement bore fruit from seeds that had been planted much earlier and nurtured in many places. The roots of concern for people in organizations may be traced to humanists of the Italian Renaissance in the late fourteenth century who questioned the Roman Catholic Church's monolithic authority, the accompanying breakup of rigid social structures, and the subsequent rediscovery of the individual as the primary unit of analysis in the study of human behavior. Throughout the preceding pages, varying views and assumptions about people and organizations have been examined. Robert Owen admonished factory owners to pay as much attention to their "vital machines" (their workers) as to their physical machines. Fred Taylor, concerned with the initiative of individual workers, understood he was dealing with humans as well as material and machinery and called for studies that would provide insights into the "motives that influence men."[1] Hugo Münsterberg answered this call, viewing the workplace as part of a broader social system in which work provides a sense of fulfillment and happiness, as well as a source of identity and self-worth. Whiting Williams extended the meaning of employee relations to include human relations. As he explained, by improving human relations at every level of an organization, all parties—workers, managers, and the public—would benefit: "The coming together of factory management and factory man for the development of both will do more than humanize and justify this factory age."[2] From these varied beginnings, the human-relations movement would spread and dominate a period in management thought.

[1] Frederick W. Taylor, *The Principles of Scientific Management* (New York: Harper & Brothers, 1911), p. 119.
[2] Whiting Williams, *Human Relations in Industry* (Washington, DC: U.S. Department of Labor, 1918), pp. 9–10.

APPLYING AND EXTENDING HUMAN RELATIONS

In the years following the Hawthorne studies, the human-relations movement took on an open-system approach and interpersonal bent as its findings were applied and extended. As recounted in Chapter 15, the Committee on Human Relations in Industry was formed in 1943. An interdisciplinary group, its members were drawn from business (Burleigh Gardner), sociology (William Foote Whyte), and anthropology (W. Lloyd Warner). In 1945, Kurt Lewin founded the Research Center for Group Dynamics at the Massachusetts Institute of Technology; following his death, the center was moved to the University of Michigan, where Rensis Likert and others would further the study of participative decision-making and the use of group intervention to achieve changes in workplace behavior. In 1947, another of Lewin's disciples, Leland P. Bradford, established the National Training Laboratory for Group Development at Bethel, Maine. Elliott Jaques's case study of the Glacier Metal Company (London) underscored the importance of studying organizations as interacting sociotechnical systems. His Tavistock colleagues Eric L. Trist and Kenneth W. Bamforth documented how changes in technology can disrupt an organization's social system.

HAWTHORNE REVISITED

As noted in Chapter 13, the Hawthorne studies were an intellectual gold mine. Although, unlike Taylorism, they did not inspire any investigating commissions, congressional inquiries, or confrontations such as occurred at the Watertown Arsenal, critics have relentlessly examined the studies' premises, methods, and results. Among early critics, Henry Landsberger critiqued four separate areas of the studies: the Hawthorne researchers' (1) view of society as characterized by anomie, social disorganization, and conflict; (2) managerial view of work and workers; (3) disregard for other alternatives for accommodating industrial conflict, such as collective bargaining; and (4) failure to take labor unions into account as a method for building social solidarity.[3] Since Landsberger's critique, other criticisms have been voiced.[4] The following comments will expand on Landsberger's critique with respect to the Hawthorne researchers' (1) premises about an industrial society and (2) methods and data interpretation.

PREMISES ABOUT AN INDUSTRIAL SOCIETY

Elton Mayo and Fritz J. Roethlisberger, the two principal Hawthorne researchers, both operated with a view of industrial society characterized by *anomie* (from the Greek word meaning "without norms"). As noted in Chapter 13, Mayo viewed anomie as leading to social disorganization in both personal lives and communities and to a general overall sense of personal futility, defeat, and disillusionment. Mayo further believed that people, bound up in their "pessimistic reveries," needed constructive outlets for their latent fears and frustrations. He felt that although industrial societies had made impressive technological advances, they had created a cultural lag by diminishing the importance of collaborative social skills. Mayo's recommended

[3] Henry A. Landsberger, *Hawthorne Revisited: Management and the Worker, Its Critics, and Developments in Human Relations in Industry* (Ithaca, NY: New York State School of Industrial and Labor Relations, Cornell University, 1958), pp. 29–30.

[4] For a review of other criticisms, see Ronald W. Korajczyk, "The Human Relations Approach and Its Critics" (Master's thesis, Loyola University, Chicago, IL, 1961); Jeffrey Muldoon, "The Hawthorne Studies: An Analysis of Critical Perspectives, 1936–1958," *Journal of Management History* 23(1) (2017), pp. 74–94; François Geoffroy, "Existe-t-il un effet Hawthorne?" ["Is There a Hawthorne Effect?"] *Annales des Mines—Gérer & Comprendre* no. 135(1) (January 2019), pp. 42–52; and Muldoon and Yaron Zoller, "Contested Paths: A Meta-Analytic Review of the Hawthorne Studies' Literature," in Kyle D. Bruce, ed., *Handbook of Research on Management and Organizational History* (Cheltenham, UK: Edward Elgar, 2020), pp. 56–79, and Muldoon, Eric W. Liguori, Steve Lovett, and Christopher Stone, "For Whom Does the Bell Toll: A Political Analysis of Criticisms of the Hawthorne Studies," *Management Research Review* 44(10) (2021), pp. 1390–1408.

response was to emphasize small-group interactions and to view people as embedded in a larger social system.

Critics have questioned Mayo's worldview. For example, Daniel Bell charged that Mayo and the other Hawthorne researchers took the goal of increasing worker productivity as a given and considered themselves to be social engineers who managed not people, but a social system intended to "adjust" workers to the demands of their jobs. Writing in 1947, Bell posited that to think of contented workers as productive workers was to equate human behavior with "cow sociology"; that is, just as contented cows give more milk, contented and satisfied workers would produce more.[5] In Bell's opinion, the interviewers at Hawthorne were "ambulatory confessors" and represented a new method of workplace control. When workers exposed their innermost doubts and fears, they were more susceptible to managerial manipulation. The socially skilled supervisor could move from using authority to elicit desired behavior to psychological manipulation "as a means of exercising dominion."[6] The personnel-counseling program that Mayo advocated to relieve workers of their "pessimistic reveries" was, in particular, seen as "a new method of human control" in the service of greater output.[7] In Bell's opinion, the counseling program was designed to shift workers' attention from legitimate workplace grievances to unhappy events in their personal lives, so that when they reconsidered their original grievances, they did not seem so grim. He recalled a folktale to make this point:

> A peasant complains to his priest that his little hut is horribly overcrowded. The priest advises him to move his cow into the house, the next week to take in his sheep, and the next week his horse. The peasant now complains even more bitterly about his lot. Then the priest advises him to let out the cow, the next week the sheep, and the next week the horse. At the end the peasant gratefully thanks the priest for lightening his burdensome life.[8]

Organized labor's perspective on organizations employing industrial psychologists to "talk workers out of their grievances" was no less subtle. In commenting on Bell's reference to "cow sociology," Lewis Carliner, in a 1949 article titled "Deep Therapy on the Assembly Line" published in the UAW-CIO publication *Ammunition*, went further in describing how the Hawthorne assemblers were (mis-)treated: "Everything you do to white mice was done to them, except their spines and skulls were not split so that the fluid could be analyzed."[9] Echoing both Bell and Carliner, Kyle D. Bruce and Chris T. Nyland have more recently argued that Mayo's perspective "provided employers with an authoritarian management model that held employees are irrational, agitation-prone individuals whose demand for better wages and working conditions was symptomatic of a deep psychosocial maladjustment."[10]

A second charge was that the Hawthorne researchers held a naive view of industrial conflict. Critics maintained that conflict is inevitable in every society and, to an extent, even necessary. The goal should not be to eliminate conflict, but to provide healthy outlets for its resolution.[11] Mayo's notion of a conflict-free state of equilibrium was a worthy goal but, in hindsight, was too idealistic. Moreover, the human-relations movement, like Fred Taylor and his followers,

---

[5] Daniel Bell, "The Study of Man: Adjusting Men to Machines," *Commentary* 3(1) (January 1947), p. 88.
[6] Daniel Bell, *Work and Its Discontents: The Cult of Efficiency in America* (Boston, MA: Beacon Press, 1956), pp. 25–28.
[7] Jeanne L. Wilensky and Harold L. Wilensky, "Personnel Counseling: The Hawthorne Case," *American Journal of Sociology* 57(3) (November 1951), pp. 265–280.
[8] *Ibid.*, p. 26n1. This story parallels the Yiddish folktale "It Could Always Be Worse," found in Nathan Ausubel, ed., *A Treasury of Jewish Folklore* (New York: Crown Publishers, 1948), pp. 69–70. See also Elford Eddy, "Stick, Dig and Save," *Sunset Magazine: The Pacific Monthly* 54(4) (April 1925), p. 14.
[9] Lewis Carliner, [Review of the book *Partners in Production*], *UAW-CIO Ammunition* 7(1) (April, 1949), p. 47. Carliner was the *UAW-CIO Ammunition*'s managing editor when this article was published.
[10] Kyle D. Bruce and Chris T. Nyland, "Human Relations," *Oxford Handbook of Management* (2017). Available online at https://www.oxfordhandbooks.com/view/10.1093/oxfordhb/9780198708612.001.0001/oxfordhb-9780198708612-e-3.
[11] Landsberger, *Hawthorne Revisited*, pp. 30–35.

attracted faddists who perverted the Hawthorne researchers' original intentions. These faddists often concluded that the goal of the human-relations movement was simply to keep employees and employers happy in a continuing state of bliss. When bliss was attained, labor-management cooperation would follow. As William M. Fox put it:

> Among the guilty are the "human relationists" with an inadequate concept of human relations, who mistakenly preach participation, permissiveness, and democracy for all, and those employers who confuse popularity with managerial effectiveness and misinterpret the Golden Rule in dealing with their subordinates. . . . Many mistakenly regard it [human relations] as an "end" toward which the organization shall endeavor rather than as what it should be—a "means" for achieving the organization's primary service objectives.[12]

Fox held that the regard for human relations as an end, rather than a means, misled managers to think that a conflict-free state and worker contentment would automatically lead to a company's success. He warned that human relations could not be substituted for well-defined goals, policies, and high-performance standards necessary for achieving an organization's goals. Or, as Malcolm P. McNair saw it, managers needed more than listening and human-relations skills to be effective in ensuring a company's success. In teaching human relations as a separate skill, McNair saw danger in compartmentalizing one aspect of managing when it should be an integral part of all a company's activities. In essence, McNair concluded: "It is not that the human relations concept is wrong; it is simply that we have blown it up too big and have placed too much emphasis on teaching human relations as such at the collegiate and early graduate level. . . . Let's treat people like people, but let's not make a big production of it."[13]

William H. Knowles also called for a better mix of managerial skills, one that would avoid the evangelism and mysticism that so often characterized human-relations training. Too often human relationists seemed to believe that only they could "save Western civilization from impending doom."[14] For social philosophers such as Émile Durkheim (and Mayo), advancing technology had destroyed the solidarity individuals found in traditional societies, creating personal and social disorganization and a general overall sense of futility, defeat, and disillusionment. The answer to the impending doom was an evangelical zeal by human-relations advocates to rebuild primary groups (the family) and teach people to love one another again. The world could be saved by a sense of belonging, and people could once more find contentment by interacting within a close-knit community that shared common sentiments and values. This mystical overtone, reflecting the Gestalt psychology of the totality, attributed collective wisdom to groups that could not be found in individuals. It was not the logic of efficiency, but the illogic of sentiments that would save the world from the brink. The moral uplift of scientific management had been efficiency; for human-relations advocates, it was belonging and solidarity.

RESEARCH METHODS AND DATA INTERPRETATION

The scientific and methodical standards of today are more rigorous than those in use when the Hawthorne studies were conducted. Over the years, the Hawthorne researchers have been criticized for their research methods and data interpretation. They have been assailed for not

---

[12] William M. Fox, "When Human Relations May Succeed and the Company Fail," *California Management Review* 8(3) (Spring 1966), p. 19.

[13] Malcolm P. McNair, "Thinking Ahead: What Price Human Relations?" *Harvard Business Review* 35(2) (March–April 1957), p. 39.

[14] William H. Knowles, "Human Relations in Industry: Research and Concepts," *California Management Review* 1(1) (Fall 1958), p. 99.

randomly selecting participants, the small size of the groups they studied, and their failure to control other variables that may have influenced their findings.[15] As Michael Kompler correctly notes, however:

> Historical studies must be understood in their "at that time" scientific and societal context. . . . Therefore, it would neither be fair nor correct to judge the Hawthorne studies by the scientific and methodological standards of today. Much of today's standard expertise (experimental and quasi-experimental designs, multivariate analyses, theories on work motivation, and group performance) was not available to these pioneers.[16]

Criticisms relating to the Hawthorne researchers' failure to use random selection to draw representative samples seem especially unjust: the Hawthorne studies were begun in 1927, and the earliest documented use of true randomization in the social sciences was not published until 1928.[17]

Moving beyond methodology to data interpretation, as noted in Chapter 13, critics have suggested that performance incentives may have accounted for the output increases that occurred throughout the Hawthorne studies. For example, Andrew Sykes has contended that though human-relations advocates believed that money does not motivate behavior, the Hawthorne results, in his opinion, lead to the opposite conclusion.[18] Alex Carey similarly criticized the Hawthorne researchers for downplaying the importance of money as a motivator in increasing output and overemphasizing the significance of "friendly supervision" in maintaining employee job satisfaction and productivity.[19] As he noted, the Hawthorne researchers selected "cooperative" workers who were willing to participate in the studies. Second, two assemblers from the original relay-assembly group "were removed for a lack of cooperation, which would have otherwise necessitated greatly increased disciplinary measures."[20] In analyzing the relay-assembly test-room production records, Carey found that output did not increase until the two defiant assemblers were replaced with "more cooperative" substitutes. Was this "friendly supervision" or the use of negative sanctions to increase output? In Carey's view, the results of the Hawthorne studies showed that performance incentives and "managerial discipline" were responsible for higher output.

Richard H. Franke and James D. Kaul likewise challenged the Hawthorne researchers' data interpretation. Reanalyzing data from the relay-assembly test-room study, they claimed that "three variables—managerial discipline, the economic adversity of the depression, and time set aside for rest"—explained most of the variance in employee output.[21] Thus, they concluded that it was not supervisory style or performance incentives, but the use of discipline, the larger economic environment, and relief from fatigue that led to increased output. In rebuttal, Robert Schlaifer alleged that Franke and Kaul had improperly analyzed the relay-assembly test-room study data. He further contended that "managerial discipline" in the test room was not harsh, as it simply involved sending two assemblers back to their original department. Schlaifer reanalyzed the relay-assembly test-room study data to show that the "passage of time" was sufficient to

---

[15] For example, see Michael Argyle, "The Relay Assembly Test Room in Retrospect," *Occupational Psychology* 27(2) (April 1953), pp. 98–103; J. Scott Armstrong, "The Ombudsman: Management Folklore and Management Science— On Portfolio Planning, Escalation Bias, and Such," *Interfaces* 26(4) (July–August 1996), pp. 25–55.

[16] Michael A. J. Kompler, "The 'Hawthorne Effect' Is a Myth, but What Keeps the Story Going?" *Scandinavian Journal of Work, Environment & Health* 32(5) (October 2006), p. 410.

[17] Louise Forsetlund, Iain Chalmers, and Arild Bjørndal, "When Was Random Allocation First Used to Generate Comparison Groups in Experiments to Assess the Effects of Social Interventions?" *Economics of Innovations and New Technology* 16(5) (July 2007), pp. 371–384. For further historical background, see Peter Gundelach, "Bringing Things Together: Developing the Sample Survey as Practice in the Late Nineteenth Century," *Journal of the History of the Behavioral Sciences* 33(1) (Winter 2017), pp. 71–89.

[18] Andrew J. M. Sykes, "Economic Interest and the Hawthorne Researchers," *Human Relations* 18(3) (August 1965), p. 253.

[19] Alex Carey, "The Hawthorne Studies: A Radical Criticism," *American Sociological Review* 32(3) (June 1967), p. 410.

[20] T. North Whitehead, *The Industrial Worker*, vol. 1 (Cambridge, MA: Harvard University Press, 1938), p. 118. In *The Human Problems of an Industrial Civilization* (New York: Macmillan, 1933), Mayo stated that they "dropped out" (p. 56).

[21] Richard H. Franke and James D. Kaul, "The Hawthorne Experiments: First Statistical Interpretation," *American Sociological Review* 43(5) (October 1978), p. 636.

explain increased output, which he concluded was "in all respects consistent with the conclusions reached by the original researchers."[22] Richard A. Toelle confirmed Schlaifer's findings and further criticized Franke and Kaul's analysis for treating the relay-assembly test-room operators as one group, when there were actually two groups: the first group of five included the two operators who were later removed and the second group comprised the original three operators, plus the two replacements. Toelle found that if the groups were analyzed separately, the passage of time accounted for over 91 percent of the total variance in their output.[23]

What happened at Hawthorne? What can 20/20 hindsight tell us about the methods and conclusions of the Hawthorne researchers? First, the researchers made conclusive statements that could be interpreted as rejecting the imaginary of the wealth-seeking and -consuming economic man, or *homo economicus*, who is generally assumed to be motivated solely by money. For example, Sykes quoted Roethlisberger and Dickson as concluding that "none of the results . . . [substantiated] the theory that the worker is primarily motivated by economic interest." Sykes did not quote, however, the following sentences: "The evidence indicated that the efficacy of a wage incentive is so dependent on its relation to other factors that it is impossible to separate it out as a thing in itself having an independent effect."[24] Thus, performance incentives should not be excluded from an explanation for increased output, but should be viewed as part of a larger, more complex equation. As Jon M. Shepard commented, Roethlisberger and Dickson saw factors such as company policies, hours of work, wages, and physical events as "carriers of social value" rather than as absolute explanations of employee behavior and motivation.[25] In short, the "social man" supplemented, but did not supplant, *homo economicus*.

Second, Schlaifer's finding that the "passage of time" was sufficient to explain increased output in the relay-assembly test-room suggests that trust is an important factor in building human relationships and that it took time for trust to develop between the Hawthorne researchers and study participants. Interviews with the surviving relay-group members and observer-supervisor Donald Chipman indicated that a rapport did develop during the studies.[26] By contrast, in situations where a friendly and respectful relationship did not develop, such as in the bank-wiring room, productivity did not increase.

Third, there is what has become known as the "science versus advocacy" distinction.[27] As Clark Kerr and Lloyd H. Fisher have noted, "no research in the social sciences can be free of value assumptions."[28] In the case of Hawthorne, as noted in Chapter 13, Roethlisberger wrote: "Mayo was an adventurer in the realm of ideas . . . the [Hawthorne] data were not his; the results were not his; but what the results meant . . . were his."[29] If Mayo's conclusions went beyond the Hawthorne data, he was speaking as an advocate, not as a scientist, leading to further criticism.

---

[22] Robert Schlaifer, "The Relay Assembly Test Room: An Alternative Statistical Interpretation," *American Sociological Review* 45(6) (December 1980), p. 1005.

[23] Richard A. Toelle, "Research Notes Concerning Franke and Kaul's Interpretation of the Hawthorne Experiments," unpublished paper, University of Oklahoma, Norman, 1982.

[24] Roethlisberger and Dickson, *Management and the Worker* (Cambridge, MA: Harvard University Press, 1939), pp. 575–576; a similar statement appears on p. 185.

[25] Jon M. Shepard, "On Alex Carey's Radical Criticism of the Hawthorne Studies," *Academy of Management Journal* 14(1) (March 1971), pp. 23–32.

[26] Alfred A. Bolton, "Relay Assembly Test Room Participants Remember: Hawthorne a Half Century Later," *International Journal of Public Administration* 17(2) (1994), p. 372.

[27] Lyle Yorks and David A. Whitsett, "Hawthorne, Topeka, and the Issue of Science versus Advocacy in Organizational Behavior," *Academy of Management Review* 10(1) (January 1985), pp. 21–30.

[28] Clark Kerr and Lloyd H. Fisher, "Plant Sociology: The Elite and the Aborigines," in Mirra Komarovsky, ed., *Common Frontiers of the Social Sciences* (Glencoe, IL: Free Press, 1954), p. 308. For a defense of Mayo's work in general, see Jeffrey Muldoon, Joshua Bendickson, Antonina A. Bauman, and Eric W. Liguori, "Reassessing Elton Mayo: Clarifying Contradictions and Context," *Journal of Management History*, in press; Muldoon, "Spontaneity Is the Spice of Management: Elton Mayo's Hunt for Cooperation," in Bradley G. Bowden, Jeffrey Muldoon, Anthony M. Gould, and Adela J. McMurray, eds., *The Palgrave Handbook of Management History* (London, UK: Palgrave Macmillan, 2020), pp. 545–564.

[29] Fritz J. Roethlisberger, *The Elusive Phenomena*, ed. George F. F. Lombard (Boston, MA: Division of Research, Graduate School of Business Administration, Harvard University, 1977), pp. 50–51. See also William Dowling, "Interview with Fritz J. Roethlisberger," *Organizational Dynamics* 1(2) (Autumn 1972), 31–45.

Richard Gillespie claimed that the Hawthorne findings were "manufactured" by Mayo and his colleagues because "in Mayo's hands, the Hawthorne experiments provided the experimental data on which he could base his political and social theory."[30] An awareness of such "investigator effects" is important in understanding when a researcher's personal beliefs and data interpretation begin to blur.[31]

Finally, John S. Hassard has claimed that the findings of the Hawthorne studies were not "enlightened" new revelations, but were judgments used to promote an underlying "hard-edged paternalism and tough-minded anti-unionism."[32] In this regard, Bruce and. Nyland have argued that Mayo's interpretation of the Hawthorne results reflected his "preformed personal views," as well as the influence of John D. Rockefeller, Jr., (Mayo's "financial and professional benefactor") and "other conservative business leaders" who were interested "in fending off the Bolshevik threat of socialism" as represented by organized labor.[33] Both of these criticisms were voiced when Roethlisberger and Dickson's account of the Hawthorne studies, *Management and the Worker,* was first published. For example, as evidence of the Hawthorne researchers' pro-management and anti-labor bias, Mary B. Gilson noted: "In all the more than six hundred pages describing the Western Electric experiment . . . no reference is made to organized labor except a short statement, unindexed, that it was so seldom mentioned by any workers that it was not considered sufficiently important to discuss."[34] Gilson acknowledged that in his preface to *Management and the Worker*, Mayo "modestly states that the authors . . . do not claim that the enlightenment that many collaborators of the scheme got from their researches was 'either very extensive or very profound.'" She nonetheless attacked the Hawthorne researchers for "discovering the obvious," and concluded that Mayo's claim "[t]hat what they learned was 'novel and unexpected' seems to me an acknowledgment of inexperience in the field of industrial practice."[35]

Although *Management and the Worker* does not refer to organized labor, it seems unfair to conclude that this constituted an anti-labor bias.[36] Until 1935, the dominant labor organizations in the United States were the American Federation of Labor, which consisted of skilled workers, and the brotherhoods that represented various groups of railroad employees. As will be seen in Chapter 18, the passage of the National Labor Relations (Wagner) Act in 1935 provided the

---

[30] Richard Gillespie, *Manufacturing Knowledge: A History of the Hawthorne Experiments* (New York: Cambridge University Press, 1991), p. 181. Other critics have even suggested that the prominence of the Hawthorne studies was due to Mayo's "talent for publicity" and having "probably suppressed" alternative interpretations of the studies' results. See Michael Rose, *Industrial Behaviour: Theoretical Development since Taylor* (London: Allen Lane, 1975), p. 106; Hugo Gaggiotti, Monika Kostera, and Paweł Krzyworzeka, "Neglecting the Anthropological Origins of Organizing: Causes and Consequences," in Tuomo Peltonen, Hugo Gaggiotti, and Peter Case, eds., *Origins of Organizing* (Cheltenham, UK: Edward Elgar, 2018), p. 54.

[31] Naomi Weiner-Levy and Ariela Popper-Giveon, "The Absent, the Hidden and the Obscured: Reflections on 'Dark Matter' in Qualitative Research," *Quality & Quantity* 47(4) (June 2013), p. 2180.

[32] John S. Hassard, "Rethinking the Hawthorne Studies: The Western Electric Research in Its Social, Political, and Historical Context," *Human Relations* 65(11) (November 2012), pp. 1431–1461.

[33] Kyle D. Bruce and Christopher T. Nyland, "Elton Mayo and the Deification of Human Relations," *Organization Studies* 32(3) (March 2011), pp. 390, 391. The Hawthorne studies received funding under a grant from the Rockefeller Foundation to the Harvard University Committee on Industrial Hazards. The Harvard group, however, always referred to itself as the "Committee on Industrial *Physiology*." For details, see Jason Oakes, "Alliances in Human Biology: The Harvard Committee on Industrial Physiology, 1929–1939," *Journal of the History of Biology* 48(3) (August 2015), pp. 365–390. Mayo received personal funds from John D. Rockefeller, Jr. On this point, see Martin Bulmer and Joan Bulmer, "Philanthropy and Social Sciences in the 1920s: Beardsley Ruml and the Laura Spelman Rockefeller Memorial, 1922–1929," *Minerva* 19(3) (September 1981), p. 383.

[34] Mary B. Gilson, [Review of the book *Management and the Worker*], *American Journal of Sociology* 46(1) (July 1940), p. 100. See also Ordway Tead, [*Review of Social Problems of an Industrial Civilization*], *Survey Graphic* 35(5) (May 1946), p. 179.

[35] Gilson, *op. cit.*, p. 101. The Mayo quotes appear on p. xii in *Management and the Worker*. For a discussion of Mayo's response that Gilson was "insane," see Christopher T. Nyland and Kyle D. Bruce, "Democracy or Seduction? The Demonization of Scientific Management and the Deification of Human Relations," in Nelson Lichtenstein and Elizabeth Tandy Shemer, eds., *The Right and Labor in America: Politics, Ideology, and Imagination* (Philadelphia, PA: University of Pennsylvania Press, 2016), p. 72.

[36] It should be noted that an independent union, which was previously a company union, did exist at the Hawthorne Works. George C. Homans, "Report of the Committee," in Committee on Work in Industry of the National Research Council, *Fatigue of Workers: Its Relation to Industrial Production* (New York: Reinhold Publishing Corporation, 1941), p. 113.

legislative basis for a surge in union membership from a turn-of-the-decade 3.5 million to almost 9 million by 1939. Given that the Hawthorne studies concluded in 1932, before organized labor made its great strides, it is not surprising to find little mention of unions in *Management and the Worker*.

Mayo and his colleagues did not draw any distinction between union-management relations and human relations, thus suggesting that in both union and nonunion employment there was an equal need for human relations–oriented supervisors. That being said, human-relations thought entered a revisionist period in the 1950s with an emphasis on "industrial human relations." Just as Morris L. Cooke tried to bring about a rapprochement between scientific management and organized labor (see Chapter 8), post-Hawthorne scholars quickly brought unions into the human-relations picture. Industrial sociologists studied the relationship between organized labor and management. Reflecting a social-systems orientation, they focused on the economic dimensions of employee–employer relations within a more encompassing societal framework.[37]

A basic assumption that appeared to prevail in this revisionist period was that there was an inherent conflict between management and labor with respect to dividing the surplus created by an advanced technological society. Increased industrial conflict was, in fact, a reality during this time. A comparison of work stoppages and their causes for the decade of the 1920s with those in the decade of the 1930s reveals dramatic differences. The 1920s, characterized by employee representation plans and union-management cooperation, showed a steady decline in work stoppages, whereas in the 1930s, this trend was reversed. Of 14,256 work stoppages during the 1920s, 51 percent were due to wages and hours of work, and 21 percent were the result of union-organized drives. From 1930 to 1934, stoppages associated with union organizing attempts increased to 34 percent, but wages and hours still accounted for 51 percent of the disruptions. For the remainder of the 1930s, however, and following the passage of the Wagner Act, a reversal occurred. Of the 14,290 work stoppages from 1935 to 1939, 31 percent concerned wages and hours, and 53 percent were due to union organizing efforts.[38] To many scholars writing during this period, the answer to industrial conflict resided not in human-relations training per se, but in overcoming the contrasting interests and ideologies of management and labor, "labor" usually meaning organized workers. It was largely believed that industrial harmony would come through collective bargaining and the efforts of professional industrial-relations specialists.

In addition to bringing unions into the picture, the human-relations textbooks of the 1940s and early 1950s typically held that the feelings of people were more important than organization charts, rules, and directives. Human relationships were based on intangibles, not on hard, scientific investigation, and there were no final answers; that is, nothing is positive or fixed in solutions to human complexities. In general, these early texts emphasized emotions, sentiments, and collaboration.[39] They were heuristic rather than specific or systematic, encouraging students to investigate and discover for themselves what worked, rather than prescribing solutions. In brief, the human-relations ethos led to a revisionist period that focused on the economic dimensions of employee–employer relations within a more encompassing societal framework. The Hawthorne researchers were not antiunion per se, but their views reflected the limited influence of organized labor during the 1920s and early 1930s. Whether organized or not, it was the individual worker who was the center of attention for management's understanding and application of human-relations skills.

---

[37] Examples of this thinking may be found in Eugene V. Schneider, *Industrial Sociology* (New York: McGraw-Hill, 1957); Delbert C. Miller and William H. Form, *Industrial Sociology: An Introduction to the Sociology of Work* (New York: Harper & Brothers, 1951). A historical perspective is provided by Bruce E. Kaufman, *The Origins & Evolution of the Field of Industrial Relations in the United States* (Ithaca, NY: ILR Press, Cornell University, 1993), pp. 75–102.

[38] U.S. Department of Commerce, Bureau of the Census, *Historical Statistics of the United States: Colonial Times to 1970.* part 1 (Washington, DC: U.S. Government Printing Office, 1974), p. 179.

[39] For example, see Schuyler D. Hoslett, ed., *Human Factors in Management* (Parkville, MO: Park College Press, 1946); Burleigh B. Gardner and David G. Moore, *Human Relations in Industry* (Homewood, IL: Richard D. Irwin, Inc., 1955).

SUMMARY

The foregoing criticisms suggest that answering the question "What happened at Hawthorne?" may be difficult, if not impossible. In his autobiography, Roethlisberger cautioned that the Hawthorne findings "have been so often restated and misstated that it [*Management and the Worker*] has a life of its own . . . human relations was first and foremost an *investigatory and diagnostic tool*. It was not a model of what an organization should be; it was a conceptual scheme for finding out what the relations in a *particular organization at a particular place and time* were, not what they should be."[40] Nonetheless, the Hawthorne studies were an important step in advancing the idea of improving human relations in all types of settings. Its emphasis on human relations was not new. Indeed, Elton Mayo recognized his work as "an extension of that begun by the pioneer [Taylor]."[41] Although Mayo's name is closely connected with the human-relations movement, he was but one person in a cast of many who were responsible for its growth. Had George Pennock, Claire Turner, and others at Western Electric not persisted in attempting to understand the puzzling results of the Illumination Study, Mayo's thoughts on the ill-effects of an industrial society may have remained the ruminations of one man. Mayo became an advocate rather than an impartial researcher, and as the Hawthorne studies' results became clouded with ideological overtones, it became easier and easier to misperceive, misquote, and misinterpret what really happened at Hawthorne.

In retrospect, certain conclusions stand out: (1) human relations was intended as a tool for understanding workplace behavior rather than as an end in itself; (2) trust was crucial in uniting the interests of management and labor; (3) performance and nonfinancial incentives played a role in productivity gains, but cannot explain all the Hawthorne results; and (4) care should be taken to avoid going beyond or selectively extracting data from a study's results to support one's "preformed" beliefs.

[40] Roethlisberger, *Elusive Phenomena*, pp. 305, 311.
[41] Elton Mayo, "The Basis of Industrial Psychology," *Bulletin of the Taylor Society* 9(6) (December 1924), p. 258.

The Social-Person Era in Retrospect

CHAPTER 18

As noted in Chapter 1, to understand the evolution of management thought, one first needs to appreciate the cultural environment within which management as an activity and as an academic discipline is situated. In the United States, scientific management found its *raison d'être* in the growth of large-scale businesses; the social sanction of individual achievement and the moral uplift of efficiency; and a concern for national productivity and the conservation of natural resources. In contrast, the "social-person era"—from the advent of the Hawthorne studies to the early 1950s—was an age in which individual hopes were dashed on the reefs of economic misfortune, social change reshaped the nation's values, and political upheaval ushered in support for government entities becoming more involved in people's lives. The social-person era heralded a transformation in the nation's traditional values and beliefs. Though treated independently here, the economic, social, and political facets underlying this transformation interacted to form the cultural environment of the era's social person.

THE ECONOMIC ENVIRONMENT: FROM DEPRESSION TO PROSPERITY

Like the Duke of Gloucester in Shakespeare's *Richard III*, the 1929 Wall Street stock-market crash found the "winter of its discontent" in earlier days.[1] The 1920s were a decade of unexampled prosperity, characterized by falling consumer prices, a near doubling of industrial productivity, and a 53 percent rise in the real earnings for nonfarm workers.[2] Mass-production technology held costs down and increased the purchasing power of the U.S. dollar. In the year preceding the market crash, the value of stocks had nearly doubled. Speculators invested in the market, buying and quickly reselling stocks in the hope of making an easy profit. Stock shares were often purchased "on margin"; that is, purchased using money borrowed from brokerage firms and banks to make a down payment equaling a fraction of the shares' cash value, anticipating that their market value would increase to cover the cost of the loan plus a profit when they were subsequently sold. All was well until informed investors noted that the aggregate market value of the 846 companies listed on the New York Stock Exchange had decreased $2.6 billion in September 1929, but

[1] William Shakespeare, *Richard III*, Act 1, Scene I. Wall Street is a thoroughfare at the southern tip of Manhattan Island and the location of the New York Stock Exchange.

[2] Stanley Lebergott, *The Americans: An Economic Record* (New York: W. W. Norton, 1984), Table 2.4, p. 390; Table 33.3, pp. 434–435.

brokers' loans had nonetheless increased by $668 million to a record high $8.5 billion.[3] These investors began selling their holdings in the belief that stocks were trading exponentially higher than their fundamental value (some were selling at more than 100 times their earnings). They realized that stock prices had reach a level that was unsustainable, causing a financial "bubble" that would soon burst, as prices hit a ceiling and plummeted sharply. The bubble first showed signs of bursting on October 24, known in the United States as "Black Thursday," the day of the largest stock sell-off in U.S. history.[4] Over two days, October 28 and 29, the decline in stock prices eliminated over $30 billion of wealth, foreshadowing the Great Depression and its ultimate spread around the world. Millions of speculators who were unable to pay back their margin loans were financially ruined, as were the brokers and banks that held the loans, depressing stock prices even further.[5] The severity of the ensuing economic disruption is suggested by an exchange between the British economist John Maynard Keynes (remembered for making the case for governments to spend their way out of recessions) and a reporter: "Can you tell us, Mr. Keynes, from your great knowledge of history, whether there has ever been a parallel to the present depression, and if so, how long did it last?" Reflecting for a moment, Keynes replied, "Yes, there was one. It was called the Dark Ages, and it lasted for five hundred years."[6]

For more than a decade, the Great Depression substantially changed life in the United States. In 1929, prior to Black Thursday, 48 million people were employed, and only about 1.5 million (3.2 percent) unemployed. By 1933, the first year of Franklin D. Roosevelt's presidency, around 12,830,000 people (nearly one-quarter of the civilian labor force) were unemployed. This number dropped below 8 million only once (in 1937) until 1941 and the beginning of World War II.[7] The nation "had never experienced unemployment of these magnitudes or of this duration."[8] Despite state and federal attempts to create jobs, banks were shuttered in 38 states (there was no Federal Deposit Insurance Corporation to secure savings until the Banking Act of 1935), businesses failed, incomes dropped, homes were lost, family savings were wiped out, and, worst of all, national morale was at an all-time low. Gone were the optimism of prosperity and the promise of material wealth; the old guideposts apparently had failed, as "rags to riches" became the "midnight pumpkin." Recovery from the economic morass was painfully slow. Socially and psychologically, it was even slower. Feeling inept in confronting economic deprivation, people turned to state and federal governments for assistance.

ATTEMPTS AT ECONOMIC RECOVERY

In November 1929, President Herbert C. Hoover had asked for labor–management cooperation in reducing employee work hours as an alternative to full layoffs.[9] Doing so would cut pay for everyone, but was preferred to leaving some without pay entirely. In the early days of the Great Depression, labor and management responded positively to such appeals, as forward-looking

---

[3] "Hugh Drop in Month in Exchange Stocks: $2,594.646,431 Decline Shown in Aggregate Market Value September," *New York Times* (October 19, 1929), p. 27; "Brokers' Loans Rise to $8,549,383,979: Increase of $667,764,553 in September Is the Fourth Consecutive Record Set" *New York Times* (October 3, 1929), p. 53.

[4] Maury Klein, "The Stock Market Crash of 1929: A Review Article," *Business History Review* 75(2) (Summer 2001), pp. 325–351.

[5] Karol Jan Borowiecki, Michał Dzieliński, and Alexander Tepper, "The Great Margin Call: The Role of Leverage in the 1929 Wall Street Crash," *Economic History Review* 76(3) (August 2023), pp. 807–826.

[6] John Maynard Keynes quoted in Vira Brittain, "Books and World Peace," *Saturday Review of Literature* 17(11) (January 8, 1938), p. 3.

[7] Stanley Lebergott, "Annual Estimates of Unemployment in the United States, 1900–1950," in Universities–National Bureau Committee for Economic Research, *The Measure and Behavior of Unemployment* (Princeton, NJ: Princeton University Press, 1957), Table 1, pp. 215–216.

[8] David M. Kennedy, *Freedom from Fear: The American People in Depression and War, 1929–1945* (New York: Oxford University Press, 1999), p. 87.

[9] Jonathan D. Rose, "Hoover's Truce: Wage Rigidity in the Onset of the Great Depression," *Journal of Economic History* 70(4) (December 2010), pp. 843–870.

policies initiated during the 1920s provided employees with a cushion against a loss in work and wages. In particular, company-sponsored thrift plans with matching employer contributions gave employees a way to get through tough economic times. Employee stock-ownership plans had been a mixed blessing: as stock prices soared in the late 1920s, some employees had sold their stock and pursued high-risk investments only to later regret doing so; other employees had held on to their stocks and, with equal regret, had seen them plummet in value. By necessity, there was a change in attitude about women working outside the home as increasing numbers of women entered the labor force to bolster family income.

In his 1941 State of the Union address, Franklin D. Roosevelt, who had succeeded Hoover in 1933, promised freedom from "fear" and "want."[10] Hoover had previously used the Reconstruction Finance Corporation to pump federal funds into state and local governments, as well as to loan money to banks, mortgage associations, railroads, and other businesses. Roosevelt went much further, endorsing the "new economics" touted by Keynes. In contrast to the Protestant ethic that emphasized frugality, thrift, and hard work, Keynes held that, during an economic downturn, a shortfall in the demand for goods and services (measured as the sum of purchases by households, businesses, and government) results in a lack of jobs for those seeking employment.[11] Therefore, governments should intervene and, as explained by Hoover, "prime the economic pump" to stimulate consumption and, in turn, economic recovery.[12]

Although Keynes believed that government spending could be used to moderate the ups and downs of a nation's economic activity, Milton Friedman later maintained that proper monetary action by the Federal Reserve System would have prevented contraction of the nation's money supply and thereby quelled the Great Depression.[13] Disagreeing with both Keynes and Friedman, Robert L. Heilbroner concluded that the massive increase in gross domestic product and decline in unemployment associated with World War II ended the Depression, not government pump priming.[14] Though economists disagree about what should have been done to spur the nation's economy, "what might have been" is a matter of speculation. The fact is that the federal government became ever more involved in the nation's economic life; though free-market capitalism was preserved (with ownership and management remaining in private hands), regulatory power became increasingly lodged in government agencies. An emerging view tied corporate actions more closely than ever to the public interest, with concomitant calls for "economic statesmanship" on the part of business and attacks on "unjust" corporate concentrations of wealth and marketplace power.

"BIG BUSINESS" AS CULPRIT

During the years following the Great Depression and those leading up to World War II, many critics saw "Big Business" as the primary culprit responsible for the nation's economic ills. It was argued that public policy should come from the grassroots up to counterbalance the undue influence of a moneyed elite and large corporations. Believing that there was a privileged class of top earners who controlled a disproportionate share of the nation's wealth, critics sought to reduce income inequality and restore the influence of those at the base of the economic pyramid. As part of a larger study on "Ethics and Economic Life" sponsored by the Federal Council of Churches,

[10] Franklin D. Roosevelt, "State of the Union Message to Congress," January 6, 1941, Washington, DC, Franklin D. Roosevelt Presidential Library and Museum, National Archives. Available online at https://www.fdrlibrary.org/address-text.

[11] John Maynard Keynes, *The General Theory of Employment, Interest, and Money* (London: Macmillan, 1936), p. 378.

[12] Herbert C. Hoover, "Consequences to Liberty of Regimentation," *Saturday Evening Post* 207(11) (1934), p. 85.

[13] Milton Friedman and Anna Jacobson Schwartz, *A Monetary History of the United States, 1867–1960* (Princeton, NJ: Princeton University Press, 1963), pp. 300–301.

[14] Robert L. Heilbroner, *The Making of Economic Society* (Englewood Cliffs, NJ: Prentice-Hall, 1962). Although labor data adjusted to include persons with temporary jobs in emergency government programs indicate that federal and state projects lessened unemployment, a substantial decline in percentage of unemployed is not apparent until the eve of the U.S. entry into World War II. See Robert A. Margo, "Employment and Unemployment in the 1930s," *Journal of Economic Perspectives* 7(2) (Spring 1993), pp. 41–59.

Kenneth E. Boulding warned in his 1953 book *The Organizational Revolution: A Study in the Ethics of Economic Organization* that the growing presence of larger and more economically powerful organizations—including labor unions, trade associations, trusts, governmental agencies, and especially corporations—risked a potential moral conflict between an aristocratic society and a democracy based on fellowship and social equality.[15] Boulding was not only interested in the growth of organizations, but also the ethics of organizations.

In his 1941 global best seller, *The Managerial Revolution*, James Burnham echoed Adolf A. Berle, Jr., and Gardiner C. Means's earlier claim that the ascendancy of professional managers with the broad spread of public ownership in the 1920s had severed corporate control from corporate ownership (see Chapter 16). He foretold a bleak future where a ruling managerial elite (neither capitalist nor socialist) would control society's means of production and distribution for its own selfish interests. Burnham labeled this new type of exploitative society "managerialism." In this transformed world, an overclass of highly credentialed professional managers who possessed technical skills would dominate economic relations, politics, and culture through corporate and government bureaucracies. Burnham argued that increasing technical complexity and the need to coordinate mass phenomena—mass production, mass consumption, mass political movements, mass education, mass labor, mass armies, and so on—made a "ruling class" of technocratic managers a necessity. Simply stated, beyond being unable to do everything on their own, few corporate owners would possess the specialized technical knowledge required to manage the complexities and scope of a modern industrial company. He warned of a collective tyranny in which these "managers will exploit the rest of society as a corporate body, their rights belonging to them not as individuals but through [the] position[s] . . . which they occupy."[16] Burnham, a former member of the Socialist Workers Party who became a leading opponent of communism in the 1940s, joined a growing line of skeptics, dating back to Adam Smith (see Chapter 2), who doubted the motives of those who managed other people's property and money. He was awarded the Presidential Medal of Freedom, the nation's highest civilian honor given to those who have "risen to the pinnacles of achievement in their fields," in 1983 by Ronald W. Reagan. The citation accompanying the medal reads in part: "Freedom, reason and decency have had few greater champions in this century than James Burnham."[17]

Although the Great Depression had stymied the nation's economic growth, mobilization for World War II had resulted in both technological and managerial advancements. Coming out of the war, occupational training within industry and the armed forces had created a deep pool of qualified employees. The postwar years found the United States with pent-up demand for formerly rationed consumer products and services. With demand outrunning productive capacity, the United States experienced an economic boom. The war effort had created new products, new technologies, and new markets. Soon, management thought was in transition, shifting from a war footing to a renewed interest in general management theory as businesses grew at home and abroad. Postwar prosperity and expansion provided a palpable impetus for the further evolution of management thinking.

---

[15] Kenneth E. Boulding, with commentary by Reinhold Niebuhr, *The Organizational Revolution: A Study of the Ethics of Economic Organization* (New York: Harper & Brothers, 1953). See also Robert H. Scott III, "Kenneth Boulding: A Friends' Economist," *Journal of Philosophical Economics* 15(1) (Spring 2022), pp. 35–61.

[16] James Burnham, *The Managerial Revolution: What Is Happening in the World* (New York: John Day Company, 1941), p. 126. See also Patricia Genoe McLaren, "James Burnham, The Managerial Revolution, and the Development of Management Theory in Post-War America," *Management & Organizational History* 6(4) (2001), pp. 411–423; Julius Krein, "James Burnham's Managerial Elite," *American Affairs* 1(1) (Spring 2017), pp. 120–151; and Francis P. Sempa, "James Burnham: The *Partisan Review* Years," *University Bookman* (August 14, 2022), accessed at https://kirkcenter.org/reviews/james-burnham-the-partisan-review-years/.

[17] Ronald W. Reagan, "Remarks at the Presentation Ceremony for the Presidential Medal of Freedom," February 23, 1983. Available online at https://www.r.eaganlibrary.gov/archives/speech/remarks-presentation-ceremony-presidential-medal-freedom.

"CREATIVE DESTRUCTION": NEW INNOVATIONS

Writing following the outbreak of World War II, Joseph A. Schumpeter (pronounced *shoompay-ter*) was pessimistic about the future of capitalism. He saw innovations in new products, new methods of production, new markets, new uses of raw materials, and new forms of organization as essential to economic growth and human progress. As Schumpeter explained, innovation "incessantly revolutionizes the economic structure *from within,* incessantly destroying the old one, incessantly creating a new one."[18] "Creative destruction," as he dubbed this process, sometimes occurs in rushes with intervening lulls, but is unceasing. In Schumpeter's account, entrepreneurs (and the novel startup companies they create) spur economic growth, as their innovations displace older technologies and methods, increasing productivity and enhancing the world's living standards. For pro–free market advocates, the capacity for disruption and innovation is the genius of capitalism. Schumpeter should have been less pessimistic given the life-changing innovations that began emerging as early as the 1920s.

In transportation, automobiles were miraculous inventions that largely replaced passenger rail service, creating a need for paved roads and garages. Enabling legislation in 1926 provided for a "national" highway—U.S. Route 66, which began on the shores of Lake Michigan in Chicago, sloped westward across Illinois and Missouri, crossed the Great Plains and deserts of the southwest, and ended on the shores of the Pacific Ocean at Santa Monica, California. All 2,448 miles were paved by 1938. In 1956, U.S. President Dwight D. Eisenhower signed the Federal-Aid Highway Act, authorizing construction of a national network of east-west and north-south freeways.

As noted in Chapter 12, on December 17, 1903, Orville and Wilbur Wright made the first heavier-than-air flight, covering 120 feet in 12 seconds. Just 24 years later, Charles Lindbergh soloed the Atlantic Ocean, traveling more than 3,600 miles in less than 34 hours. In 1939, Igor Sikorsky perfected the first helicopter. Charles E. "Chuck" Yeager broke the sound barrier in a jet-powered test plane at a speed of 640 miles per hour in 1947. A mere 65 years, 7 months, and 3 days after the Wrights' historic flight, U.S. astronauts Neil A. Armstrong and Edwin E. "Buzz" Aldrin, Jr., walked on the moon. Innovative aircraft manufacturers such as Boeing, Lockheed, and McDonnell Douglas supplied new airlines such as Delta, American, and Pan American. Piston engines, soon replaced by jet turbines, extended long-distance passenger travel from highways and railways to skyways, spurring demand for travel to global destinations. In 2018, foreign and domestic airlines carried 1,000,000,000 passengers.

In communications and entertainment, radios had become a household staple by the late 1920s. As the number of broadcasting stations multiplied, audiences grew. By the early 1930s, two-thirds of the nation's households had one or more radios and one-third had telephones. Sitting in their own living rooms, radio listeners across the country could hear the same news and music, simultaneously, for free. This even included sporting events: the first Rose Bowl football game was broadcast in 1927. In 1926, General Electric (GE) invented the first practical device for recording sound on film for Hollywood movies, and motion pictures became a growth industry, carrying American values, customs, and traditions throughout the world. True to Schumpeter's notion of creative destruction, Western Electric soon developed an electrical phonograph recording system to replace GE as the leading provider of sound recording and reproducing equipment. Beginning in 1948, Ampex reel-to-reel magnetic tape recorders allowed consumers to preserve voices and music at home. Ampex pioneered the first videotape recorder, a three-quarter-inch band of ribbon to preserve television images, in 1956. RCA provided the first glimpse of television at the 1939 World's Fair in New York City. The first

[18] Joseph A. Schumpeter, *Capitalism, Socialism, and Democracy* (New York: Harper & Brothers, 1942), p. 83. See also Timothy S. Kiessling, "Entrepreneurship and Innovation: Austrian School of Economics to Schumpeter to Drucker to Now," *Journal of Applied Management and Entrepreneurship* 9(1) (January 2004), pp. 80–92.

television commercial, a 10-second ad for Bulova watches, aired in 1941. In 1951, WCBS-TV broadcast the first baseball game in color—the Brooklyn Dodgers lost at home to the Boston Braves by the score of 8-1. Four years later, more than half the nation's homes wired for electricity had a black-and-white television set. By 1960, some 90 percent had one or more televisions, many wired for "living color." In 1980, the world's first 24-hour television news channel, CNN (Cable News Network), signed on the air.

Alan Turing, aware of Charles Babbage's idea of a general-purpose calculating machine, led the successful effort to develop the world's first programmable digital electronic computer. It went into service in 1944 and was used to break the German signal code during World War II (see Chapter 21). This was only the beginning of a revival of interest in computing machinery. Remington-Rand, IBM, Minneapolis-Honeywell, RCA, and others began making general-purpose computers. Built between 1943 and 1945 at the University of Pennsylvania, the Electronic Numerical Integrator and Computer (ENIAC) was used to calculate trajectories for artillery at the U.S. Army's Ballistic Research Laboratory at Aberdeen Proving Ground, Maryland. It was the size of a large school bus; contained 18,000 vacuum tubes, 1,500 relays, 70,000 resisters, 7,200 diodes, 10,000 capacitors, and miles of wiring; weighed 27 tons; and required an air-conditioned room to avoid meltdowns. In 1947, Bell Laboratories transformed the computer industry when it invented the first solid-state transistors, replacing vacuum tubes in most applications. Texas Instruments patented the first integrated circuits (microchips) in 1959. Integrated circuits are used today in virtually all electronic equipment, including personal computers, smart phones, automobiles, and home appliances. In 1971, Intel Corporation launched the modern computer revolution with the release of the Intel 4004 microprocessor, essentially a complete computer on a chip. Steve Jobs and Steve Wozniak transformed the computer industry in 1977 when they introduced the Apple II with the first color graphics. Bill Gates and Paul Allen released Microsoft Corporation's personal computer (PC) disk operating system (MS-DOS) in 1981. Microsoft soon dominated the PC market. It deepened its market position in 1990 when it implemented a graphical user interface in its Windows operating system. On August 6, 1991, Sir Timothy J. Berners-Lee published the first website on the World Wide Web. In 1993, after co-creating Mosaic, the first web browser, while working at the University of Illinois, Marc Andreessen headed to Silicon Valley and started Netscape. The search engine Yahoo! ("Yet Another Hierarchical Officious Oracle") was launched by Jerry Yang and David Filo in 1994 and was soon followed by more than a dozen rivals, including Lycos (1994), Excite (1995), and Google (1998). Internet-phone start-up Skype debuted in 2003, enabling users from around the globe to confer (via videoconferences) without leaving their homes or offices or incurring the cost of long-distance calls. It was followed by breakout competitor Zoom Video Communications in 2011. At about the same time, as smartphones became widespread, dialing over the mobile internet replaced landline phone service provided by legacy telecom companies such as AT&T Corporation. Considering these waves of communication and entertainment innovations, especially the advent of the internet, and cloud computing, it is hard to fathom that in 1977, speaking before the World Future Society, Digital Equipment Corporation (DEC) co-founder Kenneth H. Olsen had declared he could see "no possible reason to have a computer in the home."[19]

Additional life-changing innovations that emerged during the first half of the past century included dry-copying, or electrophotography. It combined electrostatic printing with photography. Developed in 1938 by Chester Carlson, within a decade the Haloid Photographic Company (later renamed Xerox) negotiated commercial rights for making copies at the touch of a button. Medical breakthroughs, beginning in the 1920s and extending into the 1950s, were astounding: Alexander Fleming's 1928 chance discovery of penicillin ignited research into antibiotics; the last natural outbreak of smallpox in the United States occurred in 1949; and Jonas Salk licensed the first polio vaccine in 1955. Rosalind Franklin's 1953 crystallographic X-rays of the

[19] David Ahl, "Interview with Gordon Bell," *Creative Computing* 6(4) (April 1980), p. 88.

deoxyribonucleic acid (DNA) molecule (the basis for heredity) became increasingly relevant when James Watson and Francis Crick realized it consisted of a three-dimensional double-helix polymer and offered a clue in understanding the building blocks of life. The advent of the atomic age in the 1940s lead to significant innovations such as radiation treatments that cure cancer and nuclear power for space exploration.

Developments in the public sector also led to further life-changing innovations. Created in 1933 as one of President Franklin D. Roosevelt's New Deal Programs (discussed below), the Tennessee Valley Authority (TVA) built dams along the Tennessee River, providing electricity for economic expansion and household use. By an Executive Order issued in 1935 as part of his New Deal, Roosevelt established the Rural Electrification Administration (under the direction of Morris L. Cooke), bringing electrical power to the nation's farms, which nearly 90 percent lacked. As electrical supplies increased, the home appliance industry blossomed: electric vacuum sweepers, food freezers, refrigerators, stoves, washing machines, clothes dryers, and more revolutionized the lives of the middle class. A century earlier no one could have predicted the benefits of these life-altering innovations for home and industry.

Writing following the outbreak of World War II, Schumpeter possessed an understandable pessimism about the future of capitalism and, perhaps, the world in general. If Schumpeter were alive today, looking back over the past 75-plus years, the economic growth and human progress that have resulted from innovations in new products, new methods of production, new markets, new uses of raw materials, and new forms of organization would, no doubt, change his pessimism into astonishment. His belief that the world's future prosperity requires people to think differently as they search for new ideas, however, remains just as true today as it did during his lifetime.

THE SOCIAL ENVIRONMENT: RESHAPING THE NATION'S VALUES

The economic temper of the social-person era shaped the nation's dominant social values. The Great Depression was for many a violation of the previously held precepts of abundance and success for everyone. The 1920s had brought Madison Avenue to places like Peoria and Dubuque, and U.S. productivity presaged more than the Republican Party's 1928 campaign promise of "A chicken in every pot and a car in every backyard."[20] What happened to social relationships and the assumptions that guided people's behavior in the troubled 1930s? Broadly viewed, two distinct developments were reshaping the nation's social values: (1) a questioning of the virtues found in Max Weber's Protestant ethic and a greater acceptance of secular values, and (2) a change in society's view of business and business executives.

SHIFTING SOCIAL VALUES

Robert and Helen Lynd, in their famous study of the typical U.S. city of the late 1920s (later identified as Muncie, Indiana), found a divergence in the social values of an average wage earner and the typical white-collar employee. For the average wage earner, economic motives were primary: "This dominance of the dollar appears in the apparently growing tendency among younger working class men to swap a problematic future for immediate 'big money.'"[21] Whereas the average wage earner in the Lynd study measured status by financial standing and tended to hold to the traditional virtues of individualism, including a declining interest in belonging to organized labor, white-collar employees viewed their place in society differently. The Lynds noted a decline

[20] "A Chicken in Every Pot" political ad and rebuttal article, *New York Times* (October 30, 1928), Collection HH-HOOVH: Herbert Hoover Papers. Available online at https://www.docsteach.org/documents/document/a-chicken-in-every-pot-political-ad-and-rebuttal-article-in-new-york-times.

[21] Robert S. Lynd and Helen M. Lynd, *Middletown: A Study in American Culture* (New York: Harcourt, Brace and Company, 1929), p. 81.

in individualism among white-collar employees and a rapidly increasing need to belong. In a follow-up study conducted in Muncie during the Great Depression, however, the Lynds found that "[t]he heightening of insecurity during the depression has brought with it greater insistence upon conformity and a sharpening of latent issues" on the part of both groups.[22] Average wage earners were turning to unions for collective action. Their white-collar brethren were acquiescing to the demands of corporate life as salaried managers. This resulted in a sharpening of class distinctions and generated social bitterness. The Great Depression had brought about a shift in social values for the average wage earner and the typical white-collar employee alike.

After the 1929 Wall Street stock-market crash, of what value were the Protestant-ethic virtues of frugality, thrift, and hard work? Black Thursday had apparently affected nearly every person in some way—the loss of a job here, a savings account there, or even one's home or farm. The Great Depression struck the virtuous as well as the wicked, the tycoon as well as the tyro, and the responsible as well as the feckless. People found their own fortunes intertwined with those of others in a pattern that defied reason or justice and, as a result, became more cautious: "As time went on there was a continuing disposition among Americans young and old to look with a cynical eye upon the old Horatio Alger formula for success; to be dubious about taking chances for ambition's sake; to look with a favorable eye upon a safe if unadventurous job, social insurance plans, pension plans. They had learned from bitter experience to crave security."[23]

This craving for security, this turning inward to others who shared the same tribulations, was passed from parents to their children and even, in some instances, on to further generations. Perhaps people have a natural predilection to form groups when faced with threatening circumstances. Erich S. Fromm has noted the desire of people to escape the loneliness of standing alone. In fascist Germany, to escape their loneliness, people turned to an authoritarian regime that made their decisions for them and gave them a sense of identity, however evil. According to Fromm, this need to belong also pervaded U.S. industrial life during the 1930s, and individuals were, more frequently than not, willing to give up their self-identity to conform to societal strictures. Whereas the Protestant Reformation and the Industrial Revolution drove people from the shadows of medieval life, enabling them to find freedom in the spiritual, political, and economic spheres of society, industrialization created unprecedented threats to these newfound liberties.[24] Perhaps people felt alone in a free-market system and needed something larger than themselves—God, the Nation, the Company, the Union, and so on—with which to identify and find strength.

The conditions of the troubled 1930s may have compounded this desire for group membership as a source of strength. David C. McClelland found in his studies of people's motives that the "need for achievement" increased in the United States from 1800 to 1890 but decreased thereafter. The trade-off between the need for achievement and the "need for affiliation" took a dramatic shift between 1925 and 1950. In 1925, the need for affiliation was primarily a familial concern; by 1950, affiliation had become an alternative for economic achievement. By that time, people were showing more concern for affiliation and less for achievement.[25]

David Riesman and his associates furnished additional evidence relating to the nation's change in social values, noting a shift in society from an "inner-directed" to "other-directed" culture. The inner-directed person represented the era's free-market capitalism and emphasized self-direction and control. The other-directed person was characterized by high social mobility, an emphasis on consumption rather than production, and a recognition of getting along and being accepted by others as the keys to achievement. Riesman called the inner-directed character of the scientific-management period "job-minded" and the other-directed person of the human-relations

[22] *Idem*, *Middletown in Transition: A Study in Cultural Conflicts* (New York: Harcourt, Brace and Company, 1937), p. 427.
[23] Frederick Lewis Allen, *The Big Change: America Transforms Itself, 1900–1950* (New York: Harper & Row, 1952), p. 149.
[24] Erich S. Fromm, *Escape from Freedom* (New York: Holt, Rinehart & Winston, 1941), pp. 7–10.
[25] David C. McClelland, *The Achieving Society* (Princeton, NJ: Van Nostrand, 1961), pp. 166–167; *idem*, "Business Drive and National Achievement," *Harvard Business Review* 40(4) (July–August 1962), p. 110.

era "people-minded."[26] For Riesman, the shift from what Adam Smith called the "invisible hand" to the "glad hand" began in about 1900. Up until that time, individualism had been the dominant social value. After the closing of the nation's frontier in 1890, those seeking opportunity and freedom in the West could no longer do so (see Chapter 12). The "passing of the frontier" led to a reduction in individualism and allowed "groupism," or the social nature of humans, to prevail. The inner-directed person persisted for a period after 1900, but the nation's social values had shifted. In the main, people had little choice but to live where they were, being unable to use the frontier as a "safety valve." Most of the pressing challenges of production began to disappear. The new challenges that arose in the modern industrial world were challenges that involved people. With the growth in corporate ownership, employee–employer relationships became less personal, as the engaged style of the small-business owner was replaced with the bureaucratic style of the professional manager. The hands-on touch of an owner-manager was lost, replaced with directives from technically trained specialists. Social competence, that is, influencing others, began to assume a new importance, and technical skills became less valued.

This shift in the nation's social values led to the rise of "groupism" and the social person. Self-proclaimed "progressive" educators sought to remake classroom instruction and to replace parents as the primary agents in teaching children societal norms, emphasizing the skills, habits, and shared values necessary to function within social groups. Getting along and being accepted were more important than individual accomplishments in defining one's self and aspirations. People were judged by what others thought of them, not by what they thought of themselves.

Although the Great Depression had not necessarily made people less religious, it allowed them to segment their lives more easily into secular and spiritual spheres. Many in dire economic straits found comfort in the secular values promoted by New Deal progressives who advocated using government power to mandate greater economic equality. For one authority, the Great Depression caused a spiritual "confusion of souls" and a crisis for the Protestant ethic.[27] Self-help had failed, and the notion of the successful "self-made" man or woman was no longer seen as the foundation of an orderly economic system. Charity became a public rather than private concern, and the Protestant-ethic virtues of frugality, thrift, and hard work fell into disfavor. From this confusion and crisis, the nation's moral order took on new dimensions.

Two books in particular answered the nation's thirst for moral advice and direction. Both are among the most popular books in publishing history. Almost from its initial debut in 1937, Dale Carnegie's *How to Win Friends and Influence People* was an immediate bestseller, with 250,000 copies sold in the first 3 months following its publication.[28] Emphasizing the importance of human relations, Carnegie maintained that success in life could be achieved by (1) making others feel important through a sincere appreciation of their efforts; (2) making a good first impression; (3) winning people to one's way of thinking by letting others do the talking and being sympathetic, with the caveat "never tell a man he is wrong"; and (4) changing people by praising good traits and giving the offender the opportunity to save face. Although Roethlisberger and Dickson's full report on the Hawthorne studies, *Management and the Worker*, had not been published at the time, Carnegie's advice for success bore a striking resemblance to Western Electric's rules for supervisors in interviewing employees.

A second book that offered the nation moral advice and direction was the Reverend Dr. Norman Vincent Peale's *The Power of Positive Thinking*.[29] In contrast to Carnegie's "getting along" approach, Peale "counseled readers that they could achieve better results in life by dwelling exclusively on optimistic interpretations of their circumstances" and believed it was

---

[26] David Riesman with Nathan Glazer and Reuel Denney, *The Lonely Crowd: A Study in Changing American Character* (New Haven, CT: Yale University Press, 1950), pp. 19–40, 151.

[27] Donald Meyer, *The Positive Thinkers: A Study of the American Quest for Health, Wealth and Personal Power from Mary Baker Eddy to Norman Vincent Peale* (Garden City, NY: Doubleday, 1965), pp. 233–237.

[28] Dale Carnegie, *How to Win Friends and Influence People* (New York: Simon and Schuster, 1937).

[29] Norman Vincent Peale, *The Power of Positive Thinking* (New York: Prentice-Hall, 1952).

an affront to God to have a low opinion of oneself.[30] Despite coming under criticism for their reliance on anecdotes and unsourced testimonials, the Carnegie and Peale books were hugely popular with contemporary readers and garner sales even today.

These positive thinkers stressed two ways to move from a "confusion of souls" to a "clarity of minds": (1) drawing on the inward power of faith, and (2) gaining personal strength by winning the cooperation of others through personal magnetism. The social ethic of the times deemphasized achievement by rugged individualism, as the Protestant ethic had seemingly run its course. This new ethic was other-oriented, with moral uplift coming not from efficiency, but from getting along with others. For the most part, the social person was conceived, born, and nurtured in these trying times. People sought comfort in groups, solace in association, and fulfillment in affiliation.

"ORGANIZATION MEN"

Another aspect of the social-person era relates to the image of corporate executives as reflected in popular literature. Admittedly, the fictional "bad guy" executive portrayed as a heartless agent of greed in literature (and film) may or may not be a true reflection of society's view of life behind corporate doors. Nonetheless, after surveying over 100 novels, Robert A. Kavesh warned that the fictional corporate executive is generally portrayed as flawed and cynical.[31] In film, it is evident that corporate executives are often damned for society's ills and are among Hollywood's favorite villains.[32] The 1920s had canonized business moguls as heroes and symbols of prosperity and the good life, though when times turned turbulent, these figures were cursed as the "bankster[s]" who "robbed" people of their homes and savings.

William G. Scott noted that novels of the 1930s and 1940s were characterized by a disillusionment with individualism and a plea for "humanitarianism and collectivism in the form of proletarian fiction."[33] The heroes and heroines of the early twentieth century vanished to be replaced by a "they" who did things without reason and were beyond the control of mere mortals. "They" represented power, machines, and unidentified forces, not individual managers who could be held responsible for their actions. Corporations were monsters of oppression that destroyed people and their lives piece by piece. Examples of such novels include John Steinbeck's *Grapes of Wrath* and Nathanael West's *A Cool Million: The Dismantling of Lemuel Pitkin*.[34] For Steinbeck, it was not individuals but "they" who exploited the Joads (defenseless tenant farmers escaping from Dust Bowl Oklahoma) to the point of starvation. A satire of the Horatio Alger "myth," West's hero is caught between the depravities of international bankers and world revolutionaries, who slowly destroy his spirit and quest for success.

As the 1940s and 1950s unfolded, corporate executives (as well as managers at all levels) were increasingly depicted in popular literature and film as "organization men" who cherished "belongingness" above all else. They not only worked for "The Organization," they *belonged* to it, as well.[35] In John P. Marquand's *The Point of No Return*, Ernst Pawel's *From the Dark Tower*,

---

[30] Barton Swaim, [Review of the book *Surge of Piety: Norman Vincent Peale and the Remaking of American Religious Life*], *Wall Street Journal* (December 27, 2016), p. A15.

[31] Robert A. Kavesh, *Businessmen in Fiction: The Capitalist and Executive in American Novels* (Hanover, NH: Amos Tuck School of Business Administration, Dartmouth College, 1955), p. 11.

[32] Rachel Dodes, "Hollywood's Favorite Villain," *Wall Street Journal* (October 14, 2011), p. D1. See also Algis Valiunas, "Business and the Literati," *National Affairs* no. 9 (Fall 2011), pp. 192–179.

[33] William G. Scott, *The Social Ethic in Management Literature*, Bulletin no. 4 (Atlanta, GA: Bureau of Business and Economic Research, School of Business Administration, Georgia State College of Business Administration, 1959), p. 47.

[34] John Steinbeck, *The Grapes of Wrath* (New York: Viking Press, 1939); Nathanael West, *A Cool Million: The Dismantling of Lemuel Pitkin* (New York: Covici-Friede Publishers, 1934).

[35] The term "organization man" was coined by William H. Whyte in his book *The Organization Man* (New York: Simon and Schuster, 1956), pp. 7, 15. Parts of this book were originally published in *Fortune* magazine. See also *idem*, "The Organization Man: A Rejoinder," *New York Times* (December 7, 1986), section 6, p. 98.

and Sloan Wilson's *The Man in the Gray Flannel Suit*, the emphasis is on group conformity and the collective nature of people seeking collaborative solidarity.[36] This emphasis may also be discerned in the work of Mary P. Follett, Elton Mayo, and others who stressed group responsibility and collective will. The management literature of the late 1940s and 1950s endorsed teamwork, employee participation, participative decision-making, small rather than large groups, committee management, and democratic leadership.

As many of the era's intellectuals sought to denigrate the importance of business, some idealized the agrarian lifestyle characterized by small farms and self-sufficiency. To be big was to be bad, and to live in an urban rather than rural society was a sign of decline. Why did intellectuals idealize agriculture and attack business? Kavesh has noted that "the growth of cities is the history of business: the big businessman is the symbol of the city, and the city became the symbol of degradation."[37] Loren Baritz suggests that Mayo was one of those who were committed to an "Agrarian Golden Age":

> [Mayo] believed that there was a mystical but direct relationship between farming and truth. . . . An industrial society, by definition, could not be virtuous, for as men lost sight of the soil they lost sight of nature; and in so doing, they lost sight of the meaning of life and fell victim to the glossy gadgetry of modern industrialism. For Mayo, then, the problem of the modern factory was clear: how to make possible the re-creation of Agrarian Virtue, Agrarian Loyalty, and the Agrarian Sense of Community in the twentieth century's world of skyscrapers and subways, of smoke and steam?[38]

As noted in Chapter 13, for Mayo, the answer to society's ills was to restore a collective consciousness in society that embodied shared sentiments and values. Mayo, influenced by Émile Durkheim, saw evils in industrial life much as Robert Owen had seen them in the early nineteenth century. Whereas Durkheim admonished people to love one another unselfishly, and Owen built industrial communes, Mayo accepted the parameters of industrialization and tried to rebuild people's interpersonal relations within a social framework. The gloom of the Great Depression, the horror of World War II, and the fear that nuclear war could happen at any time may have caused Mayo to harken back to an Agrarian Golden Age in which people could find stability, purpose, and established norms in small groups.

THE POLITICAL ENVIRONMENT: FDR'S PLEDGE

As the nation's economic cycle went from prosperity to depression and the social environment reflected increasing needs for affiliation, the role for government in individual and business affairs was reimagined. No other period in U.S. history has witnessed a political administration begin in such dire times, endure for such a long period, and cope with as many adversities as the tenure of President Franklin D. Roosevelt (FDR), the only president elected four times. Scion of a patrician family, cousin of former president Theodore Roosevelt, and paralyzed from the waist down by polio, Roosevelt brought hope to a nation in the depths of despair. In his 1932 acceptance speech for the Democratic presidential nomination, Roosevelt addressed the problems of the Great Depression, promising: "I pledge you, I pledge myself, to a new deal for the American people."[39] This pledge and the phrase "A New Deal," a counterpart to Theodore Roosevelt's "Square Deal," became the slogan of his election campaign and the name for his administration's legislative programs.[40]

---

[36] John P. Marquand, *Point of No Return* (Boston, MA: Little, Brown, 1949); Ernst Pawel, *From the Dark Tower* (New York: Macmillan, 1957); and Sloan Wilson, *The Man in the Gray Flannel Suit* (New York: Simon and Schuster, 1955).

[37] Kavesh, *Businessmen in Fiction*, p. 6.

[38] Loren Baritz, *The Servants of Power: A History of the Use of Social Science in American Industry* (Middletown, CT: Wesleyan University Press, 1960), p. 111.

[39] Franklin D. Roosevelt, "Address Accepting the Presidential Nomination at the Democratic National Convention in Chicago," July 2, 1932. Available online at https://www.presidency.ucsb.edu/node/275484.

[40] Stuart Chase, a member of Roosevelt's "brain trust," coined the phrase "A New Deal." See Ronald Sullivan, "Stuart Chase, 97; Coined Phrase 'a New Deal,'" *New York Times* (November 17, 1985), section 1, p. 44.

THE NEW DEAL

FDR saw restoring confidence to a stricken nation facing the imperative of economic crisis as his first task in office. In his 1933 inaugural address, he declared: "The only thing we have to fear is fear itself."[41] In enacting the New Deal, FDR issued executive orders and shepherded legislation through the U.S. Congress that created federal agencies and public works programs such as the Agricultural Adjustment Administration (AAA; 1933), Civilian Conservation Corps (CCC; 1933), Farm Credit Administration (FCA; 1933), Federal Emergency Relief Administration (FERA; 1933), Federal Deposit Insurance Corporation (FDIC; 1933), Home Owners' Loan Corporation (HOLC; 1933), Public Works Administration (PWA; 1933), and Securities and Exchange Commission (SEC; 1934). Although the U.S. Supreme Court declared parts of the New Deal unconstitutional, the day of an activist government, supported by a dizzying array of what former New York governor Alfred E. Smith ridiculed as "alphabet-soup" agencies, had arrived.[42] Foreshadowed by President Woodrow Wilson's belief in a government widely staffed by nonpartisan experts who rationally ordered public policy (see Chapter 6), an expansive administrative state grew within FDR's New Deal.

Whereas some viewed the New Deal as "creeping socialism" and prophesied the end of free-market capitalism, others saw its programs as necessary to smooth out ebbs and flows in the nation's economic activity. Free-market capitalism endured as the prevailing economic system, but critics charged that the New Deal not only prolonged the Great Depression through over-regulation, it put the nation on the road to socialism and even totalitarianism.[43] A hands-off approach to economic policy, allowing markets to regulate themselves based on Adam Smith's "invisible hand," was now over. As seen by New Deal policy advisor Rexford G. Tugwell, capitalism was wasteful and must be replaced by a more efficient economic system that incorporated central government planning.[44] Tugwell maintained that "[a]ny system that encouraged competition among companies instead of cooperation (i.e., businesses working together to increase efficiency) was inevitably destined to fail."[45] Further, given that the nation's businesses had been unable to provide security for wage earners, Tugwell argued that the government should act aggressively to alleviate widespread poverty and unemployment. Roosevelt's administration responded by supporting the Social Security Act (1935), which provided for old-age assistance, unemployment insurance, and welfare programs; the Fair Labor Standards Act (1938), which established a guaranteed minimum hourly wage of 25 cents and time-and-a-half overtime pay for more than 40 hours worked a week; and the Railroad Unemployment Insurance Act (1938), which restored lost wages due to unemployment or illness. These and other legislative acts marked a pronounced shift from Adam Smith's "invisible hand" to Riesman's "glad hand," from private to public charity, and from the Protestant ethic to the social ethic.

---

[41] *Idem*, "Inaugural Address of the President," Washington, DC, March 4, 1933, p. 1. Available online at https://www.archives.gov/education/lessons/fdr-inaugural.

[42] Alfred E. Smith quoted in "Smith Denounces Civil Works Plan as Costly 'Alibi,'" *New York Times* (December 1, 1933), p. 1. Roosevelt stretched his presidential powers to the limit and beyond, Among notable decisions, the U.S. Supreme Court ruled against the Roosevelt administration's New Deal agenda in declaring the National Industrial Recovery Act (1933), Agricultural Adjustment Act (1933), Railroad Retirement Act (1934), and Municipal Bankruptcy Act (1937) unconstitutional. In response, during the 1936 presidential campaign, Roosevelt argued for expanding the size of the court from 9 to 15 justices to gain favorable rulings. The Judicial Procedures Reform Bill of 1937, proposed by Roosevelt for this purpose, however, failed in the U.S. Senate.

[43] See, for example, Amity R. Shales, *The Forgotten Man: A New History of the Great Depression* (New York: HarperCollins, 2007) pp. 7–10.

[44] Rexford G. Tugwell and Howard C. Hill, *Our Economic Society and Its Problems: A Study of American Levels of Living and How to Improve Them* (New York: Harcourt, Brace and Company, 1934), pp. 497–505. An alternate version of this book, also published in 1934 by Harcourt, Brace, lists Hill as first author.

[45] Steven A. Chichester, "'Make America Over': Rexford Guy Tugwell and His Thoughts on Central Planning" (Master's thesis, Liberty University, Lynchburg, VA, 2011), pp. 1–2.

AUGMENTING THE POSITION OF LABOR

During the Roosevelt years, the federal government became more deeply involved in the nation's economic life than could possibly have been envisioned by earlier progressives such as Louis D. Brandeis (see Chapter 12). Of all the changes introduced by the New Deal, none had a more immediate significance for business than the newfound legitimacy enjoyed by labor unions. The 1930s witnessed the first real successes at organizing workers on a national scale by industry rather than by craft. Previous attempts to organize all workers, regardless of their profession or skill level, had met with limited success—William Sylvis's National Labor Union and Terence V. Powderly's Noble Order of the Knights of Labor had failed in the nineteenth century. The American Federation of Labor (AFL), a federation of craft workers, formed in 1886, and numerous railroad brotherhoods, emerging as early as 1863, had demonstrated that unions could be successful when workers possessed common skills. There had been some successful industrial unions (such as those of the garment, millinery, and coal industries), but they were typically small relative to craft unions, in which all members belonged to the same profession. For example, almost 60 percent of the nation's union members in 1929 were in the building trades (919,000 members) or in transportation (892,000 members) and for the most part were affiliated with the AFL or the rail brotherhoods. The largest industrial unions were in mining (271,000 members) and garments and millinery (218,000 members).[46]

The political climate of the 1930s created an opportunity for industrial unionism to flourish. The first significant piece of legislation, the Federal Anti-Injunction Act of 1932, more commonly known as the Norris–LaGuardia Act, was passed during President Hoover's administration. For all practical purposes, it completely divested federal courts of injunctive powers in cases growing out of labor disputes. In 1933, FDR's first year as president, Congress passed the National Industrial Recovery Act (NIRA). In the run-up to the 1932 presidential election, in which FDR defeated Hoover, FDR had promised to protect the jobs of union members and the right of non-union workers to organize without threats of being blacklisted.[47] Section 7a of the NIRA, in similar but stronger language than that of the Norris–LaGuardia Act, specifically guaranteed that "employees shall have the right to organize and bargain collectively through representatives of their own choosing . . . free from interference, restraint, or coercion of employers."[48]

When the U.S. Supreme Court declared the NIRA unconstitutional in 1935 for delegating too much legislative authority to the president (*United States v. A. L. A. Schechter Poultry Corporation*[49]), Congress quickly replaced it with a law that was even more pro–organized labor. The National Labor Relations Act (NLRA), more commonly known as the Wagner Act, guaranteed employees "the right to self-organization, to form, join, or assist labor organization, to bargain collectively through representatives of their own choosing, and to engage in concerted activities for the purpose of collective bargaining."[50] In addition, it placed specific restrictions on employer conduct intended to discourage workplace unionization. The NLRA established a National Labor Relations Board (NLRB) that was granted the authority to not only issue cease-and-desist letters to employers to halt purported restriction violations, but to determine appropriate bargaining units and conduct representation elections. The NLRB also limited the scope of

[46] U.S. Department of Commerce, Bureau of the Census, *Historical Statistics of the United States*, part 1, p. 178.

[47] Franklin D. Roosevelt, "History of Labor and Social Welfare Legislation: Campaign Address," in State of New York, *Public Papers of Franklin D. Roosevelt: Forty-Eighth Governor of the State of New York, 1930* (Albany, NY: J. B. Lyon, 1931), pp. 795–800. See also Eric Rauchway, "The New Deal Was on the Ballot in 1932," *Modern American History* 2(2) (July 2019), pp. 201–213.

[48] National Industrial Recovery Act, Title I, Sec. 7a, 1933. Available online at https://www.ourdocuments.gov/doc.php?doc=66.

[49] *A. L. A. Schechter Poultry Corp. v. United States*, 295 U.S. 495 (1935).

[50] National Labor Relations Act, Title 29, Chapter 7, Subchapter II, United States Code, 1935. Available online at https://www.nlrb.gov/how-we-work/national-labor-relations-act.

nonunion employee-representation plans. Organized labor bitterly opposed such plans, seeing them as "company unions" that hindered their organizing efforts. In 1938, the U.S. Supreme Court ruled that these plans were employer dominated and violated the National Labor Relations Act (*NLRB v. Pennsylvania Greyhound Lines*[51]). Thus ended one era in labor–management relations, while yet another began.[52]

The passage of the Wagner Act marked a critical turning point in labor–management relations. John L. Lewis, president of the United Mine Workers, led the fight for industrial unionism within the AFL. Rebuffed, Lewis formed the Committee for Industrial Organization (known after 1938 as the Congress of Industrial Organizations; CIO), the purpose of which was to bring workers into unions regardless of their profession or skill level. The newly founded CIO enjoyed almost instant success and was able to claim nearly 4 million members by 1937. While the CIO prospered, the AFL did as well—almost doubling its membership from 2,126,000 in 1933 to 4,000,000 in 1939. With the passage of favorable New Deal legislation, total union membership spurted from a turn-of-the-decade 3.5 million (6.8 percent of the total labor force) to almost 9 million (15.8 percent) by 1939.[53]

Labor unions gained substantial political power during the 1930s. The pro-union stance of the Roosevelt administration was an attempt to realign collective-bargaining negotiations. It meshed with calls for teamwork, employee participation, group decision-making, and democratic leadership in the workplace. During World War II, labor and management joined together to keep the wheels of industry turning, and their differences were temporarily laid aside. The National War Labor Board, created to minimize labor unrest that might stall the war effort, generally favored the interests of workers. With peacetime, however, unions feared layoffs from war work and the return of millions of veterans to civilian employment. There were 4,750 strikes involving 3,367,000 workers in 1945, the year the war ended. In 1946, there were an additional 4,985 strikes affecting some 4,6000,000 workers.[54] These strikes highlighted unfair union practices, resulting in the passage of the Labor–Management Relations Act (Taft–Hartley Act). Passed in 1947, the act placed restrictions on unions akin to those already imposed on employers. The Taft–Hartley Act sought to equalize the balance of power that formerly favored unions.

Overall, not only had the nation's labor–management relations changed throughout the social-person era, so had government involvement in the nation's marketplace. This involvement threw into relief the nature of the progressive–conservative divide that continues to this day. The era's progressives believed in the ability of a professional overclass of political appointees (presumably gifted with superior knowledge and judgment), supplemented by activist courts, to dictate the behavior of ordinary people who did not appreciate what was in their own best interest. As one observer has noted, "During the Depression, Franklin Roosevelt struck a defining bargain with the public: Cede to the government expanded powers over the details of American life, and government will administer it efficiently."[55] Toward this end, for the progressives, the central challenge was achieving an equal redistribution of income and societal wealth through government programs and regulations.

Despite Roosevelt's good intentions, the era's conservatives preferred individual liberty to enforced equality and economic freedom and limited government over the promised efficiency of a bureaucracy administered by a supposed intellectual elite. Conservatives held that people should be free to make their own private and business decisions, including taking risks

[51] *National Labor Relations Board v. Pennsylvania Greyhound Lines, Inc., et al.* 303 U.S. 261 (58 S. Ct. 571, 82 L.Ed. 831) (1938).

[52] C. Ray Gullett and Edmund R. Gray, "The Impact of Employee Representation Plans upon the Development of Management-Worker Relations in the United States," *Marquette Business Review* 20(1) (Fall 1976), pp. 85–101.

[53] U.S. Department of Commerce, Bureau of the Census, *Historical Statistics of the United States*, part 1, p. 178.

[54] "Work Stoppages Caused by Labor-Management Disputes in 1945," *Monthly Labor Review* 62(5) (May 1946), p. 718; "Work Stoppages Caused by Labor-Management Disputes in 1946," *Monthly Labor Review* 64(5) (May 1947), p. 780.

[55] Daniel Henninger, "The Incompetence Party," *Wall Street Journal* (February 13, 2020), p. A15.

in competitive markets that may lead to vastly different lifestyle outcomes. In this regard, they believed that some economic inequality was beneficial, as it encouraged individual initiative, creativity, risk-taking, and investment, which (per Schumpeter's account) propels a nation's continued economic prosperity. Taking a zero-sum view of the economy in the belief that if one person becomes rich someone else must become poor, progressives focused on income redistribution. In contrast, conservatives, recognizing that in a free-market society one person's wealth does not necessarily come at the expense of someone else's, emphasized income generation in the belief that a growing economy benefits everyone. To wit, contemporary billionaires such as Bill Gates (Microsoft), Jeff Bezos (Amazon), and Mark Zuckerberg (Facebook) did not become rich at the expense of others, but by meeting the needs of hundreds of millions of people worldwide. Moreover, by providing a good or service their users find productive, they have expanded their users' (and society's) wealth.

To redress what it saw as the worst abuses of the New Deal, the U.S. Congress passed (with unanimous consent of both the House and Senate) the Administrative Procedure Act (APA) in 1946.[56] The APA stipulates how federal agencies develop and enforce regulations. It mandates a notice-and-commentary period to permit public input before proposed and final substantive rulemaking take effect and provides standards for judicial review of agency actions.

SUMMARY OF PART III

Figure 18.1 depicts major landmarks in the social-person era. Scientific management was the dominant theme in the 1920s. Sociologists and social psychologists popularized behaviorism in the mid-1900s. Though belonging chronologically to the scientific-management era, Mary P. Follett served as an intellectual bridge to the later study of groups. The Hawthorne studies, beginning before, but enduring through, the early days of the Great Depression, brought about a shift in management focus, including (1) an increased concern for people along with production; (2) exhortations to increase the fulfillment of employee needs; (3) the use of economic incentives as but one element in motivating employees; and (4) a greater concern for the illogic of sentiments than the logic of efficiency.

Post-Hawthorne, the human-relations movement passed through micro and macro phases. The micro phase saw an outpouring of behavioral research on topics such as group dynamics, participative decision-making, leadership, and workplace motivation. On the macro side of the movement, there were a number of attempts to understand the interaction of the social and technical systems operating within organizations. Chronologically paralleling these developments in the human-relations movement, a complementary stream of management thought focused on the structure and design of organizations. Although the human element was not entirely omitted from this second stream of management thought, it was intentionally set aside for a specific purpose: to provide an analysis independent of idiosyncratic personalities and politics.

As outlined in this chapter, management thought in the social-person era was shaped by the Great Depression, which redefined the role of government in individual and business affairs. No longer would the Protestant-ethic virtues of frugality, thrift, and hard work be seen of unquestioned value. If you were down, the government helped you up; if you lost your savings in a bank failure, the government would reimburse you; if you had saved nothing for retirement, the government would provide a pension, and so on, through a host of social programs intended to take some of the sting out of life's peaks and valleys. Whereas the Depression had stalled economic growth, the postwar boom in the world economy created a need for a new view of top-level management. The Protestant ethic and the need for achievement, though not disappearing entirely, declined in significance as people sought comfort in groups, solace in association, and fulfillment in affiliation. People, not production, were a manager's main concern. A newfound legitimacy for labor unions brought success at organizing workers on a national scale by industry rather than by craft. It was out of this age of confusion, trauma, and diversity that the modern era in management was about to begin.

[56] *Administrative Procedure Act, 1946*. Available online at https://www.justice.gov/sites/default/files/jmd/legacy/2014/05/01/act-pl79-404.pdf.

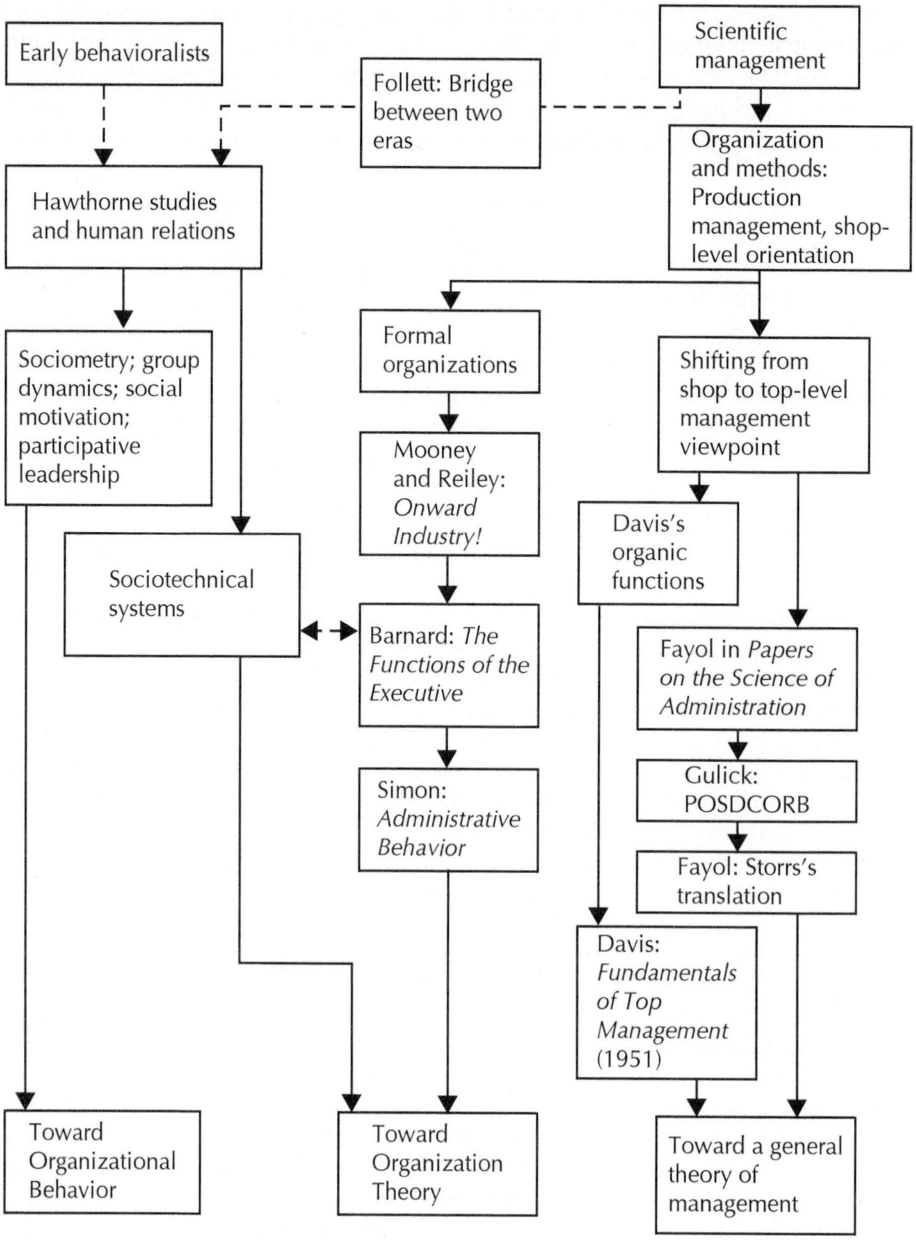

FIGURE 18.1 Synopsis of the social-person era.

Moving Onward: The Near Present

PART IV

Nestled between the knowns of yesterday and the unknowns of tomorrow, the present is the twilight of history. The zoom lens of history often leaves the near past out of focus, as recent developments and events are invariably colored by contemporary vested interests. The historian's most difficult task is to step away from the present day and place more recent developments into a balanced perspective. Simply put, history needs time to steep and settle before one can assess merit and debate legacy. Because the present-day management literature is too extensive for an in-depth analysis, we must be content to sketch the broad outlines of management thought in the post–World War II economic-expansion period.

Part IV begins by reviewing the years following World War II, when a renewed interest in general management theory emerged as businesses grew at home and abroad, fostering a need for more broadly educated managers. It then focuses on the ascent of a new generation of scholars devoted to the study of what became known as "organizational behavior." Next it traces the transformation of personnel management as a field into human-resource management and, subsequently, strategic human-resource management. It then reviews the debate beginning at roughly the same time among organization theorists concerning the effect of technology on an organization's structure and the relationship between an organization's design and its environment. The continued quest for science in management leading into the Information Age is then recounted. Part IV concludes with a consideration of how the globalization of business and society's expectation that managers will act responsibly have influenced the evolution of management thought.

Moving Onward: The Next Present

Management Theory and Practice

CHAPTER 19

Technological changes and the proliferation of multinational enterprises (MNEs) in the period following World War II led to a reevaluation of management education, a renewed interest in understanding the nature of managerial work, and a formulation of new business strategies to compete at home and abroad. It was concluded that management education programs were not providing their graduates with the skills and knowledge necessary to succeed in an ever more complex and interrelated world. Others noted the lack of relevance and growing divide between management theory and practice. Inquiries into the nature of managerial work would challenge established orthodoxies, as business strategists faced exceptional challenges and opportunities in developed and emerging nations. If any one factor explained the concern for improved management theory and practice, it would be the need for more broadly educated managers who could enhance a firm's performance in a rapidly changing global marketplace.

THE EMERGENCE OF GENERAL MANAGEMENT

Although the practice of management is rooted in antiquity, it has only been within the last century that managers have begun to systematically reflect on their experiences to sort out and identify those managerial practices that work better than others. These better practices have been articulated as "principles," but more closely resemble guides to managerial thought and action than scientific facts. The impetus for codifying these principles is a desire to transmit the knowledge necessary to be a successful manager. Those who first tilled the topsoil of this landscape were primarily practitioners. Owen, McCallum, Taylor, Gantt, Fayol, and Barnard are only a few examples of the practitioners who distilled their experiences for the benefit of others.

If not the first, Henri Fayol was one of the earliest practitioners to advance a formal statement of management principles. He believed that a lack of theory made it more difficult to teach

management because managers' experiences were limited to specific situations and not easily applied by managers in other settings. Fayol defined *theory* as "a collection of principles, rules, methods, and procedures tried and checked by general experience."[1] As outlined in Chapter 10, he used his experience as an executive to identify the elements or functions that compose a manager's job. This experience taught Fayol that "there is nothing rigid or absolute in management affairs."[2] He thus expected new principles to emerge and to be "tried and "checked" in the crucible of real-world experience.

PRINCIPLES OF MANAGEMENT AND THE FUNCTIONS OF MANAGEMENT

As has been recounted, Fayol's work only received widespread recognition outside France following World War II. Like Max Weber, Fayol and his contributions to the evolution of management thought were not fully appreciated in their own time—they had to wait until cultural conditions created the need to think in theoretical terms. To wit, the post–World War II economic expansion and the translation of Fayol's *General and Industrial Management* from its original French into English unleashed a renewed interest in Fayol's ideas about managing and spawned numerous "principles of management" textbooks. William H. Newman authored one of the earliest and most successful of these texts. His *Administrative Action: The Techniques of Organization and Management* was published in 1951. Major sections covered planning, organizing, assembling resources, directing, and controlling. Newman defined *administration* as "the guidance, leadership, and control of the efforts of a group of individuals toward some common goal."[3]

Courtesy of Arthur G. Bedeian

William H. Newman

Though Newman's description of administration resembles Fayol's "elements of management," he recalled that he was then "unacquainted" with Fayol's work. He was influenced, like so many others, by the earlier works of Taylor, Barnard, Ralph C. Davis, and Luther H. Gulick.[4] Much like Fayol, Newman noted the importance of objectives in shaping the character of an organization. He felt that an organization's basic objectives should define its place or niche in an industry, define its social philosophy as a business "citizen," and establish its general managerial philosophy.[5]

George R. Terry authored a second influential textbook from this era. Published in 1953, it was titled simply *Principles of Management.* Terry considered management to be "the activity which plans, organizes, and controls the operations of the basic elements of men, materials, machines, methods, money, and markets, providing direction and coordination, and giving leadership to human efforts, to achieve the sought objectives of the enterprise."[6] He viewed management as a "vital process" that included planning, organizing, directing, coordinating, controlling, and leading. Terry defined a *principle* as "a fundamental statement providing a guide to action," and his principles, like Fayol's, were not meant to be rigid or absolute.

[1] Henri Fayol, *General and Industrial Management*, trans. Constance Storrs (London: Sir Isaac Pitman and Sons, 1949), p. 15.
[2] *Ibid.*, p. 19.
[3] William H. Newman, *Administrative Action: The Techniques of Organization and Management* (Englewood Cliffs, NJ: Prentice-Hall, 1951), p. 1.
[4] *Idem*, "The Takeoff," in Arthur G. Bedeian, ed., *Management Laureates: A Collection of Autobiographical Essays*, vol. 2 (Greenwich, CT: JAI Press, 1993), p. 385.
[5] *Idem*, "Basic Objectives Which Shape the Character of the Company," *Journal of Business of the University of Chicago* 26(4) (October 1953), pp. 211–223.
[6] George R. Terry, *Principles of Management* (Homewood, IL: Richard D. Irwin, 1953), p. 3.

Writing in their 1955 textbook *Principles of Management: An Analysis of Managerial Functions*, Harold D. "Howdy" Koontz and Cyril J. O'Donnell defined *management* as "the function of getting things done through others."[7] According to Koontz and O'Donnell, managers were known by the basic managerial functions they performed: planning, organizing, staffing, directing, and controlling. They stressed that each of these functions promoted internal coordination. Coordination, however, was not a separate function, but was the result of effectively utilizing the five basic functions that all managers perform. Koontz and O'Donnell identified a number of management principles, including "the principle of parity of authority and responsibility," "the principle of unity of command," and "the principle of strategic factors." The Koontz and O'Donnell text became an enduring, integral part of the search for a systematic body of management knowledge.

Fayol's influence was apparent in all of these textbooks, as each viewed management as a process, or set of ongoing activities, replete with guiding principles. Although the names used to identify the various functions composing the "management process" varied across texts, they all largely followed the same framework laid out by Fayol decades earlier. Likewise, all considered management to be a distinct intellectual pursuit that could be distilled into principles and, hence, into a general theory of management.

PETER F. DRUCKER AND THE PRACTICE OF MANAGEMENT

Peter F. Drucker

Peter F. Drucker, one of the twentieth century's most influential management thinkers, titled his autobiography *Adventures of a Bystander*, which was anything but an accurate description of his life and work.[8] Drucker achieved prominence through his writings and consulting, and made significant contributions to management practice. Largely influenced by economist Joseph A. Schumpeter (see Chapter 18), a fellow Austrian, Drucker viewed free-market economies as being in a constant state of creation, growth, stagnation, and decline. What kept an organization from failing was the ability of its managers (echoing Schumpeter) to give birth to innovations in new products, new methods of production, new markets, new uses of raw materials, and new forms of organization that drive economic success.

Drucker stressed that managers should establish objectives in each area vital to an organization's existence. He identified eight "key result areas": market standing (measuring against a market's potential); innovation (in products and services, or in improving how these products and services are made or delivered); productivity (a yardstick for "constant improvement"); physical and financial resources (defining needs, planning, and acquiring); profitability (for rate of return on investment); manager performance and development ("management by objectives" and self-control); worker performance and attitude (employee relations); and public responsibility (participating "responsibly in society").[9] Before setting objectives, managers had to first ask the "right questions": What is our business? Who is our customer? What do our customers buy? What is the value of our business to our customers? What will our business be? And what should it be?[10]

Although other authors had written about the need for establishing objectives, Drucker was the first to coin the phrase "management by objectives" (MBO). According to Drucker, "A manager's job should be based on a task to be performed in order to attain the company's

[7] Harold D. Koontz and Cyril J. O'Donnell, *Principles of Management: An Analysis of Managerial Functions* (New York: McGraw-Hill, 1955), pp. v, 3.
[8] Peter F. Drucker, *Adventures of a Bystander* (New York: HarperCollins, 1991).
[9] *Idem, The Practice of Management* (New York: Harper & Row, 1954), pp. 63–84.
[10] *Ibid.*, pp. 49–61.

objectives. . . . [T]he manager should be directed and controlled by the objectives of performance rather than by his boss."[11] Management-by-objectives was to replace management-by-drive, and control was to be self-control rather than control from above. Knowing a company's objectives, and those of each of its departments, managers could direct their own activities:

> The only principle that can do this is management by objectives and self-control. . . . It substitutes for control from outside the stricter, more exacting and more effective control from the inside. It motivates the manager to action not because somebody tells him to do something . . . but because the objective needs of his task demand it.[12]

Drucker maintained that MBO was not new, having been practiced earlier at General Motors by Alfred P. Sloan and at DuPont by Pierre du Pont and Donaldson Brown. Whatever the case, Ronald G. Greenwood concluded, "[I]t took Drucker to put it all together, think through the underlying philosophy, and then explain and advocate it in a form others could use."[13]

For Drucker, 90 percent of managerial work was generic, working with and through people to lead in such a manner that they could use their individual strengths and knowledge productively. The remaining 10 percent varied according to the mission, culture, history, and vocabulary of any specific type of organization, whether for profit or not-for-profit.[14] Drucker complemented Fayol by further stressing the need to set objectives, the value of participative goal-setting, and the existential necessity of organizations to give birth to innovations that drive economic success.

MANAGEMENT EDUCATION: CHALLENGES AND CONSEQUENCES

In 1959, two reports appeared that would have a significant impact on management education. Unlike Morris L. Cooke's study for the Carnegie Foundation for the Advancement of Teaching in 1910 (see Chapter 8), educators took these new reports seriously. The Ford Foundation, the world's largest philanthropy, commissioned the first report by R. Aaron Gordon and James E. Howell.[15] The Carnegie Corporation sponsored the second report by Frank C. Pierson.[16] Although the authors of the two reports exchanged some of their findings, they reached their conclusions independently; both reports were sharp indictments of collegiate business education in the United States, noting that schools of business administration were in a state of turmoil with little agreement on what should be taught and how. The reports concluded that by adhering to outdated methods of education, the nation's business schools were not preparing competent, imaginative, and flexible managers for an ever-changing economy.[17] Courses overemphasized training for specific jobs rather than preparing broadly educated graduates with the range of intellectual skills required for a successful business career.

The reports advised that the path to preparing managers for the future resided in changing the content of the typical business-school curricula. More stress needed to be placed on providing a general education, especially in the humanities and liberal arts, mathematics, and the social sciences. The call for more instruction in mathematics and the social sciences led to an influx of specialists—including industrial engineers, operations-research analysts, communication

[11] *Ibid.*, p. 137.
[12] *Ibid.*
[13] Ronald G. Greenwood, "Management by Objectives: As Developed by Peter Drucker, Assisted by Harold Smiddy," *Academy of Management Review* 6(2) (April 1981), p. 230.
[14] Peter F. Drucker, *Management Challenges for the 21st Century* (New York: Harper Business, 1999).
[15] Robert A. Gordon and James E. Howell, *Higher Education for Business* (New York: Columbia University Press, 1959). See also Francis X. Sutton, "The Ford Foundation: The Early Years," *Dædalus* 116(1) (Winter 1987), p. 52.
[16] Frank C. Pierson, *The Education of American Businessmen: A Study of University-College Programs in Business Administration* (New York: McGraw-Hill, 1959).
[17] For an analysis of collegiate business education in the United States prior to the Gordon and Howell and Pierson reports, see James H. S. Bossard and J. Frederic Dewhurst, *University Education for Business* (Philadelphia, PA: University of Pennsylvania Press, 1931).

theorists, psychologists, and sociologists to teach these subjects.[18] For management education, in particular, Gordon and Howell noted at least four areas that required strengthening: (1) managerial problem-solving through the scientific method and quantitative analysis; (2) organization theory; (3) management principles; and (4) human relations.[19] They recommended that these areas be integrated into a sequence of courses rather than each area being covered separately. Toward this end, Gordon and Howell further proposed that Business Policy serve as a capstone course to provide an integrative experience for all business-school majors. Finally, they called for business-school faculty to engage in scholarly research. Other academic disciplines had adopted the German model of higher education (with its emphasis on research) as far back as the late 1870s.[20] It was only after the Gordon and Howell report was released that the imperative to "publish or perish" began to take hold in the nation's premier business schools, and tenure and promotions were made contingent upon establishing a national reputation based on peer-reviewed publications appearing in refereed journals. Patricia G. McLaren has argued that academics took the Gordon and Howell report out of context, interpreting it as a call for more rigorous research rather than a call for research having more relevance to students and practitioners.[21] Not coincidentally, it was also during this period that developing a lengthy publication record took precedence in business schools over undergraduate teaching.[22] It was at this time, too, that the quality and extent of faculty research became increasingly emphasized by the (then titled) American Assembly of Collegiate Schools of Business, the agency charged with accrediting university business programs.

Courtesy of Arthur G. Bedeian

Harold D. Koontz

THE "MANAGEMENT THEORY JUNGLE"

Although the Gordon and Howell report noted that there were numerous approaches to the study of management, it was Harold D. Koontz who delineated the differences between these approaches and applied the catchy label "management theory jungle" to their varying perspectives.[23] Koontz noted six main groups, or schools, of management thought: (1) the *management process school* (e.g., Fayol's principles and process); (2) the *empirical school* (e.g., case analyses/the study of experiences); (3) the *human behavior school* (e.g., human relations/behavioral sciences); (4) the *social system school* (e.g., sociological theory/cultural interrelationships); (5) the *decision theory school* (e.g., economic theory/consumer choice); and (6) the *mathematical school* (e.g., operations research/management science). Koontz acknowledged that each school had something to offer management theory but suggested that content and tools should not be confused. A familiarity with decision-making techniques or mathematical methods alone, for instance, was insufficient preparation to be a successful manager. Preferably, each school of management thought should provide managers with useful content *and* tools that, when taken together, offered a cumulative advantage.

[18] William P. Bottom, "Organizing Intelligence: Development of Behavioral Science and the Research Based Model of Business Education," *Journal of the History of the Behavioral Sciences* 45(3) (Summer 2009), pp. 253–283.

[19] Gordon and Howell, *Higher Education for Business*, pp. 179–182.

[20] Laurence R. Veysey, *The Emergence of the American University* (Chicago, IL: University of Chicago Press, 1970), p. 129.

[21] Patricia Genoe McLaren, "Stop Blaming Gordon and Howell: Unpacking the Complex History Behind the Research-Based Model of Business Education," *Academy of Management Learning and Education* 18(1) (March 2019), pp. 43–58.

[22] Rakesh Khurana, *From Higher Aims to Hired Hands: The Social Transformation of American Business Schools and the Unfulfilled Promise of Management as a Profession* (Princeton, NJ: Princeton University Press, 2010), p. 307.

[23] Harold D. Koontz, "The Management Theory Jungle," *Journal of the Academy of Management* 4(3) (December 1961), pp. 174–188; *idem*, "Making Sense of Management Theory," *Harvard Business Review* 40(4) (July–August 1962), pp. 24–46.

Revisiting the theory jungle some 20 years later, Koontz found it had become "more dense and impenetrable," having expanded from 6 to 11 schools.[24] Koontz noted, "The management theory jungle is still with us. . . . Perhaps the most effective way [out of the jungle] would be for leading managers to take a more active role in narrowing the widening gap . . . between professional practice and our college and university business [schools]." He chastised his fellow academics for failing to undertake research more relevant to practice:

> I see too many academics forgetting what I think our job is in management, and that is to organize available knowledge; develop new knowledge, of course, but organize it in such a way that it can be useful to practicing managers to underpin management . . . I think we have to agree that management theory and science should underpin practice, otherwise why develop it?[25]

Thomas J. Peters and Robert H. Waterman, McKinsey & Co. consultants, would have agreed with Koontz about theory and practice. Based on a study of 43 companies, they identified various managerial practices that lead to superior performance, including developing a corporate culture that emphasizes shared values; adopting human-resource policies and practices that promote a "we" rather than "they" mentality; and implementing "loose-tight" properties that keep a firm on target without stifling change and innovation.[26] U.S. managers responded to Peters and Waterman's book, *In Search of Excellence*, which sold three million copies within the first few years of being published. The initial academic reaction was frosty, but in retrospect it has been suggested that this response could be explained by the fact that "Peters and Waterman gave managers a genuinely new way of seeing (and of doing) while they confronted academics with the uncomfortable thought that maybe [their] carefully crafted theoretic modeling is of marginal significance to practical management."[27] It should be noted, however, that academic skepticism was well founded, as several of the companies extolled as "the best" experienced difficulties soon after the book's publication and Peters later created doubt as to whether he and Waterman "faked the data" on which their results were based.[28]

MANAGEMENT EDUCATION: THE PORTER–MCKIBBIN REPORT

The American Assembly of Collegiate Schools of Business International sponsored a 3-year comprehensive study of management education that surveyed practitioners and academics. The authors of the report, Lyman W. Porter and Lawrence E. McKibbin, noted that a breadth in knowledge and intellectual skills is required to integrate problem finding and problem solving across various business functions; yet many business-school faculty members lacked relevant work experience and were too narrowly educated to "appreciate the complexities and subtleties of business."[29] They recommended that faculty, in their teaching, should pay more attention to external factors, especially trends in international business; develop a greater ability to integrate knowledge across business functions; put more emphasis on interpersonal and communication skills; and nurture Ph.D. students who would have analytical sophistication in addition to "the sharpened and broadened perspective of real world work experience."[30]

---

[24] For a discussion on these schools circa 1961 and 1980, see Harold D. Koontz, "The Management Theory Jungle Revisited," *Academy of Management Review* 5(2) (April 1980), pp. 175–187. See also *idem*, "Toward an Operational Theory of Management," in Melvin Zimet and Ronald G. Greenwood, eds., *The Evolving Science of Management: The Collected Papers of Harold Smiddy and Papers by Others in His Honor* (New York: American Management Associations, 1979), pp. 327–347.
[25] Harold D. Koontz quoted in Ronald G. Greenwood, "Harold Koontz: A Reminiscence," unpublished paper presented at the annual meeting of the Academy of Management, Boston, MA, August 14, 1984, pp. 5–6, Ronald G. Greenwood Collection, University Archives, Alvin Sherman Library, Nova Southeastern University, Fort Lauderdale, FL.
[26] Thomas J. Peters and Robert H. Waterman, Jr., *In Search of Excellence* (New York: Harper & Row, 1982).
[27] Cliff Oswick, Tom Keenoy, and David Grant, "Metaphor and Analytical Reasoning in Organization Theory: Beyond Orthodoxy," *Academy of Management Review* 27(2) (April 2002), p. 300.
[28] Tom Peters, "Tom Peters's True Confessions," *Fast Company* no. 53 (December 2001), pp. 78–92.
[29] Lyman W. Porter and Lawrence E. McKibbin, *Management Education and Development: Drift or Thrust into the 21st Century?* (New York: McGraw-Hill, 1988), p. 132.
[30] *Ibid.*, p. 327.

In Porter and McKibbin's view, management educators needed to avoid a further proliferation of theoretical approaches, couple theory more closely with application, appreciate external factors affecting the management discipline, and study business in global settings. Writing 14 years later, Jeffrey Pfeffer and Christiana T. Fong disappointedly concluded that management research continued to have little relevance to the practice of management, placed too much emphasis on "hard" (quantitative) skills at the expense of "soft" (people) skills, and many faculty still lacked the perspective afforded by work experience.[31]

THE MANAGEMENT THEORY–PRACTICE DIVIDE

It has been acknowledged that management practitioners do not look to academic research for guidance nor do academics look to practitioners for research topics or to assist in interpreting research findings, thereby creating a "great divide" between theory and practice.[32] It would seem that practicing managers and management educators have different ideologies and different values—one seeking to solve day-to-day and bottom-line challenges and the other seeking tenure, promotions, and standing among their colleagues. A study of human-resource managers documents the lack of knowledge transfer between practitioners and educators, finding that less than 1 percent of practicing managers regularly consult the management literature and that 75 percent never do so.[33]

Donald C. Hambrick has argued that this practice–theory gap results from the desire on the part of management educators to gain academic respectability among their peers by publishing theory-laden articles in journals with a high "impact factor" (as defined by others with similar goals). These articles contrast with those published in marketing, finance, and accounting journals where the word "theory" seldom appears.[34] The infatuation of management educators with theory is compounded by a lack of theory testing. K. Michele Kacmar and J. Michael Whitfield found that less than 10 percent of the citations in the *Academy of Management Journal* and the *Academy of Management Review*, widely regarded as the discipline's most prestigious journals, were to direct tests of their authors' prior theories.[35] Ajnesh Prasad has argued that the "fetishization" of theory has thwarted rather than enabled knowledge production by encouraging both a proliferation of theoretical constructs with little analytical distinction and theory being built upon theory rather than empirical validation.[36] A 2007 study of management educators found that the relative balance between management theory and application in university instruction had tipped in favor of the former at the expense of the latter. This finding lends "credibility to the notion that theories are emphasized to a greater extent than the usefulness of those theories in practice at all levels of . . . management instruction."[37]

The *Academy of Management Executive* (*AME*) was created in 1987 as a means for management educators to reach a practitioner audience. Toward this end, *AME*'s editors elicited practice-oriented submissions, provided "executive summaries" for busy readers, and sought to

---

[31] Jeffrey Pfeffer and Christina T. Fong, "The End of Business Schools? Less Success Than Meets the Eye," *Academy of Management Learning & Education* 1(1) (September 2002), p. 91.

[32] Sara L. Rynes, Kenneth G. Brown, and Amy E. Colbert, "Seven Common Misperceptions about Human Resource Practices: Research Findings versus Practitioner Beliefs," *Academy of Management Learning & Education* 18(3) (2002), p. 100. See also Paula Ungureanu and Fabiola Bertolotti, "From Gaps to Tangles: A Relational Framework for the Future of the Theory-Practice Debate," *Futures* 118 (April 2020), pp. 1–15.

[33] Sara L. Rynes, Jean M. Bartunek, and Richard L. Daft, "Across the Great Divide: Knowledge Creation and Transfer Between Practitioners and Academics," *Academy of Management Journal* 44(2) (April 2001), pp. 340–355.

[34] Donald C. Hambrick, "The Field of Management's Devotion to Theory: Too Much of a Good Thing?" *Academy of Management Journal* 50(6) (December 2006), pp. 1346–1352.

[35] K. Michele Kacmar and J. Michael Whitfield, "An Additional Rating Method for Journal Articles in the Field of Management," *Organizational Research Methods* 3(4) (October 2000), p. 397. For a similar analysis (and similar results) of citations in *Administrative Science Quarterly*, see Gerald F. Davis and Christopher Marquis, "Prospects for Organization Theory in the Early Twenty-First Century: Institutional Fields and Mechanisms," *Organization Science* 16(4) (July–August 2005), pp. 332–343.

[36] Ajnesh Prasad, "What's Up With Our Obsession With the Theoretical Contribution: A Means to an End or an End In and Of Itself?," *Organization*, in press.

[37] Daniel A. Wren, Jonathon R. B. Halbesleben, and M. Ronald Buckley, "The Theory–Applications Balance in Management Pedagogy: A Longitudinal Update," *Academy of Management Learning & Education* 6(4) (December 2007), p. 490.

publish articles on topics of interest to a managerial audience. *AME* was superseded by the *Academy of Management Perspectives* (*AMP*) in 2005. The new editor stated, "the direction of *AME* will change. . . . We are interested in evidence-based manuscripts that rely on research findings to address the needs of Academy members outside their areas of research."[38] This restricted focus on evidenced management findings that "rely on research" contrasts with the wider view that "evidence" may also come from sources such as internal company metrics, as well as "professional experience."[39] The journal notably overlooked Henri Fayol's suggestion that management principles be "tried and checked by general experience."[40]

Denise M. Rousseau echoed *AMP*'s change in direction in her 2005 Academy Presidential Address, stating: "Evidence-based management [EBM] means translating principles based on best evidence into organizational practices."[41] She cited Edwin A. Locke and Gary P. Latham's goal-setting theory (see Chapter 20) as an illustration of a sustained research program (replete with replicated findings and practical applications) to identify the principles of task motivation. In a later article, Rousseau and Sharon McCarthy noted that EBM is a long way from being realized, lamenting: "In contrast to medicine and education, . . . EBM today is only hypothetical."[42] In making this judgment, Rousseau and McCarthy noted that management-education programs do not offer opportunities for clinical training or lab work or for students to gain mentoring experiences in non-classroom settings. Moreover, they observed that business-school students too often lack experience in reading, evaluating, and interpreting academic findings or the knowledge necessary to search for relevant information in the management literature.

What Rousseau and McCarthy lamented in 2007 continues to be true. Evidence-based management remains "hypothetical." Following a decade of concern for narrowing the theory–practice divide and fulfilling the promise of EBM, Jone L. Pearce and Laura Huang examined the *Academy of Management Journal* and *Administrative Science Quarterly* and found little "actionable" research relevant to practice and teaching. Over the past half-century, articles in both journals had become less likely to report practical applications.[43] On balance, management scholarship has produced mountains of data, but little of practical relevance. Dennis Tourish has criticized much of academic management research as often being "overblown nonsense."[44] This situation has been made worse by an increasing public skepticism toward research findings due to a growing distrust of "academics, scientific research, and professional expertise in general."[45] This distrust has grown as evidence has accumulated that questionable research practices (QRPs) such as data fabrication and data falsification are more common than previously acknowledged, and that there has been an ideological corruption of science whereby political doctrine, rather than academic rigor, determines what is published, who is promoted, and what grants are funded.[46]

---

[38] Peter Cappelli, "From the Editor," *Academy of Management Perspectives* 19(1) (February 2005), p. 5.

[39] Eric Barends, Denise M. Rousseau, and Rob B. Briner, *Evidenced-Based Management: The Basic Principles* (Amsterdam: Center for Evidence-Based Management, 2014), p. 5. Accessed at https://www.cebma.org/wp-content/uploads/Evidence-Based-Practice-The-Basic-Principles-vs-Dec-2015.pdf.

[40] Fayol, *General and Industrial Management* (Storrs translation), p. 15.

[41] Denise M. Rousseau, "Is There Such a Thing as Evidence-Based Management?" *Academy of Management Review* 31(2) (April 2006), p. 252. See also *idem*, "The Realist Rationality of Evidence-Based Management," *Academy of Management Learning & Education* 19(3) (September 2020), pp. 415–424,

[42] Denise M. Rousseau and Sharon McCarthy, "Educating Managers from an Evidence-Based Perspective," *Academy of Management Learning & Education* 6(1) (March 2007), p. 84. For a review of recent developments in evidence-based management, see Sara L. Rynes and Jean Bartunek, "Evidence-Based Management: Foundations, Development, Controversies and Future," *Annual Review of Organizational Psychology and Organizational Behavior* 4 (2017), pp. 235–261.

[43] Jone L. Pearce and Laura Huang, "The Decreasing Value of Our Research to Management Education," *Academy of Management Learning & Education* 11(2) (June 2012), pp. 247–262.

[44] Dennis Tourish, "The Triumph of Nonsense in Management Studies," *Academy of Management Learning & Education* 19(1) (March 2021), pp. 99–109.

[45] Sara L. Rynes, Amy E. Colbert, and Ernest H. O'Boyle, "When the 'Best Available Evidence' Doesn't Win: How Doubts About Science and Scientists Threaten the Future of Evidenced-Based Management," *Journal of Management* 44(8) (November 2018), p. 2995.

[46] Arthur G. Bedeian, Shannon G. Taylor, and Alan N. Miller, "Management Science on the Credibility Bubble: Cardinal Sins and Various Misdemeanors," *Academy of Management Learning & Education* 9(4) (December 2010), pp. 715–725; Lawrence Krauss, "The Ideological Corruption of Science," *Wall Street Journal* (July 13, 2020), p. A19.

Management educators have long been faulted for being more interested in their careers than in educating the constituencies of management knowledge—students, practitioners, public-policy makers, and society in general.[47] Bruce E. Kaufman has noted the resulting asymmetry in the relationship between the practitioner and academic communities. He attributes this imbalance "to the penchant of academics to view themselves as higher-positioned scientist-scholars who *talk at* and *talk down* to practitioners rather than *talk with* them."[48] Such a pretentious attitude is, of course, no basis for establishing a close working relationship. One possibility for bridging the practice–theory divide is to form mutually respectful partnerships involving managers and researchers. It has been suggested that "[m]anagement researchers must take the first step. Business firms have proven they can survive and be successful without depending on scholarly management research. Researchers must demonstrate how they can add value by offering ideas that improve organizational performance."[49] A survey of 828 academics and 939 managers has found a number of shared interests between management researchers and practicing managers. These include reducing or eliminating pay inequality, reducing or eliminating workplace discrimination, and reducing or eliminating unethical business practices.[50] History is rife with examples of executives who, drawing on personal experience, have contributed to management understanding. As a prime example, as recounted in Chapter 15, James C. Worthy, a vice president at Sears, Roebuck, served in the U.S. Commerce Department in both the Franklin D. Roosevelt and Dwight D. Eisenhower administrations; partnered with the University of Chicago Human-Relations Group in conducting seminal studies of employee morale and organization structure; became a Fellow of the Academy of Management; and, following his retirement, worked as a professor at the Kellogg School of Management at Northwestern University.[51] He had a talent for combining theory and practice, and provided a vivid example of how partnerships between practicing managers and management researchers can yield practice-relevant knowledge.

POST-FAYOL: STUDIES OF MANAGERIAL WORK

Henri Fayol was among the first to systematically reflect on his experiences and observations as a manager in an attempt to sort out and identify what managers do and what managerial practices work better than others. Although Fayol's reflections provided a conceptual basis for teaching management, alternative approaches have since been employed to analyze the nature of managerial work. In studying the CEOs of five medium to large private and semipublic organizations, Henry Mintzberg found that their daily activities were fragmented, short-term responses rather than deliberative, analytical, and logical actions, as Fayol had suggested. In contrast to engaging in Fayol's "elements of management," Mintzberg concluded that the "typical" manager performs 10 different, but highly interrelated, roles that may be grouped into three categories: (1) interpersonal, (2) informational, and (3) decisional. The interpersonal role derives from a manager's formal authority and occurs when dealing with others as a *figurehead, leader,* or *liaison*. The informational role involves a manager receiving, storing, and sending information as a *monitor,*

---

[47] See, for example, Arthur G. Bedeian, "Totems and Taboos: Undercurrents in the Management Discipline," *Academy of Management News* 19(4) (October 1989), p. 4.

[48] Bruce E. Kaufman, "The Academic–Practitioner Gap: Past Time to Bring in the Practitioner Perspective," *Human Resource Management Review* 32(2) (June 2022), article 100895.

[49] Eric W. Ford, W. Jack Duncan, Arthur G. Bedeian, Peter M. Ginter, Matthew D. Rousculp, and Alice W. Adams, "Mitigating Risks, Visible Hands, Inevitable Disasters: Management Research that Matters to Managers," *Academy of Management Executive* 17(1) (February 2003), p. 58.

[50] George C. Banks, Jeffrey M. Pollack, Jaime E. Bochantin, Bradley L. Kirkman, Christopher E. Whelphy, and Ernest H. O'Boyle, "Management's Science–Practice Gap: A Grand Challenge for All Stakeholders," *Academy of Management Journal* 59(6) (December 2016), pp. 2205–2231.

[51] James C. Worthy, "From Practice to Theory: Odyssey of a Manager," in Arthur G. Bedeian, ed., *Management Laureates*, vol. 3 (1993), pp. 375–414. See also *idem, Brushes with History: Recollections of a Many-Favored Life* (Evanston, IL: Thomson-Shore, 1998).

disseminator, or *spokesperson*. The decisional role arises when a manager commits an organization to action as an *entrepreneur, disturbance handler, resource allocator,* or *negotiator*.[52]

After extensive interviews and observations of managers at work, Rosemary Stewart offered another view of what managers do by examining: (1) demands—what had to be done in a job; (2) constraints—internal and external limits on what could be done in a job; and (3) choices—areas in which different managers could do the same job in different ways.[53] Using staffing as an example, a manager must find and select qualified employees; in doing so, a manager is restricted to a company's wage scales, the available labor supply, general economic conditions, and employment laws, and must choose one job candidate over all others. In a similar study, based on the observation of 15 general managers (GMs) at nine companies, John P. Kotter found that the best GMs (1) could be very different in terms of personal characteristics and behaviors; (2) thought of themselves as generalists, yet each had a specialty that matched a specific job's demands; and (3) had a detailed knowledge of their industry's intricacies and possessed a network of cooperative working relationships.[54] Studies of management across borders would perhaps challenge these Western-based views.

GLOBAL STUDIES OF MANAGERIAL WORK

Is a nineteenth-century theory proposed by the managing director of a French coal and iron firm appropriate for the twenty-first century? How should managers be educated and trained to succeed in a global economy? In the late 1970s, the oft-asked question "if Japan can . . . why can't we?" was a wake-up call for managers (and management educators) in the United States and around the world seeking to remain globally competitive in an increasingly complex and interrelated world (see Chapter 21).

At the mid-point of the twentieth century, the United States lagged behind other nations in international business education.[55] Universities worldwide began offering Master of Business Administration programs to prepare students to be globally competent, making "MBA" an international acronym. Fayol's reflections on what managers do and what managerial practices work better than others were pushed aside in favor of "modern" theories. Ernest R. Archer noted, "[T]he purging of Fayol's principles from the mainstream of management thought . . . in the United States is a rather peculiar phenomenon, especially when it is considered . . . that the principles were the guiding beacons for the practice of management . . . for nearly four decades prior to the 1960s."[56] Ian Smith and Trevor Boyns noted a similar turning away from Fayol's pioneering work toward an interest in observations about the nature of managerial work *à la* Mintzberg, Stewart, and Kotter: "Since 1970, the focus of management thinking has turned away from the functions of management toward trying to understand management and managing through an examination of what managers do."[57]

Michael Lubatkin and colleagues suggested that Mintzberg's analysis of the roles managers enact raised the question of whether the nature of managerial work is "universal." In an effort to answer this question, they studied seven Southern- and Central-African nations, plus Senegal and Hungary. They concluded: "[A]t some broad level, all managers, even those from non-western, non-industrialized, non–Anglo Saxon origins, face a similar set of administrative

---

[52] Henry Mintzberg, *The Nature of Managerial Work* (New York: Harper & Row, 1973).
[53] Rosemary Stewart, "A Model for Understanding Managerial Jobs and Behavior," *Academy of Management Review* 7(1) (January 1982), pp. 7–13.
[54] John P. Kotter, *The General Managers* (New York: Free Press, 1982).
[55] Chuck C. Y. Kwok and Jeffrey S. Arpan, "A Comparison of International Business Education in the U.S. and European Business Schools in the 1990s," *Management International Review* 34(4) (1999), pp. 357–379.
[56] Ernest R. Archer, "Toward a Revival of the Principles of Management," *Industrial Management* 32(1) (January–February 1990), p. 19.
[57] Ian Smith and Trevor Boyns, "British Management Theory and Practice: The Impact of Henri Fayol," *Management Decision* 43(10) (2005), p. 1331.

challenges that cause them to independently construct similar solutions, or mimic the skill activities of others."[58,59] In line with this conclusion, after reviewing the international management literature, Taïeb Hafsi and Mehda Farashahi also found that there was a "widespread applicability of western-based concepts of general management and organizational theories to developing countries."[60]

Mintzberg acknowledged that "managerial work is a fundamental practice that does not change . . . some of the factors we assume to be most significant—such as national culture (for example, managing in China versus the U.S.)—may not be that significant, while others—such as the forms of organization (professional versus machine, etc.)—may be more so than previously thought."[61] He noted that his 10 managerial roles received attention because they replaced "the tired words of 'planning, organizing, coordinating, commanding, and controlling' (all words for controlling) that had dominated the literature for the last half a century."[62] Are Fayol's reflections "tired words," or do they continue to have merit? Stephen J. Carroll and Dennis J. Gillen argued that the managerial functions Fayol identified "still represent the most useful way of conceptualizing the manager's job, especially for management education . . . [because they] provide clear and discrete methods of classifying the thousands of activities that managers carry out and the techniques they use in terms of the functions they perform for the achievement of organizational goals."[63]

MANAGING ACROSS BORDERS

Geert Hofstede was among the first to challenge the global applicability of Western-based theories with their emphasis on market processes, stress on individuals, and focus on management rather than workers. His doubt in this regard evolved from a project he began in the early 1960s for the "HERMES" corporation (later revealed to be IBM).[64] Drawing on data collected in 53 countries and regions, he identified four basic societal-level work-related values (i.e., dimensions) across which different cultures could be compared: power–distance, uncertainty avoidance, individualism–collectivism, and masculinity–femininity.

Power–distance relates to a culture's acceptance of hierarchy and the degree of power inequality that is acceptable. In cultures where equality is valued, participative management and joint decision-making are likely to be viewed favorably. In cultures where power distance is acceptable, hierarchical authority is more likely to be accepted without question. *Uncertainty–avoidance* concerns a culture's tolerance of uncertainty and ambiguity. In cultures where structured interactions are preferred over unstructured processes, seniority-based systems, for example, are more likely to be valued over performance-based outcomes. *Individualism–collectivism* reflects the tendency within a culture to act as an individual rather than as a member of a group. In cultures high in collectivism, for example, rewarding teamwork is more likely to be preferred over

---

[58] Michael Lubatkin, Momar Ndiaye, and Richard Vengroff, "The Nature of Managerial Work in Developing Countries: A Limited Test of the Universalist Hypothesis," *Journal of International Business Studies* 28(4) (1997), p. 711.

[59] *Ibid.*, p. 727.

[60] Taïeb Hafsi and Mehda Farashahi, "Applicability of Management Theories to Developing Countries: A Synthesis," *Management International Review* 45(4) (2005), p. 488.

[61] Henry Mintzberg, "*The Nature of Managerial Work* (1973) & *Simply Managing: What Managers Do—And Can Do Better* (2013)," *Management* 18(2) (2015), p. 187. Available at https://www.cairn.info/revue-management-2015-2-page-186.htm#pa11.

[62] *Ibid.*

[63] Stephen J. Carroll and Dennis J. Gillen, "Are the Classical Management Functions Useful in Describing Managerial Work?" *Academy of Management Review* 12(1) (January 1987), p. 48. See also Michael J. Fells, "Fayol Stands the Test of Time," *Journal of Management History* 6(8) (2000), pp. 345–360; David A. Lamond, "Henry Mintzberg vs. Henri Fayol: Of Lighthouses, Cubists, and the Emperor's New Clothes," *Journal of Applied Management and Entrepreneurship* 8(4) (October 2003), pp. 5–23; *idem*, "A Matter of Style: Reconciling Henry and Henri," *Management Decision* 42(2) (2004), pp. 330–356.

[64] Geert Hofstede, *Culture's Consequences: International Differences in Work-Related Values* (London: Sage, 1980); *idem*, *Culture's Consequences: Comparing Values, Behavior, Institutions, and Organizations Across Nations* (Thousand Oaks, CA: Sage, 2001).

individual rewards. *Masculinity–femininity* reflects a culture's preference for social differentiation between men and women. In a masculine culture that emphasizes differences between the sexes, assertive workplace behavior is more likely to be seen as acceptable than in a feminine culture that values quality of life and social relations.

When combined, Hofstede felt these four dimensions explained some 50 percent of the cross-cultural differences in employees' work-related values, the remainder being country specific. In a later work, Hofstede and Michael H. Bond identified a fifth dimension, which they labeled "Confucian Dynamism." This dimension was found in Eastern nations such as South Korea, Taiwan, Hong Kong, and Japan, where the teachings of Confucius were highly regarded. These nations were more long-term oriented, preferred to order relationships by status, and were persevering in working and thrift habits. These qualities were not found in Western nations, which were less accepting of hierarchy, more individualistic, and short-term oriented.[65] Hofstede and Bond did not have results on mainland China, but one study found "Confucian Dynamism" to be positively related to the virtues found in Max Weber's Protestant Work Ethic (see Chapter 2) and a contributing factor in the economic success of the "Five Asian Dragons" (China, Japan, Hong Kong, Taiwan, and Singapore).[66]

A substantial body of research emanated from Hofstede and Bond's work. For example, it was found that compensation based on seniority plans is more likely to be acceptable in cultures where there are lower levels of uncertainty–avoidance (less willing to take risks), but individualistic cultures tend to prefer pay for performance plans where the inclination to take risks is higher.[67] Quality Control Circles, as practiced in Japan, and other similar group-work arrangements are less likely to be practiced in the United States due to cultural expectations relating to work autonomy and performance feedback.[68] Jerald Greenberg reasoned that because a concern for justice is "a functional prerequisite for social life," it exists in all cultures. He warned, however, "justice standards" are "highly particularistic," reflecting the internalized norms, collective customs, and unique values that distinguish different cultures. In individualistic cultures, such as the United States, equity is preferred over equality. This contrasts with both the Netherlands, where people favor equality, and India, where people favor distributing outcomes according to need. Studies of other nations and regions reveal additional differences and similarities.[69] Some six years after the 1991 collapse of the Soviet Union, a comparison of Russian managers and business-school students with their U.S. counterparts found the Russian managers to be higher in power–distance (inequality was acceptable) and lower in uncertainty–avoidance (less tolerant of ambiguity).[70]

THE CHANGING SCENE

How managers assemble resources to accomplish a firm's objectives has been a topic of interest for many years. Various attempts have been made to understand why firms exist, how firms differ in resource acquisition and deployment, and why firms vary in corporate governance. We consider these attempts next.

[65] Geert Hofstede and Michael H. Bond, "The Confucian Connection: From Cultural Roots to Economic Growth," *Organizational Dynamics* 16(4) (Summer 1988), pp. 5–21.

[66] Suchuan Zhang, Weiqui Liu, and Xianolang Liu, "Investigating the Relationship Between Protestant Work Ethic and Confucian Dynamism: An Empirical Test in Mainland China," *Journal of Business Ethics* 106(2) (March 2012), pp. 243–252. No religious connotations were implied in this study.

[67] Randall S. Schuler and Nicolai Rogocsky, "Understanding Compensation Practice Variations Across Firms: The Impact of National Culture," *Journal of International Business Studies* 29(1) (1998), pp. 159–177.

[68] Miriam Erez, "Culture and Job Design," *Journal of Organizational Behavior* 31(2–3) (January 2010), pp. 389–400.

[69] Jerald Greenberg, "Studying Organizational Justice Cross-Culturally: Fundamental Challenges," *International Journal of Conflict Management* 12(4) (2001), p. 370.

[70] Detelin S. Elenkov, "Differences and Similarities in Managerial Values Between U.S. and Russian Managers: An Empirical Study," *International Studies of Management and Organization* 27(1) (Spring 1997), pp. 85–106.

NEW INSTITUTIONAL ECONOMICS

As recounted in Chapters 3 and 6, management, as a factor of production, provides a competitive advantage. In Chapter 16, we introduced John R. Commons's notion that *transactions* are the smallest unit of analysis in the transfer of property rights. We also discussed Ronald Coase's interest in knowing why business firms exist if markets are so efficient in allocating resources, and offered that firms come into existence when the cost of securing the resources necessary to produce a desired output is less than the cost of securing those resources on the open market. Beginning in the mid-1970s, Oliver E. Williamson extended Coase's thinking and coined the phrase "new institutional economics" to refer to the study of imperfections in markets that require a consideration of nonmarket factors.[71] These imperfections include laws, cultural constraints, and political systems under which firms must operate, as well as considerations such as "bounded rationality" (Herbert A. Simon's label for Barnard's limits to "the power of choice"[72]; see Chapter 14) and the need for monitoring mechanisms to thwart self-serving "opportunism"—the "effort to realize individual gains through a lack of candor or honesty in transactions."[73] Williamson's opportunism paralleled Barnard's "theory of opportunism,"[74] which Williamson described as "self-interest seeking with guile," as "even among the less opportunistic, most have their price."[75] As viewed by Coase and Williamson, what Alfred D. Chandler branded the "visible hand" of management is typically more efficient in allocating resources than Adam Smith's "invisible hand" of the market because, as a basic factor of production, the authority exercised by an entrepreneur–manager can provide a competitive advantage.[76] In situations where this may not be true, firms may instead elect to compete in the open market.

THE RESOURCE- AND KNOWLEDGE-BASED THEORIES OF THE FIRM

In reflecting on how firms differ, Edith T. Penrose observed, "It is the heterogeneity, and not the homogeneity, of the productive services available or potentially available from its resources that give each firm its unique character."[77] In making this observation, Penrose was emphasizing the competitive advantage afforded by sound management considered as a factor of production:

> [A] firm is more than an administrative unit; it is also a collection of productive resources the disposal of which between uses and over time is determined by administrative decision. . . . management tries to make the best use of the resources available . . . [and] a firm is essentially a pool of resources the utilization of which is organized in an administrative framework.[78]

Penrose's observation would lie fallow for a quarter century before being applied by Birger Wernerfelt in a 1984 paper, "A Resource-Based Theory of the Firm."[79] Wernerfelt reasoned:

---

[71] Oliver E. Williamson, *Markets and Hierarchies, Analysis and Antitrust Implications: A Study in the Economics of Internal Organization* (New York: Free Press, 1975).

[72] Chester I. Barnard, *The Functions of the Executive* (Cambridge, MA: Harvard University Press, 1938), p. 14; Herbert A. Simon, *Administrative Behavior: A Study of Decision-Making Processes in Administrative Organization* (New York: Macmillan, 1947), p. xxiv; and *idem*, *Models of Man: Social and Rational* (New York: John Wiley & Sons, 1957), p. 198.

[73] Oliver E. Williamson, "Markets and Hierarchies: Some Elementary Considerations," *American Economic Review* 63(3) (June 1973), p. 317.

[74] Barnard, *The Functions of the Executive*, pp. 200–211.

[75] Oliver E. Williamson, "Transaction-Cost Economics: The Governance of Contractual Relations," *Journal of Law & Economics* 22(2) (October 1979), p. 234n4.

[76] Alfred D. Chandler, *The Visible Hand: The Managerial Revolution in American Business* (Cambridge, MA: Belknap Press of the Harvard University Press, 1977).

[77] Edith Tilton Penrose, *The Theory of the Growth of the Firm* (New York: John Wiley & Sons, 1959), p. 75.

[78] Penrose, *The Theory of the Growth of the Firm*, pp. 5, 24, 149.

[79] Birger Wernerfelt, "A Resource-Based View of the Firm," *Strategic Management Journal* 5(2) (April–June 1984), pp. 171–180. The use of the definite article "the" in referring to "growth of the firm" (Penrose) or "a resource-based view of the firm" should not be taken to suggest that there is but a single independent firm. Rather, reference here is to "a theory of all firms . . ., equivalent to a psychologist talking about a theory of the mind. Or a biologist talking about a theory of the gene." Personal communication from James G. March to Arthur G. Bedeian, April 13, 2008.

"*What a firm wants is to create a situation where its own resource position directly or indirectly makes it more difficult for others to catch up*."[80] Mergers and acquisitions, for example, provide an opportunity for a firm to gain a competitive advantage by acquiring or selling resources at its disposal. Jay B. Barney has emphasized that gaining a competitive advantage in this way requires that a firm's resources be valuable, rare, inimitable, and non-substitutable (VRIN).[81] Resources are valuable if they allow a firm to minimize threats and exploit opportunities. A resource is rare if it is not possessed by a firm's competitors. "Inimitable" implies that a resource is difficult to imitate or directly replicate. A resource is non-substitutable if there are no easy or readily available substitutes.

Penrose identified an additional way to gain a competitive advantage, which became known as the "knowledge-based view." As she explained, "There is no reason to assume that the new knowledge and services [from corporate exploration and research] will be useful only in the firm's existing products; on the contrary, they may . . . provide a foundation which will give the firm an advantage in some entirely new area."[82] "Knowledge" may also be inherited, residing in the experience, education, and intuition of a firm's human resources. Penrose further held that firms could extend their capabilities through learning. Penrose's ideas have lasting value for firms seeking to acquire competitors for their technological prowess or to learn from other industries about new production methods or processes.

GOVERNANCE AND AGENCY ISSUES

By virtue of their status as owners, stockholders are responsible for selecting the members of a corporation's board of directors. In turn, the directors are responsible for hiring qualified senior managers to oversee a corporation's daily operations. In theory—and legally—a corporation's board members and senior managers are its *agents*, charged with maximizing stockholder value.[83] In practice, however, the interests of a corporation's board members and senior managers may not always align with those of stockholders, raising questions related to corporate governance.

Adam Smith expressed concerns about the intentions of those who manage "other people's money." In contrast, John Stuart Mill believed that by using monetary incentives the "zeal" of hired managers could be aligned with the interests of a corporation's stockholders (see Chapter 3). Mill erred, of course, as instances of executive rewards with little connection to a firm's performance or stockholder returns attest. Michael C. Jensen has been a perennial critic of internal control systems (such as boards of directors) for failing to deal with such situations. He has argued that board members are negligent, if (1) they have a greater allegiance to a firm's president than its stockholders; (2) they encourage a culture that favors consensus and frowns on dissent; (3) they allow a firm's president to set the agenda for board meetings and to preferentially disclose vital information to selected board members; and (4) the possibility of personal liability leads them to minimize risks and take measures to avoid being blamed or criticized if something goes wrong.[84] As noted, Barnard anticipated Williamson's "theory of opportunism." Fayol was also well acquainted with opportunistic behavior. He listed

---

[80] *Ibid.*, p. 173.

[81] Jay B. Barney, "Firm Resources and Sustained Competitive Advantage," *Journal of Management* 17(1) (March 1991), pp. 771–792. See also *idem*, "The Emergence of Resource-Based Theory: A Personal Journey," *Journal of Management* 47(7) (September 2021), pp. 1663–1676.

[82] Penrose, *Theory of the Growth of the Firm*, p. 115.

[83] Joshua Bendickson, Jeffrey Muldoon, and Eric W. Liguori, "Agency Theory: The Times, They Are A-Changin'," *Management Decision* 54(1) (2016), pp. 174–193; Joshua Bendickson, Jeffrey Muldoon, Eric W. Liguori, and Phillip E. Davis, "Agency Theory: Background and Epistemology," *Journal of Management History* 22(4) (2016), pp. 437–449.

[84] Michael C. Jensen, "The Modern Industrial Revolution, Exit, and the Failure of Internal Control Systems," *Journal of Finance* 48(3) (July 1993), pp. 831–880. See also Jensen and William H. Meckling, "Theory of the Firm: Managerial Behavior, Agency Costs and Ownership Structure," *Journal of Financial Economics* 3(4) (October 1976), pp. 305–360.

"subordination of individual interests to the general interest" among his 14 principles of management (see Chapter 10).[85]

Questions of corporate governance touch on issues such as executive compensation, the inside–outside "mix" of boards of directors, executive selection and development, and top-management leadership. At the heart of these questions, though, is an even larger question: *Whose interests are being served?* The answer to this larger question provides insight into the business strategies available for competing in domestic and international markets.

FROM BUSINESS POLICY TO STRATEGIC MANAGEMENT TO GLOBAL STRATEGY

As noted in Chapter 11, the study of business policy as a separate academic subject was pioneered by Arch W. Shaw at the Harvard University Business School in 1911. Shaw sought to develop a course for general managers that integrated knowledge across business functions. Edmund P. Learned and C. Roland Christensen were among those who followed Shaw's lead, further developing the now famous Harvard Business School case-study method.[86] William H. Newman authored the first textbook on business policy, *Business Policies and Management*, published in 1940.[87] Newman recalled, "This was the first textbook on business policy ever published (Richard D. Irwin [Inc.] did not start publishing collections of Harvard cases until after World War II)."[88] Newman traced his interest in business policy to his years serving as an assistant to James O. McKinsey, founder of the eponymous consulting firm (see Chapter 11). Through 10 editions, the last one simply titled *Strategy*, Newman's textbook bridged the years from general management as "business policy" to general management as "strategy."

Peter F. Drucker established the basic conceptual framework for business policy as an academic field in 1954:

> [T]he important decisions, the decisions that really matter, are strategic. They involve either finding out what the situation is, or changing it, either finding out what the resources are or what they should be. . . . Anyone who is a manager has to make such strategic decisions, and the higher his level in the management hierarchy, the more of them he must make. . . . Among these are all decisions on business objectives and on the means to reach them. . . . [T]he important and difficult job is never to find out the right answer, it is to find the right question.[89]

In the 1960s, the Harvard business-policy group began utilizing SWOT analysis, a basic tool for strategic management, in its classroom instruction.[90] An acronym for "strengths" and "weaknesses" (within a firm) and "opportunities" and "threats" (outside a firm), SWOT analysis provides a framework for matching a firm's strengths with market opportunities while minimizing its weaknesses. Kenneth R. Andrews cites Howard H. Stevenson's 1969 Harvard doctoral dissertation, "Defining Corporate Strengths and Weaknesses: An Exploratory Study," as "making the first formal study of management practice in defining corporate strengths and weaknesses as part of the strategic planning process."[91]

---

[85] For a history of "opportunism" in management thought, see Jeffrey Muldoon, Joshua S. Bendickson, Furkan A. Gur, and Patrick J. Murphy, "Management's Knowledge Filter: Entrepreneurship Theory and the Historic Conceptual Evolution of Opportunism in Management Studies," *Journal of Small Business and Enterprise Development* 29(3) (May 2022), pp. 402–420.

[86] Edmund P. Learned, "Reflections on Leadership, Teaching, and Problem Solving Groups," in Arthur G. Bedeian, ed., *Management Laureates*, vol. 2 (Greenwich, CT: JAI Press, 1993), pp. 149–175.

[87] William H. Newman, *Business Policies and Management* (Cincinnati, OH: South-Western Publishing Co., 1940).

[88] *Idem*, "The Takeoff," pp. 375–397.

[89] Drucker, *Practice of Management*, pp. 352–353.

[90] Pankaj Ghemawat, "Competition and Business Strategy in Historical Perspective," *Business History Review* 76(1) (Spring 2002), pp. 37–74. For a discussion of the origins of SWOT analysis, see Richard Puyt, Finn Birger Lie, Frank Jan De Graaf, and Celeste P. M. Wilderom, "Origins of SWOT Analysis," in Sonia Taneja, ed., *Proceedings of the Annual Academy of Management Meeting* (2020). Available online at https://doi.org/10.5465/AMBPP.2020.132.

[91] Kenneth R. Andrews, *The Concept of Corporate Strategy* (Homewood, IL: Dow Jones-Irwin, 1971), p. 90. See also Howard H. Stevenson, "*Defining Corporate Strengths and Weaknesses: An Exploratory Study*" (Doctoral dissertation, Harvard University, Boston, MA, 1969).

The 1959 Gordon and Howell report's recommendation that Business Policy serve as a capstone course delivering an integrative experience for all business-school majors further boosted interest in business policy as an academic subject. Published in 1962, Chandler's *Strategy and Structure* also had a profound influence on the study of business policy. "Structure follows strategy," meaning that, in effective organizations, structure is adjusted to suit strategies rather than strategies modified to match established structures—would become an enduring part of the business canon.[92] Dan E. Schendel and Charles W. Hofer rechristened "business policy," renaming it "strategic management" to signify its commitment to being a more empirically based field.[93] Subsequently, the phrase "global strategy" emerged in recognition that almost all businesses face competition from around the world.

Beginning in the late 1970s and spreading into the 1980s, a succession of approaches to strategy formulation were popularized. These included "portfolio analysis," developed by the Boston Consulting Group.[94] The basic concept is that a corporation should be managed as a portfolio of businesses based on their individual market growth rate and relative market share. A second popular approach from this time period was advanced by Raymond E. Miles and Charles C. Snow.[95] It argued that distinct strategies should be crafted for each of a corporation's operational units depending on their unique environmental challenges. A third approach from this era that gained wide popularity was introduced by Michael E. Porter.[96] It stressed that every corporation needed to have a competitive advantage tailored to its capabilities to be successful. More recently, there has been a concern that strategic-management research is no longer producing useful knowledge that addresses real-world problems. This has been attributed to an absence of a "pragmatic, engaged and problem-focused process" that, historically, had helped produce "many of the seminal works, groundbreaking concepts, and core theories in the strategic management field."[97] Moreover, it has been suggested that because strategic-management scholars have "constructed an architecture of ideas on an inherently shaky foundation," that "the future of democratic capitalism as a system for organizing social and economic life" is in jeopardy.[98]

MULTINATIONAL ENTERPRISE AND GLOBAL STRATEGY

Perhaps the business world's most profound accomplishment in the past 100-plus years has been its ability to move beyond two world wars, the Great Depression, a post–World War II expansion in science and technology, and the 2007–2008 global financial crisis to create the phenomenon known as the "multinational enterprise" (MNE). Following World War II, the victorious Allies formulated plans to rebuild war-ravaged Europe. The Marshall Plan and the Organization for European Economic Cooperation (predecessor to the European Union) were initial steps toward this end. Other agencies formed to promote global economic and social recovery included the International Monetary Fund and the General Agreement on Tariffs and Trade (predecessor to the World Trade Organization).

Regional trade alliances such as the European Union, the North American Federation Trade Agreement, and the Association of Southeast Asian Nations were also established, followed by the Organization for Economic Co-operation and Development (OECD) in 1961. OECD member

[92] Alfred D. Chandler, Jr., *Strategy and Structure: Chapters in the History of an American Industrial Enterprise* (Cambridge, MA: MIT Press, 1962), p. 14.

[93] Dan E. Schendel and Charles W. Hofer, eds., *Strategic Management: A New View of Business Policy and Planning* (Boston, MA: Little, Brown, 1979).

[94] Barry Hedley, "Strategy and the Business Portfolio," *Long Range Planning* 10(1) (February 1977), pp. 9–15.

[95] Raymond E. Miles and Charles C. Snow, *Organizational Strategy, Structure, and Process* (New York: McGraw-Hill, 1978).

[96] Michael E. Porter, *Competitive Strategy: Techniques for Analyzing Industries and Competitors* (New York: Free Press, 1980).

[97] Paul L. Drnevich, Joseph T. Mahoney, and Dan E. Schendel, "Has Strategic Management Research Lost Its Way?" *Strategic Management Review* 1(1) (2020), p. 35.

[98] Anita M. McGahan, "The State of the Union in the Field of Strategic Management: Great Theories, Imperative Problems," *Strategic Management Review* 3(1) (2022), pp. 27, 25.

nations are economically well-developed nations with higher income populations that are dedicated to political democracy and free-market economics. Global opportunities and challenges also existed in emerging nations (such as those in Asia, Latin America, Africa, and the Middle East) whose economies were underdeveloped, with lower income populations, and less political stability, thus making international direct investment a greater risk.

Although there is an extensive literature on global strategy, the history of MNEs is yet unfolding.[99] Trade alliances are fragile, and the competitive landscape is shaped by daily developments creating opportunities and challenges. The circumstances and capabilities of firms seeking to compete in global markets will vary, of course, as will the suitability of individual firm policies. Different stages of economic development, laws, culture, and customs influence a firm's ability to compete across borders.

State-owned enterprises (SOEs) present a unique risk to firms seeking to compete globally. In these cases, some central agency (or person) makes resource-allocation decisions, often based on political ideology. Firms are formed, financed, and operated by a governmental body, which can grow quite large. SOEs distort marketplace economics by protecting markets at home and subsidizing domestic firms abroad. It has been suggested that SOEs may be "motivated by political objectives, rather than normal profit considerations."[100] Firms entering foreign markets where SOEs are present encounter not only normal marketplace pressures, but also competitors backed by the financial and political clout of their home nations. In some developing and emerging countries, SOE prices are dictated by government fiat and foreign competitors face limits on their maximum profits. In a further complication, because government-controlled investors cannot allocate capital as well as free markets, state-run "economies quickly become less innovative and less transparent."[101] This, perhaps, explains why "SOEs under perform their private counterparts under almost any circumstance."[102] On balance, experience suggests that SOEs all too often emulate rather than innovate, and commonly lack transparency in governance where political connections are their principal resource.

STRATEGIC LEADERSHIP AND "DYNAMIC CAPABILITIES"

As noted, Drucker contended that what keeps an organization from failing is the ability of its managers to give birth to innovations in new products, new methods of production, new markets, new uses of raw materials, and new forms of organization that drive economic success. Nonetheless, a firm's prosperity is not assured indefinitely, as its competitive advantages may quickly evaporate. In what Schumpeter (see Chapter 18) dubbed "creative destruction," innovation "incessantly revolutionizes the economic structure from within, incessantly destroying the old one, incessantly creating a new one."[103] Evidence for this market dynamic may be found in *Fortune* magazine's yearly list of the 500 largest U.S. companies ranked by total revenues. Between 1980 and 2021, 177 newcomers were added to this list, with 40 joining since 2021.

In the Schumpeterian tradition, David J. Teece and his colleagues advise that firms must develop the capacity to create, extend, or modify their resources to rapidly address environmental

[99] See, for example, Michael A. Hitt, Daniel Li, and Kai Xu, "International Strategy: From Local to Global and Beyond," *Journal of World Business* 51(1) (January 2016), pp. 58–73; Robert E. Hoskisson, Lorraine Eden, Chung Ming Lau, and Mike Wright, "Strategy in Emerging Economies," *Academy of Management Journal* 43(3) (June 2000), pp. 249–267.

[100] Organization for Economic Co-operation and Development, "International Investment of Sovereign Wealth Funds: Are New Rules Needed?" *OCED Newsletter* 5(4) (October 2007), p. 4. See also Garry D. Bruton, Mike W. Peng, David Ahlstrom, Ciprian V. Stan, and Kehan Xu, "State-Owned Enterprises Around the World as Hybrid Organizations," *Academy of Management Perspectives* 29(1) (February 2015), pp. 92–114; Mike W. Peng, Garry D. Bruton, Ciprian V. Stan, and Yuanyuan Huang, "Theories of the (State–Owned) Firm," *Asia Pacific Journal of Management* 33(2) (June 2016), pp. 293–317.

[101] Ian Bremmer, "The New Rules of Globalization," *Harvard Business Review* 92(1–2) (January–February 2014), p. 103.

[102] Aldo Musacchio, Sergio G. Lazzoni, and Ruth V. Aguilera, "New Varieties of State Capitalism: Strategic and Governance Implications," *Academy of Management Perspectives* 29(1) (May 2015), p. 116.

[103] Joseph A. Schumpeter, *Capitalism, Socialism, and Democracy* (New York: Harper & Brothers, 1942), p. 83.

threats. They refer to this capacity as a firm's "dynamic capability," which is enhanced by its manager's (as a factor of production) abilities to innovate. They suggest that a firm must develop "dynamic capabilities" that allow it to "integrate, build, and reconfigure internal and external competencies to address rapidly changing environments. Dynamic capabilities thus reflect an organization's ability to achieve new and innovative forms of competitive advantage, given path dependencies and market positions."[104]

Teece and his colleagues consider it the responsibility of a firm's general managers to implement incentives, policies, and actions necessary to develop a firm's dynamic capabilities. This general-management task has been termed "strategic leadership" to distinguish the work of chief executives, directors, and other top-siders from the leadership activities of lower-level managers.[105] The root of the word "strategy" comes from the Greek word *strategos*, meaning "a military general."[106] Moving from ancient Greece to the modern business world, the word retains much of its original meaning. As a general in command of an army is charged with successfully "meeting and defeating" a country's foes, general managers are charged with developing and implementing plans (strategic and operational) to successfully compete in the marketplace.

Free-Market Capitalism

The central lesson of the dynamic-capabilities literature is that to safeguard its long-term survival, a firm must not only achieve its current objectives, but also engage in the continuous learning necessary for ongoing innovation and renewal. Indeed, at the center of free-market capitalism is the notion that the most successful firms are those that fulfill the needs and desires of the public with innovative products and services at competitive prices. In this regard, the beauty of free-market economies—based solely on voluntary exchange—is that buyers get something they value more than whatever they give up and so do sellers. Voluntary commerce results in cooperation without coercion for the mutual gain of all market participants. Buyers choose sellers because sellers offer what they want at a price they are willing to pay. Thus, free-market transactions in which fair value is exchanged for fair value benefit both buyer and seller: "The genius of free exchange is not that one party gains more than the other, but that both gain more than they had before."[107] This simple concept explains why the owner of your corner diner was open this morning and ready to prepare your favorite breakfast. A win–win result for you both. This is the free-market miracle of Adam Smith's "invisible hand" in action. What Smith wrote almost 250 years ago is still true: "It is not from the benevolence of the butcher, the brewer, or the baker that we expect our dinner, but from their regard to their own interest."[108]

Note, too, that market prices are the efficient synthesis of hundreds of billions of daily decisions willingly made by hundreds of millions of "self-interested" consumers (i.e., buyers) based on their needs/desires matched against the current and anticipated availability of goods and services. Prices, thus, communicate to buyers and sellers the scarcity or surplus of goods and services and are the basis by which a free-market economy organizes itself, removing the need for central planners. In this sense, so long as personal and property rights are respected,

[104] David J. Teece, Gary Pisano, and Amy Shuen, "Dynamic Capabilities and Strategic Management," *Strategic Management Journal* 18(7) (August 1997), p. 516. See also Teece, "The Foundations of Enterprise Performance: Dynamic and Ordinary Capabilities in an (Economic) Theory of Firms," *Academy of Management Perspectives* 28(4) (November 2014), pp. 328–352.
[105] Sydney Finkelstein, Donald C. Hambrick, and Albert A. Cannella, *Strategic Leadership: Theory and Research on Executives, Top Management Teams, and Boards* (New York: Oxford University Press, 2009), p. 4.
[106] Jeffrey Bracker, "The Historical Development of the Strategic Management Concept," *Academy of Management Review* 5(2) (April 1980), p. 219.
[107] William White, "Letters to the Editor: Greed, Self-interest and Capitalist Virtues," *Wall Street Journal* (February 23, 2022), p. A16.
[108] Adam Smith, *An Inquiry into the Nature and Causes of the Wealth of Nations* (London: W. Strahan and T. Cadell in the Strand, 1776), vol. 1, bk. I, ch. 2, p. 17.

"[t]he market is a democracy where every penny gives a right of vote."[109] With their dollar "votes," buyers rather than government edicts determine marketplace winners and losers, and prices adjust spontaneously.

History has amply documented that centralized economic planning and the concentration of power such planning gives to the state leads not only to higher prices and fewer consumer options, but to widespread corruption and the misallocation of resources. Capitalism is the only economic system that allows buyers to make their own decisions on what goods and services to consume, as sellers invest their own money, going head-to-head to attract customers. It thus succeeds not only because the private allocation of resources is more efficient than central planning, but because "it drives [sellers] to innovate and to provide consumers with less costly and better products" lest, as recognized by Drucker and noted above, they risk becoming a loser in the never-ending battle for customers.[110]

Whether referred to as "business policy" or rechristened as "strategic management," the notion that firms are in a constant state of creation, growth, stagnation, and decline is essential in understanding how to survive in a globally competitive environment. Wisdom and experience cannot be taught, but an appreciation of management theory provides the foundation for assessing a firm's strengths and weaknesses and heightening its ability to innovative.

SUMMARY

A renewed interest in general management theory occurred as businesses grew domestically and beyond, fostering a need for more broadly educated managers. Studies of business education led to a reformulation of business-school curricula and an emphasis on creating new knowledge. This emphasis on academic research created a divide between management theory and its relevance to students and those who practiced the art of management.

Various attempts have been made to understand why firms exist, how firms differ in resource acquisition and deployment, and why firms vary in corporate governance. Foundational work in business policy, strategic management, and Hofstede's initial findings on the nature of managerial work across nations would evolve as the need to meet global challenges and, in turn, capitalize on worldwide opportunities in developing and emerging nations mounted. This required that firms match their capabilities with opportunities and learn to work in other nations with differing histories, institutions, and cultures.

[109] Frank A. Fetter, *The Principles of Economics with Applications to Practical Problems* (New York: Century Co., 1904), p. 394.

[110] Marian L. Tupy and Gale L. Pooley, *Superabundance: The Story of Population Growth, Innovation, and Human Flourishing on an Infinitely Bountiful Planet* (Washington, DC: Cato Institute, 2022), p. 350.

CHAPTER 20

Organizational Behavior and Organization Theory

Part III began by examining the Hawthorne studies and the previously unappreciated patterns of employee behavior that they revealed. It then discussed the lives and thoughts of two individuals—Mary P. Follett and Chester I. Barnard—who bridged the scientific-management and social-person eras. It next reviewed the growth and refinement of the human-relations movement as it moved through micro and macro phases, from roughly 1930 into the early 1950s, and concluded with a look at human relations in theory and practice and a consideration of the economic, social, technological, and political environment of the social-person era.

Beginning in the 1950s, the human-relations movement was overtaken by a new generation of scholars devoted to the study of what became known as "organizational behavior." Shunning the "feel-good" reputation of human relationists, organizational-behavior researchers addressed issues such as job design, work motivation, and effective leadership. Personnel management as a field began to build a firmer empirical base and evolved into human-resource management (HRM) and, then, strategic human-resource management (SHRM). At about the same time, organization theorists began to debate the effect of technology on an organization's structure and the relationship between an organization's design and its environment. With the globalization of business following World War II, there was also a growing focus on differences in workplace dynamics across borders and on how national cultures influence management theory and practice. This chapter reviews each of these developments.

THE HUMAN SIDE OF MANAGEMENT

Until the 1960s, psychologists, sociologists, and anthropologists had little impact on general management theory. As noted in Chapter 19, the Gordon and Howell report on the status of U.S. business education called for a greater emphasis on the social sciences: "Of all the subjects which he might undertake formally, none is more appropriate for the businessman-to-be than human behavior . . . . The very nature of the firm and of the manager's role in the firm suggests that every

person anticipating a responsible position in a modern business enterprise needs a substantial amount of knowledge about human behavior."[1]

THE TRANSITION FROM HUMAN RELATIONS TO ORGANIZATIONAL BEHAVIOR

Scornful of the feel-good reputation associated with the human-relations movement, the social scientists entering business schools following the Gordon and Howell report applied more powerful analytical and conceptual tools for addressing employee–employer relations. One of the earliest, if not the first, uses of the phrase "organizational behavior" appeared in a 1948 paper by Philip Selznick published in the *American Sociological Review*.[2] By 1951, supported by a Ford Foundation grant, Princeton University had initiated an organizational-behavior research program under the direction of sociologist Wilbert E. Moore.[3] A year later, Yale University's Labor and Management Center began a publication series titled "Studies in Organizational Behavior." Its first volume was Chris Argyris's *Organization of a Bank: A Study of the Nature of Organization and the Fusion Process*, published in 1954. Argyris sought to integrate "the individual and the organization." He proposed a "personality versus organization" hypothesis based on an "immaturity–maturity" theory of human behavior.[4] According to Argyris, there was an incongruence between the demands of formal organizations (with their extreme division of labor and close oversight and control) and the needs of healthy, mature individuals. Argyris argued that from infancy to adulthood, there was a tendency for the healthy personality to develop along a continuum from immaturity to maturity by moving from being passive to being active, from dependence to independence, from a lack of awareness of self to an awareness and control over self, and so on. In Argyris's view, when the needs of healthy personalities conflicted with the requirements of formal organizations, individuals naturally protected themselves by responding defensively (e.g., by becoming aggressive or apathetic, or restricting output). All too often, managers responded by either becoming autocratic and directive or, alternatively, turning to human relations. With regard to the latter, it was Argyris's opinion that many managers turned to pseudo-human-relations programs to sugarcoat workplace realities rather than address the actual causes of employee discontent.

Argyris (together with Donald Schön) also popularized the notion of "organizational learning," which grew from his views on individual needs and the demands of modern organizations. The question was, "Why do individuals (and groups) use 'defensive reasoning' to resist organizational changes?" The answer, according to Argyris and Schön, echoed Kurt Lewin's findings on introducing change and resided in "unfreezing" and altering individuals' "defensive reasoning" patterns and encouraging reasoning that led to "double-loop" learning; that is, learning by doing and making corrections as needed based on information fed back from different action strategies. This contrasted with "single-loop" learning that did not question the status quo and inhibited learning from experience.[5] Argyris and Schön's thoughts on organizational learning complemented Edith T. Penrose's knowledge-based view of the firm (see Chapter 19) and stimulated further interest in organizational change and development.

The insights of Keith Davis marked the beginning of a philosophically broader understanding of workplace interactions. Focusing on work organizations, Davis defined human relations as "the integration of people into a work situation that motivates them to work together productively,

[1] Robert A. Gordon and James E. Howell, *Higher Education for Business* (New York: Columbia University Press, 1959), p. 166.
[2] Philip Selznick, "Foundations of the Theory of Organization," *American Sociological Review* 13(1) (February 1948), p. 25.
[3] Foreign Policy Analysis Project, Organizational Behavior Section, Princeton University, *Organizational Behavior: Report on a Research Program* (Princeton, NJ: The Author, 1953), p. 21.
[4] Chris Argyris, *Personality and Organization: The Conflict between System and the Individual* (New York: Harper & Brothers, 1957), p. 50.
[5] Chris Argyris and Donald A. Schön, *Organizational Learning II* (Reading, MA: Addison-Wesley, 1996). See also Argyris, "Double-Loop Learning, Teaching, and Research," *Academy of Management Learning & Education* 1(2) (December 2002), pp. 206–218.

cooperatively, and with economic, psychological, and social satisfactions."[6] He held that human relations in the workplace had two underlying facets: (1) a concern with understanding and describing human behavior in organizations by identifying causes and effects of that behavior, and (2) the application of behavioral knowledge to further human cooperation. The first facet could be termed *organizational behavior* and the second *human relations*. These facets were complementary, in that one investigates and explains while the other applies knowledge gained from the study of human behavior to benefit society. Davis stressed the importance of appreciating how economic, psychological, and social factors influence work relationships. In doing so, he moved the study of workplace behavior from its "feelings" base toward a more analytical foundation.

THEORIES X AND Y

Douglas McGregor taught in the Sloan School of Management at the Massachusetts Institute of Technology from 1937 until his death in 1964, with the exception of the 6 years he served as president of Antioch College. As president of Antioch College (1948–1954), McGregor found that contemporary human-relations theory was inadequate for coping with the realities of organizational life:

> It took the direct experience of becoming a line executive . . . to teach me what no amount of observation of other people could have taught.
>
> I believed, for example, that a leader could operate successfully as a kind of adviser to his organization. I thought I could avoid being a "boss." Unconsciously, I suspect, I hoped to duck the unpleasant necessity of making difficult decisions, of taking the responsibility for one course of action among many uncertain alternatives, of making mistakes and taking the consequences. I thought that maybe I could operate so that everyone would like me—that "good human relations" would eliminate all discord and disagreement.
>
> I couldn't have been more wrong. It took a couple of years, but I finally began to realize that a leader cannot avoid the exercise of authority any more than he can avoid responsibility for what happens to his organization.[7]

Based on his experiences at Antioch, McGregor began to formulate a set of ideas that would have a profound influence on management education, such as the notion that "[a] manager who believes that people in general are lazy, untrustworthy, and antagonistic toward him will make very different decisions [from] a manager who regards people generally as cooperative and friendly."[8] In *The Human Side of Enterprise,* McGregor expanded on the idea that one's underlying assumptions about human nature were all-important in determining one's approach to managing. He identified two fundamental management styles: Theory X and Theory Y. Theory X represented the "traditional view of direction and control." It assumed:

1. *The average human being has an inherent dislike of work and will avoid it if he can . . . .*
2. *Because of this human characteristic of dislike of work, most people must be coerced, controlled, directed, and threatened with punishment to get them to put forth adequate effort toward the achievement of organizational objectives. . . .*
3. *The average human being prefers to be directed, wishes to avoid responsibility, has relatively little ambition,* [and] *wants security above all.*[9]

---

[6] Keith Davis, *Human Behavior at Work: The Dynamics of Organizational Behavior*, 3rd. ed. (New York: McGraw-Hill, 1967), p. 5.

[7] Douglas McGregor, "On Leadership," *Antioch Notes* 31(9) (May 1, 1954), p. 3.

[8] Douglas McGregor and Joseph N. Scanlon, *The Dewey and Almy Chemical Company and the International Chemical Workers Union* (Washington, DC: National Planning Association, 1948), p. 72.

[9] Douglas McGregor, *The Human Side of Enterprise* (New York: McGraw-Hill, 1960), pp. 33–34. See also *idem*, "The Human Side of Enterprise," *Management Review* 46(11) (November 1957), pp. 22–28.

In contrast, Theory Y assumed:

1. *The expenditure of physical and mental effort in work is as natural as play or rest. The average human being does not inherently dislike work.*
2. *External control and the threat of punishment are not the only means for bringing about effort toward organizational objectives. Man will exercise self-direction and self-control in the service of objectives to which he is committed.*
3. *Commitment to objectives is a function of the rewards associated with their achievement. The most significant of such rewards, for example, the satisfaction of ego and self-actualization needs, can be direct products of effort directed toward organizational objectives.*
4. *The average human being learns, under proper conditions, not only to accept but also to seek responsibility. Avoidance of responsibility, lack of ambition, and emphasis on security are generally consequences of experience, not inherent human characteristics.*
5. *The capacity to exercise a relatively high degree of imagination, ingenuity, and creativity in the solution of organizational problems is widely, not narrowly, distributed in the population.*
6. *Under the conditions of modern industrial life, the intellectual potentialities of the average human being are only partially utilized.*[10]

For McGregor, the central principle that derives from Theory Y is the importance of creating "conditions such that the members of [an] organization can achieve their own goals *best* by directing their efforts toward the success of the enterprise."[11] Managers accepting the Theory Y assumptions of human nature would not structure, control, or closely supervise the work environment. Instead, they would give their subordinates wider latitude in their work, encourage creativity, use fewer external controls, foster self-control, and motivate through the satisfaction that comes from the challenge of work itself. McGregor hoped that, in adopting Theory Y, employers and employees would come together to advance their common interests. It should be stressed that McGregor did not view Theory X and Theory Y as "polar opposites . . . at the extremes of a scale," but "simply *different* cosmologies."[12]

HUMAN-RESOURCE MANAGEMENT AND INDUSTRIAL RELATIONS: THE CHANGING SCENE

Employees as willing contributors to the accomplishment of an organization's goals is, of course, not a new idea. Whereas classical economists in the seventeenth and eighteenth centuries believed that work was without intrinsic reward and, thus, employees must be coerced by extrinsic motives to perform, in the late nineteenth century, neo-classical economists began to appreciate that work was much more than a means of survival and, indeed, could be personally fulfilling.[13] As noted in Chapter 9, at the gates of many factories across the country at the turn of the twentieth century, unskilled workers would line up each morning and a foreman would appear to hire the day's labor. This often, however, amounted to little more than hiring friends or the well-connected or, in some cases, even selling jobs. Frederick W. Taylor denounced this practice and replaced it with the position of functional foremen, who evolved into specialists to aid in making hiring decisions. For Henri Fayol, staffing was simply part of organizing. From these rudimentary beginnings, "personnel management" gradually evolved as a standard label for the practice of advising managers about employee recruitment, selection, and so forth.

Early personnel-management practices borrowed from many academic disciplines, including industrial psychology (personnel testing), labor economics (for understanding labor market factors as they affected the supply of employees and wage rates), and industrial relations

[10] *Ibid.*, pp. 47–48.
[11] *Ibid.*, p. 49.
[12] Douglas McGregor, *The Professional Manager*, eds. Caroline McGregor and Warren G. Bennis (New York: McGraw-Hill, 1967), p. 80.
[13] For a review of early economic theories of work, see David A. Spencer, "Work Is a Four-Letter Word: The Economics of Work in Historical and Critical Perspective," *American Journal of Economics and Sociology* 70(3) (July 2011), pp. 563–586.

(for promoting better union–management relations). Collegiate-level personnel-management instruction, however, was all too often regarded as less than adequate. In their report on the status of U.S. business education, Gordon and Howell charged: "Next to the course in production, perhaps more educational sins have been committed in the name of personnel management than in any other required course in the business curriculum. Personnel management is a field which has had a particularly small base of significant generalization with which to work (beyond what is important in the area of human relations), and, partly for this reason, it is an area which has not been held in high regard in the better schools."[14] In response, a growing number of social scientists were recruited into U.S. business schools (see Chapter 19). They brought with them more powerful analytical tools for addressing employee–employer relations, and, with the continued growth of university programs in labor studies, personnel-management instruction began to develop a broader scientific base and enhanced respect.

The labor economist John R. Commons appears to have been the first person to use the phrase "human resources" in an industrial context.[15] E. Wight Bakke stressed that more emphasis had to be placed on the human element to elevate its importance relative to other inputs used in the production of goods and services. The central concern of the human-resource function was not "personal happiness," but "productive work" and the belief that humans had to be integrated into an organization's corporate culture. Maintaining an organization's human resources, however, was the responsibility of all managers, not just those in personnel or labor-relations departments.[16] Wendell L. French seems to have been the first author to add "human resources" to the title of a personnel-management textbook.[17] The notion that an organization's human resources could be "managed" carried a certain dignity, and the term itself gave personnel management a new legitimacy. This legitimacy was further heightened when, beginning in the 1960s and accelerating thereafter, federal and state laws concerning equal-employment opportunity, occupational safety and health, employment testing, compensation practices, and retirement plans gave rise to a new breed of "personnel specialists" trained in both business and law.

By the 1980s, human-resource management, "challenged by heightened competitive pressure and a fast changing business environment," adopted a strategic orientation.[18] The label "strategic human-resource management" (SHRM) subsequently appeared in the management literature. The stated goal of SHRM is to develop employment practices that create a sustainable performance advantage.[19] According to Bruce E. Kaufman, however, "[m]odern HRM and SHRM . . . appear to have dressed up many old ideas in new garb and claimed a new discovery for things known and practiced by earlier generations."[20] In a three-decade review, Kaufman criticized SHRM researchers for failing to add to management science; being too focused on the internal dimension of organizations (such as strategy, organizational behavior, and psychology) to the neglect of external dimensions (such as economics and industrial/employment law); harboring an inability to develop actionable findings; and disregarding anything outside the "Anglo-American orbit." The full benefit of SHRM remains unclear, and moving beyond a predominantly Western-based research literature will not be easy.

---

[14] Gordon and Howell, *Higher Education for Business,* p. 189.

[15] John R. Commons, *Industrial Goodwill* (New York: McGraw-Hill, 1919), pp. 129–130.

[16] E. Wight Bakke, *The Human Resources Function* (New Haven, CT: Yale University Labor-Management Center, 1958).

[17] Wendell L. French, *The Personnel Management Process: Human Resources Administration* (Boston, MA: Houghton Mifflin, 1964).

[18] Bruce E. Kaufman, *Managing the Human Factor: The Early Years of Human Resource Management in American Industry* (Ithaca, NY: Cornell University Press, 2008), p. 42.

[19] James G. Combs, Yongmei Liu, Angela T. Hall, and David J. Ketchen, Jr., "How Much Do High-Performance Work Practices Matter? A Meta-Analysis of Their Effects on Organizational Performance," *Personnel Psychology* 59(3) (Autumn 2006), pp. 501–528.

[20] Bruce E. Kaufman, "Strategic Human Resource Management Research in the United States: A Failing Grade after 30 Years?" *Academy of Management Perspectives* 26(2) (May 2012), p. 22.

JOB DESIGN

How to design jobs for maximum effectiveness and efficiency has been a concern of long-standing interest. Taylor, the Gilbreths, and other scientific-management pioneers studied job design in hopes of reducing fatigue and increasing efficiency (see Part II). Beginning in the early 1950s, Allan H. Mogensen pioneered the work-simplification movement in the belief that jobs could be designed so that people could work smarter, not harder.[21] Following Charles R. Walker and Robert H. Guest's 1952 study of assembly-line workers (see Chapter 15), the belief that management has a responsibility to design jobs so that they are more meaningful and personally fulfilling (and, therefore, motivating) gathered momentum.

In the late 1950s, Frederick I. Herzberg sought to discover which job-related factors motivate employees.[22] He asked employees to provide examples of times when they felt exceptionally good or exceptionally bad about their jobs. The examples revealed that the factors producing job satisfaction were distinct from those producing job dissatisfaction. That is, although an unpleasant work environment might be a reason given for job dissatisfaction, a pleasant work environment was rarely cited as a reason for job satisfaction. This finding contrasted with the traditional view that job satisfaction and job dissatisfaction are opposite ends of the same continuum. Herzberg labeled the factors that produced job satisfaction "motivators." His analysis indicated that these factors were directly related to *job content*, reflecting a need for personal fulfillment. Motivators included feelings of achievement, recognition, and responsibility; the work being performed; opportunities for advancement; and job growth. He labeled the factors that led to job dissatisfaction "hygienes" and found that they were more related to environment or setting in which work is performed, or *job context*, than to job content. Hygiene factors included company policies and administration, supervision, relations with one's peers, working conditions, pay, and job security. Based on this dichotomy, Herzberg and his colleagues declared that only motivators produce job satisfaction, whereas hygienes, when sufficient, merely prevent job dissatisfaction. In other words:

1. To the degree that hygienes are absent from a job, dissatisfaction will occur. When present, hygienes prevent dissatisfaction, but do not lead to satisfaction.
2. To the degree that motivators are present in a job, satisfaction will occur. When absent, motivators do not lead to dissatisfaction.

Hygienes thus provide a platform that must be present before satisfaction can take place. Stated more directly, employers must prevent employee job dissatisfaction by providing hygienes before they can address employee job satisfaction using motivators.

As noted in Chapter 9, Herzberg's "two-factor theory" of job satisfaction is remarkably similar to Hendrik de Man's conclusion that a worker's mental attitude toward work is a mix of "pleasurable and unpleasurable elements."[23] Despite Herzberg's insights, scholars noted several difficulties with his findings. For example, doubts have been raised about Herzberg's data-collection methods. Rather than asking employees to provide examples of times when they felt exceptionally good or exceptionally bad about their jobs, researchers used techniques less susceptible to respondent bias and failed to replicate his findings. In this regard, critics noted that people are more likely to credit their own achievements as reasons for job satisfaction. Similarly, they are more likely to blame poor policies or supervision for their dissatisfaction. This suggests that Herzberg's results may have been attributable to the way he gathered his data. Indeed, other

[21] Allan H. Mogensen, "Work Simplification," *Electrical Engineering* 71(3) (March 1952), pp. 237–238.
[22] Frederick I. Herzberg, Bernard Mausner, and Barbara B. Snyderman, *The Motivation to Work* (New York: John Wiley & Sons, 1959), p. 141.
[23] Hendrik de Man, *Joy in Work*, trans. Eden and Cedar Paul (London: G. Allen & Unwin, 1929), p. 9. German edition published in 1927.

investigators using different methods obtained findings contrary to what Herzberg's theory would predict. In addition, although Herzberg reported replications of his original study in Europe, Africa, the Middle East, and Asia, research conducted by other investigators has shown a wide diversity in the work preferences of different people in different cultures, thus casting doubt on whether his findings extend across cultures.

Herzberg's research stimulated an increased interest in job design. Arthur N. Turner and Paul R. Lawrence investigated "requisite task attributes," or RTAs (namely, *task variety*, *work autonomy, required interaction*, *optional interaction*, *required knowledge and skill*, and *responsibility*), related to job satisfaction and attendance.[24] A significant aspect of Turner and Lawrence's research was their finding that employees from varying cultural backgrounds (small towns versus urban cities) responded differently to high RTA jobs. A summary index of the six requisite task attributes was positively related to job satisfaction and attendance for employees in small towns and negatively related for those in urban areas.

J. Richard Hackman and Edward E. Lawler III extended Turner and Lawrence's work.[25] They identified four job characteristics, termed *core dimensions*, which could be modified to "enrich jobs" (see Chapter 15). The core dimensions were *skill variety*, *work autonomy*, *task identity*, and *performance feedback*. Hackman and Lawler reasoned that the more a job activated these core dimensions, the more likely it would be to provide employees with feelings of satisfaction and motivation. In turn, higher-quality performance and lower absenteeism and turnover would be more likely.

Hackman would later join with Greg R. Oldham to argue that *task significance* should be considered a fifth core dimension. Hackman and Oldham urged managers to determine the quantity and quality of the different core dimensions present in the jobs they supervised. They believed that if these characteristics could be expanded, for example, by increasing the range of skills and creativity required by a job or by providing performance feedback, then employees would be more likely to find their jobs more meaningful. Recognizing that there would be large individual differences in how employees reacted to the five core dimensions, Hackman and Oldham acknowledged that the success of this approach depended on an employee's "growth-need strength." If an employee already felt sufficiently challenged and experienced a job as meaningful, growth-need strength would be low, and further efforts to enrich a job would be less effective. Some individuals seek more freedom and challenge in their jobs, and others do not; further, some jobs can be made more meaningful, and others cannot. Thus, Hackman and Oldham did not present job design as a universal panacea for all work-related challenges. Indeed, they advised, "the redesign of work is much more a *way of managing* than it is a prepackaged 'fix' for problems of employee motivation and satisfaction."[26]

This advice is a reminder that job design is a part of the management process, involving motivating and leading employees to achieve an organization's goals. Other considerations may also come into play. For instance, advances in communication technology, including electronic mail, social-media sites, news and instant messaging services, and innumerable websites devoted to an endless list of subjects, have altered the means whereby work is accomplished. In addition, the growing use of self-employed "independent contractors" may limit the extent to which a firm can control the way a job is designed and performed. Finally, Miriam Erez has warned

[24] Arthur N. Turner and Paul R. Lawrence, *Industrial Jobs and the Worker: An Investigation of Response to Task Attributes* (Boston, MA: Division of Research, Graduate School of Business Administration, Harvard University, 1965).

[25] J. Richard Hackman and Edward E. Lawler III, "Employee Reactions to Job Characteristics," *Journal of Applied Psychology* 55(3) (June 1971), pp. 259–286.

[26] J. Richard Hackman and Greg R. Oldham, *Work Redesign* (Reading, MA: Addison-Wesley, 1980), p. 249. For a complete historical review of the job-design literature, see Greg R. Oldham and Yitzhak Fried, "Job Design Research and Theory: Past, Present, and Future," *Organizational Behavior and Human Decision Processes* 136 (September 2016), pp. 20–35; Sharon K. Parker, Frederick P. Morgeson, and Gary Johns, "One Hundred Years of Work Design Research: Looking Back and Looking Forward," *Journal of Applied Psychology* 102(3) (March 2017), pp. 403–420.

that a job-design model appropriate in an organization's home country may be ineffective in other countries. For example, workers in the United States are known for placing a high value on autonomy and personal responsibility and, thus, embrace job enrichment. In northern Europe, where collectivism is valued, workers are more comfortable with autonomous work groups and codetermination (i.e., cooperation between management and workers in decision-making). In Japan, cultural values align with group rewards and quality circles.[27] The frontier for understanding work and its potential for making management practices "practical" is vast.

WORK MOTIVATION

The next two topics, work motivation and leadership, are closely related, though are discussed separately here to highlight the contributions different individuals made to our general understanding of each. Motivation is a central issue that pervades all aspects of human behavior: "The question, 'How can I motivate my people?' has been philosophically and practically posed in many eras and many tongues."[28] Classical economists argued that because work was an irksome activity, employees had to be compelled or coerced to work hard. As detailed in Chapters 2 and 15, this line of thinking was challenged by psychologists such as Henry A. Murray, Abraham H. Maslow, and David C. McClelland. As a group, these and other psychologists were primarily focused on needs, motives, and wants to discover *what* motivates people. Maslow, for example, identified five categories of inborn needs, whereas McClelland, building on the work of Murray, gave primacy to the needs for *power*, *affiliation*, and *achievement*. It soon became apparent, however, that in applied settings, a full understanding of motivation requires an appreciation of both *what* motivates people and *how* people are motivated. With regard to the latter, three motivation theories (developed beginning in the early 1960s) that focus on *how* behavior is energized, *how* it is directed, *how* it is sustained, and *how* it is stopped generated the greatest interest: Vroom's expectancy theory, Adams's equity theory, and Locke and Latham's goal-setting theory.[29]

Expectancy theory, one of the most influential work-motivation theories of the mid-to-late twentieth-century, was popularized by Victor H. Vroom.[30] Based on the belief that people will act to maximize their rewards, expectancy theory holds that motivation is determined by (1) *expectancies*, or the belief that effort will be rewarded, and (2) *valences*, or the value attached to specific rewards. In brief, the motivation to behave in a certain way will be greatest when individuals believe their behavior will lead to outcomes (e.g., a raise or a promotion) that they value. Expectancy theory underscores the realization that different people have different desires and that they are likely to perceive different connections between actions and the fulfillment of these desires. In doing so, it highlights important factors (i.e., expectancies and valences) that influence behavioral intentions and suggests ways in which these factors alone and in combination can be used to predict behavior.

Championed by J. Stacy Adams, equity theory attempts to explain satisfaction with outcomes (e.g., pay, promotion opportunities, and increased status) and to predict changes in behavior.[31] It defines motivation in terms of the perceived equity between the effort one puts into a job and what one receives in return, especially compared to others in similar positions. Equity theory holds that perceived inequity creates tension within a person, and this tension in turn motivates

[27] Miriam Erez, "Culture and Job Design," *Journal of Organizational Behavior*, 31(2–3) (2010), pp. 389–400.
[28] David E. Terpstra, "Theories of Motivation—Borrowing the Best," *Personnel Journal* 58(6) (June 1979), p. 376.
[29] For a 100-year review of work-motivation research, see Ruth Kanfer, Michael Frese, and Russell E. Johnson, "Motivation Related to Work: A Century of Progress," *Journal of Applied Psychology* 102(3) (March 2017), pp. 338–355.
[30] Victor H. Vroom, *Work and Motivation* (New York: John Wiley & Sons, 1964).
[31] J. Stacy Adams, "Toward an Understanding of Inequity," *Journal of Abnormal and Social Psychology* 67(5) (November 1963), pp. 422–436.

a drive to restore equity. The greater the tension one feels, the harder one will work to restore equity and, thereby, reduce the tension. According to equity theory, the "other person" an individual compares themselves to could be one person (e.g., a coworker), a group (e.g., workers on another shift), or someone from a previous, or even hypothetical, work situation. Two points are key to understanding equity theory: (1) it emphasizes "perceived" as compared to "actual" equity; it matters little whether an individual's comparisons are based on subjective perception or objective reality, and (2) equity and equality are not the same. Equality is said to exist when one perceives the outcomes they receive as being equal to the outcomes received by another person. Equity is attained when the ratio of an individual's perceived outcomes to inputs equals the ratio of the other person's outcomes to inputs. Thus, perceived inequity may exist in either of two cases: (1) when individuals judge the ratio of their perceived outcomes to inputs as being too low relative to another's, or (2) when individuals feel the ratio of their perceived outcomes to inputs is excessive relative to another's. The notion that individuals seek fairness is, of course, not a new finding. It is the basis for Whiting Williams's 1920 conclusion that the pay a worker receives is considered not in absolute terms, but in terms of what others receive.[32] It is also the basis for the first-century biblical parable (Matt. 20: 1–16) in which a group of workers laboring in a vineyard since sunrise are upset at receiving the same pay as others who had been hired late in the day. It seems that a desire for equity is timeless.

Goal-setting theory is primarily the work of Edwin A. Locke and Gary P. Latham. It focuses on the causal effects of developing and setting specific work goals on job performance, holding that conscious goals are the most proximal determinant of motivation.[33] The more specific a goal, the better: aim to "produce one hundred units that will pass the quality inspection" rather than "do the best you can today." Further, difficult goals are better than easy goals—goals should challenge (but not exceed) an individual's abilities. Locke and Latham's research supports a positive relationship between goal difficulty and job performance. It further indicates that goal setting as a motivational tool works equally well whether goals are assigned or determined by group participation. According to Locke and Latham, assigned goals work best with employees already internally motivated to perform at a high level, such as employees with a high need for achievement or high self-efficacy. In contrast, they found that when employees are familiar with and at ease with participative techniques, and when their need for achievement is lower, participative goal setting is likely to be more effective. Locke and Latham's research also revealed that employee acceptance of goals depends on several factors, including the extent to which employees trust a company's managers, the fairness and difficulty of goals, and the perceived legitimacy of workplace demands. In general, 40 years of research has provided robust support for a positive relationship between goal difficulty and job performance.

Courtesy of Edwin A. Locke

Edwin A. Locke

As Ruth Kanfer and Gilad Chen have noted, "For much of the mid- to late-20th century, expectancy-value and goal setting models dominated the work-motivation literature."[34] At the same time, given an increasing integration of national markets and a growing workforce diversity

[32] Whiting Williams, *What's on the Worker's Mind? By One Who Put on Overalls to Find Out* (New York: Charles Scribner's Sons, 1920), p. 323.

[33] Edwin A. Locke and Gary P. Latham, *A Theory of Goal Setting and Task Performance* (Englewood Cliffs, NJ: Prentice Hall, 1990); Gary P. Latham and Edwin A. Locke, "Self-Regulation Through Goal Setting," *Organizational Behavior and Human Decision Processes* 50(2) (December 1991), pp. 212–247.

[34] Ruth Kanfer and Gilad Chen, "Motivation in Organizational Behavior: History, Advances and Prospects," *Organizational Behavior and Human Performance* 136 (September 2016), p. 12.

throughout the world, it is apparent that research is needed to establish whether Western-based theories of motivation are applicable across cultures. Geert Hofstede chided Maslow, Herzberg, and McClelland for their Freudian inclinations about the nature of human needs and aspirations, arguing that Freudian thinking does not fit other cultural patterns.[35] He also noted that Maslow's hierarchy of needs emphasizes self-actualization as a supreme need. This, however, presumes an individualist culture that emphasizes the self over the group and, thus, overlooks collectivist cultures where maintaining group harmony is the ultimate need. Similarly, Herzberg assumed job content to be a universal motivator, whereas teamwork, status, and power are more highly prized in many non-Western cultures. The upshot is clear: culture matters, and Western-based theories of work motivation are not universally valid.[36]

EFFECTIVE LEADERSHIP

Leadership has been studied for thousands of years. The continued importance of contemporary leadership research is reflected in a recent review that identified 49 leadership theories.[37] Space and time constraints do not allow us to comment on each theory individually. In general, leadership research has addressed three questions: "who" leads; "how" do they lead; and "when," or under what circumstances, are they effective? We will discuss the most frequently cited theories associated with each approach in chronological order. This does not suggest that one has replaced another, but rather reflects changes over time. We will conclude with a comment on leadership research conducted in a global context.

THE TRAIT APPROACH

Leadership as a concept has played a fundamental role in human thought. Good or bad, the leadership of great people has shaped the history of the world. Without Moses, the Jews would have remained captive in Egypt. Without Winston Churchill, the British may have succumbed to the German bombing campaign carried out by the Luftwaffe during World War II. Considering we have all marveled at the achievements of certain people, it is not surprising that the first attempts to understand leadership centered on determining what specific traits make a person an effective leader. Consequently, early investigations sought to discover how people in leadership positions had attained them and whether these people had certain traits in common. In general, these investigations defined a trait as a distinctive physical or psychological characteristic that accounts for a person's behavior. In its pure form, the trait approach grew out of the "great-man" theory of leadership, which held individuals were leaders either because of heredity (as evidenced by royal dynasties) or because they possessed some genetic trait; that is, leaders were born and not made. Thus, leadership was thought to be derived from nature; biology alone explained who would and who would not become a leader. Learned behavior was considered irrelevant. People such as Alexander the Great, Julius Caesar, Charlemagne, Hannibal, Joan of Arc, and Napoleon Bonaparte were said to be "natural leaders" who were born to lead. It was believed they came into the world endowed with certain inborn qualities that enabled them to be effective leaders in any situation. Books such as Plutarch's *Lives of the Noble Greeks and Romans* and Charles F. Horne's

[35] Geert Hofstede, "Motivation, Leadership, and Organizations: Do American Theories Apply Abroad?" *Organizational Dynamics* 9(1) (Summer 1980), pp. 50, 55.
[36] *Idem*, "Think Locally, Act Globally: Cultural Constraints in Personnel Management," special issue, *Management International Review* 38(2) (1998), pp. 16–17.
[37] Jeremy D. Meuser, William L. Gardner, Jessica E. Dinh, Jinyu Hu, Robert C. Liden, and Robert G. Lord, "A Network Analysis of Leadership Theory: The Infancy of Integration," *Journal of Management* 42(5) (July 2016), pp. 1374–1403. For a 100-year review of leadership research, see Robert G. Lord, David. V. Day, Stephen J. Zaccaro, Bruce J. Avolio, and Alice H. Eagly, "Leadership in Applied Psychology: Three Waves of Theory and Research," *Journal of Applied Psychology* 102(3) (March 2017), pp. 434–451. Murillo de Oliveira Dias, Juliana Pan, Patrícia Vieira, and Leonardo José Dias Pereira have more recently identified 105 "leadership theories and styles." See their "From Plato to e-Leaders: The Evolution of Leadership Theories and Styles," *Economics and Business Quarterly Review* 5(2) (June 2022), p. 134.

eight-volume *Great Men and Famous Women* were read by generations of youth to determine whether they possessed the traits required to be a leader.[38]

The great-man theory held sway well into the early 1900s. As Lillian M. Gilbreth noted (see Chapter 8), scientific management challenged this view by showing that "ordinary" people who were properly trained could succeed as leaders. Under the influence of Gilbreth and others, the great-man theory began to be reevaluated for, at least, two reasons: (1) it was contended that if there were indeed "great men," or "natural leaders," it should be possible to investigate the traits that set them apart from the masses, and (2) it was believed that if these unique traits could be identified, other individuals should be able to acquire them through learning and experience. It is, perhaps, no consequence that it was during this period that groups such as the Girl Guides (1909), Boy Scouts (1910), and Girl Scouts (1912) were founded. The creeds of all these groups stressed the importance of traits such as kindness, reverence, obedience, and loyalty for success in life.

This logic prompted a wave of studies to discover the traits that, if acquired, would transform followers into leaders. Between 1904 and 1948, some 125 studies were conducted to compare traits of successful leaders with those of their unsuccessful counterparts in the hope that the unique traits of the former could be identified. A wide range of what are essentially personality traits were investigated, including assertiveness, enthusiasm, persistence, self-confidence, dependability, need for achievement, and social maturity. Physical attributes such as height, weight, energy, athletic ability, and attractiveness were also studied. Overall, the results were disappointing. Though certain relationships were found, these findings were generally weak, suggesting that these relationships were likely more incidental to leadership than central.[39]

THE BEHAVIORAL APPROACH

Because the study of traits offered little evidence for distinguishing leaders from followers or for making the latter into the former, researchers in the 1940s began to doubt the existence of unique leader traits and shifted their attention instead to leader behavior. This shift marked the beginning of a new approach which held leaders may be best characterized by "how" they behave, rather than by their personal traits. Underlying this approach was the assumption that leaders use a particular behavioral style that causes others to follow them. The behavioral approach is represented best by the Ohio State University Leadership Studies, conducted under the primary direction of Ralph M. Stogdill and Carroll L. Shartle, and the University of Michigan Leadership Studies, conducted under the direction of Rensis Likert, both discussed at length in Chapter 15.

THE SITUATIONAL APPROACH

By the late 1960s, it had become increasingly clear that there was no one best style of leadership. Recognizing that situational differences influence leader effectiveness, researchers began to explore "when," or under what circumstances, different leadership styles were most effective. The first situational theory to be advanced was the "contingency theory of leadership," developed by Fred E. Fiedler.[40] This theory defines leader effectiveness in terms of work group performance. It holds that work group performance depends (or is contingent) upon the match between a person's leadership style and the "favorableness" of the specific situation. Fiedler identified leadership style, or manner of acting in a situation, using a simple measure called the "least-preferred coworker," or LPC, scale. The LPC asks respondents to think of all the individuals with whom they

[38] Plutarch, *Plutarch's Lives*, trans. André Dacier, 6 vols. (London: Jacob Tonson, 1758) [written ca. 200 CE]; Charles F. Horne, ed., *Great Men and Famous Women: A Series of Pen and Pencil Sketches of the Lives of More than 200 of the Most Prominent Personages in History*, 8 vols. (New York: Selmar Hess, 1894).

[39] Ralph M. Stogdill, "Personal Factors Associated with Leadership: A Survey of the Literature," *Journal of Psychology* 25(1) (January 1948), pp. 35–71.

[40] Fred E. Fiedler, *A Theory of Leadership Effectiveness* (New York: McGraw-Hill, 1967).

have ever worked and, using the scale, rate the one person with whom they worked *least well*. LPC items deal with personality attributes such as "friendly–unfriendly," "rejecting–accepting," and "distant–close." People who rate their least-preferred coworker in a relatively unfavorable manner are described as "task-oriented." Conversely, people who rate their least-preferred coworker in a relatively favorable manner are described as "relationship oriented." Fiedler also identified three factors that determined a situation's "favorableness": (1) "leader–member relations," or the degree to which a group trusted, liked, or was willing to follow a leader; (2) the "task structure," or the degree to which a task assignment was ill- or well-defined; and (3) "leader position power," or the formal authority as distinct from the personal power of a leader. Fiedler concluded that, judged on group performance, leaders who are task-oriented tended to be most effective in situations that are either very favorable or very unfavorable. They are more effective in favorable situations because relationship-oriented behaviors are superfluous. They are also the most effective in unfavorable situations because at least they get the job done. It is only in moderately favorable situations that leaders who are relationship-oriented tended to be the most effective because interpersonal relations are especially important. Although Fiedler's conclusions have been criticized, his findings imply that there is no such thing as a perfect leader for every situation and that anyone can be a leader by carefully selecting those situations that match one's leadership style.

FURTHER THEORETICAL DEVELOPMENTS

The proliferation of literature on leaders and leadership requires us to limit our discussion of further theoretical developments: "who" leads is the focus of charismatic and transformational theories; "how" they lead is the basis for leader–member exchange theory; and we will subsume authentic, servant, and ethical leadership theories under the notion of "moral leadership," which tends to emphasize "who" and "how."

Taking its name from the Greek word *charismata*, meaning "divine gift," charisma and its role in leadership and "who" leads may be traced to the work of Max Weber.[41] In distinguishing among types of authority, Weber discussed not only legal and traditional authority, but also the authority that derives from the charisma of a leader. Charismatic leadership relies on attracting followers who trust, share the vision of, often attribute mystical powers to, and offer blind obedience to a leader. A special quality, charisma reaches people on an emotional, non-rational level, motivating them to extraordinary efforts. U.S. Presidents John F. Kennedy and Ronald Reagan are frequently cited examples of charismatic leaders. Both possessed an intense magnetic charm that set them apart from others. In general, it has been suggested that when a leader possesses charisma, followers perform better. Charismatic leaders engender favorable outcomes by modeling a value system for followers, exuding competence and success, articulating an inspirational goal that is ideological rather than pragmatic, establishing high expectations, showing confidence in followers, and arousing followers' motivation. Whatever the consequences, charisma is likely a complex interaction of leader and follower characteristics, together with situational factors. Critics note, however, that effective leadership does not depend on charisma. U.S. Presidents Dwight D. Eisenhower and Harry S. Truman were singularly effective leaders, but neither was especially charismatic.

In the leadership literature, charismatic and transformational leadership are often discussed interchangeably.[42] This may be explained by the fact that in Bernard M. Bass's model of

[41] Max Weber, *The Theory of Social and Economic Organization*, trans. Alexander M. Henderson and ed. and trans. Talcott Parsons (New York: Free Press, 1947), p. 328. German edition published in 1922. Weber borrowed the notion of charisma from Sohm's studies of early Christianity. See Rudolph Sohm, *Kirchenrecht: Die geschichtlichen Grundlegen* [*Canon Law: The Historical Basis*], vol. 1 (Leipzig: Verlag von Duncker & Humblot, 1892), p. 6. See also Christopher Adair-Toteff, "Max Weber's Charisma," *Journal of Classical Sociology* 5(2) (July 2005), pp. 189–204.

[42] Meuser et al., "A Network Analysis of Leadership Theory: The Infancy of Integration," p. 1383.

transformational leadership, the dominant research framework, developing charisma is but one part of becoming a transformational leader, which involves inspiring followers to adopt more challenging goals, focusing efforts, and expressing important goals in influential ways.[43] The term *transformational* as applied to a form of leadership was coined by James MacGregor Burns to describe types of political leaders.[44] Research suggests that transformational-charismatic leaders emerge at particular times, such as when an organization is in decline and, consequently, revitalization and a renewed vision are required. For this reason, transformational-charismatic leaders are often described as offering a vision of the major changes needed in an organization's structure, culture, market, and so on. It is unclear, however, what would happen if a transformational-charismatic leader's intentions were not socially desirable; for instance, some historical figures (Adolf Hitler comes to mind) have demonstrated a personal magnetism and have led others in blind obedience toward evil ends. Transformational-charismatic leadership research has come under increasing criticism. Perhaps the most fundamental objection is that there is no clear "conceptual definition" of transformational-charismatic leadership, making it impossible to compare results from different studies. This has led some to conclude that the notion of transformational-charismatic leadership should be abandoned.[45]

Leader–member exchange theory addresses the "how" of leadership. Most leadership theories assume that a leader behaves in much the same way toward all followers. In contrast, leader–member exchange theory holds that leadership is a one-on-one exchange in which leaders behave differently with different work group members.[46] It further holds that followers, based on the quality of their interpersonal relationships (exchanges) with a leader, form different groups: an in-group (higher quality) and an out-group (lower quality). Insiders and outsiders experience very different work outcomes. Leader interactions with insiders resemble social transactions, with leaders and followers exchanging resources and enjoying higher levels of trust and support. In this way, leader and follower become reciprocally interdependent. In contrast, in exchanges with outsiders, leaders act as supervisors, relying on formal authority to extract follower performance. At the extreme, leader exchanges with outsiders can be very mechanistic, arising from workplace rules, policies, and procedures rather than spontaneous interaction. Such exchanges are typically characterized by low levels of trust, interaction, support, and leader-provided rewards. Research suggests that, because of such differing treatments, in-group members perform better and are more satisfied than out-group members. Leader–member exchange theory underscores the fact that leader behavior originates, in part, in followers. That is, leadership is a mutual influence process. Leaders respond differently to different followers, and both leaders and followers alter their behavior depending on the performance of the other.

Like other theories of leadership, leader–member exchange theory has not escaped criticism. For example, critics have taken exception to various methodological aspects of how leader–member exchanges are measured. Although leader–member exchange theory has already been extended to investigate individual differences such as gender, Bruce J. Avolio and colleagues note that one promising area for future research would be to explore the implications of national culture on the development and quality of leader–member relationships and their resulting influence on workplace outcomes such as job satisfaction and performance.[47] Leader–member exchange theory may also run contrary to more recent ideas concerning "moral leadership," as expressed in authentic, servant, and ethical leadership theories.

---

[43] Bernard M. Bass, *Leadership and Performance Beyond Expectations* (New York: Free Press, 1985).

[44] James M. Burns, *Leadership* (New York: Harper & Row, 1978).

[45] Daan Van Knippenberg and Sim Sitkin, "A Critical Assessment of Charismatic-Transformational Leadership Research: Back to the Drawing Board?" *Academy of Management Annals* 7(1) (June 2013), p. 45.

[46] George B. Graen and Terri A. Scandura, "Toward a Psychology of Dyadic Organizing," *Research in Organizational Behavior* 9 (1987), pp. 175–208.

[47] Bruce J. Avolio, O. Fred Walumbwa, and Todd J. Weber, "Leadership: Current Theories, Research, and Future Directions," *Annual Review of Psychology* 60 (2009), p. 434.

Some 80-plus years after Chester I. Barnard first wrote of "moral leadership" (see Chapter 9), leadership researchers turned their focus to whether leaders' moral behavior contributes to leader effectiveness. In general, their research has concentrated on whether leaders are *authentic*, *serve* others, and maintain high standards of *ethical* behavior. Barnard based his idea of moral leadership on his practical experiences as president of New Jersey Bell Telephone, chairman of the National Science Foundation, president of the Rockefeller Foundation, and president of the United Service Organization, to name a few. As recounted previously, Barnard observed, "[T]he endurance of an organization depends upon the quality of leadership; and that quality derives from the breadth of morality upon which it rests. . . . A low morality will not sustain leadership long, its influence quickly vanishes, it cannot produce its own succession."[48] In line with Barnard's thinking, high standards of ethical conduct are seen as essential in authentic, servant, and ethical forms of leadership. Authentic leaders possess an internalized self-awareness and moral courage, are transparent in dealings with others, and objectively think through all side of issues. Servant leaders are altruistic, put others before themselves, empower others to help them grow, and focus on the needs of multiple stakeholders in making decisions. Ethical leaders follow societal norms, engage in two-way communication to encourage employee engagement, and are "credible role models." These descriptions are brief but illustrate the characteristics and behavior of "moral leaders."[49]

Attempts to summarize the evolution of leadership theory and research can be bewildering. In 1974, after reviewing some 3,000 studies, Stogdill lamented, "Four decades of research on leadership have produced a bewildering mass of findings. . . . The endless accumulation of empirical data has not produced an integrated understanding of leadership."[50] Nearly four more decades would pass, and Gary A. Yukl would similarly despair, "Thousands of studies on leader behavior and its effects have been conducted over the past half century, but the bewildering variety of behavior constructs used for this research makes it difficult to compare and integrate the findings."[51] A little over a decade later, Thomas Fisher and Sim B. Sitkin reviewed the leadership literature and lamented a perpetuation of the same limitations, including an overlap or redundancy in the descriptions of leader behaviors and the impossibility of establishing whether a link between leadership behaviors and intended outcomes is causal or due to other factors.[52] To add to the confusion, it should be noted that the majority of leadership approaches and theories that we have discussed to this point may be culturally constrained, having been predominantly developed by scholars based in Western cultures. Bearing this in mind, the next section reviews management research conducted in a non-Western context.

PROJECT GLOBE

Project Global Leadership and Organizational Behavior Effectiveness (GLOBE) was a cross-cultural study involving more than 200 researchers.[53] Conceived in the early 1990s, GLOBE's 25-plus-year study of 17,300 middle managers in 950 organizations in 62 societies was a long-term

---

[48] Chester I. Barnard, *The Functions of the Executive* (Cambridge, MA: Harvard University Press, 1938), pp. 282–283. See also *idem*, "Elementary Conditions of Business Morals," *California Management Review* 1(1) (Fall 1958), pp. 1–13.

[49] G. James Lemoine, Chad A. Hartwell, and Hannes Leroy, "Taking Stock of Moral Approaches to Leadership: An Integrative Review of Ethical, Authentic, and Servant Leadership," *Academy of Management Annals* 13(1) (January 2019), pp. 148–187.

[50] Ralph M. Stogdill, *Handbook of Leadership: A Survey of Theory and Research* (New York: Free Press, 1974), p. xvii.

[51] Gary A. Yukl, "Effective Leadership Behavior: What We Know and What Questions Need More Attention," *Academy of Management Perspectives* 26(4) (November 2012), p. 66.

[52] Thomas Fischer and Sim B. Sitkin, "Leadership Styles: A Comprehensive Assessment and Way Forward," *Academy of Management Annals* 17(1) (January 2023), pp. 331–372.

[53] Robert J. House and Mansour Javidan, "Overview of GLOBE," in Robert J. House, Paul J. Hanges, Mansour Javidan, Peter W. Dorfman, and Vipin Gupta, eds., *Leadership, Culture, and Organizations: The GLOBE Study of 62 Societies* (London: Sage, 2004), pp. 11–16. See also Jagdeep S. Chhokar, Felix C. Brodbeck, and Robert J. House, eds., *Culture and Leadership across the World: The GLOBE Book of In-Depth Studies of 25 Societies* (Rahway, NJ: Lawrence Erlbaum Associates, 2007).

program to discover differences in societal-level work-related cultural values or dimensions that influence leader–follower behavior and relationships. The GLOBE Project incorporated both Geert Hofstede's power–distance and uncertainty–avoidance dimensions (though relabeled long-term orientation to "future orientation"). The GLOBE researchers split Hofstede's individualism–collectivism dimension into institutional-level collectivism (organizational and societal) and in-group collectivism (individual cohesiveness in their organizations/families). They also expanded his masculinity–femininity dimensions to include assertiveness and gender egalitarianism, as well as humane orientation (the degree to which members of a collective reward others for caring, fairness, altruism, and so on) and performance orientation (the degree to which members of a collective reward individuals for improved performance and excellence). The GLOBE researchers identified 6 higher-order global leadership dimensions, comprised of various primary dimensions: (1) *Charismatic/Value-Based Leadership* (including the primary dimensions: visionary, inspirational, integrity); (2) *Team-Oriented Leadership* (including the primary dimensions: collaborative team orientation, team integrator, diplomatic); (3) *Participative Leadership* (primary dimensions: nonparticipative and autocratic); (4) *Humane-Oriented Leadership* (primary dimensions: modesty and humane orientation); (5) *Autonomous Leadership* (a single dimension consisting of individualistic independence, autonomy, and unique attributes); and (6) *Self-Protective Leadership* (including the primary dimensions: self-centered, conflict inducer, face-saving orientation).[54] They clustered the societies being studied by the degree to which they were similar in preference for each leader dimension and categorized them into higher, middle, and lower groups based on the extent to which each dimension contributed to outstanding leadership. Charismatic/value-based leaders were preferred in Anglo countries such as England and the United States; team-oriented leaders in Latin American countries such as Bolivia and Brazil; humane-oriented leaders in South Asian countries such as India and Indonesia; autonomous leaders in Eastern European countries such Albania and Russia; and self-protective leaders in Middle Eastern countries such as Egypt and Turkey. Leadership attributes such as "trustworthy, just, and honest" were shown to be "universally desirable." Conversely, leadership attributes such as "irritable" and "ruthless" were found to be universally undesirable. The GLOBE researchers uncovered one constant: "In all cultures, leader team orientation and the communication of vision, values, and confidence in followers are reported to be highly effective leader behaviors."[55]

Although the notion that there are leaders who can be successful across cultures might be appealing, the GLOBE Project indicates that there are substantial differences in the attributes that managers need to be effective in different cultures. In brief, culture matters. A broad set of experiences and competencies is necessary for a manager to be a global leader. The GLOBE Project remains one of the most ambitious cross-cultural studies of leadership ever undertaken.

ORGANIZATION THEORY: A CONTINUING VENTURE

In the preceding chapters, we have seen how management practitioners and scholars, including Henri Fayol, Max Weber, Lyndall F. Urwick, James D. Mooney, and Chester I. Barnard, sought to understand the basic elements of organization design. For the most part, they drew from their practical experiences to understand task specialization, authority, coordination, and other principles of organization. By the late 1950s, "academics were making a distinction between 'organization theory' and 'organizational behavior,'" the former referring to "a collection of general propositions about organizations."[56] Around the same time, various scholars in Great Britain and the United States were embarking on a series of studies into the effect of technology on an

[54] Peter W. Dorfman, Mansour Javidan, Paul Hanges, Ali Dastmalchian, and Robert A. House, "GLOBE: A Twenty Year Journey into the Intriguing World of Culture and Leadership," *Journal of World Business* 47(4) (October 2012), pp. 504–518.

[55] Robert J. House, "Illustrative Examples of GLOBE Findings," in House, Hanges, Javidan, et al., *Leadership, Culture, and Organizations*, p. 7.

[56] William H. Starbuck, "The Origins of Organization Theory," in Haridimos Tsoukas and Christian Knudsen, eds., *The Oxford Handbook of Organization Theory* (Oxford: Oxford University Press, 2004), pp. 143, 144.

organization's structure and the relationship between an organization's design and its environment. We will now turn to a review of these studies.

ASTON STUDIES: WORKFLOW INTEGRATION AND PRODUCTION CONTINUITY

Beginning in the 1960s, a group of English researchers known as the Aston Group began an ambitious study of the relationship between an organization's structure and technology.[57] Under the direction of Derek Pugh and David Hickson, they studied the structural and technological characteristics of 52 firms located in Birmingham (England) and focused on two major facets of what they termed "operation technology," meaning the equipping and sequencing of activities in a workflow.[58] These facets were *workflow integration* and *production continuity*. In contrast to Joan Woodward's earlier work, which concluded that a firm's success is directly related to a proper match between its technology and certain structural characteristics,[59] they found only a weak relationship between workflow integration and various structural variables. The researchers observed that organization size moderated the relationship between technology and structure, which, to reconcile their result with Woodward's conclusions, led them to conclude that her findings were valid only for smaller organizations. This, the researchers believed, was contrary to the situation in larger organizations where "managers and administrators are buffered from the technology itself by the specialized departments, standard procedures, and formalized paperwork that size brings with it." An organization's size, not its technology, was therefore the primary determinant of its structure.

TECHNOLOGICAL INTERDEPENDENCE

James D. Thompson offered an alternative view of technology, incorporating the notion of *technological interdependence*.[60] Thompson's work focused on how organizations cope with uncertainties created by a manager's cognitive limits and by events and influences that cannot be controlled or predicted. He developed a classification of three technologies—mediating, long-linked, and intensive—based on the mechanisms used to coordinate different types of workflow interdependence. Generally, the greater the problem-solving behavior required by a workflow, the more extensive the coordinating mechanism required to satisfy coordination needs. *Mediating technology* entails the joining of independent clients or customers where subunits within an organization may not directly interact, but are interdependent and must perform adequately or other subunits falter, such as in post offices, auction houses, and online dating services. *Long-linked technology* is characterized by the *sequential interdependence* of tasks or operations. The procedures necessary to complete a good or service are highly uniform and must be performed in a specified serial order, such as in relay teams and assembly lines. *Intensive technology* is characterized by *reciprocal interdependence* and is exemplified by the use of different technologies and skills required to produce a good. The selection, mix, and sequence of techniques and skills used at one stage of production are contingent on feedback from earlier production stages. Thus, the sequence of operations required to produce a good or service cannot be predetermined, such

[57] This section is adapted from Arthur G. Bedeian and Raymond F. Zammuto, *Organizations: Theory and Design* (Hinsdale, IL: Dryden Press, 1991). See also Donald Gerwin, "Relationships Between Structure and Technology," in Paul C. Nystrom and William H. Starbuck, eds., *Handbook of Organizational Design, vol. 2: Remodeling Organizations and Their Environments* (Oxford: Oxford University Press, 1981), pp. 3–38.

[58] David J. Hickson, Derek S. Pugh, and Diane Phessey, "Operations Technology and Organization Structure: An Empirical Appraisal," *Administrative Science Quarterly* 14(3) (September 1969), pp. 394–395.

[59] Joan Woodward, *Management and Technology* (London: Her Majesty's Stationery Office, 1958); *idem*, *Industrial Organization: Theory and Practice* (London: Oxford University Press, 1965). See also Carolyn P. Garrity, Eric W. Liguori, and Jeffrey Muldoon, "Woodward's Aegis: A Critical Biography of Joan Woodward," *Journal of Management History* 24(4) (2018), pp. 457–475.

[60] James D. Thompson, *Organizations in Action* (New York: McGraw-Hill, 1967), pp. 15–18.

as with military combat units, mental-health centers, basketball teams, and certain research and development projects. Of the various technological typologies that have been developed, Thompson's is generally considered the richest conceptually and has the advantage of being applicable to a wide variety of manufacturing and service organizations.

CONTINGENCY THEORY AND ITS COROLLARIES

Contingency theory was developed around the late 1950s and 1960s as an outgrowth of the application of systems theory (see Chapter 21) to the social sciences. Contingency theorists examined whether some organization designs fit different environmental conditions better than others and concluded that managers should choose the design that best fits a firm's environment. A study by Tom Burns and George M. Stalker was the first major attempt to identify the types of organization structures and managerial practices appropriate for different environmental conditions.[61] Reminiscent of a metaphor used by Émile Durkheim to differentiate two modes for maintaining social order (i.e., "organic solidarity" and "mechanical solidarity"),[62] Burns and Stalker identified two "divergent systems of management practice": *organic* and *mechanistic*. In organic systems, structure is flexible, tasks are loosely defined, and communication resembles consultation rather than order giving. Organic systems are especially appropriate for changing environments in which novel problems continually arise. In contrast, organizations with mechanistic systems are characterized by distinct functional specialties, precisely defined tasks and responsibilities, and a well-defined chain of command. Mechanistic systems, containing many bureaucratic elements, are particularly appropriate for stable environments. Burns and Stalker viewed organic and mechanistic systems as ideal types defining two ends of a continuum. They suggested that few, if any, management systems are purely mechanistic or purely organic; most combine characteristics of both. In addition, no part of their research indicated that one system is superior to the other. Rather, the nature of an organization's environment determines which system is appropriate.

ORGANIZATIONS AND THEIR ENVIRONMENTS

Paul R. Lawrence and Jay W. Lorsch built on Burns and Stalker's findings and studied 10 U.S. firms experiencing varying levels of economic effectiveness in three different industry environments: plastics, consumer foods, and containers. The plastics industry was chosen because, at the time, it operated in a dynamic environment characterized by high rates of technological and scientific innovation and by rapidly changing customer needs and preferences. The container industry, on the other hand, had a stable environment, where customer needs were predictable and technical requirements were constant. Finally, the environment of the consumer foods industry was of intermediate stability, characterized by a moderate rate of change—slower than the plastics industry but faster than the container industry. Lawrence and Lorsch argued that as an organization's environment becomes more complex and uncertain, it tends to differentiate into subunits. This structural differentiation leads to differences in subunit goals and structure, time perspectives, and interpersonal orientations, reflecting the task and environmental uncertainties with which each unit copes. They found that it is more difficult to integrate functional subunits' efforts as differentiation increases. *Integration* is "the process of achieving unity of effort among various subsystems in the accomplishment of [an] organization's tasks."[63] Perhaps most important, Lawrence and Lorsch reported that the most economically effective organizations in each industry, with one exception, exhibited a higher degree of integration. A higher degree

---

[61] Tom Burns and George M. Stalker, *The Management of Innovation* (London: Tavistock Publications, 1961), p. 5.

[62] Émile Durkheim, *The Division of Labor in Society*, trans. George Simpson (Glencoe, IL: Free Press, 1933), pp. 70, 105. French edition published in 1893.

[63] Paul R. Lawrence and Jay W. Lorsch, "Differentiation and Integration in Complex Organizations," *Administrative Science Quarterly* 12(1) (June 1967), pp. 3–4.

of differentiation was needed to deal with diverse and uncertain environmental demands and needed a matching degree of integration to achieve effective performance. Consistent with Burns and Stalker's results, Lawrence and Lorsch's study implies that there is no universal best way to design an organization. The specific design of an organization and its subunits must "fit" its environment. Successful organizations are those able to diagnose and meet environmental requirements for differentiation and integration. Thus, appropriate patterns of structure vary, and they are contingent on the relationship between an organization and its environment.

STRATEGIC CHOICE

John Child coined the term "strategic choice" and argued that contingency theory "is inadequate, primarily because it fails to give due attention to the agency of choice by whoever have the power to direct [an] organization."[64] According to Child, through strategy formulation and implementation, a management team can take steps to define and manipulate an organization's domains, thereby choosing to ignore or restrain environmental effects that might require modification of existing structural arrangements. In commenting further, Child noted, "In view of these essentially strategic and political factors, environmental conditions cannot be regarded as a direct source of variation in organizational structure, as [contingency] theorists often imply."[65] Child's notion of strategic choice emphasizes that managers act in response to events in their organizations' environments. Such actions extend "to the context within which [their] organization is operating, to the standards of performance against which the pressure of economic constraints has to be evaluated, and to the design of the organization's structure itself."[66]

POPULATION ECOLOGY

In the late 1970s, a broader approach to the study of organization–environment relations, known as *population ecology*, was proposed by Michael T. Hannan and John Freeman.[67] Population ecologists are interested in the processes that generate organizational diversity, and in how the diversity of organizational structures within industries and societies changes in response to long-term environmental pressures. Drawing heavily from the biological ecology literature, Hannan and Freeman suggested looking at changes in organizational populations rather than studying individual organizations to examine organizational adaptation. They stated that adaptation to changing environmental conditions takes place primarily through the creation of organizations with new forms that replace existing organizations. They reasoned that this occurs because there are strong inertial forces (such as sunk costs in plants, equipment, and personnel) in existing organizations that make it difficult for them to change.[68] As existing organizations change slowly, new organizations taking advantage of emerging environmental opportunities have an opening to gain a foothold in an industry. The result is the replacement of existing organizations by new ones better suited to altered environmental conditions. A shortcoming of this perspective, however, is that it fails to account for changes in the population of organizations such as occurred with the rise of new firms and industries in areas like biotechnology, pharmaceuticals, and information technology—changes that occurred several years after the authors stated their thesis. Nevertheless, the notion of firms and industries as changing populations is an interesting view of the dynamic competitive arena.

---

[64] John Child, "Organizational Structure, Environment, and Performance: The Role of Strategic Choice," *Sociology* 6(1) (January 1972), p. 3.
[65] *Ibid.*, p. 10.
[66] *Ibid.*, p. 2.
[67] Michael T. Hannan and John Freeman, "The Population Ecology of Organizations," *American Journal of Sociology* 82(5) (March 1977), pp. 929–963.
[68] *Idem*, "Structural Inertia and Organizational Change," *American Sociological Review* 49(2) (April 1984), pp. 155–156.

INSTITUTIONAL THEORY

In addition to being considered the Father of Industrial Relations (see Chapter 9), John R. Commons is also regarded as a founder of the "institutional school of economics." His views on the role of collective action (in the form of business corporations, labor unions, farmers' cooperatives, political parties, courts, churches and so on) in furthering a nation's economic development are the basis for what is known as "institutional theory."[69] Commons viewed society *in toto* as a social organization composed of purposeful individuals whose interests conflict, but whose actions are mutually dependent in a "world of scarcity," where one party *may* injure others if it takes all it wants.[70] Consequently, a central concern of collective activities is the control of differences in degrees of power that enable individuals to impose their will on others. For Commons, the control necessary to decide conflicts and maintain order is achieved through "institutions," or what he termed "rules of action" or "working rules of collective action."[71] Examples of working rules include statutory laws, court decisions, contracts, corporate charters, collective-bargaining agreements, and cultural norms. Working rules derive their authority from customs, practices, and societal conventions that define acceptable behavior within a civil society. They are enforced through three categories of sanctions: physical (e.g., seizure of property), economic (e.g., financial penalties), and moral (e.g., public ridicule). When applied, these sanctions are a means of controlling individual actions for the good of society.

In an essay reflecting on the development of institutional theory, sociologist Philip Selznick, who considered himself to be a member of the "old" school that included Commons, expressed doubt about the contributions of "new" institutionalists in addressing "the central problems of organization and governance."[72] Building on the argument that "social science should be guided by problems of life and practice," Selznick quoted philosopher and educator John Dewey: "Any problem of scientific inquiry that does not grow out of actual (or 'practical') social conditions is factitious; it is arbitrarily set by the inquirer instead of being objectively produced and controlled."[73] Selznick felt that "new" institutionalists had replaced "rational-actors models" with "supraindividual" explanations disassociated from the "direct consequences of individuals' attributes or motives." He thus called for a renewed focus on the "genuine problems of institutional life" rather than what he saw as the irrelevant interests of new institutionalism.

What Selznick considered "new" institutionalism is, perhaps, most closely associated with a 1977 paper by John W. Meyer and Brian Rowan. The authors acknowledge that "[m]any formal organizational structures arise as reflections of rationalized institutional rules." They, however, argue that many of these rules are "rationalized myths" (members' shared beliefs) that are used to seek legitimacy, stability, and resources. Meyer and Rowan maintain that, as a consequence, modern societies are filled with organizations structured according to the myths of the institutional environment in which they are embedded rather than being "primarily structured by the demands of technical production and exchange."[74] Whether this conclusion addresses, per Selznick's terms, a "genuine problem of institutional life" or is otherwise "irrelevant" is left to the reader's judgment. Writing in 1993, Andrew H. Van de Ven lamented that the then "new generation of institutional scholars" had "largely ignored" Commons's pioneering ideas.[75] The absence of a single reference to Commons's work in a recent review of institutional theory sadly confirms that this continues to be the case.[76]

---

[69] John R. Commons, *Institutional Economics: Its Place in Political Economy* (New York: Macmillan, 1934), p. 1.

[70] *Ibid.*, p. 225.

[71] *Idem, The Economics of Collective Action,* ed. Kenneth H. Parsons (New York: Macmillan, 1951), p. 26.

[72] Philip Selznick, "Institutionalists 'Old' and 'New,'" *Administrative Science Quarterly* 41(2) (June 1996), pp. 270–277.

[73] John Dewey, *Logic, The Theory of Inquiry* (New York: Henry Holt, 1938), p. 499.

[74] John W. Meyer and Brian Rowan, "Institutionalized Organizations: Formal Structure as Myth and Ceremony," *American Journal of Sociology* 83(2) (September 1977), p. 340.

[75] Andrew H. Van de Ven, "The Institutional Theory of John R. Commons: A Review and Commentary," *Academy of Management Review* 18(1) (January 1993), p. 139.

[76] Mary Ann Glynn and Thomas D'Aunno, "An Intellectual History of Institutional Theory: Looking Back to Move Forward," *Academy of Management Annals* 17(1) (January 2023), pp. 301–330.

WHEN ENDS BECOME MEANS

By 2005, Mie Augier and James G. March were able to declare that between 1945 and 2000, the field of organization theory in Anglophone North America had become a "scholarly community" and had "moved from being a combination of established disciplines to becoming a quasi-discipline of its own, with its own journals and professional associations."[77] In large measure, however, organization theory, much like the management discipline as a whole (see Chapter 19), had turned inward to theorizing rather than outward to applied practice. William McKinley contended that, within the field of organization theory, a preoccupation with "new theory development" had become the "ultimate goal of the discipline" rather than a means to further an end, meaning "the production of a consensus about the validity or invalidity of the theories . . . that . . . represent organizations."[78] Robert K. Merton long ago observed that such inversions occur when the methods of doing work (the means) become substituted for output (the ends) in such a way that means become ends in themselves.[79] In short, McKinley believed that a "scholarly community" had formed in which new theory development had become the overriding goal without reference to real-world challenges facing practicing managers. Robert E. Ployhart and Jean M. Bartunek subsequently encouraged academics, in general, to recognize that their relationship with practitioners is two-sided, and that they "can and should make more explicit use of what [they] can learn from practitioners."[80]

DIFFERENT COUNTRIES, DIFFERENT CULTURES

Reflecting on the history of organization studies, James G. March noted: "By 1970, European universities had largely recovered from the ravages of the Second World War and had started to experience the same kind of exceptional growth that had profoundly affected North American universities 20 years earlier." He pointed out, however, that "European organizations scholarship followed different paths in different countries, particularly across different linguistic groups."[81] Underscoring and expanding this point to a global level, Geert Hofstede, writing at the end of the 1970s, observed: "Many of the differences in employee motivation, management styles, and organizational structures of companies throughout the world can be traced to differences in the collective mental programming of people in different national cultures."[82] Hofstede likewise observed that organization theorists, like organizations themselves, are culture bound: he wrote, "Give me a new theory and I will tell you the nationality of its author."[83] In Hofstede's opinion at the time, the North American organization theorists were driven by free markets, the French by power, the Germans by rules, the Dutch by consensus, and the Chinese by family. As such, he concluded there will be no universal theory of organizations because of cultural differences. Hofstede added: "More and more organizations are crossing national borders, and thus differences in nationality are increasingly a source of conflicts and contradictions in organizations."[84] Consequently, as subsequent experience has shown, negotiations between representatives from different countries are almost certain to be difficult unless an appreciation of cultural differences is front and center in any such situations.

[77] Mie Augier, James G. March, and Bilian Ni Sullivan "Notes on the Evolution of a Research Community: Organization Studies in Anglophone North America, 1945–2000," *Organization Science* 16(1) (January–February 2005), p. 5.
[78] William McKinley, "Organization Theory Development: Displacement of Ends?" *Organization Studies* 31(1) (January 2010), p. 48.
[79] Robert K. Merton, "Bureaucratic Structure and Personality," *Social Forces* 18(4) (May 1940), p. 563n11.
[80] Robert E. Ployhart and Jean M. Bartunek, "Editors' Comments: There Is Nothing So Theoretical As Good Practice—A Call for Phenomenal Theory," *Academy of Management Review* 44(3) (July 2019), p. 496.
[81] James G. March, "The Study of Organizations and Organizing Since 1945," *Organization Studies* 28(1) (January 2007), p. 13.
[82] Geert Hofstede, "Motivation, Leadership, and Organization: Do American Theories Apply Abroad?" *Organizational Dynamics* 9(1) (Summer 1980), p. 42.
[83] *Idem*, "An American in Paris: The Influence of Nationality on Organization Theories," *Organization Studies* 17(3) (May 1996), p. 531.
[84] *Ibid.*, p. 535.

In an interesting aside, Hofstede noted that although East Asia was fully developed economically, there were still a few "native theories" of organization, most having been formulated by individuals from Europe, the United States, and other non–East Asian countries. For instance, in 1990, Richard D. Whitley, an Englishman, argued that the dominant forms of organizing in Japan, South Korea, and Taiwan reflect the values of a long-term orientation, desire for stability (uncertainty avoidance), group rewards (collectivism), personal authority relationships, and loyalty to an enterprise as a whole. Similar values shaped the powerful Japanese business alliances known as *keiretsu*, family-owned conglomerates (*chaebol*) in South Korea, and Chinese family businesses in Taiwan. Despite some variations, the basic form of organizing expatriate Chinese family businesses was similar in countries such as Taiwan, Hong Kong, and Thailand. Whitley concluded that "(a) there are a variety of forms of business organization which are competitive in world markets; (b) these vary in certain basic characteristics because of the institutional environment in which they become established; and (c) to a considerable extent, they are societally specific in that they would not function as effectively in different societal contexts."[85] All this suggested, and continues to suggest, that managers of multinational firms should carefully consider where and when different forms of organization might be the most successful.

It is encouraging that a study of articles published in 88 leading journals between 1980 and 2020 reveals that management scholarship has become more internationalized. Although management research continues to be concentrated in North America, the geographical diversity of authorships has increased from 35 to 91 countries. Indicative of a growing cooperation among scholars across cultures, the increase in publications by non–North American authors has been driven by papers coauthored by North American scholars. As the author of this study observes, more nations than ever are contributing to our understanding of managerial practices.[86]

SUMMARY

As we have moved toward the present day in understanding people and organizations, it has become increasingly clear that numerous developments have shaped the evolution of management thought. The human-relations movement was overtaken by the emergence of a new generation of scholars devoted to the study of what became known as "organizational behavior." Shunning the "feel-good" reputation of the human relationists, organizational-behavior researchers addressed issues such as job design, work motivation, and effective leadership. Personnel management as a field began to build a firmer empirical base and over time evolved into HRM and, then, SHRM. Early writers on organization structure were practitioners or consultants. By the late 1950s, scholars in Great Britain and the United States embarked on a series of studies into the effect of technology on an organization's structure and the relationship between an organization's design and its environment . Between 1945 and 2000, the field of organization theory in Anglophone North America became a "scholarly community." Contemporary critics contended that within the field of organization theory, "new theory development" had become the "ultimate goal of the discipline" rather than a means to further an end, thus contributing to a widening of the gap between management theory and practice. With the growing globalization of business following World War II, there was also a growing understanding that Western-based organization theories were not universally applicable. This chapter reviewed each of these developments.

[85] Richard D. Whitley, "East Asian Enterprise Structures and the Comparative Analysis of Forms of Business Organization," *Organization Studies* 11(1) (January 1990), p. 69.
[86] Przemysław G. Hensel, "Geographical Diversity of Management and Organization Research," *OSF Preprints* (January 10, 2023), p. 7. Accessible at https://osf.io/3zmjf.

Science and Systems in an Information Age

CHAPTER 21

Numbers have always held a special fascination for humans; people have ascribed mystical powers to some numbers, malignant qualities to others, and, throughout history, have used numbers to tally flocks of sheep as well as to reach for the stars. Though numbers have no intrinsic value in themselves, by lending a preciseness and orderliness to the world, they have become symbols of the continued quest for knowledge. An inborn inquisitiveness has led humans to explore, to attempt to explain the inexplicable, and to search for a force that binds the complexities observed in nature into some logical scheme. Since time immemorial, humans have sought to bring order from chaos by searching for patterns in environmental events.

Organizations have also long sought to track events in their environments. Notably, in earlier chapters, we saw how managers used new technologies, such as the electric telegraph, to monitor environmental events and make informed decisions. This chapter extends these deep roots to trace the emergence of operations research and management science, the new language of production/operations management, the rise of Japanese industry following World War II, and the search for world-class manufacturing. The chapter concludes with a discussion of general systems theory, cybernetics, and the arrival of the "digital hand" of the Information Age.

THE QUEST FOR SCIENCE IN MANAGEMENT

The scientific method represents an objective approach to problem-solving that involves clearly stated hypotheses, data collection and analysis, and the selection of a course of action based on the ensuing results. In breaking with the mystics who held that reality was unknowable, in his 350 BCE book *Prior Analytics*, Aristotle defined the conditions under which scientific arguments provide true knowledge.[1] His *syllogistic logic*, in which premises are manipulated to produce conclusions, laid the foundation for modern scientific inquiry. During the so-called Dark Ages—the roughly five-hundred years of cultural stagnation after 476 CE when Rome fell to Germanic invaders—the masterpieces of the Greco-Roman world were largely lost. The wisdom of the ancient world, however, was rediscovered by Renaissance intellectuals in the fourteenth, fifteenth, and sixteenth centuries (see Chapter 2), leading to a renewed interest in scientific experiment and mathematics, and preparing the way for the 1600s and what philosopher

[1] Aristotle, "Analytica Priora," ["Prior Analytics"], trans. Arthur J. J. Jenkinson in W. David Ross, ed., *The Works of Aristotle*, vol. 1 (Oxford, England: Clarendon Press, 1908). Written circa 350 BCE.

Alfred North Whitehead celebrated as the "century of genius."[2] Over this period of one hundred years, Copernicus (1473–1543) posited that the Earth is not the center of the universe and revolves around the Sun; Galileo (1546–1642) revolutionized astronomy and physics; Johannes Kepler (1571–1630) advanced laws of planetary motion; René Descartes (1596–1650) invented analytical geometry; and Isaac Newton (1642–1727), one of the most influential scientists of all time, developed calculus and universal laws of motion and gravitation. Other seventeenth-century polymaths who helped lay the foundations of modern science by making seminal contributions in chemistry, physics, and mathematics included Blaise Pascal (1623–1662), Robert Boyle (1627–1691), Christiaan Huygens (1629–1695), and Gottfried W. Leibniz (1646–1716). In the mid- to late-eighteenth century, inventors such as John Kay, James Hargreaves, Richard Arkwright, Samuel Crompton, Thomas Newcomen, and James Watt applied the scientific methods of these and other thinkers to solve the challenges of the burgeoning factory system that began during the Industrial Revolution (see Chapter 3). Industrialization demanded order and predictability, and in the early twentieth century, engineers such as Frederick W. Taylor, Carl G. Barth, Henry L. Gantt, Frank B. Gilbreth, and Harrington Emerson led the way in the scientific study and systematization of work (see Chapters 7 and 8). The seeds of the modern industrial corporation—the forerunner of today's *Fortune* 500 company—were sown during this era.

OPERATIONS RESEARCH (OR)

World War I gave widespread recognition and acceptance to the application of the scientific method to management, as evidenced in Gantt's work for the Emergency Fleet Corporation and Wallace Clark's efforts for the U.S. Shipping Board (see Chapter 8). For more than three decades, the work of Gantt, Taylor, and other scientific-management proponents was carried forward and known as "industrial administration" or (more commonly) "production management." The focus during these years was on expanding output to minimize unit costs rather than maintaining a commitment to high quality at a low cost. Outside events would soon intervene, however, giving rise to a competitive challenge from abroad that would move production/operations management to a new stage of development that emphasized both low cost and high quality.

World War II brought managers, government officials, and scientists together to introduce order and rationality to the logistics of global hostilities. The British formed the first operations-research (OR) groups comprised of various specialists to bring their diverse knowledge together to develop radar systems, perfect ground-to-air and air-to-air gunnery, design antisubmarine measures, guide bombing runs, and provide civilian defense.[3] One of the best known OR groups was under the direction of future Nobel laureate Patrick M. S. Blackett, an experimental physicist. Called "Blackett's circus," the interdisciplinary group included three physiologists, two mathematical physicists, one astrophysicist, one army officer, one surveyor, one general physicist, and two mathematicians. It was in such groups that diverse specialists were brought together to solve the complex challenges of "modern" warfare. OR was conceived as the application of scientific knowledge and methods to the study of complex problems with the stated purpose of deriving a quantitative basis for decisions. The British formed the first OR groups, though U.S. industrial organizations and private consulting firms, such as Arthur D. Little, Inc., as well as nonprofit institutions such as RAND Corporation, soon followed suit.[4] The Operations Research Society

[2] Alfred North Whitehead, *Science and the Modern World* (New York: Macmillan, 1925), p. 57. For a discussion of the search for "lost" classical manuscripts, beginning with Petrarch's (1304–1374) exploits in the fourteenth century, see Martin L. McLaughlin, "The Rediscovery of Classical Texts," in Angus Mackay with David Ditchburn, eds., *Atlas of Medieval Europe* (London: Routledge, 1997), pp. 239–241.

[3] Joseph F. McCloskey, "The Beginnings of Operations Research: 1934–1941," *Operations Research* 35(1) (January–February 1987), pp. 143–152.

[4] William Thomas, "Operations Research vis-à-vis Management at Arthur D. Little and the Massachusetts Institute of Technology in the 1950s," *Business History Review* 86(1) (Spring 2012), pp. 99–122.

of America (ORSA) was founded in 1952. It began publishing its flagship journal, *Operations Research,* the same year. Formed the next year, The Institute of Management Sciences (TIMS) sought "to identify, extend, and unify scientific knowledge that contributes to the understanding of the practice of management."[5] It began publishing the journal *Management Science* in 1954. ORSA and TIMS merged in 1995 to form the Institute for Operations Research and the Management Sciences (INFORMS).

The application of OR techniques came very naturally to production management, an area with structured problems (such as optimizing economic order quantities for inventories, service scheduling and dispatching, determining economic batch sizes, and quality control) where decision rules could be rationally devised. The Gilbreths spoke of the "one best way" as the objective of their scientific analysis (see Chapter 8). The "management scientists" merely put the quest in more euphemistic terms: "The approach of optimality analysis is to take various alternatives into account and to ask which of these possible sets of decisions will come closest to meeting the businessman's objectives (i.e., which decisions will be best or optimal)."[6] The old school and the "new" management scientists both sought to apply the scientific method when evaluating alternatives in an effort to make the best possible decisions. Operations research and management science were not so much the search for a science of management as a striving for the use of science *in* management. In this endeavor, the tools of mathematics and science were enlisted to solve the age-old challenge of optimally allocating society's scarce resources. This would reshape the prevailing view of production management.

PRODUCTION MANAGEMENT IN TRANSITION

The Gordon and Howell report on the status of U.S. business education had few kind words for production management. It concluded: "Production management courses are often the repository for some of the most inappropriate and intellectually stultifying materials to be found in the business curriculum . . . many faculty members have little respect for such courses . . . and students complained more strongly to us about the pointlessness of the production requirement than of any other."[7] How had production management fallen into such ill repute? In the years following World War II, it had academically taken a back seat to the rising human-relations movement with its emphasis on employee satisfaction and study of work group behavior. Production management had forgotten the lessons of Babbage, Ure, Taylor, Gantt, and others who had taught that something to be consumed first had to be produced. James M. Wilson observed, "It is perverse that OM [Operations Management] does not fully embrace Taylor's . . . *Shop Management*. . . . By the 1970s, Scientific Management had been virtually banished from OM."[8] The Gordon and Howell report was also critical of the typical business school's failure to require baseline math skills for a degree. In response, business schools began to incorporate statistics and mathematics into their curricula, and a new genre of production-management textbooks emerged that heavily emphasized operations-research techniques. The outcome for management education was a blend of the old and the new that became known as "production/operations management."

The new language of production/operations management was heavily oriented toward statistics and mathematics. With the scientific method as its base, its body was comprised of specific techniques for quantifying variables and relationships; at its apex were models for optimally allocating scarce resources. Techniques such as probability theory, linear programming, queuing theory, decision trees, and simulation were an essential part of the new language. Probability theory was

[5] Merrill M. Flood, "The Objectives of TIMS," *Management Science* 2(2) (January 1956), p. 178.

[6] William J. Baumol, *Economic Theory and Operations Analysis* (Englewood Cliffs, NJ: Prentice-Hall, 1961), p. 4.

[7] Robert A. Gordon and James E. Howell, *Higher Education for Business* (New York: Columbia University Press, 1959), p. 190.

[8] James M. Wilson "Deconstructing the Reinvention of Operations Management," *Journal of Management History* 24(2) (2018), p. 134.

used in drawing random samples for quality control; linear programming facilitated the allocation of limited resources among competing uses to maximize benefits or minimize losses; and queuing theory helped achieve an optimal balance between the cost of increasing service and the amount of time individuals, machines, or materials must wait for service. Decision trees could be created to calculate the benefits or costs likely to result from alternative courses of action. Simulation could be used to imitate different conditions so that the likely outcomes of different competitive strategies (developed using game theory) could be compared.

Along with applying these techniques, "decision theorists" sought to combine economic concepts such as utility and choice with probability theory to assess conditions of risk and uncertainty.[9] These applications also reshaped business-school curricula and created a new set of staff specialists with whom managers had to communicate. Postwar developments in computer technology furthered Gantt's early work with progress and performance bar charts (see Chapter 8). Beginning in 1956, the DuPont Company developed a computerized network method for planning and controlling, which became known as the Critical Path Method (CPM). At about the same time, the U.S. Navy, Lockheed Aircraft Corporation, and management consultants Booz Allen Hamilton created the Program Evaluation and Review Technique (PERT) for mapping the activities necessary for constructing the Polaris missile. PERT and CPM rely on diagrams depicting the relationships between the events and activities that compose a project across time. These diagrams, called "networks," allow managers to total the required time for each activity along every sequence—or path—of activities necessary for a project's completion. The path having the longest time is the "critical path," indicating the earliest date that a project can be completed. Having identified the critical path, project managers can focus their attention on reducing the time of activities in this path or, at minimum, watching closely for any delays. Although PERT and CPM are more complex than this brief description implies, they are little more than Gantt's pioneering bar charts enriched by increased computing power.

In brief, operations researchers, management scientists, and decision theorists reshaped the earlier notions of "industrial administration" or "production management." The techniques that they developed and applied enhanced the academic credibility of production/operations management in U.S. business schools. It would take a competitive challenge from abroad, however, to move production/operations management to a new stage of development.

"IF JAPAN CAN . . . WHY CAN'T WE?"

On June 24, 1980, the NBC television documentary titled *If Japan Can . . . Why Can't We?* was aired in the United States. It highlighted Japan's rise, following World War II, as a leader in the production of high-quality goods, and is considered one of the most important events in the U.S. quality movement. Of note, the documentary credited U.S. engineer W. Edwards Deming as the major force behind Japan's post–World War II economic success.

QUALITY AND QUALITY CIRCLES

After World War II, as part of U.S. efforts to revive the Japanese economy, a series of events occurred that would make Japan an industrial phoenix. The Japanese productivity "miracle" was based on ideas introduced by two U.S. civilian communication engineers given the task of helping Japanese industry rebuild. Charles W. Protzman, Sr., and Homer M. Sarasohn, assigned to the Civil Communications Section, Supreme Command for the Allied Powers, presented two

[9] See, for example, David W. Miller and Martin K. Starr, *Executive Decisions and Operations Research* (Englewood Cliffs, NJ: Prentice-Hall, 1960); *idem*, *The Structure of Human Decisions* (Englewood Cliffs, NJ: Prentice-Hall, 1967).

four-month seminars (Tokyo in 1949 and Osaka in 1950) for Japanese executives on "the fundamentals of industrial management."[10] Thereafter, the seminars were conducted by Nikkeiren, the federation of Japanese employers' associations. They continued until 1974. As Protzman was "on loan" from the Hawthorne Works of the Western Electric Company, his understanding of statistical quality control was based on the work of Walter A. Shewhart.[11]

Shewhart had begun working on quality-control problems at the Hawthorne Works in 1918. He moved to the new Bell Telephone Laboratories (owned by Bell Telephone and Western Electric) at Murray Hill, New Jersey, in 1925. His goal was to replace the phrase "as alike as two peas in a pod" with "as alike as two telephones."[12] He took samples of output and used statistical methods to assess and control variations in quality. Shewhart understood there would always be some random variation in output. There would, however, be limits to this variation. It was what happened outside these limits that could be examined for corrective action. Shewhart is often referred to as the "Father of Statistical Quality Control." He described the basic principles of this new field in his 1931 book, *Economic Control of Quality of Manufactured Product*.[13] It would be one of Shewhart's followers, however, who would popularize statistical quality control in Japan during the post–World War II years.

W. Edwards Deming received his Ph.D. in mathematical physics from Yale University in 1928. In 1925 and 1926, Deming spent his summer months employed in the Inspection Statistical Department at the Hawthorne Works, where he first met his future mentor, Shewhart.[14] An expert on statistical sampling, Deming was employed by the War Department during World War II to teach engineers how to use Shewhart's quality-control techniques in the production of war matériel. In 1947, he went to Japan to advise General Douglas MacArthur's Supreme Command of Allied Powers on sampling techniques to be used in the 1951 population census. Deming was pleased when Kenichi Koyanagi, managing director of the Union of Japanese Scientists and Engineers (JUSE), invited him to present a series of lectures in 1950 on statistical quality control. Koyanagi and his colleagues had continued their study of U.S. manufacturing methods after Sarasohn and Protzman's departure and had read Shewhart's 1931 book, as well as a set of lectures he had given at the U.S. Department of Agriculture, edited by Deming.[15]

Deming lectured and consulted in Japan for three decades.[16] When U.S. audiences first became aware of Deming through the 1980 NBC documentary, they did not find a smiling face. Deming was critical of U.S. management, perhaps because he had been ignored for so long, but more likely because U.S. firms were losing market share to other more quality- oriented and productive foreign competitors. As he explained: "The wealth of a nation depends on its people, management, and government, more than its natural resources. The problem is where to find good management. It would be a mistake to export American management to a friendly country."[17]

---

[10] Kenneth Hopper and William Hopper, *The Puritan Gift: Reclaiming the American Dream Amidst Global Financial Chaos* (London: I. B. Taurus, 2009), pp. 290–327. See also Robert C. Wood, "A Lesson Learned and a Lesson Forgotten," *Forbes* (February 6, 1989), pp. 70–78, for Sarasohn's recollections of these events.

[11] Hopper and Hopper, *The Puritan Gift*, p. 442.

[12] Mark A. Best and Daniel Neuhauser, "Walter A. Shewhart, 1924, and the Hawthorne Factory," *BMJ Quality & Safety* 15(2) (April 2006), p. 142.

[13] Walter A. Shewhart, *Economic Control of Quality of Manufactured Product* (New York: D. Van Nostrand, 1931).

[14] Mark A. Best and Daniel Neuhauser, "W. Edwards Deming: Father of Quality Management, Patient and Composer," *Quality & Safety in Health Care* 14(4) (August 2005), pp. 310–312.

[15] Walter A. Shewhart, with the editorial assistance of W. Edwards Deming, *Statistical Method from the Viewpoint of Quality Control* (Washington, DC: Graduate School, Department of Agriculture, 1939).

[16] For a discussion of Deming's work in Japan, see Peter B. Petersen, "The Contributions of W. Edwards Deming to Japanese Management Theory and Practice," in Frank S. Hoy, ed., *Proceedings of the Annual Meeting of the Academy of Management* (1987), pp. 133–137; Beth Blankenship and Peter B. Petersen, "W. Edwards Deming's Mentor and Others Who Made a Significant Impact on His Views During the 1920s and 1930s," *Journal of Management Inquiry* 5(8) (1999), pp. 454–467.

[17] W. Edwards Deming, *Out of the Crisis* (Cambridge, MA: Center for Advanced Engineering Study, Massachusetts Institute of Technology, 1986), p. 6.

Deming identified Seven Deadly Diseases of Management that were barriers to improved quality:

1. Lack of constancy of purpose to plan product and service that will have a market and keep the company in business, and provide jobs.
2. Emphasis on short-term profits: short-term thinking (just the opposite from constancy of purpose to stay in business), fed by fear of unfriendly takeover, and by push from bankers and owners for dividends.
3. Evaluation of performance, merit rating, or annual review.
4. Mobility of management; job hopping.
5. Management by use only of visible figures, with little or no consideration of figures that are unknown or unknowable.
6. Excessive medical costs.
7. Excessive costs of liability, swelled by lawyers that work on contingency fees.[18]

Deming attributed 95 percent of all errors to the systems under which people worked, not the people themselves. He believed that quality control began with an organization's top managers, not with its lower-level employees. The goal was the reduction of variations in quality through continuous improvement (*Kaizen*). Deming's slogan was "Plan-Do-Act," an iterative cycle that provides feedback for continual improvement. Deming repeatedly berated U.S. managers for their faults, igniting a quality-control revolution.[19]

Joseph M. Juran was another significant contributor to the early quality-control movement. Juran had worked at the Western Electric Company's Hawthorne Works from 1924 to 1941, and, like Deming, was taken with Shewhart's ideas on statistical quality control. After World War II, Juran resigned from Western Electric to become a quality-control consultant for Wallace Clark & Co. He subsequently formed his own consulting firm.[20] In 1954, JUSE invited Juran to Japan to aid in its rebuilding efforts. Expanding on the work of Vilfredo Pareto, Juran popularized the notion that 80 percent of the defects in production are due to 20 percent of the causes of all defects.[21] Juran thus advised managers to work on their most critical problems first, which he called the "vital few," before moving on to resolve the "trivial many."

Kaoru Ishikawa

Courtesy of Ichiro Kotsuka, Managing Director, Union of Japanese Scientists and Engineers (JUSE) Odakyu Daiichi Seimei Building 4F2-7-1 Nishi-Shinjuku, Shinjuku-ku, Tokyo 163-0704, JAPAN

Kaoru Ishikawa was a professor of engineering at the University of Tokyo. He gave voice to Shewhart, Deming, and Juran, and is generally considered a key figure in developing "quality circles."[22] Quality circles are comprised of a group of employees who are brought together to discuss ways to improve the quality of a product or service. Ishikawa's work at the U.S. Kawasaki Plant in Lincoln, Nebraska, led to the adoption of quality circles at Hewlett-Packard Company and a host of additional firms.

[18] *Ibid.*, pp. 97–98.
[19] For more on Deming, see Peter B. Petersen, "Library of Congress Archives: Additional Information about W. Edwards Deming (1900–1993) Now Available," *Journal of Management History* 3(2) (1997), pp. 98–119.
[20] John Butman, *Juran: A Lifetime of Influence* (New York: John Wiley & Sons, 1997), pp. 75–76.
[21] See Vilfredo Pareto, *Cours d'économie politique* [*A Course on Political Economics*], 2 vols. (Lausanne: F. Rouge, 1896–1897).
[22] Greg Watson, "The Legacy of Ishikawa," *Quality Progress* 39(4) (April 2004), pp. 54–57.

Others would advance the quality-control mantle, including Armand V. Feigenbaum, who began his career at General Electric Co. and coined the phrase "total quality control," forerunner of GE's well-known "six sigma" quality program. Philip Crosby originated the "zero defects" concept, believing that the benefits derived from implementing a quality philosophy far outweighed its costs, declaring: "[q]uality is free." Those in Japan that continued Ishikawa's work included Genichi Taguchi, director of the Japan Industrial Technology Institute; Taiichi Ohno and Shigeo Shingo at Toyota Motor Corporation; and Ichiro Ueno, son of Yōichi Ueno, who promoted scientific management in Japan (see Chapter 11).

THE TOYOTA PRODUCTION SYSTEM AND LEAN MANUFACTURING

Following Henry Ford's development of the automobile assembly line (see Chapter 12), it was generally held that the inventory methods required by mass production were only appropriate for firms manufacturing a high volume of similar goods. Frank G. Woollard, general manager of Morris Motor Cars (Coventry, England), however, challenged this view. Compared to Ford Motors, Morris operated on a much smaller volume, but Woollard devised a system of raw-material deliveries and inventory control to achieve continuous production while minimizing parts inventories and capital outlays. Kiichiro Toyoda visited the Morris assembly plant in 1930 and may have become aware of Woollard's new inventory control system that assured there was neither a shortage nor glut of raw materials. Although the evidence is circumstantial, Mario L. Emiliano and Peter J. Seymour suggest that Woollard's work may have influenced the thinking of Toyoda and his colleagues Taiichi Ohno and Shigeo Shingo in developing Toyota Motors' "just-in-time" (*Kanban*) inventory-management system.[23] The origins of Material Requirements Planning (MRP), an extended form of inventory control, are even less clear. Vince A. Mabert attributes the spread of MRP in the early 1960s to Joseph Orlicky, Oliver Wight, and George W. Plossl.[24] Orlicky, an immigrant from Czechoslovakia, worked for J. I. Case Company before joining IBM to become its Manufacturing Industry Education Manager. Wight worked first with Orlicky at IBM and then with Ploosl at the Stanley Works (now Stanley Black & Decker). Published in 1975, Orlicky's book *Material Requirements Planning: The New Way of Life in Production and Inventory Management* is considered the definitive text on the subject.[25]

GLOBALIZATION AND THE INTERNATIONAL ORGANIZATION FOR STANDARDIZATION

Although the efforts of Deming, Juran, and others in the years following World War II highlighted the competitive advantage to be gained by global corporations bringing lower prices and quality products to an expanding share of the world's population, an interest in quality standards may be traced to the early twentieth century: the British Engineering Standards Committee was established in 1901, and the American Engineering Standards Committee in 1916.[26] Both groups sought to develop quality standards applicable across products, industries, and nations.

---

[23] Mario L. Emiliano and Peter J. Seymour, "Frank George Woollard: Forgotten Pioneer of Flow Production," *Journal of Management History* 17(1) (2011), p. 77.

[24] Vincent A. Mabert, "The Early Road to Material Requirements Planning," *Journal of Operations Management* 25(2) (March 2007), pp. 346–356. For evidence that the underpinning of MRP systems may be traced to Fred Taylor's Planning Office, see James W. Wilson, "The Origin of Material Requirements Planning in Frederick W. Taylor's Planning Office," *International Journal of Production Research* 54(5) (March 2016), pp. 1535–1553.

[25] Joseph Orlicky, *Material Requirements Planning: The New Way of Life in Production and Inventory Management* (New York: McGraw-Hill, 1975).

[26] JoAnne Yates and Craig N. Murphy, "From Setting National Standards to Coordinating International Standards: The Foundation of the ISO," *Business and Economic History On-line* 4 (2006). See also *idem*, *The International Organization for Standardization (ISO): Global Governance through Voluntary Consensus* (London: Routledge Press, 2009).

The British Engineering Standards Committee is now known as the BSI Group, and the American Engineering Standards Committee has become the American National Standards Institute. On the international front, the International Federation of the National Standardizing Associations (ISA) was organized in 1926. In 1947, the ISA joined with the newly formed United Nations Standards Coordinating Committee to create the International Organization for Standardization (ISO), based in Geneva. The ISO provides companies with standards to ensure that their products and services meet customer requirements. The latest standards, ISO 9000, were published in 2010 following 10 years of transnational negotiations.

SYSTEMS AND INFORMATION

Throughout history, people have observed order in nature. They saw an ecological balance in plant and animal life; noted that the planets and stars moved in predictable patterns and used them to chart their lives; and followed a rhythm in the coming and going of seasons to plant and harvest their crops. Early people built their lives around rituals that were a part of this natural order; such ceremonies gave them a sense of security.

As people designed organizations, they sought the same order they observed in nature. Early factory managers followed the dictates of systematic management to arrange their workplaces, assure the proper flow of materials, and facilitate the accomplishment of desired goals. Social scientists spoke of social systems, studied workplaces as sociotechnical systems, and noted the need for equilibrium both within an organization and in relation to its surrounding environment. Each of these applications shares several common characteristics: (1) a goal or purpose; (2) presumed inputs, or what we have termed factors of production, which may include people, materials, money, or information; (3) transformation of these inputs into goods or services; and (4) feedback about whether the intended goal or purpose is met. This cycle of inputs, transformations, outputs, and feedback must be maintained if an organization is to exist over time. That is to say, an organization can only survive if it is capable of producing outputs that can be exchanged for the energy necessary to obtain new inputs and to maintain itself in operating order. In a business setting, the value of the outputs an organization produces is measured by the amount that buyers are willing to pay for the goods and services it provides. A business is considered profitable if this value exceeds the collective cost of procuring and transforming inputs into outputs. If excess profits exist, they can be held in reserve for hard times or used to finance growth.

GENERAL SYSTEMS THEORY AND CYBERNETICS

Although Chester I. Barnard (see Chapter 14) viewed organizations as open systems that included investors, suppliers, customers, and others, it was not until the 1960s that systems theory made an impact on management thought. K. Ludwig von Bertalanffy, a biologist, is credited with coining the phrase "general systems theory."[27] He noted the "openness" of all systems; that is, all organisms are both affected by and, in turn, affect their environment. "Organism" has the same Greek and Latin roots as "organization," and both deal with the function, structure, and relationship of parts to a whole. It became appropriate, then, to think of an organization in terms of an open system, meaning a system that depends on other systems for its inputs (people, money, materials, and so forth) and, thus, cannot exist in isolation. An organization's managers cannot solve a production problem, for example, without considering whether supplier organizations (systems) will ship necessary materials on time or at a mutually acceptable price.

Bertalanffy's efforts were an initial piece in a jigsaw puzzle that others began to build upon. Norbert Wiener derived the word *cybernetics* from the Greek *kubernētēs*, meaning pilot or person

[27] K. Ludwig von Bertalanffy, "General Systems Theory: A New Approach to the Unity of Science," *Human Biology* 23(4) (December 1951), pp. 302–361.

at the helm, to label the study of organisms and machines as self-regulating systems.[28] Being self-regulating, the human body is, technically speaking, a cybernetic system. By contrast, artificially created systems, such as business firms, health-care facilities, and educational institutions, do not have automatic controls. Their performance must be monitored continually to detect and adjust for deviations from established standards. From a cybernetics perspective, an organization's performance can be monitored and adjusted at three points: before, during, or after an activity is completed. Each of these points matches a different aspect of the input → transformation → output → feedback cycle that must be maintained if an organization is to exist over time. Wiener developed his theory of cybernetics while exploring interactions between humans and machines. He found that both rapidly adjusted to changing conditions based on feedback about whether an intended goal or purpose was met, indicating that both could "learn" to adapt to their environment. This suggests a rather startling conclusion: "In tandem, humans and machines could form a dynamic and powerful system; left to themselves, machines could, in principle, develop intelligence and the ability to self-replicate. They might even replace humanity."[29]

Inspired by Wiener's thinking, Claude E. Shannon developed a general theory of information.[30] Drawing on the work of English mathematician George Boole, Shannon treated "communicated signals as streams of binary alternatives—dots and dashes, or zeros and ones—that were soon christened . . . bits." He "derived explicit formulas for rates of transmission, the capacity of an ideal channel, ability to correct errors and coding efficiency . . . bringing us the age of digital machines."[31] On the heels of Shannon's pioneering work, the field of "artificial intelligence" (AI) emerged in the mid-1950s, when John McCarthy (considered the "Father of Artificial Intelligence") coined the term to describe computers capable of doing things that were formerly thought to require the natural intelligence of humans.[32] AI combines the reasoning ability of the human mind with the processing power of computers.

Herbert A. Simon, Allen Newell, and J. Cliff Shaw were among the early pioneers in AI research.[33] By simulating human-information processing using "expert systems," they programmed a computer to play chess and prove mathematical theorems taken from Alfred North Whitehead and Bertrand A. W. Russell's *Principia Mathematica*.[34] As early as 1960, Simon predicted, "[M]achines will be capable, within twenty years, of doing any work that a man can do."[35]

[28] Norbert Wiener, *Cybernetics, Or Control and Communication in the Animal and the Machine* (Cambridge, MA: MIT Press, 1948), p. 23. Although Wiener claimed to have "invented" the word "cybernetics," it appears throughout ancient Greek writings dating back to Plato's *First Alcibiades*. On this point, see Pesi R. Masani, *Norbert Wiener, 1894–1964* (Basel, Switzerland: Birkhauser, 1989), p. 259. In claiming to have invented the term cybernetics, Wiener does note that "incidentally" he later learned that "the word had already been used by [André-Marie] Ampère . . . [and] a Polish scientist" (pp. 23–24). Ampère used the term *cybernétique* in his *Essai sur la philosophie des sciences* [*Essay on the Philosophy of Science*] (Paris: Bachelier, 1834), p. 140, to refer to a new science of government. The unnamed Polish scientist appears to have been Bronisław F. Trentowski, who wrote of cybernetyka or the "art of governing a nation" in his book *Stosunek filozofii do cybernetyki czyli sztuki rządzenia narodem* [*The Relationship of Philosophy to Cybernetics, Or the Art of Ruling a Nation*] (Poznań, Poland: J. K. Żupańskiego, 1843), p. 9. See also Plato, *The Dialogues of Plato*, 3rd ed., vol. 2, trans. Benjamin Jowett (Oxford, England: Clarendon Press, 1892), p. 508. Written circa 350 BCE. The passage in question reads: "SOC.[RATES]: Or again, in a ship, if a man having the power to do what he likes, has no intelligence or skill in navigation [*kubernētēs*], do you see what will happen to him and to his fellow-sailors?" See also Michele Kennerly, "Cybernetics in the *Republic*," *History of the Human Sciences*, 36(1) (February 2023), pp. 80–102.

[29] Michael Saler, [Review of the book *Rise of the Machines: A Cybernetic History*], *Wall Street Journal* (September 3–4, 2016), p. C6.

[30] Claude E. Shannon. "A Mathematical Theory of Communication," *Bell System Technical Journal* 27(3) (July 1948), pp. 379–423; *idem*, "A Mathematical Theory of Communication," *Bell System Technical Journal* 27(4) (October 1948), pp. 623–666.

[31] George Dyson, [Review of the book *A Mind at Play: How Claude Shannon Invented the Information Age*], *Wall Street Journal* (July 22–23, 2017), p. C7.

[32] Elaine Woo, "John McCarthy Dies at 84; The Father of Artificial Intelligence," *Los Angeles Times* (October 27, 2011), p. 2.

[33] Herbert A. Simon, *The Sciences of the Artificial* (Cambridge, MA: MIT Press, 1969); Allen Newell and Herbert A. Simon, *Human Problem Solving* (Englewood Cliffs, NJ: Prentice-Hall, 1972).

[34] Alfred North Whitehead and Bertrand Russell, *Principia Mathematica*, vols. 1–3 (Cambridge, England: Cambridge University Press, 1910–1913).

[35] Herbert A. Simon, *The New Science of the Management Decision* (New York: Harper & Brothers, 1960), p. 38. On May 11, 1997, Garry Kasparov was the first world-chess champion to be beat by a computer, IBM's Deep Blue.

Although AI could not account for unique parts of human existence such as ethics or aesthetics, it marked the beginning of computers designed to guide robots, drive automobiles, answer questions through smartphones, render medical diagnoses, and make "virtual reality" a reality. Apple, Inc.'s Siri and Amazon.com Inc.'s Alexa digital assistants are AI applications, as are navigation apps that help plan the most efficient route to a destination or allow online retailers to recommend products and services based on past purchases. In 1975, Simon and Newell received the Turing Award from the Association for Computing Machinery for their contributions to artificial intelligence.

Marvin L. Minsky developed the first artificial neural network, SNARC (for stochastic neural-analog reinforcement calculator), in 1951. Neural networks, an AI approach to problem solving, mimic the architecture of biological nervous systems and are used to model the brain to understand intelligence. In a strange twist, Isaac Asimov's science fiction short story, "Runaround,"[36] published in 1942, was the impetus for Minksy's interest in building a machine that could think. Minksy told a *New York Times* reporter, "After 'Runaround' appeared in the March 1942 issue of *Astounding*, I never stopped thinking about how minds might work."[37] The "Roundabout" plot involves two engineers who design a robot to follow the Three Laws: (1) it must not harm a human or allow a human to be injured; (2) it must obey orders given by humans unless they violate the First Law; and (3) it must protect its own existence as long as doing so does not in conflict with the First and Second laws.

The move from science fiction to reality came quickly. In 1950, British mathematician Alan M. Turing asked, "Can a machine think?" and created the "imitation game," a test of a machine's ability to generate human-like behavior.[38]

FROM THE "INVISIBLE HAND" TO THE "DIGITAL HAND"

Imagine that it is 1960 and you are the director of the Data Processing Department in your firm. When you arrive at work, you see numerous people operating keypunch machines to make tiny holes in 80-column cards that carry a printed admonishment that they should not be folded, spindled, or mutilated. A person is running a sorter to arrange these cards into various categories; another is operating a tabulator that reads these tiny holes and prints the results on long sheets of continuous paper. Assured that work is proceeding smoothly, you enter your office, check your flip-the-page paper calendar for your appointments, and, finding some spare time, you check the financial pages of the *Wall Street Journal*. You see ads for computers made by International Business Machines (IBM), Sperry Rand, Minneapolis-Honeywell, RCA, National Cash Register, and a few other firms, but IBM is number one in the information-technology industry. You begin thinking about taking a vacation and use your black rotary dial phone to call your local travel agent, who can make plane, hotel, and rental-car arrangements and mail you some brochures describing how to find your destination, your accommodations, and other matters. Seeking additional information about your destination, you go to your bookshelves and pull out the appropriate volume of your encyclopedia. Just in case you wish to verify the spelling or meaning of a word, you also have a dictionary handy.

Fast-forward to the present, and the world you know is quite different. You can accomplish all these tasks with a mobile device you carry in your pocket, as you wait to order lunch or commute to work. Reading the *Wall Street Journal,* you now see advertisements for Dell, Microsoft, Cisco, Intel, Apple, and other companies prominent in the computer industry. You use search engines such as Google to locate information instantly on arcane subjects such as the Boer War or

---

[36] Isaac Asimov, "Runaround," *Astounding Stories of Super-Science* 29(3) (March 1942), pp. 94–103.

[37] Marvin L. Minksy quoted in John Markoff, "A Celebration of Isaac Asimov," *New York Times* (April 12, 1992), p. 117.

[38] Alan M. Turing, "Computing Machinery and Intelligence," *Mind: A Quarterly Review of Psychology and Philosophy* 59(236) (October 1950), p. 433.

the Battle of Waterloo. For your vacation, you arrange your own transportation, compare airfares, locate accommodations, and view the dining room, sleeping area, or other facilities in the hotel you have chosen; you are virtually there. What happened in the intervening 60 years?

IT IS A SMALL, SMALLER WORLD

You have entered the Information Age, enabled by advancing computer technology. Of the ten forces that Thomas L. Friedman identified as "flattening the world," eight are related directly to the Information Age: workflow software, uploading, outsourcing, offshoring, supply-chaining, insourcing, informing, and steroids.[39] James W. Cortada has characterized this flattening as an evolution from Adam Smith's "invisible hand" of the marketplace to Alfred D. Chandler's "visible hand" of management to the "digital hand" of the Information Age.[40] In Chapter 4, we discussed Charles Babbage's vision of a machine capable of performing any calculation. He encountered so many problems in constructing his Analytical Engine, however, he was never able to build a full-scale model.

Some 90 years later, Alan M. Turing (mentioned above) took a step toward fulfilling Babbage's vision. In 1938, as the armies of Adolf Hitler's Third Reich (Empire) threatened Europe, the British Secret Intelligence Service (commonly known as MI6) became aware of improvements to the German message-encoding machine named Enigma. If the strengthened Enigma cipher codes, which changed daily, could be broken, MI6 could decrypt intercepted radio messages sent by the German High Command to anticipate the movement of Hitler's armies and ships. Cryptology (the devising and breaking of coded messages) was a complicated process, and Enigma-coded messages had defied all traditional cryptanalysis. Building on the efforts of mathematician Marian A. Rejewski and his colleagues Jerzy Różycki and Henryk Zygalski at the Polish General Staff's Cipher Bureau headquartered in Warsaw, Turing, working at the ultrasecret Government Code and Cipher School at Bletchley Park in southern England, helped crack the Enigma cipher-machine codes in 1940 and end World War II. At its peak, some 10,000 codebreakers, mostly women, were employed at the school. As almost all codes depend on the substitution of numbers for letters in various ways, and because millions of combinations are possible, only a machine that processed masses of numbers could hope to succeed. Turing led the successful effort to develop the world's first fully electronic digital computer (Colossus) to handle the necessary calculations.[41]

As also noted in Chapter 4, Herman Hollerith created a punched-card tabulating machine to input data for the 1890 U.S. Census. In 1896, he formed the Tabulating Machine Company, which, after merging with three other companies that made complementary equipment, would in 1924 become known as International Business Machines Corporation (IBM).[42] During 1937–1944, with funding from IBM, Howard H. Aiken designed and built the Harvard University–based electromechanical computer called Mark I, which was used during the Manhattan Project for designing an atomic bomb to help end World War II. U.S. Navy Lieutenant (later Rear Admiral) Grace Murray Hopper, who developed the computer programming language COBOL, was the lead programmer for Mark I. What makes computers, as mere machines (hardware), useful is "software," general-purpose symbols providing instructions. The Electronic Numerical Integrator and Computer (ENIAC) was programmed by a team that included Jean Jennings Bartik,

[39] Thomas L. Friedman, *The World Is Flat: A Brief History of the Twenty-First Century* (New York: Farrar, Straus, and Giroux, 2005), pp. 48–172. Friedman uses the term "steroids" to reference increased computing power and capabilities rather than to describe a class of organic compounds.

[40] James W. Cortada, *The Digital Hand: How Computers Changed the Work of American Manufacturing, Transportation, and Retail Industries*, vol. 1 (New York: Oxford University Press, 2004), p. viii.

[41] Andrew Hodges, *Alan Turing: The Enigma* (New York: Simon & Schuster, 1983), p. 268.

[42] George E. Biles, Alfred A. Bolton, and Bernadette DiRe, "Herman Hollerith: Inventor, Manager, Entrepreneur—A Centennial Remembrance," *Journal of Management* 15(4) (December 1989), pp. 603–615.

Marlyn Wescoff Meltzer, Ruth Lichterman Teitelbaum, Elizabeth Snyder Holberton, Frances Bilas Spence, Kathleen McNulty Mauchly, Shirley Blumberg Melvin, and Doris Blumberg Polsky.[43] The ENIAC, built between 1943 and 1945 at the University of Pennsylvania's Moore School of Electrical Engineering under the direction of John Mauchly (a physicist), Herman Goldstine (a mathematician), and J. Presper Eckert, Jr. (an engineer), was the world's first all-electronic, general-purpose, programmable computer. A thousand times faster than any other computer in the world, the ENIAC could complete 5,000 additions and 500 multiple additions (multiplications) in a single second. Mauchly and Eckert's underlying patents, however, were disputed in a lawsuit filed by Honeywell and Control Data Corporation. John V. Atanasoff, working with graduate student Clifford Berry, had built an automatic electronic digital computer at Iowa State University, beginning work in 1939. Mauchly had visited Iowa State as Atanasoff's guest for four days in 1943 and had taken notes on what is now known as the Atanasoff–Berry Computer. Although neither Atanasoff nor Iowa State had applied for patent protection, the U.S. District Court for the District of Minnesota upheld Atanasoff's patent rights on the basis that he was the first person to both conceive and build "the calculating device that led to the invention of the computer."[44] As a result, royalties that had been going to computer manufacturer Sperry Rand (today's Unisys), which had acquired Mauchly and Eckert's patents, were discontinued in April 1973. Worthy of mention, in the early 1980s, the computer programming language Ada, named after Lady Ada Lovelace, Babbage's close friend and collaborator (see Chapter 4), was developed by the U.S. Department of Defense.

During the century or so that had elapsed from Charles Babbage's vision to Atanasoff's reality, computers had advanced rapidly in technological capability, allowing hitherto unrealized applications. The first computers were monster mainframes; it was thought that only a few computers would be necessary to handle the U.S. census, scientific calculations, and perhaps, someday, accounting, payroll, and inventory problems. "Electronic data processing" was the term used to refer to the automated methods used by computers to process data, with "automation" referring to each step in a sequence controlling the next.

In 1960, IBM's revenues were twice the total of all other firms' revenues in the computer industry. Threats to break up the alleged IBM "monopoly" were, however, made unnecessary by advancing computer technology that moved from vacuum tubes to transistors to integrated circuits (the latter co-invented by Robert N. Noyce of Fairchild Semiconductor and Texas Instruments' Jack S. Kilby in 1958).[45] Integrated circuits triggered a host of changes in both hardware (equipment) and software (operating systems). "Microcomputers," which used circuit boards, became popular in the early 1970s. By 1977, three firms held some 72 percent of the microcomputer market: Apple, Commodore, and Tandy. Commodore declared bankruptcy in 1995 and was acquired by Tulip, a Dutch computer firm; Tandy acquired RadioShack in 1963 and continued to sell the TR-80 Micro Computer System and other electronic equipment until declaring bankruptcy in 2015. William H. Gates and Paul Allen had founded Microsoft in 1975. IBM entered the microcomputer market in 1980, and personal computers, laptops, and mobile devices inexorably followed.

Profound changes in science and technology in the next two decades dramatically changed *Fortune* magazine's yearly list of the largest U.S. companies ranked by total revenues. In 2022, four health care/pharmaceutical firms were in the top 10 (CVS Health, UnitedHealth Group, McKesson, and AmerisourceBergen). In computers and computer-mediated applications,

---

[43] Walter Isaacson, "The Women of ENIAC," *Fortune* (October 6, 2014), pp. 160–165. See also Claire L. Evans, *The Broad Band: The Untold Story of the Women Who Made the Internet* (New York: Portfolio/Penguin, 2018); Kathy Kleiman, *Proving Ground: The Untold Story of the Six Women Who Programmed the World's First Modern Computer* (New York: Grand Central Publishing, 2022).

[44] Jane Smiley, *The Man Who Invented the Computer: The Biography of John Atanasoff, Digital Pioneer* (New York: Doubleday, 2010), p. 80.

[45] Leslie Berlin, *The Man Behind the Microchip: Robert Noyce and the Invention of Silicon Valley* (New York: Oxford University Press, 2005), p. 3.

Amazon was #2, Apple #3, and Alphabet (Google) #8.[46] In just over a quarter century, the nation's largest firms no longer made automobiles, electrical equipment, or delivered petroleum products. The only constant was Walmart, a retailing firm.

ENABLING GLOBAL TRADE THROUGH INFORMATION AND COMMUNICATION

Tom Standage reminded us (see Chapter 5) that the Victorians had an internet of their own: the electric telegraph, which fostered romances, facilitated commercial transactions, reshaped distribution strategies, and swept away local trade barriers.[47] ARPANET (Advanced Research Projects Agency Network), the precursor of today's internet, was developed by the U.S. Department of Defense beginning in 1960. The internet as we know it was privatized starting in 1993. With the internet's commercialization, a borderless economy emerged as goods and services could be bought and sold worldwide. True to Joseph A. Schumpeter's notion of "creative destruction" (see Chapter 18), the internet abounded with innovations, including e-mail, social-media platforms, news and instant messaging services, and websites devoted to an endless list of subjects.

Technology is the handmaiden of management theory and practice. Information technology can provide a firm with an initial, but not necessarily unassailable, competitive advantage. Based on an analysis of the development of communications in corporations prior to the widespread introduction of computer-information technology, JoAnne Yates concluded, "[T]echnologies were adopted, not necessarily when they were invented, but when a shift or advance in managerial theory led managers to see an application for them. . . . The technology alone was not enough—the vision to use it in new ways was needed as well."[48] This conclusion appears to hold with respect to the Information Age, as computers have become more than giant electronic calculating machines, fulfilling information needs across continents, oceans, and time zones. Information is distributed globally through network systems, stored in the "cloud" on virtual servers, input into decision support systems, and accessed remotely so that group members can work "together" from their own homes. Enabled by digital crowdsourcing, Wikipedia (launched in 2001) and other online encyclopedias now provide access to information on millions of topics to internet users throughout the world.

Reliable and valid information has always been essential for effective managerial decision-making. Over time, however, as transactions and interactions within organizations became more complex, information was needed for internal uses as well as for reporting to external constituents and regulatory agencies. As information-providing capabilities advanced, managers mastered, as well as developed, innovative workplace applications for new information technologies. Alfred D. Chandler commented on the importance of developing an information-rich "integrated learning base" that is rooted in the technical, functional, and managerial capabilities of an organization as a whole rather than in individual managers.[49] These capabilities provide the basis for an organization's continued growth and competitiveness. *Technical capabilities* develop by learning from new and existing knowledge bases, which may be firm or industry specific. This involves gathering knowledge related to basic and applied research to improve existing products or to introduce new products. *Functional capabilities* refer to those activities in which an organization must successfully engage to acquire, transform, and market its products. These activities are essential for an organization's survival. *Managerial capabilities* are required to administer an organization's operational units, integrate its activities, and coordinate the flow of goods and services

---

[46] "Largest U.S. Corporations," *Fortune*. Available online at https://fortune.com/fortune500/.

[47] Tom Standage, *The Victorian Internet: The Remarkable Story of the Telegraph and the Nineteenth Century's On-Line Pioneers* (New York: Walker and Company, 1998), p. 213.

[48] JoAnne Yates, *Control through Communications: The Rise of System in American Management* (Baltimore, MD: Johns Hopkins University Press, 1989), pp. 274–275.

[49] Alfred D. Chandler, Jr., *Inventing the Electronic Century: The Epic Story of the Consumer Electronics and Computer Industries* (New York: Free Press, 2001), pp. 2–5.

through the input → transformation → output → feedback cycle to retailers and final customers. Chandler's appreciation of the importance of developing an information-rich integrated learning base that is rooted in an organization's technical, functional, and managerial capabilities aligns with Edith T. Penrose's view that the productive services available (or potentially available) from an organization's resources give it a unique character (see Chapter 19).

SUMMARY

The post–World War II era posed new opportunities in the global arena that would transform old ideas about markets and manufacturing. Japanese industry led the way in improving product quality and reliability with quality circles, just-in-time inventory management, and lean manufacturing. General systems theory and cybernetics underscored that organizations are open systems that interact with their surrounding environment. With the dawning of the Information Age, computer technology advanced rapidly from vacuum-tube mainframes to lithium-powered miniature chips loaded with computing and information capabilities for mobile devices. This computational power enabled the testing of advanced mathematical models, reshaped production management, and created opportunities for innovative ventures in technology. The internet has enabled unlimited communication around the world, opened markets, and created applications for multiple purposes. From the "invisible hand" of Adam Smith to Alfred D. Chandler's "visible hand of management" to the "digital hand" of the Information Age, our daily and work lives were changed. Perhaps only the Industrial Revolution rivals the social change experienced during this period.

Obligations and Opportunities

CHAPTER 22

Managers face daily challenges as they make decisions within a framework of cultural values and institutions. This chapter considers the increasing globalization of business and how competition in international markets with contrasting cultural values and institutions has influenced the evolution of management thought. It also discusses business ethics and society's wider expectation that managers will act responsibly beyond legal or regulatory requirements.

MANAGING IN A GLOBAL ARENA

As the spice trade between Asia, Africa, and Europe (dating back to at least 1500 BCE) and the Silk Road (established in 130 BCE, when the Han Dynasty in China opened trade with the West) can attest, the exchange of goods between civilizations located in different parts of the world—what today is called the *globalization of business*—has a rich history. Coins, clay tablets, and the remains of once mighty trading forts tell the story of ancient empires engaged in exchanging gold, ivory, precious stones, spices, and textiles. Commerce, whether by land or sea, bound early civilizations, and placed them in economic competition with one other.[1]

THE GLOBALIZATION OF BUSINESS

In past centuries, trade among nations was often initiated and pursued as an economic strategy; this still remains true today. Although many early adventurers were motivated by natural curiosity, the economic interests of kings, queens, and potentates provided the main driving force behind the great discoveries of unknown lands and peoples, with national treasuries financing the explorers who sailed uncharted waters to ply new trade routes, establish colonies, bring home exotic goods, and expand empires. As discussed in Chapter 2, the economic philosophy known as mercantilism held that governments should play a central role in financing and protecting trade to build strong national economies in which exports exceed imports. Mercantilists used import quotas, embargoes, tariffs, and (if necessary) military force to protect domestic producers.

[1] Miriam Beard, *A History of the Business Man* (New York: Macmillan, 1938), p. 199. See also Robert Fitzgerald, *The Rise of the Global Company: Multinationals and the Making of the Modern World* (Cambridge, England: Cambridge University Press, 2015), pp. 24–155.

Trading companies—such as the British East India Company, the Muscovy Company, the French East India Company, Hudson's Bay Company, and the Dutch East India Company—were state-sponsored monopolies that dominated trade in specific areas or items such as furs or spices. As also noted in Chapter 2, these companies were established by either royal charter or by an act of Parliament and represented the kind of joint-stock (limited liability) companies for which Adam Smith expressed the greatest concern because of their separation of ownership from management. India, provinces in Canada, and the original 13 United States of America were British colonies; France, Belgium, Portugal, and Germany controlled colonies in Africa; Indonesia was a Dutch colony (called the Dutch East Indies); and French Indochina (today's Vietnam, Laos, and Cambodia) was a colony ruled by France. In each case, these colonies provided the country that controlled them with markets, raw materials, and labor, and are early examples of global business.

Adam Smith believed that the protectionist policies advocated by mercantilism harmed a nation's productivity and economic growth; as a result, he held that trade between nations should be regulated solely by marketplace forces. He contended that the "invisible hand" of the marketplace would ensure that resources flowed to their most efficient use and yielded the greatest return. In this way, the separate interests of each person and nation, acting in a fully competitive market, would bring about the greatest prosperity for all.[2] The economist David Ricardo suggested that what was needed was not a national economic policy, such as mercantilism, but rather a free market that allowed each nation to find its *comparative advantage* over others in producing a particular good.[3] He realized that if one nation can produce a good at a comparative advantage *relative* to another, and the other has a comparative advantage in producing a second good, both nations gain from trading with each other by concentrating on what they do best and trading for other goods. Ricardo further recognized that if either of the two nations has an *absolute advantage* in producing both goods, they can still benefit by trading with one another if they have different *relative* costs of production (or, to put it another way, different *relative* efficiencies).

To illustrate this point, Ricardo gave an example involving England and Portugal.[4] He noted that the costs of producing wine and manufacturing cloth were different in the two countries. In England, then and now, it is quite expensive to produce wine and somewhat expensive to manufacture cloth. By comparison, in Portugal, cloth is less expensive to make and wine even less costly than that. Because Portugal can produce wine cheaper than it can manufacture cloth, however, it is to Portugal's advantage to exchange wine for English cloth. England likewise gains from this trade, as its cost of manufacturing cloth remains the same, and it can enjoy wine at a lower price. Each country is, thereby, able to increase its total consumption by exporting the good for which it has the greatest *relative* efficiency and importing the other. By producing the most benefit for the greatest number of people, this would also be the best way to use the available resources of both countries. With this example, Ricardo provided a rationale for free trade and, conversely, an argument against protectionist policies such as import quotas, embargos, and tariffs that replace markets with government dictates. Simply put, by specializing in producing the good for which it has the greatest *relative* efficiency, each nation increases the total output, and both have more to consume. A win-win proposition.[5]

As colonialism and mercantilism faded, trade among nations continued to thrive. In its early economic development, the United States was a debtor nation, depending on capital from abroad. J. & W. Seligman & Co., a New York investment bank founded in 1864, had branches in London, Paris, and Frankfurt. Members of the Seligman family and other domestic bankers sold

---

[2] Adam Smith, *An Inquiry into the Nature and Causes of the Wealth of Nations*, vol. 2 (London: W. Strahan, and T. Cadell in the Strand, 1776), pp. 351–356.

[3] David Ricardo, *On the Principles of Political Economy and Taxation* (London: John Murray, 1817), pp. 156–161, 273.

[4] For the sake of simplicity, this example does not consider transportation expenses and assumes an absence of restrictions on international trade.

[5] For an understanding of the limiting assumptions underlying the "comparative advantage" concept, see Clyde Prestowitz, "Industrial Policy Comes Full Circle," *Wall Street Journal* (December 15, 2022), p. R17.

securities abroad to finance the growth of U.S. businesses. Mira Wilkins observed that as late as 1914, the United States still had a balance of payment deficit, borrowing more from abroad than it invested worldwide. Although the United States maintained trade relations in the Pacific (some 80 U.S. firms had branches in China alone), South America, Africa, continental Europe, and Great Britain, it still had to import capital to finance the growth of its own industries.[6]

Technology has always been an important factor in growing world markets. Early trade routes hugged the world's shorelines because of fragile ships and poor navigational aids. Stronger masts, larger sails, and advances in navigation techniques broadened trade horizons. Centuries passed before humans used hydrocarbons for energy: steam power came first, developed for the Industrial Revolution and for travel, and was later used to generate electricity for illumination and communication, and, subsequently, to drive internal combustion engines. Steam-powered ships and railroads, the electric telegraph, and transoceanic cables improved communication and reduced travel time. Faster ships and railroads, aircraft, and the wireless radio presaged the coming of jet travel and global communication by sky-based and orbiting satellites. The title of the book *The Lexus and the Olive Tree* is a metaphor for the globalization of business. The olive tree symbolizes cultural identity, old ways, ritual, and nationalism. The Lexus symbolizes the marvels of modern technology and global integration.[7] According to the book's author, Thomas L. Friedman, modern societies can either move toward free worldwide trade or engage in economic protectionism based on tribalism and nationalism. Friedman sees globalization as the only alternative that supports economic viability.

What some scholars refer to as the "new" global competition is, in a historical perspective, an extension of the past. The primary differences are improvements in communication and transportation that enable almost immediate international exchanges of products, services, and information. The United States' experience with multinational enterprise began in the 1850s, but did not grow rapidly until after World War II, when the book value of its direct investments abroad increased some 10-fold by 1970.[8] During the same period, other nations established manufacturing, distribution, and sales facilitates in the United States for products such as automobiles, tires, electronics, and pharmaceuticals. At present, the United States is the world's biggest importer as well as exporter of goods, with trillions of dollars in play annually.

INDIVIDUALS AND ORGANIZATIONS: EVOLVING EXPECTATIONS

Niccolò di Bernardo dei Machiavelli wrote "there is nothing more difficult to carry out, nor more doubtful of success, nor more dangerous to handle, than to initiate a new order of things. For the reformer has enemies in all those who profit by the older order, and only lukewarm defenders in all those who would profit by the new order."[9] Change can come from within, but it is far more likely to come from without. A firm's economic environment can bring new opportunities as well as unanticipated challenges; technology can alter how people live and earn a living; political disruptions may lead to greater freedom or place limits on individuals and organizations; and evolving social norms can redefine appropriate behavior.

BUSINESS ETHICS

Ethics, or questions of human moral conduct, have occupied the thoughts of theologians and philosophers since antiquity. Broadly viewed, ethics are the moral "oughts" that enable a society

[6] Mira Wilkins, *The Emergence of Multinational Enterprise: American Business Abroad from the Colonial Era to 1914* (Cambridge, MA: Harvard University Press, 1970), pp. 201–207.

[7] Thomas L. Friedman, *The Lexus and the Olive Tree: Understanding Globalization* (New York: Farrar, Straus and Giroux, 1999).

[8] Mira Wilkins, *The Maturing of Multinational Enterprise: American Business Abroad from 1914–1970* (Cambridge, MA: Harvard University Press, 1974), Table XIII, p. 329.

[9] Niccolò di Bernardo Machiavelli, *The Prince*, trans. Luigi Ricci (London: Grant Richards, 1903), pp. 49–50. Written in 1513, but not published until 1532 because of its controversial nature.

to function. In the present context, "business ethics is an integral part of the Western ethical tradition."[10] Greek philosopher Aristotle (384–322 BCE) is credited with the search for "virtuous behavior" in one's moral character and justice in one's relations with others. His notion of "commutative justice" addresses the voluntary exchange of goods and services, an important element in a free society. His concept of "distributive justice" relates to the distribution of wealth and income within a society and forms the basis for contemporary discussions of economic inequality.[11]

The notion of a "just price" has been debated since at least the ninth century.[12] Building on Aristotle's notion of commutative justice, Saint Thomas Aquinas, writing in thirteenth-century Italy, addressed the issue of justice in trade matters with the idea of a "just price" (see Chapter 2).[13] In Chapter 2, we also examined how the expansion of trade promoted the need for business ethics, and how Dominican Friar Johannes Nider, active in early fifteenth-century Germany, declared that goods should be "lawful, honorable, and useful"; prices should be just; sellers should beware (*caveat venditor*) and not engage in "trickery" or "intimidation" or sell to "simpletons," who would not be informed buyers; and those who buy "looking for nothing but a rise in prices [i.e., financial speculators], sin most gravely."[14]

As early as the beginning of the eighteenth century, moral-philosophy courses emphasizing "natural, rational ethics" were taught in both U.S. Christian and secular institutions of higher education.[15] Following this tradition, Joseph Wharton, who donated $100,000 in 1881 to establish the University of Pennsylvania's school of business, felt that an effort should be made "to inculcate and impress upon the students: The immorality and practical inexpediency of seeking to acquire wealth by winning it from another rather than earning it through some sort of service to one's fellowmen. . . . [and] the necessity of rigorously punishing by legal penalties and social exclusion, those persons who commit frauds, betray trusts, or steal public funds, directly or indirectly."[16] Wharton set his ethical standards high, hoping they would be attained in practice.

The Wharton School became a model for other collegiate programs. Instruction in business ethics began as early as 1904 at the University of California (today's University of California—Berkeley), Yale University, the University of Chicago, and Northwestern University. Economics departments in colleges of business offered courses in sociology or social work and emphasized service and moral obligations. Other universities would follow with business-ethics courses and lectures. In a historical account of the business-ethics field and the people responsible for its development, Gabriel Abend noted the failure of succeeding generations to recognize that episodes of business misconduct are seldom without precedent: "[E]arly twentieth century concerns and arguments were not all that different from early twenty-first century ones. . . . [Yet] each generation of business ethicists, politicians, and journalists seems to represent certain business ethics problems as novel problems . . . unique to their own age. But this is just mistaken. . . . [H]istorical research shows this novelty and uniqueness to be illusory."[17]

---

[10] David J. Vogel, "Business Ethics Past and Present," *Public Interest* 102 (Winter 1991), p. 49. For an intellectual history of business ethics, see Bernard Mees, *The Rise of Business Ethics* (New York: Routledge, 2020), pp. 1-11.

[11] Aristotle, *The Nicomachean Ethics*, trans. Robert Williams (London: Longmans, Green and Co., 1876), pp. 115–150. Written ca. 350 BCE.

[12] Raymond de Roover, "The Concept of Just Price: Theory and Economic Policy," *Journal of Economic History* 18(4) (December 1958), especially pp. 420–423.

[13] Thomas Aquinas, *The "Summa Theologica"* ["Sum Total of Theology"] *of St. Thomas Aquinas*, trans. Fathers of the English Dominican Province (New York: Benziger Brothers, 1911), vol. 2, part II, second number, pp. 317–320. Written between 1259 and 1272.

[14] Johannes Nider, *On the Contracts of Merchants*, trans. Charles H. Reeves and ed. Ronald B. Shuman (Norman, OK: University of Oklahoma Press, 1966), pp. 38–45. Written ca. 1430 and published ca. 1468.

[15] Perry Glanzer and Todd C. Ream, *Christianity and Moral Identity in Higher Education* (New York: Palgrave Macmillan, 2010), p. 39.

[16] Joseph Wharton quoted in Fairman Rogers, "The Wharton School of Finance and Economy," *The Penn Monthly* 12(1) (May 1881), p. 359.

[17] Gabriel Abend, "The Origins of Business Ethics in American Universities, 1902–1936," *Business Ethics Quarterly* 23(2) (April 2013), p. 172.

Robert Wood Johnson II wrote the initial Johnson & Johnson Company Credo in 1943.[18] The credo is a statement of the values that guide the company's decision-making. It currently reads:

> We believe our first responsibility is to the patients, doctors and nurses, to mothers and fathers and all others who use our products and services. In meeting their needs everything we do must be of high quality. We must constantly strive to provide value, reduce our costs and maintain reasonable prices. Customers' orders must be serviced promptly and accurately. Our business partners must have an opportunity to make a fair profit.
>
> We are responsible to our employees who work with us throughout the world. We must provide an inclusive work environment where each person must be considered as an individual. We must respect their diversity and dignity and recognize their merit. They must have a sense of security, fulfillment and purpose in their jobs. Compensation must be fair and adequate and working conditions clean, orderly and safe. We must support the health and well-being of our employees and help them fulfill their family and other personal responsibilities. Employees must feel free to make suggestions and complaints. There must be equal opportunity for employment, development and advancement for those qualified. We must provide highly capable leaders and their actions must be just and ethical.
>
> We are responsible to the communities in which we live and work and to the world community as well. We must help people be healthier by supporting better access and care in more places around the world. We must be good citizens—support good works and charities, better health and education, and bear our fair share of taxes. We must maintain in good order the property we are privileged to use, protecting the environment and natural resources.
>
> Our final responsibility is to our stockholders. Business must make a sound profit. We must experiment with new ideas. Research must be carried on, innovative programs developed, investments made for the future and mistakes paid for. New equipment must be purchased, new facilities provided and new products launched. Reserves must be created to provide for adverse times. When we operate according to these principles, the stockholders should realize a fair return.[19]

The 1960s witnessed renewed interest in business ethics when the Reverend Raymond C. Baumhart, S.J., asked, "How ethical are businessmen?" More than half the approximately 1,700 readers of the *Harvard Business Review* he polled indicated they believed that business operators "would violate a code of ethics whenever they thought they could avoid detection."[20] *Business and Society Review*, the first journal entirely devoted to business ethics, began publication in 1972.[21] Other business-ethics journals followed, including *Business & Professional Ethics Journal* (1981), *Journal of Business Ethics* (1982), and *Business Ethics Quarterly* (1991).

When John Shad, chairman of the Securities and Exchange Commission from 1981 to 1987, donated $23 million to the Harvard Graduate School of Business Administration for the teaching of business ethics, he called for knowledge accompanied by conscience: "It is not enough for these [business] schools to certify that their graduates have mastered the fundamentals of their profession. The schools must hone their ability to certify that their graduates have the character and integrity to use the knowledge gained for the benefit—rather than the abuse—of society."[22] Business schools do have an opportunity to influence the character and integrity of their graduates. Less evident in Shad's comment is the responsibility of parents, schools, religious groups, and communities to inculcate the moral "oughts" that sustain a civilized society.

---

[18] Robert Wood Johnson II, *Robert Johnson Talks It Over* (New Brunswick, NJ: Johnson and Johnson, 1949), p. 168.

[19] Available online at http://www.jnj.com/sites/default/files/pdf/jnj_ourcredo_english_us_8.5x11_cmyk.pdf. As this is being written, Johnson & Johnson is facing multiple lawsuits in various states alleging unethical marketing practices promoting pain-killing opioids. The outcomes in all the cases have yet to be determined but may serve as a test for executives trying to implement ethical credos.

[20] Raymond C. Baumhart, "How Ethical Are Businessmen?" *Harvard Business Review* 39(4) (July–August 1961), p. 19.

[21] Theodore Cross, "Why *Business and Society Review*?" *Business and Society Review* 1(1) (Spring 1972), p. 4.

[22] John S. R. Shad, "Business's Bottom Line: Ethics," *New York Times* (July 27, 1987), p. A19.

The Interstate Commerce Act (1887), the Sherman Antitrust Act (1890), the Federal Reserve Act (1913), the Clayton Antitrust Act (1914), and the Federal Trade Commission Act (1914) were early actions to control business practices (see Chapter 12). The Securities and Exchange Commission was established in 1934 to implement the Securities Act of 1933 and the Securities Exchange Act of 1934, which required full financial disclosure and independent audits of financial statements and prohibited "insider trading." The Sarbanes–Oxley Act (2002) created a board to oversee public auditing firms, mandated new financial disclosure requirements, imposed stronger criminal penalties for fraud, and prohibited public-accounting firms from serving as a consultant to the businesses they audit. Section 406 of the Sarbanes–Oxley Act requires publicly traded firms to prepare and make public a code of ethics. One study has found, however, the result of this requirement to be "cut and paste" documents, in which the "content and language converge" in boilerplate language and provide little guidance tailored to ethical issues unique to firms or their industry.[23] This should remind us that laws alone cannot overcome human frailties or prevent dishonesty; that ultimate responsibility for one's actions cannot be avoided; and that history's lesson is to be skeptical in legislating ethical conduct.

ACTING ETHICALLY AND GLOBALLY

History is replete with examples of unethical behavior in business, politics, religion, education, sports, and all other human endeavors. As events around the world have shown, unethical behavior knows no national boundaries. Ethical behavior, whether in business or life, is not bounded by borders, ethnicity, religious beliefs, or other aspects of human experience.

There have been attempts to define "hypernorms," certain standards to be respected across cultures: the rights to freedom of movement, freedom from torture, private property, physical security, a fair trial, freedom of speech and association, subsistence, a minimal education, political participation, and nondiscriminatory treatment based on traits such as gender.[24] A study of normative guidelines endorsed by various international groups reveals some agreed-upon standards: adequate health and safety protections; the rights of all persons to life, liberty, personal security, and privacy; and environmental standards regarding pollution.[25]

The U.S. Foreign Corrupt Practices Act (FCPA, 1977; amended 1988) forbids publicly traded companies from making illicit payments to foreign government officials, to foreign political parties or their officials, and to intermediaries for acquiring or retaining business. The FCPA has been controversial. It makes relatively small payments (called "grease") to expedite activities such as obtaining a work permit or visa legal, but forbids relatively large payments to political figures or their intermediaries to gain or retain business—this is considered bribery. The line between grease and bribery can be very thin. Such efforts to legislate ethical behavior make Aristotle's "virtuous conduct" a statute and a matter of advocacy, not morality.

The search for hypernorms may be a worthy endeavor, but ethics (like management) is culturally bound. Hypernorms are advocated by North Americans and Western Europeans espousing individual rights. Western cultural tradition is indebted to John Locke, who challenged the supposed divine right of kings to rule without the consent of the governed (see Chapter 2). As one observer has noted, however, "[s]ome non-Western world views question the *primacy* of the 'inalienable dignity of the individual' as being a threat to the community or religious tradition. Sometimes, religion or a religious leader trumps individual rights."[26] Constitutional guarantees to

---

[23] Lori Holder-Webb and Jeffrey Cohen, "The Cut and Paste Society: Isomorphism in Codes of Ethics," *Journal of Business Ethics* 107(4) (June 2012), pp. 485–509.

[24] Thomas Donaldson, *The Ethics of International Business* (New York: Oxford University Press, 1989), p. 81.

[25] Christian J. Resick, Paul J. Hanges, Marcus W. Dickson, and Jacqueline K. Mitchelson, "A Cross-Cultural Examination of the Endorsement of Ethical Leadership," *Journal of Business Ethics* 63(3) (February 2006), pp. 345–359.

[26] Patricia H. Werhane, "Principles and Practices of Corporate Responsibilities," *Business Ethics Quarterly* 20(4) (October 2010), p. 699.

promote universal and inalienable rights are a part of a Western heritage that reflects an age-old struggle between autocracy, theocracy, and democracy.

BUSINESS AND SOCIETY

The line between ethics and the social responsibility of business firms is likewise not always clear. Johnson & Johnson's Credo specifies how its employees ought to behave, but also recognizes that the broader community in which they and the company operate plays a role in supporting ethical behavior. "Ethics" refers to the moral conduct of individuals, whereas "social responsibility" addresses society's wider expectations for business. Judgments relating to a person's moral conduct and acceptable corporate behavior rest on social values and legal requirements that evolve over time.

THE STEWARDSHIP OF WEALTH

As noted in Chapter 6, business operators throughout history have been benefactors of literature, music, and art. Legal precedents in the nineteenth century narrowly defined the extent to which managers and directors could engage in corporate philanthropy to further corporate (and not personal) ends. This legal straitjacket did not preclude individuals from engaging in philanthropic activities. Indeed, business philanthropists funded a great part of our nation's heritage, affirming that private wealth can benefit society in ways government spending cannot: for instance, "The money of steel tycoon Andrew Carnegie built 1,689 public libraries, Julius Rosenwald, the genius behind Sears, Roebuck, devoted much of his fortune to funding [more than 5,000] schools for African-American children in the rural South. Oil magnate John D. Rockefeller gave vast sums to medical research, higher education and Baptist missions."[27] Carnegie gave all his money away because he believed that wealth imposed a duty:

> [T]o set an example of modest, unostentatious living, shunning display or extravagance; to provide moderately for the legitimate wants of those dependent upon him; and after doing so, to consider all surplus revenues which come to him simply as trust funds, which he is called upon to administer, and strictly bound as a matter of duty to administer in the manner which, in his judgment, is best calculated to produce the most beneficial results for the community—the man of wealth thus becoming the mere trustee and agent for his poorer brethren.[28]

Carnegie's belief that wealth imposes a duty underscores that we all (both rich and poor) have a social responsibility to use our material resources wisely. In a review of the social role of business (and business operators such as Carnegie), historian Morrell Heald concluded:

> American businessmen fully shared the social concerns and preoccupations of their fellow citizens. Although they have often been depicted—indeed, caricatured—as single-minded pursuers of profit, the facts are quite otherwise. . . . Like others, they were frequently troubled by the conditions they saw; and, also like others, they numbered in their ranks men who contributed both of their ideas and their resources to redress social imbalance and disorganization.[29]

Moreover, as economist W. Philip Gramm recognizes, it should not be forgotten that "Henry Ford, Andrew Carnegie, Thomas Edison, Sam Walton, and Bill Gates all became rich by producing

---

[27] Marc Levinson [Review of the book *J. C. Penney: The Man, the Store, and American Agriculture*], *Wall Street Journal* (September 25, 2017), p. A19. See also Daniel A. Wren, "American Business Philanthropy and Higher Education in the Nineteenth Century," *Business History Review* 57(3) (Autumn 1983), pp. 321–346.

[28] Andrew Carnegie, "The Gospel of Wealth," *North American Review* 148(391) (June 1889), pp. 661–662.

[29] Morrell Heald, *The Social Responsibilities of Business: Company and Community 1900–1960* (Cleveland, OH: Press of Case Western Reserve University, 1970), p. 1.

goods and services we chose to buy because they enriched our lives" and, in actuality, "received only a small share of the bounty that their drive and genius created."[30]

Donna J. Wood provided an example of how food and drug manufacturers united to become stewards of our nation's health, as well as its wealth. In a study of the forces behind the passage of the Meat Inspection Act (1906) and the Pure Food and Drug Act (1906), Wood found that business interests were proactive, desiring legislation to protect both themselves and consumers. The passage of these acts has often been attributed to Upton B. Sinclair's nausea-inducing book on the Chicago (IL) stockyards, *The Jungle*.[31] The book's title reflects Sinclair's view of the brutality workers faced in the meat-packing industry. The facts, however, do not support Sinclair's portrayal. Manufacturers and producers such as Henry J. Heinz, Frederick Pabst, and Edward R. Squibb from the food processing, pharmaceutical, brewing, baking, and distilling industries joined together to support consumer protection laws.[32] They understood that these laws protected the honest seller from the adulterer and were in the interest of business, in addition to being sound public policy. Indeed, meatpackers favored the Meat Inspection Act: it helped market their products by giving them the federal government's mark of approval. An ensuing U.S. Department of Agriculture report on the Chicago stockyards debunked the harshest of Sinclair's claims, calling them "wilful and deliberate misrepresentations of fact" and "atrocious exaggeration."[33] The Meat Inspection Act and the Pure Food and Drug Act were signed into law by President Theodore Roosevelt on the same day, June 30, 1906. The latter act led to the establishment of the federal Food and Drug Administration (FDA).

CORPORATE SOCIAL RESPONSIBILITY AND PERFORMANCE

The idea that businesses have a role to play as a force for the good of society has deep roots. In the early years of the Industrial Revolution, Robert Owen (see Chapter 4) advanced new ideas for addressing the novel challenges posed by the factory system of production. Leading into World War I, Henry L. Gantt, irked by the failure of U.S. industrial leadership, called for an industrial democracy based on equality of opportunity (see Chapter 8). Writing in the late 1920s, Oliver Sheldon held that managers should adopt practices conducive to communal well-being (see Chapter 11). Merten J. "Mandy" Mandeville and John M. Anderson argued that managers have a responsibility to promote both economic and social progress through productive and distributive efficiency, as well as through an emphasis on human relations in business (see Chapter 16). It was not until the mid-twentieth century, however, that the *A. P. Smith Manufacturing Co. v. Barlow* decision (see Chapter 6) legitimized corporations engaging in general philanthropy for the public good.[34] Was it only a coincidence that what followed was an outpouring of corporate giving? Academic interest likewise grew, as new journals devoted to social issues appeared (viz., *Society* in 1963 and *Business and Society Review* in 1974).

Howard R. Bowen, erstwhile president of the University of Iowa, spearheaded the modern concern for how business behaves toward society. In his 1953 book sponsored by the Federal Council of the Churches, *Social Responsibilities of the Businessman*, Bowen defined "social responsibility" as "the obligations of businessmen to pursue those policies, to make those decisions, or to follow those lines of action which are desirable in terms of the objectives and values

[30] W. Philip Gramm, "The GOP's 'Tax the Rich' Temptation," *Wall Street Journal* (October 9, 2017), p. A17.

[31] Upton B. Sinclair, *The Jungle* (New York: Grosset & Dunlap Publishers, 1906). Originally serialized under the title "The Jungle: A Story of Chicago" in the newspaper *Appeal to Reason* from February 25 to November 4, 1905. Sinclair's intention was to highlight the plight of immigrant workers, but later acknowledged, "I aimed for the public's heart, and by accident hit it in the stomach." See Sinclair, "What Life Means to Me," *Cosmopolitan* 41(6) (October 31, 1906), p. 594.

[32] Donna J. Wood, "The Strategic Use of Public Policy: Business Support for the 1906 Food and Drug Act," *Business History Review* 59(3) (Autumn 1985), pp. 403–432.

[33] U.S. Congress, House of Representatives, *Hearings before the Committee on Agriculture on the So-called "Beveridge Amendment" to the Agricultural Appropriation Bill*, 59th Congress, 1st Session (Washington, DC: Government Printing Office, 1906), pp. 350, 349.

[34] *A. P. Smith Manufacturing Co. v. Barlow, 98 A.2d 581 (NJ) 1953.*

of our society."[35] Synonymous with this definition were the phrases "public responsibility," "social obligations," and "business morality." Bowen was the first writer to frame the "social responsibilities of the businessman" as a moral imperative. He recognized, however, that businesses could not solve the problems of economic life alone: "Such an assumption would be unwise and dangerous not only for society . . . but also for businesses themselves. They cannot be saddled with responsibilities which they cannot hope to discharge effectively."[36] Drawing this distinction between what businesses could do and should do sparked a debate that continues today.

Courtesy of Arthur G. Bedeian

Keith Davis

Keith Davis recalled that Bowen's book "crystallized" his thinking about social issues in management. "If you mess it up, you clean it up," a lesson from Davis's childhood, led him to the conclusion that because business influenced society, it had to accept the social responsibilities that followed.[37] In a widely cited article, Davis stated the pros and cons of social responsibility for business. Arguments in favor of social responsibility include: (1) it serves the long-run interest of business; (2) it improves the public image of business and increases its legitimacy in society; (3) socially responsible corporations can avoid government regulation; and (4) corporations have the resources and expertise to apply to social problems. Arguments against include: (1) as a trustee for a corporation's stockholders, management should optimize corporate return; (2) social involvement is costly and dilutes the primary economic purpose of corporations; and (3) corporations should not be given social responsibilities for which they cannot be held accountable.[38] On balance, Davis favored social responsibility for business, but acknowledged Bowen's caveat that certain social challenges should be the province of others better equipped to meet them.

STAKEHOLDERS: ECONOMIC AND NONECONOMIC RESPONSIBILITIES

The belief that corporations have "stakeholders," or various constituencies whose interests should be considered in making decisions, became popular in the early 1960s. As traditionally defined, a stakeholder is "any group or individual who can affect or is affected by the achievement of [an] organization's objectives."[39] In line with this definition, Igor Ansoff, Vice President of Planning and Director of Diversification at Lockheed Aircraft, agreed that a corporation's "objectives" could not be accomplished if stakeholders did not provide the necessary support. He distinguished, however, between "economic objectives" and "social or noneconomic objectives":

> The firm has both (a) "economic" objectives aimed at optimizing the efficiency of its total resource conversion process and (b) "social" or noneconomic objectives. . . . In most firms the economic objectives exert the primary influence on the firm's behavior and form the main body of explicit goals used by management for guidance and control of the firm . . . [whereas] the social objectives exert a modifying and constraining influence on management behavior.[40]

---

[35] Howard R. Bowen, *Social Responsibilities of the Businessman* (New York: Harper & Brothers, 1953), p. 6.

[36] *Ibid.*, p. 7.

[37] Keith Davis, "A Journey through Management in Transition," in Arthur G. Bedeian, ed., *Management Laureates: A Collection of Autobiographical Essays*, vol. 1 (Greenwich, CT: JAI Press, 1992), p. 285. See also Keith Davis and Robert L. Blomstrom, *Business and Its Environment* (New York: McGraw-Hill, 1966).

[38] Keith Davis, "The Case for and against Business Assumptions of Social Responsibilities," *Academy of Management Journal* 16(2) (June 1973), pp. 312–322.

[39] R. Edward Freeman, *Strategic Management: A Stakeholder Approach* (Boston, MA: Pitman, 1984), p. 46. See also *idem.*, "Stakeholder Theory," *Philosophy of Management* 8(3) (September 2009), pp. 97–107.

[40] H. Igor Ansoff, *Corporate Strategy: An Analytic Approach to Business Policy for Growth and Expansion* (New York: McGraw-Hill, 1965), pp. 37–38.

For Ansoff, the purpose of a firm was to maximize long-term return on investments; secondary responsibilities could not be met unless a firm's economic objectives had been achieved. He acknowledged the earlier view of Peter F. Drucker that managers must put economic considerations first and could justify a firm's existence only through the economic results it produced. As Drucker explained:

> [M]anagement has failed if it fails to produce economic results. It has failed if it has not supplied goods and services desired by the consumer at a price the consumer is willing to pay. It has failed if it does not improve or at least maintain the wealth producing capacity of the economic resources entrusted to it.[41]

Drucker recognized that there could be noneconomic consequences of managerial decisions, such as improved community well-being, but these were by-products made possible only by an emphasis on economic performance. Drucker and Ansoff agreed that economic results (i.e., meeting the demands of customers while providing a competitive return to investors) must take priority, as social or noneconomic objectives can be pursued only if a firm's primary objectives are attained.

Although the stakeholder approach provides useful guidance in a changing economic, social, and political environment, issues remain with respect to determining primary claimants and who will be considered secondary. Archie B. Carroll and Kareem M. Shabana helped clarify this issue by describing four categories of business responsibilities: economic, legal, ethical, and discretionary (later labeled philanthropic). These were "not mutually exclusive, nor . . . intended to portray a continuum with economic concerns on one end and social concerns on the other. . . . They are neither cumulative nor additive . . . [but] are simply [reminders] that motives or actions can be categorized as primarily one or another of these four kinds."[42] Economic responsibilities are primary, because before all else a business has an obligation to produce and sell products and services society wants at a profit. Legal responsibilities are those regulations and rules created by political institutions to legitimize and govern business activities. Ethical responsibilities are expectations of how a firm should conduct its business beyond what the law requires. Philanthropic responsibilities are voluntary. The intent of these categories is to show that corporate social responsibility is not an either-or proposition; that is, a firm's economic responsibility to earn a profit for its owners interacts with, rather than excludes, its other stakeholder responsibilities.[43]

CAN YOU HAVE YOUR CAKE AND EAT IT TOO?

In Voltaire's satire *Candide, ou l'Optimisme* [*Candide, or, All for the Best*] (1759), the character Professor Pangloss is the eternal optimist, who claims that all is for the best "in this best of all possible worlds."[44] Can this ever be true at a for-profit business? Can it be profitable while being socially responsible? Carroll and Shabana state the case positively: "The right corporate social responsibility is the one which pursues issues which demonstrate a convergence between economic and social goals."[45] Although institutions shape decisions, all the members of a firm's management team must engage in a coordinated effort to make socially responsible choices.

---

[41] Peter F. Drucker, *The Practice of Management* (New York: Harper & Row, 1954), p. 8.
[42] Archie B. Carroll, "A Three-Dimensional Conceptual Model of Corporate Performance," *Academy of Management Review* 4(4) (October 1979), pp. 499–500.
[43] Mark Schwartz and Archie B. Carroll, "Corporate Social Responsibility: A Three Domain Approach," *Business Ethics Quarterly* 13(4) (October 2003), pp. 503–530.
[44] Voltaire, *Candide, ou l'Optimisme* [*Candide, or, All for the Best*] (Geneva: Chez les frères Cramer, 1759), p. 26.
[45] Archie B. Carroll and Kareem M. Shabana, "The Business Case for Corporate Social Responsibility: A Review of the Concepts, Research, and Practice," *International Journal of Management Reviews* 12(1) (March 2010), p. 101.

SOCIAL ENTREPRENEURSHIP

Social entrepreneurship has been proposed as a way to match business capabilities with socially responsible opportunities. Gregory Dees has suggested creating social value along with economic benefits by adopting an entrepreneurial approach to social problems. Entrepreneurship, of course, is not a new phenomenon. Social entrepreneurship, however, provides opportunities for firms to introduce fresh ideas, resources, and capabilities for solving social issues that governments have been unable to successfully address. In Dees's view, "Government alone is not the answer."[46] "Top-down," bureaucratic, governmental approaches too often fail, leaving in place dependency and a sense of entitlement. Beyond "innovative not-for-profit ventures, social entrepreneurship can include social purpose business ventures, such as for-profit community development banks, and hybrid organizations mixing not-for-profit and for-profit elements, such as homeless shelters that start businesses to train and employ their residents."[47] Prominent social entrepreneurs include Victoria Hale, who founded the nonprofit pharmaceutical company OneWorld Health to provide safe, effective, and affordable medicines for developing countries, and Jim Fruchterman, a Silicon Valley engineer, who created the nonprofit Benetech to provide technological solutions to such challenges as landmine detection, illiteracy, and civil rights. Médecins Sans Frontières [Doctors Without Borders], Alcoholics Anonymous, and the Sierra Club are other examples of social entrepreneurship.

Michael E. Porter and Mark R. Kramer have suggested that social entrepreneurship can "enhance the competitiveness of a company while simultaneously advancing the economic and social conditions in the communities in which it operates."[48] This may involve rethinking all facets of a company's operations, including employee wellness and safety, product packaging, plant and distribution locations, supply-chain management, environmental impact, and energy and water usage. Social entrepreneurship proponents recognize that businesses cannot do everything, but believe that what businesses *can* do to enhance their competitiveness while also improving economic and social conditions in their communities, they *should* do. This moves the discourse about corporate social responsibility to another level, with the emphasis on "Doing Good" rather than simply "Looking Good."

BUSINESS AND ITS ENVIRONMENT

Expectations about the role of business in conserving the earth's natural resources have also changed over time. The Yellowstone Act, passed by the U.S. Congress in 1872, established the first national park in the world. By 1916, the year the National Park Service was created, there were 14 national parks in the United States, including Yosemite and Sequoia in California, Glacier in Montana, and Rocky Mountain in Colorado. There are now 61 national parks in the United States. Global concern for environmental matters escalated in the 1990s, and the terms "ecology," "greening," "sustainability," and "climate change" became more common. Nongovernmental groups such as the Caux Round Table (1994), the Coalition for Environmentally Responsible Economies (CERES; 1999), and the United Nations Global Compact (2000) reflected this concern. The International Organization for Standardization (ISO) published the world's first standards on environmental management in 1992 and released its ISO 14000 Environmental Management System standards in 1996. ISO 14000 is a family of environmental standards that offers world-class specifications for products, services, systems, and waste reduction in energy

---

[46] J. Gregory Dees, "Taking Social Entrepreneurship Seriously," *Society* 44(3) (March 2007), p. 25.

[47] *Idem*, "The Meaning of 'Social Entrepreneurship,'" original draft: October 31, 1998; reformatted and revised: May 30, 2001. Available online at https://entrepreneurship.duke.edu/news-item/the-meaning-of-social-entrepreneurship/.

[48] Michael E. Porter and Mark R. Kramer, "Creating Shared Value," *Harvard Business Review* 89(1–2) (January–February 2011), p. 66. See also Michael A. Driver, "An Interview with Michael Porter: Social Entrepreneurship and the Transformation of Capitalism," *Academy of Management Learning & Education* 11(3) (September 2012), pp. 421–431.

and materials.[49] The same challenges associated with defining hypernorms for corporate social performance, however, apply to setting standards for environmental performance. Nevertheless, it may be easier to define standards for air and water quality and product safety and performance than social responsibility, which is less quantifiable. After nearly a decade of transnational negotiations, the ISO released international standards (ISO 26000) in 2010 to guide organizations in responsibly contributing to society's health and welfare.[50]

SUMMARY OF PART IV

Part IV begins by reviewing the post–World War II years, during which a revived interest in general management theory arose as businesses grew domestically and internationally, creating a need for more widely educated managers. Next it focuses on the emergence of a new generation of scholars interested in studying what is now known as "organizational behavior." Then it examines the transition of the field of personnel management into human-resource management and, subsequently, strategic human-resource management. It also considers the debate among organization theorists concerning the effect of technology on an organization's structure and the relationship between an organization's design and its environment. It then follows the ongoing quest for science in management into the Information Age. Part IV closes with a consideration of how the globalization of business and society's expectation that managers will act responsibly have shaped the evolution of management thought.

[49] JoAnne Yates and Craig N. Murphy, "From Setting National Standards to Coordinating International Standards," *Business and Economic History On-Line* 4 (2006), pp. 1–25. See also *idem, Engineering Rules: Global Standard Setting since 1880* (Baltimore, MD: Johns Hopkins University Press, 2019).

[50] See S. Prakash Sethi, Janet L. Rovenpor, and Mert Demir, "Enhancing the Quality of Reporting in Corporate Social Responsibility Guidance Documents: The Roles for ISO 26000, Global Reporting Initiative, and CSR-Sustainability Monitor," *Business and Society Review* 122(2) (Summer 2017), pp. 139–163.

Epilogue: A Commerce Across the Ages

Our goal throughout the preceding chapters has been to trace the many roots of modern management thought. In doing so, we have focused on how ideas about management as an academic discipline and management as an activity have developed over time. We believe that to understand management thought in its broadest sense, one must also understand it historically. The historical record provides a bridge across time, uniting the past and present as they lead into the future.

Contemporary management theory and practice are quite literally what the past—as received and interpreted by the present—has made them. The past repeatedly informs and reinforms the present such that the search for understanding is never finished. In this sense, the past exists in a reciprocal relationship with the present. Moreover, just as the past is seen through the eyes of the present, the present is judged in an unending dialogue with the past. Today is not like yesterday, nor will tomorrow be like today, yet today is a synergism of all our yesterdays.

A free commerce across the ages cements our kinship with times and places past and allows us to more fully appreciate our own time and place in the parade of history. It also permits us to reach across the years and repeatedly tap the past's greatest minds. With only the cost of one's intellectual effort, the insights of the past are available to repeatedly engage, delight, and pique one's curiosity at a moment's notice. It is hoped that at least some of our readers are prompted to search out the writings of the various personalities to whom they have now been introduced.

Our expedition into the past is concluded. We trust that you have enjoyed the journey and will continue to benefit from having explored the management discipline's intellectual roots and having become acquainted with the work and lives of its many contributors from around the world.

Name Index

C

D

T

U

V

W

X

Y

Z

Subject Index